DECODING INTERNATIONAL LAW

DECODING INTERNATIONAL LAW

SEMIOTICS AND THE HUMANITIES

SUSAN TIEFENBRUN

OXFORD
UNIVERSITY PRESS

OXFORD
UNIVERSITY PRESS

Oxford University Press, Inc., publishes works that further Oxford University's objective of excellence in research, scholarship, and education.

Oxford New York
Auckland Cape Town Dar es Salaam Hong Kong Karachi Kuala Lumpur Madrid Melbourne Mexico City Nairobi New Delhi Shanghai Taipei Toronto

With offices in
Argentina Austria Brazil Chile Czech Republic France Greece Guatemala Hungary Italy Japan Poland Portugal Singapore South Korea Switzerland Thailand Turkey Ukraine Vietnam

Published by Oxford University Press, Inc.
198 Madison Avenue, New York, New York 10016

Library of Congress Cataloging-in-Publication Data

Tiefenbrun, Susan
Decoding international law : semiotics and the humanities / Susan Tiefenbrun.
p. cm.
Includes bibliographical references and index.
ISBN 978-0-19-538577-9 ((hardback) : alk. paper)
1. Semiotics (Law) 2. Civil rights. 3. International law.
4. Culture—Semiotic models. I. Title.
K213.T53 2010
341.4'8—dc22

2009043475

1 2 3 4 5 6 7 8 9
Printed in the United States of America on acid-free paper

Note to Readers
This publication is designed to provide accurate and authoritative information in regard to the subject matter covered. It is based upon sources believed to be accurate and reliable and is intended to be current as of the time it was written. It is sold with the understanding that the publisher is not engaged in rendering legal, accounting, or other professional services. If legal advice or other expert assistance is required, the services of a competent professional person should be sought. Also, to confirm that the information has not been affected or changed by recent developments, traditional legal research techniques should be used, including checking primary sources where appropriate.

(Based on the Declaration of Principles jointly adopted by a Committee of the American Bar Association and a Committee of Publishers and Associations.)

To my husband, Jonathan, who is my best friend,
the smartest person I know, and the one who has encouraged me for the past
forty years to read, study, and write this book

CONTENTS

Acknowledgments xi

A. INTRODUCTION TO SEMIOTICS AND THE LAW

Chapter 1. Introduction 3

Chapter 2. Legal Semiotics 19

- I. Introduction 19
- II. Sources of Semiotics 28
- III. Conclusion 79

B. TERRORISM

Chapter 3. A Semiotic Approach to a Legal Definition of Terrorism 83

- I. Introduction 83
- II. Elements of the Crime of Terrorism 87
- III. The Many Definitions of Terrorism 89
- IV. What is the Difference Between International and Domestic Terrorism? 108
- V. Terrorism is not only a Crime but a Method to Achieve Self-Determination 109
- VI. International Crimes are also Methods of Committing Terrorism 111
- VII. If Terrorism is not only a Crime, but a Method or an Act of War, Then What Court Should Try International Terrorists? 113
- VIII. The Paradoxes Inherent in the Meaning of Terrorism 113
- IX. Literary and Cinematographic Representations of Terrorism 114
- X. Conclusion 125

Chapter 4. State-Sponsored Terrorism, the Laws of War, and the Role of Storytelling as a Self-Help Remedy: Law, Literature, and Semiotics 127

- I. Introduction 127
- II. The Legitimacy of an Interdisciplinary Method 133

III. Laws of Armed Conflict Represented in *The Pianist* 144
IV. Retributive Justice After World War II and the Nuremberg Trials 158
V. Restorative Justice and the Power of Art as Self-Help Remedy 159
VI. Conclusion 164

C. CIVIL DISOBEDIENCE

Chapter 5. Deconstructing *Civil Disobedience*: A Semiotic Definition 169

I. Introduction 169
II. The Deep Structure of Civil Disobedience 175
III. Civil Disobedience and Terrorism 178
IV. Arguments for and Against Civil Disobedience 181
V. Civil Disobedience is not Protected by the Constitutional Right to Dissent or Free Speech 185
VI. Conclusion and the Delicate Balance 189

Chapter 6. Semiotics and Martin Luther King's *Letter from Birmingham Jail* 191

I. Introduction: *The Letter* 191
II. Semiotics 193
III. Role of the Reader 196
IV. Genre of the *Letter* 199
V. Intertextuality and the *Letter*: Biblical Allusions 200
VI. Biblical Underpinnings of Martin Luther King's Anti-Law Stance 201
VII. Plato's *Allegory of the Cave* 202
VIII. Historical and Legal Context of the *Letter* 203
IX. Narrative Structure of the *Letter* 205
X. The Notion of Difference and "Différance" 211
XI. Natural Law Theory and Civil Disobedience 213
XII. For and Against Civil Disobedience: Dworkin and Bork 216
XIII. Conclusion 220

Chapter 7. On Civil Disobedience, Jurisprudence, Feminism, and the Law in the *Antigones* of Sophocles and Anouilh 221

I. Introduction 221
II. What is Civil Disobedience? 223
III. Civil Disobedience and Jurisprudence 228
IV. Hegel's Reading of Sophocles' *Antigone* 239

v. Antigone and Feminism 242
vi. Civil Disobedience in Sophocles' *Antigone* 244
vii. Civil Disobedience and Jean Anouilh's *Antigone*: A Parody 251
viii. Conclusion 258

D. WOMEN'S HUMAN RIGHTS

Chapter 8. The Semiotics of Women's Human Rights in Iran 263

i. Introduction 263
ii. History of Women's Rights in Iran 265
iii. Semiotics of *Hejab*, the Veil, and Women's Dress Code 280
iv. Signs of Women's Rights in Iran as Represented in the Humanities 294
v. Iranian Family Laws: Then and Now 321
vi. International Human Rights Laws Protecting Women's Rights and their Representation in the Humanities 326
vii. Conclusion 341

Chapter 9. Gendercide and the Cultural Context of Sex Trafficking in China 347

i. Introduction 347
ii. Laws Protecting Women in China From Trafficking 354
iii. Sex Trafficking in China 364
iv. Root Causes of Trafficking 369
v. Changing Role of Women in Chinese Society 383
vi. Policy Suggestions to Combat Sex Trafficking in China 387
vii. Lisa See, *Snow Flower and the Secret Fan* 389
viii. Conclusion 393

E. CHILDREN'S HUMAN RIGHTS

Chapter 10. The Culture of Violence: Child Soldiers, Slavery, and the Trafficking of Children 397

i. Introduction 397
ii. The Root Causes of the Use of Child Soldiers 405
iii. Laws Relating to the Use of Child Soldiers 412
iv. Literary Representations of Child Soldiers 436
v. Conclusion and Proposals for Solutions 450

F. CULTURE AND SEMIOTICS

Chapter 11. The Japanese Culture, Copyright Infringement, Defamation, and Sex Trafficking: A Study of the Fictional Life of a Geisha 459

I. Introduction 459
II. Text 463
III. Context 479
IV. Subtext 492
V. Post-Text: The Complaint Iwasaki v. Arthur Golden and Publishers 499
VI. Pretext 519
VII. Conclusion 522

Chapter 12. The Impact of Culture on the Semiotics of Treaty Interpretation: How Pirates Read and Misread the Berne Convention 527

I. Introduction 527
II. Hermeneutics and Reader-Response Theory 530
III. Arguments for and Against Protecting Authors' Rights 531
IV. Piracy, The Berne Convention and Dramatic Irony 533
V. History of Copyright 535
VI. Copyright Theories and the Berne Convention 536
VII. Clashes of Culture 540
VIII. Berne Convention: Underlying Principles and Rights Theories 541
IX. U.S. and Chinese Compliance with the Berne Convention's Minimum Standards 542
X. U.S. Responses to the Berne Convention 543
XI. How the United States Reads the Berne Convention 545
XII. China's Responses to the Berne Convention 547
XIII. Hermeneutics and Cultural Difference 549
XIV. How China Reads the Berne Convention 550
XV. U.S. Views on Piracy of Patented Inventions as Expressed in Film: *Flash of Genius* 552
XVI. Conclusion 553

G. CONCLUSION

Index 559

ACKNOWLEDGMENTS

How do I begin to thank the people in my life who have supported my research for the past forty years, inspired me to write, and provided me with the information and insight to find relationships among so many different fields of learning: literature, art, music, philosophy, history, feminism, semiotics, linguistics, stylistics, rhetoric, on the one hand, and international law on the other hand? I must begin by thanking my own literature professors as well as my humanities professors at Wisconsin University where I obtained my Bachelor of Arts degree and a Master of Arts degree in French. I would like to thank my professors at Columbia University where I obtained my Ph.D. in French and where I had the great pleasure and privilege of working with such eminent literary scholars as Gerard Genette, Michael Riffaterre, Julia Kristeva, Tzvetan Todorov, Umberto Eco, Jacques Derrida, and many others during the heyday of structuralism and post-structuralism. This was a period of intense intellectual excitement about literature that was catalytic and energizing. I would like to thank my law professors at New York University School of Law where I obtained my J.D. degree with a concentration in international law. The late Professor Thomas Franck and Professor Andreas Lowenfeld as well as Professor Theodor Meron formed me and inspired me to engage in this interdisciplinary study of international law and the humanities. I was lucky because I learned about international law from the greats! I would also like to thank The Thomas Jefferson School of Law for supporting my research and enabling me to put together this life's work into a book that can serve as an introduction to the many facets of international and comparative law. Special thanks to Michelle Hoskinson, my research assistant, who worked tirelessly and effectively to make editorial changes. This book is a journey into international human rights law, women's international human rights laws, children's human rights laws, international humanitarian law, public and private international law, international business, intellectual property law, jurisprudence, and comparative law. In the course of my real journey into many foreign countries, I have met many illustrious scholars of law and scholars of literature who have given me inspiration and whom I would like to thank. But most of all, I would like to thank my family, my daughter Michele, my sons Jeremy and Gregory, and my husband Jonathan who have had to put up with my many hours of research and writing. I could not have written this work without their encouragement and moral support.

PART A

INTRODUCTION TO SEMIOTICS AND THE LAW

1. INTRODUCTION

Violations of international law and human rights laws are the plague of the twentieth and twenty-first centuries. Man's inhumanity to man seems to be epidemic, especially as wars proliferate and warriors abandon respect for human rights and the laws of war. Witnessing mass violence and violations of human rights has a powerful and dramatic effect. Writers, filmmakers, artists, philosophers, historians, and legal scholars deeply affected by the horrors of human rights violations occurring all over the world respond by representing them indirectly through the humanities. The hidden meanings and the international law issues embedded in these artistic representations of international human rights violations are the subject of this book.

To delve more deeply into the underlying international human rights laws represented in the humanities, I use an interdisciplinary method based on semiotic theory. Semiotics is the science of signs. When applied, sign theory can effectively unravel the complexities of such controversial issues as terrorism, civil disobedience, women's human rights, children's human rights, and the impact of culture on the interpretation of international law. These complex issues are represented indirectly, visually, and dramatically in works of art, film, literature, and the humanities, which I study in detail in this book.

Semiotics is a mysterious term to some but a household word to others, especially Europeans in the fields of art, music, literature, medicine, and now, the law. Sign theory was originally a European phenomenon founded by Ferdinand De Saussure and advanced by Charles Sanders Peirce. Semiotics has developed internationally; it is applied most frequently in the fields of literature and interpretation.

Semiotics is a vast branch of knowledge encompassing many different investigatory fields such as linguistics, philosophy, stylistics, hermeneutics, cultural anthropology, and many others, all involving interpretation. Because law is very definitely about the interpretation of legal discourse, semiotics is a very useful tool to facilitate legal interpretation. Semiotics helps readers go beyond the mere surface of a text. Lawyers; diagnosticians; interpreters of art, music, and dance; doctors examining body signs and symptoms; and judges reading legal documents all use semiotics without knowing it to see between the lines and thereby excavate hidden meanings or obscure but significant phenomena not always visible to the naked eye. Semiotics is to readers what the microscope is to scientists.

Semiotics is also called *sign theory*. The letters of the word on a page are called the *signifiers*, and the meanings hidden below the written letters are called the *signifieds*. The relationship between the signifier and the signified is the sign itself. Thus, a word is a sign that has both a physical presence on the surface of the text (signifier) and meanings hidden below the text and within the connotations and cultural contexts of the word (signifieds). Semiotics, then, is by definition interdisciplinary and highly dynamic because the reader or legal scholar trying to interpret a text must determine the relationship between the signifier and the signified to derive the latent meanings of the sign. Furthermore, semiotics is interdisciplinary because it is a science built on elements from many different fields of investigative research.

Umberto Eco defined *semiotics* as "the discipline studying everything which can be used in order to lie."[1] The deception Eco refers to when he speaks of lies is the duplicity implicit in words themselves that, by their very relational nature, are designed to hide some meanings while representing others. We all know that words can say one thing and mean something else. Semiotics allows researchers to excavate hidden meanings and thereby illuminate a literary or legal text.

Because of the vastness of the field and the many areas of knowledge semiotics encompasses, confusion seems to surround the term—and some people even get frightened when they hear the word! Some call it *semiotics* while others call it *semiology* (and may even spell it *semeiology*). Some refer to it as *semiotics* in the plural, or *semiotic* in the singular or as another lexical monstrosity coined *sematology*. This terminological confusion that plagues the field of semiotics is due in part to the breadth of its subject matter and to the subdivision of the field into syntactics, semantics, and pragmatics, to name but a few.

In this book I apply semiotics to illuminate, not obfuscate, the intricacies of international law and international human rights laws as represented in the humanities. Examples of some of the literary and cinematographic works that contain hidden international law issues are Joseph Conrad's *The Secret Agent* and the movie *Hotel Rwanda* (both representing terrorism); Roman Polanski's film *The Pianist* (representing State-sponsored terrorism and violations of the laws of war); Martin Luther King's *Letter from Birmingham Jail* (defining civil disobedience and its link to natural law); Sophocles' *Antigone* as compared to Anouilh's more recent *Antigone* (representing civil disobedience and women's rights in two different cultural milieux and two different periods of time); Azar Nafisi's memoir, *Reading Lolita in Tehran;* Shirin Ebadi's memoir, *Iran Awakening*; two powerful documentary films about women and family law in Iran: *Divorce Iranian Style* and *Two Women* (all four focusing on different aspects of the violation of women's human rights in Iran); Lisa See's *Snow Flower and the Secret Fan* (representing women's human rights violations in China); Uzodinnma Iweala's *Beasts of No Nation* and Ahmadou Kourouma's *Allah is Not Obliged* (both depicting the life of child soldiers, trafficking of humans, and the violation of children's human rights in Africa); Arthur Golden's *Memoirs of a Geisha* (illustrating a case

1. Umberto Eco, A Theory of Semiotics 7 (1976).

of copyright infringement, defamation, and sex trafficking in Japan), and *Flash of Genius* (a movie about the piracy of patented inventions).

Part A of the book provides an introduction to the relationships between semiotics and the law. Chapter 2 is an in-depth study of semiotics as it is applied to the law. It can be used as a manual of legal semiotics. This chapter explores the basic elements of semiotics, the role sign theory plays in the law, and the potential use of the semiotic method for legal scholars and practitioners. It defines the term *legal semiotics* and traces the history and development of semiotics as it grew out of the varied disciplines of medicine, philosophy, linguistics, anthropology, and literature. This chapter also sketches the basic principles of the sign classification system proposed by Charles Sanders Pierce, whose theories influenced the legal academic community especially in the development of the legal realism movement. Semiotics is the overarching science encompassing linguistics. In this chapter, I discuss the semiotic theories of certain key figures in linguistics such as Ferdinand De Saussure, the father of modern linguistics, including his view of the scope of semiotics and its relation to the development of legal positivist theory. The semiotic theories of Charles Sanders Pierce influenced the legal realists. In the field of cultural anthropology, I look at the work of Claude Levi-Strauss who adopted Saussure's semiotic principles and developed a structural method used successfully by legal scholars (mainly in Europe). Through the fertile connection of literature and the law, legal scholars have become aware of the potential of semiotics.

Chapter 2 also traces the sources of semiotics in different schools of literary theory ranging from Russian formalism to post-structuralism, including the specific contributions of these literary theories to legal interpretive theory. Roman Jakobson, for example, is a major contributor to semiotics and to communication theory in general, and his work has significant implications for legal interpretive practice. It is interesting to see that the literary schools of new criticism, structuralism, post-structuralism, and deconstructionism have made a mark on American and European legal scholarship, especially in the development of the critical legal studies movement. This chapter will isolate and describe the specific influence of these literary schools on the law and on the critical legal studies movement in particular. I look at the work of three eminent European structuralists (Algirdas Greimas, Tzvetan Todorov, and Roland Barthes) and their influence on legal semiotics in the United States. Semiotics plays a significant role in the "opening up" of the legal text, as discussed by Ronald Dworkin. Similarly, there is a fertile relationship between H.L.A. Hart's theory on legal positivism and semiotic theory. The interdisciplinary nature of semiotics has promoted much dialogue among researchers from many different areas of knowledge and has helped breathe life into the interpretation of literary and legal texts. This chapter attempts to draw analogies between the structural method of Saussure and the empirical models adopted by the legal positivists, the open-ended semiotic process proposed by Peirce and espoused by the legal realism movement, and the role that contradiction and demystification play in the deconstructionist and critical legal studies movement. Each of these legal movements has adopted the semiotic theories of Saussure, Peirce, and the post-structuralists respectively.

Once the elements of semiotic theory are exposed, the rest of the book is basically an application of semiotic theory to international law in order to unravel particularly complex and compelling international law issues represented vividly in the humanities.

Part B of the book focuses on the very controversial question of a definition of *terrorism*, which very few of our most learned international law scholars are willing to provide. In the U.N. debate about the definition of terrorism, the West has been worried that any proposed definition could be used to include State-sponsored terrorism, while the Third World has been worried that a definition which emphasizes non-State actors might fail to differentiate between terrorism per se and the struggle for national liberation. As a result of this interesting dialogue, there remains no real definition of terrorism to guide us in a world that fears terrorists.

Chapter 3 proposes a definition of terrorism based on semiotic principles. Terrorism must be deconstructed to distinguish between domestic and international terrorism, State-sponsored terrorism and non-State-sponsored terrorism, and terrorism per se and revolutionary violence that arguably falls afoul of the laws of war. The basic problem in the quest for a definition of terrorism is the lack of a single criterion determining the fundamental component elements of the term. Semiotics enables us to uncover the basic structural elements of terrorism.

One obstacle to arriving at a universally accepted definition of the word is the need to resolve its underlying paradoxes and conflicting political and ideological premises. Is terrorism legitimate if it is perpetrated in self-defense or in an attempt to achieve self-determination? This chapter will uncover five basic elements of the crime of terrorism. Under certain circumstances terrorism can be included in other specifically defined international crimes such as war crimes, crimes against humanity, and genocide. Chapter 3 looks comparatively at definitions of terrorism provided by the United States, England, France, the European Union, Canada, and the United Nations. Terrorism is conceived of by some as a crime, by others as a method, and by still others as an act of war. The paradoxical nature of terrorism complicates the establishment of a universally accepted definition of the term. A brief analysis of the book *The Secret Agent* by Joseph Conrad and the more recent movie *Hotel Rwanda* (depicting the despicable acts of terrorism that preceded the genocide in Rwanda) dramatically illustrate the complexities of defining terrorism.

Despite the definitional difficulties, there is no justification for terrorism. It is not defensible to argue that terrorism needs to be viewed from a political context and that the motivation of the actor and the sociological and cultural contexts in which the act occurs must be taken into consideration. Such a relativistic approach would legitimize terrorist acts via the claim that the end justifies the means. This simply does not comport with generally accepted principles of the rule of law.

Chapter 4 looks more closely at State-sponsored terrorism by analyzing *The Pianist*, a film directed by Roman Polanski based on a book by Wladyslaw Szpilman. This chapter decodes the legal principles of international humanitarian law illustrated dramatically in the narrative and cinematic representations of the life of a famous Polish pianist who recounts in his memoirs his horrifying experience in and out of the Warsaw Ghetto. Both the book and the movie shed light on the lack of effectiveness of unenforced international laws of war and international human rights laws in our global society. The chapter summarizes the personal history of Szpilman's ordeal; the historical basis for the Warsaw Ghetto uprising; the manner in which the film and book depict international humanitarian laws and international human rights laws being flagrantly violated by the Nazis during the Warsaw occupation, the Warsaw Ghetto, and the Warsaw uprisings; and the differences between the book and the film. This chapter examines the special role of music in the book and film and the role that art can play during catastrophic events to prevent further atrocities, assuage victims of horrific events, inspire the collective conscience of perpetrators, and protect victims from the reality of pain caused by war and the failure to enforce international laws of armed combat. Art can distance the victims from the reality of pain caused by the war and the violation of international laws of armed combat and human rights.

But can art offer a form of self-help remedy to the victims of massive violence and atrocities without offering retribution to the perpetrator or revenge to the victim? What is the power of art to transcend the ugliness and brutality of war, especially if the combatants and other actors refuse to play by the internationally accepted rules of war? Recognizing through past experience that art cannot prevent atrocities, this chapter reexamines art's power of effective communication, education, and edification. Is the widespread dissemination of information through artistic media about wartime brutality and futility able to constitute a long-term preventive or palliative measure against the further commission of genocide, war crimes, and human rights violations? International human rights violations and war crimes are being committed today; they are increasing in number and degree of atrocity despite the peace-loving nature of our global society. These crimes may be reduced by the interplay of traditional retributive justice and a newly proposed restorative justice. However, the international community should not treat the perpetrators with impunity. Instead, a new form of restorative justice is discussed that may not focus on retribution, but rather emphasizes the personhood of the victim through language and expression.

Part C of this book examines the subtle relationship between civil disobedience and terrorism. Chapter 5 provides a semiotic definition of the term *civil disobedience*, which like the term *terrorism* has been misapplied in recent years. The chapter reviews the history of civil disobedience in the United States and how it grew out of resistance and revolution. Basic tensions exist between the rights of resistance and national security and the origins of a constitutional protection of resistance. After the Revolutionary War, American leaders sought to dampen the prevailing "spirit of resistance" by giving the national government the power to suppress unlawful resistance.

The term *civil disobedience* is built on an oxymoron that reflects its positive and negative aspects. Some will even say that "civil disobedience" is semantically inaccurate because disobedience to the law cannot be "civil"! Civil disobedience is not the use of violence to compel the government to grant autonomy to a specific group. That is *rebellion* or *revolution*, with the aim of rebels seeking change by destroying the system. In contrast, Martin Luther King and other civil disobedients sought reform within the established order. The oxymoron reflects a basic duality in the term *civil disobedience* that denotes both obedience and disobedience of the law. Gandhi was a great proponent of violating laws in order to publicize a protest and bring pressure on the public or the government to accomplish purposes that had little to do with the law being breached.

Generally speaking, an act of civil disobedience must be nonviolent, open and visible, illegal, and performed for a moral purpose to protest an unjust law or to object to the status quo; it must also be done with the expectation of receiving punishment. Thus, there are both positive and negative connotations of the term *civil disobedience*, which is often associated with the term *terrorism*. But civil disobedience is clearly not terrorism although there are certain similarities between the two concepts. Both are associated with anarchy and chaos. Both are about protest. Terrorists and civil disobedients both have an overarching cause that they want to publicize by their symbolic acts. Terrorists and civil disobedients are both sometimes viewed as heroes. But unlike civil disobedience, terrorism works on the principle of fear.

The U.S. Constitution probably will not, and should not, protect nonviolent civil disobedience by exempting it from punishment because that would undermine the respect for the rule of law and erode the effectiveness of the very act of civil disobedience itself. The U.S. Constitution seeks to accommodate two conflicting values: (1) the need for the right to speak freely, to protest effectively, to organize, and to demonstrate; and (2) the need to maintain order so that other people's rights and the peace and security of the State will not be impaired. The State is obligated constitutionally to protect protestors who march peaceably as in the famous Selma march. However, civil disobedience (which is the act of breaking the law) is not protected by the constitutional right to dissent or right to free speech. The use of impermissible means of dissent is an act of civil disobedience done intentionally and for moral purposes, and the disobedient expects to be punished for the unlawful act irrespective of any noble motivation. Similarly, there are limitations on the right to free speech. Good motives do not excuse speech acts or actions that will injure some and diminish the rights of others.

In Chapter 6, the book delves more deeply into Martin Luther King's views on civil disobedience as expressed in the memorable *Letter from Birmingham Jail.* This text is one of the classics in the literature of civil disobedience along with Sophocles' *Antigone,* Thoreau's *Walden and Civil Disobedience,* Gandhi's writings, and Jean Anouilh's *Antigone.* King wrote this *Letter* on the margins of a newspaper from his prison cell after he was jailed on April 12, 1963. He was arrested for failing to obtain a parade permit from the Birmingham city commission and for disobeying a court order forbidding civil rights leaders from taking part in or encouraging demonstrations. The *Letter* ranks high among masterpieces of prison literature, like the philosophy of Gramsci and the poems of Verlaine. The *Letter* is a call to arms without violence, a plea for freedom, and a cry for communal brotherhood. King proclaims that man's failure to disobey an unjust law is as evil as resisting justice. These words rang true during the Nuremberg trials with the Nuremberg court holding that a soldier or officer is individually responsible for committing crimes during wartime, even if these crimes were ordered by a superior.

In this chapter I decode the *Letter* to penetrate the surface of the text and excavate its many rich and hidden allusions to important legal issues. King's readers are initially eight white moderate clergymen of different religious backgrounds. King's readership expands to include the public at large and anyone concerned about human rights. The *Letter* is an apology for the values of the Christian religion. King's *Letter* is designed to disturb, and it does so by engaging in linguistic gymnastics and by depolarizing obvious oppositions. The *Letter* resembles a legal brief where King presents arguments convincingly for and against immediate nonviolent direct action in order to protest racial discrimination and to enforce the right of equality. But unlike a good brief, King's *Letter* is contradictory and ambiguous—and purposely so. The semantic and stylistic dissonance he creates with words is designed to wrench conservative white moderates out of their political and legal indifference.

The *Letter* has biblical underpinnings, especially related to Martin Luther King's anti-law stance. King's *Letter* is also full of literary and philosophical references to Plato's *Allegory of the Cave,* Socrates, and Sophocles. King believes the eternal law and natural law will be fulfilled only when sinful separation of human beings in the act of segregation finally ends.

King's views on civil disobedience are complex and contradictory. Parts of his theory resemble the conservative views of Robert H. Bork while others resemble the more radical views of Ronald Dworkin. Basically, a close reading of the *Letter* reveals that King was ahead of his time. He replaced the conservative evangelical conception of a fundamentally evil human nature with the view of man as fundamentally good. He synthesized opposites and embraced a Christian existentialism advocating individual nonviolent direct action and a struggle for the goal of community.

Chapter 7 continues the theme of civil disobedience as represented in the play *Antigone* written by Sophocles in Athens in fifth century B.C. as compared to the more modern rendition by Jean Anouilh, which was written during the Nazi occupation of Paris. The character Antigone is the symbol of civil disobedience. She is the inspiration of resistance movements against tyranny and probably one of the first feminists who heroically resisted against the oppression of women and unjust laws. The study of this play in Chapter 7 reveals the differences between natural law and legal positivism as well as the effectiveness of civil disobedience for legal reform. The study focuses on the connection between civil disobedience, jurisprudence, and feminism in ancient and modern comparative legal systems as viewed from a postmodernist perspective.

The critics of natural law led the way toward the development of legal positivism. *Antigone* was the philosopher Hegel's favorite Greek drama; Hegel saw in the main character the representation of obedience to a higher order. Hegel's particular reading of Sophocles' *Antigone* focuses on the legality of Creon's harsh decrees that may be justified in order to preserve the authority of the State and the sanctity of its laws. Hegel was a statist who believed in preserving the *polis*, but he still extolled the virtues of the heroine Antigone, calling her the "noblest of figures that ever appeared on earth." For Hegel, Antigone's act of defiance was based not on personal desire, but on a belief that she had a higher duty to bury her brother. Burial of a family member was her God-given right that conflicted with Creon's law banning it. Antigone defies Creon's law and willingly accepts her cruel punishment to be buried alive in a cave with only enough food to prolong her agony. Creon stands for the principles of law and order, allegiance to the public order and to the State, and the superiority of men over women in a universe governed by gender difference.

Jean Anouilh was a French playwright known for his rebellious spirit. Anouilh's *Antigone* is based on but differs very much from Sophocles' Greek tragedy, which Anouilh knew by heart. Anouilh's play reflects the horrific events of World War II. He expressed his views cautiously because he lived in an atmosphere of censorship and repression. He participated in the theatre of revolt and expressed his ideas through the medium of the absurd. The play was performed in 1944 in German-occupied France. Existential philosophy was in the air, which is reflected in this play's tragic and comic tense interplay. Anouilh's play is a parody that attacks vice and folly by the use of satire and irony to mask the author's subversive message. The playwright is a French postmodernist who debunks the virtues of the tragic heroine, calls into question tragedy itself, and raises serious doubts about the effectiveness of civil disobedience for legal reform. Nevertheless, by Anouilh's recreation of the classical Greek tragedy, the modern play allowed the public at large in war-torn Europe to rethink the underlying issues of civil disobedience and its ability to influence real change in the French legal system that was intricately connected to its political environment.

Part D of the book focuses more on comparative women's human rights: women's right to freedom of speech, freedom of association, freedom to control their own bodies, and freedom from slavery. Women in many Middle Eastern countries are being denied the right to wear their clothing of choice, and Muslim women in Europe and Turkey are being forced to remove their headscarf (worn for religious reasons) in public institutions such as elementary schools and medical schools. Women in Iran have had their human rights systematically curtailed since the fall of the Shah in 1979. Women in China are discriminated against and subject to serious injury due to the one-child policy that has given rise to infanticide of girl babies and the trafficking of women into China.

Chapter 8 looks at the contradictory and paradoxical status of women's human rights in Iran today. The Iranian society and language reflect this paradox because words reportedly have double meanings that produce vagueness and intentional ambiguity, resulting in misunderstandings for some and advantages for others engaged in the fine art of hiding what they really mean to say. This linguistic deception is not unusual, especially for Iranian women who must behave one way publicly and another privately, even though society in the Islamist State has been forced to adopt a universalist moral code that militates against relativist ethics.

Human rights abuses are prevalent in Iran today with women suffering the most from this deplorable condition. The following serious human rights abuses exist in Iran and detrimentally impact women: summary executions; disappearances; widespread use of torture and other degrading treatment including rape; severe punishments including stoning to death and public flogging; harsh prison conditions; arbitrary arrests and detention; prolonged and incommunicado detention; impunity of government officials accused of misconduct in judicial proceedings; influence of conservative government clerics in the judiciary preventing citizens from due process or fair trials; governmental restriction of the freedom of religion; flagrant discrimination against religious minorities; governmental control over the selection of candidates for elections; governmental restriction of the work of human rights groups in Iran; domestic and public violence against women; increase in women and children runaways, prostitution and sex trafficking; and increased poverty in Iran where 29 percent of the families below the poverty line are single mothers.

Women's human rights and the role of women in Iranian society are tied up in a thick web of historical, political, cultural, economic, social, and legal factors, all of which work together in an intricate contextual system resembling a structural puzzle whose parts or elements can be identified and analyzed. Each of these elements is itself a sign system with complex underlying mechanisms. Each sign system plays a significant role in the development and continuation of human rights abuses of women in Iran. Classical structural analysis provides insights into surface and deep meanings. Semiotic analysis studies the signs of women's human rights that can reveal hidden, deeper structures unknown even to the women themselves. This semiotic study will examine various types of coded sign systems that, when decoded and interpreted contextually, reveal hidden realities about women's human rights in Iran. The analyst will attempt to determine how and to what extent basic human rights are being denied to women in Iran today and whether there is hope for more justice and gender equality in Iran in the future.

The first part of this study examines the historic and political contexts of women's human rights in Iran and the sign system of wearing women's Islamic garb known as the *hejab* or veil so as to uncover the meaning of the many different messages this act conveys. I discuss the significance of the French headscarf case and the Turkish headscarf case decided finally in the European Court of Human Rights. That court, based on pure semiotics, and in an almost unanimous decision denied women the right to wear a headscarf in public schools and universities.

Chapter 8 investigates various cultural manifestations of women's human rights abuses in Iran by studying the memoirs and films of four Iranian women. Azar Nafisi's best-selling memoir, *Reading Lolita in Tehran,* was written by an Iranian woman who is a literature professor who lived in Iran both before and after the Shah's fall. The second memoir is *Iran Awakening,* written by Shirin Ebadi, a Nobel Peace Prize winner and former Iranian female judge, who is currently a lawyer and a women's rights activist working within the Iranian system to change it. The powerful documentary film *Divorce Iranian Style* sheds light on the institution of marriage in Iran and the deficiencies of its family laws and legal system, especially for women seeking a divorce. The popular Iranian film *Two Women* juxtaposes one modern woman (allowed by her "liberal" husband to flourish in Iranian society) against another woman who is virtually enslaved by a tyrannical husband who denies her even the most basic human rights of freedom of movement. This film represents the paradoxes in Iranian society today. These contradictions and blatant human rights violations have resulted in a series of protests by the people of Iran who fear the abuse of power by the Guardian Council and the conservative clerics.

This chapter also investigates the Iranian family laws as a sign system that reflects the culture in Iran and the status of women's rights today in that country. The inadequacies of the Iranian legal system, which is caught up in a difficult relationship with Islam and with differing views of Koranic interpretation, negatively impact women. This chapter also examines some of the international human rights laws and instruments that, if enforced, do protect gender equality. Finally, this chapter will try to look at the future of women's rights in Iran.

Chapter 9 reveals a demographic crisis that rises to the level of *gendercide* in China where women are bought and sold, murdered, and made to disappear to comply with a governmental policy that coincides with a cultural phenomenon of male-child preference. To comply with the One-Child Policy instituted in 1979 and to ensure that the family has a coveted boy child, millions of people in China have committed sex-selective abortions, infanticide of their own baby girls, non-registration of the first or second infant in the family, and abandonment or sale of their own girls. Government officials have instituted forced abortions, forced sterilizations, and financial penalties for noncompliance with the One-Child Policy. There are more than one hundred million missing women in China today. Infant murder is caused by parents who want a son or by obstetricians who kill unauthorized babies by injection, strangulation, and other inhumane practices. Although these practices are illegal, successful prosecutions and sentencing of these perpetrators are rare. Accordingly, women are disappearing because of the social pressures of male-child preference, the zealous enforcement of the One-Child Policy by local government authorities, and the murderous responses to this policy undertaken by millions of ordinary parents in China who are desperate to have a son. The scarcity of women in China has produced a gender imbalance and an increase in prostitution and human trafficking. The traffic of women has many forms in China: the purchase of women for brides, the abduction and/or purchase of a male son, and the sale of unwanted female children.

Human trafficking is one of the most profitable big businesses in the world; it earns more than $7 billion annually. Trafficking is the purchase and sale of human beings for the purpose of exploitation of forced labor, such as sex work or participation in armed conflict. The trafficking of women and children in and to China is one of China's most serious human rights violations. The prevalence of sex trafficking in China and the disappearance of Chinese women are due to a deeply ingrained culture of women's inferiority that is reflected in Confucius' *Five Classics*. Lisa See's wonderful book, *Snow Flower and the Secret Fan*, vividly represents the plight of women in China in the nineteenth century, including the horrors and pains of forced foot binding that crippled women, and the utter isolation of the typical Chinese woman brought up in a patriarchal society.

Despite many international instruments regulating trafficking, and even Chinese domestic anti-trafficking laws, the business of sex trafficking and human trafficking is on the rise in China. Even the powerful American anti-trafficking law that has an international prong and extraterritorial reach cannot control the chronic discrimination against women in China and the development of its human trafficking industry. Corrupt local officials participate and exploit women through trafficking and prostitution, thus making it difficult to combat the trafficking industry there. This chapter discusses the interconnection of historic, legal, and cultural contexts resulting in the continued discrimination against women in Chinese society, including the increase in trafficking and the concomitant deplorable human rights violations committed in China.

Part E focuses on children's rights and the relationship between women and children. There is a serious need to protect children from the abuse and human rights violations now occurring all over the world. Children are forced to work in slave-like conditions because of poverty, greed, and the general devaluing of children in certain cultures. Human rights violations of children are exacerbated during wartime conditions, especially with the recent development of the practice of brutally forcing children to fight as soldiers. Child soldiering is a form of trafficking, a deplorable human rights violation, an international crime, and a contemporary form of slavery.

Chapter 10 focuses on the development of a culture of violence in many parts of the world, especially Africa, which has given rise to genocide, mass violence, and child soldiering. As described above, child soldiering is a variant of human trafficking that is one of the worst human rights violations as it rises to the level of slavery (a universal crime). The recruitment of a child (a person under age eighteen) for the purpose of participation in armed conflict is considered trafficking in persons.

Although child participation in armed conflict is not new, child soldiering today is a widespread phenomenon, prevalent particularly in developing countries where political, economic, and social instability are more commonplace and where approximately half the population consists of children. In 2000, it was estimated that thirteen million children were displaced as a result of warring conflicts all over the world. During the civil war in Sierra Leone, more than one million children were displaced, and twenty-five thousand children (some as young as eight) were abducted and forced to become members of armed groups. Currently, over three hundred thousand children are serving as child soldiers in fifty countries in every region of the world. These children are subjected daily to dehumanizing atrocities.

Children who are trafficked into child soldiering—girls as well as boys—are often abducted from their homes, tortured, brutally indoctrinated, forced to become intoxicated with mind-altering drugs, threatened with death or dismemberment if they do not fight, forced to return to their homes to witness or participate in the death or disfigurement of their own family members, required to kill friends who do not obey their commanders, and forced to watch the punishment of other child soldiers who attempt to escape. Some children who tried to escape have reportedly been boiled alive, and other child soldiers have been forced to eat the human flesh as part of their training. Girls are often raped, enslaved, and victimized by sexual violence on a daily basis. These children are drugged to make them fearless, empowered with small weapons, and indoctrinated brutally to commit atrocities.

Despite a proliferation of international human rights treaties, labor laws, and humanitarian laws that should provide children with special protection from this heinous form of abuse, the trafficking of children and their use as soldiers are increasing. Chapter 10 examines the relationship between human trafficking, slavery, and child soldiering, and analyzes the root causes of child soldiering. The international and domestic laws designed to protect children from this kind of abuse are also analyzed. Finally, this chapter examines two literary representations of child soldiering (Iweala's *Beasts of No Nation* and Kourouma's

Allah is Not Obliged) and the significant insights such representations can provide to the international community. I also propose some cultural and economic solutions to the global failure to implement the many legal instruments that should protect children from being abducted and used as child soldiers.

Part F studies the intricate relationship between semiotics and culture. Semiotics involves the decoding of cultural signs. Umberto Eco referred to semiotics as a "substitute for cultural anthropology." Signs exist in society, and each society has its own culture. Moreover, culture is one of the contexts that impacts the interpretation of texts. Sometimes we read, interpret, and understand laws, treaties, and texts in accordance with our own cultural traditions. If we are asked to interpret a foreign or ancient law or text, it is necessary to understand the cultural context in which this law is framed.

Chapter 11 delves into the Japanese culture, the Japanese people, and their views on copyright infringement, defamation, and sex trafficking as represented in the memoirs of a fictional geisha. This chapter delves into the geisha tradition, which is clearly a significant part of the Japanese culture and history. In it I explore some of the legal issues embedded in Arthur Golden's *Memoirs of a Geisha*. The geisha tradition has been alternately glorified by Japanese society and outlawed by Japanese law as a form of prostitution. The duality of the geisha as both artisan and courtesan is a leitmotif of Golden's famous and beautifully written novel. At its worst, the geisha tradition involves force, fraud, and deception, and the horrifying practice of selling one's own children into slavery for purposes of sexual exploitation.

In striving for historical accuracy, Golden obtained an intimate interview with a real geisha named Mineko Iwasaki, who consented to reveal to him valuable secrets about the closed geisha society. Using her narrative as source material, Golden wrote a fictional biography of a little girl named Chiyo-chan who is sold by her own father at the age of nine into debt bondage. Like many Japanese girls sold by their parents into forced prostitution and slavery, Chiyo-chan endures a harsh indoctrination and eventually becomes a famous geisha known as Nitta Sayuri. The essence of the novel is the transformation of Chiyo-chan into Nitta Sayuri.

The poetic, fairy-tale quality of Golden's prose and his unusual narrative style made the novel a literary and financial success upon its publication in 1997. In 2001, however, Mineko Iwasaki shocked the literary world by filing a lawsuit against Golden and his publishers in New York under Japanese and New York law, claiming breach of contract, quantum meruit, copyright infringement, unjust enrichment, defamation of character, and violation of her rights to privacy and publicity. It seems that Iwasaki became outraged by the discrepancies between her own life and that of Golden's purportedly fictional geisha. This chapter asks—and seeks to answer—two questions: First, is the geisha tradition as described by Golden a variant of sex trafficking and sexual slavery, which, despite possible cultural justifications, should be abolished by law? Second, did Iwasaki's lawsuit have any merit?

To answer these questions, I proceed in accordance with structuralist and post-structuralist literary critical methods by looking first at the *text* itself and then its *context*, *subtext*, and *post-text* in order to explain the plaintiff's *pre-text* for suing. I analyze the narrative structures and style of the text; the legal and historic context of the novel (i.e., Japanese laws on prostitution and on protection of the geisha); the legal issues hidden in the subtext, which include sex trafficking, feminist legal theory, and the role of cultural relativism as a justification for the geisha tradition; the *post-text*, which are the merits (if any) of Iwasaki's legal claims in the Complaint she filed four years after the publication of the fictional biography; and finally, the big issue, the *pre-text*, or why the real geisha sued Golden and his publishers for copyright infringement. In view of the famous Hemingway copyright case involving taped interviews, the geisha had very little chance of success in her suit.

Chapter 12 addresses the impact of culture on the semiotics of treaty interpretation. Using hermeneutics, semiotics, and reader-response theory, I look closely at *how* the Chinese read and misread the Berne Convention to explain why they pirate intellectual property.

Yuri Lotman was the great Russian formalist who understood the importance of culture and its relationship to semiotics. He tried to define a typology of cultures across time, understanding that there is a multiplicity of codes in any given culture, as well as a multiplicity of valid interpretations. He led the way to an acceptance of a multiplicity of interpretations based on cultural differences and codes.

China's rampant piracy of American intellectual property costs the United States billions of dollars a year. The causes and effects of intellectual property piracy are intricately connected to—and affected by—many factors, including the economy of the country in which the piracy is committed, the political history and ideology of the pirating nation, the culture of the people engaged in the piracy, and the adequacy of the legal system to enforce domestic and international intellectual property laws. I examine the effect of these interrelated factors on China's interpretation of the Berne Convention, an international treaty designed to protect intellectual property rights of authors and artists. A nation's possible responses to an international treaty include its recognition of and decision to adhere to the treaty, its implementation of domestic laws in compliance with the international treaty, and its success or failure to enforce these domestic and international laws. These responses are also signs indicating the manner in which a nation reads, interprets, and possibly misreads the legal discourse of an international treaty.

The average Chinese reader understands the Berne Convention against a backdrop of communist ideology that overdetermines their interpretation of the Berne Convention. The ownership of private property and of intellectual property are contrary to the fundamental principles of communist ideology in which the State owns property. Chinese readers read the treaty in its own idiom and interpret the legal discourse of the Berne Convention in a manner inconsistent with the spirit and intent of the treaty.

In this chapter, I review the history and development of intellectual property protection; the advantages and disadvantages of protecting creative works, inventions, and names; the history of American piracy of intellectual property (including explaining why the United States did not sign the Berne Convention for 103 years after it was enacted); the history of copyright law itself, and different copyright theories associated with the Berne Convention (natural rights, economic rights, moral rights, agency, privacy, personality rights, and market theories).

Finally, I uncover the clashes of culture, explaining the difference between the Chinese and American interpretation of and responses to the Berne Convention. These responses enable us to analyze *how* the United States reads the Berne Convention and why the Chinese read it differently. A study of the Chinese Authorship Right Law and its terminology sheds light on the Chinese understanding of the basic concept of copyright. The Chinese Computer Software Protection Regulations appear to address every mode of piratical activity, but for various reasons which I discuss, as well as the cultural and political overdetermination of this law that implicitly places power in the hands of State agencies, this law has failed to protect against piracy of computer software.

The Chinese perception of copyright protection is summed up in an ancient Chinese proverb: "To steal a book is an elegant offense." This metaphoric oxymoron crystallizes the concept that the Chinese read and interpret the Berne Convention in their own idiom and in accordance with their own cultural traditions. Unfortunately, this behavior results in the loss of millions of dollars to businesspeople dealing with the sale of goods in China.

I predict that the Chinese will stop pirating when they develop their own intellectual property and start to fear the piracy of their own protected works. This is happening already, as China's patent office now leads the world in patent applications, more than eight hundred thousand of which were filed in 2008.[2] Chinese firms are increasingly filing invention patents that are rigorously scrutinized and receive twenty years of protection (as in the West). This year Chinese companies are going to surpass foreign ones in receiving invention patents in China. The rush for patent protection by the Chinese in China has resulted in an increase in disputes. "Since 2006 more patent lawsuits have been filed in China than anywhere else, even litigious America."[3] The Chinese are also seeking patents abroad. This is a sign that China plans to protect its own technology, especially when China exports it to developed countries. It is common knowledge that countries developing intellectual property eventually enforce laws protecting it as well. Therefore, I believe that as China continues to develop its own

2. *Chinese Companies are Enforcing Patents against Foreign Firms*, The Economist 68 (2009).

3. *Id.*

intellectual property, China's piracy will decrease, as did the piracy of European works and inventions by the United States once the United States joined the Berne Convention and needed protection of its own intellectual property.

The film, *Flash of Genius*, uncovers the pain and suffering of an American inventor who patents his windshield wiper invention and then experiences the piracy of his invention by a big American manufacturing car company whom he seeks successfully to sue on principle alone. His ordeal lasts more than ten years, but he wins in the end. The film seems to point in the direction of an implicit adoption by the United States of moral rights principles and a return to the European doctrine of the romantic author or the mad scientist whose ambitious and noble endeavors need incentivization and recognition as well as financial remuneration. The legal community needs to engage in continued efforts to educate the people in foreign countries and in our own country about international intellectual property laws and to enforce the laws in order to realign deep-rooted cultural practices that determine a nation's interpretation of—and responses to—a widely accepted international treaty such as the Berne Convention.

2. LEGAL SEMIOTICS*

I. INTRODUCTION

Semiotics is the science of signs.[1] As mysterious as the word may seem,[2] *semiotics* has become a household term among interpreters of art, music, literature, and now, the law.[3] Although sign theory is predominantly a European phenomenon,

---

* The original version of this chapter appeared in Volume 5 of the CARDOZO ARTS & ENTERTAINMENT LAW JOURNAL 89–156 (1986), but it has been revised and updated. For their willingness to read and comment on this study, I would like to thank Professor Lewis Kornhauser of the New York University School of Law; Bernard Jackson, Professor of Law at the University of Kent at Canterbury; and Paul Robertshaw, Assistant Dean of the Faculty of Law at University College, Cardiff. Their suggestions were invaluable to me.

1. Any attempt at defining semiotics is at best a preliminary and partial effort. Eco proposed an explanation of semiotics as *"the discipline studying everything which can be used in order to lie."* UMBERTO ECO, A THEORY OF SEMIOTICS 7 (1976). Later Eco offered Saussure's definition of semiotics: *"une science qui étudie, la vie des signes au sein de la vie sociale." Id.* at 14 (quoting Saussure) ("a science that studies signs as they function in society"). For a discussion of Saussure's sign theory, *see infra* text accompanying notes 120–31. Eco is more satisfied with Peirce's definition: "*[S]emiotic* . . . the doctrine of the essential nature and fundamental varieties of possible semiosis . . . " CHARLES SANDERS PEIRCE, COLLECTED PAPERS 5:488 (Charles Hartshorne & Paul Weiss eds., 1958). By semiosis, Peirce means an action involving "a cooperation of *three* subjects, such as a sign, its object, and its interpretant . . . " *Id.* at 5:484. For a discussion of Peirce's semiotic and the role of the interpretant, *see infra* text accompanying notes 79–85.

2. Confusion surrounding the term *semiotics* is legendary. For Peirce the term was *semiotic* in the singular; for Saussure it was *sémiologie*. Americans now use semiotics in the plural, while the French have adopted the term in the singular, *la sémiotique. See* Thomas A. Sebeok, *The Semiotic Web: A Chronical of Prejudices*, 2 BULL. OF LITERARY SEMIOTICS 1, 8–15 (1976) (discussion of the terminological confusion that plagues the field of semiotics). This is due in part to the breadth of the subject matter and the subdivision of the field into syntactics, semantics, and pragmatics. According to Eco, it was resolved at the International Association of Semiotics that the term *semiotics* should be used as a translation of *semiology. Id.* at 10 (citing Eco). Eco also reported in a humorous vein that until a few years ago, Anglo-Saxons said *semiotics* and Continentals *semiology*. In more recent times however, Anglo-Saxons have come to prefer *semiology*, and Continentals have adopted *semiotics* after the unanimous exclusion of *semeiotic, semiotic, semeiology, sematology*, and other lexical monstrosities. *Id.; see also* UMBERTO ECO, LA STRUCTURE ABSENTE 1 (1972) for a discussion of the difference in meaning between *semiotics*, the term adopted by the American school under the influence of Peirce, and *semiology*, coined by Saussure and adopted primarily by the French and European scholars.

3. Eco, *supra* note 1, at 9–13.

semiotics has developed internationally[4] especially in the field of literature. Curiously, despite the nexus among literature, law, and interpretive theories, only a handful of legal scholars have consciously adopted the principles of sign theory.[5] And yet, without knowing it, lawyers constantly make use of semiotics in their everyday legal activities.[6] Reading, writing, interpreting documents and cases, negotiating, interviewing, and selecting jurors are merely a few of the lawyerly tasks that involve the fundamental elements of semiotics: an exchange between two or more speakers through the medium of coded language.[7]

Legal practice is a general exercise in interpretation.[8] Whenever lawyers attempt to determine the meaning of a verbal exchange, they face the semiotic task of unlocking a key to a legal code. To complete the task in a valid manner, the lawyers must know how to read and interpret the words or "signs" of the code that are governed by a particular convention.[9] This decoding process, better known as interpretation,[10] is lawyer's work that constitutes the very essence of

---

4. *See* Sebeok, *supra* note 2, at 2–8 for a brief history and development of the international scope of semiotics; Eco, *supra* note 1, at 5–16; Susan W. Tiefenbrun, *The State of Literary Semiotics: 1983*, 51 SEMIOTICA 7 (1984) (containing an extensive bibliography of semiotic studies undertaken in the field of literary theory and practice); *see also* SUSAN W. TIEFENBRUN, SIGNS OF THE HIDDEN: SEMIOTIC STUDIES (1980) (introduction to semiotic theory and its application to literary texts of the seventeenth century); *see also* Charles Pearson, *Beyond Peirce: The New Science of Semiotics and the Semiotics of Law*, 21 INT'L J. SEMIOT. LAW 247 (2008).

5. *See infra* text accompanying notes 94–119, 132–39, 175–79, 186–90, 251–86, 314–34. Recently a small number of legal scholars have been applying semiotics in the analysis of legal doctrine, such as in SEMIOTICS AND LEGISLATION: JURISPRUDENTIAL, INSTITUTIONAL AND SOCIOLOGICAL PERSPECTIVES, (Hannecke Van Schooten ed., 1991), in which Schooten states in the Preface, "Language is central to the nature of law. For that reason, law may be regarded as a semiotic system". *Id.* at 1. *See* ROBERTA KEVELSON, THE EYES OF JUSTICE: SEVENTH ROUND TABLE IN LAW AND SEMIOTICS (1994); International Journal for the Semiotics of Law;NEW APPROACHES TO SEMIOTICS AND THE HUMAN SCIENCES: ESSAYS IN HONOR OF ROBERTA KEVELSON (William Pencak & J. Ralph Lindgren eds., 1998); Barton Beebe, *The Semiotic Analysis of Trademark Law*, 51 UCLA L. REV. 621 (2003); Llewelyn Gibbons, *Semiotics of the Scandalous and the Immoral and the Disparaging: Section 2(A) Trademark Law After Lawrence v. Texas*, 9 MARQ. INTELL. PROP. L. REV. 187 (2005) (viewing trademark law through the lens of semiotics); Sonia K. Katyal, *Semiotic Disobedience*, 84 WASH. U. L.R. 489 (2006) (contrasting the notion of semiotic democracy and semiotic disobedience and applying the theory of semiotics to intellectual property); Douglas J. Goodman, *Approaches to Law and Popular Culture*, 31 LAW & SOC. INQUIRY 757 (2006) (applying a semiotic approach to study the proliferation of diverse meanings of law found in popular culture).

6. *See infra* text accompanying notes 48–59.

7. *See infra* text accompanying notes 40–47.

8. *See generally* Ronald Dworkin, *Law as Interpretation*, 60 TEX. L. REV. 527 (1982).

9. *See infra* text accompanying notes 90–91.

10. BERNARD S. JACKSON, SEMIOTICS AND LEGAL THEORY 19–21 (1985). Jackson draws a distinction between decoding and interpretation.

semiotics. If the lawyer's goal is to communicate information persuasively and to defend a certain interpretation contained in legal discourse, he will certainly benefit from a deeper understanding of semiotic theory.

This chapter explores the basic elements of semiotics, the role that sign theory has played in the law, and the potential use of the semiotic method yet untapped by the legal community. In Part I, I shall broadly define *semiotics,*[11] propose a definition of *legal semiotics,*[12] and discuss some of its frequent uses in everyday legal practice.[13] In Part II, I shall trace the history and development of semiotics as it grew out of the varied disciplines of medicine,[14] philosophy,[15] linguistics,[16] anthropology,[17] and literature.[18] A goal of this chapter is to determine the extent to which these disciplines have made specific contributions to the field of semiotics and the manner in which they have been applied to the law.

In Part II(B), which provides an overview of the development of semiotics in philosophy, I will sketch the basic principles of sign theory and the sign classification system proposed by Charles Sanders Peirce,[19] whose theories have influenced the legal academic community,[20] especially in the development of legal realism.[21]

Like philosophy, linguistics is a major branch of semiotics. Linguistics has undisputedly influenced the perceptions, creations, and communication skills of the legal world.[22] In Part II(C), I will discuss the semiotic theories of certain key figures in linguistics,[23] especially Ferdinand De Saussure, the father of modern linguistics, including his view of the scope of semiotics and its relation to the development of legal positivist theory.[24]

In the field of anthropology, which is discussed briefly in Part II (D), Claude Levi-Strauss[25] adopted Saussure's semiotic principles and developed a structural

---

11. *See infra* text accompanying notes 37–39.

12. *See infra* text accompanying notes 40–47.

13. *See infra* text accompanying notes 48–59.

14. *See infra* text accompanying note 68.

15. *See infra* text accompanying notes 69–119.

16. *See infra* text accompanying notes 120–73.

17. *See infra* text accompanying notes 174–79.

18. *See infra* text accompanying notes 180–309.

19. *See infra* text accompanying notes 79–93.

20. *See infra* text accompanying notes 94–119.

21. For a discussion of Peirce's role in the development of legal realism, *see infra* text accompanying notes 107–19.

22. *See infra* text accompanying notes 145–61.

23. *See, e.g.*, the linguistic theories proposed by: Charles Morris, *infra* text accompanying notes 162–66; Eric Buyssens, *infra* text accompanying notes 167–68; Louis Hjelmslev, *infra* text accompanying notes 169–71; and the Soviet semioticians, *infra* text accompanying notes 172–73.

24. *See infra* text accompanying notes 120–39.

25. *See infra* text accompanying notes 174–76.

method that has been successfully applied to various aspects of the legal process by scholars mainly abroad.[26]

Semiotics has seen its most significant impact in the area of literary criticism. Through the fertile connection of literature and the law, the legal community has become aware of the potential of semiotics. In Part II(E), I will trace the sources of semiotics in the different schools of literary theory ranging from the Russian formalists to the post-structuralists and comment on their specific contributions to legal interpretive theory. I will explore in some detail the work of Roman Jakobson,[27] a member of the Prague Schoo1,[28] and his catalytic description of the six constituent factors of a speech event.[29] Jakobson is a major contributor to semiotics and to communication theory in general, and his work has significant implications for legal interpretive practice. Similarly, the literary schools of new criticism,[30] structuralism,[31] and post-structuralism[32] have each made a mark on American and European legal scholarship, especially in the development of the critical legal studies movement.[33] I intend to isolate and describe the specific semiotic influence of these literary schools on the law and on the critical legal studies movement in particular. I will also discuss the semiotic theories of three structuralists who have played an important role in the development of semiotics abroad and whose works will continue to influence legal semiotics in the United States in the future: Algirdas Greimas,[34] Tzvetan Todorov,[35] and Roland Barthes.[36]

---

26. *E.g.*, André-Jean Arnaud, *Structuralisme et Droit*, 13 ARCHIV. DE PHILOS. DU DROIT 283 (1968).

27. *See infra* text accompanying notes 196–203.

28. *See infra* text accompanying notes 191–95.

29. *See infra* text accompanying notes 202–03.

30. *See infra* text accompanying notes 204–08.

31. *See infra* text accompanying notes 246–96.

32. The post-structuralist movement (otherwise termed *deconstructionism*) is associated with Derrida, Foucault, and others such as Lacan, whose theories are discussed. *See infra* text accompanying notes 297–313.

33. *See infra* text accompanying notes 314–34.

34. Greimasian narrative structures have been applied to the law and analyzed in detail by Bernard Jackson in *Semiotics and Legal Theory*. JACKSON, *supra* note 10, at 31–143. *See infra* text accompanying notes 186–90 for a brief discussion of Greimasian methodology.

35. Todorov's theory of narrative grammar and his other related theories have been influential in the area of literary interpretation as it is practiced in the United States. His theories are applicable to the analysis of legal discourse. *See infra* text accompanying notes 286–91. Robin West, *Jurisprudence as Narrative: An Aesthetic Analysis of Modern Legal Theory*, 60 N.Y.U. L. REV. 145 (1985) (attempting to apply Northrup Frye's literary theories to the law on the assumption that law, itself, is a narrative. If we accept her assumption, then Todorov's theories on the grammar of narrative become eminently useful to the legal community).

36. Roland Barthes' little book, *Éléments de Sémiologie*, which appeared originally in 1964 as an article in the influential journal *Communications*, was the gunshot that set the

Semiotics is only at the infant stage in its adoption by the legal community as a workable theory and method. Therefore, I will undertake as a major goal the suggestion of future applications of semiotics to the law.

A. Definition of Semiotics

What is semiotics? Derived from the Greek word *semion* or sign, semiotics is the scientific study of communication and signification. It has been defined as "the exchange of any messages whatever and of the systems of signs which underlie them."[37] Words, the basic tools of communication, are at best mere representations of reality, signs of the thing itself, and mediators between the perception and verbal expression of an event. Signs—be they words, gestures, or the dots and dashes of Morse Code—are the means by which an exchange of information takes place.

Exchange, or the process of communication, is characterized by mediation. Signs, which can do no more than mediate between the perception and expression of an event, lead ineluctably to distortion. The distortion of an observed reality might occur during the communication process due to memory lapses, variations in the expressive competency of speakers reporting the observed event, perceptual interference, lying, or a speaker's failure to properly interpret the observed reality. As words are nothing more than signs that mediate between the observed event and our expression of that event, we can conclude that the fundamental linguistic basis of communication is mediation itself. Because mediation engenders distortion, it is easy to understand why meaningful communication is difficult to achieve. Semiotics is intricately bound up in culture, and semioticians consider all cultural processes as processes of communication. A word or gesture may have one meaning in one culture but a different meaning in another. This further complicates the goal of communication and interpretation of meaning. The fundamental mediational property of language allows speakers to mask their intentions by the mere manipulation of words possessing the potential for multiple meanings, metaphoric expansion,[38] and ambiguity. Because signs are indirect and intermediary, language is fraught with uncertainties inviting and

---

literary world off on a major quest for signs and their various manifestations in literary works. For a discussion of Barthesian semiotics and the law, *see infra* text accompanying notes 292–96.

37. Thomas A. Sebeok, *Semiotics: A Survey of the State of the Art*, 12 Current Trends in Linguistics 211 (1974).

38. *See* Eco, *supra* note 1, at 8, 26–28, 66 for a discussion of the role of culture in semiotics. *See also* Lawrence Rosen, Law as Culture: An Invitation (2006); Clifford Geertz, *Application of Cultural Analysis to the Law, in* Local Knowledge 182 (1983) ("The creation of legal meaning takes place always through an essentially cultural medium"). *See infra* text accompanying notes 140–44 for a discussion of the incidence of metaphor in legal discourse, and in particular, Paul Robertshaw's study of the use of metaphor in a British case. *See infra* text accompanying notes 269–73.

necessitating interpretation. With its rich history steeped in linguistics, the theory of knowledge,[39] and literary interpretive techniques, semiotics can provide the tools for more defensible interpretations of sign systems based on mediation.

B. Definition of Legal Semiotics

The semiotics of law is a specialized study of sign systems underlying legal informational exchanges.[40] Law, like literature, culture, art, music, mathematics, Morse Code, or even traffic signs, is a communication system composed of elements called *signs* (or more familiarly *words*) that convey a coded message.[41]

A legal code is a language made up of signs and sign relationships governed by convention. There are many codes in the law, and the receiver of the coded message will understand its signs only if she is privy to the conventions of that particular code. The lawyer's attempt to understand the signs of a code is called interpretation, a process that is undertaken to resolve the problems of distortion and masked intentions created by the nature of language itself.[42]

Interpretation (known in semiotic terms as decoding) is the systematic process of finding keys to hidden codes that unlock the doors to meaning. Interpretation is a major part of the legal process because of the volume and complexity of its codes and because of the indirect nature of legal language that, like ordinary language, merely represents reality through the mediation of words. Mediation, then, is a fundamental linguistic property of the law, which is explored in semiotics.

The semiotics of law would attempt to identify, classify, and describe in a systematic fashion—and in standardized language—modes of signification present in legal discourse that give rise to interpretation.[43] But the semiotics of law is still in the process of formation.[44] Legal semiotics has been undertaken

---

39. For a study of the philosophical sources of semiotics, *see infra* text accompanying notes 69–78.

40. *See supra* text accompanying note 7. This definition is adapted from Sebeok's basic definition of semiotics. Sebeok, *supra* note 37, at 211.

41. *See* Eco, *supra* note 1, at 48–150 (detailed discussion of a theory of codes). "[C]odes provide the rules which *generate* signs as concrete occurrences in communicative intercourse." *Id.* at 49.

42. Other sources of distortion are discussed in the context of evidentiary theory. *See infra* text accompanying notes 52–53.

43. Jonathan Culler, The Pursuit of Signs: Semiotics, Literature, Deconstruction 12 (1981) (definition adapted from Culler).

44. *"La sémiotique du langage du droit est seulement en train de se former."* Georges Kalinowski, Introduction à la Logique Juridique: Éléments de Sémiotique Juridique, Logique des Normes et Logique Juridique 53 (1965) ("Legal semiotics is only in the process of formation.").

abroad only by a very courageous few[45] who have studied the language of the law and lawyers[46] as a system of communication. Legal semiotics is at the infant stage, but I predict on the basis of its rapid development in the field of literature[47] that the law will soon actively adopt the principles and methods of semiotics.

C. The Role of Semiotics in the Legal Process

Even though most lawyers are not consciously aware of the fundamentals of sign theory, semiotics does play an important but implicit role in many aspects of the legal system. In the legal academic community, the use of semiotics is more explicit. Legal hermeneutics[48] has been influenced by semiotic theory on an international scale.[49] The development of two major theories of legal interpretation—positivism and realism—has a direct parallel in the different semiotic approaches of Saussure and Peirce, respectively.[50] The critical legal studies movement adopted the semiotic theories that grew out of structuralism and post-structuralism.[51]

In legal practice, semiotics plays an active role in the courtroom. Juror selection, as seen through a semiotic lens, is a process by which a litigator reads the signs of prospective jurors: their words, gestures, verbal, and nonverbal communication acts. Using semiotic skills, the litigator determines whether the juror will work for or against the client. Moreover, semiotic principles of communication guide the use of interpreters in the courtroom in cases involving international law and speakers from different linguistic systems.

---

45. J. Rey, L'Essai sur la structure logique du code civil français (structure of the language of the French Civil Code examined from a semiotic perspective), *cited in* Kalinowski, *supra* note 44, at 53; *see also* André-Jean Arnaud, Essai d'analyse structurale du Code Civil Français (1973).

46. *See, e.g.*, B. Wroblewski, Jezyk Prawny I prawniczy (Language of the Law and of Lawyers), *cited in* Kalinowski, *supra* note 44, at 53; J. Wroblewski, Zagadnienia teorii interpretacji prawa ludowego (Problems of the Theory of Interpretation of Popular Law), *cited in* Kalinowski, *supra* note 44, at 53 (European scholarly studies investigating the language of the law and lawyers).

47. *See infra* text accompanying notes 180–311 for a discussion of semiotics and literature.

48. *See infra* note 119 for a discussion of legal hermeneutics and the role that semiotics played in the work of Francis Lieber.

49. Among the primary contributors to the field of legal hermeneutics are: Edward Beal, Cardinal Rules of Legal Interpretation (2d ed. 1908); R. Ross, The Law of Discovery (1912); Francois Gény, Méthode d'Interprétation et Sources en Droit Privé Positif (1899) (Jaro Mayda trans., 1963); Hans Georg Gadamer, Wahreit Une Methode (1960); Emilio Betti, Le Categorie Civilistiche Dell'Interpretazione (1948); *see also* Francis Lieber, Legal and Political Hermeneutics (3d ed. 1880).

50. *See infra* text accompanying notes 107–19 for a discussion of legal realism and the influence of Peirce. In contrast, legal positivism, discussed *infra* at text accompanying notes 224–45, has been allied with the theories of Saussure.

51. *See infra* text accompanying notes 314–34.

Semiotics directs the use and misuse of controversial terms in the general practice of the law. The differences between the legal, medical, and lay definitions of *death* or *right to life* are phenomena rooted in the semiotics of code theory. Another important practical result of the application of semiotics to the law is the widespread use of computer systems such as Lexis and Westlaw that have revolutionized legal research. The simple fact is that semiotics is a body of knowlwedge that has and will continue to play a quiet but major part in the everyday affairs of the law.

1. Semiotics and Evidentiary Theory Evidentiary theory and hearsay rules are founded on the semiotic principle of mediation. In a seminal study on the derivation of hearsay objections, Professor Laurence Tribe has described the process by which information is communicated as a triangle whose two main legs are perception and expression.[52] When a witness perceives an event or hears an utterance, the witness develops a mind picture of that objective reality that is then relayed to a receiver (the jury) by means of the witness' own language. Distortion of this objective reality can result from ambiguity, insincerity, erroneous memory, or faulty perception. The receiver of the information (the juror) must decode the message sent by the witness in order to arrive at as accurate a reconstruction of the reality as words will allow.

The nature of this communication is indirect, and the distortion level increases as the link between the perception of the reality and its expression is weakened by mediation. When the linkage between the objective reality and the juror is further weakened by hearsay, distortion increases. The semiotic principle of mediation, which is the primary cause of informational distortion, constitutes the basis of hearsay objections.

2. Sign Theory and the Law The words with which we give testimony, draft documents, negotiate deals, interview clients, and interpret legal texts are mere signs—only indirect expressions of a reality at least one step removed from the thing itself. Therefore, speakers and listeners in a legal context are constantly engaged in a kind of informal interpretation process that can be described as semiotic analysis. Interpretation enables the parties to decode the messages and understand the explicit or implicit signs embedded in the legal discourse that confronts them and produces confusion.

An explicit sign is an easy sign to read and to understand because a one-to-one correspondence exists between the word and the reality the word is designed to represent. The letters *t-r-e-e*, called a signifier, mean tree and not dog, and there is a conventional agreement about what the coded word *tree* means. The conventional agreement of the meaning is called the *signified*. The word *tree* is coded because its reality or referent is communicated by means of a fundamentally

52. Laurence Tribe, *Triangulatory Hearsay*, 87 HARV. L. REV. 957, 959 (1974).

arbitrary[53] sign whose meaning is determined by convention alone. The sign *tree* belongs to a field of words—types of trees—of which the term *tree* is the abstraction and the types its variants.[54] This field of words is called the *code*, or more precisely the *metaphoric code*, whose sign is the substitute for the reality the speaker intends to communicate. When I say *tree*, all of us know more or less what a tree is and communication is simple, unambiguous, and free from multiplicity of meanings necessitating interpretation. In other words, the sign is explicit. However, if the convention of the code *tree* is not understood, or if one speaker has in mind a spruce while the other is thinking of an elm, the intended communication of meaning will not take place.

The problem in law is that some words look like they are explicit signs governed by universally accepted convention but, in fact, they are false friends—words governed by a hidden code known only to the initiated. A good example of this type of explicit sign is the layman's definition of a sale in the ordinary course of business, which turns out to be otherwise for lawyers following the conventions of either the Uniform Commercial Code or the Internal Revenue Code.

Injustice can result from the failure to recognize a false friend or deceptive explicit sign. A case taken from the commercial law context will serve as an illustration. A buyer of sand paid for his goods, but left them at the premises of the seller, who subsequently defaulted on a loan from a bank that had a security interest in the seller's inventory.[55] To protect his purchased property, the buyer actually placed signs on the sandpiles saying they were the property of Martin Marietta Aggregates. Despite the explicitness of this sign (intended as an identification of ownership), the bank took over the seller's premises and sold the sand. According to the Uniform Commercial Code § 2-501(b), identification requires designation

---

53. *See infra* text accompanying notes 123–24 for the meaning of an *arbitrary sign* as elaborated by Saussure.

54. Structuralism involves the study of invariants and variants. The invariant is an abstraction, called a *structure*; the variants are the concrete and variable manifestations in the text of the abstraction that is itself invisible. The structuralist, then, is constantly trying to determine how one or another form of the invariant structure is manifested, and how this individual manifestation fits into the pattern of the whole. Structuralists analyze textual variants of an abstract and hidden structure to determine (1) the relation of that particular variant to the whole picture or the system of the text, and (2) the specific quality of that variant which makes it different from the other variants of the structure. A structural analysis can be undertaken on different levels of the text, such as on segments of the text that are smaller than a sentence and suprasegmental portions analyzing blocks of discourse. *See* SUSAN W. TIEFENBRUN, A STRUCTURAL STYLISTIC ANALYSIS OF LA PRINCESSE DE CLÈVES (1976) (example of a structural analysis of literature that investigates structures within and beyond the sentence of a classical French novel). *Compare* Susan W. Tiefenbrun, *Mathurin, Regnier's Macette: A Semiotic Study in Satire*, 13 SEMIOTICA 131 (1975) for a more semiotically oriented approach to structural and stylistic analysis of a shorter literary segment (*i.e.*, a poem).

55. Martin Marietta Corp. v. New Jersey Nat'l Bank, 505 F. Supp. 946 (D.N.J. 1981).

by the seller not the buyer. Because the buyer in this instance was not privy to the conventions of the Uniform Commercial Code and its own sign system, the buyer's sign had little if any significance in a court of law.

When the correspondence between the word and the reality is either not clear or not limited to one immediately apparent meaning, the sign is implicit. A 1984 creche case[56] is an example of the multiplicity of meaning created by the use of an implicit sign. In that case the court debated whether the creche, which is an iconical sign[57] customarily displayed around Christmas time, constituted a religious symbol as opposed to a sign of winter festivity enjoyed by all and not limited to a specific religious group.[58] Without expressly acknowledging the fundamentals of semiotic theory, the court in its discussion of the distinction between sign and symbol was actually adopting a semiotic argument and contributing to a major debate that continues unresolved among Peircean and Saussurean semioticians today.[59]

In the course of this brief attempt in Part I to define semiotics and legal semiotics, I have shown that semiotics and sign theory play a significant role (if not consciously than at least indirectly) in the everyday practice of the law that involves verbal exchanges mediated by signs. Semiotics plays a particularly vital role in the lawyer's task of interpretation. Here a more conscious application of semiotic theory has been attempted by legal scholars whose work will be examined in Part II.

II. SOURCES OF SEMIOTICS

How did semiotics develop? At the turn of the twentieth century, Charles Sanders Peirce and Ferdinand De Saussure, two scholars in different fields of philosophy and linguistics, were investigating the elements of meaning or what is referred to as *signification*. Peirce, who considered semiotics a branch of logic, studied

---

56. Lynch v. Donnelly, 465 U.S. 668 (1984).

57. *See infra* text accompanying notes 89–91 for a discussion of icons, indices, and symbols as elaborated by Peirce.

58. *Lynch*, *supra* note 56, at 685–86. In his dissent, Justice Brennan spoke the language of semiotics when he drew attention to the motivation of the sign, the creche. *Id.* at 708–13 (Brennan, J., dissenting). It is precisely because the creche here is not an arbitrary but a motivated sign that it should be considered as a symbol in Saussurean terms. A creche is tied to the concept of religion by its contiguous relation to the Christ figure, which symbolizes Christianity. Justice Brennan in dissent said that to label the creche a secular element of Christmas is a corruption of the very concept of religion and would be tantamount to state support of religion. *Id.* at 725–26 (Brennan, J., dissenting).

59. *See infra* text accompanying notes 123–24 for a discussion of the contrast between Peirce's definition of the symbol and Saussure's more radical distinction between sign and symbol based on the notion of the arbitrariness of the sign.

legisigns or signs of the law as a special category of semiotics.[60] Saussure viewed *semiology*[61] as an all-encompassing science that would someday include linguistics, psychology, and anthropology.[62] Saussure did not specifically investigate signs of the law, but we can assume that he considered legal language (like literature, art, music, and dance) a complex variant of ordinary language.[63]

Semiotics is vast in scope.[64] Umberto Eco has proposed a list of the many areas of investigation undertaken in the name of semiotics: zoosemiotics, olfactory signs, tactile communication, codes of taste, paralinguistics, medical semiotics, kinesics and proxemics, musical codes, formalized languages, written language, unknown alphabets and secret codes, natural languages, visual communication, systems of objects, plot structure, text theory, cultural codes, aesthetic texts, mass communication, and rhetoric.[65] To this list Eco later added psychoanalysis, motor signs, grammatology, traffic signs, and semiotics of architecture and literature.[66]

Legal language should be added as well, for it is a particular form of communication whose complexity attracted the attention of no less a prominent philosopher and semiotician than Charles Sanders Peirce.[67] To determine how semiotics developed into this broad-based, widely applied discipline, I will trace the sources of its development from such divergent fields as medicine, philosophy, linguistics, anthropology, and literature.

A. Medicine

1. Signs and Symptoms Semiotics was one of the three main branches of Greek medicine, constituting the study of detectable indications of changes in the human body. The modern equivalent of semiotics in medicine is the study of signs and symptoms, which all doctors continue to learn throughout

---

60. *See infra* text accompanying notes 86–88.

61. *See supra* note 2 for a detailed analysis of the different uses of the terms *semiotics* and *semiology*.

62. *See infra* text accompanying notes 130–38.

63. *See infra* note 120 for Saussure's famous definition of *semiology*.

64. This brief excursion into the sources of semiotics will explain why semiotics has been applied to many different avenues of inquiry. Even though both Peirce and Saussure perceived the breadth of the field, neither possibly could have imagined that semiotics would someday include the study of linguistics, speech act theory, formalism, structuralism, semantics, stylistics, rhetoric, psychoanalytic approaches to discourse analysis, structural and cultural anthropology, reader-response theory, deconstruction, and post-modernism (among others).

65. Eco, *supra* note 1, at 13.

66. *Id.*

67. Informal discussions with Umberto Eco at a semiotics conference at the University of Indiana at Bloomington confirmed my belief that Eco would now add law to the fields of investigation undertaken in the name of semiotics.

their careers. Although the word *semiotics* has almost totally disappeared from the basic vocabulary of the medical profession, at least in the United States, the study of signs and symptoms continues to be a fundamental course in the typical medical school curriculum.[68]

B. Philosophy

1. Sign, Signifier, Signified, Referent, and Context The Greek philosophers (namely the Stoics, Epicureans, and Skeptics) studied theories of signs and considered semiotics a basic division of philosophy, including logic and theory of knowledge.[69]

The early philosophers grappled with the basic elements of semiotic theory: the sign, the signifier, the signified, and its referent.[70] Aristotle conceived of the sign as a relation between words and mental events (the referent) rather than things. According to Aristotle, a word is the name of the referent or the mental picture the receiver has of the thing expressed in words. Stoic theory differed in terminology and in context from Aristotelian semiotics with the Stoics believing that meanings are distinguishable from the referent or mental event.[71]

The Stoic Sextus Empiricus identified three aspects of the sign: the signified, the signifier, and the referent. The signified, or the thing itself to which the words refer, is often compared to the content level of a discussion or discourse. The signifier, the actual word or physical presence of the letters on the page, is more akin to the style of a discourse. The referent is the speaker's own conception of the thing itself, which is culturally variable. Content analysis, which is the type most often performed by lawyers, deals primarily with the signified. Stylistic analysis, which literary scholars often undertake, mainly involves the signifier. The sign itself is the relationship of the signifier (*signifiant*—symbolically referred to as *Sa*) to the signified (*signifiee*—symbolically referred to as *Se*). The sign is represented as the equation of Sa/Se. Because the sign is basically a relationship of form to content, both stylistic and content analysis should be undertaken in any interpretive endeavor. Considering both the form and content of the words to be interpreted would better reflect the basic nature of the sign and would help the interpreter arrive at a more valid description of the discourse under investigation. Thus, it is hoped that those reading cases and interpreting

68. The fact the medical profession studies signs and symptoms without calling this semiotics is another illustration of the basic premise of Part I of this chapter: people in both the law and other fields are making use of semiotic theory without even knowing it.

69. G. Bursill-Hall, Speculative Grammars of the Middle Ages (1971) (detailed discussion of the Greek philosophers as a source of semiotics).

70. *See* Roland Barthes, Éléments de Sémiologie *supra* note 36, at 106–30 (elaborate discussion of *signifier*, *signified*, and *referent*).

71. *See* Charlotte l. Stough, Greek Skepticism: A Study in Epistemology (1969) (offering an interesting view of the sign theories of the Stoics and Epicureans).

legal discourse will take into account the interplay of style and content in the search for the hidden or intended meanings of a legal text.

It is in the intricate relation of signifier, signified, and referent that meaning as well as misunderstanding is located. A signifier devoid of a signified is a nonsense utterance having no conventional meaning, such as the term *Jabberwocky*. A signifier whose signified varies greatly from the referent creates misunderstanding necessitating interpretation. For example, when I write *dog* in the sentence "she's a dog," one person may understand a furry animal as the referent and another may understand an ugly woman. The disparity here between the signified and the referent would be clarified by an examination of the context of the utterance. This utterance is a metaphor requiring knowledge of the equivalence between the word *dog* and the concept of *ugliness*. But some people think dogs are beautiful! Thus, confusion reigns. The interpretation, which should be limited by an examination of the context of the utterance, yields one of several possible solutions to the initial misunderstanding created by the use of metaphor in the relation of signifier, signified, and referent.

2. *Bedeutung* and *Sinn*: Denotation and Connotation Semiotics continued to grow from the time of the Greek philosophers up until the present.[72] In the middle of the nineteenth century, Bernard Bolzano, a Prague philosopher,

72. In the Middle Ages, a theory of signs developed known as *scientia sermocinales* that included grammar, logic, and rhetoric. The scholars who proposed this theory followed one of two directions: either Aristotelian and Platonic metaphysics (Leibniz) or the assimilation of semiotics into empirical science and philosophy. CHARLES MORRIS, SIGNS, LANGUAGE AND BEHAVIOR 286 (1946). This led to the more specialized study of the syntax of sign structures and the eventual proposal of a universal system of signs. The British empiricists, notably John Locke, were more concerned with the semantic aspect of sign systems.

In the Renaissance, the English philosopher and empiricist Hobbes, who drew the distinction between *marks* and *signs*, developed a conceptualist theory of semiotics in which words have no similarity to things. But later in the nineteenth century, Mill would argue strongly in favor of a referential view: "Names are names of things themselves and not merely our ideas of things." JOHN STUART MILL, A SYSTEM OF LOGIC 24 (1851).

Following the line of philosophers engaged in semiotic theory (Aristotle, Sextus Empiricus, Ockham, Hobbes, and Mill), we should cite Gottlob Frege, who in his 1893 *Grundgesetze der Aritmetic*, distinguished between what words actually express (their sense) and what these words stand for (their reference). This distinction is similar to the concepts of connotation and denotation often used in legal contexts.

In the middle of the seventeenth century, Poinsot created the link between scholastic semiotics and the theory of John Locke. JEAN POINSOT, TREATISE ON SIGNS (TRACTATUS DE SIGNIS) 9 (John Deely ed., 1986), *cited in* Sebeok, *supra* note 2, at 3. John Locke greatly influenced the development of semiotics. In the final chapter of his *Essay Concerning Human Understanding* in 1690, Locke called the complex problem of the sign one of the "three great provinces of the intellectual world." He named this province *Metov* or the "doctrine of signs."

broached a theory of signs[73] in which he distinguished between *Bedeutung* (the meaning of a sign) and its *Sinn* (the sense of the sign obtained from the context). This distinction is vital to the law and relates to the notions of denotation and connotation often referred to by legal interpreters attempting to tease out some implicit meaning from the use of a given word.[74]

Umberto Eco defined the *Bedeutung* or meaning of a word in terms of denotation: "The *Bedeutung* is intended as the definition of a historical entity that a culture recognizes as a single person, and is therefore a denoted content."[75] He defined the *Sinn* or contextual sense of a word in terms of connotation: "The *Sinn* is a particular way of considering a given content, according to other cultural conventions, thereby including within one's consideration some of the connotated contents of the first denoted content."[76] The main point of this rather technical definition is that certainty of uniform interpretation is reduced because one person's sense of the meaning of a term (which is developed from the context and cultural convention of which he may or may not be a part) will not be the same as another person's sense of the meaning of that same term. To arrive at a more certain and uniform interpretation, connotational factors should be taken into consideration: the historical period in which the utterance is made, the special meaning the term might have had at the time it was first made, the intention of the speaker as evidenced by other related documents, and the linguistic context of the utterance itself.

The nineteenth and twentieth centuries saw inroads being made in the theory of semiotics, especially in the area of the classification of signs. In his classification system,[77] Bolzano distinguished between universal and particular signs, natural and accidental signs, arbitrary and spontaneous signs, visual and auditory signs, simple and complex signs, and signs and indices. Edmund Husserl

---

In the eighteenth century Jean-Henri Lambert, who was significantly influenced by Locke, devoted an entire section to semiotics in his two-volume work *Neues Organon* (1764). Hoene-Wronsky, also familiar with Locke's work, wrote *La Philosophie du Langage* in which he examined the nature of signs. JOSEPH MARIE HOENE-WRONSKY, LA PHILOSOPHIE DU LANGAGE (1879).

73. Bolzano was familiar with the work of Locke and Lambert. He wrote a book about semiotics entitled *Wissenschaftslehre* in 1837.

74. Eco defined the concepts of denotation and connotation in his *Theory of Semiotics*. "[A] denotation is a cultural unit or semantic property of a given sememe which is at the same time a culturally recognized property of its possible referents; . . . a connotation is a cultural unit or semantic property of a given sememe conveyed by its denotation and not necessarily corresponding to a culturally recognized property of the possible referent." Eco, *supra* note 1, at 86.

75. *Id.* at 61.

76. *Id.*

77. BERNARD BOLZANO, WISSENSCHAFTSLEHRE (1837).

made yet another attempt to classify signs,[78] but none would equal the great classification system proposed by Charles Sanders Peirce at the beginning of the twentieth century.

3. Charles Sanders Peirce

a. Peirce's Definition of the Sign and the Interpretant. Few would argue that Peirce is the father and "fountainhead" of modern semiotics.[79] Peirce's semiotic involves "a cooperation of *three* subjects, such as a sign, its object, and its interpretant . . . "[80] Peirce conceived of the sign in terms of a dynamic process, a "referring back" of the signifier to the signified. His celebrated reformulation of the classical definition of the *sign—aliquid stat aliquo*—is that a sign is "something which stands to somebody for something in some respects or capacity."[81] Thus, the sign can only be a sign if it is taken to be one by a receiver.

The sign is always taken as "standing for" something in some way that Peirce calls its *ground.* A sign creates in the mind of someone an equivalent sign called an interpretant of the first sign. Whatever the sign stands for is its *object.* A sign can have varying meanings to different people because the relation between the reality observed and the sign used to designate it is mediated by what Peirce calls an *interpretant.* The interpretant[82] is merely another sign that translates and explains the first one, but which is governed by the interpreter's personal conception of the observed reality.[83]

---

78. EDMUND HUSSERL, ZUR LOGIK DER ZEICHEN (SEMIOTIK) (1890).

79. Sebeok, *supra* note 2, at 6.

80. PEIRCE, *supra* note 1, at 5:484.

81. *Id.* at 2:228.

82. *See supra* text accompanying notes 79–85.

83. Peirce conceived of the doctrine of signs as an integral part of logic. "Logic, in the general sense, is, as I believe I have shown, only another name for semiotic, the quasi-necessary, or formal doctrine of signs." PEIRCE, *supra* note 1, at 2:227.

> Borrowing the term "semiotic" from Locke, Peirce then postulated a triadic relation for the sign:
>
> A Sign or Representamen, is a First, which stands in such a genuine triadic relation to a Second, called its Object, as to be capable of determining a Third, called its Interpretant, to assume the same triadic relation to its Object, in which it stands itself to the same Object. The triadic relation is genuine, that is its three members are bound together by it in a way that does not consist in any complexus of dyadic relation.

Id. at 2:274.

Peirce's emphasis on the triadic relationship constitutes a basic difference between Peirce's semiotic and Saussure's semiology. Peirce conceives of the semiotic system as a fundamentally triadic interaction of sign, object, and interpretant, whereas Saussure's conception is largely binary with a concentration on the interaction between signifier and signified and other binary oppositions that are inherent to the structure of language. *See* JACKSON, *supra* note 10, at 14–15.

Peirce's concept of the interpretant has been misunderstood by many. The interpretant (not to be confused with the interpreter) is a sign itself. The interpretant "addresses somebody, creates in the mind of a person an equivalent sign, a more developed sign."[84] The fact that an interpretant or individualized conception of an event exists in every verbal exchange explains the need for interpretation.[85]

b. Peirce's Classification of Signs. Peirce coined the phrase that all semioticians repeat: "The entire universe is perfused with signs, if it is not composed exclusively of signs"[86] In fact, "every thought . . . is in itself essentially of the nature of a sign."[87] Peirce tried to put some order in a universe flooded with signs by developing a classification system. He identified sixty-six different kinds of signs based on a trichotomy.

Qualisigns, Sinsigns, and Legisigns. The first classification depends on the sign itself, which can be a duality, an existent, or a general law. In this division there are *qualisigns* (a qualitative possibility), *sinsigns* (an actual existent), and *legisigns* (a general or repeatable sign). All linguistic signs fall into the category of legisigns.[88]

Icon, Index, and Symbol. Peirce's second classification of signs is dependent on the type of relation that exists between the sign and its object or interpretant. In this division there are *icons, indices,* and *symbols.* A diagram is an example of an icon. The nature of the iconic relationship between the sign and its object is one of similarity.[89] Lawyers often make use of diagrams and various types of

---

Mediation or Thirdness is essential to the understanding of Peirce's semiotic theory and its processes, which he called *semiosis*:

> All dynamical action, or action of brute force, physical or psychical, either takes place between two subjects, or at any rate is a resultant of such actions between pairs. But by "semiosis" I mean, on the contrary, an action, or influence, which is, or involves, a cooperation of three subjects, such as a sign, its object, and its interpretant. This tri-relative influence not being in any way resolvable into actions between pairs . . . my definition confers on anything that so acts the title of a "sign."

PEIRCE, *supra* note 1, at 2:484. The sign is inseparable from semiosis or from the unlimited referring back of sign to sign. Mediation, then, is the source of the essentially dynamic quality of the Peircean semiotic that is conceived of in terms of a process.

84. PEIRCE, *supra* note 1, at 2:228.

85. Eco explained the relationship of the interpretant to the sign in this way: "The fundamental characteristic of the sign is that I can use it to lie . . . The fact that a sign can be used to lie means that it does not necessarily have to be explained by showing the thing, the object to which it corresponds; it can be explained by using another sign, and so on and so forth. This is Peirce's theory of interpretants . . . " Eco, *Looking for a Logic of Culture, in* THE TELL-TALE SIGN: A SURVEY OF SEMIOTICS 12 (Thomas Sebeok ed., 1975).

86. PEIRCE, *supra* note 1, at 2:448.

87. *Id.* at 2:594.

88. *See* ECO, THE ROLE OF THE READER 175–99 (1979) for a discussion of Peirce's use of the terms *ground, interpretant,* and *object,* as well as an in-depth exploration of Peirce's classification system.

89. The icon, which Peirce calls a sign, is based on a relationship of similarity derived from the platonic notion that the signifier imitates the signified. Peirce identified three subclasses of icons: images, diagrams, and metaphors. PEIRCE, *supra* note 1, at 2:277.

iconical signs to illustrate a point on the basis that a picture is worth a thousand words. The use of iconical signs is particularly prevalent in products liability cases. Warnings on consumer products are often accompanied with illustrations or icons of the product to avoid liability for inadequacy of the warning and to prevent lack of comprehension if foreign language speakers or children use the product.

The index is a sign that stands in a physical relation to its object, such as a weather vane, a shout, or an act of pointing. When I say, "Where there is smoke there is fire," I am referring to the indexical sign of smoke that bears a cause-and-effect relationship to the fire. The relationship between sign and object here is based on contiguity rather than similarity. The indexical sign is particularly important in evidentiary inquiries. As the nature of the relationship of an indexical sign is more complex than the icon, the lawyer is required to offer a sufficient explanation for the basis of the contiguity to convince the court that the evidence is relevant. The explanation of the relevance of a shout to a case involving an alleged act of violence would involve incursions into the cause and effect, effect and cause, or part/whole relationship of the shout to the violence.

Unlike the iconical and indexical signs in Peirce's classification that are based respectively on relationships of similarity and contiguity, a symbol has only a conventional relation to the object it represents. According to Peirce, linguistic signs are symbols inasmuch as they represent objects by linguistic convention. The word *dog* means dog only because convention says so. However, it should be noted that Saussurean semioticians prefer to distinguish the sign from the symbol more radically than Peirce has done.[90] According to Saussurean semiotics, the sign is arbitrary or nonmotivated, whereas the symbol is motivated by relationships of contiguity or similarity.[91]

Rhemes, Dicents, and Arguments. Peirce's third classification of signs is based upon the relation of the sign to its interpretant. He identified *rhemes, dicents,* and *arguments.* The rheme is a "Sign which, for its interpretant, is a Sign of qualitative Possibility, that is, is understood as representing such and such a kind of possible

---

90. *See* Oswald Ducrot & Tzvetan Todorov, Dictionnaire encyclopédique des sciences du langage 124–25 (1972) for a discussion of the confusion between Peirce's and Saussure's definitions of the sign. Peirce recognized the subtlety involved in a study of signs and symbols. He stressed the blending of index, icon, and symbol in a given sign. Roman Jakobson, Coup d'oeil sur le développement de la sémiotique 9 (1975). Peirce believed that the most perfect signs are those in which the iconic, indicative, and symbolic characters are blended as equally as possible. Peirce, *supra* note 1, at 4:448.

91. *See supra* text accompanying notes 56–59 (discussion of the creche as a religious symbol as it grew out of Lynch v. Donnelly, 465 U.S. 668 (1984)). According to the Saussurean conception of the symbol (i.e., a motivated sign), the creche would constitute a symbol because of the contiguous relationship of the Christ figure to Christianity. The creche would also be a symbol according to Peirce because there is a conventional link between the creche and Christianity.

Object."[92] Thus, the rheme is either a term or propositional function. A dicent is a "Sign, which for its Interpretant, is a Sign of actual existence," notably a proposition. An argument is a "Sign which, for its Interpretant, is a Sign of Law."[93] These three types of signs are relevant to logicians and interpreters of legal texts.

c. The Influence of Peirce's Semiotic on the Law. It is evident throughout Peirce's writing that he considered the concept of law to be a major issue in each part of his philosophy.[94] Peirce maintained that law is an element in every rational and meaningful experience. He defined law in different terms derived from sign theory: in phenomenology, law is the continuity of experience; in logic, law is an operative symbol; in metaphysics, law is efficient reasonableness or what Peirce calls *thirdness*. Thirdness is the concept of mediation or representation that characterizes the indirect nature of the law and constitutes the very principle on which semiotics is built. Although some continue to question the validity of Peirce's typologies,[95] there is no doubt that Peirce was a pioneer who had considerable impact on the law.

The next section of this study will investigate the influence of Peirce's semiotic on such key legal figures as Oliver Wendell Holmes, Jerome Frank, François Gény, and John Dewey. I will also propose the theory that Peirce's semiotic influenced[96] the development of the legal realist movement.

Peirce's Influence on Oliver Wendell Holmes. Few are aware of the extent to which the father of semiotics, Charles Sanders Peirce, directly influenced legal

---

92. PEIRCE, *supra* note 1, at 2:250–52.

93. *Id.*

94. WILLIAM P. HAAS, THE CONCEPTION OF LAW AND THE UNITY OF PEIRCE'S PHILOSOPHY 22 (1964).

95. Arthur Skidmore, *Peirce and Semiotics: An Introduction to Peirce's Theory of Signs, in* SEMIOTIC THEMES 33, 46–49 (Richard De George ed., 1981). Even though some question Peirce's classification system, others recognize the significant influence Peirce's semiotic theory has had on many fields of investigation. Roman Jakobson described Peirce as "the most inventive, the most universal among the American thinkers." JAKOBSON, *supra* note 90, at 6, *citing* Roman Jakobson, *A La Recherche de L'Essence du Langage*, 51 DIOGENE 346 (1965). Similarly, Charles Morris, another major contributor to the field of semiotics, remarked that Peirce's:

> classification of signs, his refusal to separate completely animal and human sign-processes, his often penetrating remarks in linguistic categories, his application of semiotic to the problems of logic and philosophy, and the general acumen of his observations and distinctions, make work in a semiotic source of stimulation that has few equals in the history of the field.

MORRIS, WRITINGS ON THE GENERAL THEORY OF SIGNS 340 (1971).

96. I am aware of the weaknesses inherent in any hypothesis concerning "influences" of one man's work on another. It is my goal merely to report the findings of researchers investigating Peirce's so-called influence on legal figures and legal movements.

theory and interpretive practice.[97] Some scholars claim that Peirce had considerable impact on the development of a radically new approach to legal discovery and interpretation.[98] It is generally believed that Oliver Wendell Holmes was profoundly influenced by his friend Peirce and Pierce's philosophy of signs and sign interpretation. In fact, Holmes and Peirce were comembers of the famous Metaphysical Club where legal debates and the burgeoning of legal theory are said to have taken place.[99] Scholars have sought to establish a link between Peirce's pragmatism and Holmes' prediction theory in law.[100] Holmes viewed the law as a "great anthropological document," the indicator of evolving social ideals, and the "morphology and transformation of human ideas."[101] Peirce held similar views regarding the dynamic nature of language.[102]

Peirce's Semiotic and Jerome Frank. Like Peirce, Jerome Frank supported the controversial theory that rules are not the law, but only one source to which judges may turn in making law.[103] In fact, Frank went so far as to say there was a myth of certainty in rules of law, and he opposed the legal absolutism of Joseph Beale who had proposed the famous conflict of laws rules.[104] Without calling himself a semiotician, Frank defined legal decisions in distinctly semiotic terms, referring to them as mere signs that point to future decisions. In other words, Frank conceived of legal decisions as Peircean indexical signs,[105] a concept that would have a profound effect on legal realist thinkers both here and abroad.[106]

The Influence of Peirce's Semiotic on François Gény and Legal Realism. Scholars have attempted to show a parallel between Peirce's semiotic logic and the

97. Roberta Kevelson, *Comparative Legal Cultures and Semiotics: An Introduction,* 1 AMER. J. OF SEMIOTIOCS 63, 64 (1982) (discussing Peirce's influence on the law).

98. Roberta Kevelson, *Semiotics and Methods of Legal Inquiry: Interpretation and Discovery, in* LAW FROM THE PERSPECTIVE OF PEIRCE'S SPECULATIVE RHETORIC 2 (Oct. 13, 1984) (unpublished manuscript).

99. Max H. Fisch, *Was There a Metaphysical Club in Cambridge?,* in STUDIES IN THE PHILOSOPHY OF CHARLES SANDERS PEIRCE (Edward C. Moore & Richard S. Robin eds., 1964).

100. Max H. Fisch, *Justice Holmes, The Prediction Theory of Law and Pragmatism,* 39 J. OF PHILO. 85 (1942).

101. Oliver Wendell Holmes, *Law in Science and Science in Law,* in COLLECTED LEGAL PAPERS (Peter Smith ed., 1952), *cited in* Roberta Kevelson, *Peirce as Catalyst in Modem Legal Science: Consequences, in* SEMIOTICS 1980, 241, 249 (Michael Herzfeld & Margot D. Lenhart eds., 1982).

102. *See infra* text accompanying notes 117–18.

103. JEROME FRANK, LAW AND THE MODERN MIND 127–28 (1930).

104. Beale was of the opinion that one of the most important features of law is that "it is not a mere collection of arbitrary rules, but a body of scientific principle [sic]." 11 JOSEPH H. BEALE, A TREATISE ON THE CONFLICT OF LAWS § 3.4, at 24 (1935); JOSEPH H. BEALE, *Summary of the Conflict of Laws, in* 3 CASES ON THE CONFLICT OF LAWS 501 (1902).

105. *See supra* text accompanying notes 89–90.

106. Kevelson, *supra* note 98, at 3.

jurisprudential concepts of François Gény.[107] Gény's influence on continental and Anglo-American law, especially on the school of legal realism, has just recently been recognized and explored.[108] The speculation is that Peirce was the connecting link between Gény, Holmes, and the legal realist movement in general.[109] Like Peirce, Gény believed in living law. Thus, for Gény a statute is only a provisional kind of law subject to reinterpretation and modification. Gény's "provisional law," stated in Peircean terms is a legisign[110] or one of the major classifications of signs.

Gény applied his method to the French Civil Code, which is a body of fixed law deductively interpreted to solve legal problems. Before Gény breathed life into the Civil Code with his concept of provisional law, the whole system of *positive law*, which was contained in a limited number of categories, was "predetermined in essence and regulated by inflexible dogma."[111] Anglo-American law was similarly ideal up to the end of the eighteenth century when the validity of the concept of discovering law, the "brooding omnipresence," was questioned. Gény's influence changed the conceptualization of the practice of Continental law from a nominalist to a realist system, a phenomenon that would be paralleled in Anglo-American law between 1870 and 1930 by the development of the movement of legal realism. Gény was no doubt a vanguard in the legal realism movement.[112]

The Influence of Peirce's Semiotic on John Dewey and Legal Realism. Both Dewey[113] and Peirce had a strong impact on the legal realists' belief that the logic of rigid demonstration is inadequate to account for legal decisions. Like Peirce, the legal realists sought out an experimental logic of search and discovery, a logic of inquiry, where rules were only provisional and where law was a system in the process of formation. Even more radical than Dewey, Peirce believed that traditional laws are inherently inadequate to describe evolving legal and social ideas. Law for Peirce is provisional, subject to developing doubts,[114] because only in its provisional nature can law account for the "contradiction and paradox"[115] inherent in language and in human relations.

Peirce's semiotic accounts for a legal system which, in its evolution, is sensitive to social change. The legal realists have adopted this philosophy in their

---

107. Gény, *supra* note 49.

108. Kevelson, *supra* note 101, at 241.

109. *Id.* at 249.

110. *See supra* text accompanying notes 86–93 for a discussion of Peirce's classification system and the place of legisigns.

111. Gény, *supra* note 49, at 129, *quoted in* Kevelson, *supra* note 101, at 244.

112. Kevelson, *supra* note 101, at 244–45.

113. John Dewey, Philosophy and Civilization 126–34 (1931).

114. Kevelson, *supra* note 101, at 251.

115. *See infra* text accompanying notes 297–98 for a discussion of the role of contradiction and paradox in the post-structuralist movement.

description of the law. Lon Fuller[116] holds a view of the role of the judge that is very close to the Peircean notion of the interpretant. For Fuller, the judge deliberately evolves rules so that the earlier rule is subsumed in the latter. Thus, the very notion of stability in law is threatened as every case carries the seeds of doubt that can develop into further inquiry and the establishment of new law. Fuller believes that through the interpretive process the judge plays an active role in shaping society and responding to the changing values of the community.

Peirce's Semiotic and Legal Realism: An Historical Perspective. What was Peirce's role in the development of legal theory as it progressed from the earlier Austinian view of law as a closed system to the legal realist's view of law as an incomplete, open-ended, and dynamic process?[117] Rules for legal interpretation were developing in the nineteenth century in civil and common law countries to reflect the emergence of a social conscience, as seen in Bentham's theory of utilitarianism and John Stuart Mill's theory of social and economic justice. Peirce played a part in the elaboration of a method of legal interpretation, proposing hermeneutics as the "method of methods."

Peirce maintained that in society the communication of social values results in a constant emergence of new values, new signs, and new sign-systems. For this reason—and in contrast to the more prevalent nineteenth century Austinian view of law as the inviolable command of the sovereign to be discovered and described—Peirce proposed a more open-ended view of the law. He envisaged the law as an incomplete code, prescriptive rather than descriptive, reinterpretable and essentially provisional. His method of methods was in consonance with what he saw as a dynamic process inherent in all systems of thought.[118]

---

116. Lon L. Fuller, The Law in Quest of Itself (1940).

117. *See generally* Haas, *supra* note 94.

118. Peirce's work is found in the eight-volume collection Charles Sanders Peirce, Collected Papers (vols. I–VI, Charles Hartshorne & Paul Weiss eds., 1960, vols. VII–VIII, Arthur W. Burks ed., 1958). The identification of Peircean semiotics with an open-ended system has resulted in the adoption of Peirce by the legal realists and the frequent association of the term *semiotics* with open-ended systems in general. Even Roberta Kevelson, one of the greatest contributors to the field of semiotics, said, "The greatest thing about semiotics is the recognition that . . . we are open to the world; the self is a dynamic sign in play that continually creates something genuinely new. Semiotics can keep freedom alive . . . it is experimental and anti-authoritarian." *See* New Approaches to Semiotics and the Human Sciences: Essays in Honor of Roberta Kevelson ix (William Pencak & J. Ralph Lindgren eds., 1998). Willem J. Witteveen describes a semiotics of law that "refuses to accept the claims of positivism and natural law." *Id.* at x. In contrast to the openness of semiotics, the term *structuralism*, or what some refer to as Saussurean semiotics, is sometimes identified with closed systems such as Austin's view of the law. Bernard Jackson draws interesting parallels between Saussure's semiotics, legal positivism, and legal realism. Jackson, *supra* note 10; *see infra* text accompanying notes 261–67 for a discussion of Jackson's study.

Thus, this brief excursion into Peirce's contribution to semiotics and his influence on the law has demonstrated that Peirce established an elaborate sign classification system and a definition of the sign in terms of a dynamic process. The open-ended quality of Peirce's semiotic was in consonance with the theories of Holmes, Dewey, Gény, and Lieber[119] and influenced the development of the legal realist movement.

C. Linguistics

1. Ferdinand De Saussure

a. Semiology. Ferdinand De Saussure has been the leading force in European structuralism and semiotics. While Peirce was actively engaged in formulating a theory of semiotics, Saussure was postulating a dream of the future: a science which he named *sémiologie* from the Greek word for *sign.*[120]

---

119. An overview of the interplay of Peirce's semiotic and the law would not be complete without mention of Francis Lieber, an authority on domestic and international law and the author of the early code of the rules of war. Lieber spoke the language of semiotics when he expressed the view that law is a system of signs in which "[t]here is no direct communion between the minds of men . . . without resorting to the outward manifestations of that which moves us inwardly, that is, to signs." FRANCIS LIEBER, LEGAL AND POLITICAL HERMENEUTICS 13 (Roy M. Mersky & J. Myron Jacobstein eds., 1970). By drawing attention to the speaker's linguistic selection as an index of meaning, Lieber's semiotic concepts have had a lasting impact on the lawyer's everyday practice of interpretation. Lieber literally enunciated a theory of modern semiotics in 1839 when he declared "[t]he signs which man uses . . . are very various, for instance, gestures, signals, telegraphs, monuments, sculptures of all kinds, pictorial and hieroglyphic signs, the stamp on coins, seals, beacons, buoys, insignia, ejaculations, articulate sounds, or their representations, that is phonetic characters on stones, wood, leaves, paper, etc., entire periods, or single words, such as names in a particular place, and whatever other signs, even the flowers in the flower language of the East, might be enumerated." *Id.* at 17.

Lieber, who wrote thirty years before Peirce, was unwittingly dependent upon semiotic principles for his work on legal and political hermeneutics. Moreover, Lieber's hermeneutic theory complements Peirce's semiotic theory and may even have contributed to major aspects of Peirce's thought. *See* Roberta Kevelson, *Francis Lieber and the Semiotics of Law and Politics, in* SEMIOTICS (1981) 167, 193 (John N. Deely & Margot D. Lenhart eds., 1983).

Lieber defined and described the role of signs in legal hermeneutics. LIEBER, *supra* at 17–18. The use of signs implies a speaker's intention to convey a particular idea; the sign the speaker chooses is a key to the essence of that particular thought. In other words, interpretation is the process of discovery and recreation in different words of true meaning of the speaker's chosen sign.

120. FERDINAND DE SAUSSURE, COURS DE LINGUISTIQUE GÉNÉRALE 16 (1955) (COURSE IN GENERAL LINGUISTICS (Wade Baskin trans., 1966), *cited in* ROBERT E. SCHOLES, STRUCTURALISM IN LITERATURE: AN INTRODUCTION 16 (1974) ("Since the science does not yet exist, no one can say what it would be, but it has a right to existence, a place staked out in advance.").

For the European world, Saussure is the father of modern linguistics who clarified the relation of linguistics to semiology.[121] Saussure conceived of semiology as the science that would investigate the nature and laws governing signs. These laws would then be applicable to linguistics. Saussure's very conception of language was in semiotic terms as he compared language to writing, military signals, gestures, ceremonials, rituals, forms of etiquette, and other customs. Language is the most important system of signs that expresses ideas.[122] To communicate with signs, we must understand the convention underlying their use. This is particularly true of specialized languages such as law or literature. As Saussure conceived it, the primary goal of semiology was to uncover the codes and conventions of language—the gateways to meaningful communication. Thus, Saussurean semiotics is a science in which language is the center of attention of a wider framework that he called semiology.

b. The Arbitrary Sign. Probably the most important feature of Saussure's theory of language is his conception of the arbitrary nature of the sign. Arbitrariness in linguistics means simply that there is no natural link between the signifier and the signified, only a relationship of convention. There is no particular reason why we use the letters *d-o-g* to mean a furry little animal. Stated otherwise, there is no *motivation* between the signifier and signified. (The obvious exception to this rule is the onomatopoeia in which the sound of the signifier imitates the signified.[123]) The concept of motivation is essential to the distinction Saussure draws between signs and symbols, with a symbol being a motivated

---

121. "Linguistics is only a part of the general science of semiology: the laws discovered by semiology will be applicable to linguistics, and the latter will circumscribe a well-defined area within the mass of anthropological facts." SAUSSURE, *supra* note 120, at 16 (also cited in Eco, *supra* note 1, at 14).

122. Roland Barthes expanded and reversed Saussure's conception of semiology in relation to linguistics by coining the notion of translinguistics:

> Linguistics is not a part of the general science of signs, even a privileged part, it is semiology which is a part of linguistics: to be precise, it is that part covering the great signifying unities of discourse. By this inversion we may expect to bring to light the unity of research being done in anthropology, sociology, psychoanalysis, and stylistics round the concept of signification.

Barthes, *supra* note 36, at 81 (author's translation).

Barthes' influence in bringing semiotics to the attention of the scholarly public cannot be stressed enough. His work, *Éléments de Sémiologie,* is a good starting point for the understanding of basic principles of semiotic theory. Moreover, Barthes' applied semiotics demonstrates the bountiful fruits that a rigorous application of the semiotic method can reap. *See, e.g.,* ROLAND BARTHES, SYSTÈME DE LA MODE (1967), in which Barthes uncovers the hidden mechanisms at work in the complex system of the fashion industry. Barthes' method is eminently applicable to the analysis of legal discourse.

123. However, there are words with partial motivation such as *lawful* whose motivation is contained in the root *law.* But the term *law* by itself is arbitrary.

sign that is never entirely arbitrary. Thus, for Saussure conventional signs are arbitrary, whereas for Peirce they are labeled as symbols or legisigns.[124]

c. Langue/Parole: *Language as Norm and Individual Speech Act; Legal Positivism.* Saussure draws an important distinction between individualized speech acts (*parole*), otherwise termed *performance* by the celebrated linguist Noam Chomsky, and the system of language (*langue*), or abstract set of rules and conventions a speaker must know in order to communicate successfully. Chomsky refers to this generalized awareness of language rules as *competence,* which is both a "social product of the faculty of speech and a collection of necessary conventions that have been adopted by a social body to permit individuals to exercise that faculty."[125] Saussure considered competence (the law or general rules), not individual performance (the acts), to be the proper object of linguistics. The Saussurean conception of the language system—the code or semiotic of linguistic laws—can be compared to the Kelsenian grammar of legal structure.[126] As with Saussure's distinction between *langue* and *parole,* Kelsen distinguishes between legal validity (*langue*) and legal volition (*parole,* an individual act in deviation of the norm), or stated differently, between positive law and the judicial application of legal norms.[127] In the minds of some legal scholars applying semiotics, Saussure's interest in the general rules of language has allied him with the legal positivist school.

d. Synchronic/Diachronic Study of Language. A synchronic study of language attempts to reconstruct the system as a whole, whereas a diachronic study traces the historical evolution of its elements through different stages. Because the sign is arbitrary (i.e., contingent), Saussure believed it could only be defined in its relation to other signs, and therefore should be studied synchronically. One of the major features of Saussure's linguistic theory is his insistence on the relational quality of the sign, a point of view that will influence structural analysis in literature and the law. Structuralists in the Saussurean school study a literary or legal phenomenon not from the historical perspective, but as a system of interrelated parts that fit together as a puzzle.[128] Saussure's departure from

---

124. *Cf. supra* text accompanying notes 89–91 for a discussion of the symbol in Peirce's semiotic.

125. Saussure, *supra* note 120, at 16.

126. Peter Goodrich, *Law and Language: An Historical and Critical Introduction,* J. OF. L. & SOC'Y 173, 181 (1984). *See also* JACKSON, *supra* note 10, at 225–62 (detailed analysis of Kelsen's legal theory and its semiotic underpinnings).

127. Goodrich, *supra* note 126, at 181, *citing* HANS KELSEN, PURE THEORY OF LAW 349–52 (Max Knight trans., 2d ed. 1970).

128. According to Saussure, language is an abstraction, a system of interdependent, related values characterized by form rather than substance. *See* JONATHAN CULLER, FERDINAND DE SAUSSURE 42 (1972). Language can be explained in terms of syntagmatic and paradigmatic relations. Within the linguistic system there are various levels of structure. At any given level, there are elements which differ or contrast with one another and

historical linguistics is one of the reasons he has been called the father of modern linguistics.

e. Semiology and Society. Saussure continually stressed the importance of seeing language as a system of socially determined values.[129] In fact, Saussure conceived of semiology as a "science that studies the life of signs within society; it would be part of social psychology and consequently of general psychology."[130]

f. Semiology and Linguistics. In Saussure's perception of the relation between semiology and linguistics, he viewed linguistics as a model for semiology:

> (W)holly arbitrary signs are those which come closest to the semiological ideal. This is why language, the most complex and widespread of systems of expression, is also the most characteristic. And for this reason, linguistics can serve as a model for semiology as a whole, though language is only one of its systems.[131]

Unfortunately Saussure's proposals about semiology were not taken up until many years after the publication of the *Cours*. Anthropologists, sociologists,

---

combine with other elements to form units. The combinatory possibility of words and their contiguity constitute the syntagmatic relations of language. Paradigmatic relationships determine the possibility of substitutions.

129. The ultimate law of language is, dare we say, that nothing can ever reside in a single term.

> This is a direct consequence of the fact that linguistic signs are unrelated to what they designate. And that *a* cannot designate anything without the aid of *b* and vice versa, or in other words, that both have value only by the differences between them, or that neither has value, in any of its constituents, except through this same network of forever negative differences.

Id. at 49 (translating and citing Saussure).

130. Saussure's original and complete enunciation of the science of semiology and its relation to linguistics and psychology is cited below:

> On peut done concevoir *une science qui étudie la vie des signes au sein de la vie sociale;* elle formerait une partie de la psychologie sociale, et par conséquent de la psychologie générale; nous la nommerons *sémiologie* (du grec semeion, "signe"). Elle nous apprendrait en quoi consistent les signes, quelles lois les régissent . . . La linguistique n'est qu'une partie de cette science générale, les lois que découvrira la sémiologie seront applicables à la linguistique, et celle-ci se trouvera ainsi rattachée à un domaine bien défini dans l'ensemble des faits humains.
>
> C'est au psychologue à déterminer la place exacte de la sémiologie; la tâche du linguiste est de définir ce qui fait de la langue un système spécial dans l'ensemble des faits sémiologiques . . . si pour la première fois nous avons pu assigner à la linguistique une place parmi les sciences, c'est parce que nous l'avons rattachée à la sémiologie.

SAUSSURE, *supra* note 120, at 33–34.

131. Culler, *supra* note 128, at 68 (citing Saussure).

literary critics, and legal scholars slowly began to use linguistics as a model for their own disciplines, and it was in this way that structuralism was born.

g. Semiology and the Law. The sociological leanings of the Saussurean system have been understated by those who see Saussure as a mere positivist imbued with the scientific spirit. Some have characterized him as a "crude, early" semiotician able to provide a descriptive overview of linguistic and legal rationality and certainty that is "comforting to those within the legal institution who have a professional interest in the belief or mythology of legal determinacy."[132] Thus, Saussure has been linked with legal positivism whereas Peirce remains the fountainhead of legal realism.[133]

Saussurean semiotics has been particularly influential in Europe on a small but growing number of modern legal scholars who have readily adopted the structuralist approach to legal interpretation.[134] The legal profession's incursions into structuralism[135] are a natural and inevitable development because of the systematized nature of the law and the scientifically inspired systems' analysis approach that constitutes the very stuff of structuralist inquiry. It is my belief that the legal profession will also take the inevitable leap from structuralism to semiotics that has already occurred in the field of literature because structuralism and semiotics are deeply intertwined.[136] Law is a system of communication,

---

132. Goodrich, *supra* note 126, at 181.

133. *See supra* text accompanying notes 107–19 for a discussion of Peirce and legal realism.

134. Bernard S. Jackson, *Towards a Structuralist Theory of Law*, 2 LIVERPOOL L. REV. 5 (1980) [hereinafter cited as Jackson, *Towards a Structuralist Theory*]; Bernard S. Jackson, *Structuralisme et "sources du droit,"* 27 ARCHIV. DE PHILOS. DU DROIT 147 (1982) [hereinafter cited as Jackson, *Structuralisme et "sources du droit"*]; Arnaud, *supra* note 26, at 283; ARNAUD, *supra* note 45; Paul Robertshaw, *Structuralism and Law: Some Comments*, 2 LIVERPOOL L. REV. 31 (1980). *See* Thomas C. Heller, *Structuralism and Critique*, 36 STAN. L. REV. 127 (1984) for an American scholar's view of structuralism and the law; KALINOWSKY, *supra* note 44 (with a special chapter devoted to semiotics and the law at 41–69) for works devoted to semiotics and the law per se, with a Saussurean bent; Christophe Grzegorczyk, *Le rôle du performatif dans le langage du droit*, 20 ARCHIV. DE PHILOS. DU DROIT 229 (1974); Georges Kalinowski, *La loqique juridique, sémiotique et la rhétorique*, 20 ARCHIV. DE PHILOS. DU DROIT 455 (1974); André-Jean Arnaud, *Autopsie d'un juge: Etude sémiologique de la jurisprudence Aixoise en matière de divorce*, 20 ARCHIV. DE PHILOS. DU DROIT 197 (1974). The major work in the field that appeared felicitously as this chapter was in its early draft is *Semiotics and Legal Theory*. JACKSON, *supra* note 10.

135. *See infra* text accompanying notes 251–85 for a discussion of structuralism and the law.

136. Structuralism and post-structuralism, better known as *deconstruction*, grew out of linguistics and its affiliation with semiotic theory. *See infra* text accompanying notes 246–50 for a discussion of this interdisciplinary relationship.

and as such benefits from "whatever contribution structuralism has made to the science of semiotics . . . "[137]

Saussure, then, was the modern thinking linguist who postulated a dream of the future that he called semiology, an all-encompassing science designed according to linguistic theory to investigate the laws of signs. Saussure's revolutionary notion of the arbitrary nature of the sign has drawn attention to the study of the conventions governing sign use. Insistence on language laws rather than individual speech acts has linked Saussure with the legal positivist school and its search for a grammar of legal structure.[138] This analogy between Saussurean semiology and legal positivism stops short of recognizing the considerable role society played in Saussure's conception of language as a system of socially determined values. Moreover, those who see semiotics as a theory of communication cannot disregard Saussure's semiology, which is eminently applicable to legal discourse.[139]

2. Ogden and Richards' Context Theory of Meaning

a. Metaphor and Legal Language. After Peirce and Saussure formulated a theory of semiotics, the science of signs continued to evolve under the direction of Ogden and Richards.[140] They developed the notion of a context theory of meaning and differentiated between scientific discourse, which is characterized by a predominance of referential or *symbolic* terms, and nonscientific discourse, which contains emotive or expressive terms. Included within expressive terms are rhetorical figures such as metaphor and metonymy.

The distinction between scientific and nonscientific discourse is important to the characterization and differentiation of literary and legal discourses. In legal discourse, there is a conventional preference for referential terms. In contrast, literary discourse is characterized by a predominance of metaphor and metonymy. Students of law are taught early in law school to avoid the use of emotive or metaphoric language in legal brief writing. Yet despite the generally held belief in this convention, metaphors are commonly found in legal cases. Ironically, the use of metaphor is especially prevalent in the free speech area. For example, Justice Brandeis used the highly charged metaphor of slavery to describe the emotional state of fear: "It is the function of speech to free men from the bondage of irrational fears."[141] Justice Harlan's metaphor in *Cohen v. California* is memorable: "One man's vulgarity is another's lyric."[142] Thus, legal language is not the scientific discourse ideally composed of referential terms that it is thought to be.

---

137. Jackson, *Towards a Structuralist Theory*, *supra* note 134, at 5.

138. *See* JACKSON, *supra* note 10, at 124–30.

139. Eco, *supra* note 1, at 14.

140. *See* CHARLES K. OGDEN & I.A. RICHARDS, THE MEANING OF MEANING (1972).

141. Whitney v. California, 274 U.S. 357, 376 (1927) (Brandeis, J., concurring).

142. Cohen v. California, 403 U.S. 15, 25 (1971).

The courts are now sensitive to the emotive function of words. In *Cohen v. California*, the court arrived at criteria for protected speech on the basis of semiotic theory. Cohen was convicted of violating the California Penal Code section prohibiting "maliciously and willfully disturb[ing] the peace or quiet of any neighborhood or person . . . by . . . offensive conduct . . . " Cohen publicly wore a jacket bearing the words *Fuck the Draft*. The court considered several issues in this case, all of which are distinctly semiotic concerns. Is it conduct or speech which is offensive? Is this a case of obscenity? Are these fighting words?[143] The court finally reversed the conviction on the basis of semiotic principles, drawing attention to the distinction between content and expression (i.e., signifier and signified in semiotic terms) and the emotive function of the chosen words of the communication.[144]

3. Law as a Sublanguage Despite all efforts at achieving objectivity in legal language[145] through a general use of referential terms, there is no doubt that the language of law is a distinct sublanguage, a special case of ordinary language that can and often does baffle nonlawyers.[146] In *Semiotics and Legal Theory*, Professor Jackson draws interesting conclusions about the specificity of law achieved through its language:[147] "It is neither the syntax nor semantics of legal statements which make them special, but rather the particular 'force' which is attributable to them."[148] Law has the peculiar trait of claiming to regulate its own creation[149] by what Greimas and other structuralists would call a grammar of law that seeks to be explicit. The law acquires the power to regulate its own meaning by enacting statutes that provide legal self-interpretation.

Legal language differs from ordinary language by the nature of the semantic changes that take place within it. Semantic change is institutionally controlled and immediate in legal language, whereas in natural language semantic change occurs gradually and almost imperceptibly.[150]

---

143. *See* Chaplinsky v. New Hampshire, 315 U.S. 568, 572 (1942) for the elaboration of the "fighting words" doctrine in protected speech.

144. *Cohen, supra* note 142, 403 U.S. at 26 ("We cannot sanction the view that the Constitution while solicitous of the cognitive content of individual speech has little or no regard for that emotive function which, practically speaking, may often be the more important element of the overall message sought to be communicated.").

145. Peter Goodrich, *The Role of Linguistics in Legal Analysis*, 47 Mod. L. Rev. 523 (1984).

146. Veda R. Charrow, JoAnn Crandall, & Robert P. Charrow, *Characteristics and Functions of Legal Language*, *in* Sublanguage, Studies of Language in Restricted Semantic Domains 175 (Richard Kittredge & John Lehrberger eds., 1982).

147. Jackson, *supra* note 10, at 306–10.

148. *Id.* at 306.

149. *Id.*

150. Domenico Carzo, I Segni del Potero 88 (1981), *cited in* Jackson, *supra* note 10, at 307.

Scientific language in general, and legal language in particular, have a higher incidence of monosemicity—one word, one meaning—and an "appearance of restricted connotations" when the context is foregrounded.[151] However, judges have a higher degree of choice in their use of legal language by virtue of the flexibility legal interpretation affords.[152]

Legal language is particularly puzzling in its inability to define its own crucial words in terms of ordinary factual counterparts.[153] Notwithstanding the beneficial effects of vagueness in legal terminology, William Charron has attempted to shed some light on the meaning of some particularly controversial terms by comparing their legal, medical, and lay usages in the light of semiotics. Charron claims that in the legal definition of death, priority is given to the folk psychology perception of a persistent vegetative state. In the debate on the definition of death—one that is carried over into the definition of life and the abortion issue—Charron believes that the "informed preference of the public" should be sought.[154]

4. Linguistics and the Law: Peter Goodrich The influence of modern linguistics on legal studies has been significant.[155] Law libraries contain works on phonetics, phonology, morphology, syntax, semantics, pragmatics, speech act theory, sociolinguistics,[156] psycholinguistics, and rhetoric. Linguists in the law have been particularly interested in the nature of legal language per se[157] and in the language of courtroom transactions, especially the reliability of eyewitness testimony, the effects of language variation in courtroom testimony, and the comprehensibility of jury instructions.[158]

Within the field of legal linguistics, there is a dichotomy that mirrors the split between positivists and realists existing in jurisprudence. Linguists advocate

---

151. ALGIRDAS JULIEN GREIMAS & J. COURTÈS, SÉMIOTIQUE ET SCIENCES SOCIALES 85 (1976), *cited in* JACKSON, *supra* note 10, at 308.

152. Jerzy Wroblewski, *Semantic Basis of the Theory of Legal Interpretation, in* 21 LOGIQUE ET ANALYSE 414 (1963), *cited in* JACKSON, *supra* note 10, at 308.

153. H.L.A. HART, *Definition & Theory in Jurisprudence, in* ESSAYS IN JURISPRUDENCE AND PHILOSOPHY 21, 23 (1983).

154. William C. Charron, *Death: A Philosophical Perspective on the Legal Definition,* 4 WASH. U.L.Q. 979 (1976); *see also* William C. Charron, *Some Legal Definitions and Semiotic: Toward a General Theory,* 32 SEMIOTICA (1980).

155. A bibliography on linguistic studies in the law has been compiled by Levi in JUDITH N. LEVI, LINGUISTICS, LANGUAGE, AND LAW: A TOPICAL BIBLIOGRAPHY (1982) (available at the Department of Linguistics of Northwestern University).

156. *E.g.*, Douglas W. Maynard, *Person-Descriptions in Plea Bargaining,* 42 SEMIOTICA 195 (1982) (a semiotic perspective on sociolinguistics and the law).

157. *See* DAVID MELLINKOFF, THE LANGUAGE OF THE LAW (1978) for the bible on this subject. *See also* William C. Charrow, *Linguistic Theory and the Study of Legal and Bureaucratic Language, in* EXCEPTIONAL LANGUAGE AND LINGUISTICS 81 (1982).

158. Robert P. Charrow & Veda R. Charrow, *Making Legal Language Understandable: A Psycholinguistic Study of Jury Instructions,* 79 COLUM. L. REV. 1306 (1979).

either a Saussurean, normative, empirical brand of linguistics, or a more open-ended Peircean brand of semiotics. This split is also manifested in the adoption of the Peircean view of semiotics by the post-structuralists in preference to Saussurean semiotics. Peter Goodrich summed up the conflict in approaches when he stated that his goal as a legal realist was to "criticise (sic) the dominant view within both linguistics and jurisprudence, that . . . language as well as legal communication are to be understood best as structurally determined activities, as specialised (sic) normative enterprises that can be studied scientifically according to the internal laws, or grammar, of a static, governing, code."[159] Instead, Goodrich urged a more flexible, interdisciplinary approach to legal studies, one which would "include the study of the rhetoric of law, the analysis of the context and pragmatics of legal speaker and legal institution, the empirical examination of the functions and affinities of law viewed as communication and as function."[160] Goodrich applied this interdisciplinary and eminently semiotic approach to the analysis of an English case, *Bromley London Borough Council v. Greater London Council*, and studied the interplay of stylistics and semantics, connotations, and economic theories behind the decision.[161] His approach to case analysis is noteworthy and can guide the way toward future legal studies applying linguistics.

5. Charles Morris and Behaviorist Semiotics Charles Morris has contributed significantly to the dissemination of Peirce's theory of semiotics and to the establishment of a behavioristic direction for the science of signs. Morris described semiotics as a behavioral process in which something takes account of something else mediately. The first element is the *interpretant*,[162] the second is the *designatum*, and the mediator is the *sign* (vehicle).[163]

In his *Foundation of the Theory of Signs*,[164] Morris identified the Peircean trichotomy of syntactics, semantics, and pragmatics as a useful division of semiotics. *Syntactics* is that branch of semiotics that studies the way signs of various classes are combined to form compound signs. *Semantics* is the study of the signification of signs. Finally, *pragmatics* studies the origin, the uses, and the effects of signs. Legal semiotics often falls under the category of semantic analysis. Thus, indexes to legal studies may only contain indirect references to semiotic studies under the narrow heading of semantics.

---

159. Goodrich, *supra* note 126, at 191.

160. *Id.*

161. *Id.* at 192–200.

162. *See supra* text accompanying notes 79–85 for a discussion of Peirce's meaning of the interpretant.

163. *See* Alain Rey, *Communication vs. Semiosis: Two Conceptions of Semiotics*, *in* SIGHT, SOUND AND SENSE 102 (Thomas A. Sebeok ed., 1978).

164. CHARLES MORRIS, FOUNDATIONS OF THE THEORY OF SIGNS (1938).

Morris also distinguished between pure, descriptive, and applied semiotics which utilizes knowledge about signs for the accomplishment of various purposes. Legal semiotics would clearly fall into the category of an applied semiotics. Kalinowski's study of legal semiotics outlines the direction in which a semiotic analysis of legal language might be going: pragmatics, semantics, and syntactics.[165] He also stated categorically that law is like a science. It is not a language; it only possesses one that can be analyzed semiotically.[166]

6. Eric Buyssens and Functional Linguistics Eric Buyssens, a Belgian linguist, continued to develop Saussure's concept of semiology by confronting language with other sign systems.[167] He introduced the term *seme*, the basic element of meaning, and distinguished between intrinsic and extrinsic semes. For Buyssens the seme cannot be isolated; it can only be defined in terms of a semic function—hence the term *functional linguistics*.[168]

7. Louis Hjelmslev and Glossematics: Content and Expression Hjelmslev, a Danish linguist, developed the *glossematic* theory.[169] According to glossematics, the semiotic system is based on a small set of primes, such as class and component function, necessary and non-necessary function, both/and either/or functions, content and expression, form, and substance. Hjelmslev's distinction between content and expression, or style and substance, is particularly useful in the analysis of free speech cases. For example, in the application of the "clear and present danger" test, the court has sometimes failed to identify the real source of danger that resides in the choice of a speaker's style rather than the actual content of speech.[170] On a more practical level, courts will distinguish between form and substance when considering whether a pleading fails to state a cause of action. Looseness, verbosity, and excursiveness (i.e., form) are overlooked on a motion to dismiss if any cause of action (i.e., substance) can be ascertained from the four corners of the pleading.[171]

---

165. KALINOWSKI, *supra* note 44, at 56.

166. *Id.* Moreover, Horovitz shares the view that legal logic is a pure semiotics of scientific language in the manner of Carnap, which should be studied from the point of view of syntactics and semantics (excluding pragmatics). *See* KALINOWSKI, *supra* note 44, at 455 (Kalinowski's review of Joseph Horovitz's LAW AND LOGIC (1972)).

167. ERIC BUYSSENS, LES LANGAGES ET LES DISCOURS: ESSAI DE LINGUISTIQUE FONCTIONELLE DANS LE CADRE DE LA SÉMIOLOGIE (1948).

168. Buyssens, as well as Prieto (in *Messages et Signaux)*, views semiology as the study of voluntary messages transmitted by signals rather than indices. Functional linguists such as André Martinet established the semiology of communication in contrast to the semiology of signification practiced by Roland Barthes. *Compare* BARTHES, *supra* note 36, *with* André MARTINET, LE LANGAGE 93 (1968).

169. LOUIS HJELMSLEV, PROLOGOMENA TO A THEORY OF LANGUAGE 80 (2d ed. 1963).

170. *See supra* text accompanying notes 142–44.

171. OSCAR G. CHASE, CIVIL LITIGATION IN NEW YORK 495 (1983) (citing David D. Siegel, *Introducing: A Biannual Survey of New York Practice*, 38 ST. JOHN'S L. REV. 190, 205 (1963)).

8. Soviet Semioticians Soviet scholars, the descendants of the Russian formalist movement, have made significant contributions to the field of semiotics, especially in the area of secondary modeling systems and the study of the poetic function of language. Much of the work conducted by Soviet semioticians has been inspired by Juri Lotman.[172] To study art, music, literature, or law, Lotman examined the place and effect of these secondary modeling systems in and on the general system of culture. Lotman believed that culture is an interrelated semiotic system in which typologies of culture should be drawn up on the basis of norms, rules, and signs. A structural analysis of a secondary modeling system would account for the language level of the text, the structure of the writer's consciousness, and the structure of the world reflected in the text. A modeling system is therefore an apparatus through which a person perceives and actually models the world.

Lotman's interest in the effect of secondary modeling systems on the general system of culture has its analogy in the field of legal studies with the recent emphasis on the development of a social consciousness in the law. A work of art is as much a secondary modeling system as a carefully drawn contract or a curiously decided legal case that when studied in detail from the point of view of its linguistic elements, can reveal a world view.[173]

In conclusion, this section on linguistics has attempted to tease out of this vast field of knowledge the semiotic elements that have influenced the thinking of legal scholars in the past and their potential uses in the law in the future. It is hoped a greater awareness of the work done abroad by legal linguists imbued with the spirit and the laws of semiotics will inspire a more active application of this method to the law in the United States.

D. Anthropology

1. Claude Lévi-Strauss

a. Semiology and Structuralism. In his inaugural lecture at the Collège de France in 1961, Claude Lévi-Strauss defined *anthropology* as a branch of semiology. Lévi-Strauss was influenced by Saussure and conscientiously applied linguistic

---

172. Jurij Lotman, Lekcii po structural noj Poètike: Vvedenie, teorija stixa (Lectures on structural poetics: introduction, theory of verse) (1964); Jurij Lotman, Trudy po Znakovym sistemam (Studies in sign systems) (1964); Jurij Lotman, Stat'i po tipologii kul'tury: Materialy k kursu teorii literartury (Essays on the typology of culture: materials for a course on the theory of literature) (1973); Jurij Lotman, Sbornik state po vtoricnym modelirujuscim sistemam (Collected essays on secondary modeling systems) (1973).

173. In studying the British legal conception of woman revealed in the structural analysis of sex discrimination cases, Robertshaw makes reference to the "world-view" that is built up in the linguistic structure of the cases. Paul Robertshaw, *Contemporary Legal Constitution of Woman: Categories, Classifications, Dichotomy*, *in* Revue de la Recherche Juridique and the Oxford Review of Literature.

concepts as he set out to identify the elements of the rich and complex systems of anthropology. The main goal of his structural method is to identify constants in order to reduce the complexities of such seemingly diverse phenomena as cultural behavior, marriage laws, kinship relations, totemic systems, and cooking methods. The structural approach is applicable to most complex systems including the law.

Lévi-Strauss viewed the constitutive elements of the system at issue as relational phenomena, not intrinsic entities of substances. Thus, he examined elements in terms of their contrastive relationship to other elements. It is precisely this notion of a relationship that constitutes a *structure*. Structural analysis is by definition a study of the relationship between two or more elements. According to Lévi-Strauss, "the error of traditional anthropology, like that of traditional linguistics, was to consider the terms and not the relations between the terms."[174]

2. Structural Anthropology and the Law Lévi-Strauss' methodical approach to systems and his clear formulation of structuralist principles have had a catalytic effect on literary studies;[175] the impact on legal studies has been only faint, but lasting.[176]

Arnaud's interesting analysis of matrimonial and family structure in Aix en Provence combines the Lévi-Strauss structural approach with a sophisticated linguistic analysis of legal discourse.[177] Arnaud studied divorce decrees during January 1968 and December 1971 to arrive at the latent structures of family relations. In his goal to discover the meanings or signification behind the divorce decrees, Arnaud has clearly caught the pulse of the law by studying its language and rhetoric.

In Arnaud's analysis of matrimonial and family structure, he observed that there is a basic difference between the written stylistic structure of divorce law and the logic of family relations. He debunked the French concept of spousal equality,[178] and proved by studying judicial metaphors that judges do not really believe in spousal equality at all. Moreover, his study of judicial language reveals an unsettling oscillation between law and reality—a preference by judges for the

174. Claude Lévi-Strauss, Structural Anthropology 46 (Claire Jacobson & Brooke Grundfest Schoepf trans., 1963).

175. Roman Jakobson & Lévi-Strauss, *Les Chats de Baudelaire*, 2 L'Homme 5 (1962), *reprinted in* Introduction to Structuralism 202 (Michael Lane ed., 1970). This text-centered analysis of Baudelaire's poem served as the catalyst for a steady stream of critical commentary that remains in the annals of literary history as a primary source of structuralist theory and praxis.

176. On the legal scene, several scholars (mainly abroad) have illustrated in their varied approaches to legal texts the extent to which Lévi-Strauss' structuralist theory (inspired by Saussure) has influenced legal studies. *See* the works of Arnaud, Kalinowski, Jackson, and Robertshaw cited *supra* note 134. *See also* Goodrich, *supra* note 145.

177. Arnaud, *supra* note 134.

178. *Id.* at 217.

image of the *haus-frau* balanced against their recognition of the legal equality of the wife.

Arnaud's study rests on the structural principle that relationships, not elements, are the key to uncovering the hidden mechanisms of complex legal systems. This principle concern with relationships is based on the nature of the sign itself, which is a constant interaction between signifier, signified, and referent. As Arnaud aptly observed, a computerized study of French family structure as seen in the law could only identify key words.[179] The computer could not study the significant relationships that exist between the words used and the reality hidden within and below the rhetoric. Notwithstanding the vital function of the computer for certain kinds of data collection, we cannot help but agree with Arnaud that meaning is found through language study in the interstices of complex relationships such as law and reality.

Structural anthropology and its application in the law have demonstrated the benefits of adopting a clearly defined system's approach to solving legal problems. As law is moving in the direction of relational analysis with emphasis on law as social change, the structural and semiotic principles outlined by Lévi-Strauss should prove to be of major importance.

E. Literary Criticism

1. Russian Formalism Russian formalism flourished at the Moscow Linguistic Circle and the Petrograd Society for the Study of Poetic Language (OPOYAZ) from 1915 to 1930; it had a direct influence on the development of structuralism and semiotics in Western Europe and the United States.[180] The early Russian formalists were text-centered critics who wrote primarily about the specificity of poetic language and devices of style. They considered literature outside the realm of social consciousness and thereby continued the symbolists' emphasis on form over content. They believed that literature was fundamentally autonomous, self-expressive, and intrinsically different from ordinary language. Disassociating themselves from aesthetic theoreticians and philosophers, the formalists advocated a scientific, objective investigation of the facts in and of themselves. Excursions into extratextual matters were not within the purview of a formalist method. As with the structural linguists, their purpose was to study the laws of

---

179. *Id.* at 224.

180. *See* Terence Hawkes, Structuralism & Semiotics 59–73 (1977) (discussion of Russian Formalism). Roman Jakobson, Boris Eichenbaum, Victor Shklovsky, Boris Tomashjevsky, and Juni Tynjanov are primary contributors to Russian Formalism. Tzvetan Todorov's publication of translated formalist criticism in *Théorie de la Littérature* in 1965 is an indication of the importance of formalist theories to literary criticism of the Western world. It is also a sign pointing to the methodological relationship that exists between formalists and structuralists. *See* Lee Lemon & Marian J. Reis, Russian Formalist Criticism (1965); Victor Erlich, Russian Formalism (1954).

literary production, and they concentrated on the uses of phonemic devices. Unlike the structuralists who studied the relationship of form and content, formalists believed in the dominance of form. Echoes of the formalist text-centered approach to literature are heard in some rule-based legal circles by those who object to the study of law as a social phenomenon.

a. Defamiliarization and the Law. Victor Shklovsky's provocative notion of *defamiliarization* or "making strange"[181] is of particular interest to lawyers analyzing and presenting a sequence of events or facts to a judge or jury. Shklovsky believed the essential function of poetry or art is to attack routinization in the reader's modes of perception. Art shocks the observer the way illegal acts shock the people because art deviates from the norm. In other words, art defamiliarizes that which is overly familiar and forces us into an awareness of its very existence. Shklovsky focused his attention on that aspect of a novel's narrative structure in which the process of defamiliarization is most obvious—the plot—and investigated the means by which the shock takes place.

Defamiliarization is a concept that applies on many levels of the law, not the least important of which is the drafting of a document and the use of words that shock the judge and jury into awareness without creating a sense of impropriety. This shock can be accomplished rhetorically (or simply grammatically) by contrast from a context.[182] Defamiliarization is also important in the interpretation of legal texts. Even though the immediate purpose of the law differs from that of literature, both are analyzable discourses in which "shocking" or unexpected terms, "unconventional" language,[183] and nonnormative constructions play a similar role. These defamiliarizing techniques in the law can be further examined from the point of view of their stylistic effects and persuasiveness.

b. Narrative Structures and the Law: Vladimir Propp and Algirdas Greimas. The full implications of Shklovsky's theory of defamiliarization and the conventions on which narrative structures are built are illustrated in Vladimir Propp's *Morphology of the Folktale.*[184] Propp's work is a major contribution to formalist theory and narrative syntax. In the course of his incisive analysis of the folktale, Propp identified thirty-one constant functions distributed among seven "spheres of action:" the villain, the donor, the helper, the princess, the dispatcher, the hero, and the false hero. This type of categorization is not without interest to lawyers intent on analyzing a fact pattern in criminal law. For example, the

---

181. *See* Hawkes, *supra* note 180, *at* 65; Victor Shklovsky, Oteorii prozy (On the Theory of prose) (1973).

182. Echoes of this formalist concept can be heard in Brooks' *The Well Wrought Urn* where he introduces the notion of stylistic contrast from a context. Cleanth Brooks, The Well Wrought Urn (1947).

183. *See* Ronald Dworkin, Law's Empire 114–50 (1986) (discussion of the role of conventionalism and shared expectation in the law).

184. Vladimir Propp, Morphologie du conte (1965).

particular function of each player in a criminal Racketeer Influenced and Corrupt Organizations (RICO)[185] action could be reduced to categories of actors performing a similar function in the pattern of activity or enterprise.

Greimas[186] made significant modifications on Propp's distribution of actors' functions.[187] In fact, Greimas applied his brand of semiotics to legal texts relying on the belief that semiotics is a method applicable to any discourse.[188] Greimas viewed legal language as a variant of natural language. When approaching a legal text, he considered the levels of its linguistic code, legal code (norms or grammar), and legal judgment.[189] Like Chomsky, Greimas is in search of a legal grammar, and his view of legal language as a "logic" is like that of the positivists. Goodrich has commented on the limits of Greimasian semiotics as applied to legal texts: "Greimas' analysis adds nothing of substance to the commonplaces of legal positivism—it adds linguistic refinement and precision. In a sense it represents the apotheosis of positivism. . . ."[190]

2. The Prague School: The Development of Social Consciousness The Prague School continued in the tradition of the formalists but attempted to integrate the study of sound and meaning into the social consciousness.[191] This development in literary theory is analogous to the movement in law from positivism to realism. Legal exegetes have profited from the notion of a social consciousness in the text, and a rich brand of legal interpretation known as law and society developed and flourished into legal realism.

Mukarovsky, who rejected the formalist concept of art as a solely autonomous sign, insisted on the semiotic function of art, which he viewed as being both

---

185. Racketeer Influenced and Corrupt Organizations Act, Pub. L. No. 91–452, 84 Stat. 941 (codified at 18 U.S.C. §§ 1961–1968 (1982)).

186. *See supra* text accompanying notes 186–90 for a discussion of Greimasian structuralism.

187. ALGIRDAS JULIEN GREIMAS, SÉMANTIQUE STRUCTURALE: RECHERCHE DE MÉTHODE (1966).

188. *See* JACKSON, *supra* note 10, at 31–147 (detailed discussion of Greimasian semiotics applied to the law). Greimas, in collaboration with Landowski, analyzed legal discourse in a chapter entitled "Analyse sémiotique d'un discours juridique." GREIMAS &COURTÈS, *supra* note 151, at 79–128.

189. GREIMAS & COURTÈS, *supra* note 151, at 90–94.

190. Goodrich, *supra* note 126, at 183.

191. The *Theses* of the Prague Linguistic Circle contain the connections among linguistics, semiotics, society, and the study of literature. "Everything in the work of art and its relation to the outside world . . . can be discussed in terms of sign and meaning; in this sense aesthetics can be regarded as a part of the modern science of signs or semiotics." Edward Stankiewicz, *Structural Poetics and Linguistics*, 12 CURRENT TRENDS IN LINGUISTICS 629, 630 (1974) (quotation omitted). The path toward social consciousness was laid by the early formalists in the 1920s when Tynyanov and Jakobson attempted to create a more integrated school of criticism belonging to the collective consciousness.

autonomous and communicative.[192] "It is the total context of so-called social phenomena—for example, philosophy, politics, religion, and economics that constitutes the reality which art must represent."[193] Mukarovsky believed that only a semiotic point of view could permit theoreticians to account for both the autonomous nature of art and its essentially dynamic structure. Semiotics, then, would help theoreticians understand artistic structure "which is imminent but in constant dialectic relation to the development of other spheres of culture."[194]

The development of a social consciousness grew out of the Prague School and its insistence on the dynamic nature of artistic structure. These ideas are shared by legal realists who, like Mukarovsky, would greatly benefit by the adoption of a semiotic orientation in their legal analyses.

3. Roman Jakobson

a. Metaphor, Metonymy, and the Law. Roman Jakobson's linguistic and literary theories grew out of his affiliation with the Prague School, and he has played a major role in orienting literary interpretation toward linguistics and semiotics. Jakobson attempted to describe the poetic function of language,[195] pursuing this goal as a formalist, linguist, and semiotician. His two basic notions of *polarity* and *equivalence*[196] are derived from Saussure's concepts of the syntagmatic and paradigmatic planes of linguistic performance. Extending these ideas to literary language, Jakobson identified metaphor and metonymy as the basic rhetorical figures in poetry and prose.[197]

---

192. J. Mukarovsky, Structure, Sign, and Function (J. Burbank & P. Steiner trans. 1978).

193. *Id.* at 84. Realizing that the formalists needed a truly semiotic orientation (and by that he meant being socially aware in both the Saussurean and Peircean senses), Mukarovsky proclaimed that "as long as the semiotic character of art is insufficiently illuminated, the study of the structure of the work will necessarily remain incomplete." *Id.* at 87. As with the new critics, who follow the formalists both chronologically and philosophically, Mukarovsky rejects purely formal analysis. He will also reject analysis that considers the work a direct reflection of either its author's psyche or the ideological, economic, social, or cultural milieu.

194. *Id.*

195. *See* Roman Jakobson, *Closing Statement: Linguistics and Poetics, in* Style in Language (Thomas Sebeok ed. 1960).

196. *See* Scholes, *supra* note 120, at 19 (discussion of Jakobson's study of language loss among aphasiacs in which the concepts of equivalence and polarity in linguistic performance are elaborated).

197. Roman Jakobson & Morris Halle, Fundamentals of Language 69, 75 (1956). These modes of binary opposition correspond respectively to the process of selection and combination. *See* Jakobson, *supra* note 195, at 370. The combinative or syntagmatic process proceeds by contiguity (i.e., one word is placed next to another). This mode, which is metonymic, is more frequently associated with prose. The selective or associative process is characterized by similarity and occurs more frequently in poetry than prose.

Today we recognize the ever-presence of metaphor in ordinary language as well as in poetry and prose.[198] Reflecting on Jakobson's discovery, some legal scholars observe that legal discourse is predominantly denotative (i.e., referential rather than emotive).[199] The time has come to debunk the notion that legal language is ordinary, objective, and ideally nonmetaphoric. As with ordinary language, legal language cannot escape metaphor, and much of its inscrutable ambiguity is the result of metaphoric usage. Words are freighted with political, ideological, cultural, and literary overtones that aid in a speaker's subconscious selection. Freighted language is even more complicated due to cultural diversity that increases the possibility for interference with communication or understanding.[200]

b. The Act of Communication. Jakobson's work on the nature of the communicative act is probably the starting point for any introduction to semiotics. From his diagram of the six constituent factors that make up a speech event,[201] we can plot the direction that studies in legal semiotics might take in the near future:

context
message
addresser —— —— addressee
contact
code

Communication consists of a message sent by an addresser to an addressee. The message, sent in code, requires a contact between addresser and addressee that may be made orally, visually, or otherwise. If the message does not refer to a context that is mutually understood between the addressee and the addresser (who presumably share the convention upon which this code depends), the message will not make sense.

The meaning of a text can be found by considering the total act of communication and each of the six elements possessing its own special function. The nature of a particular message will depend on the functional character of the dominant element.[202] If the communication is mainly concerned with the addresser of the message, the emotive function will predominate. This is rare in

---

198. *See supra* text accompanying notes 140–44 for a discussion of metaphors in the law.

199. *See* KALINOWSKI, *supra* note 44, at 52 (*"Il est évident que le langage du droit n'est pas appelé à remplir la fonction d'expression, mais celle de communication"*) ("It is obvious that the purpose of legal language is not to fulfill an expressive function but rather one of communication.").

200. During an informal discussion held on Mar. 26, 1985 with the late Thomas Franck, Professor of International Law at New York University School of Law, Professor Franck confirmed that the frequent and unavoidable use of metaphor in international legal contexts was of legitimate semiotic concern for the accurate transmission and reception of information.

201. Jakobson, *supra* note 195, at 353.

202. *Id.* at 357.

legal language that is primarily concerned with the communication of the message to the addressee. However, emotive language is used for emphasis and persuasion in argumentation.

If the message is oriented toward the addressee, the *conative* function will dominate. The conative function is manifested by the vocative or imperative mode of address ("Look," or "I say," or "Oyez"). For a communication oriented toward its context, the referential function will dominate; the phatic function is designed to establish contact with the addressee, as with small talk that does nothing more than establish a rapport between speakers.

When speakers want to make sure they are using the same code, the *metalingual* function will dominate ("Do you see?" or "Understand?"). In legal contexts, the frequent presence of the adverb *clearly* or *obviously* performs a subtle metalingual function when lawyers are communicating with lawyers. When lawyers are communicating with lay people, the metalingual function is more direct because the conventions of the legal codes are not shared by all laymen.

If the communication is dominated by the message for its own sake, the poetic or aesthetic function dominates. As legal language is designed to communicate a message (less for its own sake than for the sake of the addressee), legal language has a reduced poetic function. Thus, semiotics and the dominance of certain constituent functions making up a speech event enable us to identify in a more precise manner the major difference between literary and legal language.

4. The New Criticism

a. The Text-Centered Approach and Its Application to the Law. In Britain and America around the 1930s and 1940s, the new literary critics rose up in arms against traditional literary criticism that was then oriented toward such extratextual matters as biography, the author's psyche, and literary history. But as with the formalists before them, the new critics viewed the work of art as autonomous. They coined the phrase "the intentional fallacy" and rejected hypotheses about what an author really meant.[203] Justice Antonin Scalia's legal analytical method, which he applies rigorously in statutory and constitutional interpretation, is a text-centered approach that he calls *originalism* and *textualism*.[204] Justice Scalia opposes the popular idea that judicial interpretation should be guided by legislative intent.[205]

The new critics argued that the literary work is "bounded," self-sufficient, and free of authorial intention, historical necessity, and reader prejudices. Therefore, the literary text should be examined in and for itself, on its own terms, without

---

203. *See* Susan W. Tiefenbrun, *The Secret of Irony: Apollo and Isis in Rabelais*, XI Oeuvres et Critiques 15, 18 (1986) for a discussion of the intentional fallacy, originally proposed by Wimsatt and Beardsley, and its use or misuse in literary interpretation

204. Antonin Scalia, A Matter of Interpretation: Federal Courts and the Law 132 (1997).

205. *Id.*

any special method or system.[206] Art, they argued, is separate from science, and only natural intelligence is necessary to fathom a text's hidden meanings. However, interpretive legal theory has never thoroughly adopted this antiscientific view because of the significant role that history and authorial intention play in both positivist and realist interpretive techniques.[207]

b. The New Criticism and Semiotics. Despite an almost wholesale rejection of sign theory by the new critics, some active participants of this school were important contributors to the development of semiotic theory.[208] Early structuralists[209] opposed the new critics, arguing that their conception of a totally objective reader devoid of subconsciously held ideological principles is an impossible goal.[210] Structuralists say the new critics turned literature into an abstraction divorced from reality. An infusion of semiotic orientation into this school of literary interpretation would have avoided these criticisms, which are no doubt shared by the legal realists against the text-centered approach and false purity of the positivists.

c. Semiotics and the Opening Up of the Text Semiotic theory focuses attention away from the literary work as a divinely inspired "book" to be discovered. Instead, the semiotician studies "the text" which is considered, for the most part, as open and incomplete. Semioticians are very much at home with the goal of demystifying literature and the law. Many semioticians, as with the legal realists who object to the closed system of legal positivism, welcome the indeterminacy of legal language and attempt to fill in communication gaps with references to sociological, psychological, and anthropological phenomena that aid in the establishment of meaning.

However, some semioticians are closely allied to the traditions of new criticism, and they retain the notion of the bounded, self-sufficient, self-referential, and nonmimetic text. With the help of a rich background in literary

---

206. The new critics were particularly interested in questions of ambiguity, irony, paradox, and wit. Their primary thrust was the sanctity of the text and the informality of its interpretive process.

207. *See generally* Dworkin, *supra* note 8, at 536–39.

208. I.A. Richards wrote not only about the psychological complexities at work in poetry and in experience, but he produced *The Meaning of Meaning* with Charles K. Ogden, in which Richards studied the influence of language upon thought and the science of symbolism. Cleanth Brooks and William Empson, refusing the idea of a single meaning for a poem, investigated the notions of beneficial ambiguity and multiplicity of meaning—concepts that are critical to the broad interpretation of legal texts. *See supra* note 140.

209. An example of the early structuralist approach is found in the works of Roland Barthes and Serge Doubrovsky. *See, e.g.*, SERGE DOUBROVSKY, POURQUOI LA NOUVELLE CRITIQUE (1966).

210. Scholes called new criticism a "scandal" because critics subconsciously use cultural codes to interpret texts while insisting these codes are irrelevant for analytical purposes. ROBERT SCHOLES, SEMIOTICS AND INTERPRETATION 15 (1982).

conventions, these semioticians produce insightful and innovative interpretations.[211] Saussurean legal semioticians such as Kalinowski[212] and Arnaud[213] would be representative of this group of semioticians who retain the notion of the bounded text, but who rely on a background of legal conventions rooted in reality to inform their insightful exegeses.[214]

d. Objectivity and Subjectivity in Legal Interpretation: Ronald Dworkin. Semiotics teaches us that words are merely arbitrary.[215] However, applied to legal language, this concept threatens the very stability of the legal system. If the words used have no rational basis other than convention, where does the lawyer look to determine the meaning of a legal text? For some, such as the legal positivists allied with the Saussurean brand of semiotics, the text has objective, determinate meaning within it and needs only to be identified.[216] For others more in line with Peirce's notion of semiotics as an open-ended process, the law is not a system of rules or commands having an invariable meaning. Rather, a rule is a range of culturally possible results that lawyers and judges must argue out.[217] For these legal realists, law is the culture of legal argument.[218] Thus, we have two camps in legal interpretive theory: one which is objective and limits interpretation to that which is strictly in the text, and one which is subjective and relatively free.

Ronald Dworkin holds the intermediary position that legal and critical practice is not totally free. Law is "deeply and thoroughly political . . . [but it] is not a matter of personal or partisan politics . . . "[219] Law is like a "chain enterprise," both objective and subjective, and dependent on history.[220] Dworkin's theory of literary interpretation begins with the "aesthetic hypothesis" that "[a]n interpretation of a text should attempt to show it as the best work of art it can be . . . "[221]

---

211. Michael Riffaterre, *The Self-Sufficient Text*, DIACRITICS 39 (Fall, 1973).

212. *See supra* note 134.

213. *See infra* text accompanying notes 274–75.

214. "When a semiotician starts examining laws as a patterned system of meaning, their insubstantiality becomes evident and the inquiry presses on both jurisprudence and epistemology." Gerald Graff, *"Keep off the Grass," "Drop Dead," and other Indeterminancies: A Response to Sanford Levinson*, 60 TEX. L. REV. 405 (1982) (quoting Mary Douglas, The Future of Semiotics (1982) (unpublished manuscript)).

215. *See infra* text accompanying notes 123–24 for a discussion of the arbitrary sign.

216. H.L.A. HART, THE CONCEPT OF LAW (1961).

217. *See* James Boyd White, *Law as Language: Reading Law and Reading Literature*, 60 TEX. L. REV. 415, 436 (1982).

218. A good example of the culture of legal argument is found in Chief Justice Marshall's interpretation of the meaning of the word *necessary* in *McCulloch v. Maryland*: "This word, then, like others, is used in various senses; and in its construction, the subject, the context, the intention of the person using them, are all to be taken into view." McCulloch v. Maryland, 17 U.S. (4 Wheat.) 316, 415 (1819).

219. Dworkin, *supra* note 8, at 527.

220. *See id.* at 542–43.

221. *Id.* at 531 (emphasis in original).

He then proposes the analogy between legal interpretation, which is a social practice involving judicial decision making, limited by principles of fitness, and the writing of a chain novel.[222] Implicit in Dworkin's conception of law as interpretation is a view of judicial authority that is grounded not in rules as the positivists would have it, but in an articulate consistency epitomized by the global rationality of a Herculean judge.

H.L.A. Hart: Legal Positivism and Semiotics. H.L.A. Hart is the positivist who proposed the theory that law is an interplay of primary and secondary rules.[223] Unlike the naturalists who claim that mankind through a common human nature perceives certain basic norms as universals in the law, the positivists adhere "to the view that there is no necessary connection between law and morality."[224] Rather, law for the positivists is a matter of human choice. The source of that element of human choice is located in the interaction between primary and secondary rules in Hart's legal theory, in which "[p]rimary rules concern the behaviour of the subjects of the [legal] system . . . " Secondary rules take into account the recognition and change of primary rules as well as the manner of dispute adjudication.[225] Because secondary rules for Hart depend on convention and not nature, their content reflects the positivists' view that law is based on human choice.[226]

According to Bernard Jackson, who has studied Hart's legal theory from the point of view of semiotics,[227] Hart is the contemporary positivist and legal philosopher who has dealt most explicitly with law as a semiotic system.[228] Hart is interested in communication as an intentional act, not as signification.[229] His account of a central "'core of settled meaning'[230] is predominantly pragmatic

---

222. *Id.* at 542.

> Deciding hard cases at law is rather like this strange literary exercise . . . Each judge is then like a novelist in the chain. He or she must read through what other judges in the past have written not simply to discover what these judges have said, or their state of mind when they said it, but to reach an opinion about what these judges collectively have done, in the way that each of our novelists formed an opinion about the collective novel so far written . . . Each judge must regard himself, in deciding the new case before him, as a partner in a complex chain enterprise of which these innumerable decisions, structures, conventions, and practices are the history; it is his job to continue that history into the future through what he does on that day. . . .

Id. at 542–43.

223. Hart, *supra* note 216.

224. *See* Jackson, *supra* note 10, at 5.

225. *Id.* at 6.

226. *Id.*

227. *Id.* at 147–66.

228. *Id.* at 148.

229. *Id.*

230. *Id.* at 147. *See* H.L.A. Hart, *Positivism and the Separation of Law and Morals*, 71 Harv. L. Rev. 593, 607 (1958).

rather than semantic" in nature, and it assumes an activity of interpretation.[231] It is in Hart's concept of the penumbra of linguistic uncertainty[232] that his communicational model is most clearly demonstrated. Hart identifies two principal devices used "to communicate general standards of conduct which multitudes of individuals could understand"—legislation and precedent.[233] To communicate these general standards of conduct, there "must be a core of settled meaning, but there will be, as well, a penumbra of debatable cases in which words are neither obviously applicable nor obviously ruled out."[234]

Although according to Hart, most cases fall within the core of settled meaning, legal language is at times indeterminate and suffers from multiple meanings or *polysemy*. Hart aptly called the cases that fall outside the core a crisis in communication requiring judicial discretion,[235] which is the result of what Hart called the "open texture" of legal language. To limit the problem of polysemy, Hart created the model of core and penumbral cases. Although meaning is generally determinative for Hart, he recognized that in certain penumbral cases judges will have to use their subjective decision-making powers.[236]

Few would consider Hart to be allied in any way with the theory of semiotics, and yet he spoke the language of signs as early as 1952.[237] Communication for Hart is the intentional transmission of a message. In a penumbral question, the plain meaning does not generate certainty of the intention, and the judge must decide this question. Often this judicial discretion will be facilitated by a semiotic argument. For example, in *Griswold v. Connecticut*,[238] Justice Douglas found the right of association hidden in the penumbra of the Bill of Rights. He also discovered the right of privacy lurking in the Third Amendment. These discoveries, which have had profound effects on the development of constitutional law, have come about (probably without conscious attempt) in accordance with the most basic semiotic principles. *Griswold* is a case that was decided semiotically, and unsurprisingly one of the opinion's last words refers to "telltale signs."[239]

---

231. Jackson, *supra* note 10, at 148.

232. Hart, *supra* note 216, at 12.

233. *Id.* at 121.

234. *Id.* at 123.

235. *Id. See* Ronald Dworkin, Taking Rights Seriously 31 (1978) for Dworkin's account of positivism and Hart's notion of judicial discretion.

236. Hart, *supra* note 216, at 123; *cf.* Dworkin, *supra* note 8, at 536–39.

237. Before we speak of a person meaning something by a statement, it must be true not merely (i) that he uttered noises and those were in fact interpreted as signs and not merely (ii) that he intended the noises to be interpreted as signs, but that he should intend the listener not merely to believe or to do something but to recognise [sic] from the utterance that *he intended* the listener to believe or do something. Hart, *supra* note 216, at 62.

238. 381 U.S. 479, 484 (1965).

239. *Id.* at 485.

Hart appears to have been well-informed about speech act theory, another branch of semiotics.[240] He looked into the role of performatives in a famous article in which he proposed the theory that man is responsible for his acts and that the language of rights is attributive rather than descriptive.[241] Hart explained that when a man says, "I did that," this language is not a description of a physical act, but an attribution of the man's responsibility for the act, which is a "performative utterance."[242]

Thus, this current study has attempted to draw an analogy between the open-ended approach of Peircean semiotics and the reality-based perspective of the legal realist tradition that has been identified as subjectivist. I have also shown that a goal of objectivity is shared by legal positivists and the new critics using a text-centered approach. But labels are misleading. A brief look at Hart's evolution from objectivist to subjectivist,[243] the unexpected role that semiotics played in the elaboration of his legal positivist theories, and his enunciation of the "open texture" of language[244] (which allies him with the ideology of the realist school despite his explicit criticism of the realist position) demonstrates the dangers of applying labels to legal theories. Analogies are at best fraught with distortions, but categories and analogy are the cornerstones of structural and semiotic studies of the type undertaken here. It is hoped these inevitable distortions will somehow be corrected by reference to the specialized studies cited. The identification of a harmonious interdependence of many disciplines at work in the quest for validity in interpretation and meaning may even justify the distortion.

5. Structural Poetics

a. Structuralists vs. Deconstructionists. Structural poetics is the application of the basic principles of structuralism to the analysis of literary texts.[245] Early in the development of this literary theory, which was firmly rooted in linguistics and anthropology,[246] structuralists branched out into several schools differing either as to their conception of literary language or their allegiance to the principle of a

---

240. *See* J.L. AUSTIN, HOW TO DO THINGS WITH WORDS (1962); John Searle, *What is a Speech Act?, in* PHILOSOPHY IN AMERICA 223 (Max. Black ed., 1984) (introduction to speech theory).

241. H.L.A. Hart, *The Assumption of Responsibility and Rights, in* LOGIC AND LANGUAGE 145 (A. Flew ed., 1951).

242. *See* Grzegorczyk, *supra* note 134, at 229.

243. JACKSON, *supra* note 10, at 155.

244. *Id.* at 161, *citing* HART, *supra* note 216, at 121.

245. According to Edward Stankiewicz in 1974, structural poetics was a "trend in modern literary theory and practice which tries to apply to the study of literature strict and objective methods and which starts with the premise that literary works, as verbal art, cannot be studied without reference to the linguistic material of which they are made." Stanckiewicz, *supra* note 191, at 629.

246. *See* text accompanying notes 174–76; *see also* note 54 that discusses the fundamentals of structuralist theory.

bounded text. This proliferation of schools of structuralist persuasion accounts for the confusion surrounding the term *structuralism.* The confusion is exacerbated by the fact that many call structuralist theory what is now referred to as post-structuralist or deconstructionist theory.

Deconstructionists both accept and reject structural analysis. As Jonathan Culler put it: [S]tructuralists take linguistics as a model and attempt to develop "grammars" [to] account for the form and meaning of literary works; post-structuralists investigate the way in which this project is subverted by the workings of the texts themselves. Structuralists are convinced that systematic knowledge is possible; post-structuralists claim to know only the impossibility of this knowledge.[247]

Thus, a self-critical awareness has punctuated the development of structuralism from the very start and may have reinforced the scientific spirit of the whole enterprise.[248] The same self-critical awareness is characteristic of semiotics in general.[249] This similarity may explain why, despite their philosophical differences, both structuralists and post-structuralists have adopted semiotics as a theory with which to approach the analysis of discourse.

b. Structuralist Theories and the Law. Diversity among structuralists is legion. Some are deviationists, others are pragmatic, and still others are neo-formalist. Deviationists believe the essence of poetic language is its violation of the norm.[250] This theory is particularly suited to the analysis of legal discourse; it has been expressed by Kelsen in the distinction he drew between legal validity and volition, the latter being likened to the deviation by an individual in the creation of norms.[251] Those who object to the deviation theory because of the ill-defined nature of the norm propose a more flexible approach based on stylistic and semantic contrasts from a context.[252] This approach is particularly suited to the interpretive legal theory that views the law as prescriptive rather than descriptive. Thus, the legality of an act, viewed not as a deviation from black letter law but

---

247. JONATHAN D. CULLER, ON DECONSTRUCTION, THEORY AND CRITICISM AFTER STRUCTURALISM 22 (1982).

248. Philip Lewis, *The Post-Structuralist Condition,* DIACRITICS 2, 8–9 (Spring, 1982).

249. Julia Kristeva, one of the pioneers in literary semiotics, remarked in the development of structuralist criticism that:

> [S]emiotics cannot develop except as a critique of semiotics. At every moment in its development semiotics must theorize its object, its own method, and the relationship between them; it therefore theorizes itself and becomes, by thus turning back on itself, the theory of its own scientific practice . . . It is a direction for research, always open, a theoretical enterprise which turns back upon itself, a perpetual self-criticism.

JULIA KRISTEVA, SEMIOTIKÈ: RECHERCHES POUR UNE SÉMANALYSE 30 (1969) (author's translation).

250. Tzvetan Todorov, *Les Poètes devant "le bon usage,"* 314 REVUE D'ESTHÉTIQUE 301, 305 (1965); *see also* PIERRE GUIRAUD, LA SÉMIOLOGIE (Que sais-je edit. 1971).

251. *See supra* text accompanying note 126.

252. MICHAEL RIFFATERRE, ESSAIS DE STYLISTIQUE STRUCTURALE 64–94 (1971).

rather as a contrast from the context, might depend on the degree of contrast, the manner in which the contrast is executed, and the effect of the contrast on the public. This approach would retain some of the certainty associated with a rules-based system and promote justice for the individual.

Some structuralists view the structures of the text and its underlying codes as residing within a hermetically closed system.[253] Others conceive of the text as open and ready to be completed by the reader.[254] The same dichotomy exists in legal theory. Legal structuralists such as Arnaud, who have adopted a Lévi-Straussian model, are perplexed by the closedness of the system and seek ways to justify it.[255] Arnaud has incorporated semiotics in his structuralist approach to legal texts. He believes that law can be studied as the development of underlying structures and not of a conscious construction. As law is included within a general theory of communication, the understanding of the structures of the legal system will come about only through an attentive examination of signs.[256] Arnaud perceives semiotics as providing the link with society that can open up the fundamentally closed system of the structuralists.

In keeping with the rejection of early formalism and its static text-centered perspective, some structuralists began to view the reading process as one involved in history and society.[257] Thus, Marxist critics,[258] psychoanalytic critics, and sociologic critics, whether their text is literary or legal, are still classified as structuralist if their perception of the text is a fundamentally relational one in which individual elements have no significance in and of themselves, but take on significance in relation to other elements in the text's structural system.

Before discussing the particular contribution of scholars applying structuralist methods to the law, it might be useful to summarize the somewhat confused global picture of structural theory. Without oversimplifying the diversity of structuralist

---

253. Riffaterre elaborates a literary theory based on a closed text but which incorporates an interpretive method rich enough to produce rather extraordinary insights into the hidden mechanisms of literary texts. Riffaterre, *supra* note 211, *passim*.

254. Umberto Eco and Roland Barthes are structuralists who envisaged an open text.

255. Arnaud, *supra* note 26, at 300.

256. *Id.* at 299.

257. The confusion of identity between structuralists and post-structuralists began when the reality-based structuralists questioned the closedness of the systems analysis traditionally undertaken by Saussurean structuralists. This confusion has led Jonathan Culler to conclude "the distinction between structuralism and post-structuralism is highly unreliable." CULLER, *supra* note 247, at 30. De Man described the changes that were taking place early in the development of structuralist thought: "The spirit of the times is not blowing in the direction of formalist and intrinsic criticism . . . [W]e do continue to hear a great deal about reference, about the non verbal 'outside' to which language refers." Paul De Man, *Semiology and Rhetoric*, *in* TEXTUAL STRATEGIES 121 (Josué V Harari ed., 1979).

258. André-Jean Arnaud studies the relationship between Marxism and structuralism in the analysis of legal discourse in *Structuralisme et Droit*. Arnaud, *supra* note 26, at 300.

persuasions, let us say there are basically two waves of structuralist thought. The first group of text analysts remains formalistic, stressing style over content. They concentrate on either a bounded or unbounded text as a phenomenon of linguistic game playing or as the disruption of a particular norm or convention. The second group, adopting the notion of an open text, is interdisciplinary. These text analysts attempt to reach out into the fields of psychoanalysis, Marxism, anthropology, and philosophy to determine how meaning is conveyed through a structural system. This group's emphasis on language as a social phenomenon has had particular appeal among the legal realists and the critical legal studies movement.[259] Both groups of structuralists are united by their adoption of semiotic theory.

Bernard Jackson. What has structuralism contributed to legal studies? As Bernard Jackson put it, "legal philosophy cannot remain immune from the structuralist approach for two reasons: first, law partakes . . . of a system of communication and . . . is subject to whatever contribution structuralism has made to the science of semiotics; second, structuralism [is] a challenge to the positivist metaphysic . . . underlying legal philosophy."[260]

Jackson has attempted a systematic analysis of the relationship between contemporary semiotic theory and modern jurisprudence in his challenging book, *Semiotics and Legal Theory*,[261] which is weighted toward structural semiotics of the Saussurean or European school. Jackson juxtaposes Greimasian structural theory and the mainly positivist legal theories of Hart, Dworkin, MacCormick, and Kelsen to lay the foundation for a semiotic theory of law. The intriguing parallels he draws between the jurisprudential divisions of naturalism, positivism, and realism[262] and their counterparts in semiotics reflect the implication of language in the legal process and a grammar of language common to both ordinary and legal language.[263] Jackson manages to crack through the barriers of conventional wisdom by demonstrating with conviction and persuasiveness that Greimasian methodology, long since considered by most to be a bastion of restrictive normativity that is isolated from a sociocultural context, has an affinity to the legal realism movement.[264] Similarly striking is Jackson's

259. Roberto M. Unger, *The Critical Legal Studies Movement*, 96 HARV. L. REV. 561 (1983). *See infra* text accompanying notes 314–35 for a discussion of the role of semiotics in the critical legal studies movement.

260. Jackson, *Towards a Structuralist Theory*, *supra* note 134, at 5.

261. *See supra* note 10.

262. *Id.* at 4.

263. *See* West, *supra* note 35 for an interesting account of the relationship between literary theory and jurisprudence. West relies on Northrup Frye's literary theories and applies them to the law as narrative.

264. JACKSON, *supra* note 10, at 137.

attempt to uncover the semiotic basis of Hart's positivism[265] and "[t]he [s]emiotic [c]haracter of Dworkinian logic."[266]

Donald Hermann. In his overview of meritorious legal structuralist studies, Jackson draws our attention to the work of Donald Hermann,[267] who views such legal phenomena as electronic surveillance, monopolization, and products liability in terms of Saussure's binary oppositions. Hermann's aim is purely structuralist; that is, he tries to distinguish the limited number of constants from the multiple variants in a complex field.

Paul Robertshaw. Of particular interest is Paul Robertshaw's structural analysis of a single House of Lords' case.[268] In attempting to apply the structuralist method to the facts of the case, Robertshaw has succeeded in elucidating the otherwise inexplicable or hidden. Robertshaw has also applied Piaget's basic laws of transformation[269] to the evolution of the concept of an "equitable mortgage" in the chancery courts and in the common law courts[270] relating legal changes to societal transformation.

In Robertshaw's structural analysis[271] of all of the reported British sex discrimination cases, he drew an important distinction between legal discourse and "folk talk."[272] He identified the latter as the organizing mode of the legal outcomes. *Folk talk* consists of references to tigers, fables, parables, and proverbs occurring in the cases that share a zoological unity. Robertshaw's structural analysis of the zoological unity of the folk talk in these cases reflects the approaches of both Saussure and Lévi-Strauss. He studied the surface and deep structures of the figures, identified five different levels of inquiry, and provided real insights into the British perception of equality between the sexes. Furthermore, Robertshaw was able to define the characteristics of the nature of "woman" in contrast to

265. *Id.* at 147–66.

266. *Id.* at 192–224.

267. Donald H. J. Hermann, *A Structuralist Approach to Legal Reasoning*, 48 S. Cal. L. Rev. 1131 (1975).

268. Paul Robertshaw, *Unreasonableness and Judicial Control of Administrative Discretion: The Geology of the Chertsey Caravans Case*, Pub. L. 113 (1975) [hereinafter cited as Robertshaw, *Unreasonableness and Judicial Control*]; *see* Paul Robertshaw, *Structuralisim and Law: Some Comments*, 2 Liverpool L. Rev. 31 (1980) (critique of Jackson's essay on structuralism and the law).

269. Jean Piaget, Structuralism (1971).

270. Robertshaw, *supra* note 268, at 36.

271. *See supra* text accompanying notes 307–10 for Robertshaw's post-structuralist developments in semiotics and the law.

272. Robertshaw, *supra* note 268. This article is a reworking of Robertshaw's original study of metaphor in the sex discrimination cases. Paul Robertshaw, *Semantic and Linguistic Aspects of Sex Discrimination Decisions: Dichotomised Woman*, *in* Semiotics, Law, and Social Science, Liverpool L. Rev. 203 (Domenico Carzo & Bernard S. Jackson eds., 1984 spec. issue).

"man" as constituted in seventy-six printed items called Law Reports. Through a study of the binary opposition of the male-to-the-female paradigm and the relations among the paradigmatic elements, Robertshaw observed that females are characterized in the folk talk by reproduction, consumption, leisure, play, passivity, and preoccupation with the past (chivalry). In contrast, males are characterized by production, work, activity, and preoccupation with the present (equality).

André-Jean Arnaud. Arnaud, another structuralist in the Lévi-Straussian tradition, has drawn our attention to the difference between the surface (explicit) structures of legal writing and the implicit or subconscious structures hidden in the legal text.[273] While remaining faithful to the structural method, Arnaud also managed to stress the role of reality located at a level even deeper than the implicit abstractions he sought to extract from the text. Arnaud incorporated Foucault's theory of signification with the theories of Lévi-Strauss, Althusser, Barthes, and Lacan in a curiously modern, post-structuralist, and eminently semiotic approach.[274] Arnaud's approach to legal analysis mirrors the imperceptible passage from structuralism to semiotics that has taken place in the literary scene.

Thomas Heller. In his comprehensive study of structuralism and the law, Heller equates structuralism with "objectivism" and "pure scientific positivism" tempered only by the rare post-structuralist assertion that unexplainable events sometimes do exist.[275] Heller's view of structuralism takes into account the very early split that took place among structuralists.[276] His linking of the structuralists and post-structuralists supports our contention that post-structuralism is a movement that both accepts and rejects the doctrines of structuralism.

In Heller's view, the structuralist is so purely objective that the individual subject ceases to exist as the collective is stressed. As the structuralist is intent on finding the constants beneath the variants, discontinuity is stressed over evolution. Heller classifies the structuralist as a rational materialist sometimes labeled as antihumanist. Post-structuralists reintroduce the liberal image of the subject, thereby injecting more flexibility into the analysis of discourse.

Heller then relates the phenomenon of the loss of the subject to structural analysis of the law. He views the law as predominantly subjectivist. Thus, he considers that the analysis of American legal categories as a structural discourse is an undertaking that would put order in an orderless "chronicle of aggregated wills."[277] Any purely structuralist account of a uniform production of legal practices would miss the complexity of the legal landscape and paint so false a

273. André-Jean Arnaud, *Du bon usage du discours juridique*, 12 Langages 123 (1979).

274. *See* Arnaud, *supra* note 26, at 283.

275. Thomas Heller, *Structuralism and Critique*, *supra* note 134, at 147.

276. *See infra* text accompanying notes 251–60 for a discussion of the diversity among structuralists.

277. Heller, *supra* note 134, at 173.

picture of the reproduction of theory in practice that it would strain the credibility of the entire account.[278]

Although structuralism gets some rather bad press in Heller's view of its application to the law, few could argue with Heller's desire for a more integrated view that would incorporate both subjective and objective approaches to discourse analysis. Semiotics, "a science that studies the life of signs within society,"[279] would no doubt breathe life into the objectivist approach of the structuralists whom Heller criticizes. In other words, semiotics would incorporate extratextual factors from reality into the analysis of legal discourse.[280]

Prior to a discussion of post-structural theory, the contributions of three particular structuralists who have significantly advanced and applied semiotic theory to literary texts will be noted: Greimas,[281] Todorov, and Barthes. Of these three, only Greimas[282] has actually applied his structural semiotic approach to legal texts.[283] Bernard Jackson's detailed study of Greimasian structural semantics as applied to legal discourse is a convincing demonstration of the manner in which Greimas integrated three different jurisprudential theories (positivism, naturalism, and realism) to produce new insights into the specificity of legal language.[284] It is hoped the theories of Barthes and Todorov (broadly sketched below) will provide legal interpreters with finer tools with which to approach their endeavor.

c. Tzvetan Todorov's Grammar of Narrative and Its Application to the Law. Todorov was in search of a grammar of narrative from which all stories can be derived. Legal realists would object to this view as overly determinant and static, similar

278. *Id.* at 184.

279. *See* SAUSSURE, *supra* note 120, at 33–34.

280. Heller, *supra* note 134, at 189.

281. *See supra* text accompanying notes 187–90 for a discussion of Greimasian theory applied to the law.

282. In his books, *Sémantique Structurale* and *Du Sens: Essais Sémiotique*, Greimas developed a theory of narrative structures in terms of an established linguistic model derived from Saussure. Greimas and other structuralists such as Claude Lévi-Strauss relied on the Saussurean concepts of *langue* and *parole* and upon Jakobson's notion of binary oppositions. JAKOBSON & HALLE, *supra* note 197, at 75. Following in the footsteps of Vladimir Propp and inspired by the Prague circle's orientation toward functional linguistics, Greimas perceived a story as if it were a sentence having a semantic structure. When analyzing the structure of a story, Greimas made use of spheres of action that he reduced to three pairs of opposed categories called *actants*. Many *acteurs* can perform one function or action. The functions are the following: (1) subject vs. object; (2) sender vs. receiver; and (3) helper vs. opponent. Algirdas Greimas and Bernard Jackson have reported on the application of Greimasian narrative structures to the law and shown how these categories and their combination can be useful for the description of a series of events in a legal setting. JACKSON, *supra* note 10, at 31–143.

283. GREIMAS & COURTÈS, *supra* note 151.

284. JACKSON, *supra* note 10.

to the grammar of legal structure proposed by Kelsen[285] in response to social studies of law that threatened to uproot "the scientific status of legal dogmatics."[286] Todorov described the workings of the universal grammar to which not only all languages but all signifying systems conform.[287] Legal language is a signifying system governed by this universal grammar. Todorov's grammar, which is on the level of syntax, is complex and almost totally detached from the content level of the text. Legal science studies the law as a grammar; as a "system of norms"; and as a structure free of any reference to historical, political, or ethical values.[288] In the grammar of law, meaning is conceived of in terms of a syntax. In other words, what "should be" is the positive law (*langue*), and what deviates from that norm is the illegal act (*parole*).

According to Todorov, interpretation should not be the mere servile application of the instruments of textual analysis to a particular discourse. Instead of engaging in a futile search for hidden meanings, the interpreter should be concerned with the relationships between the various levels of meaning within the text (i.e., with the multiplicity of meanings within the text as a system).[289]

Todorov, like many theoreticians of discourse analysis, was interested in what constitutes a literary act. The mere examination of the contents of literary writing cannot bring us closer to the understanding of the literary phenomenon itself. The essence of literature is found in its difference from ordinary language—"literature is like a deadly weapon with which language commits suicide."[290] The simile of literature to an illegal act is not fortuitous and points toward the applicability of Todorov's theories to legal discourse. Legal language is highly specialized, coded, and dependent on a separate set of conventions from that of ordinary language. One of the critical differences between law and literature is that literature seeks out difference consciously whereas law resists it, striving with frustration both to uphold legal precedent, certainty, and predictability and to communicate its coded language to the layman for whom it is intended to apply.

d. Roland Barthes' Structural Semiotics and Its Application to the Law. There is a constantly operating contradiction in Roland Barthes' work that mediates between the hermeneutic and structural approaches to the languages of literary and nonliterary texts.[291] His style is both scientific and poetic, as with legal

285. Hans Kelsen, General Theory of Law and State (1945); Hans Kelsen, What is Justice? (1957); Hans Kelsen, Pure Theory of Law (1970) [hereinafter cited as Pure Theory].

286. Goodrich, *supra* note 126, at 180.

287. Tzvetan Todorov, Grammaire du Décaméron 15 (1969).

288. *See* Kelsen, Pure Theory, *supra* note 285, at 191.

289. Tzvetan Todorov, *The Analysis of Literature: The Tales of Henry James*, *in* Structuralism, An Introduction 73 (David Robey ed., 1973).

290. Tzvetan Todorov, Introduction à la Littérature Fantastique 91 (1970) (author's translation).

291. *See* Julia Kristeva, *Matière, Sens, Dialectique*, 44 Tel Quel 17, 33 (1971).

discourse at its best. As Barthes' writing contributes to furthering the development of the philosophy, sociology, and psychology of language, it naturally fulfills Saussure's conception of semiology.[292]

Barthes' semiotic theory[293] stresses the importance of the signifier. He claims that the purpose of semiotic analysis is to move beyond the level of mere content analysis (the signified) to the level of form and style (the signifier). This point of view will engender a revision by the deconstructionists of the traditional definition of semiotics as the interplay between signifier and signified: "Semiology, as opposed to semantics, is the science or study of signs as signifiers."[294] Peter Goodrich elaborated on this distinction in his introductory study of law and language. Semiotics does not:

> study meaning as actually realised (sic) or manifested in text or utterance as historical and local events. Semiotics studies the internal coherence of the object utterance, or the immanent logic of the text. . . . The predominant characteristic of post-Saussurian semiotics has indeed been precisely the development of numerous and diffuse metalanguages or second order descriptive theories of semiotic systems.[295]

---

292. *See supra* text accompanying notes 129–30 for a discussion of the social function of Saussurean semiology.

293. *See* Susan W. Tiefenbrun, *The Third Degree of Language: Mediation and Roland Barthes' Semiotic Productions*, 34 SEMIOTICA 143 (1981). Around 1954, Barthes envisaged a science of signs intrinsically involved with sociology and with the theories of Sartre, Brecht, and Saussure. Barthesian semiotics varies in response to political and social changes that were taking place at the time of the 1968 events in France. At that point, semiotics became a passionate return to the text. Of particular merit is Barthes' early study of Racinian tragedy that literally overturned the views of Racinian dramaturgy held by the French literary establishment for centuries and provoked a scandal. *See* ROLAND BARTHES, SUR RACINE (1963); *see also* ROLAND BARTHES, CRITIQUE ET VÉRITÉ (1966) (response to RAYMOND PICARD, NOUVELLE CRITIQUE OU NOUVEL IMPOSTEUR (1965)).

Despite the threatening effect that Barthes' literary criticism had on the French in the early sixties, his espousal of the self-contained text, its plurality of meaning, and the beneficial effects of textual ambiguity were already quite familiar to the American school of new criticism. Barthes added a rigorous method and a semiotic dimension to the principles of new criticism. His responsiveness to social change, his iconoclastic approach to the interpretation of classical texts, and his flirtation with the notion of textual indeterminacy should make his work particularly appealing to the critical legal studies movement.

Of particular interest is Barthes' analysis of the interplay of codes at work in literary texts—a notion eminently applicable to legal discourse. *See* ROLAND BARTHES, S/Z (1970). In *S/Z*, Barthes identified and described the function of at least five codes at work in the novel: the hermeneutical, the code of semes or signifiers, the symbolic code, the proairetic code, and the cultural code. *See* SCHOLES, *supra* note 120, at 148–57 (discussion of the meaning of these codes).

294. De Man, *supra* note 257, at 123.

295. Goodrich, *supra* note 126, at 181.

Barthes occupies a special place in the history and development of semiotics. He was one of the early structuralists who was influential in bringing forth a more generally open-ended approach to textual analysis.

6. Post-Structuralism The period of literary critical thought dominated by Derrida and the Yale School is characterized by diverse approaches united only by the common name of post-structuralism.[296] The bond that unites these apparently warring factions in the post-structuralist school is their perception of literature as signification and/or communication—in short, semiotics. Nothing like this quagmire of literary critical approaches exists in legal interpretive theory, but it may be on its way. An excursion into the history of the literary tradition that produced the quagmire may relieve the effects on legal scholars.

Post-structuralists, obsessed with the inherent paradoxes of language, are convinced that systematic knowledge is impossible. Although they are united in their opposition to a strictly scientific approach to textual analysis, post-structuralists have not refused the tools of semiotics.[297]

---

296. The post-structuralists include: reader-response critics (*e.g.*, HANS ROBERT JAUSS, LITERATURGESCHICTE ALS PROVOKATION (1970); Hans Robert Jauss, *Literary History as a Challenge to Literary Theory*, *in* NEW DIRECTIONS IN LITERARY HISTORY 11-41 (Ralph Cohen ed., 1974); HANS ROBERT JAUSS, AESTHETISCHE ERFAHRUNG UND LITERARISCHE HERMENEUTIK (1977); STANLEY EUGENE FISH, IS THERE A TEXT IN THIS CLASS? THE AUTHORITY OF INTERPRETIVE COMMUNITIES (1980); NORMAN N. HOLLAND, FIVE READERS READING (1975); RIFFATERRE, *supra* note 252, at 87); *Rezeptionsaesthetik* critics (*e.g.*, Wolfgang Iser, *The Reading Process: Phenomenological Approach*, 3 NEW LITERARY HISTORY 279 (1972)); feminist critics (*e.g.*, ROBIN LAKOFF, LANGUAGE AND WOMAN'S PLACE (1975); Jean Bethke Elshtains, *Feminist Discourse and its Discontents: Language, Power and Meaning*, 7 SIGNS 603 (1982); D. DALE SPENDER, MAN MADE LANGUAGE (1980); and CULLER, *supra* note 128, at 43–64. To this list we can add phenomenological, Marxist, and psychoanalytic critics. Hermeneutics and pluralism also compete with traditional approaches to text analysis in this highly diversified school of literary criticism. The theory of communication or *hermeneutic* is contained in the celebrated work of Hart; *see* H.L.A. Hart, *Signs and Words*, 2 PHILO. Q. 59 (1952). For a discussion of pluralism, *see* Steven Knapp & Walter Benn Michaels, *Against Theory*, 8 CRITICAL INQUIRY 723, 737–42 (1982) (they attack Fish's pluralistic view of interpretation: "There are as many plausible readings of the United States Constitution as there are versions of Hamlet. . . ." Stanley Fish, *Interpretation and the Pluralist Vision*, 60 TEX. L. REV. 495 (1982)).

297. Turning away from the positivistic approach in Saussure's *Cours*, the post-structuralists now rely on Saussure's *Anagrammes* for advice and direction in their search for meaning. Sylvère Lotringer, *Introduction, Saussure's Anagrammes*, *in* 2 SEMIOTEXT(E) 7 (1974). Hillis Miller explained the difference between structuralists and post-structuralists in rather colorful terms:

> Socratic critics are those who are lulled by the promise of a rational ordering of literary study on the basis of solid advances in scientific knowledge about language. They are likely to speak of themselves as "scientists" and to group their collective enterprise under some term like "the human sciences" . . . Such an enterprise is represented by the discipline called "semiotics," or by new work in the exploration and exploitation of

a. Deconstruction and Semiotics. The distinction between the scientific approach of the structuralists, who are allied to semiotics by tradition, and the antiscientific approach of the deconstructionists might leave us with the false impression that semiotics is the adversary of post-structuralism. Nothing could be further from the truth. The interplay between semiotics and deconstruction is tense and highly productive. Based on the unresolvable paradoxes inherent in language—paradoxes that deconstructionists believe can only be revealed by a systematic semiotic analysis of signs and signification—deconstructionists adopt the curiously ambivalent position of both accepting and rejecting the principles and practice of semiotics.[298]

Derrida has explained the conflict inherent in the deconstructionists' simultaneous acceptance and rejection of semiotics.[299] For Derrida, semiotics is the logical culmination of the faith that the Western culture has placed in science and rationality, which he called *logocentrism*. Logocentrism is based on the assumption that concepts exist independently of their expression and can be examined as logical representations. Derrida admits that semiotics began as a critique of the very notion of logocentrism. Saussure, the founder of semiotics, was the first to insist that the sign is a relational union between signifier and signified—an arbitrary phenomenon at best. However, Derrida concluded that semiotics cannot escape logocentrism because it assumes that expression depends on conventions and the prior existence of a system of signs. Literature and the law, for example, are constantly accepting and rejecting preestablished conventions and codes. According to Derrida, it is precisely this paradox that

---

> rhetorical terms. Included would be aspects of the work of Gérard Genette, Roland Barthes, and Roman Jakobson . . . This would be a discipline bringing literature out into the sunlight in a "happy positivism". . . .
>
> Opposed to these are the critics who might be called "uncanny" . . . One feature of Derrida's criticism is a patient and minutely philological "explication de texte." Nevertheless, the thread of logic leads . . . into regions which are alogical, absurd.

Joseph Hillis Miller, *Stevens' Rock and Criticism as Cure II*, 30 GA. REV. 330, 335–36 (1976), *cited in* CULLER, *supra* note 128, at 23.

298. Johnson, one of Derrida's most faithful translators and interpreters, defined *deconstruction* as "the careful teasing out of warring forces of signification within the text itself." Barbara Johnson, *The Critical Difference*, DIACRITICS 2, 3 (Summer, 1978).

299. Jacques Derrida, *Sémiologie et grammatologie*, in POSITIONS (1972) (trans. 1981) (good discussion of the theory of signs and Derrida's critique of it). Derrida's readings of Rousseau, Saussure, Freud, Austin, Hegel, and Husserl can be found in JACQUES DERRIDA, DE LA GRAMMATOLOGIE (1967) (OF GRAMMATOLOGY (Gavatri Spivak trans., 1976)); *see also* JACQUES DERRIDA, L'ÉCRITURE ET LA DIFFÉRENCE (1967) (WRITING AND DIFFERENCE (Alan Bass trans., 1978)); JACQUES DERRIDA, MARGES DE LA PHILOSOPHIE (1972); JACQUES DERRIDA, *"Differance" and Form and Meaning: A Note in the Phenomenology of Language, in* JACQUES DERRIDA, SPEECH AND PHENOMENA 107–60 (1973).

makes the goal of semiotics—the establishment of a theory of signification and communication—virtually impossible.

b. Deconstructionist Notion of Difference and Its Application to the Law. Deconstructionists define the act of writing as *semiosis.* Writing is made up of signs that facilitate the recreation of reality. This recreation is possible only with the help of a reader or receiver of the message. If the message is in the form of literary discourse, the reader must simultaneously remember and then temporarily forget the conventions and codes that constitute expectation. It is only by virtue of the trait of forgetfulness that the writer as well as the reader can experience the "difference" that characterizes the literary act. Literary discourse thrives on difference or contrasts from a context or convention made possible by the reader's temporary abandonment of a past tradition.

Like literature, the law also depends on shared expectations, but legal analysis resists the abandonment of convention. Precedent and stare decisis are pervasive forces aimed at promoting predictability and uniformity in the law. In response to this resistance to the abandonment of past tradition, deconstructionists would insist that the very act of writing:

> destabilizes words, in the sense that it makes us aware at one and the same time of their alien frame of reference (they are words of the other or come to us already interpreted, trailing clouds of meaning, each one a representamen) and of the active power of forgetfulness (a kind of silencing) which it enables and which, in turn, enables us to write.[300]

Derrida's notion of difference[301] and his theory of signs is firmly rooted in Saussurean semiotics. Although Derrida found in Saussure a compatriot, a critique of the "metaphysics of presence," or logocentrism, he and other post-structuralists criticized Saussure's theory of the sign, objecting in particular to the necessary relation of signifier to signified.[302]

c. Michel Foucault, Literal and Figurative Language, and the Law. Foucault has a unique perception of language that has come to be shared by post-structuralists. For him language is *catachresis,* abuse and misuse, or deviations from the norm. Foucault maintained that language is a conscious failure to

---

300. Geoffrey H. Hartman, Saving the Text: Literature/Derrida/Philosophy xxi–ii (1981) (emphasis added).

301. For Derrida the notion of "différance" [sic] is key. He defined it in terms that remind us of Saussure's concept of the arbitrary and relational nature of the sign. No element can function as a sign without relating to another element that is itself not present. Jacques Derrida, Writing and Difference, *supra* note 299, *passim.*

302. For example, Foucault stated "there is no distinction between signifier and signified, subject and object, sign and meaning." Michel Foucault, The Archeology of Knowledge 86 (trans. 1972).

live up to shared expectations.[303] On the theory that all language is by nature catachretic, Foucault rejected the traditional distinction between literal and figurative language.

Applying Foucault's conception of the nature of language to the law, I believe he would reject the notion of two competing types of language in legal discourse, one based on similarity and the other on difference. The first type of legal language (the approved kind directed toward the signified or the communication of content in and for itself) simply does not exist in Foucault's theory. This ideal type of language, which never shocks due to its conscious similarity to the defined norm, is designed to promote prediction by adherence to convention. The other type of language based on the principle of difference is directed toward the signifier in and for itself. This form of discourse is designed to persuade by the careful manipulation of signifiers—words chosen for their formal and stylistic effects. Rhetorical figures such as metaphor are only one of a myriad of devices to which lawyers may resort in order to persuade.[304] Lawyers then must balance the goal of content-based discourse with the reality of the persuasive effects of style or catachresis.

Following in the post-structuralist tradition that saw metaphor as a natural phenomenon of language itself, Paul Robertshaw has been particularly successful in adopting semiotic principles in his study of metaphors in the law.[305] Professor Robertshaw has proposed an important method for the analysis of metaphors occurring in British cases. He deconstructs the language of the case in order to expose a deep design hidden by the use of style or surface structures such as metaphor, metonymy, or simile; he calls these the signals of deeper realities within. Robertshaw studies judicial metaphors as semantic transformations of a hidden reality, an abstraction, and/or a rule. The basic proposition of the method, which stems from Nietzche, is that language is constitutive of reality. As language is intrinsically metaphoric, a study of metaphor will necessarily reach to the core of meaning.[306] Nietzche is the patron saint of close textual analysts and interpreters of legal texts who do not move far from the words themselves for the source of hidden meaning.[307] Robertshaw studies the audience in

303. Foucault's own style is a demonstration of catachresis in which a profusion of rhetorical figures, (such as oxymoron, paradox, chiasmus, antiphrasis, hyperbole, and others) are designed to communicate information.

304. *See* Foucault's study of figuration that he limits to metaphor, metonymy, synechdoche, and irony. MICHEL FOUCAULT, LES MOTS ET LES CHOSES (1966) (THE ORDER OF THINGS (trans. 1970)).

305. Paul Robertshaw, *Hierarchies, Metaphors and Judicial Decisions* (1986) (unpublished manuscript).

306. *Id.* at 1.

307. *See* Levinson's discussion of strong and weak textualists who interpret the Constitution. Sanford Levinson, *Law as Literature*, 60 TEX. L. REV. 373, 378–84 (1982). The weak textualist will emphasize the plain words of the text while the strong textualist will

legal decisions and concludes that in cases which are fully reported and have a large perceived audience, the court is more likely to use language figures and tropes that attempt to bridge the various audiences.[308]

d. Post-Structuralism and Psychoanalysis. Jacques Lacan is a psychoanalyst who had roots in the early structuralist movement.[309] Modern psychoanalytic critics cannot disregard the impact of this controversial figure who concentrated on the linguistic intricacies of his patients' speech. Lacan believed the unconscious, which is structured like a language, is governed by the principle of paradox. Language is overdetermined and polyphonic, like poetry. Lacan believed that studying the overlapping and interweaving of signifiers within a written chain of words can lead to the discovery of the very nature of the unconscious and how it is structured. Lacan's major contribution to psychoanalytic theory is his insistence on a close linguistic analysis of the patients' words themselves. In this regard, Lacan was indebted to the semiotic theories of Saussure.[310]

In a language unique in its own combination of art and science, Lacan advocated the supremacy of the signifier and the quest for the signified in its pure form. This concept of hidden meanings and the distortion that comes about by the use or misuse of words is the very stuff with which lawyers grapple on a daily basis. Legal scholars have made significant inroads into the psycholinguistic effects of legal language on the layman. For example, studies have been undertaken to determine whether jury instructions are clear enough to promote meaningful communication and justice.[311] The law, which has begun to adopt if not a Lacanian then a psycholinguistic approach to legal issues,[312] could benefit from more explicit applications of semiotic principles.

---

emphasize the meaning to be given to the words of the text by historical reconstruction. This approach is limited by the validity of authorial intent. Ely is an example of a weak textualist who attempts to crack the code of a text by considering the overall structure in which individual words fit. *See* John Hart Ely, Democracy and Distrust (1980). Strong textualists do not discover hidden meanings—instead they create meanings. As Fish put it, "[i]nterpretation is not the art of construing but the art of constructing. Interpreters do not decode poems, they make them." Stanley Fish, *supra* note 296, at 327. Fish's pluralism has been criticized as nihilistic; *see* Owen M. Fiss, *Objectivity and Interpretations*, 34 Stan. L. Rev. 739 (1982).

308. *See* Robertshaw, *supra* note 305, at 17.

309. Jacques Lacan, Écrits (1966).

310. *See* Charrow & Charrow, *supra* note 158.

311. *See* Levi, *supra* note 155, at 3 (studies relating to the reliability of eyewitness testimony), 3–4 (issues in memory acquisition, retention, and retrieval for courtroom use), 4–6 (the social psychology of courtroom behavior/forms of questioning and their psychological effects), 6–7 (other related psycholinguistic research done on legal matters).

312. *Id.* at 6–7.

7. Critical Legal Studies and Semiotics The critical legal studies (CLS) movement has been characterized as "one third legal realism, one third anarchism, and one third Marxism."[313] Proponents of the CLS movement are direct descendants of legal realists[314] and share with them three basic tenets: skepticism about the pretensions of legal institutions,[315] belief in the indeterminacy of law, and belief in the inseparability of law and politics. The CLS movement is an attempt to carry out in an even more radical manner the reformist ideals of the legal realist movement that somehow got thwarted in the 1970s.

As do the realists, CLS scholars deny that law is either autonomous or determinate. Legal doctrine exists, but it is not a system, and therefore cannot provide definitive answers to all the variants of the pattern of cases.[316] "[W]hen you situate law in a social context, it varies . . . in that context . . . law is indeterminate at its core, in its inception, not just in its applications. This indeterminacy exists because legal rules derive from structures of thought, the collective constructs of many minds, that are fundamentally contradictory."[317]

Like the realists, CLS scholars "regard law *primarily* as a social institution rather than *primarily* as a normative study."[318] Because law is indeterminate, CLS scholars believe it cannot be analyzed by means of the empirical, scientific, behaviorist model elaborated by the positivists.[319] While the positivists attempt to predict how courts will decide cases on the basis of social science, the CLS movement seeks out the social values expressed by the law.[320] This anti-normative attitude could preclude the application of a Saussurean brand of semiotics to the law and explain why CLS scholars have adopted the post-structuralist theories of Jacques Derrida, Michel Foucault, and Roland Barthes,[321] who despite their roots in Saussurean structuralist tradition are more in league with the openness of Peircean semiotics. Even though CLS scholars reject normative study and empirical models, they use the language of structuralist semiotics in

---

313. Norman Dorsen reported this description at a session of the Federalist Society of New York University School of Law devoted to the CLS movement (Feb. 20, 1986).

314. Mark Tushnet, *Critical Legal Studies and Constitutional Law: An Essay in Deconstruction*, 36 STAN. L. REV. 623, 626 (1984).

315. Phillip Johnson, *Do You Sincerely Want To Be Radical?*, 36 STAN. L. REV. 247, 261 (1984).

316. David Trubek, *Where the Action Is: Critical Legal Studies and Empiricism*, 36 STAN. L. REV. 575, 578 (1984).

317. Robert W. Gordon, *Critical Legal Histories*, 36 STAN. L. REV. 57, 114 (1984).

318. Lewis A. Kornhauser, *The Great Image of Authority*, 36 STAN. L. REV. 349, 365 (1984).

319. Trubek, *supra* note 316, at 579–80.

320. Kornhauser, *supra* note 318, at 367.

321. The CLS scholars "draw on critics of the feminist, structuralist, and deconstructionist schools." Jerry Frug, *Henry James, Lee Marvin and the Law*, N.Y. TIMES, Feb. 16, 1986 (Book Review), at 1, col. 1.

their interpretivist investigation of legal issues.[322] For example, to determine the role of law in society, the CLS scholar would investigate how this "complex cultural code . . . explains the social world[,] how it fits together, and [how it] forms part of the structure in which action is embedded."[323] Willingly or not, this is a systems approach to discourse and one envisaged by Saussurean semiotics. Moreover, to determine what constitutes valid social knowledge about the law, the CLS scholar would decode or explicate "the deep structures of law and demonstrat[e] the relationship between these structures[,] action[,] and order in society."[324] This approach, rooted in a concept of law as social institution, is derived from the Saussurean structuralist branch of semiotics that Claude Lévi-Strauss applied in his structural anthropology[325] and that Noam Chomsky later developed into a normative grammar.

Because law is inseparable from politics in the CLS tradition, proponents of this movement (along with the realists) deny that law is formally analyzable[326] by means of a neutral mode of legal reasoning.[327] The attempt by a legal scholar to apply doctrine to hard cases in an objective manner that is independent of personal ideals, passions, or political persuasions is simply impossible in the CLS perception of the law. The interpretation of law must, therefore, engage people's passion and politics as well as their reason.[328] Law is not inseparable from society, but rather is a product of and a contributor to the way people understand themselves and their society. This point of view, which is at the heart of the CLS movement, is in consonance with the semiotic system envisaged by Saussure, practiced by Barthes, and continued by the reality-based post-structuralists. The CLS scholars have, therefore, adopted the liberalizing theories of Barthes and the post-structuralists in preference to text-centered literary theorists such as E.D. Hirsch, Wayne Booth, or the new critics. The more traditional legal scholars have followed the text-centered literary theorists who emphasize the limits of interpretation rather than the openness of the text.[329]

Critical legal scholars believe that legal doctrine reflects the basic contradictions in human relations and as such does not constitute a coherent body of

---

322. Trubek, *supra* note 316, at 605.

323. *Id.* at 601.

324. *Id.*

325. *See supra* text accompanying notes 174–79.

326. *See* Duncan Kennedy, *Toward an Historical Understanding of Legal Consciousness: The Case of Classical Legal Thought in America 1850–1940*, 3 Research L. & Soc. 3 (1980); Duncan Kennedy, *Legal Formality*, 2 J. Legal Stud. 351 (1973) (principle of indeterminacy of legal doctrine), *cited* in Trubek, *supra* note 316, at 578.

327. Trubek, *supra* note 316, at 578.

328. Frug, *supra* note 321, at 28.

329. *Id.*

knowledge.[330] Their emphasis on contradiction and paradox in law, and their attempt to demystify the law (which they consider to be a marginal factor in social behavior)[331] allies the CLS movement with the post-structuralist theories of Derrida and Foucault. And like post-structuralism, the CLS movement is often accused of anarchy and nihilism.[332] The movement has an affinity to postmodernism that is "an elusive idea that is not easily defined." Postmodernism is neither a theory nor a concept; it is rather a skeptical attitude or aesthetic that "distrusts all attempts to create large-scale, totalizing theories in order to explain social phenomena."[333] If an interpreter engages in an open-ended interpretive approach to the meanings of an utterance in legal discourse, without invoking the restraints imposed by the linguistic, historical, or social context in which the utterance is embedded, the CLS method can produce a limitless number of interpretations. Such an approach is creation, not "interpretation" in the traditional sense[334] (i.e., an attempt to uncover hidden meanings textually rooted and verifiable as existing both in the text and in the mind of the observer). Semiotics, which orients the investigator toward a close and concrete study of language as a sign system in society, provides beneficial boundaries of interpretation. The CLS movement could, therefore, greatly expand its potential by a more conscientious adoption of the minutely philological and semiotically based explications that Derrida's deconstructionist method requires.

---

330. Duncan Kennedy, *The Structure of Blackstone's Commentaries*, 28 BUFFALO L. REV. 205 (1979).

331. Trubek, *supra* note 316, at 585.

332. Allan C. Hutchinson & Patrick J. Monahan, *Law, Politics, and the Critical Legal Scholars: The Unfolding Drama of American Legal Thought*, 36 STAN. L. REV. 199, 236 (1984).

333. *See* GARY MINDA, POSTMODERN LEGAL MOVEMENTS: LAW AND JURISPRUDENCE AT CENTURY'S END 224 (1995). Minda's book is very informative, and in it he distinguishes between modernity and postmodernity: "While the distinctive discourse of modernity is aimed at prediction and control, postmodernism brings out the diversity of multiple discourses and is skeptical of all universal knowledge claims. Postmodernism rejects the belief in stable, transcontextual foundations . . . Postmodernists deny . . . that we can rely on theory and language to objectively fix the meaning of reality." *Id.* at 225.

334. Dworkin draws the distinction between creation and interpretation, between interpreters who interpret and those who invent, and between artists and critics. An inventor is the skeptic who believes there are limitless interpretations possible and no right answer. "The artist can create nothing without interpreting as he creates . . . The critic, for his part, creates as he interprets . . . A judge's duty is to interpret the legal history he finds, not to invent a better history." RONALD DWORKIN, *How Law is Like Literature*, *in* MATTER OF PRINCIPLE 146, 158–60 (1985).

III. CONCLUSION

In reviewing the sources of semiotics, its relation to literary criticism, and the application of semiotics to the law, I have attempted to show that semiotics is an ancient discipline stemming from pre-Socratic sources and branching off into at least five different fields: medicine, philosophy, linguistics, anthropology, and literature. The interdisciplinary nature of semiotics has promoted dialogue among researchers from many different areas of knowledge and has helped to breathe life into the interpretation of literary and legal texts. The most important contributors to the development of semiotics are Saussure (in linguistics), Peirce (in philosophy), and Lévi-Strauss (in anthropology). Each of the major schools of literary theory from Russian formalism to the most recent deconstructionism has adopted semiotic principles in various ways to further particular goals. These literary applications have served as a catalyst for the analysis of legal discourse. An examination of the history and development of various semiotic approaches to literary interpretation provides insight into the source of certain parallels that exist between literature and the law. The current study has attempted to draw analogies between the structural method of Saussure and empirical models adopted by the legal positivists, the open-ended semiotic process proposed by Peirce and espoused by the legal realism movement, and the role that contradiction and demystification play in the deconstructionist and CLS movements. This study has also tried to show how each of these legal movements has adopted the semiotic theories of Saussure, Peirce, and the poststructuralists, respectively.

Semiotics has and will continue to play an increasingly important role in both the everyday practice of law and the elaboration of legal interpretive theory. Semiotics is the link between the system of law under investigation and the reality that produced it. A better understanding of the elements of semiotics will provide the lawyer with the key to the communication and discovery of meaning hidden under the weight of coded language and conventions that go beyond the four corners of the legal text.

PART B

TERRORISM

3. A SEMIOTIC APPROACH TO A LEGAL DEFINITION OF TERRORISM*

I. INTRODUCTION

Terrorism is not a new phenomenon. It has appeared in many different forms throughout the ages and become one of the "plagues of modern society."[1] It is hard to believe that a word like *terrorism*, which is used so frequently these days in different contexts (including casual, colloquial, political, and legal discourses) does not have a universally accepted definition.[2] The academic literature on defining terrorism is vast.[3] At the United Nations, an unending debate has

---

* This chapter originally appeared as an article in 9 ILSA Journal of International and Comparative Law 357–89 (Spring 2003), The original article has been revised, updated, and expanded to include analyses and interpretations of literary representations of terrorism such as Joseph Conrad's classic novel, *The Secret Agent*, written in 1907 concerning terrorist acts committed in 1894, and cinematographic representations of terrorism such as the movie *Hotel Rwanda* that appeared in 2005 covering the recent genocide and terrorist acts in Rwanda in 1994 . . . I would like to thank Professors Aaron Schwabach and Richard Scott of the Thomas Jefferson School of Law and Professor Malvina Halberstam of the Benjamin N. Cardozo School of Law for reading earlier drafts of the original article. Special thanks to Professor Cherif Bassiouni for his insightful comments about the article. I delivered a shorter version of that article for a War, Crimes, and Terrorism Conference: The Role of International Courts and Tribunals that I organized at the University of Nice School of Law in France on July 17, 2002. The conference included Judge Claude Jorda of the International Criminal Tribunal of the Former Yugoslavia, Judge Lucius Caflisch of the European Court of Human Rights, and Judge Rosalyn Higgins of the International Court of Justice, as well as leading scholars in the field such as Professors Catharine MacKinnon, Malvina Halberstam, William Ginsberg, and Norman Silber. A different version of that article was also delivered at the American Branch of the International Law Association on Oct. 24, 2002 in New York for a panel devoted to September 11th and the War on Terrorism.

1. Jacques Bourrinet, *The Economic Analysis of Terrorism*, *in* Terrorism and International Law 3, 4 (Rosalyn Higgins & Maurice Flory eds., 1997).

2. M. Cherif Bassiouni, International Terrorism; Multilateral Conventions (1937–2001) 14, n.48 (2001). *See also* Kevin J. Greene, *Terrorism as Impermissible Political Violence: An International Law Framework*, 16 Vt. L. Rev. 461 (1992) ("Terrorism has 'no precise or widely accepted definition.'"). *See also* Rosalyn Higgins, *The General International Law of Terrorism*, *in* Terrorism and International Law 13, 14 (Rosalyn Higgins & Maurice Flory eds., 1997) ("Furthermore, the difficulties of definition are objective and not just subjective. The technical problems of definition are prodigious").

3. Alex Houen, Terrorism and Modern Literature, From Joseph Conrad to Ciaran Carson 7 (2002) (Footnote 19 lists the following sources dealing with terrorism:

focused on whether terrorism should or can be defined. Some argue that as there is no agreement about what conduct is prohibited or what uses of force, by whom, and in what circumstances certain acts are considered to be terrorism, any attempt at a definition is doomed to failure. Others argue more rationally that normative responses to prohibited conduct can only be devised with agreement or consensus as to what conduct is actually prohibited. It is not enough to say, as U.S. Supreme Court Justice Potter Stewart once did of pornography, "we know it when we see it."[4] Terrorism must be deconstructed[5] to distinguish between domestic and international terrorism,[6] State-sponsored and non-State sponsored terrorism, and terrorism per se and revolutionary violence[7] that

---

Alex Schmid & Albert Jongman, Political Terrorism: A New Guide to Actors, Authors, Concepts, Data Bases, Theories and Literature (1988); Walter Laqueur, The Age of Terrorism (1987); Terrorism (Conor Gearty ed., 1996); Grant Wardlaw, Political Terrorism: Theory, Tactics, and Counter-Measures ch. I (1989); Michel Wieviorka, The Making of Terrorism ch. I (David Gordon White trans., 1993); William Perdue, Terrorism and the State: A Critique of Domination through Fear ch. I (1989); Terrorism: Interdisciplinary Perspectives (Yonah Alexander & Seymour Maxwell Finger eds., 1977); and Conor Gearty, The Future of Terrorism (1997). *See also* more recent works on the definition of terrorism: Beth Van Schaack, *Finding the Tort of Terrorism in International Law,* 28 rev. litigation. 381 (2008). John D. Shipman, *Taking Terrorism to Court: A Legal Examination of the New Front in the War on Terrorism,* 86 N.C.L. Rev. 526 (2008); Debra M. Strauss, *Reaching Out to the International Community: Civil Lawsuits as the Common Ground in the War on Terror,* 19 Duke J. Comp. Int'l. L. 307 (2009); George P. Fletcher, *The Indefinable Concept of Terrorism,* 45 J. int'l. crim. Just. 894 (2006), (addressing criminal terrorism, but also includes an interesting discussion of the definition of terrorism).

4. *See* Stephen Yagman, *Defining the Weapon of Terrorism: Frustrated People Without Another Method Resort to "Politico-Military" Violence Instead,* L.A. Daily J. 6 (Mar. 12, 2002).

5. See Susan Tiefenbrun, *Legal Semiotics, supra* Chapter 2 of this book and earlier in 5 Cardozo Arts & Ent. L.J. 89 (1986) (discussing the application of semiotics to the law and the meaning of *deconstruction*).

6. In the US Antiterrorism Act of 1990, the United States defines the term *international terrorism* to mean activities that: "(A) involve violent acts or acts dangerous to human life that are a violation of the criminal laws of the United States or of any state, or that would be a criminal violation if committed within the jurisdiction of the United States or of any State; (B) appear to be intended (i) to intimidate or coerce a civilian population; (ii) to influence the policy of a government by intimidation or coercion; or (iii) to affect the conduct of a government by assassination or kidnapping; and (C) occur primarily outside the territorial jurisdiction of the United States, or transcend national boundaries in terms of the means by which they are accomplished, the persons they appear intended to intimidate or coerce, or the locale in which their perpetrators operate or seek asylum." (US Antiterrorism Act of 1990, Pub. L. No. 101-519, 104 St. 2250 (codified at 18 U.S.C. § 2331 (Supp. 1991), cited in U.S. Federal Legal Responses to Terrorism 74–75 (Yonah Alexander & Edgar H. Brenner eds., 2002).

7. Yonah Alexander et al.. ETA: Profile of a Terrorist Group 4 (2001). "The ETA proclaims the right of the Basque people to self-rule and the use of the most appropriate

arguably falls within the laws of war.[8] In the U.N. debate about the definition of terrorism, the West was—and still is—concerned that a definition could be used to include State-sponsored terrorism, while the Third World is concerned that a definition emphasizing non-State actors might fail to differentiate between terrorism per se and the struggle for national liberation.[9] Clearly, the basic problem in this quest for a definition "is the lack of a single criterion determining the fundamental component elements of the definition of the term 'terrorism.'"[10]

A semiotic approach to defining terrorism is designed to uncover the basic structural elements of the meaning of the term. As previously noted in Chapter 2, semiotics is the science of signs.[11] A semiotic approach to the meaning of the term *terrorism* involves decoding its multiple codes and includes an investigation of its hidden meanings and connotations as well as denotations in order to

---

means to achieve its goal." *Id.* at 4. Recently a terrorist attack occurred in Madrid, and the Spanish government blamed the Basque separatist group ETA for a car bomb that exploded outside the Madrid office of a unit of infrastructure company Grupo Ferrorvial SA. This was the latest apparent flare-up in ETA's violent campaign against a planned bullet train linking the Basque region to Madrid. The bomb shattered windows and destroyed parked cars, but no one was hurt. *See* Thomas Catan, *Madrid Blames Bomb on ETA,* WALL STREET J., Feb. 10, 2009, at A12.

8. CHRISTOPHER L. BLAKESLEY, TERRORISM, DRUGS, INTERNATIONAL LAW, AND THE PROTECTION OF HUMAN LIBERTY 17, 20 (1992). Blakesley defines *terrorism* as "violence aimed at innocents (or non-combatants) to gain an edge over, or to coerce, a third party. This is different from justifiable and legal revolutionary violence, which seeks liberation from oppression or restriction on one's own sovereignty (assuming such acts of revolutionary violence fall within the laws of war)" (cited in DOUGLAS J. DAVIDS, NARCO-TERRORISM: A UNIFIED STRATEGY TO FIGHT A GROWING TERRORIST MENACE 2 (2002)). *See also* Louis Rene Beres, *The Legal Meaning of Terrorism for the Military Commander,* CONN. J. INT'L. L. 9 (1995), with Beres arguing that the failure of insurgents to comply with the laws of war does not convert these military forces into terrorists, but it does make them guilty of war crimes and possibly even crimes against humanity. Cherif Bassiouni argues convincingly that terrorist methods can occur during armed conflict; therefore, terrorism can be included under war crimes. I maintain that terrorism can be included under war crimes only if the five elements of the definition of terrorism (discussed in this chapter) are present.

9. Higgins, *supra* note 2, at 17. Higgins concludes that the term *terrorism* has no specific legal meaning. *Id.* at 27.

10. *Id.* at 16. Statement cited in Higgins by the representative of Mexico to the United Nations during the U.N. debate on the definition of terrorism.

11. Any attempt here at a definition of semiotics is at best preliminary and partial. *See* Tiefenbrun, *supra* note 5, for a history of semiotics as it applies to the law. *See also* COLLECTED PAPERS OF CHARLES SANDERS PEIRCE 335 (Charles Harshone & Paul Weiss eds., 1960). By *semiotics* or *semiosis,* Peirce means the interplay of three subjects: a sign, its object, and its interpretant. *See also* UMBERTO ECO, A THEORY OF SEMIOTICS 7 (1976), *citing* Ferdinand de Saussure's definition of semiotics: "a science that studies the life of signs at the heart of society."

expose the deep structure of the term and unravel its complexities. Each element of the definition would act as a sign for the identification of a terrorist act. The elements of the definition are either necessary or sufficient for the act to be deemed a terrorist act.

At least two major obstacles must be overcome to arrive at a universally accepted definition of the term. First, it is necessary to distinguish between three different conceptions of terrorism: terrorism as a crime in itself, terrorism as a method to perpetrate other crimes, and terrorism as an act of war. When terrorism is conceived of as a crime, its elements and defenses can be identified and analyzed. When terrorism is conceived of as a method to perpetrate other crimes, terrorism will sometimes overlap with other crimes such as crimes against humanity, genocide, war crimes, rape, etc. When terrorism is conceived of as an act of war, the laws of war will cover the legal responses to it. State responses to terrorism require the balancing of a State's right to defend itself proportionally against threats of the illegal use of force or acts of aggression, as included under the U.N. Charter norms.[12]

The second obstacle is the need to resolve the term's underlying paradoxes. Terrorism is a phenomenon steeped in varying and often conflicting political and ideological beliefs. Given that States have fundamental rights to self-defense and self-determination, we can ask whether terrorism is legitimate if it is perpetrated in self-defense or in an attempt to achieve self-determination.

This chapter will uncover five basic elements of the crime of terrorism that are deeply embedded in each of the many definitions proposed by the United States in its laws, and by many other nations, scholars, and international organizations such as the United Nations. This chapter will attempt to show that under certain circumstances requiring the presence of the basic five elements of the crime, terrorism can be included in other specifically defined international crimes such as war crimes, crimes against humanity, and genocide. I will also look comparatively at the U.S., English, French, European, and Canadian definitions of terrorism as well as the U.N.'s attempt to define terrorism in its seventeen multilateral conventions. I will also examine different definitions proposed by leading scholars in the field of international law and the law of terrorism. Finally, I will look at two different literary and cinematographic representations

12. *See* U.N. Charter art. 2, para. 4: "All members shall refrain in their international relations from the threat or use of force against the territorial integrity or political independence of any state, or in any other manner inconsistent with the Purposes of the United Nations," http://www.un.org/Overview/Charter/chapter1.html (last visited Jan. 31, 2003). *See also* U.N. Charter art. 51: "Nothing in the present Charter shall impair the inherent right of individual or collective self-defense if an armed attack occurs against a Member of the United Nations, until the Security Council has taken measures necessary to maintain international peace and security," http://www.un.org/Overview/Charter/chapter7.html (last visited Jan. 31, 2003).

of terrorism: Joseph Conrad's novel *The Secret Agent* (1907) and the more recent movie *Hotel Rwanda*. By applying semiotic analysis to these literary texts, I will attempt to tease out their hidden legal issues in order to shed light on the complex problem of terrorism.

This chapter will distinguish between international and domestic terrorism and will uncover the existence of three different conceptions of terrorism that have profound implications for the adjudication of terrorist acts. Terrorism is conceived of as a crime, as a method, and as an act of war. These different conceptions of terrorism lead us to question which tribunal would be appropriate to try international terrorists. Finally, I will focus on the paradoxical nature of terrorism which complicates the establishment of a universally accepted definition of the term.

II. ELEMENTS OF THE CRIME OF TERRORISM

Black's Law Dictionary defines *terrorism* as: "the use or threat of violence to intimidate or cause panic, especially as a means of affecting political conduct."[13] Scholars have attempted to further define the term,[14] resulting in many different definitions[15] that can all be reduced to five basic structural elements:[16]

1. The perpetration of violence by whatever means;
2. The targeting of innocent civilians;
3. The intent to cause violence or with wanton disregard for its consequences;
4. The purpose of causing fear, coercing, or intimidating an enemy;
5. The undertaking in order to achieve some political, military, ethnic, ideological, or religious goal.[17]

---

13. Black's Law Dictionary 1484 (7th ed. 1999).

14. Davids, *supra* note 8, at 2.

15. *See* Emanuel Gross, *Legal Aspects of Tackling Terrorism: The Balance Between the Right of a Democracy to Defend Itself and the Protection of Human Rights*, 6 UCLA J. Int'l L. & For. Aff. 89 (2001).

16. *See id.* "It is difficult to classify the term 'terrorism' or provide it with a clear definition or interpretation . . . Nonetheless, the majority of the definitions have a common basis–terrorism is the use of violence and the imposition of fear to achieve a particular purpose, generally entailing the aspiration to overthrow an existing regime, or fight it, and where the persons forming the group organize in a tightly controlled structure . . . need to determine whether the activities of the particular group are morally supported by the state."

17. These basic five elements are a variation of Blakesley's elements. Blakesley, *supra* note 8, at 37. Blakesley's five elements include "conducting the above acts without justification or excuse" but do not include "ethnic or ideological" goals (termed "benefits" in

Normally the violence associated with terrorism is perpetrated without justification or excuse in an aim to gain publicity for the cause.[18] The European anarchists at the end of the nineteenth century called their violent acts "propaganda by the fact,"[19] thus describing their own bloody deeds with euphemistic irony. In this sense terrorism is similar to extreme forms of civil disobedience[20] in which the perpetrators resort to violence to gain publicity for a cause that is presumably their objection to an unjust law or an example of societal oppression. Normally State-sponsored terrorists do not seek publicity, but individual terrorists thrive on publicity for their cause.[21] State responses to acts of civil disobedience have sometimes resulted in the use of force. Similarly, the peacetime use of terrorism by a State against passive resistance is arguably justified in order to maximize compliance to a new State policy.[22] However, I will attempt to show that terrorism in any form and for whatever reason is unjustified.

The structural elements of the definition of terrorism need further analysis. What actually constitutes violence? The dictionary definition of *violence* includes unjust or unwarranted use of force (usually accompanied by fury, vehemence, or outrage), as well as physical force unlawfully exercised with the intent to harm.[23] But there is a broad spectrum to the definition of *violence*. Some courts have held that violence is not limited to physical contact or injury, but may also include picketing in a labor dispute conducted with misleading signs, false statements, erroneous publicity, and veiled threats by words and acts.[24] Violence has many forms and degrees of severity. An act is violent only if it causes harm to persons and things,[25] but violence in any form can inspire terror in its victims and in those people who are indirectly affected by it.

What is an "innocent civilian?" There is no agreement as to who is actually included in this category,[26] but we are tempted to say "we know an innocent civilian when we see one." If only one innocent civilian is killed or seriously injured

---

Blakesley's listing). Blakesley's elements also do not include the word *fear*, which is key to the definition of the term *terrorism*.

18. *See* Walter Laqueur, *Reflections on Terrorism*, FOREIGN AFFAIRS 65 (1986), at 86–88 (cited in DAVIDS, *supra* note 8, at 2).

19. Bourrinet, *supra* note 1, at 4.

20. *See infra* Chapters 6, 7, and 8 on the nature of civil disobedience. *See also* Susan W. Tiefenbrun, *Classic Greek Themes in Contemporary Law: On Civil Disobedience, Jurisprudence, Feminism and the Law in the Antigones of Sophocles and Anouilh*, 11 CARDOZO STUD. L. & LIT. 35 (1999); *see also* Susan Tiefenbrun, *Semiotics and Martin Luther King's "Letter from Birmingham Jail,"* 2 CARDOZO STUD. L. & LIT. 255 (1992).

21. BASSIOUNI, *supra* note 2, at 29.

22. *Id.* at 32.

23. BLACK'S LAW DICTIONARY, *supra* note 13, at 1564.

24. *Id.*

25. BASSIOUNI, *supra* note 2, at 8.

26. *Id.* at 15.

during an act of war motivated by self-defense, will this be enough to call it a terrorist act? What are the legitimate defenses to the unintentional killing of an innocent civilian during wartime? Is collateral damage from the use of force during wartime a legitimate defense to killing innocent civilians? These are only some of the questions that the element of violence against innocent civilians raises as we attempt to propose a universally accepted definition of terrorism.

The element of *intent* or *wanton disregard* is less troublesome because of established definitions used by the courts to determine the mental state of an accused. What is more troublesome is the element of *fear*, which is not a legal term but a psychological phenomenon manifested by various signs and symptoms such as trembling, shaking, sweaty palms, etc. Intimidation, which was established as a common law tort in England in 1964,[27] is unlawful coercion that produces harm.

The manifold purposes of terrorism include the accomplishment of a political, military, ethnic, ideological, or religious cause. The overriding purpose is a necessary element of the definition. Political, ethnic, ideological, and religious goals are not troublesome within the definition of terrorism. However, the accomplishment of a *military goal* is controversial. If a military goal is added to the definition of terrorism, this places a burden on combatants never to use terrorism during wartime. Individuals, small groups, and States have been known to commit terrorist acts in the context of wars of national liberation.[28]

III. THE MANY DEFINITIONS OF TERRORISM

Even though there are many definitions of terrorism[29] available for legislative purposes, terrorism per se has never been explicitly defined in any of the seventeen existing multilateral anti-terrorism conventions.[30] Moreover, the multilateral conventions are not applicable to State-sponsored terrorism—they apply only to

---

27. Rookes v. Barnard, 1 Lloyd's Rep 28 (H.L. 1964).

28. BASSIOUNI, *supra* note 2, at 19.

29. *Id.* at 15 (Bassiouni provides a long list of scholarly articles that attempt to define the term *terrorism*). *See also* John F. Murphy, *The Future of Multilateralism and Efforts to Combat International Terrorism*, 25 COL. J. TRANS'L L. 35 (1986); Thomas M. Franck & Bert B. Lockwood, *Preliminary Thoughts Towards an International Convention on Terrorism*, 68 AM J. INT'L L. 69, 70–72 (1974).

30. Bassiouni, *supra* note 2, at xxvi. The Convention for the Suppression of the Financing of Terrorism, Article 2.1 (b), U.N. Doc. A/54/109 (Dec. 9, 1999) proposes an indirect definition of *terrorism:* "Any other act intended to cause death or serious bodily injury to a civilian, or to any other person not taking an active part in the hostilities in a situation of armed conflict, when the purpose of such act, by its nature or context, is to intimidate a population, or to compel a government or an international organization to do or to abstain from doing any act." *Id.*

terrorism committed by individual actors. The absence of a universally accepted definition of terrorism and the inapplicability of multilateral anti-terrorism legislation to State-sponsored terrorism reflect the deeply political nature of the term and the absence among nations of commonly shared values[31] about the rule of law, the legitimacy of goals, and the means to achieve these goals. For example, the international community cannot agree on whether the intimidation or actual attack on an "innocent civilian" is a necessary or simply a sufficient element of the definition. It also cannot agree on who should be included in the category of "innocent civilians" or "diplomats" or "civilian installations" or "legitimate targets."[32] Finally, the international community cannot agree on whether terrorism is illegal under all situations or whether it is sometimes permissible to achieve a legitimate goal. Some international organizations proclaim that the right to self-rule legitimizes the use of the most appropriate means (including terrorism) to achieve the goals of liberation and independence.[33]

A. U.S. Definitions of Terrorism

In the United States there is general confusion about what constitutes terrorism.[34] The United States has shifted its conception of terrorism as a "crime" to terrorism as an "act of war."[35] In the past, the United States classified international terrorism as a crime and applied legal means as the primary tool to fight it.[36] More recently however, the United States has moved away from reactive counter-terrorism law enforcement methods towards more proactive techniques to fight international terrorism. This shift has occurred because the United States now perceives terrorist acts as acts of war.[37] In its "war against terrorism,"

---

31. *Id.* at 15.

32. *Id.*

33. ALEXANDER ET AL., *supra* note 7, at 4; *see also id.* at 6 ("Between 1963 and 1965 the terrorist organization adopted the principles of revolutionary war because it was influenced by the successes of the independence war in Algeria and the Cuban revolution. Marxist theory was predominant in its ideology. ETA's purpose was to change the state through an uprising of the people, the destruction of the oppressor state, and finally, the assault to power").

34. TERRORISM AND THE LAW 3 (Yonah Alexander & Edgar H. Brenner eds., 2001).

35. Malvina Halberstam, *The US Right to Use Force in Response to the Attacks on the Pentagon and the World Trade Center*, 9 CARDOZO J. INT'L & COMP. L. 101 (2001), "Terrorism is a form of war, probably the most serious form of war used against the United States since World War II, if not ever." *See also* Malvina Halberstam, *Terrorist Acts Against and On Board Ships*, 331 ISR. Y.B. HUM. RTS. (1987); Malvina Halberstam, *Terrorism on the High Seas: The* Achille Lauro, *Piracy and the IMO Convention on Maritime Safety*, 82 AM. J. INT'L L. 269 (1988).

36. Tyler Raimo, *Notes and Comments, Winning at the Expense of Law: The Ramifications of Expanding Counter-Terrorism Law Enforcement Jurisdiction Overseas*, 14 AM. U. INT'L. L. REV. 1473, 1474 (1999).

37. *Id.*

the United States uses expanded law enforcement and intelligence agencies such as the FBI and CIA to fight terrorism—and these agencies have their own definitions of the term.

In the U.S. federal system, each state determines what constitutes an offense under its domestic criminal or penal code. States define terrorism generically as a crime. For example, the Arkansas Criminal Code provides that "a person commits the offense of terroristic[sic] threatening if, with the purpose of terrorizing another person, he threatens to cause death or serious physical injury or substantial property damage to another person."[38]

The U.S. Congress has not been able to reach a consensus on a working definition of terrorism.[39] The executive branch has also not developed a coordinated position on the meaning of the term.[40] The absence of a generally accepted definition of terrorism in the United States allows the government to craft variant and vague definitions that can result in an erosion of civil rights and the possible abuse of power by the State in the name of fighting terrorism and protecting national security.

1. U.S. 1996 Anti-Terrorism Act's Definition of Terrorism In the 1996 U.S. Anti-Terrorism Act and Effective Death Penalty Act,[41] the United States defines international terrorism as:

> [T]he unlawful use of violence against the United States, citizens of the United States or any other nation, outside the boundaries of the Unites States, apparently intended to intimidate or coerce a civilian population, influence government policy, or to affect the conduct of a government for political or social objectives.[42]

This definition includes the five basic elements outlined above, but does not list specific terrorist acts that can be classified as criminal.[43] The advantage of not listing specific acts as terrorist acts is that as new forms of technology are created, new forms of terrorist acts are likely to develop, and this law will still cover these new modalities. The disadvantage of not listing specific acts as terrorist acts is that it will be left up to policy makers to determine who is and who is not committing terrorist acts. A subjective definition leaves too much room for political bias to affect the decision.

---

38. ARK. CODE ANN. § 5-13-301 (Michie 2002).

39. Raimo, *supra* note 36, at 1481.

40. *Id.*

41. Jason Binimow & Amy Bunk, Annotation, *Validity, Construction, and Operation of "Foreign Terrorist Organization" Provision of Anti-Terrorism and Effective Death Penalty Act (AEDPA), 8 U.S.C.A. § 1189*, 178 A.L.R. FED. 535 (2002); *see* Nicholas J. Perry, *The Numerous Federal Definitions of Terrorism: The Problem of Too Many Grails*, 30 J. LEGIS. 249 (2004). *See also* U.S. Antiterrorism Act of 1990, 18 U.S.C. § 2331 (1991).

42. Riamo, *supra* note 36, at 1481.

43. *Id.* at n.46.

Despite the inclusion of a definition of terrorism in the U.S. 1996 Anti-Terrorism Act, some civil libertarians have attacked this law, basing their objection on a dubious claim that the Act does not contain a definition of terrorism. A more valid claim might be that the Act does not explicitly designate specific acts constituting terrorism. Civil libertarians have expressed a legitimate fear that the alleged absence of a definition will have the following deleterious result: that "terrorism" will be whatever the Secretary of State decides it is, with the possibility the Secretary may designate a foreign group as a terrorist organization if the Secretary "finds that the group 'engages in terrorist activity' that threatens the security of United States nationals or the national security of the United States."[44] The absence of a universally accepted definition of terrorism and the failure to list specific acts as terrorist acts could cause this bad result in other countries besides the United States.

2. The 2001 United and Strengthening American by Providing Appropriate Tools Required to Intercept and Obstruct Terrorism Act (U.S. Patriot Act)[45] President George Bush of the United States actually defined the term *terrorism* in an anti-terrorism act known as the U.S. Patriot Act: "For crimes to be defined as 'terrorist acts' the government must show that they were calculated to influence or affect the conduct of government by intimidation or coercion or to retaliate against government conduct."[46] However, this definition requires insight into the mental state of the perpetrator, does not specifically identify the necessary element of violence, and reduces the purpose clause to achieving political goals (i.e., influencing government conduct).

Some civil libertarians have objected to the erosion of civil liberties in the 2001 Patriot Act because it authorizes executive detention on the mere suspicion that an immigrant has at some point engaged in a violent crime or provided humanitarian aid to a proscribed organization. It is noteworthy and highly symbolic that President Barack Obama ordered the closing of Guantanamo Detention Center within one year as one of his very first executive acts because of the perceived abuse of power allowed by the Patriot Act. Provisions in this Act authorize guilt by association and give the government power to deny entry to aliens for reasons that are arguably "pure speech" acts.[47]

3. The International Money Laundering Abatement and Financial Anti-Terrorism Act of 2001 The U.S. Financial Anti-Terrorism Act of 2001, which is the counterpart of the U.N. International Convention for the Suppression of the

---

44. James X. Dempsey & David Cole, Terrorism & the Constitution: Sacrificing Civil Liberties in the Name of National Security 119 (1999). *See also* Binimow & Bunk, *supra* note 41.

45. USA Patriot Act, Pub.L.No. 107-56, 115 Stat. 296-342 (2001).

46. *Id. at* §802 (9) (5)(b), p. 396. *See also* 18 U.S.C.A. section 2331 (i) (B).

47. Dempsey & Cole, *supra* note 44.

Financing of Terrorism (1999),[48] was signed into law on October 26, 2001 as Title III of the U.S. Patriot Act. This statute requires the Secretary of the Treasury to implement numerous changes under a strict timetable in order to follow the trail of those who finance terrorism. Due diligence measures require the identification of the beneficial owners of bank accounts.[49]

The United States has designated a variation on the domestic form of terrorism called *global terrorism*. For example, President George Bush signed Executive Order 13244 on September 23, 2001 requiring U.S. persons to block the assets of a new category of sanctioned parties, known as "specially designated global terrorists" (SDGTS). This category includes individuals, organizations, charities, and business entities as well as U.S. persons, U.S. citizens and permanent residents, and both U.S. corporations and their non-U.S. branches. The Office of Foreign Assets Control of the U.S. Department of the Treasury implements the executive order. President Bush threatened to freeze assets and transactions of banks and other financial institutions that refuse to share information about terrorists.[50] An action to freeze assets was also taken by the U.N. Security Council on October 15, 1999 under Chapter VII of the U.N. Charter via Resolution 1267. Similar actions were taken against Osama bin Laden on December 19, 2000 pursuant to Security Council Resolution 1333.[51]

4. FBI's Definition of Terrorism Since 1980, the Federal Bureau of Investigation (FBI) has defined terrorism as: "the unlawful use of force or violence against persons or property to intimidate or coerce a government, the civilian population, or any segment thereof, in the furtherance of political or social objectives."[52]

The FBI definition does not include the basic five elements because it omits the necessary element of intent and limits the purpose to the achievement of "political or social objectives." Moreover, the definition does not specifically include or exclude State-sponsored terrorism. If the definition of terrorism does not include the element of intent to coerce or intimidate, then any criminal (such as the Son of Sam) who kills just for the sake of bloodthirsty violence could be deemed a terrorist.

---

48. *See* International Convention for the Suppression of the Financing of Terrorism, adopted Dec. 9, 1999, 39 I.L.M. 270 (2000).

49. Edward J. Krauland & Stephane Lagonico, *The New Counter-Money Laundering and Anti-Terrorism Financing Law,* INT'L L. NEWS 1 (2002).

50. Executive Order on Terrorist Financing, http://www.whitehouse.gov/news/releases /2001/09/ 20010924-1.html (last visited Jan. 31, 2003).

51. Peter D. Trooboff, *Antiterrorism Measures,* THE NAT'L L.J. A19 (2001).

52. United States Department of Justice, FBI, *Terrorism in the United States,* 1988 (Terrorist Research and Analytical Center, Counter-Terrorism Section, Criminal Investigative Division, Dec. 31, 1988), at 34, *cited in* TERRORISM AND THE LAW, *supra* note 34, at 4, n.7.

5. U.S. State Department's Definition of Terrorism The U.S. Department of State defines *terrorism* as: "premeditated, politically motivated violence perpetrated against noncombatant targets by sub-national groups or clandestine agents, usually intended to influence an audience."[53] This definition includes all five elements and the requisite intent, but it limits the purpose to "politically motivated" goals. The U.S. State Department's definition arguably excludes terrorism committed by a State because it lists only "sub-national groups or clandestine agents." However, if the term *agents* refers to "agents of the State," then State-sponsored terrorism is included in this definition.

6. U.S. Department of State's Definition of International Terrorism The U.S. Department of State defines the term *international terrorism* as: "terrorism involving citizens of the territory of more than one country."[54] The requirement of more than one country in this definition refers to both perpetrators and victims. The U.S. Department of State also defines the term *terrorist group* to mean "any group practicing, or that has significant subgroups that practice international terrorism".[55] Because international terrorism refers back to terrorism, which includes only subnational groups or clandestine agents, arguably the Department of State's definition of international terrorism does not cover State-sponsored terrorist acts, unless the term *agents* refers to the State.

B. England's Definition of Terrorism

The United Kingdom has undergone an evolutionary process in defining terrorism. England defined *terrorism* in the English Prevention of Terrorism (Temporary Provision) Act of 1984[56] and in the English Prevention of Terrorism (Temporary Provision) Act of 1989 as follows: "Terrorism means the use of violence for political ends and includes any use of violence for the purpose of putting the public or any section of the public in fear."[57] However, this definition is overly broad, does not include the element of intent, expansively includes "civilians" in the category of "any section of the public" (which could include combatants), and limits the goal to "political" benefit. The perpetration of violence without the requirement of intent could produce odd results. For example, demonstrators for a politial cause who end up in a brawl might be deemed

---

53. 22 U.S.C. § 2656f(d), *cited in* Terrorism and the Law, *supra* note 34, at 4.

54. *Id.*

55. *Id. See* 17 Yonah Alexander & Donald J. Musch, Terrorism Documents of International and Local Control, 170–71 (1999).

56. English Prevention of Terrorism (Temporary Provision) Act of 1984, Section 14(1).

57. English Prevention of Terrorism Act of 1989, Section 20(1), http://www.hmso.gov.uk/acts/acts1989/ Ukpga_19890004_en_6.htm (last visited Feb. 1, 2003); *see* Gross, *supra* note 15, at n.20.

terrorists. An accidental killing by the police or the army, which is hardly an act of terror, might still fall within this definition.[58]

In 1996, Lord Lloyd defined *terrorism* as "the use of serious violence against persons or property or the threat to use such violence, to intimidate or coerce a government, the public, or any section of the public, in order to promote political, social, or ideological objectives."[59] This definition remedies the deficiencies of the earlier one that placed limitations on goals and modifies the act of violence by describing it as "serious violence." However, it maintains the element of "civilians" in the broad category of "any section of the public" and still falls short of including an element of intent.

In the 1999 Prevention of Terrorism Bill, the British government defined terrorism even more broadly to include expressions of extremism by groups such as the Animal Liberation Front that had only one issue as its cause.

The more recent United Kingdom Terrorism Act of 2000[60] defines terrorism in Section (1):

> Terrorism means the use or threat of action where the action falls within subsection (2) (i.e. violence, serious damage, endangering life, etc.) and (b) the use or threat is designed to influence the government or to intimidate the public or a section of the public, and (c) the use or threat is made for the purpose of advancing a political, religious or ideological cause.

Terrorist action is further defined in Section 1(2) as:

> Acts involving serious violence against a person, serious damage to property, acts that endanger a person's life, other than that of the person committing the action; acts that create a serious risk to the health or safety of the public or a section of the public, or acts designed seriously to interfere with or disrupt an electronic system.[61]

Thus, English law continues to omit the element of intent in its definition of terrorism. Moreover, it specifically lists certain acts as being terrorist acts, such as environmental terrorism, biological terrorism, and even computer hacking. English law on terrorism is extraterritorial and covers terrorist actions outside the United Kingdom and those committed by the government of a country outside of the United Kingdom.[62]

As a matter of comparative law, U.S. law and UK law are quite different with regard to the definition of terrorism. The UK Terrorism Act of 2000 provides a

58. *See* Gross, *supra* note 15, at n.20.

59. *See* Lord Lloyd, *Inquiry into Legislation Against Terrorism*, H.L., Mar. 1996 (*cited in* Terrorism and the Law, *supra* note 34, at 4–5).

60. United Kingdom Terrorism Act of 2000, Ch. 11 § 1(1) (July 20, 2002).

61. Terrorism and the Law, *supra* note 34, at 4–5.

62. *Id.* at 6.

broad definition of the criminal act of terrorism ("serious violence against a person, serious damage to property, acts that endanger a person's life") and also specifically names certain terrorist acts ("acts that create a serious risk to the health or safety of the public . . . or disrupt an electronic system"). In contrast, the U.S. 1996 Anti-Terrorism Act includes the element of intent but softens the requirement by adding the adverb *apparently* to the element of intent ("apparently intended to intimidate or coerce a civilian population. . . ."). As previously noted, the U.S. law on terrorism does not specifically list the acts that constitute terrorist criminal acts.

The English approach to terrorism may have odd but beneficial results. If Greenpeace were to threaten to disrupt a government computer system (e.g., to put pressure on Iraq for dealing with its Kurd population in an inhumane manner), the Greenpeace movement would be committing an act of terrorism.[63] As odd as this result may seem given its laudable purpose, in my view the identification of the Greenpeace organization's act as a terrorist act would be correct in this instance because terrorist acts are not justified, even if they are committed for humanitarian purposes.

C. France's Definition of Terrorism

The French coined the term *terrorisme* during the French revolution[64] in the period following the fall of Robespierre in 1793–94 under the infamous Reign of Terror.[65] The French dictionary definition of terrorism is "violence committed by an organization in order to create a climate of insecurity or in order to overthrow the established government."[66] This definition eliminates the elements of intent and harm to innocent civilians and limits the purpose to the achievement of political goals. In France, the term *terrorism* is also included under the definition of crimes against humanity. As a result of the famous Klaus Barbie case,[67] a new

---

63. *Id.*

64. David B. Kopel & Joseph Olson, *Preventing a Reign of Terror: Civil Liberties Implications of Terrorism Legislation*, 21 OKLA. CITY U.L. REV. 247, 251 (1996). The term *terrorism* was conceived during the French Revolution when the government created a reign of terror to execute political opponents, requisition their property, and impose terror over the remainder of the population until they yielded to the government.

65. LE PETIT LAROUSSE (1991 ed.) and LE PETIT ROBERT (1972 ed.).

66. *Id.*

67. *See* Leila Sadat Wexler, *The Interpretation of the Nuremberg Principles by the French Court of Cassation: From Touvier to Barbie and Back Again*, 32 COLUM. J. TRANSNAT'L L. 289 (1994). As a result of the French court's decision in the *Barbie* case, the court found that to be guilty of a crime against humanity, a person had to intend to take part in carrying out a common plan by systematically committing inhumane acts and illegal persecutions in the name of a state practicing a hegemonic political ideology. Because Vichy, France could not be considered a hegemonic state, Touvier could not, as a matter of law, have committed a crime against humanity. Sadat points out that there is no requirement to prove a

law defining crimes against humanity had to be adopted in the French Criminal Code. The term *terrorism* is specifically defined in the French Criminal Code:[68] "Acts are terrorist acts when they are intentionally committed by an individual entity or by a collective entity in order to seriously disturb law and order by intimidation or by terror."[69]

Unlike the U.S. law, which does not list particular acts as being terrorist acts, the French law specifically names and describes the acts constituting terrorism. Article 421-1 of the French Criminal Code lists the following acts as terrorist acts:

> Attempted murder, assault, kidnapping, hostage-taking on airplanes, ships, all means of transport, theft, extortion, destructions, and crimes committed during group combat, the production or ownership of weapons of destruction and explosives including the production, sale, import and export of explosives, the acquisition, ownership, transport of illegal explosive substances, the production, ownership, storage, or acquisition of biological or chemical weapons, and money laundering.

Article 421-2 of the French Criminal Code[70] continues the list of terrorist acts to include environmental terrorism: ". . . Placing in the air, on the ground, under the ground and in the water (including territorial water) any substance that would put the health of man and animals or the environment in danger."

Article 421-2-1 of the French Criminal Code[71] makes it illegal to belong to or participate in a group formed for the purpose of planning one of the terrorist acts named above.

Article 421-2-2 of the French Criminal Code[72] makes it illegal for anyone to finance a terrorist organization by intentionally providing, collecting, or managing funds of any value whatsoever—or by giving advice for the purpose of

---

"hegemonic state." As a result of this case, a new French Criminal Code was adopted defining crimes against humanity. However, nowhere in this definition is terrorism specifically mentioned.

68. French Criminal Code, Article 421-1 (Loi No. 96-647 du 22 juillet 1996 art. 1 Journal Officiel du 23 juillet 1996) (Loi No. 98-467 du 17 juin 1998 art. 84 Journal Officiel du 18 juin 1998) (Loi No. 2001-1062 du 15 novembre 2001 art. 33 Journal Officiel du 16 novembre 2001). *See* http://222.1egigrance.gouv.fr/html/frame_codes 1.htm.

69. Translations of Article 421-1 and other pertinent Articles of the French Criminal Code are provided by Susan Tiefenbrun. The term *ordre public* refers to "public policy" or to "law and order."

70. Article 421-2 of the French Criminal Code (Loi No. 96-647 du 22 juillet 1996 art. 2 Journal Officiel du 23 juillet 1996).

71. Article 421-2-1 of the French Criminal Code (Loi No. 96-746 du 22 juillet 1996 art. 3 Journal Officiel du 23 juillet 1996).

72. Article 421-2-2 of the French Criminal Code (Loi No. 2001-1062 du 15 novembre 2001 art. 33 Journal Officiel du 16 novembre 2001).

financing terrorism—if that person knows these funds are going to be used fully or partially for the purpose of committing terrorist acts, whether or not the terrorist act actually occurs.

Article 421-3 of the French Criminal Code[73] sets forth penalties ranging from six years to life imprisonment for the commission of a terrorist act. Article 421-4 of the French Criminal Code[74] adds monetary penalties to the prison sentence. For example, a convicted terrorist imprisoned for fifteen years might also be required to pay a monetary penalty of 225,000 Euros. If an alleged terrorist is convicted of killing one or several people, the terrorist would be sentenced to imprisonment for life and would be required to pay a penalty of 750,000 Euros. Article 421-5 of the French Criminal Code[75] provides that an alleged terrorist who is sentenced to ten years of imprisonment must also pay a penalty of 225,000 Euros.

Article 422-1 of the French Criminal Code provides an exemption for informants. Anyone who has attempted to commit a terrorist act, but who informs the administrative and judicial authorities in advance of the commission of the act and facilitates the avoidance of the terrorist act and the identification of the other guilty parties will be immune from imprisonment and penalties.

Article 422-2 of the French Criminal Code permits the reduction of a prison sentence by half for anyone who committed a terrorist act or aided a terrorist act if that person, either by warning or informing the administrative or judiciary authorities, enabled the terrorist act to be avoided, enabled anyone's death or permanent injury to be avoided, or provided the names of the other guilty parties. A life sentence will be reduced to twenty years for such assistance.

Article 422-5 of the French Criminal Code expressly requires that corporations (*personnes morales*) engaging in terrorist activities pay monetary penalties. Article 422-6 of the French Criminal Code[76] includes confiscation of property as a penalty for any person or corporation engaging in terrorist activity.

Article 422-7 of the French Criminal Code[77] provides that any financial penalties imposed on the terrorists will be given to the victims' funds.

---

73. Article 421-3 of the French Criminal Code (Loi No 96-647 du 22 juillet 1996 art. 4 Journal Officiel du 23 juillet 1996).

74. Article 421-4 of the French Criminal Code (Ordonnance No. 2000-916 du 19 septembre 2000 art. 3 Journal Officiel du 22 septembre 2000 en vigueur le 1er janvier 2002).

75. Article 421-5 of the French Criminal Code (Loi No. 96-647 du 22 juillet 1996 art. 5 Journal Officiel du 23 juillet 1996) (Loi No. 2001-1062 du 15 novembre 2001 art. 33 Journal Officiel du 16 novembre 2001) (Ordonnance No 2000-916 du 19 septembre 2000 art. 3 Journal Officiel du 22 septembre 2000 en vigueur le 1er janvier 2002).

76. Article 422-6 of the French Criminal Code (Loi No. 2001-1062 du 15 novembre 2001 art. 33 Journal Officiel du 16 novembre 2001).

77. Article 422-7 (Loi No. 2001-1062 du 15 novembre 2001 art. 33 Journal Officiel du 16 novembre 2001).

Article 434-2 of the French Criminal Code[78] imposes a five-year prison sentence and a fine of 75,000 Euros on anyone attempting to harm the fundamental interests of the nation by a terrorist act.

Article 434-6 of the French Criminal Code[79] imposes a penalty of three years imprisonment and 45,000 Euros for anyone aiding a terrorist who receives a ten-year prison sentence. Aiding and abetting may be found if a person simply offers a terrorist lodging, subsidies, means of subsistence, or any other form of assistance. The penalty for aiding and abetting can be increased to five years of imprisonment and 75,000 Euros. However, relatives of the terrorist (parents, brothers, sisters and their spouse) and the spouse of the terrorist or the person with whom the terrorist is living are not included in the list of potential aiders and abetters.

D. European Nations' Definitions of Terrorism

The European Convention on the Suppression of Terrorism[80] was signed by 17 out of 19 Member States of the Council of Europe in January 1977. According to this treaty, all States must treat assassination, hostage taking, bomb attacks, and hijacking (major terrorist offenses) as "common crimes" and cannot refuse extradition. However, an escape clause was inserted into the European Convention on the Suppression of Terrorism permitting the contacting State to reserve the right to regard a certain offense as a political one. This escape clause would enable that State to withhold extradition. The Member States of the European Union strengthened this provision via the European Convention on Extradition.[81]

E. Canada's Definition of Terrorism

Canada has recently made strong legislative proposals in an attempt to combat terrorism. The Canadian Anti-Terrorism Act takes aim at terrorist groups, but also seeks to strike an appropriate balance between respecting Canadian values of fairness and respect for human rights and protecting Canadians and the global community from terrorism. This balance is accomplished by providing what

---

78. Article 434-2 (Ordonnance No. 2000-916 du 19 septembre 2000 art. 3 Journal Officiel du 22 septembre 2000 en vigueur le 1er janvier 2002).

79. Article 434-6 (Loi No. 96-647 du 22 juillet 1996 art. 7 Journal Officiel du 23 juillet 1996) (Ordonnance No. 200-916 du 19 septembre 2000 art. 3 Journal Officiel du 22 septembre 2000 en vigueur le 1er janvier 2002).

80. European Convention on Suppression of Terrorism (Jan. 27, 1977), http://www.ciaonet.org/cbr/cbr00/ video/cbr_ctd/cbr_ctd_39.html (last visited Feb. 1, 2003).

81. Paul Wilkinson, Terrorism Versus Democracy: The Liberal State Response 193 (2001).

the Canadian Department of Justice refers to as checks and balances in the form of "clear definitions"[82] of terrorism.

Terrorist activities in Canada have always been treated as criminal offenses. Under the Canadian Criminal Code, terrorists can be prosecuted for hijacking, murder, and other acts of violence. The Canadian government has signed twelve U.N. conventions and protocols[83] related to terrorism and has ratified ten, including those that protect against harming aircraft, civil aviation and airports, international shipping, and internationally protected persons and diplomats. They also address the safety of nuclear material and the prevention of taking of hostages and terrorist bombings. According to its Department of Justice, Canada plans to ratify the remaining two U.N. counter-terrorism conventions dealing with the suppression of both terrorist financing and terrorist bombings. Canada also expects to ratify the Convention on the Safety of United Nations and Associated Personnel Convention (1994), ensuring the safety of U.N. personnel (including peacekeepers) from attacks against their person, official premises, private accommodations, and modes of transport. Canada proposes to amend its Criminal Code to implement these U.N. conventions and to establish provisions aimed at disabling and dismantling the activities of terrorist groups and those who support them.

Canadian law defines a *terrorist activity* in its Criminal Code as an action taking place either within or outside of Canada that "is an offense under one of the ten United Nations anti-terrorism conventions and protocols"[84] or is an "act or omission, in or outside Canada, that is committed for a political, religious, or ideological purpose, objective or cause" and that "intentionally causes death or serious bodily harm to a person by the use of violence, endangers a person's life, causes serious risk to the health and safety of the public, etc."[85]

This Canadian definition of terrorism does not explicitly include the word *violence,* but it is implied in the descriptive term "seriously harming or endangering." Although the element of "innocent civilians" is not designated with particularity, the broad terms *a person* and *people* imply civilians.

The element of intent is also not specified but merely implied vaguely in the words "an action is taken." Some insight into the element of intent implied in these words can be gleaned by looking at the list that Canadian law provides of specific acts of terrorism. Unlike the definition of terrorism in U.S. law, the Canadian law lists specific terrorist acts, including the disruption of an essential

---

82. *See* Report from Department of Justice, Oct. 15, 2001, on "Highlights of Anti-Terrorism Act" from the Minister of Justice of Canada, http://www.canada.justice.gc.ca/en/news/nr/2001/doc_27787.html (last visited Feb. 1, 2003).

83. *See infra* Part III(F) for discussion of UN Definitions of Terrorism in Conventions, Protocols, and Resolutions.

84. Canadian Criminal Code, R.S., 1985, C-46, Section 83.01 (1)(a) contains the definition of the "terrorist activities" under the United Nations anti terrorism conventions.

85. Section 83.01 (1) (b), *supra* note 84, defines the term "terrorism".

service, facility, or system. It is interesting to note that in an effort to balance civil rights with the protection of national security, Canadian law does not include under the definition of a terrorist act the disruption of an essential service during a lawful protest or a work strike, if the action does not intend to cause serious harm to persons. The emphasis on intent as a condition of terrorist activity in this context strongly supports the view that the element of intent is implied in the definition of terrorism under Canadian law. The element of "fear, coercion or intimidation" is not specified explicitly, but implied in the term *threatens*. The Canadian definition specifically designates the purpose of the terrorist action as political, religious, or ideological and omits military and ethnic purposes.

Canadian law permits the designation of groups as terrorist groups if their activities meet the definition of terrorist activity.

The Canadian Criminal Code makes it a crime to knowingly collect or provide funds (either directly or indirectly) to carry out terrorist crimes. The maximum sentence for this offense is ten years. It is also a crime to knowingly participate in, contribute to, or facilitate the activities of a terrorist group. Participation or contribution can include knowingly recruiting into the group new individuals for the purpose of enhancing the ability of the group to aid, abet, or commit indictable offences. The maximum prison sentence for the offense of participating or contributing is ten years while the maximum for facilitating is fourteen years. Anyone who instructs another to carry out a terrorist act or an activity on behalf of a terrorist group ("leadership" offense) carries a maximum life sentence. Finally, anyone knowingly harboring or concealing a terrorist can receive a maximum ten-year sentence.

A careful analysis of the Canadian definition of terrorism with respect to the five necessary elements shows that the definition is not as clear as the Canadian Department of Justice would have us believe. It is, however, more specific than U.S. law, which does not list with particularity any acts of terrorism.

F. U.N. Definitions of Terrorism

The United Nations and other international organizations have failed for decades to reach agreement on a common universal definition of terrorism. Nonetheless, U.N. General Assembly and Security Council resolutions repeatedly affirm the U.N.'s determination to combat terrorism in all its forms "irrespective of motive, whenever and by whomever committed."[86]

---

86. G.A. Res. 1269, U.N. GAOR Security Council, 4053rd mtg. at 1, U.N. Doc. S/RES/1269 (1999). *See* G.A. Res. 1373, U.N. GAOR Security Council, 4385th mtg. at ¶¶ 7,8, U.N. Doc. S/RES/1373 (2001), which mandates that U.N. member states take measures to combat terrorism; it also creates a Counter Terrorism Committee to monitor the implementation of that resolution. *See* Jennifer Trahan, *Terrorism Conventions: Existing Gaps and Different Approaches*, 8 NEW ENG. J. INT'L & COMP. L. ANN. 215, 239 (2002).

The U.N. definition of terrorism contained in a critical 1991 General Assembly Resolution reflects the consensus of the General Assembly and resolves the issue of whether terrorism constitutes a legal response by a State to safeguard its undeniable right to self-determination and self-defense. The General Assembly Resolution "unequivocally condemns, as criminal and unjustifiable, all acts, methods and practices of terrorism, wherever and by whoever [sic] committed."[87]

The U.N. General Assembly's definition contained in its Resolution 1991 has reappeared in several subsequent resolutions. This definition makes it clear that even though all people have certain rights (the right under racist regimes or alien domination to self-determination, the right to freedom and independence, and the right to struggle legitimately to achieve this end), people fighting against colonial domination may not resort to the acts proscribed in the antiterrorism conventions.[88]

In December 1999, the U.N. General Assembly Resolution 54/109[89] defined terrorism as:

> Criminal acts intended or calculated to provoke a state of terror in the general public, a group of persons or particular persons for political purposes are in any circumstances unjustifiable, whatever the considerations of a political, philosophical, ideological, racial, ethnic, religious or other nature, that may be invoked to justify them.[90]

Kofi Annan further reinforced the U.N. blanket prohibition of terrorism: "Terrorism strikes at the very heart of everything the United Nations stands for. It presents a global threat to democracy, the rule of law, human rights and stability . . . the methods and practices of terrorism [are] criminal and unjustifiable—whoever commits them and wherever they occur."[91]

The coexistence of a proliferation of antiterrorism conventions and the increase in terrorist acts in 2001 and 2002 indicate the legislative failure by the United Nations to deter acts of terrorism. The international community has been trying to define terrorism since 1937 when the League of Nations first drafted the Convention for the Prevention and Punishment of Terrorism[92] that was signed by twenty-four nations, but ultimately ratified by only India. The United Nations began drafting antiterrorism conventions in the 1960s because of a high

---

87. Michael P. Scharf, Book Review: *Rebels With a Cause: The Minds and Morality of Political Offenders*, 96, A.J.I.L. 276, 278 (Jan. 2002).

88. *Id.* at 278.

89. U.N. GAOR, 54th Sess., 76th mtg. at art. 6, U.N. Doc. A/RES/54/109 (1999).

90. *Id.*

91. "International Instruments Related to the Prevention and Suppression of International Terrorism, (United Nations 2001), in Preface".

92. League of Nations, Convention for the Prevention and Punishment of Terrorism, O.J. 19 at 23 (1938), League of Nations Doc. C. 546 (I). M.383 (1),1937,V(1938).

incidence of aircraft hijackings. The United Nations has continued to draft specific antiterrorism conventions for the past sixty-two years to respond to different kinds of terrorist attacks against civilians, diplomats, civilian aircrafts, commercial maritime navigation, and sea-based platforms involving the use of explosives and weapons of mass destruction.[93]

There are currently seventeen specialized international U.N. conventions on terrorism,[94] three international conventions on the control of weapons of mass

---

93. Bassiouni, *supra* note 2, at 1.

94. The U.N. conventions on terrorism, and one draft convention on the Suppression of Acts of Nuclear Terrorism are as follows:

Convention on the High Seas, Apr. 29, 1958, 13 U.S.T. 2312;

United Nations Convention on Law of the Sea, Dec. 10, 1982, 21 I.L.M. 1261;

Convention for the Suppression of Unlawful Acts Against the Safety of Maritime Navigation, Mar. 10, 1988, 27 I.L.M. 668;

Protocol for the Suppression of Unlawful Acts Against the Safety of Fixed Platforms Located on the Continental Shelf, IMO. Doc. Sua/Con/16/ Rev.1; 27 I.L.M. 685 (Mar. 10, 1988);

Convention on Offences and Certain Other Acts Committed on Board Aircraft, Sept. 14, 1963, 2 I.L.M. 1042;

Convention for the Suppression of Unlawful Seizure of Aircrafts (Hijacking), Dec. 16, 1970, 18 I.L.M. 1419;

Convention on the Prohibition of the Development, Production, Stockpiling and Use of Chemical Weapons and on their Destruction (CWC Convention), Jan. 13, 1993, 32 I.L.M. 800;

Draft Convention on the Suppression of Acts of Nuclear Terrorism [Nuclear Terrorism], http://www.undcp.org/odccp/terrorism_convention_nuclear_material.html (last visited Feb. 1, 2003).

Convention for the Suppression of the Financing of Terrorism [Terrorism Financing Convention]; U.N. Doc. a/54/109 (Dec. 9, 1999) 133 (Dec. 16, 1970);

Convention for the Suppression of Unlawful Acts Against the Safety of Civil Aviation, Jan. 26, 1973, 10 I.L.M. 1151;

Protocol for the Suppression of Unlawful Acts of Violence at Airports Serving Civil Aviation [Montreal Protocol], Jan. 12, 1988, 27 I.L.M. 627;

Convention on the Prevention and Punishment of Crimes Against Internationally Protected Persons, Including Diplomatic Agents [Diplomats Convention], Dec. 14, 1973, 13 I.L.M. 41;

Convention Against the Taking of Hostages [Hostage-Taking Convention], Dec. 17, 1979, 18 I.L.M. 1456;

Convention on the Safety of United Nations and Associated Personnel [U.N. Personnel Convention], http://www.un.org/law/cod/safety.htm (last visited Feb. 1, 2003);

Convention on the Marking of Plastic Explosives for the Purpose of Detection, Mar. 1, 1991, 30 I.L.M. 721;

Convention for the Suppression of Terrorist Bombings [Terrorist Bombing Convention], U.N. Doc. A/Res/52/164 (Jan. 9, 1998);

Convention on the Prohibition of the Development, Production and Stockpiling of Bacteriological (Biological) and Toxic Weapons and on Their Destruction [BWC Convention], Apr. 10, 1972, 11 I.L.M. 309;

destruction; two international conventions containing general U.N. provisions; two U.N. draft comprehensive conventions on terrorism; and eight regional conventions against terrorism that have been developed by the Organization of American States, the Council of Europe, the South Asian Association for Regional Cooperation, the League of Arab States, the Organization of African Unity, the Commonwealth of Independent States, and the Organization of the Islamic Conference.[95] There are also international humanitarian law conventions on the prevention and punishment of torture related to terrorist acts. In addition, there are twenty-one international crimes conventions whose commission involves terrorism. Thus, terrorism is included in many different laws prohibiting crimes and human rights violations and covered under international humanitarian law conventions. Nevertheless, the increase in international terrorism and the magnitude of the tragic events that occurred in the years 2001 and 2002 bear witness to the failure of these international conventions to deter the crime.

What is needed is not more laws but better enforcement of existing norms. Due to the political nature of terrorism, States have not been able to reach an agreement on a comprehensive convention that would include all types of terrorist acts and that would apply to State-sponsored terrorism.[96] Moreover, as terrorism has been committed in the past by many State actors during the time of war or revolution, many States prefer to leave the definition of terrorism as vague as possible. More conventions will have to be adopted in the future to prevent against the threat or use of weapons of mass destruction, cyberterrorism, and other new forms of terrorism.[97] The many existing terrorism laws would be more efficiently collected in one comprehensive multilateral convention.

Nevertheless, the protections that are needed against terrorism will not be adequately provided simply by the creation of new norms. What is needed is the effective enforcement of existing laws, the adoption of one universally accepted definition of terrorism, the agreement by all nations that terrorism must be prohibited irrespective of its motivation, and the application of the existing laws to State-sponsored terrorist acts.[98]

Convention on the Physical Protection of Nuclear Material, IAEA Doc. C/225;1456 U.N.T.S. 101; 18 I.L.M. 1419 (Mar. 3, 1980)

Convention on the Prohibition of the Development, Production, Stockpiling and Use of Chemical Weapons and on their Destruction (CWC Convention), U.N. Doc. A/Res/47/39; 1974 U.N.T.S. 3; 32 I.L.M. 800 (Jan. 13, 1993)

Draft Convention on the Suppression of Acts of Nuclear Terrorism [Nuclear Terrorism], U.N. Doc. A/AC.252/L.3 (Jan. 28, 1997).

95. Bassiouni, *supra* note 2, at xxviii.

96. *Id.* at xxv.

97. *Id.* at xxvi–xxvii.

98. WILKINSON, *supra* note 81, at 13: "The difference between state and factional terrorism is that the former is more lethal and may be antecedent to, and a contributory

In December 1999, the U.N. General Assembly adopted by consensus the text of a draft of the International Convention for the Suppression of the Financing of Terrorism in which terrorism was indirectly defined in the same terms as the U.N. General Assembly Resolution 54/109 described above:

> Criminal acts intended or calculated to provoke a state of terror in the general public, a group of persons or particular persons for political purposes are in any circumstances unjustifiable, whatever the considerations of a political, philosophical, ideological, racial, ethnic, religious, or other nature, that may be invoked to justify them.[99]

This definition in the U.N. Convention for the Suppression of the Financing of Terrorism does not specifically refer to acts of violence but refers instead to "criminal acts." The definition arguably includes the element of targeting innocent civilians in the term *general public*. It includes the element of intent via the words "intended or calculated to provoke." The requirement of coercion or intimidation is included in the term *terror*. However, this definition does not include State-sponsored actors. Moreover, the definition expands the motivation of terrorism to almost any possible cause other than military. The definition does convey very clearly that the root cause or motivation of the terrorist act does not provide any justification whatsoever for terrorism. In other words, according to the United Nations, the ends do not justify the means.

G. Scholars' Attempts at A Definition of Terrorism

One terrorism expert has produced a working definition of terrorism that still falls short of including all five elements: "Terrorism is defined as the calculated employment or the threat of violence by individuals, sub-national groups, and state actors to attain political, social, and economic objectives in the violation of law, intended to create an overwhelming fear in a target area greater than the victims attacked or threatened."[100]

This definition does not specifically include the targeting of innocent civilians and limits the perpetrator's motivations to illegal political, social, and economic purposes. This definition opens the door for States to engage in terrorism by simply declaring that the purpose of the terrorist activity is justified by a legal political, social, or economic goal.

Cherif Bassiouni, who is one of the world's leading experts in the field of international criminal law, has proposed a definition of terrorism that specifically includes State-sponsored terrorism, which is conceived of not explicitly as a

---

cause of, factional terrorism. . . . Guerrilla insurgents often use terrorism . . . States conduct "terror" and substate organizations conduct "terrorism." *Id.* at 19.

99. UN GAOR, 54th Sess., 76th mtg. at art. 6, U.N. Doc. A/RES/54/109 (1999).

100. Terrorism and the Law, *supra* note 34, at 7.

crime but rather as a "strategy," and which specifically excludes the intent of the perpetrator and the targeting of innocent civilians:

> Terrorism is an ideologically-motivated strategy of internationally proscribed violence designed to inspire terror within a particular segment of a given society in order to achieve a power-outcome or to propagandize a claim or grievance, irrespective of whether its perpetrators are acting for and on behalf of themselves, or on behalf of a state.[101]

By referring to the "ends" as a "power outcome," a "claim," or a "grievance," Bassiouni's definition cleverly eliminates the consideration of the worthiness of the goals or the claimed justifications for terrorist acts. Arguably, the definition does not specifically include the element of intent. However, as the act is conceived of as a "strategy," which requires a mental process, the intent element is presumed. Moreover, the phrase "designed to inspire terror" evokes the premeditated intent of the actor. If the element of intent were absent from this definition, a person could presumably be condemned as a terrorist if, in the course of a carefully conducted attack not specifically intended to produce fear and not specifically targeted at innocent civilians, a bomb blast did cause fear in the population and the accidental injury of one or two civilians. The element of intent should be a necessary requirement in the definition of terrorism in order to exclude justifiable attempts at self-defense not involving intentional terrorist acts.

Bassiouni's definition also does not include the targeting of innocent civilians but refers instead to "a particular segment of a given society." This broad designation of a particular segment of the population could include the military, especially if acts of international terrorism are claimed to arise in the context of a conventional war or armed conflict of either an international or a non-international character. Bassiouni specifically states that international terrorism arises in the following contexts:

1. Armed conflicts of an international character or of a non-international character:
   a) conventional wars;
   b) wars of national liberation;
   c) conflicts against settler regimes, when the intended power outcomes is either the removal of the settlers or transfer of power from settler group to indigenous population;
   d) resistance against foreign occupation and/or colonial regimes.
2. International political conflicts, which may or may not involve armed conflict or non-international character.[102]

---

101. BASSIOUNI, *supra* note 2, at 16–17.
102. *Id.* at 18.

By excluding the innocent civilian element, Bassiouni's definition of international terrorism would include an attack on combatants as well as noncombatants during an armed conflict. Arguably, an intentional attack on combatants during an armed conflict with the aim of inspiring fear (or terror) within the population of combatants should not be deemed terrorism—rather it is war, pure and simple. Bassiouni's definition of international terrorism is brilliantly articulated, but would be enhanced if it included the element of innocent civilians[103] in peacetime as well as wartime. Bassiouni uses the word *terror* rather than *fear* to define international terrorism, thereby preserving the original denotation of the Latin word *terrore* (fear producing).

Bassiouni's definition of terrorism requires the act of violence to be "internationally proscribed." He carefully lists fourteen specific acts of terrorism (including aggression, war crimes, crimes against humanity, genocide, apartheid, unlawful human experimentation, torture, slavery and slave-related practices, piracy, unlawful acts against the safety of maritime navigation, kidnapping of diplomats and other internationally protected persons, taking of civilian hostages, serious environmental damage, or serious violations of fundamental human rights).[104]

---

103. Many scholars and journalists include innocent civilians in their definition of terrorism. *See* Caleb Carr, The Lessons of Terror (2002). Carr is a military historian who defines terrorism as "the contemporary name given to, and the modern permutation of, warfare, deliberately waged against civilians with the purpose of destroying their will to support either leaders or policies that the agents of such violence find objectionable" (cited in Stephen Yagman, *Defining the Weapon of Terrorism, supra* note 4. *See also* William Pfaff, *The Politics of Terrorism, or Civilians vs. Civilians,* Int'l Herald Trib. 8, (Jan. 10, 2002), at op ed page. Pfaff defines as "a form of politico-military combat that attacks civilians . . . because terrorists can't get at the political and military figures they really want to kill. Terrorism is the weapon that oppressed populations have always employed against those they consider their oppressors, usually because it is the only weapon available." Note that Yagman objects to Carr's insistence on "civilians":

> There have been numerous attacks on the military that surely can be characterized as terrorism: the Japanese attack on Pearl Harbor, the attack on the American garrison at Kobat Towers in Saudi Arabia, the terrorist attack on the U.S.S. Cole, while it was moored in Yemen . . . during France's horrific repression in Algeria, France regularly and openly employed military terrorism against innocent civilians to make concessions to France. American military bombing of a mental hospital in Grenada in . . . 1984 was allegedly fought to free American medical students studying in Grenada. America's bombing, with Thatcher's assistance, of Libyan Col Muammar Al al Qaddafi's family's home in Tripoli to get even for what Reagan claimed was Qaddafi's terrorism in which one of Qaddafi's small children was murdered; President Clinton's bombing of a pharmaceutical factory in Sudan, where an innocent night watchman was murdered.

These are all military terrorist acts conducted upon innocent civilians.

104. Bassiouni, *supra* note 2, at 18.

The advantage of this specific listing is the establishment of clarity and certainty in the law. However, the disadvantages are important to recognize. New forms of terrorist acts that develop with the advancement of technology (such as computer hacking) are not specifically included and may fall afoul of the definition, although this list is very broad and seems to cover the unanticipated act of terrorism under such umbrella categories as "aggression," or "serious violation of fundamental human rights." Yet absent from this list is "the use of weapons of mass destruction," which will necessarily (if not intentionally) inflict harm on innocent civilians. Does that mean that the use of the A-bomb during wartime is a terrorist act because it necessarily resulted in the killing of innocent civilians? There may be a political reason to exclude the use of weapons of mass destruction from the list of proscribed terrorist acts.

IV. WHAT IS THE DIFFERENCE BETWEEN INTERNATIONAL AND DOMESTIC TERRORISM?

International terrorism is covered under the seventeen U.N. multilateral antiterrorism conventions that provide legal measures (albeit in a piecemeal and ad hoc fashion) against different manifestations of international terrorist conduct such as hijacking, hostage taking, and violence against diplomats or internationally protected persons. For a terrorist act to be deemed *international*, the act of violence must contain an international element, be directed against an internationally protected target, or violate an international norm.[105] Internationally proscribed conduct applicable to terrorist violence includes aggression, war crimes, crimes against humanity, genocide, apartheid, unlawful human experimentation, torture, slavery, piracy,[106] hijacking and sabotage of aircraft, kidnapping of diplomats, taking of civilian hostages, serious environmental damage, or serious violations of fundamental human rights.[107]

Domestic terrorism is harder to define than international terrorism because it is usually included in State criminal statutes under acts committed by common criminals.[108] Some States define terrorism as a crime, while others define it as an "act of war,"[109] and most States consider terrorism to be a

105. *Id.* at 17.

106. MARITIME TERRORISM AND INTERNATIONAL LAW 43 (Natalino Ronzitti, ed., 1990) (discussing the legal relationship between piracy and maritime terrorism).

107. BASSIOUNI, *supra* note 2, at 18.

108. *Id.* at 19.

109. Raimo, *supra* note 36, at 1481 (discussing the shift in the United States away from reactive counter-terrorism law enforcement methods and towards more proactive techniques to fight international terrorism because the United States now perceives of terrorist acts as acts of war).

method used to commit other more specifically defined crimes against the person or against property.

International terrorism, like domestic terrorism, is a method used to perpetrate other crimes, and as such, it is arguably included under the category of other international crimes—but only if the five necessary structural elements of terrorism are present. Typical tools of modern international terrorism are explosive and incendiary bombings; shooting attacks and assassinations; hostage taking and kidnapping; hijacking; narco-terrorism;[110] cyberterrorism information warfare;[111] and the use of nuclear, chemical, or bacteriological weapons.[112] Terrorists can be convicted of committing war crimes, crimes against humanity, genocide, torture, and even piracy (i.e., the *Achille Lauro* incident) if they committed these crimes by using terrorist methods. Thus, international terrorism is an elusive concept that overlaps with other international crimes, but that can be included in the definitions of these other crimes if the five necessary elements are present (such as the intentional use or threat of violence for political, religious, or ideological purposes resulting in innocent civilians being harmed).

V. TERRORISM IS NOT ONLY A CRIME BUT A METHOD TO ACHIEVE SELF-DETERMINATION

One of the underlying causes of the resurgence of terrorism in the 1960s and 1970s was the development of social movements dedicated to achieving self-determination or the revolutionary transformation of the socioeconomic order and the concomitant belief by these groups that terrorism was an effective and legitimate weapon to realize their goals.[113] In the 1990s during the course of tragic ethnic wars in the Balkans and in Rwanda, mass terror was used as a weapon on both sides of the respective conflicts, requiring the establishment of

---

110. DAVIDS, *supra* note 8, at 2.

111. *See* CYBER TERRORISM AND INFORMATION WARFARE: THREATS AND RESPONSES (Yonah Alexander & Michael S. Swetnam eds., 2001).

112. WILKINSON, *supra* note 81, at 13. *See also* SUPERTERRORISM: BIOLOGICAL, CHEMICAL, AND NUCLEAR (Yonah Alexander & Milton Hoenig eds., 2001).

113. WILKINSON, *supra* note 81, at 13.

ad hoc international tribunals[114] (and later an international criminal court)[115] to bring to justice the perpetrators of genocide, crimes against humanity, and war crimes.[116]

Terrorism per se is not listed as a crime under the subject matter jurisdiction of the ad hoc tribunals.[117] In the Statute of the International Criminal Tribunal for the Former Yugoslavia (ICTY), Article 5 defines crimes against humanity, including "crimes committed in armed conflict, whether international or internal in character, and directed against any civilian population, including murder, extermination, enslavement, deportation, imprisonment, torture, rape, persecutions on political, racial and religious grounds and other inhumane acts." Even though this description of crimes against humanity contains all five elements of the definition of terrorism, it fails to name or include terrorism as a crime against humanity.

Similarly, the Statute of the ICTY at Article 3 defines war crimes or "violations of laws or customs of war," but it does not include the term *terrorism* per se. Nevertheless, under the definition of war crimes, the Statute of the ICTY proscribes the "employment of poisonous weapons, the wanton destruction of cities, towns or villages, or devastation not justified by military necessity; an attack, or bombardment, by whatever means, of undefended towns, villages, dwellings, or buildings; and the seizure or destruction or willful damage done to institutions dedicated to religions, charity, and education, the arts and sciences, historic monuments and works of art and science." This definition of war crimes also contains most of the elements of terrorism, including the use of violence with intent to harm innocent civilians (i.e., "undefended towns"), but does not include the necessary elements of fear, intimidation, and coercion for the purpose of accomplishing a political, military, ethnic, ideological, or religious goal. Moreover, in order for terrorism to be a war crime, the terrorist act has to be perpetrated during an armed conflict. If these last two elements plus the requirement of an armed conflict were included in the act constituting a war crime, that war crime as defined above could also be deemed a terrorist act.

---

114. The Statute of the International Criminal Tribunal for the Former Yugoslavia (ICTY) was established by the Security Council Resolution of May 25, 1993, following its consideration of the Report of the Secretary General (U.N. Doc. S/25704 (1993)). Secretary-General's Report on Aspects of Establishing an International Tribunal for the Prosecution of Persons Responsible for Serious Violations of International Humanitarian Law Committed in the Territory of the Former Yugoslavia, May 3, 1993, 32 I.L.M. 1159 establishing the Statute of the ICTY; *see also* International Tribunal for Rwanda, Nov. 8, 1994, 33 I.L.M. 1598 establishing the Statute of the ICTR.

115. Rome Statute of the International Criminal Court, art. 1, http://www.un.org/law/icc/statute/ 99_corr/1.htm (last visited Feb. 1, 2003).

116. Wilkinson, *supra* note 80, at 48.

117. *See* Statute of the ICTY, *supra* note 114, at Art. 5 defining "Crimes Against Humanity."

The Statute of the ICTY at Article 4 defines *genocide* as "acts committed with intent to destroy in whole or in part, a national, ethnical, racial or religious group." The definition of genocide does not specifically include terrorism per se. Nevertheless, if a genocidal act were perpetrated with the intent of furthering a cause by intentionally inspiring fear through violence committed on an innocent civilian population, such a genocidal act would necessarily also be a terrorist act.

Similarly, the Rome Statute of the International Criminal Court[118] has long lists of elements of different crimes such as crimes of aggression, war crimes, crimes against humanity, and genocide, but terrorism per se is not specifically listed as a crime. Nevertheless, many of the criminal acts listed that can cause terror among the civilian population could arguably be included under the categories of aggression, war crimes, crimes against humanity, and genocide, such as enforced disappearance of persons, rape, apartheid, and other inhumane acts of a similar character intentionally causing great suffering or serious injury to a person including both physical and mental health.[119]

The implication of conceiving terrorism as a method (i.e., strategy or tool) rather than as a crime is that terrorism can be included in other international crimes of aggression, war crimes, crimes against humanity, genocide and piracy, or torture if the acts of terror and violence also fulfill the five structural elements of the definition of terrorism.

VI. INTERNATIONAL CRIMES ARE ALSO METHODS OF COMMITTING TERRORISM

Just as terrorism is both a crime and a method to perpetrate other crimes, the reverse is true—under certain circumstances, international crimes of genocide, war crimes, and crimes against humanity can also be considered methods of terrorism intentionally designed to intimidate and cause fear in a given civilian population.[120] The right circumstances constitute the presence of the five

---

118. Rome Statute of the International Criminal Court, *supra* note 115, and Preparatory Commission on the International Criminal Court, Finalized Draft of the Elements of Crimes, U.N. Doc PCNICC/2000/1/Add.2 (2000), http://www1.umn.edu/humanrts/instree/iccelementsofcrimes.html (last visited Feb. 1, 2003).

119. Rome Statute of International Criminal Court, *supra* 115, at Article 7.

120. Bassiouni, *supra* note 2, at xxvi:

> International crimes such as genocide, crimes against humanity, war crimes, and torture are strategies of terror violence designed to instill terror within a given civilian population. How else could one describe the policies and practices carried out in Cambodia, the former Yugoslavia, Rwanda, and Sierra Leone, to name only a few of the most egregious examples. However, these international crimes are a result of state

structural elements of terrorism. Unless a genocidal act includes acts of violence and the intent to inspire fear in the civilian population for the purpose of accomplishing a political cause, the genocidal act will not be deemed a terrorist act. Similarly, rape,[121] torture, piracy, and other crimes can also be deemed methods of accomplishing terrorism only if the five elements of terrorism are present. Arguably, even if the subject matter jurisdiction of the ad hoc tribunals does not specifically cover terrorism under the list of triable crimes, terrorism as a method may nevertheless be included under the subject matter jurisdiction of the tribunal because it provides the means to perpetrate the specifically delineated crimes.[122] This is also true of the International Criminal Court. But without a consensus as to what terrorism means and without a commonality of values, some States prefer to keep the definition of terrorism in multilateral and domestic legislation as vague and ambiguous as possible.[123] This will not prove to be an effective legal response to terrorism. This indeterminacy in the law brought about by a vague or nonexistent definition of terrorism can result in a multiplicity of interpretations and the instability of the legal system.

> policy and which are committed by state officials, i.e. the military, the police, other forces under the command of public officials. The commission of these crimes depends on the availability of state resources, financial and otherwise. Yet, these crimes are not considered part of what is commonly referred to as "terrorism" by the international community. The reason, as mentioned above, is that states, which are the regulators, have seen fit to not include themselves in the context of "terrorism." Nevertheless, international crimes committed by states which constitute terror-violence should be deemed part of that category.

Id.

121. Catharine A. MacKinnon, Sex Equality: Rape Law 906 (2001): "Rape in conflict is also used as a weapon to terrorize and degrade a particular community and to achieve a specific political end. In these situations, gender intersects with other aspects of a woman's identity such as ethnicity, religion, social class or political affiliation. The humiliation of pain and terror inflicted by the rapist is meant to degrade not just the individual woman but also to strip the humanity from the larger group of which she is a part." *Id.*

122. *See* Michael P. Scharf, Editorial: *The Case for an International Trial of the Al-Qaeda and Taliban Perpetrators of the 9/11 Attacks*, Newsletter of the Interest Group on International Organizations of the ASIL, at 12–15 (Spring 2002) (discussing the advantages and disadvantages of expanding the jurisdiction of the ICTY to cover terrorist acts committed on Sept. 11, 2001 in the United States and to include them under war crimes, crimes against humanity, and genocide by simply amending the temporal and geographic jurisdictional limitation).

123. Bassiouni, *supra* note 2, at xxvi.

VII. IF TERRORISM IS NOT ONLY A CRIME, BUT A METHOD OR AN ACT OF WAR, THEN WHAT COURT SHOULD TRY INTERNATIONAL TERRORISTS?

Should international terrorists be tried in a military court, a U.S. district court, ad hoc international tribunal, or permanent international criminal court?[124] This question is left open by the failure of the international community to define terrorism or to include it as a crime in the jurisdiction of existing international courts. If terrorism is not listed specifically as a crime in the statutes of either of the two ad hoc tribunals (ICTY and ICTR) or in the statute of the new International Criminal Court, the question remains as to where international terrorists can be tried.

In order to try terrorists in either of the two ad hoc international tribunals, the temporal and geographic limitations imposed on the subject matter jurisdiction of these tribunals would have to be expanded by amendment, and terrorism would have to be presumptively included under the definitions of crimes. Even if the International Criminal Court included terrorist acts as crimes, the terrorist act of September 11, 2001 committed in the United States could not be adjudicated there for at least two good reasons: (1) the United States has not ratified the Rome Treaty establishing the International Criminal Court, and (2) the terrorist act occurred before the actual establishment of the International Criminal Court.

Trying terrorists in the U.S. district courts may be a viable solution, but one not without problems, including the potential for undesirable disclosure of sensitive evidence that might endanger national security. Other issues include the security of judges and witnesses and the fairness of trying foreigners in an American court when a heinous terrorist act is committed on U.S. soil.

It is beyond the scope of this study to analyze the relative merits of adjudicating international terrorist suits in each of these tribunals, but it is noteworthy to recognize that the problem of where to try terrorists has arisen primarily because of the failure of the international community to establish a universally accepted definition of terrorism and the failure of the courts to recognize that terrorism is actually included in other defined international crimes.

VIII. THE PARADOXES INHERENT IN THE MEANING OF TERRORISM

The main problem in defining the term *terrorism* is not its overlap with other crimes but the paradox inherent in the meaning of the word. President Ronald Reagan noted this paradox when he coined the proverbial statement: “One man’s terrorism is another man’s freedom fighter”; there is also the poetic parallelism

124. *See* Jennifer Trahan, *Trying a Bin Laden and Others: Evaluating the Options for Terrorist trials*, 24, 3 Hous. J. of Int’l. L. 475 (2002).

articulated by the international law scholar Cherif Bassiouni: "What is terrorism to some is heroism to others."[125] The paradox is related to the distinction between terrorism (which is illegal) and revolutionary violence (which some will argue is justifiable and inevitable to achieve self-determination). The antinomy in the term *terrorism* is based on the coexistence of the conflicting rights of self-defense and self-determination on the one hand, and the fundamental right to the protection of human rights on the other. Another manifestation of this paradox is the State's obligation to protect the national security of its people, which, if zealously enforced through overly broad legislation, may be in direct conflict with the State's obligation to protect its citizens' civil liberties.

Article 51 of the U.N. Charter provides the right to individual or collective self-defense if an armed attack occurs against a member of the United Nations. Moreover, every nation has a right to self-determination. In 1979, Algeria, Libya, and a few other countries wanted the United Nations to make an exception in one of its multilateral conventions[126] against hostage taking for national liberation movements[127] in which peoples are fighting against colonial domination, alien occupation, and racist regimes in the exercise of their right of self-determination. However, the Western countries rejected this demand on the grounds that even armies may not take civilian hostages because such an act would violate the Geneva Convention. A balance must be established between the right of a democracy to defend itself against terrorism and the duty of the State to preserve civil liberties and human rights.[128] The difficulty of achieving this delicate balance has resulted in the proliferation of global treaties and declarations aimed at combating international terrorism despite the abysmal failure by the international community to define terrorism and prohibit State-sponsored terrorist acts. The time has come to take a more active approach to defining terrorism.

IX. LITERARY AND CINEMATOGRAPHIC REPRESENTATIONS OF TERRORISM

A. Joseph Conrad, *The Secret Agent* (1907)

1. An Ironic Method Ever since 9/11 and the devastating terrorist attack on the World Trade Center in New York and on the Pentagon in Washington, more

125. Bassiouni, *supra* note 2, at 15.

126. International Convention Against the Taking of Hostages, U.N. Doc. A/Res/34/146(1979), Art. 12.

127. *See* Malvina Halberstam, *How Serious Are We About Prohibiting International Terrorism and Punishing Terrorists?* 11 The Jewish Lawyer 1 (1996) (discussing the exception for national liberation movements in Art. 12 of the International Convention Against the Taking of Hostages, U.N. Doc. A/Res/34/146 (1979)).

128. *See* Gross, *supra* note 15, at 89.

and more people are reading Joseph Conrad's classic and prophetic novel about anarchists, terrorists, and secret agents who plotted to cause violent destruction around the world at the turn of the century. Theodore Kaczynski, the infamous Unabomber, actually kept a copy of *The Secret Agent* at his bedside.[129] *The Secret Agent* is a book that illustrates not only the five structural elements of terrorism described above, but the complex workings of semiotics.

In the Author's Note,[130] Conrad explains his artistic purpose and his intentional use of irony to convey indirectly and through his own highly mediated messages the paradoxical nature of terrorism: "Even the purely artistic purpose, that of applying *an ironic method* [emphasis added] to a subject of that kind [the bombing of the Royal Observatory in Greenwich in 1894 by the anarchist Martial Bourdin] was formulated with deliberation and in the earnest belief that ironic treatment alone would enable me to say all I felt I would have to say in scorn as well as in pity."[131]

Irony is the appropriate rhetorical device to convey the semiotic and symbolic essence of terrorism. Both irony and terrorism have many different forms or signifiers. Irony uses words that say one thing, but mean another, thus requiring interpretation and decoding (which is the essence of semiotics). Irony enables the author and the narrator to gain distance from the events described by the use of double intention, paradox,[132] and satire, among many other tropes and figures that Conrad deftly uses. In the Author's Note of 1920, Conrad's insistence on telling merely a "simple tale" reveals his own uneasiness about the reception of his book and the possible perception of his own involvement with characters of this morally reprehensible type.[133] As the Royal Greenwich Observatory represents the sacred values of science, any effort to blow it up is a symbol of throwing "a bomb into pure mathematics."[134]

Recently the devastating terrorist bomb attacks on seven targets in Mumbai, India (including the Taj Mahal Palace and Towers, which is a well-known luxury hotel) reflect the semiotic and symbolic nature of terrorism. After the attack, the owner of the Taj Mahal Palace said, "I have a feeling that our hotel was one of the targets specifically because the terrorists know the *iconic* [emphasis added] role it plays for Indians."[135] Apparently this hotel that first opened in 1903 was

---

129. Joseph Conrad, The Secret Agent: A Simple Tale xvii (Barnes and Noble Classics 2007). *See* Introduction by Steven Marcus for an insightful discussion of Conrad's book.

130. Conrad, *supra* note 129, at 3.

131. *Id.* at 8.

132. *Id.* at xxxv. Stephen Marcus refers to the "satire" in Conrad's novel at xxxi.

133. Jacques Berthoud, *The Secret Agent*, *in* The Cambridge Companion to Joseph Conrad 100, 102 (J.H. Stape ed., 1996).

134. Conrad, *supra* note 129, at 35.

135. The Boss: *Our Hotel Was Attacked*, N. Y. Times, Feb. 8, 2009, at 15.

built by a Parsi industrialist Jamsetji Tata after he was refused entry to a Mumbai hotel with a strict Europeans-only policy. Ironically, it was built precisely to counter ethnic and racial oppression—the very ideals motivating the terrorists to attack innocent civilians inside the hotel.

Conrad's prevailing ironic method is to focus on the differences between appearances and reality, and to make "a very large distance between the way things appear to the persons in the story and the way they are made to appear to the reader."[136] For example, Verloc's hat and heavy overcoat, which he wears even inside the house, are symbols of his physical and mental "frowstiness."[137] People think he wears his coat inside because he likes the outdoor life, but it is due to his frequentation of foreign cafes. The hat appears and reappears throughout the novel as a symbol, even transforming itself into a beggar's pot to receive coins. Ossipon decodes the hat to signify "chaos," but it could mean something else. Thus, using symbols creates room for multiplicity of meaning and indeterminacy of interpretation.

Conrad's irony is manifested in the setting up of great plans that lead to nothing, such as the failed bomb that manages to blow up only the bomber. This kind of irony is also close to another that creates expectations which are falsified.[138] In the opening scene at the Embassy, Privy Councillor Wurmt questions the effectiveness of the English police, but their vigilance turns out to be greater than Wurmt had ever expected.

Another form of irony used by Conrad is foreshadowing, in which he makes an earlier passage or episode presage a later one. For example, when Stevie has an office job, the office boys induce him to let off fireworks on the stairs. Their persuasiveness forebodes Verloc's influence on Stevie, and the fireworks foreshadow the explosive Stevie will end up carrying that ends up causing his death.

Conrad insists with irony that he is merely telling a "simple" tale of a very complex, contradictory, and ambiguous phenomenon known as terrorism. The source of this tale is a terrorist act that actually occurred at the end of the nineteenth century at the time of the anarchist movement in Europe and the United States. Conrad recalls in the Author's Note: "'The Secret Agent'—I mean the tale—came to me in the shape of a few words uttered by a friend in a casual conversation about anarchists or rather anarchist activities."[139]

---

136. E.M.W. Tillyard, *The Secret Agent, in* CONRAD: A COLLECTION OF CRITICAL ESSAYS 103 (Marvin Mudrick ed., 1966).

137. *Id.* at 103.

138. *Id.* at 106.

139. CONRAD, *supra* note 129, at 5.

Anarchism originated after the French Revolution and is often associated with the name of Mikhail Bakunin,[140] who is considered to be its founder.[141] Bakunin was expelled in September 1872 from the International Working Men's Association because he opposed the running of the organization and objected to the Marxist belief that a proletarian revolution could happen without incendiary acts.[142] Bakunin insisted that "the passion for destruction is a creative passion,"[143] a theory adopted by the Professor in Conrad's novel.

Conrad invented imaginary characters who, like Moliere's stereotypes, actually represent certain people in English society, as well as certain social and cultural ideas of Conrad's time. One critic argues that Conrad's characters represent national mentalities: Vladimir is the Russian; The Professor is the American; Winnie Verloc and the Assistant Commissioner are British.[144] The central focus of *The Secret Agent* is based on a real historical event that is shrouded in a literary and satiric representation. "It is almost a parody of Dostoevsky. . . ."[145] In fact, the whole novel is based on an interplay of truth and fiction, reality and fantasy, in which stylistically lighthearted comedy combine with the power of ironic tension to convey a deeply tragic message about the instability and disintegration of European society by the spread of terrorism.

Conrad paints comedic caricatures of British aristocracy as well as not-so-funny and very dangerous anarchists, secret agents, terrorists, nihilists, spies, double agents, counter spies, police spies, and agents provocateurs, all of whom terrorize the people by the frequency of their dynamite "outrages," (which is what revolutionary and terrorist assassinations and bombings were called at that time).[146] Many of the characters in the novel have comic names based on the rhetorical device of play on words. For example, Stott-Wartenheim's name in German suggests a stutterer staying at home; Verloc in French is "syphilitic." The German Chancelier d'Ambassade Wurmt is in fact a worm, and finally Ossipon is a medical student whose name in Latin means "old bones."[147]

Conrad's story depicts the inanity of a faulty bombing that results in destroying nothing more than the man who carried the bomb. Vladimir is the instigator of the bombing, who says that "the attack must have all the shocking senselessness of gratuitous blasphemy"[148] (in the manner of André Gide's famous *acte gratuit*).

---

140. *Id.* at. xlii
141. *See* HOUEN, *supra* note 3, at 30 for a history of anarchism.
142. *Id.*
143. CONRAD, *supra* note 129, at lxxiv.
144. Bertoud, *supra* note 133, at 104.
145. ELOISE KNAPP HAY, THE POLITICAL NOVELS OF JOSEPH CONRAD: A CRITICAL STUDY 235 (1963).
146. CONRAD, *supra* note 129, at xxxii.
147. HAY, *supra* note 145, at n.44 p. 237.
148. CONRAD, *supra* note 129, at 34.

Like the faulty terrorist bombing that accomplishes almost nothing, Conrad compares himself to the absurd existentialist hero, Sisyphus, "who did get periodically his stone to the top only to see it roll down again."[149] Thus, in Conrad's idiom, the act of terrorism is represented as being intricately allied to the notions of absurdity, senselessness, and meaningless violence.

2. The Symbols of Terrorism Terrorist attacks such as the one on September 11, 2001 have an intensely symbolic nature. "The Pentagon is a symbol, and the World Trade Center is, or was, a symbol, and an American passenger jet is also a symbol—of indigenous mobility and zest, and of the galaxy of glittering destinations."[150] The September 11 attacks "were not targeted at women and children. The real targets were America's *icons* of military and economic power."[151] Osama bin Laden's name is a "stock symbol of everything loathsome and hateful to the collective imagination."[152] Arguably, the "entire event of September 11 amounted essentially to a monumental collision of symbols, metaphors and other shadowy 'figures.'"[153] The terrorist attack of 9/11 was experienced and expressed in the media most frequently through symbolism, especially by the rhetorical figure of hyperbole.[154] Writers are interested in terrorism because of its symbolic nature and its mediation through a profusion of dramatic literary tropes and figures.[155]

Conrad's *The Secret Agent* reveals the semiotic nature and symbolic world of terrorism. The very fabric of the novel is made up of signs, symbols, and icons that formally represent hidden meanings. Verloc's code designation is the triangle or delta, which becomes his sign of secrecy and enclosure.[156] The triangle is also the device of safety that Verloc seeks in isolation and hiding; it symbolizes human solitude and indifference. For example, Winnie looks at Ossipon "under the falling mist in the darkness and solitude of Brett Place, in which all sounds of life seemed lost as if in a *triangular* well of asphalt and bricks, of blind houses and unfeeling stones."[157] [emphasis added]. In contrast to Verloc's triangular symbol, Stevie (Winnie's half-witted brother) continuously draws concentric circles as if he wants to bring order and arrangement into the fragmented society where he is an outsider. The circle is a symbol of perfection and infinity, and Stevie's ideal world is one of disorganized perfection, an irrational harmony, a

---

149. *Id.* at lxv.

150. Houen, *supra* note 3, at 2.

151. *Id.* at 3.

152. Edward Said, *Islam and the West are Inadequate Banners*, The Observer, Sept. 17, 2001, at 27.

153. Houen, *supra* note 3, at 4.

154. *Id.* at 5.

155. *Id.* at 7.

156. Avrom Fleishman, Conrad's Politics: Community and anarchy in the Fiction of Joseph Conrad 197 (1967).

157. Conrad, *supra* note 129, at 276.

plan of a utopia.[158] Thus, the two symbols (the circle and the triangle) may be the two poles of an axis on which the world of the novel revolves.[159]

Conrad paints portraits of anarchists and pictures of terrorists who symbolize different types or subcategories of terrorism. His imagery is the "symbolic equivalent of the theme of fragmentation" of London in particular and of European society in general. This theme of fragmentation is expressed in the novel by "the varied forms of self-enclosure (secrecy, ignorance, foolishness, madness, etc) and of physical dismembering (explosion, butchering, islands, etc.)."[160] Conrad uses the words *secret, knowledge, private,* and *fool* so often that they come to symbolize man's very condition in London at the turn of the century.[161] The title of the novel focuses the reader's attention on the word *secret*, which occurs in the novel with noticeable frequency.[162] Repetition in literary discourse is a sign of a significant theme. Secrecy and deception are an integral part of terrorist acts, and, ironically, secrecy is a necessary feature of semiotics where deeper meanings (signifieds) are hidden below the deceptive surface of the signifier or actual physical form of the word. To arrive at the deeper meanings, we must decode and interpret the surface; to understand the meaning of the terrorist act, we must uncover the plot shrouded in mystery and secrecy. Terrorist language is riddled with the word *secrecy*. For example, when Verloc responds to his wife's accusation of his having killed the boy who carried the bomb, Verloc repeats the word *secrecy* at least three times:

> In sincerity of feeling and openness of statement, these words went far beyond anything that had ever been said in this home, kept up on the wages of a *secret* industry eked out by the sale of more or less *secret* wares: the poor expedients devised by a mediocre mankind for preserving an imperfect society from the dangers of moral and physical corruption, both *secret*, too, of their kind.[163]

Who are these people who Conrad caricaturizes in the novel and who symbolize terrorists? Mr. Verloc is a shopkeeper who does business in pornography in London and who is also a professional spy in the pay of the Russian Embassy. He keeps the Russians informed about any anarchist plots in London, and he also informs the English police about Russian anti-anarchist plots. Ironically, the

158. FLEISHMAN, *supra* note 156, at 197.

159. *Id.* at 198. Fleishman's brilliant analysis of the symbolic world of *The Secret Agent* must be read by all those who enjoy literature, appreciate semiotics, and want to learn more about symbolism.

160. *Id.* at 189.

161. *Id.*

162. *Id.* at 190: (citing all the repetitions of the word *secret* in the novel): "secret ardor," "secret scorn," "secretly much affected," "secret griefs," "secretly outspoken thought," "secrecy of his heart," "secret liberation," "secret weakness," "secret fear," "secret of good nature," "secret of guilty breasts," and "secret habits of mind."

163. CONRAD, *supra* note 129, at 258.

household of this spy Verloc is "a bastion of British upper-working class/lower-middle class respectability." Verloc is described by Conrad as a "fat pig," endowed with an "air of moral nihilism common to keepers of gambling hells and disorderly houses."[164] Verloc is the two-sided contradictory character who is both a family man and a terrorist. He is deeply involved with the anarchists in plotting revolution and committing acts of violence, terrorism, and oppression of the weak—all in the name of helping the oppressed and the weak. Verloc's duality is the fruitful creation of Conrad's ironic method, which is in itself a metaphor of terrorism.

Who are some of Verloc's cronies? Michaelis is Conrad's true anarchist.[165] He frequents Verloc's shop when released on parole after having spent fifteen years of his life sentence in solitary confinement as punishment for the small part he played in a terrorist escape from jail in which a policeman was killed. Michaelis' complicity in the terrorist crime was negligible, and he did not kill the policeman.[166] Nevertheless, he received a life sentence. As a result of his arguably unjust and harsh punishment, Michaelis is now withdrawn and writing "night and day in a shaky, slanting hand an Autobiography of a Prisoner which was to be like a Book of Revelation in the history of mankind."[167] He has become a writer, living in his "tiny cage in a litter of manuscript," and he looks "angelic." He has a "Marxian, Utopian, Anarchistic, and Socialistic spirit and lives only on raw carrots and milk."[168] He reminds one of Strelnikov, the perfect, politically driven Marxist revolutionary in Pasternak's novel *Doctor Zhivago*. Strelnikov also lives only on bread and water like Mohatma Gandhi, the vegetarian civil disobedient. Michaelis is a revolutionary optimist who, like Verloc, is very fat. He wants the "end of all private property because the (inherent viciousness) of private property can lead only to further oppression."[169] Michaelis says "Capitalism [is] doomed in its cradle, born with the poison of the principle of competition in its system. The great capitalists devouring the little capitalists . . . and in the madness of self-aggrandisement only preparing, organizing . . . making ready the lawful inheritance of the suffering proletariat."[170]

---

164. *Id.* at 18–19. *See also* BARBARA ARNETT MELCHIORI, TERRORISM IN THE LATE VICTORIAN NOVEL 74–83 (1985) for an interesting analysis of Conrad's *The Secret Agent*, Conrad's use of irony and caricature, and why Conrad renders the London anarchists as "physically repulsive."

165. HOUEN, *supra* note 3, at 40. Michaelis claims, "History is dominated and determined by the tool and production—by the force of economic conditions. Capitalism has made socialism, and the laws made by the capitalist for the socialist are responsible for anarchism." CONRAD, *supra* note 129, at 73.

166. CONRAD, *supra* note 129, at 91.

167. *Id.* at 102.

168. *Id.* at 244.

169. *Id.* at xliii.

170. *Id.* at 47.

Karl Yundt is the prototype of the "old terrorist" with a foreign accent, "dried throat and toothless gums"[171] who is possibly a caricature of Bakunin himself and clearly one of Verloc's cronies. He is and has been an "all-but moribund veteran of dynamite wars," who once "had been a great actor in his time . . . the famous terrorist" who "never in his life raised personally as much as his little finger against the social edifice . . . no man of action . . . an orator of torrential eloquence, sweeping the masses along in the rushing noise and foam of a great enthusiasm."[172] Yundt is bloodthirsty and full of talk about destruction: "I have always dreamed . . . of a band of men absolute in their resolve to discard all scruples in the choice of means, strong enough to give themselves frankly the name of destroyers, and free from the taint of that resigned pessimism which rots the world. No pity for anything on earth, including themselves, and death enlisted for good and all in the service of humanity. . . ." [173] Yundt is like any good novelist, not a man of action but a gifted orator with the capacity to corrupt via the power of words.

Ossipon is the youngest of the terrorists who is also the principal writer of propagandist leaflets. He is a former student of science whom Conrad satirically describes as a "mongrel" physical type, a mixture of the Negro and the Mongoloid. He is nothing at all like the pure terrorist Vladimir who is contrastingly represented by Conrad as a man of breeding.[174] Both these characters are parodies of types drawn from the scientific theories prevalent at the time. In his own writings and pamphlets, Ossipon exposes the hypocrisies and vices of middle-class morality. He describes prostitution as the enslavement of working–class girls and the exploitation of women in the service of bourgeois, unfaithful men. But in the end Ossipon also ends up hypocritically living off of "silly girls with savings-bank books."[175]

The Professor is the terrorist par excellence who builds the bomb Stevie drops in the Royal Greenwich Observatory. The Professor is a solitary figure, undernourished and unhealthy but "supremely self-confident."[176] He is a scientist, and *The Secret Agent* is arguably a critique of science itself.[177] The Professor is like H.G. Wells' creatures (Conrad dedicated his book to Wells). He is an agent of destruction, always carrying a detonator with him, working to improve the mechanism that would cause the explosion. He is a man of science, an inventor trying to invent a detonator that "would adjust itself to all conditions of action,

171. *Id.* at 42.
172. *Id.* at 46.
173. *Id.* at 42.
174. *Id.* at 35.
175. *Id.* at 249.
176. *Id.* at 59.
177. HOUEN, *supra* note 3, at 41.

and even to unexpected changes of conditions."[178] He is the perfect nihilist who despises everyone, including the revolutionists.[179] He is the agent of death. The Professor says that ordinary people "depend on life, which . . . is . . . open to attack at every point; whereas I depend on death, which knows no restraint and cannot be attacked."[180] The Professor is not an advocate of intimidation—he wants total destruction, a true terrorist. His dream is "of a world like shambles, where the weak would be taken in hand for utter Extermination . . . Exterminate, Exterminate! That is the only way of progress . . . First the great multitude of the weak must go, then the only relatively strong . . . Every taint, every vice, every prejudice, every convention must meet its doom."[181] The Professor's insidious belief is prophetic of the dangerous theory of eugenics that Hitler relied on to exterminate the Jews and all those whom Hitler believed were physiologically and "scientifically" inferior. The Professor believes "the world is mediocre, limp, without force. And madness and despair are a force. And force is a crime in the eyes of the fools . . . who rule the roost. You are mediocre . . . Everybody is mediocre. Madness and despair! Give me that for a lever, and I'll move the world."[182]

The Professor's words echo the famous *Catechism of the Revolutionist* (possibly written by Bakunin and clearly read by the Professor): "The revolutionary enters into the world of the state, of class, and of so-called culture, and lives in it only because he has faith in its speedy and total destruction."[183] The Professor, then, is the ultimate terrorist who incorporates the beliefs of anarchists and nihilists. He is a remnant of Robespierre, the product of Nietzsche who was arguably "one of the earliest and certainly the greatest of modern intellectual terrorists."[184] Nietzsche believed the fulfillment of nihilism is achieved with the advent of the active terrorist.[185] Like Conrad who contrasts the man of words (Verloc) and the man of action (the Professor), Nietzsche distinguishes the "Propagandist" who is committed to a "sublime test of the power of words" from the "Terrorist" who is "committed to "Acts." [186]

---

178. CONRAD, *supra* note 129, at 61.

179. HAY, *supra* note 145, at 251.

180. CONRAD, *supra* note 129, at 63.

181. *Id.* at 244.

182. *Id.* at 248–49.

183. *Id.* at lxxxv.

184. *Id.* at lxxix. *See also* HOUEN, *supra* note 3, at 54 (citing FRIEDRICH NIETZSCHE, THE WILL TO POWER 35 (Walter Kaufman & R.J. Hollingdale trans., 1968)). In this work written between 1883 and 1888, Nietzsche discusses "the most terrifying form of Nihilism" which is "existence without meaning or aim, recurring inevitably without any finale of nothingness: the 'eternal recurrence.'"

185. HOUEN, *supra* note 3, at 56 (citing SERGEI KRAVCHINSKY, UNDERGROUND RUSSIA 4 (Smith & Elder, trans. 1883)).

186. KRAVCHINSKY, *supra* note 185, at 33.

3. Representation of the Five Elements of the Crime of Terrorism in *The Secret Agent* The first element of the crime of terrorism is the perpetration of violence by whatever means. The band of anarchists, nihilists, and terrorists in *The Secret Agent* are all united by one singular aim: the commission of violence by throwing a bomb in a public place to generate publicity for their political and social causes.

The second element of the crime of terrorism is the targeting of innocent civilians. In the novel, the anarchists do so by aiming the bomb not at a military target in a time of war, but at the Royal Conservatory in a time of peace.

The third element of the crime of terrorism focuses on intentionality. The intention of the terrorists is to cause serious violence and destruction without any regard for the consequences. Even though the bomb created by the Professor actually and ironically hurts only the bomber (and eventually his sister, who commits suicide), the intent of all the conspirators is to cause much wider damage.

Fear is the fourth element of the crime of terrorism. For some of the conspirators, the purpose of this bomb outrage is to cause the public to be frightened enough to think about the social ills that are being perpetrated upon them by the government leaders in the very same society these terrorists abhor. For others, the goal is total destruction, with this bomb being just one of a series that will soon follow.

The last element of the definition is the achievement of an ideological goal. Here the terrorists' arguably laudable goal is to wipe out the oppression of the masses. Vladimir and Privy Councillor [sic] Wurmt, for example, object to the "general leniency of the judicial procedure"[187] in Britain. "This country is absurd with its regard for individual liberty,"[188] decries Vladimir. But how can this goal to wipe out the oppression of the masses possibly be accomplished by detonating bombs in public places that result in harm to the innocent, the oppressed, and the weak? This is the great irony inherent in terrorism itself.

B. Hotel Rwanda

Hotel Rwanda is a film directed by Terry George and written by Keir Pearson and Terry George. It is the story of the savage and terrifying genocide that took place in Rwanda in 1994 when in ninety days more than eight hundred thousand people were slaughtered. The cause of this genocide was ethnic differences between the Tutsis and the Hutus who were forced to be friends, neighbors, and even husbands and wives under the European rule.

The trouble started when the European colonial powers put certain people in power without recognizing traditional tribal boundaries. The Belgians favored

---

187. CONRAD, *supra* note 129, at 55.

188. *Id.* at 64.

the Tutsis, who were in the minority, because they were taller, thinner, and more handsome people than the Hutus, who were in the vast majority. For years in Rwanda under the rule of the Belgians, Tutsis were in minority rule, and Tutsis killed Hutus from time to time. Now due to the power of the media, the Hutus were in control. Armed troops prowled the nation for the sole purpose of killing Tutsis, and people were in mortal fear for their lives. Hatred between the Hutus and the Tutsis festered, exacerbated by blaring radio propaganda to wipe out "the cockroaches" (the Tutsis). When the president of Rwanda's plane was shot down from the skies over Kigali, his death marked the start of an orchestrated campaign of terror leading to genocide. "It is time to cut the tall trees," called out the voices on the radio, encouraging the Hutus to wield clubs and machetes to kill Tutsis and rape their women.

A U.N. peacekeeping force was present (represented by Colonel Oliver, played by Nick Nolte), but even though he begged his U.N. superiors for help and intervention, he was largely ignored. Paul Rusesabagina, the manager of the Hotel des Mille Collines, a luxury hotel that was the best establishment in the Rwandan capital frequented by generals and dignitaries visiting Kigali, informed the corporate headquarters in Brussels of the growing tragedy and chronic terrorist attacks on innocent civilians, but Brussels also simply ignored his pleas.

This is a movie about grandiose indifference toward the people of the Third World and the horrors of terrorist attacks on innocent civilians by other civilians of a different tribe living together in Rwanda. Despite many signs that a genocide was about to occur, including the extensive and vicious terrorist attacks with machetes and axes perpetrated upon the citizens of Rwanda, the international community refused to undertake a humanitarian intervention that could have saved the lives of these innocent victims.

Hotel Rwanda is not only the vivid depiction of the massacre per se, but also the tale of one man, a hero who saved the lives of over 1,200 people by being selfless. Paul Rusesabagina (played by Don Cheadle) is a quiet, steady, competent, and even elegant man living in a time of utter turmoil and chaos in his country. Paul is a Hutu, married to a Tutsi named Tatiana (played by Sophie Okonedo). He speaks French and was trained well in hotel management in Belgium. People come to be "guests" in the Hotel Des Mille Collines by the chance of war. Paul is greatly concerned about his own family, but he manages to save as many people as he possibly can from the terrorist attacks by hiding them in his hotel. He is pragmatic and uses his skills of diplomacy, bribery, lying, blackmail, flattery, and pure deception to save his family and those who come to his hotel for help.

Hotel Rwanda is a riveting drama about the horrors of terrorism that result in almost unimaginable atrocities. In this film we see Rwanda through the eyes of its good citizens, including their powerlessness in the face of an overwhelming evil and the difficulties they experience when normalcy is restored once again after the terrorism is over.

X. CONCLUSION

Terrorism is a term that exists in a context of signs and symbols producing vagueness and indeterminacy. For example, it is quite common to say that since September 2001 a "war on terrorism" has been led by the United States supported by a coalition of over one hundred countries.[189] We use the term *terrorism* frequently but without knowing what it means. A semiotic approach used to define terrorism has uncovered five basic and necessary structural elements that must be present to identify a violent or aggressive act as terrorism. The paradoxical nature of the concept of terrorism renders the establishment of an acceptable definition difficult, but not much different from the work that judges must do in the typical "hard case," as defined by Ronald Dworkin.[190] Balance is the essence of the law iconographically represented by the scales of justice. Judges understand the sensitive nature of prioritizing two conflicting rights of equal importance. Who is to say that the right of self-determination or the right of self-defense against an armed attack is more important than the right of civilians to live in a safe environment or to enjoy their own fundamental human rights and basic civil liberties?

It is possible to decenter this paradox and to reduce the definitional difficulty by proposing a categorical prohibition on the use of terrorism, no matter how lofty the purpose may be and no matter how worthy the political or ideological cause may seem to those oppressed by tyrannical regimes. There is no justification for terrorism. It is not defensible to argue that terrorism needs to be viewed from a political context and that the "motivation" of the actor and the sociological context in which the act occurs must be taken into consideration. Such an approach would legitimize terrorist acts by claiming that the ends justify the means when this Macchiavelian principle simply does not comport with the generally accepted principles of the rule of law.

---

189. *See* Dominic McGoldrick, From "9-11" To the Iraq War 2003: International Law in an Age of Complexity 24 (2004). *See also* Richard Falk, The Great Terror War (2003).

190. Ronald Dworkin, Taking Rights Seriously 81–130 (1977).

4. STATE-SPONSORED TERRORISM, THE LAWS OF WAR, AND THE ROLE OF STORYTELLING AS A SELF-HELP REMEDY

Law, Literature, and Semiotics*

Dedicated to Alex Petrushka, who survived years in Auschwitz, and who taught me to play the piano.

I. INTRODUCTION

A. Law is not Literature . . . and Yet . . .

Lawyers are like writers and filmmakers because all are seriously engaged in the art of *representation*. Lawyers represent the interests of their clients; they aim to defend their clients zealously through the art of persuasion and ethically in accordance with the Rules of Professional Responsibility.[1] Writing memoirs, reading a book, making a movie, and watching a film are different acts of the same process known as representation, which is presentation again and anew

---

* A shorter version of this chapter was presented at a Conference on Law and the Humanities' Representation of the Holocaust, Genocide and Other Human Rights Violations at Thomas Jefferson School of Law on January 16–17, 2005. An article entitled *The Failure of the International Laws of War and the Role of Art and Story-Telling as a Self-Help Remedy for Restorative Justice* was published in 12 Tex. Wesleyan L. Rev. 91–129 (2005). That article has been completely revised and adapted to the themes of this book. I wish to thank my research assistants, Mr. Chris Ramey and Miss Michelle Hoskinson, for their invaluable assistance with the research for this chapter. I also wish to thank Professor Jordan Paust, Justice Richard Goldstone (formerly of the Supreme Court of South Africa), and Judge Theodor Meron (formerly president of the International Criminal Tribunal for Crimes against the Former Yugoslavia) for their comments on earlier drafts of this chapter. Special thanks to Alex Petrushka, a pianist and my piano teacher, whose survival story during the Holocaust helped to inspire this chapter.

1. *See* Model Rules of Professional Conduct R.1. 3 cmt 1 (2005), *reprinted in* Professional Responsibility Standards, Rules & Statutes: 2005–06 Abridged Edition 13 (John S. Dzienkowsky ed., 2005) ("A lawyer shall act with reasonable diligence and promptness in representing a client . . . A lawyer must also act with commitment and dedication to the interests of the client and *with zeal* in advocacy upon the client's behalf" (emphasis added)). The lawyer's duty to defend with zeal is analogous to the artist's endeavor to communicate persuasively through rhetorical figures and literary style.

with persuasion. Like novelists and filmmakers, lawyers must communicate information clearly and persuasively,[2] and they must defend their own interpretation[3] of the meaning of a specific passage in a legal text.[4]

Whether they are primarily legal or artistic in nature, messages are carried by different media[5] such as legal opinions, laws, cases, contracts, books, and movies. Writers and filmmakers typically communicate messages via a literary or cinematographic discourse that contains a preponderance of rhetorical tropes and figures along with other types of stylistic devices and visual effects. These various modes of concretization transmit meaning indirectly through an emphasis on style rather than content.[6] Literary discourse produces in the reader's mind a heightened awareness of an author working behind the scenes to create and convey meaning artfully through a skillful manipulation of form and subtle delivery of content. Thus, artistic discourse is dominated by form rather than content in the constant interplay of style and meaning.

In contrast, legislators and lawyers typically try to keep legal discourse in the realm of content, shunning style and literary intrusions that bring vagueness and multiplicity of meaning to a legal document. Thus, legal discourse is dominated by content rather than form. Lawyers are taught to avoid metaphor and other rhetorical devices in their legal writing to achieve clarity and reduce ambiguity. In other words, lawyers are taught to remain on the solid ground of scientific language, which is purportedly more quantitative, direct, clear, and precise while being less encumbered by indeterminacy and the multiplicity of meaning created by the use of tropes, symbols, rhetorical figures, and stylistic devices.

This simplified and admittedly reductionist dichotomy between literary and legal language is misguided because it focuses only on the differences between the two disciplines of law and literature without recognizing their similarities. Literary discourse is not strictly artistic, and legal discourse is not strictly scientific.

---

2. *See* Susan Tiefenbrun, Chapter 2 of this book, and *Legal Semiotics*, 5, CARDOZO ARTS & ENT. L.J. 89, 92 (1986).

3. *See generally* Ronald Dworkin, *Law as Interpretation*, 60 TEX. L. REV. 527 (1982) (discussing the exercise of interpretation in legal practice).

4. *See generally*, BERNARD JACKSON, SEMIOTICS AND LEGAL THEORY 19–21 (1985) (differentiating between decoding and interpretation.); *See* Tiefenbrun, *Legal Semiotics, supra* note 2, at 92 (applying semiotics to legal discourse).

5. Marshall McLuhan's proverbial remark, "The medium is the message," emphasizes the importance of media and the role that form plays in the communication of the message. *See* MARSHALL MCLUHAN, UNDERSTANDING MEDIA: THE EXTENSIONS OF MAN 7 (1965); *see also*, MARSHALL MCLUHAN & QUENTIN FIORE, THE MEDIUM IS THE MESSAGE 8 (1967) (discussing the influence of style over content).

6. *See generally* SUSAN TIEFENBRUN, A STRUCTURAL AND STYLISTIC ANALYSIS OF LA PRINCESSE DE CLEVES (1979) (discussing the nature of literary discourse, the role of style, the predominance of rhetorical devices in literary language, and the concentration of form over content in literary discourse).

Although some judges enjoy using metaphor and literary or rhetorical flourishes to persuade readers of the validity of their legal opinions,[7] others actually deny the benefits of looking at law through the lens of literature because of their belief in the essentially different natures of literary and legal discourse.[8] Law is not literature, they say with conviction! Nevertheless, as do readers of books and viewers of film, lawyers too must interpret, and they do so by means of theories of interpretation often borrowed from literature (e.g., historical analysis, structuralism, post-structuralism, deconstructionism, linguistics, semiotics, stylistics, narrativity, and postmodernism, to name but a few). Messages in books are hidden in the interstices of literary discourse. Their underlying meanings are conveyed indirectly to the reader through the reader's own perception of the interplay of signifiers and signifieds, style and content, form and meaning. Thus, lawyers, readers of literature, and viewers of film are all deeply involved in the semiotic process as they engage actively in interpretation and in the unraveling of a tightly knit relationship between style and content. This is the semiotic experience par excellence. According to Saussure, linguistics, stylistics, hermeneutics, and the study of culture are all subsets of the vast branch of scientific investigation known as semiotics. Similarly, law and literature are also subsumed under the umbrella of semiotics.

Hidden meanings are uncovered by a process of decoding.[9] Meanings may be intentional or unintentional, and they are usually embedded in the deep, narrative structures of the artistic discourse.[10] Even though legal discourse is supposed to be direct, clear, and unambiguous, it, too, requires interpretation, especially when the words used to convey the legal messages have more than one meaning. Lawyers and judges often resort to various interpretive theories known as hermeneutics, original intent, textualism,[11] and many others (also used by literary scholars) to clarify the meaning of ambiguous constructions in legal

---

7. *See* Julie Stone Peters, *Review Essay*, 9 Cardozo Stud. L. & Literature 259, 264 (1997): "Storytelling and rhetoric are central to law practice and study . . . the reading of literature has something to say to the reading of law. In fact, defense is not really necessary, because neither the study of literature as window on the law nor the claim that rhetoric and narrative are essential components of legal argument are really under attack."

8. *See* Richard A. Posner, Law and Literature 7 (rev. ed. 1998). Judge Pierre Leval has also expressed reluctance to consider legal opinions as literature. At a Yale symposium, Judge Leval stated: "I will use the occasion to object to a movement that tells judges we should consider our opinions literature and invest them with the power of literary and dramatic rhetoric." Peters, *supra* note 7, at 264.

9. Jackson, *supra* note 4, at 19–21 (distinguishing between decoding and interpretation).

10. *See* Tiefenbrun, *supra* note 2, at 92.

11. Antonin Scalia, A Matter of Interpretation: Federal Courts and the Law 23 (1997) (discussing "textualism" which Scalia distinguishes from "strict constructionism"). Scalia correctly emphasizes the role of *context* in textual interpretation. *Id.* at 37.

texts. Because the processes of persuasive representation and interpretation are the essence of lawyer's work as well as the work of literary writers and filmmakers, it is no wonder the market is glutted with novels about the law and with films about trials or hot legal topics. The relationship of law and the humanities is an international and interdisciplinary movement called *law and literature.*[12]

Proponents of the law and literature movement look at law through the lens of the humanities with an aim toward humanizing the judicial system. The laudable aims of the law and literature movement happen to coincide with a similar trend in public international law designed to humanize the laws and customs of war.[13] International humanitarian law,[14] also known as the laws of armed conflict[15] or the laws of war,[16] is evolving and "acquiring a more humane face."[17] After 1945 and the aftermath of the Holocaust, a global and unsettling awareness arose of the atrocities that a world war could wreak upon humanity. Hitler violated every law of war in the book—and civilians no longer were protected by the long-standing military codes! At that horrifying moment of awareness in

---

12. *See* POSNER, *supra* note 8, at 4, for a history of the law and literature movement beginning with the publication of JAMES BOYD WHITE, THE LEGAL IMAGINATION (1973) and continuing with RICHARD WEISBERG, THE FAILURE OF THE WORD (1984) and the establishment of the Law and Humanities' Institute (LHI) in 1979 devoted to research and writing in the area of law and the humanities. I was the President of LHI for more than eight years and have served on its Board of Directors for decades.

13. THEODOR MERON, *International Law in the Age of Human Rights: General Course on Public International Law, in* 301 RECUEIL DES COURS: COLLECTED COURSES OF THE HAGUE ACADEMY OF INTERNATIONAL LAW, 24 (2003). *See also* Society of Professional Journalists, *A Brief History of the Laws of War (2003)*, http://www.globalissuesgroup.com/geneva/history.html (last visited Sept. 24, 2005) (presenting a time line of the history of the laws of war).

14. *See* Johannes Chan, *Implementation of International Humanitarian Law*, 8 ASIA PAC. L. REV. 211–28 (2000) (introducing the concept, its development, and its implementation in Asia, particularly Hong Kong). *See generally* THE NEW HUMANITARIAN LAW OF ARMED CONFLICT (Antonio Cassese ed., 1979) (presenting several different perspectives on the development of humanitarian law and its problems).

15. *See generally* THE HANDBOOK OF HUMANITARIAN LAW IN ARMED CONFLICTS (Dieter Fleck et al. eds., 1995).

16. *See* THE LAW OF WAR: A DOCUMENTARY HISTORY (Leon Friedman ed., 1972); *see generally* Chris Jochnick & Roger Norman, *The Legitimation of Violence: A Critical History of the Laws of War*, 35 HARV. INT'L L.J. 49 (1994). *See generally* Elliott L. Meyrowitz et al., *The Past 75 Years and the Laws of War*, 75 AM. SOC'Y INT'L L. PROC. 214 (1981) (discussing the failure to incorporate restrictions on nuclear weapons in the laws of war). For a brief history of the laws of war, which have been around since the beginning of recorded history, *see* Society of Professional Journalists, *supra* note 13. For a bibliography of the laws of war, *see* Cynthia Pittson's "Bibliography on International Law and the Law of War," part of "The Law & Terrorism: A Three-Part Discussion Series" sponsored by Pace Law School and the International Law Society on Oct. 18, Oct. 25, and Nov. 7, 2001.

17. MERON, *supra* note 13, at 24.

history, the international legal community felt compelled to adopt and apply human rights law[18] and the general principles of humanity.[19]

B. Law and Literature and Semiotics

This chapter analyzes the principles of international humanitarian law as exemplified in the book and film called *The Pianist*. This method of analysis relating international law and literature is a variant form of semiotic analysis focusing on the signifier (the film and the novel) and on *how* the texts illustrate the signified (the international laws of war). In other words, the movie and the book are signifiers (like the letters of a word that are the outward representation of messages or signifieds). Within the texts there are many levels of relationships between the signifier and the signified that the reader and the movie viewer must work hard to identify in order to perceive the meanings of the texts. Thus, the reader and the movie viewer are creatively and actively involved in producing meaning. The international laws of war are the signifieds that can be perceived in many different variant art forms. The law and literature approach considers the artistic text as an illustration of legal principles according to basic semiotic principles.

The book and movie *The Pianist* dramatically represent the life of one special man, Wladyslaw Szpilman, a famous pianist from Warsaw, Poland and a Holocaust survivor, who lived to tell his story in the memoirs he wrote shortly after the war. Szpilman's memoirs became a book and later a film directed by Roman Polanski and starring Adrien Brody, who won an Oscar for his performance in that spellbinding movie.

The book and the film represent more than just the story of one survivor of a devastating world war. These two art forms reflect in different ways the failure of

---

18. *See generally* Jordan J. Paust, International Law as Law of the United States (2d ed. 2003) (discussing the human rights movement said to have been born in 1945 out of the disasters of World War II, although human rights laws had a rich history prior to the war). *Id.* at Chapters 5–6. Reaction to the horrors of the Holocaust and other war crimes and crimes against humanity during World War II contributed to the reaffirmation of human rights and human dignity through international agreements and institutions. Human rights include civil, political, social, economic, and cultural rights enshrined in post-1945 treaties and international instruments, including (but not limited to) the Charter of the United Nations; the Universal Declaration of Human Rights; the International Covenant on Civil and Political Rights; the International Covenant on Economic, Social and Cultural Rights; the Convention Against All Forms of Racial Discrimination; the Convention on the Elimination of All Forms of Discrimination Against Women; the Convention Against Torture; and the Convention on the Rights of the Child. *See generally*, International Human Rights in Context: Law, Politics, and Morals 99–100, 118–22 (Henry J. Steiner & Philip Alston eds., 1996) (discussing how the atrocities committed during World War II helped create the above-mentioned treaties and international instruments).

19. *See* Meron, *supra* note 13, at 24. *See infra* text accompanying notes 142–43 for a discussion of the principle of humanity.

nations to enforce international humanitarian laws.[20] The Nazis, under orders from Hitler and his henchmen, systematically and ruthlessly violated the laws of war during the Warsaw occupation, the Warsaw Ghetto uprising, and the Warsaw rising. In the movie the unforgettable scene of Warsaw after the Germans bombed and razed this once-elegant city is a picture that tells more than a thousand words about the total destruction and inhumanity of war.

The book and the film also reveal and represent the power of art, the therapeutic and curative effect that music can have on a victim's life during war,and the beneficial role literature and film can play as self-help remedies in a system of *restorative* rather than *retributive* justice. We have all heard stories about the Nazis listening to and appreciating great classical music as they coldly and inhumanly exterminated the Jews. Nevertheless, I will try to show that art can arguably serve as a preventive measure to deter the commission of atrocities in the future by educating society about history and moral values.

This chapter poses several questions that seem particularly relevant in view of the current state of war in which our peace-loving society is engaged today. What is the role of the laws and customs of war if the warriors do not play by the rules? What is the role of art and music during and after the commission of atrocities? Can art prevent further atrocities, assuage victims of catastrophic events, inspire the collective conscience of perpetrators, and protect victims from the reality of pain caused by war and the violations of the international laws of armed combat? Can a book or a film that substantially recreates and authentically memorializes large-scale violations of the law act in the interests of justice? Can art provide a form of self-help equitable remedy such as a declaratory judgment that offers nonmonetary compensation and restorative justice to the victim, as well as moral education to society, with an aim toward preventing further atrocities? This challenging issue is of critical importance today as the twenty-first century finds itself once again caught up in wars, genocides, and inhumane acts.

This chapter discusses the following four issues: (1) the legitimacy of an interdisciplinary approach to the study of the laws and customs of war; (2) the failure of international humanitarian laws to deter the large-scale perpetration of inhumane acts committed during World War II as represented in the film and book *The Pianist;* and (3) the role of retributive justice after World War II and the Nuremberg trials, as compared to (4) the role of restorative justice that stories

20. This chapter discusses the failure to implement laws of war during the World War II. For a more recent assessment of the adequacy of the laws of war enacted after World War II, *see* Mark L. Sacharoff, *Problems and Paradoxes of the Laws of Warfare (The Aftermath of the Persian Gulf War: Strengthening the Laws of Warfare)* 6 TEMPLE INT'L & COMP. L.J. 71, 71–79 (Spring 1992). *See generally* Marco Sassoli & Laura M. Olson, *International Humanitarian Law,* 94 AM. J. INT'L L. 571 (2000) (discussing the 1949 Geneva Conventions, international criminal law, and the conflict in Bosnia and Herzegovina).

told in artistic representations of massive violations of the laws of war can provide. In this chapter I argue that storytelling through art is a form of self-help remedy provided to the victims of atrocities. Art that produces a historic and authentic record provides society at large with a form of moral education. Art, then, has the capacity to be a long-term preventive measure against the commission of genocide, war crimes, and human rights violations in the future.

II. THE LEGITIMACY OF AN INTERDISCIPLINARY METHOD

A. The Law and Literature Movement

This book, and in particular this chapter uses an interdisciplinary method (semiotics and the law, law and literature) that looks at law through the point of view of another discipline (the humanities) in the hopes of humanizing the law and uncovering some of its complex hidden meanings. The law and literature movement has been adopted by some of the most highly respected legal scholars and judges.[21] I adopt this approach here in order to examine the laws and customs of war during World War II, as represented in *The Pianist*, a book written by the famous Polish pianist, Wladyslaw Szpilman, who was a survivor of the Warsaw Ghetto. The story was illustrated in a film of the same name directed by Roman Polanski, who also survived the horrors of the Holocaust and the discrimination of the Cracow Ghetto. Both Szpilman and Polanski were eyewitnesses to the horrors of war and the failure to enforce international laws of war.

1. Three Analytical Approaches to Law and Literature: Law-in-Literature, Law-as-Literature, and the Impact of Law on Literature Law and literature is an interdisciplinary field of investigative research that has been classified into three different types of analytical approaches: the study of law-in-literature, the study of law-as-literature, and the study of the impact of law on literature and on the arts in general.[22] For example, some scholars in the law and literature movement examine classical literary works that embody and reflect the law with an aim toward humanizing the law (i.e., the law-in-literature approach). These law-in-literature scholars look closely at the great works of literature that feature lawyers as protagonists or trials as drama in order to decode the author's particular point

---

21. *See generally* Robin West, *The Literary Lawyer*, 27 PAC. L.J. 1188 (1995–96) (discussing the history and development of the law and literature movement). *See generally*, JAMES BOYD WHITE, ACTS OF HOPE: CREATING AUTHORITY IN LITERATURE, LAW AND POLITICS (1994) (discussing the creation of authority in literature, law, and politics). *See generally* JAMES BOYD WHITE, HERACLES' BOW: ESSAYS ON THE RHETORIC AND POETICS OF THE LAW (1985) (discussing the movement of literature and the laws).

22. *See generally* Gary Minda, *Law and Literature at Century's End*, 9 CARDOZO STUD. L. & LITERATURE 245 (Fall 1997) (discussing the three analytical approaches to law and literature).

of view of the legal system or to decipher the role that lawyers play in society.[23] This book is primarily in the tradition of the law-in-literature approach. However, several chapters of this book do address the impact of law on literature, and one chapter looks specifically at legal documents (i.e., the Berne Convention) through the point of view of hermeneutics and culture.

Other scholars in the law and literature movement choose to examine and interpret legal texts such as legislative enactments, cases, contracts, or judicial opinions as if they were literary texts (i.e., the law-as-literature approach). In other words, these law-as-literature scholars look at legal texts as if they were literary discourses capable of being analyzed and interpreted by the careful application of well-known literary theories of interpretation such as structuralism or deconstructionism to the language of legal documents.

Other scholars in the law-and-literature movement prefer to look at areas of the law that have an important impact on the arts, such as intellectual property law, copyright regulations (including the role of parody in copyright protection), censorship of fiction, and the constitutional protection of freedom of speech. These three different types of investigative research have one element in common: each of these analytical approaches uses an interdisciplinary method that enables the researcher to see issues in one field (the law) from a new and enriching perspective of a different field (literature).

This chapter adopts the law-in-literature approach by uncovering international legal principles and laws of war hidden in the interstices of the literary and cinematographic narratives of *The Pianist*.

2. The History of the Law and Literature Movement At first glance, the history of the law and literature movement may appear to be rather short and simple, as it began as recently as 1973. However, the law and literature movement is actually a complex field that has developed over the years into an intellectually diverse[24] hydra with its tentacles firmly planted in antiquity. Seeing the obvious interconnection between law and literature, classical poets, playwrights, novelists such as Homer, the Greek tragedians, Shakespeare, Moliere, Dostoevsky, Kafka, Melville, Camus, and many other literary giants have written expressively and extensively about the law, about trials, about natural law, and about the drama of revenge.[25] As many famous people in the arts were actually practicing lawyers or at least legally trained, it is no wonder that legal reasoning permeates their artistic works.[26] John Donne, Henry Fielding, Sir Walter Scott, Honore de

23. *See generally* RICHARD H. WEISBERG, FAILURE OF THE WORD: THE PROTAGONIST AS LAWYER IN MODERN FICTION (1984) (analyzing the lawyer's role in society).

24. *See* Minda, *supra* note 22, at 245.

25. POSNER, *supra* note 8, at 5.

26. *See* DANIEL KORNSTEIN, THE MUSIC OF THE LAWS 107–10 (1982), with forward by Hon. Robert H. Bork (discussing why legal interpretation is like musical interpretation). Writers also reflect legal reasoning. For example, many of the plays of Corneille are often

Balzac, James Fenimore Cooper, Gustave Flaubert, Leo Tolstoy, Franz Kafka, John Galsworthy, Wallace Stevens, Peter Tchaikovsky, Robert Schumann, Hoagy Carmichael, and Cole Porter are just a few of the many artists, musicians, and writers who were either practicing lawyers or had legal training.

The law and literature movement began as an interdisciplinary field of organized scholarship with the publication in 1973 of James Boyd White's book, *The Legal Imagination*,[27] which established the legitimacy of the law-in-literature approach. Unlike many legal positivists who conceive of the law and of legal language as a science rather than an art, White views the law as an *art* and the lawyer as an *artist*.[28] He sees the value of constructing a conception of the law and of the "good lawyer" as reflections of a humanistic and literary tradition.[29]

In contrast to White's optimistic view of the legal profession, Richard Weisberg's groundbreaking work in law-in-literature, *The Failure of the Word*,[30] presents the lawyer as a "pontificating" protagonist who "makes linguistic promises with neither the intent nor the effect of enhancing social life or strengthening community."[31] Weisberg's view of lawyers and the law is also expressed in his book *Vichy Laws and the Holocaust*,[32] which exposes the casuistic legal reasoning and justification that lawyers found for drafting patently discriminatory laws denying Jews the right to fundamental human rights during World War II.

In the late 1970s and 1980s, some scholars in the law and literature movement turned away from the law-in-literature approach that views literary texts as embodiments of the law and began instead to study legal texts as a unique genre of literature.[33] This phenomenon is known as the *law-as-literature* approach. These law-as-literature scholars believe that law can be translated, deconstructed, interpreted, and decoded in accordance with different interpretive theories

---

structured like a succession of arguments for the defense followed by arguments for the prosecution. Corneille, as with most French writers before the eighteenth century, had a typically classical education, which amounted to an education in the law and in legal reasoning. This legal education is reflected in Corneille's writing style. *See* Susan Tiefenbrun, *The Big Switch: A Study of (Corneille) Cinna's Reversals*, *in* SUSAN TIEFENBRUN, SIGNS OF THE HIDDEN: SEMIOTIC STUDIES (1980) (examining Corneille's tragedy *Cinna*). *See also* CHRISTIEN BIET, DROIT ET LITTERATURE SOUS L'ANCIEN REGIME: LE JEU DE LA VALEUR ET DE LA LOI (2002).

27. JAMES BOYD WHITE, THE LEGAL IMAGINATION: THE LEGAL IMAGINATION: STUDIES IN THE NATURE OF LEGAL THOUGHT AND EXPRESSION (1973).

28. West, *supra* note 21, at 1189.

29. *Id.*

30. WEISBERG, *supra* note 23.

31. West, *supra* note 21 at 1204.

32. RICHARD H. WEISBERG, VICHY LAWS AND THE HOLOCAUST (1996).

33. Minda, *supra* note 22, at 245.

borrowed from literature, such as structuralism,[34] deconstruction,[35] linguistics, semiotics,[36] stylistics,[37] and postmodernism. It is my contention, however, that all these approaches are subsets of semiotics.

The legitimacy of the law-as-literature approach has been the subject of much debate. Although some lawyers and judges remain committed to the recognition of irreconcilable differences between literature and the law, scholars adopting the law-as-literature approach focus instead on the similarities between law and literature. The law-as-literature scholars consider the fields of law and literature to be similar because they are both composed of languages, discourses, cultures, and interpretable narratives. These scholars examine the complex and mutually beneficial relationships between the two disciplines. Thus, law-as-literature involves the study of legal and literary texts as languages that reflect ethical, political, and cultural values as well as meanings.[38]

In defense of the law-as-literature approach, proponents claim that the more traditional approaches to the law (known as rights theory, legal process, neutral principles, and pragmatism) have resulted in subtle forms of discrimination against nontraditional cultures. Adoption of a more interdisciplinary approach to the analysis of the law, such as the law-as-literature method, may have the beneficial effect of humanizing the law by focusing lawyers' attention on cultural differences.[39] But others reject outright the study of law-as-literature and prefer to remain in the literature-in-law tradition, believing that law was never meant to be a literary discourse fraught with multiple meanings, indeterminacy, or infinite interpretations.[40] Those who reject the study of law-as-literature claim that

---

34. *See generally* JONATHAN CULLER, STRUCTURALIST POETICS: STRUCTURALISM, LINGUISTICS, AND THE STUDY OF LITERATURE (1975) (discussing structuralism in linguistics and literature); FREDERIC JAMESON, THE PRISON HOUSE OF LANGUAGE; A CRITICAL ACCOUNT OF STRUCTURALISM AND RUSSIAN FORMALISM (1972) (illustrating the application of structuralism).

35. *See generally* JACQUES DERRIDA, DE LA GRAMMATOLOGIE (1967) (showing that Jacques Derrida is the father of the Deconstructionist movement); JACQUES DERRIDA, LA DISSEMINATION (1972) (illustrating the technique of deconstruction); L'ECRITURE ET LA DIFFERENCE (1967) (providing another look at Derrida's early deconstruction work); GEOFFREY H. HARTMAN, SAVING THE TEXT: LITERATURE, DERRIDA, PHILOSOPHY (1981) (discussing Derrida's work); Thomas Keenan, *Deconstruction and the Possibility of Justice*, 11 CARDOZO L. REV. 1675 (1989–90) (providing an explanation of Derrida's role in the law and the use of deconstructionism in legal interpretation).

36. *See generally* JACKSON, *supra* note 4; *see generally* Tiefenbrun, *supra* note 2 (discussing the use of semiotics in legal analysis).

37. *See generally* STANLEY FISH, IS THERE A TEXT IN THIS CLASS? 68–97, 246–68 (1980) (discussing stylistics).

38. Minda, *supra* note 22, at 248.

39. *See id.* at 251.

40. *See generally* Michel Rosenfeld, *Deconstruction and Legal Interpretation: Conflict, Indeterminacy and the Temptations of the New Legal Formalism*, 11 CARDOZO L. REV. 1211 (1990) (showing Jacques Derrida was the original proponent of deconstructionism).

law must aim at clarity, persuasion through precision, and determinacy.[41] Richard Weisberg, who pioneered the law and literature movement, holds a more balanced view, arguing this movement is sufficiently broad to encompass all these different theoretical perspectives.[42]

As the studies of law-in-literature and law-as-literature developed in the 1970s and 1980s, many law schools began to offer courses called "Law and Literature"[43] or "Law and Film" in which students were asked to read literature and view films to discover the legal principles embedded in the narratives. In some of these courses, students might also be asked to examine hermeneutics and theories of literary interpretation as applied to the interpretation of legal documents. Many scholars in the critical legal studies movement[44] have embraced these diverse theories of literary interpretation, applied them to the law, and adopted an interdisciplinary approach to the study of the law.[45]

In 1979 during the heyday of the law and literature movement, the Law and Humanities Institute (LHI) was formed to support the law and literature movement, encourage interdisciplinary research and writing in this burgeoning field, hold literary and law salons, and organize national and international conferences devoted to the study of law and the humanities in general. The pioneers of the law and literature movement were and still remain on the Board of Governors of LHI, including Professor Richard Weisberg, Professor Stanley Fish, and Judge Richard Posner. The law and literature movement has grown since 1979, much attributable to the efforts of LHI and its expanding membership. LHI[46] has now become an international institution that holds conferences on the East and West Coasts of the United States, Europe, and Asia; it also fosters interdisciplinary

---

41. *See* POSNER, *supra* note 8, at 7. Posner states: "Law and literature have significant commonalities and intersections, but the differences are as important. Law is a system of social control as well as a body of texts, and its operation is illuminated by the social sciences and judged by ethical criteria. Literature is an art, and the best methods for interpreting and evaluating it are esthetic." *Id.*

42. Richard H. Weisberg, *Family Feud: A Response to Robert Weisberg on Law and Literature*, 1 YALE J.L. & HUMAN. 69, 76 (1988).

43. Minda, *supra* note 22, at 245.

44. *See generally* Mark Tushnet, *Critical Legal Studies and Constitutional Law: An Essay in Deconstruction*, 36 STAN. L. REV. 623 (1984) (discussing the critical legal studies movement); *see also* David M. Trubek, *Where the Action Is: Critical Legal Studies and Empiricism*, 36 STAN. L. REV. 575 (1984). *See generally* Mitchell Lasser et al., *Critical Legal Theory*, *in* LAW AND THE ARTS 115, 115–45 (Susan Tiefenbrun ed., 1999) (discussion of the role of CLS in the law among Duncan Kennedy, David Kennedy, Nathaniel Berman, Mitchell Lasser, Norman Silber, and Lawrence Kessler).

45. *See* Tiefenbrun, *supra* note 2, at 153–55 (discussing the critical legal studies movement and its use of literary theories for legal interpretation).

46. I was president of LHI from 1998–2005 and was a long-standing member of LHI's Board of Governors for decades.

research, focusing particular attention on human rights issues represented in the arts.

This chapter will look at the international laws and customs of war as represented in the literary and cinematographic narratives of Wladyslaw Szpilman and Roman Polanski in the tradition of law-in-literature and film. I will examine some of the causes of the failure of the enforcement of international humanitarian law to prevent serious war crimes, crimes against humanity, genocide, and human rights violations committed during World War II.

B. What is Representation?

Books and film can represent legal principles. Representation is a complex process located in a system of signs.[47] Semiotics, which is the science of signs, is offered as a fundamental course in many fields of study such as medicine, law, and literature. Signs are words or images that can send (*rep-re-sent*) clear or vague, direct or indirect messages to a receiver, who might be a listener, reader, or viewer. The clarity and understanding of the messages depend upon many variables, including the mode and effectiveness of the connection between the sender and the receiver and the type of communication medium chosen by the sender.

Representation is a *re-presentation* of reality, a step removed from the thing itself (*rep-res-ent* (*res* in Latin meaning "thing"); therefore, the representation of an event or an idea is always partially fictional and never totally factual.[48] This gap between truth and fiction is referred to in semiotic theory as the *referential fallacy*.[49] Testimony in court is a form of representation of reality, and the farther the witness deviates from recreating the actual thing itself, the less authentic is that witness's representation—and the less valuable is the testimony.

Representation is also arguably the reenactment of resentment (*rep-resent*), the expression of deep-seated and hidden emotions (*ressentiment* in French) that can surface after the bitter experience of a catastrophe. The book and film *The Pianist* are literary and cinematic representations of Szpilman's secret thoughts and emotions, which the author expresses in a coded language in the book and which the filmmaker expresses somewhat differently in the movie (despite attempts by Polanski to remain close to Szpilman's original depiction in the book). During the processes of reading the book and viewing the film, both the reader and the viewer are naturally induced to decode or interpret the

---

47. *See* Tiefenbrun, *supra* note 2, at 89–156 (discussing semiotics and a bibliography related to semiotics and the law); *see also* UMBERTO ECO, A THEORY OF SEMIOTICS 3–31 (1979) (offering an informed overview of the field of semiotics).

48. Witness testimony, which is a representation of reality from the witness's point of view, also lies somewhere between fact and fiction, and therefore, is not totally reliable.

49. *See* Eco, *supra* note 47, at 58 for a discussion of the referential fallacy and the role of the "representamen" in Pierce's semiotic theory.

representations of these hidden emotions to find meaning in the narratives. Out of fear, embarrassment, denial, or the desire to identify with the aggressor, the victim as writer has consciously and unconsciously hidden his forbidden thoughts and feelings between the lines of his memoirs, and the film director has similarly buried these horrifying thoughts and emotions behind the scenes, so to speak, of his movie. But the victim's frightening thoughts and emotions are not lost forever, only temporarily buried, waiting for the reader to excavate them from the deep structures of the narratives. A good reader and a good movie viewer can unravel these secrets by studying the language of the narratives, including the denotation and connotation of the words, and by taking into consideration the context and placement of the words and images on the page and on the screen.

The craftsman, writer, and filmmaker arrange their respective narratives carefully into segments known as chapters or scenes, like parts of a puzzle in which each piece plays an integral and structural role in delivering significant messages.[50] Understanding the relationships among these segments, the placement of the chapters in the whole book, or the arrangement of the scenes in the movie constitute a kind of structural analysis of the narrative that, if done systematically, can unearth hidden messages. Once decoded, these messages further reveal a system of paradoxical thought and emotion that plagues victims of torture and prolonged enslavement.

The paradox in Szpilman's life is expressed in his curiously antithetical mode of feeling both pain and pleasure during his long and symbolic ordeal in the Warsaw Ghetto. Szpilman experiences physical and psychological pain as he becomes more and more aware of the nihilism of destructive war. But he also experiences a kind of forbidden pleasure by living in the memory of his recent past when he was the great Polish concert pianist, basking in the glory of fame and personhood. His identity and personhood are systematically removed during his dehumanizing and humiliating life in occupied Poland especially in the Warsaw Ghetto. He is just one of many victims wearing a blue armband, like the nameless prisoners in Nazi concentration camps who wore tattooed numbers on their forearms to identify themselves. During his ordeal, Szpilman tries continuously and vicariously to relive the joys of his past life through the beauty of transcendent music.

Music is another medium of communication or form of representation that is expressive and nonverbal, and therefore more open to interpretation than written language; nevertheless, as with literature or law, the interpretation of music is not indeterminate, but limited by the confines of musical notation, historical context, culture and tradition. Music for Szpilman is a form of representation

50. *See* Tiefenbrun, *supra* note 2, at 125–29 (discussing structuralism and its application to the law and legal discourse).

that has the power to revive his weakened body and revitalize his spirit. Music keeps Szpilman alive.

C. The Narratives in the Book and the Film *The Pianist*

1. Szpilman Symbolizes All Oppressed People in Occupied Territories The central figure in the book and film is Wladyslaw Szpilman, who recounts his horrifying experiences in and out of the Warsaw Ghetto[51] in memoirs he wrote shortly after the war. The fact that Szpilman wrote these memoirs so soon after he experienced and witnessed these actual events increases the authenticity of his representation of reality. Szpilman published his memoirs under a different title in Poland in 1946, with these memoirs becoming a book subsequently called *The Pianist.*[52] Years later in 2003, Roman Polanski, also a Polish survivor, used a more visual medium of communication to retell Szpilman's story (but anew) in the film *The Pianist.*

Szpilman's experience is unique but also representative of a large population of victims of the Holocaust because Warsaw possessed the largest Jewish community in the world.[53] Therefore, Szpilman's story is that of one man and every man, *Jederman,* who suffered during the war and survived.

2. History is Recounted as Personal Testimony in Memoirs and in Film Events in the book and the film cover Szpilman's personal experiences and ultimate survival during 1939–1945 when Germany invaded Poland, occupied Warsaw, and created the infamous Warsaw Ghetto. During this period the Polish Jews established an underground resistance and engaged heroically but tragically in the Warsaw Ghetto uprising, followed by the equally heroic and tragic rising[54] in the city of Warsaw by the Polish underground resistance. Because Szpilman's representation of his own personal experiences is done with authenticity, veracity, and sincerity, his memoirs and book serve as a source of history.

---

51. Norman Davies, Rising '44: The Battle for Warsaw 97 (2004) (discussing similar experiences in the Warsaw Ghetto): "The Ghetto functioned from November 1939 to May 1943 . . . From 15 October 1941 the gates were permanently closed, inmates were subject to immediate execution if discovered outside, and the Ghetto gradually assumed the characteristics of a concentration camp. From January 1942, the Ghetto began to be emptied by regular, forced deportations to the death camps, principally to Treblinka. After an armed uprising in April and May 1943, it became a silent, smouldering (sic) graveyard inhabited only by a handful of SS guards and a body of prisoners detailed to tidy up the ruins. It was an unspoken warning of what could happen to the city as a whole." *Id.*

52. Wladyslaw Szpilman, The Pianist (Anthea Bell trans., 1999), originally published in Poland in 1946 under the title Death of a City.

53. Davies, *supra* note 51, at 75.

54. *See generally id,* (distinguishing between the term *uprising* and *rising* to differentiate the events of the Warsaw Ghetto resistance and the resistance by citizens of the whole city of Warsaw).

3. Differences between the Representation in the Book and in the Film In interviews[55] about the making of the film, Roman Polanski claims that he tried to be as faithful as possible to the original book. Nevertheless, every artist, writer, and filmmaker inevitably puts his own imprimatur on the work he produces. Therefore, Polanski uses poetic license to make some justifiable changes from the book, especially in the selection of the musical pieces actually played by Szpilman. For example, Polanski shows Szpilman playing for his life in front of a somewhat enlightened German officer who understands the principle of humanity, appreciates music, and ultimately saves Szpilman's life. Towards the end of the film, when Szpilman is thoroughly exhausted from starvation and the travails he has had to endure for years, he chooses unrealistically to play for this German officer the technically demanding Chopin Ballade in G Minor. He plays this piece flawlessly on a miraculously clean and perfectly tuned piano that suddenly appears in the midst of the rubble and chaos around him. Conversely in the book, Szpilman more realistically plays on "the glassy, tinkling sound of the untuned strings"[56] of a piano whose "action was swollen by the damp and resisted the pressure of the keys."[57] Szpilman tells us that he actually played the Chopin C-sharp Minor Posthumous Nocturne, which is much shorter and less technically challenging than the Ballade. However, both the Nocturne and Ballade are brooding and dark. Moreover, in the book Szpilman admits that in this very exceptional moment of survival, he played the Nocturne with difficulty after not touching the piano for two-and-a-half years and not having cut his nails for a long time.[58]

This alteration of the truth between Szpilman's and Polanski's representation of reality is an example of poetic license. Polanski changes the choice of music to better convey the role of hope in times of despair. Polanski understood intuitively that at this time in his life, Szpilman needed to believe that a miracle could actually happen to save him. Polanski's poetic fantasy corresponds with Szpilman's use of music throughout his ordeal. Music has the power to change Szpilman's reality into fantasy. Music enables him to escape or at least minimize the pain by remaining somewhat removed from the slaughter of the Poles and the absurdist nihilism surrounding him in his beloved Warsaw, reduced to ruins by the excesses of war.

---

55. The DVD version of the film, *The Pianist*, is followed by an interesting interview with Roman Polanski who explains how he made the film, including his intentions to remain as close to the original book as possible, and his credentials as a filmmaker of this particular subject because of his personal experience as a Holocaust survivor in Poland. DVD: The Pianist (Universal 2002).

56. Szpilman, *supra* note 52, at 178.

57. *Id.*

58. *Id.*

Polanski's film, which he produced more than fifty years after publication of the book, is a more visual representation of reality that the filmmaker achieves with artistry, authenticity, and immediacy. Like Szpilman who lived in the Warsaw Ghetto as a young adult, Polanski grew up as a Jew in the Cracow Ghetto. Like Szpilman, Polanski was separated from his parents when he was very young. Polanski found out secondhand that his mother had died in a Nazi concentration camp, and he wandered among supporters in Catholic homes for years seeking shelter and protection until the ghetto was ultimately destroyed.[59] Polanski reports being used by German soldiers as target practice. Thus, Polanski the filmmaker was quite familiar with the complex emotions of survivors and the particular customs of occupied Warsaw. In interviews, Polanski expressed a keen desire to remain very close to the depiction in Szpilman's book and to the reality of the Warsaw Ghetto, its uprising, and the destruction of Warsaw after its own rising during the Nazi occupation. The film is a work of art, and its visual depiction of historical events shall remain in the annals of cinematic history as one of the greats.

4. The Empowerment and Remedial Effects of Writing Memoirs and Making Films The Nazi occupiers of the Warsaw Ghetto systematically deprived Jews of their human rights, dignity, humanity, and basic necessities of survival in order to strip them of their personhood. It is no wonder, then, that Wladyslaw Szpilman chose to write his memoirs after his experience in the Warsaw Ghetto. Memoirs are a literary genre that significantly gives power to the writer-narrator whose voice is represented frequently on the pages of the text by the *I* of the first-person narration. The empowerment of the narrator by memoir writing is also arguably an attempt by the victim to identify with the aggressor who has assumed power over the victim throughout the ordeal. The writing of memoirs also has a cathartic and restorative effect on Szpilman in light of the years of dehumanization and self-effacement that this well-known Polish pianist was forced to endure in the Warsaw Ghetto under Nazi occupation.

Szpilman memorializes his thoughts, feelings, and recollections of past events dramatically, and with both authenticity and poignancy in the form of memoirs that serve an important purpose for the victim, for other victims in the same situation as the memorialist, for the perpetrators, and for society. The act of writing memoirs is an attempt to immortalize events of the past, to create a written record, and to provide a therapeutic remedy to the memorialist by a process of self-help. It is well-known that Holocaust survivors rarely want to or are even able to "speak" about their ordeal, but many did and do continue to write about the atrocities they suffered. There is a swelling body of literature of

---

59. Harvey Karen, Review of *The Pianist* (2002), http://www.all-reviews.com/videos-5/pianist.htm (last visited Sept. 16, 2005).

the Holocaust,[60] with authors such as Primo Levi and Elie Wiesel being just two of the many writers whose great works about the Holocaust come to mind. Thus, the act of writing memoirs not only valorizes the narrator but provides the victim with a catharsis, a therapeutic remedy, or a form of self-help. The memoirs provide care for the victim's deep and festering psychological wounds that continue to drain in the memories of the survivors of catastrophe and their families.[61]

But memoirs do more than assuage the pain of the victim: they help to establish a historic record, induce empathy for the victim from the readers, and raise the consciousness of society about the atrocities that ordinary people can perpetrate on other ordinary people during wartime,[62] especially if the laws of war are neither enforced nor obeyed. Memoirs and other similar literary works may have inspired the collective conscience of the perpetrators and their families to feel shame and guilt that lasted in Germany for many long years after the war. Germans were reportedly in a state of guilt or abject denial for years about the atrocities their people perpetrated on the Jews. Many visitors intent on seeing the German concentration camps in Dachau or Matthausen report that the local townspeople refuse to admit that a concentration camp was once actually located there or to give directions as to its location. Whether the beneficial effects of this guilt and shame inspired by books and films about the Holocaust can prevent future genocides is a question that must be asked, but cannot easily be answered.

---

60. *See generally* Eva Hoffman, After Such Knowledge (2004) (referring to stories about the Holocaust); *see generally* Geoffrey H. Hartman, Scars of the Spirit: The Struggle Against Inauthenticity (2002) (depicting other stories of the Holocaust) [hereinafter Scars of the Spirit]; *see generally* Geoffrey H. Hartman, The Longest Shadow: In the Aftermath of the Holocaust (1996) (discussing the role of artistic responses to the Holocaust and the links between representational techniques and ethical concerns); *see also* Thane Rosenbaum, The Golems of Gotham (2002) (discussing Jewish persecution during the Holocaust); *see also* Thane Rosenbaum, Second Hand Smoke (1999) (illustrating literature of the Holocaust).

61. *See generally* Hoffman, *supra* note 60 (showing that children of survivors, known as the Second Generation, have also written extensively about the effects of the Holocaust on the survivors of their family). *See generally* Bernhard Schlink, The Reader (1997) (giving a stunning portrayal of the guilt of a young German boy who, after the war, falls in love with an older woman who turns out to have been a Nazi concentration camp guard and executioner). Schlink's superb book has been made into a 2008 award-winning film.

62. *See generally* Daniel Goldhagen, Hitler's Willing Executioners: Ordinary Germans and the Holocaust (1996) (examining motivations of ordinary people in committing extraordinary horrors).

III. LAWS OF ARMED CONFLICT REPRESENTED IN *THE PIANIST*

A. Brief History of the Laws of War Before 1939

Long before the start of World War II, numerous attempts were made to codify the rules of appropriate military behavior during armed conflict. Laws of war putting limits on wartime conduct date back to the beginning of recorded history.[63] For example, in the sixth century B.C., Chinese warrior Sun Tzu suggested regulating the way wars are conducted.[64] The notion of war crimes appeared as early as 200 B.C. in the Hindu code of Manu.[65] The ancient Greeks fought many wars in which they observed rules of battle prohibiting summary execution of prisoners, attacks on noncombatants, pursuit of defeated opponents beyond a limited duration, and many other forms of warfare that are also condemned and codified today.[66]

Various efforts to codify laws of armed combat continued in the Middle Ages through the nineteenth century. In 1305, the Scottish national hero Sir William Wallace was tried for the wartime murder of civilians.[67] In 1625, Hugo Grotius wrote *On the Law of War and Peace*,[68] focusing on the humanitarian treatment of civilians. In the eighteenth and nineteenth centuries, scholars such as De Vattel in France created rules regulating the conduct of armed conflict.[69] The most important early codification of the customs and usages of war was the Lieber Code[70] issued by President Lincoln to the Union forces in the American Civil

---

63. For a time line covering the history of the laws of war, see Society of Professional Journalists, *supra* note 13.

64. *Id.*

65. *Id.*

66. Eric A. Posner, *A Theory of the Laws of War* (John M. Olin Law & Econ., Working Paper No. 160, 2002), http://www.law.uchicago.edu/Lawecon/WkngPprs_151-175/160.eap.laws-of-war.pdf.

67. Society of Professional Journalists, *supra* note 13.

68. James Brown Scott, *Introduction* to 2 HUGO GROTIUS, DE JURE BELLI AC PACIS LIBRI TREX IX, IX-X (Francis W. Kelsey trans., Clarendon Press 1925) (1625).

69. *See, e.g.*, EMERICH DE VATTEL, LE DROIT DES GENS [THE LAW OF NATIONS] (Luke White trans., 1792) (1758).

70. *See generally* WAR DEPARTMENT, GENERAL ORDERS NO. 100, INSTRUCTIONS FOR THE GOVERNMENT OF ARMIES OF THE UNITED STATES IN THE FIELD (1863) [hereinafter the Lieber Code] (discussing the Instructions for the Government of Armies of the United States in the Field and the President of the United States' desire to have these instructions published); Theodor Meron, *Francis Lieber Code and Principles of Humanity*, 36 COLUM. J. TRANSNAT'L L. 269 (discussing extracts of the Lieber Code). For extracts of the Lieber Code, *see* JORDAN J. PAUST ET AL., INTERNATIONAL CRIMINAL LAW DOCUMENTS SUPPLEMENT 94 (2000). *See also* Jordan J. Paust, *Dr. Francis Lieber and the Lieber Code*, 95 AM. SOC'Y INT'L L. PROC. 112, 112–14 (2001). Lieber was not only an eminent international law scholar but a learned practitioner of semiotics.

War in 1863. The first Geneva Convention (which was inspired by Henri Dunant, the founder of the Red Cross) was signed in 1864[71] to protect the sick and wounded in wartime. Ever since, the Red Cross has played an integral part in the drafting and enforcement of the Geneva Conventions.[72] The St. Petersburg Declaration Renouncing the Use, In Time of War, of Explosive Projectiles Under 400 Grammes Weight[73] was enacted in 1868.

The twentieth century was a banner year for the regulation of armed conflict. The Hague Peace Conferences of 1899 and 1907 were initiated by Russian Tsar Nicholas II to avoid a large outbreak of war by regulating the manner in which war could be fought. These two peace conferences resulted in the enactment of the Hague Convention of 1899[74] and the Hague Convention of 1907,[75] along with their implementing regulations. These treaties are commonly referred to as the *Hague Regulations*[76] that were an official effort at the beginning of the twentieth century to codify the rules of war. Thus, the First Peace Conference at The Hague occurred on July 29, 1899 and resulted in four Hague Rules, three Declarations, and one Final Act[77] concerning, among other issues, the use of asphyxiating

---

71. The Geneva Convention was revised in 1906, 1929, and 1949. *See, e.g.*, American Red Cross, *The American Red Cross: The Geneva Conventions, the International Committee of the Red Cross and the Rights of Prisoners of War*, http://www.redcross.org/museum/gc.html (last visited Oct. 14, 2005).

72. Society of Professional Journalists, *supra* note 13.

73. *See generally* UK MINISTRY OF DEFENCE, THE MANUAL OF THE LAWS OF ARMED CONFLICT (2004) (dealing with the means and methods of warfare). Principles of armed conflict are set out in the Preamble:

> That the progress of civilization should have the effect of alleviating as much as possible the calamities of war;
> That the only legitimate object which States should endeavour (sic) to accomplish during war is to weaken the military forces of the enemy;
> That for this purpose it is sufficient to disable the greatest possible number of men;
> That this object would be exceeded by the employment of arms which uselessly aggravate the sufferings of disabled men, or render their death inevitable;
> That the employment of such arms would, therefore, be contrary to the laws of humanity.

Id. at 8.

74. Convention with Respect to the Laws and Customs of War on Land, with annex of regulations 32 Stat. 1803, July 29, 1899, 1 Bevans 247 [hereinafter Hague Convention of 1899]. *See also* The Avalon Project–Laws of War: Laws and Customs of War on Land (Hague II); July 29, 1899, http://www.yale.edu/lawweb/avalon/lawofwar/hague02.htm.

75. Convention Respecting the Laws and Customs of War on Land, 36 Stat. 2277, Oct. 18, 1907, l Bevans 631 (hereinafter Hague Convention of 1907 or Hague Regulations).

76. *See id.*

77. Hague Convention of 1899, *supra* note 74, It consists of four Rules and three Declarations, and regulates the following issues of wartime conduct: Hague I: Pacific

gases and expanding bullets and a general prohibition on weapons that cause "unnecessary suffering."[78] The Second Peace Conference at The Hague occurred on October 18, 1907 where thirteen treaties and one declaration regulating the laws of war[79] were signed and entered into force on January 26, 1910.

During World War I (commonly referred to as "the Great War"), the laws of armed conflict were adequate with respect to the treatment of the sick, wounded, and prisoners of war, but training, supervision, and enforcement of the laws were inadequate. The laws of armed conflict were inadequate especially for the protection of civilians and as regards to the widespread use of aerial bombardment and gas.[80] Aerial bombardment and its problems had been forbidden for a period of five years after the First Hague Peace Conference in 1899, and the Hague Convention of 1907 also prohibited bombing of undefended places.[81] Nevertheless, in World War I bombarding the enemy on his own territory became the strategy of all States capable of undertaking it.[82] Even though belligerents in World War I claimed they were obeying the principles of the laws of war by restricting air bombardment to military objectives, the techniques available to them at that time prevented accurate bombing.[83] This resulted in the loss of

---

Settlement of International Disputes; Hague II: Laws and Customs of War on Land; Hague III: Adaptation to Maritime Warfare of Principles of Geneva Convention of 1864; and Hague IV: Prohibiting Launching of Projectiles and Explosives from Balloons; The Declarations include: Declaration I: On the Launching of Projectiles and Explosives from Balloons; Declaration II: On the Use of Projectiles the Object of Which is the Diffusion of Asphyxiating or Deleterious Gases; Declaration III: On the Use of Bullets Which Expand or Flatten Easily in the Human Body.The Final Act of the International Peace Conference was signed on July 29, 1899. *Id.*

78. Posner, *supra* note 66, at 2.

79. Hague Convention of 1907, *supra* note 75. The Hague Convention of 1907 regulates the following conduct during war: Hague I: The Pacific Settlement of International Disputes; Hague II: The Limitation of Employment of Force for Recovery of Contract Debts; Hague III: The Opening of Hostilities; Hague IV: The Laws and Customs of War on Land; Hague V: The Rights and Duties of Neutral Powers and Persons in Case of War on Land; Hague VI: The Status of Enemy Merchant Ships at the Outbreak of Hostilities; Hague VII: The Conversion of Merchant Ships into War-Ships; Hague VIII: The Laying of Automatic Submarine Contact Mines: Hague IX: Bombardment by Naval Forces in Time of War; Hague X: Adaptation to Maritime War of the Principles of the Geneva Convention; Hague Convention XI: Certain Restrictions with Regard to the Exercise of the Right of Capture in Naval War; Hague XII: The Creation of an International Prize Court (never ratified); and Hague Convention XIII: The Rights and Duties of Neutral Powers in Naval War. *See generally 1899–1954: The Hague Convention*, http://www.lib.byu.edu/~rdh/wwi/hague.html (last visited Sept. 26, 2005) (discussing the above-mentioned policies).

80. The UK Manual of the Law of Armed Conflict, *supra* note 73, at 10.

81. Hague Convention of 1899, *supra* note 74, art 25.

82. *See* UK Manual of the Law of Armed Conflict, *supra* note 73, at 10 .

83. *Id.*

civilian life and damage to civilian objects that were disproportionate to the military advantage gained[84] and a serious violation of the principles of military necessity, humanity, distinction and proportionality.[85]

Accordingly, many treaties were enacted after World War I to provide more protection to the sick and wounded prisoners of war, to regulate the use of gas, and to prohibit slave labor. The Treaty of Versailles,[86] which was a treaty of peace between the Allied and associated powers and Germany, was signed in 1919. The draft of the Hague Rules of Air Warfare,[87] which reflect general principles and customary rules regarding aerial bombardment, was published in December 1922–February 1923 but never adopted by States.[88] In 1925, the Geneva Gas Protocol[89] was signed prohibiting the use of poison gas and the practice of bacteriological warfare.[90] The Slavery Convention[91] was adopted in 1926. In 1929, two more Geneva Conventions were enacted to regulate the treatment of the sick and wounded and prisoners of war:[92] (1) the Geneva Convention for the Amelioration of the Condition of the Wounded and Sick in the Armies in the Field, and (2) the Geneva Convention Relative to the Treatment of Prisoners of War.

Because of the extensive destruction of artistic historic monuments during World War I, the Treaty on the Protection of Artistic and Scientific Institutions

---

84. *Id.*

85. *See infra* text accompanying footnotes 137–48 for a discussion of the principles of military necessity, humanity, distinction, and proportionality.

86. Treaty of Peace with Germany, June 28, 1919, 2 Bevans 43 (better known as "Treaty of Versailles"). *See also* The Avalon Project: The Versailles Treaty June 28, 1919, http://www.yale.edu/lawweb/avalon/imt/parti.htm.

87. First British Delegate to the International Commission, General Report of the Commission of Jurists to Consider and Report Upon the Revision of the Rules of Warfare, 1924, Cmd. 2201 (draft coverage of the Hague Rules on Air Warfare, Dec. 1922–Feb1923) [hereinafter Hague Rules of Air Warfare]. *See also* International Committee of the Red Cross, International Humanitarian Law—Hague Rules 1923, http://www.icrc.org/ihl.nsf/FULL/275?Open Document.

88. UK Manual of the Law of Armed Conflict, *supra* note 73, at 10.

89. Protocol for the Prohibition of the Use in War of Asphyxiating, Poisonous or Other Gases, and of Bacteriological Methods of Warfare. June 17, 1925, 26 U.S.T.571, 94 L.N. T.S. 65.

90. Society of Professional Journalists, *supra* note 13, at 1.

91. Slavery, Servitude, Forced Labour and Similar Institutions and Practices Convention of 1926 (Slavery Convention of 1926), *adopted* Sept. 25, 1926, 60 L.N. T.S. 253.

92. *See* Geneva Convention Relative to the Treatment of Prisoners of War, July 27, 1929, 6 U.S. T. 3316, 75 U.N. T.S. 135; Geneva Convention for the Amelioration of the Condition of the Wounded and Sick in Armies in the Field, July 27, 1929, 6 U.S. T. 3114, 75 U.N.T.S. 31 [hereinafter the Geneva Convention of 1929]. *See also* Geoffrey Best, Humanity in Warfare (1980).

and Historic Monuments (Roerich Pact)[93] was enacted on April 15, 1935. Rules against perfidy were also recognized before 1939 and reflect "chivalric values" that date back to medieval times.[94] These were some of the treaties, rules of law, and values that existed before World War II, and which, if implemented, could have prevented the atrocities that took place between 1939 and 1945. World War II proved once again that these laws of war as applied failed to protect combatants, noncombatants, and property outside military targets. Thus, after World War II, the Nuremberg Charter,[95] the Genocide Convention,[96] four 1949 Geneva Conventions[97] and two 1977 Protocols,[98] human rights laws that apply during war, the Charter of the International Military Tribunal for the Far East, and other laws were enacted to include most of the common protections and prohibitions during wartime conduct we know of today.

B. Causes of the Failure of International Laws of War in World War II

This very brief survey demonstrates that even though laws and rules of war reflecting common values were encoded long before 1939 in treaties, in customary

93. Treaty on the Protection of Artistic and Scientific Institutions and Historic Monuments (Roerich Pact), *done* April 15, 1935, 167 L.N.T.S. 289.

94. *See generally* Theodor Meron, *The Humanization of Humanitarian Law*, 94 AM. J. INT'L L. 239 (2000) (illustrating the evolution of humanitarian law).

95. Charter of the International Military Tribunal, Annexed to the London Agreement of Aug. 8, 1945, 58 Stat. 1544, 82 U.N.T.S. 279 [hereinafter the Nuremberg Charter].

96. Convention on the Prevention and Punishment of the Crime of Genocide, Dec. 9, 1948, 78 U.N.T.S. 277 *reprinted in* PAUST ET AL., INTERNATIONAL CRIMINAL LAW: DOCUMENTS SUPPLEMENT, *supra* note 70, at 263 (2000) [hereinafter Genocide Convention].

97. Convention for the Amelioration of the Condition of the Wounded and the Sick in Armed Forces in the Field, *adopted* Aug. 12, 1949, 6 U.S.T. 3114, 75 U.N.T.S. 31; *see also* Convention for the Amelioration of the Condition of Wounded, Sick and Shipwrecked Members of Armed Forces at Sea, *adopted* Aug.12, 1949, 6 U.S.T. 3217, 75 U.N.T.S. 135; Convention Relative to the Treatment of Prisoners of War, *adopted* July 27, 1949, 6 U.S.T. 3316, 75 U.N.T.S. 135; and Convention (IV) Relative to the Protection of Civilian Persons in Time of War, *adopted* Aug.12, 1949, 6 U.S. T. 3516, 75 U.N.T.S. 287 [hereinafter the Geneva Conventions of 1949].

98. Protocol (I) Additional to the Geneva Conventions of August 12, 1949, and Relating to the Protection of Victims of International Armed Conflicts, June 8, 1977, *reprinted in* PAUST ET AL., *supra* note 70, at 124 [hereinafter Protocol I];. Protocol (II) Additional to the Geneva Conventions of 12 August 1949, and Relating to the Protection of Victims of Non-international Armed Conflicts, June 8, 1977, *reprinted in* PAUST ET AL., *supra* note 70, at 135 [hereinafter Protocol II].

laws,[99] and in other international instruments,[100] the Third Reich, Hitler and his officers, and others widely disregarded these norms and violated many (if not all) of the existing laws of war during World War II.[101] Some attribute the cause of this conduct on the inadequacies of the existing laws of war[102] while others claim the technology of the period was insufficient to protect civilians, especially with regard to aerial bombardment.[103] Furthermore, not all belligerents in World War II were parties to the Hague Convention of 1907 and its Regulations,[104] nor were all of them parties to the existing Geneva Conventions of 1864 and 1929

---

99. H. Victor Conde, A Handbook of International Human Rights Terminology 180 (2d ed. 2004). Discussing the applicability of crimes against peace, war crimes, and crimes against humanity, as set forth in the Nuremberg Charter, Conde writes: "These criminal norms . . . were largely based on the Hague Conventions of 1899/1907 as customary international law. Later the United Nations reaffirmed these rules as being declaratory of customary international law." *Id. See* UK Manual of the Law of Armed Conflict, *supra* note 73, at 5, further explaining customary laws:

> Customary international law consists of the rules which, as a result of state practice over a period of time, have become accepted as legally binding. A rule of customary law is created by widespread state practice coupled with what is known as *opinio juris,* namely, a belief on the part of the state [and other actors] concerned that international law obliges it, or gives it a right, to act in a particular way.

Id. See also Jordan J. Paust, International Law as Law of the United States, 3–16 (2nd ed. 2003) for an in-depth discussion of "customary international law." *Opinio juris* involves expectations that something is legally appropriate or required. *See* Hague Conventions of 1907, *supra* note 75, at n. 106.

100. *See* United Nations, Historical Review of Developments Relating to Aggression 29 (2003).

101. Posner, *supra* note 66, at 2. *See generally* Jordan J. Paust, *There is No Need to Revise the Laws of War in Light of September llth,* Am. Soc'y Int'l L. Task Force on Terrorism, Nov. 2002, http://www.asil.org/taskforce/paust.pdf, for an explanation of the Laws of War in light of recent world events.

102. UK Manual of the Law of Armed Conflict, *supra* note 73, at 12.

103. *See id.* at 10.

104. *See* Meron, Hague Academy, *supra* note 13, at 34: "The Fourth Hague Conventions' *si omnes clause* threatened the integrity of Nuremberg prosecutions. In the *Trial of German Major War Criminals* (Nuremberg 1946), the defence raised the argument that the [Hague] Convention and its Regulations did not apply because several of the belligerents were not parties to it." *Id.* The Nuremberg Tribunal held that "by 1939 these rules laid down in the [Hague] Convention were recognized by all civilized nations, and were regarded as being declaratory of the laws and customs of war." *Id.*, n. 28, citing *Trial of German Major War Criminals,* Cmd. 6924, Misc. No. 12, at 65 (1946). In other words, the Nuremberg Tribunal ruled that because the rights, duties, and protections reflected in the Hague Convention No. IV were universally applicable customary international law, any limitations in the treaty (such as the general participation clause that provided the treaty as such only applied among signatories and their nationals) became irrelevant. *Id.*

that dealt with the treatment of the sick and wounded and prisoners of war.[105] The Hague Regulations were arguably insufficient to guide the conduct of authorities in control of vast areas of occupied territory, and they were systematically violated during World War II.[106] Moreover, the Hague Regulations were frequently ignored with excessively harsh measures being adopted by the occupying powers to counter activities of partisans.[107] Treatment accorded to prisoners of war during World War II was far below acceptable international standards.[108] Hitler's notion of a total war resulted in civilians being heavily involved in war-supporting industries, area bombing methods, siege warfare, long-range rockets, and atomic weapons that resulted in extremely heavy civilian casualties.[109] Furthermore, between 1930 and 1945 there were few treaty provisions to protect civilians subjected to deportation and extermination as part of a concerted policy of genocide.[110] In World War II, extensive bombing offensives resulted in the destruction of many civilian areas because there was no written code of law specifically governing air warfare that was binding on the belligerents during this period.[111] Moreover, customary prohibitions broke down as violations by different sides intensified and States engaged in reprisals (which are now impermissible). Arguably, air operations directed against ground targets were subject to the same general principles of customary international law and certain treaty obligations that bound armed forces on land.[112]

In 1949, after great damage and destruction had been perpetrated in the face of existing law, the hope was that the Nuremberg Charter,[113] the Genocide

---

105. *See* Geneva Convention of 1929, *supra* note 92, for a discussion of the Geneva Conventions of 1929. The term *Geneva Conventions,* as we know it, today refers to four conventions of 1949; *see supra* note 100.

106. UK Manual of the Law of Armed Conflict, *supra* note 73, at 12. *See* Hague Convention No. IV, Annex, arts 42–56 (exemplifying the regulation of occupied territory), *reprinted in* U.S. Navy Department, Hague and Geneva Conventions 64–65 (1911). These articles are not extensive, but they were violated during World War II.

107. UK Manual of the Law of Armed Conflict, *supra* note 73, at 12.

108. *See, e.g., id.* at 12, n. 35 (citing The Nuremberg Judgment: XXII International Military Tribunal 451–53 (1947).

109. UK Manual of the Law of Armed Conflict, *supra* note 73, at 12 (2004). *See* Hague Convention No. IV, Annex, arts. 46–47, 50 (exemplifying treaty provisions protecting civilians), *reprinted in* U.S. Navy Department, Hague and Geneva Conventions, 64–65 (1911).

110. UK Manual of the Law of Armed Conflict, *supra* note 73, at 12.

111. The Draft Hague Rules of Aerial Warfare (1923) were never adopted by States. *See* Hague Rules of Air Warfare, *supra* note 87.

112. UK Manual of the Law of Armed Conflict, *supra* note 73, at 12. The Nuremberg Charter, *supra* note 98, declared indiscriminate bombardment to be a crime cognizable by the tribunal.

113. The Nuremberg Charter, *supra* note 95.

Convention of 1948,[114] the four Geneva Conventions of 1949,[115] the two 1977 Protocols,[116] and the establishment of the United Nations would provide the protections, prohibitions, and enforcement that were lacking in the laws as implemented during World War II.

C. Illustrations of the Inadequate Implementation of Laws of War in the Book and the Film

The impact of the inadequate implementation of existing laws of armed conflict during World War II is vividly illustrated in the film *The Pianist,* especially during the brutal and disproportionate siege on Warsaw by the German army. Laws prohibiting genocide were not yet written in 1939–45,[117] and existing laws of armed conflict were generally not enforced by the Third Reich, Hitler, or his German officers.

In a briefing to his generals at Obersalzburg on the event of the invasion of Poland, Hitler revealed his intention to commit genocide on the Poles and Jews:

> I have sent my Death's Head units to the East with the order to kill without mercy men, women and children of the Polish race or language. Only in such a way will we win the *Lebensraum* that we need. Who, after all, speaks today of the annihilation of the Armenians?[118] (emphasis added)

This quote by Hitler reveals two important points: first, he intended to wipe out the Poles, whom he despised and classified in the Nazi handbooks as *Untermenschen,* or "subhumans" simply because the Polish people were not a pure race but rather a mixture of Slavs and Jews.[119] Hitler's quote also reveals that very few people had ever heard of the Armenian genocide, which, had it been disseminated widely as information to the public through books and films, perhaps could have prevented the Holocaust. As Hitler launched a total war violating every existing custom, rule, and law of armed conflict, the victims did not realize that the arguable inadequacy of the laws of war and the general failure to enforce them would result in their destruction.

Viewers of the *The Pianist* can witness the impact of inadequate legal protection of civilians as hundreds of thousands of Jewish people are herded like animals into the Warsaw Ghetto, made to dance like clowns, walk in the gutter, and suffer public humiliation and starvation before they are deported to Treblinka

---

114. Genocide Convention, *supra* note 96.

115. The Geneva Conventions of 1949, *supra* note 97.

116. Protocol I, *supra* note 98; Protocol II, *supra* note 98.

117. Genocide Convention, *supra* note 96. *See generally* WILLIAM A. SCHABAS, INTERNATIONAL LAW: THE CRIME OF CRIMES (2000) (discussing the law regarding genocide prior to World War II); ENCYCLOPEDIA OF GENOCIDE AND CRIMES AGAINST HUMANITY 483 (Diana L. Shelton ed., 2005) ("The defining feature of the crime of genocide is the deliberate destruction of a group").

118. DAVIES, *supra* note 51, at 84.

119. *Id.* at 83.

where they are mistreated and eventually exterminated in gas chambers. In this cinematic depiction of war, viewers see no justice, no honor, and no humanity, even though according to the existing laws of war (and especially the Lieber Code of 1863)[120] "martial law" must be "strictly guided by the principles of justice, honor, and humanity."[121] The Lieber Code states clearly that "men who take up arms against one another in public war do not cease on this account to be moral beings, responsible to one another and to God."[122]

1. Illustration of War Crimes Readers and viewers of *The Pianist* act as witnesses to the flagrant violations of the laws of war represented in the tragic siege on Warsaw. They see the unprecedented scale of deportation of Jews and Poles in cattle cars, mass murders, sadistic treatment of civilians, long hours of slave labor, and systematic persecution of the Jews in the Warsaw Ghetto. These cinematic representations illustrate the commission of war crimes that are clearly delineated and defined in the Nuremberg Charter:[123]

> . . . violations of the laws of customs of war. Such violations shall include, but not be limited to, murder, ill-treatment or deportation to slave labor or for any other purpose of civilian population of or in occupied territory, murder or ill-treatment of prisoners of war or persons on the seas, killing of hostages, plunder of public or private property, wanton destruction of cities, towns or villages, or devastation not justified by military necessity.[124]

2. Illustration of Crimes against Humanity *The Pianist* illustrates the widespread commission of crimes against humanity[125] as defined in the Nuremberg Charter:

> . . . murder, extermination, enslavement, deportation and other inhumane acts committed against civilian populations, before or during the war; or

---

120. *See generally* the Lieber Code, *supra* note 70 (referring to the existing policies set forth by the Instructions for the Government of Armies of the United States in the Field).

121. THEODOR MERON, BLOODY CONSTRAINT: WAR AND CHIVALRY IN SHAKESPEARE 13 (1998) (quoting the Lieber Code); *see also* THEODOR MERON, HENRY'S WARS AND SHAKESPEARE'S LAWS: PERSPECTIVES ON THE LAW OF WAR IN THE LATER MIDDLE AGES 112 (1993) (discussing the Lieber Code and martial law). Meron's books cited in this note are among the best examples of the study of international law through literature.

122. The Lieber Code, *supra* note 70, art. 15, at 4.

123. *See* the Nuremberg Charter, *see supra* note 95, art. 6.

124. *Id.* art. 6(b). *See infra* text accompanying note 142 for a discussion of military necessity.

125. Crimes against humanity are listed in the Nuremberg Charter. *See* the Nuremberg Charter, *supra* note 95, art 6(c); *see id.* art. 6 (a)–(c), for the listing of three categories of crimes applicable to the defendants at the Nuremberg Trials ("crimes against the peace," "crimes against humanity," and "war crimes"). *See also* CONDE, *supra* note 99, at 53 (discussing crimes against humanity, which used to require a nexus with an armed conflict for applicability). Note that crimes against humanity in some Charters do not require a link with an armed conflict. *See, e.g.*, the International Military Tribunal at Nuremberg, which specifies that the crimes must be committed either "before or during the war." *Id.*

persecutions on political, racial or religious grounds in execution of or in connection with any crime within the jurisdiction of the Tribunal, whether or not in violation of the domestic law of the country where perpetrated.[126]

Crimes against humanity or inhumane acts committed in the context of a widespread or systematic attack against civilian populations are vividly demonstrated in the film as we see women shot in the back for no reason while walking in the street, Jews reduced to speechlessness when they are told by other Jews about thousands of people being "exterminated" in Treblinka, and Jews forced to do long hours of backbreaking manual labor in slave-like conditions where a small infraction of a person's unpaid forced labor would result in excessive punishment. Szpilman is beaten viciously until unconsciousness by a sadistic German guard when Szpilman looks up at the sky for hope and then accidentally drops some heavy bricks that he is forced to carry mindlessly on his back.

In the absence of a law against genocide, crimes against humanity were the claims brought against the German officers at the Nuremberg trials.

3. Illustration of Human Rights Violations Violations of human rights laws committed by the occupying Nazi power against the Polish people and especially the Jews are represented dramatically in the film. Human rights laws were codified after World War II in the U.N. Charter (1945),[127] the Universal Declaration of Human Rights (1948),[128] the Convention on the Elimination of All Forms of Racial Discrimination (1965),[129] the International Covenant on Civil and Political Rights (1966),[130] the International Covenant on Economic, Social and Cultural Rights (1966),[131] the Convention on the Elimination of Discrimination Against Women (1979),[132] the Convention Against Torture

126. The Nuremberg Charter, *supra* note 95, art. 6(c).

127. Charter of the United Nations, June 26, 1945, 59 Stat. 1031, 1976 Y.B. U.N. 1043, *reprinted in* Paust et al., *supra* note 70, at 5.

128. Universal Declaration of Human Rights, G/A/ Res/ 217A. at 71. U.N. GAOR, 3d Sess. 1st plen. mtg., U.N. Doc. A/810 (Dec. 12, 1948) *reprinted in* Paust et al., *supra* note 70, at 29.

129. International Convention on the Elimination of All Forms of Racial Discrimination, *opened for signature* Mar. 7, 1966, 660 U.N.T.S. 195, *reprinted in* Paust et al., *supra* note 70, at 267.

130. International Covenant on Civil and Political Rights, Dec. 9, 1966, 999 U.N. T.S. 171, *reprinted in* Paust et al., *supra* note 70, at 43; Optional Protocol to the International Covenant on Civil and Political Rights, *adopted* Dec. 16, 1966, 999 U.N. T.S. 17.

131. International Covenant on Economic, Social and Cultural Rights, *adopted* Dec. 16, 1966, 993 U.N.T.S. 3.

132. Convention on the Elimination of All Forms of Discrimination Against Women, G.A. Res. 34/180, at 193, U.N. GAOR, 34th Sess., Supp. No. 46, U.N. Doc. A/34/830 (Dec. 18, 1979).

(1984),[133] and the Convention on the Rights of the Child (1989),[134] among others.

In scene after scene of *The Pianist*, like stanzas of an epic poem, viewers observe collective executions and denial to the Jews of their fundamental rights to life, liberty, and fair trial along with their freedom from torture, freedom to enjoy cultural activities, freedom to earn a living, and freedom to practice and manifest their religion. In this movie, the cinematic technique of piling one horrific short scene on top of another enhances the emotional impact and captures the enormity of the human rights violations committed by the occupying Nazi power. With varying degrees of authenticity[135] viewers of the film witness six hundred thousand Jews being persecuted and segregated into a ghetto where they are beaten, defamed, humiliated, starved, and subjected to patently discriminatory laws[136] that denied them the right to work, the right to walk on the street as other citizens, and the right to protection under the law. These racist laws deprived Jews of the right to earn and save money and required them

---

133. Convention Against Torture and Other Cruel, Inhuman and Degrading Treatment, G.A. Res. 39/46, at 197 U.N. GAOR, 30th Sess., Supp. No. 51, U.N. Doc. A/39/708 (Dec. 10, 1984).

134. Convention on the Rights of the Child, G.A. Res. 44/25, at 166, U.N. GAOR 44th Sess., Supp. No. 49, U.N. Doc. A/44/736.

135. The question of the authenticity of representations of the Holocaust and other atrocities is a much-debated subject. Some famous writers of the Holocaust, such as Thane Rosenbaum, believe that film cannot and should not attempt to recreate the reality of the Holocaust because this reenactment cannot be historically accurate. *See* Thane Rosenbaum, *When the Truth is Too Traumatic: From "The Diary of Anne Frank" to "Schindler's List" to "Amistad" and"Anastasia,"' American Dramatizations Put a Feel-Good Spin on Barbarity*, NEWSDAY, Jan. 4, 1998, at D.16, http://pqasb.pqarchiver.com/newsday/search.html.; *see generally* SCARS OF THE SPIRIT, *supra* note 60 (discussing the difficulty and necessity of the search for authenticity of Holocaust stories); Hartman discusses the role of art in the representation of the Holocaust, recognizing that "art. . .is under heavy pressure when it comes to Holocaust representation, a pressure amounting almost to an interdiction . . ." Hartman, *supra* note 60, at 8; Claude Lanzmann, the famous filmmaker of the now classical movie, *Shoah*, "believe[s] that there are some things that cannot and should not be represented." *Id.* at 84.

While I appreciate deeply the uniqueness of the Holocaust, I disagree with the view that limits the role that art and films should play in representing the Holocaust. Preferring silence to artistic representation of the Holocaust is not a viable choice. The need to validate the historic event and to memorialize it outweighs the elements of inauthenticity lurking in all forms of representation. To reject films of the Holocaust is to reject the power of art itself. Nevertheless, it is important to recognize that art has the power to disseminate information widely and to enable the information to enter the popular culture, which can have the negative effect of trivializing the very subject of the representation art seeks to memorialize.

136. *See generally* Weisberg, *supra* note 32 (analyzing the discriminatory laws passed in Vichy, France and elsewhere under the supervision of lawyers who justified these laws by pure casuistry).

to wear a blue star of David visibly on their arm to distinguish them from the Aryans or Polish non-Jews. This blue star enabled the occupying power to identify the Jews as a group more easily. The Jews were then violated, dehumanized, and killed in a concerted plan to exterminate the entire Jewish population.

4. Illustration of Basic Principles of Military Necessity, Humanity, Distinction, and Proportionality The book and the film also provide vivid examples of the systematic violation of basic principles of the laws of armed conflict,[137] including military necessity,[138] humanity,[139] distinction,[140] and proportionality.[141]

---

137. *See generally* UK Ministry of Defence, *supra* note 73, at 21–27 (discussing the basic principles of armed conflict).

138. *See id.* at 21 ("Military necessity permits a state engaged in an armed conflict to use only that degree and kind of force, not otherwise prohibited by the law of armed conflict, that is required in order to achieve the legitimate purpose of the conflict, namely the complete or partial submission of the enemy at the earliest possible moment with the minimum expenditure of life and resources.").

> Military necessity was defined as long ago as 1863 in the Lieber Code as "those measures which are indispensable for securing the ends of the war, and which are lawful according to the modern law and usages of war."

Id. at 22, (quoting the Lieber Code, *supra* note 70, art. 14, at 3–4). The general principle of military necessity is firmly rooted in the law of armed conflict. *See* Hague Convention of 1907, *supra* note 75, art. 22 and Protocol I, *supra* note 101, art. 35 (1).

139. *See* UK Manual of the Law of Armed Conflict, *supra* note 73, at 23 ("Humanity forbids the infliction of suffering, injury, or destruction not actually necessary for the accomplishment of legitimate military purposes . . . [T]he principle of humanity confirms the basic immunity of civilian populations and civilian objects from attack because civilians and civilian objects make no contribution to military action.").

"The principle of humanity can be found in the Martens Clause in the Preamble to Hague Convention IV (1907). . . : '[I]n cases not included in the Regulations . . . the inhabitants and the belligerents remain under the protection and the rule of the principles of the law of nations, as they result from the usages established among civilized peoples, from the laws of humanity, and the dictates of the public conscience'" *Id.* at 23–24 & n.9. A more recent version of the Martens clause can be found in Protocol I, *see supra* note 98, art. 1(2) and Protocol II, *supra* note 98, Preamble. *See also* Meron, *supra* note 13, at 41–47 (discussing the principle of humanity and the dictates of public conscience in the Martens Clause and its significance today).

140. *See* UK Manual of the Law of Armed Conflict, *supra* note 73, at 24. "The principle of distinction, sometimes referred to as the principle of discrimination or identification, separates combatants from non-combatants and legitimate military targets from civilian objects." Protocol I, *supra* note 98, arts. 48 and 49(3). The principle of discrimination is inherent in customary law. *See* Manual of the Law of Armed Conflict, *supra* note 73, at 24 ("Since military operations are to be conducted only against the enemy's armed forces and military objectives, there must be a clear distinction between the armed forces and civilians, or between combatants and non-combatants, and between objects that might legitimately be attacked and those that are protected from attack").

141. *See id.* at 25 ("The principle of proportionality requires that the losses resulting from a military action should not be excessive in relation to the expected military advantage.")

a. The Principle of Military Necessity. Military necessity requires the State engaged in war to use only enough force to achieve the legitimate aims of the war; it is not an excuse for violations of other laws of war prohibitions. Germany through Hitler and his officers violated the principle of the laws of armed conflict when the Nazis went beyond military necessity[142] by burning up and totally destroying Warsaw. In the film, the scene of Warsaw reduced to flames by the Nazis who left the once-glorious city in ruins is an image that Roman Polanski captures by filming a real city in East Berlin that was recently totally destroyed with the intention of rebuilding it. Polanski communicates the unforgettable image of the power of war to cause unnecessary massive destruction of a once-beautiful city. The horrific effect of Germany's failure to obey the principle of military necessity is memorialized in the film and communicated persuasively to vast numbers of people through the ages in an attempt to prevent such a disaster in the future.

b. The Principle of Humanity. The principle of humanity prohibits the infliction of suffering, injury, or destruction that is not actually necessary for the accomplishment of a legitimate military purpose; it also immunizes the civilian population and civilian objects from attack.[143] In the film, viewers can observe countless examples of the flagrant violation of the principle of humanity when SS guards inflict excessive injury and suffering upon civilians, who are viciously beaten to death and executed collectively without trial, for no reason (or perhaps

---

"The principle of proportionality is a link between the principles of military necessity and humanity, and it is most evident in connection with the reduction of incidental damage caused by military operations." *Id.* The principle of proportionality is set forth for the first time in a treaty in Protocol I, *see supra* note 98, art 51(5)(b): "[A]n attack which may be expected to cause incidental loss of civilian life, injury to civilians, damage to civilian objects, or a combination thereof, which would be excessive in relation to the concrete and direct military advantage anticipated." UK MANUAL OF THE LAW OF ARMED CONFLICT, *supra* note 73, at 25. *Cf.* PAUST ET AL., *supra* note 70, at 837. *See generally* Paust, *Weapons Regulation, Military Necessity and Legal Standards: Are Contemporary Department of Defense "Practices" Inconsistent with Legal Norms?*, 4 DENV. J. INT'L L. & POL'Y 229 (1974) (discussing proportionality as a basic principle of the laws of armed conflict).

142. MERON, *supra* note 121, at 13. Military necessity is clearly defined in the Lieber Code (Apr. 24, 1863). *See supra* note 70, art 16 ("Military necessity does not admit of cruelty—that is, the infliction of suffering for the sake of suffering or for revenge, nor of maiming or wounding except in fight, nor of torture to extort confessions. It does not admit of the use of poison in any way, nor of the wanton devastation of a district. It admits of deception, but disclaims acts of perfidy. . ."). *See also, id.* at *supra* note 70, art 44, at 9 (discussing what acts of war are punishable by death). "All wanton violence committed against persons in the invaded country, all destruction of property not commanded by the authorized officer, all robbery, all pillage or sacking, even after taking a place by main force, all rape, wounding, maiming, or killing of such inhabitants, are prohibited under the penalty of death." *Id.*

143. UK MANUAL OF THE LAW OF ARMED CONFLICT, *supra* note 73, at 23.

only for the unjustified and utilitarian reasons of old age, but more likely as a policy of terror intentionally inflicted). One of the most vivid examples of the violation of the principle of humanity is the scene in which an old man in a wheelchair is thrown out of the window by the Nazi guards who are terrorizing his family in their apartment. The Nazis looted homes, destroyed personal property, and stole valuable objects such as one man's precious violin just before he is herded into the train to the infamous concentration camp in Treblinka. During World War II, civilians were very much at the eye of the storm because of the systematic violation of the principle of humanity in one of the most horrific examples of State-inflicted terrorism.

c. The Principle of Distinction. The principle of distinction is related to the principle of humanity in that both require the State to recognize a difference between the civilian and the military population. The principle of distinction requires military operations to be conducted only against the enemy's armed forces and against military objectives—and there must be a clear distinction between the armed forces and the civilians.[144] Szpilman's suffering on screen is actually the suffering of all civilians during the siege of Warsaw by the unrelenting military might of the Third Reich. The violation of the principle of distinction is another element of State-inflicted terrorism by Nazi Germany.

d. The Principle of Proportionality. The principle of proportionality requires that losses resulting from a military action should not be excessive in relation to the expected military goal. The principle of proportionality also requires the reduction of incidental damage caused by military operations.[145] The violation of the principle of proportionality is illustrated dramatically in the film when more than 600,000 people, forced into the Warsaw Ghetto, are reduced slowly and systematically to a mere 60,000, and then to one sole survivor. The annihilation of the population of a vibrant city is achieved by infliction of fear, starvation, unnecessary force, cruelty to women and children, and the overwhelming might of the German army that resulted in extensive destruction to the city in accordance with a planned policy of scorched earth[146] and State-sponsored terrorism. During the German occupation of Poland, people in Warsaw were illegally deprived of basic necessities such as food and drinking water that are indispensable to the survival of the civilian population.[147] The violation of this principle of proportionality is illustrated in the tragic scene where the once-elegant and

---

144. *Id.* at 24.

145. *See* UK Manual of the Law of Armed Conflict, *supra* note 73, at 25.

146. *See id.* at 305.

147. *See* the Geneva Conventions of 1949, *supra* note 97, art 147 (codifying the illegality of general devastation or the "scorched earth policy" in occupied territory); *see also* UK Manual of the Law of Armed Conflict, *supra* note 73, at 305 (discussing the destruction of basic necessity by military that was not justified).

almost aristocratic Szpilman is reduced to groveling for food, drinking dirty water full of flies and mouse droppings, and trying desperately to open a can of cucumbers to avoid death from starvation.

IV. RETRIBUTIVE JUSTICE AFTER WORLD WAR II AND THE NUREMBERG TRIALS

After World War II, the victors and victims expressed an urgent and human need to redress their grievances, to deter future acts of massive war crimes, and to punish the perpetrators in the traditional form of retributive justice that would hopefully not perpetuate cycles of more violence and revenge.[148] It was understood that the State "must do something in response to wrongs against its people,"[149] and that peace without justice is no peace at all.[150] Crimes of massive violence must not go unpunished, and the culture of impunity for perpetrators of high rank and office must be eradicated. If we ignore the need of victims to seek revenge and retribution, which is a "deeply-rooted human need that cannot be moralized away,"[151] the failure to provide retributive justice will only perpetuate more violence.[152] Thus, soon after World War II, the London Agreement was reached establishing the Nuremberg Charter,[153] which codified and compiled existing customary laws, rules, regulations, and treaties on the laws of armed conflict applicable to the defendants at the Nuremberg Trials. The Nuremberg Charter also defined *crimes against the peace* (aggression),[154] *war crimes,*[155] and

---

148. *See generally* TELFORD TAYLOR, THE ANATOMY OF THE NUREMBERG TRIALS: A PERSONAL MEMOIR (1992) (depicting the personal memoirs of Telford Taylor, the chief prosecutor of the Nuremberg Trials). *See generally* TERESA GODWIN PHELPS, SHATTERED VOICES: LANGUAGE, VIOLENCE, AND THE WORK OF TRUTH COMMISSIONS (2004) (discussing the difference between traditional justice, which is achieved through trials and punishment, and restorative justice, which is achieved through language and truth commissions. This very important book questions the legitimacy of the claim that language or narrative stories can alone substitute for the violence associated with traditional justice).

149. PHELPS, *supra* note 148, at 7.

150. *See Peace with Justice, in* WAR CRIMES AND WAR CRIMES TRIBUNALS: PAST, PRESENT, AND FUTURE, THE HOFSTRA LAW & POLICY SYMPOSIUM 1–8 (Leon Friedman & Susan Tiefenbrun eds., 1999).

151. PHELPS, *supra* note 148, at 6.

152. *Id.* at 7.

153. The Nuremberg Charter, *supra* note 95, art. 6 (a)–(c) defined three categories of crimes: crimes against peace, war crimes, and crimes against humanity. *See also* UK MANUAL OF THE LAW OF ARMED CONFLICT, *supra* note 73, at 12 n.35 (citing *The Nuremberg Judgment* (1947) XXII International Military Tribunal 451–53).

154. The Nuremberg Charter, *supra* note 95, art. 6(a).

155. *Id.*

crimes against humanity,[156] all of which were committed by the vanquished enemy.

Some argue that the Nuremberg trials are an example of "victor's justice" and are flawed by retroactivity problems. I have tried to show that norms relating to conduct during war were clearly in place before World War II; however, they were systematically violated and poorly enforced during the war. Nevertheless, Supreme Court Justice Robert H. Jackson, who served as the chief U.S. prosecutor at the Nuremberg trials, claimed that some of the norms guiding the prosecution were not explicitly or specifically in place at the time of the offenses. The framers of the Nuremberg Charter stated that they were committed to apply only preexisting laws to particular cases.[157] For example, the Kellogg-Briand Pact,[158] a treaty providing for the renunciation of war as an instrument of national policy, gave some context to the principles of crimes against peace, but did not fully articulate these crimes.[159] Crimes against humanity had other historic bases, such as in the 1919 Report of the Responsibilities Commission of the Paris Peace Conference.[160] The German defense lawyers at the Nuremberg trials made a strong case for the illegality of the application of the Nuremberg Charter because of retroactivity or ex post facto laws; however, the defense lost as the Nuremberg Court held that the more compelling argument prevailed in the end that the defendants had failed to properly execute their duty of fairness and obedience to customary laws.

V. RESTORATIVE JUSTICE AND THE POWER OF ART AS SELF-HELP REMEDY

Does art have any real power in society or any real place in the judicial system? History tells us that the Germans and Nazis used the power of art and aesthetic pleasure to harness their political goals.[161] Yet many claim that art has no power to stop the horrors of genocidal war. Ironically, many even celebrated Hitler, Mussolini, and other political leaders as "great poets."[162] Films from the Nazi period often depict elegant, cultured people (both military and civilians)

---

156. *Id.* at. 6(c).

157. Martha Minow, Between Violence and Forgiveness, 32 (1998).

158. General Treaty for Renunciation of War as an Instrument of National Policy, Aug. 27, 1928, 46 Stat. 2343, 94 L.N.T.S. 57 [hereinafter Kellogg-Briand Pact].

159. Minow, *supra* note 157, at 32.

160. *See* Paust et al., *supra* note 70, at 741–47, 857.

161. *See* Geoffrey Hartman, *Is an Aesthetic Ethos Possible? Night Thoughts After Auschwitz*, 6 Cardozo Stud. L. & Literature 135, 138 (1994) ("The complaint, therefore, that art proved powerless is mistaken in so far as art was only too effective when harnessed to political ends.").

162. *Id.*

listening intensely to Mozart and Bach at concerts, then standing by as millions are slaughtered. No one expects art to prevent terror,[163] yet art does have a role in society and even in the legal process. Art is arguably a kind of self-help remedy for the victim and a form of restorative justice.

Many have noticed that Holocaust survivors rarely speak of their past experiences, as if they have literally lost their language. Many survivors of concentration camps rarely go to movies about the war because they do not dare relive the memory of such personal horrors. A representation of the atrocities of the past may actually offend the victims and appear as an attempt to trivialize the reality. With regard to the Holocaust, some writers refuse to give any role at all to the arts even in mourning the destruction because art might stylize the event too much and thereby distort its reality.[164] In this spirit, Theodor Adorno said that it is a sign of the barbaric to write poetry after Auschwitz.[165]

Nevertheless, it is undeniable that art creates "an unreality effect in a way that is not alienating or desensitizing. At best, it also provides something of a safe-house for emotion and empathy. The tears we shed, like those of Aeneas when he sees the destruction of Troy depicted on the walls of Carthage, are an acknowledgment and not an exploitation of the past."[166] Legal scholars and psychologists report the therapeutic benefits of retelling the story of violence and torture perpetrated on the victim.[167] Storytelling through art can restore the loss of language brought about by oppression and violence. Narration through art provides communication between victor and vanquished who would not normally be able to understand each other. Storytelling through art can reveal truth, encourage empathy for the victim by the perpetrators and society at large, and help to heal victims by liberating deeply repressed fears and traumas and by offering what one scholar has referred to as "a visible manifestation of the invisible."[168] Storytelling through artistic representation can make the victim whole again by helping her "to re-member that which is fragmentary"[169] in the minds of those who have experienced oppression, torture, dehumanization, and violence. Art disseminates the story to the public and thereby induces others to empathize with the victim. The production of art empowers the creative artist, and if the artist is a victim of oppression and atrocity, the art form enables the victim to identify with the aggressor by simulating his power.

---

163. *Id.* at 139.

164. Hartman, *supra* note 161, at 157.

165. *Id.*, citing Theodor Adorno, *Commitment* (1962), *in* THE ESSENTIAL FRANKFURT SCHOOL READER (A. Arato & E. Gebhardt eds., 1982).

166. *Id.*

167. *See* PHELPS, *supra* note 148, at 8.

168. *Id.* at 70, 72.

169. *Id.* at 71.

Art therapy and music therapy exist as healing or remedial professions today because the acts of writing, telling stories, playing or listening to music, and shooting or seeing films is part of a restorative process. Remedies[170] in the judicial system are not designed to rectify the wrong done to a victim and to correct injustice,[171] but to place an aggrieved party in the same position as she would have been had no injury occurred. Remedies in law are thus classifiable as either retributive or restorative (they are otherwise referred to as legal or equitable remedies). Thus, remedies reflect two different kinds of justice. "Central to both retributive and restorative justice is a concern with righting wrongs and restoring equilibrium to a moral order upturned by criminal wrongdoing."[172] Restorative justice emphasizes "the communication process in which the victim tells her story and the offender acknowledges wrongdoing, and makes amends."[173] Restorativists are concerned with meeting the victim's needs rather than engaging in revenge and retaliation.[174]

Legal remedies, which reflect both the retributive and restorative justice systems, consist of damages that can be compensatory, punitive (retributive), exemplary, or statutory, or can take the form of restitution or specific relief (replevin or ejectment). Equitable, nonmonetary remedies may take the form of an injunction, specific performance of contracts, declaratory judgments, constructive trusts, equitable liens, or subrogation. Rehabilitation, truth-telling, truth and reconciliation commissions, and international investigations can also provide restorative justice to the victim. Self-help is also a kind of remedy in which the plaintiff or injured party takes steps to stop the harm from happening or to reduce the effects of bad behavior.

The International Criminal Court (ICC) at The Hague has investigated atrocities committed in Uganda. The ICC was close to issuing warrants for rebel leaders, but some war victims in Uganda urged the ICC to turn a blind eye to the perpetrators to avoid reprisals against the local people. The Ugandan victims argued in favor of local solutions and "foregiveness"[175]—thus, in a kind of restorative justice that may or may not legitimize a culture of impunity that can only invite more atrocities. Despite frequent attempts to bring an end to the fighting, Uganda has had three decades of massive crimes of violence. Its first

170. *See generally*, DINAH SHELTON, REMEDIES IN INTERNATIONAL HUMAN RIGHTS LAW (2nd ed. 2005) (examining the breadth and depth of remedies available under national and international law).

171. *Id.* at 38.

172. Ellen A. Waldman, *Healing Hearts or Rights Wrongs?: A Mediation on the Goals of "Restorative Justice,"* 25 HAMLINE J.PUB. L. & POL'Y 355, 356 (2004).

173. *Id.* at 356.

174. *Id.* at 359.

175. Marc Lacey, *Atrocity Victims in Uganda Choose Forgiveness*, N.Y. TIMES, Apr. 18, 2005, at A1.

truth commission was established in 1974, and a second one issued a report in 1994. Uganda issued an amnesty in 2000 and merely exiled Ugandan leaders rather than punish them. However, this form of transitional justice did not bring about peace or reconciliation in Uganda. In contrast to Uganda, the South African Truth and Reconciliation Commission was a success. There is no doubt that restorative justice has a place in society and a value in the legal system, but it cannot replace the traditional form of retributive justice that satisfies the victim's need for revenge.

Art therapy is a form of self-help remedy by which the victim relives a horrific experience and empowers herself through the healing properties of artistic representation. It is well-known that calamity inspires art, and art heals suffering. The book and film of *The Pianist* are works of art, fictional representations of reality infused with enough fantasy to distance the writer and the filmmaker from the painful realities of the ghetto and war that both Szpilman and Polanski may unconsciously have wanted to forget. Nevertheless, writing the memoirs and making this film had beneficial and liberating effects on both Szpilman and Polanski, who personally chose this form of self-help remedy. But art helps restore more than just the artist. Readers and viewers of works of art also experience a kind of liberation that comes from the revelation of hidden truths about the horrors of war and the human capability to achieve mass violence and destruction when unchecked by the rule of law.

In fact, Szpilman's method of survival throughout the war is based on a very subtle psychological technique of approach and avoidance that writing and interpreting music necessarily involves. Throughout his ordeal, Szpilman relies on his instincts to "stay put" in Warsaw and thereby approach the enemy, even though others around him decide to flee. Szpilman also withdraws from the chaos of war and avoids reality by remaining literally and figuratively *outside* the maelstrom, living both *inside* and *outside* the pain of the Warsaw Ghetto, of the war, and of his once beautiful and culturally alive city of Warsaw that is in the end in ruins. Thus, Szpilman avoids engagement and escapes the pain of reality literally by living in hiding on the Aryan side of the ghetto and figuratively by listening to familiar classical music playing in his head. This is Szpilman's form of self-help. For example, while watching out of his window from a room on the other side of the ghetto wall, Szpilman sees the Warsaw Ghetto burning; he sees the flames and the smoke; he hears the gunfire; he smells the smoke bombs; and he hears the screams of burning bodies falling from windows with broken glass and debris flying everywhere, while he remains *outside* the ghetto, suffering silently, alone and in hiding.

Szpilman is always "outside" because he is different. Polanski, too, is outside, having been banished from moviemaking in the United States for his admittedly illegal activities for which Polanski is now, in 2010, under house arrest in Switzerland and about to be tried in a U.S. Court. Szpilman is different from the others around him because he is an artist, a pianist, a celebrity, a star, and a survivor who remains outside looking in but agonizing, and, nevertheless, heroic in his solitude, starvation, and utter desperation. Yet Szpilman does his part in the underground resistance—he risks his life daily by participating in a clandestine weapon collection operation to supply the resistance with ammunition for the Warsaw Ghetto uprising. Szpilman even tries to save a very young boy who is smuggling food into the ghetto. But when the boy is caught, he is savagely beaten to death while Szpilman, risking his own life, tries to drag the little boy out through a low hole in the ghetto wall; screaming in pain, the little boy dies in Szpilman's arms. In the book Szpilman describes this scene poignantly and effectively, and in the film Polanski shows us an even more vivid picture of the flagrant violation of the principle of humanity.

Art keeps Szpilman alive. Music and his passion for artistry give Szpilman a reason for being. He hears music in his head throughout the film, and the viewer hears this music as the backdrop of the film. This is the familiar and comforting music he once played. He feels the music in his fingers that keep moving throughout the film as he plays an imaginary piano. Szpilman's salvation is the music of Chopin's[176] C-sharp minor Posthumous Nocturne, Chopin's Gb minor Ballade,[177] Beethoven's Moonlight Sonata in C-sharp Minor, Chopin's F Minor Concerto Opus 21, Bach's Suite #1 for solo cello, and other pieces, which are all in the minor and very dark mode except for Chopin's Grande Polonaise Brillante Opus 22 in Eb major, which depicts in a very heroic fashion the glory of Polish nationalism and the hope for survival. The music is a metaphor for the war. Like the movie in general and the choice of music in particular, the war is overwhelmingly dark with only an occasional glimmer of hope. During the Warsaw Rising, Warsaw Radio played the Grande Polonaise Brillante every thirty seconds to tell the world that the capital was still in Polish hands.[178] In his agonizing isolation in the Warsaw Ghetto, Szpilman longs for the kind of jubilant victory artistically expressed in the Grande Polonaise. It is that piece of uplifting music that is significantly chosen by Polanski to be the last piece Szpilman plays in the film. In the end, Szpilman is victorious and no longer alone, as he is now surrounded by the harmonious Polish orchestra where he distinguishes himself once again as "the Pianist."

---

176. *See* JIM SAMSON, CHOPIN: THE FOUR BALLADES (1992). Chopin was born on Feb. 22, 1810 in Zelazowa Wola, Poland. His early development as a composer took place in Warsaw during the 1820s. For more information about his life, *see generally* JEREMY SIEPMANN, CHOPIN: THE RELUCTANT ROMANTIC (1995) and THE CHOPIN COMPANION; PROFILES OF THE MAN AND THE MUSICIAN (Alan Walker ed., 1973) (illustrating Chopin's life and work as a composer).

177. A ballade is a folktale told in song, a narrative model based on songs and poetic forms, a story in sound, such as Roman Polanski's film *The Pianist*. *See generally*, JAMES PARAKILAS, BALLADS WITHOUT WORDS; CHOPIN AND THE TRADITION OF THE INSTRUMENTAL BALLADE (1992).

178. DAVIES, *supra* note 51, at 85.

Szpilman's fame and artistry as a composer and pianist inspired both those in the ghetto and on the Aryan side of Warsaw to keep Szpilman alive, in accordance with the laws of war that prohibit the destruction of national treasures and art.[179] Szpilman was a national treasure to Poland, and the Poles sought to protect him, even though one evil Polish woman in the film almost succeeds in betraying him when she suspects Szpilman is a Jew hiding in her building. Szpilman's deeply embedded message, which ends on a positive note, is not only about representing good and bad Germans or good and bad Poles or good and bad Jews. The film and the book do represent a balanced view of mankind. Szpilman's message is about the futility of war, the unimaginable suffering war causes, and the unnecessary and irreparable destruction of life and physical beauty in a world at war without rules of law to guide the warriors and protect the civilians.

VI. CONCLUSION

The film *The Pianist* shall remain in the annals of cinematic history as one of the greats. The beauty of the film is in its depiction of the ugliness of war. This ironic duality is expressed linguistically in the Latin word *bellum*, which means "war," and comes from the same root as *bellus* or beautiful.[180] The film is a representation of reality, but it is also an artful blend of fiction and fantasy, imbued with the rhetorical power of persuasion that only the immediacy of cinematic imagery can deliver. The film has a dual message. On the one hand, the film reveals Szpilman's deep despair through the constant and almost relentless presentation of dark images that depict the evils of total war waged in violation of the laws of war. On the other hand, the film is about hope and the power of art (especially music) to transcend the ugliness of warfare and the extreme brutality that war provokes.

Music assuages Szpilman's pain and awakens the conscience of one German officer who ultimately saves the musician's life. The book and the film say nothing about the possibility of art preventing atrocity, which clearly cannot be claimed in the face of the generally high level of culture existing in prewar Germany. Nevertheless, art is a form of restorative justice because it informs the public about the realities of war. Art raises the collective conscience of the perpetrators to the purposelessness of the destruction they cause by their failure to obey existing laws of war. Art creates a historic record that can educate society now and in the future about the horrors of war and the risk of a world that does not live by the rules of law.

---

179. *See* Convention for the Protection of Cultural Property in the Event of Armed Conflict, *done* May 14, 1954, 249 U.N.T.S. 215.

180. HOFFMAN, *supra* note 60, at 43.

Art is a self-help remedy that provides therapy for the victim as it soothes the victim's pain during the perpetration of unspeakable atrocities. But remedies typically involve retribution for the perpetrator in order to render justice to the victim. As art memorializes the catastrophic events of World War II and disseminates authentic facts to the public at large, art can pique the conscience of the perpetrators, inculcate moral values for society, and possibly prevent further atrocities. If the artist creates an authentic historic record of the wartime events and disseminates this history through the transmission capabilities of media, then art can also possibly result in a deterrence of these war crimes in the future. The artistic and persuasive reenactment of the crimes through narratives has the effect of educating society about the evils of war and the need to obey the laws of war that establish limits and protections for the combatants as well as the civilians. Thus art, through persuasive storytelling, can provide restorative justice to the victim without necessarily providing retribution to the perpetrators.

For example, the German officer who finds Szpilman hiding in the rubble of a bombed-out apartment asks him to play the piano. The officer is visibly moved by the music and shows his appreciation for Szpilman's interpretation of the Chopin Ballade by offering him safe shelter and food that Szpilman eats ravenously with his long, slender fingers. The perpetrator as well as the victim crave the escape that art alone can provide. In this critical moment, after not practicing for two-and-a-half years, the pianist manages to play perfectly and expressively a difficult ballade, a folk narrative told in song, on a perfectly tuned Steinway grand piano that miraculously appears at the end of the film and at the end of the Warsaw siege. This finale is an intentional fantasy that reflects Szpilman's never-ending hope and the restorative value of artistic narration. In the very last triumphant scene of the movie, the pianist smiles to his friend and to the audience while playing the victorious, heroic, and joyous Grande Polonaise Brillante by Chopin, Poland's greatest composer.

In the end, music saves Szpilman from the horrors of war and from life in a world without rules or laws of war to guide the combatants or protect the civilians. Words alone cannot adequately express the horrors of such a world in utter chaos. We have to read Szpilman's book and then see it represented vividly and persuasively in the film *The Pianist* to actually believe it.

PART C

CIVIL DISOBEDIENCE

5. DECONSTRUCTING *CIVIL DISOBEDIENCE*
A Semiotic Definition*

I. INTRODUCTION

A. History of the Spirit of Resistance and Revolution in the United States

The United States was founded on the principles of resistance and revolution.[1] Decades before the Revolutionary War, Americans in all the colonies protested unlawful acts of the British government, including colonists resisting British efforts to enforce the Stamp Act in 1765. Henry David Thoreau stated that "all men recognize the right of revolution: that is, the right to refuse allegiance to and to resist the government, when its tyranny or its inefficiency is great and unendurable."[2] During the revolutionary period "the right, the need, the absolute obligation to disobey legally constituted authority had become the universal cry."[3] Many of our Founding Fathers believed that civil disobedience, resistance, and revolution were inalienable rights that they wrote into the Declaration of Independence. One of the most famous Founding Fathers, Thomas Jefferson, asked rhetorically, "What country can preserve its liberties if their rulers are not warned from time to time that their people preserve the spirit of resistance?"[4]

---

* This paper was first presented at a Conference on The Right of Resistance on Dec. 13, 2002 in Dijon, France at the University of Bourgogne School of Law and published in French as "La Désobeissance Civile et la Constitution des Etats-Unis" in Le Droit de Resistance a L'Oppression, collection "Le Genre Humain," (Editions du Seuil, Paris), 159–82 (Sept. 2005). It was published in English as an article entitled *Civil Disobedience and the U.S. Constitution*, 32 Sw. U. L. Rev. 677 (2003). This article has been extensively revised. I would like to thank Dorothy Hampton and Debora Gerads of Thomas Jefferson School of Law for their assistance in the research on this paper. I also wish to thank Professor Bryan Wildenthal of Thomas Jefferson School of Law for reading and commenting on early drafts of this chapter.

1. Harris G. Mirkin, *Rebellion, Revolution, and the Constitution: Thomas Jefferson's Theory of Civil Disobedience* 13 Am.Stud.61 (1972) (arguing that Jefferson saw resistance as beneficial to society because it prevented the need for full-scale revolution. Acts of resistance "forced the society to deal with problems before they assumed proportions that would justify real revolution").

2. Henry David Thoreau, Walden and Civil Disobedience 227 (Owen Thomas ed., Norton Critical Editions 1966).

3. Pamphlets of the American Revolution 191–93 (Bernard Bailyn ed., 1965), *cited in* Mirkin, *supra* note 1, at n.1.

4. Letter from Thomas Jefferson to William Smith (Nov. 13, 1787), *in* 12 The Papers of Thomas Jefferson 356 (Julian P. Boyd ed., 1955).

Jefferson's "spirit of resistance" refers to both the rights of revolution and of civil disobedience. Nonviolent resistance is a compromise, a way to safely vent emotion about unjust laws, a middle ground between blind obedience to tyrannical rulers or unjust laws and outright revolution.[5] Before the American Revolution, the Founding Fathers reasoned that resistance to unlawful acts could not be deemed per se illegal, but they also understood resistance and revolution were not legally available to them within the judicial procedure for redress of grievances set up by the British government. Even after the Revolution, the spirit of resistance continued. It was particularly noticeable in Massachusetts, where throughout the 1780s citizens set up committees and conventions to protest high taxes and urge reform of their state constitution.[6] When the committees failed, the people turned to mob action, and actually closed down the state courts in the famous Shays' Rebellion of 1786–87.

Following the Revolution, American leaders both accepted and feared the spirit of resistance. Thomas Jefferson, who never completely renounced the right of revolution, included the doctrine of nullification and implied threat of secession when writing the Virginia and Kentucky Resolutions. Jefferson won his election to the presidency of the United States in 1800 partially based on his continued belief in the right of revolution, even though he actually assumed an antirevolutionary stance during his term of office.[7]

Unlike Jefferson, Alexander Hamilton was very suspicious of the right of resistance and revolution "by the multitude, who have not a sufficient stock of reason and knowledge to guide them, for opposition to tyranny and oppression, very naturally leads them to a contempt and disregard of all authority . . . and are apt more or less to run into anarchy."[8] Hamilton ultimately renounced the idea that people had the right to overthrow the central government.

After the Revolution, when mobs turned against the newborn American government, many American leaders began to question the appropriateness of the old "spirit of resistance." At this point, resistance clashed with the need for a stable, strong government in a new republic.[9] Upon the founding of the United States of America as one nation, even the radical Bostonian Samuel Adams (once the most vocal proponent of resistance and revolution)[10] revised his views about the right to revolt. He now saw the inherent dangers of too much resistance

---

5. Paul M. Thompson, *Is There Anything "Legal" About ExtraLegal Action? The Debate Over Dorr's Rebellion*, 36 New Eng. L.Rev. 385, 387 (Winter 2002) (discussing the difference between resistance, revolution, and civil disobedience).

6. *Id.* at 392.

7. Mirkin, *supra* note 1, at 62.

8. Letter to John Jay (Nov. 27, 1775), *in* The Papers of Alexander Hamilton 176 (Harold C. Syrett ed., 1961), *cited in* Mirkin, *supra* note 1, at n.1.

9. Thompson, *supra* note 5, at 393.

10. *Id.* at 390.

leading to a breakdown of the rule of law in society. James Madison, who did not renounce the right of revolution and originally included it as one of the rights protected by the Bill of Rights, actually feared revolution.[11] And George Washington, the father of the United States, prayed that God "would incline the hearts of the citizens to cultivate a spirit of subordination and obedience to government."[12]

Among the Founding Fathers of America, Jefferson best typifies the duality inherent in the right of resistance and revolution. He believed rebellion was a protection of freedom, a "medicine necessary for the sound health of government."[13] Among the Founding Fathers, Jefferson was the least fearful of the right of resistance and revolution, and he supported populist rebellions such as Shays' Rebellion and the effectiveness of a threat of rebellion such as the Virginia and Kentucky Resolutions.[14] Jefferson was an ardent supporter of the French Revolution, maintaining his support after both the Terror[15] and his presidency. Jefferson also continued to support the radical natural rights philosophy enunciated in the Declaration of Independence, implying in a 1799 letter to Edmund Randolph that the nation retains the right of revolution because it is the people's will "which creates or annihilates the organ which is to declare and announce it."[16] Jefferson is most remembered for his revolutionary statements: "The tree of liberty must be refreshed from time to time with the blood of patriots and tyrants" and "If the happiness of the mass of the people can be secured at the expense of a little tempest now and then, or even a little blood, it will be a precious purchase."[17]

However, despite Jefferson's continued belief in the right of revolution, he was not willing to see the American constitutional system destroyed by rebellion and resistance.[18] He was suspicious of revolt by the masses or the mob, and ideally, Jeffersonian revolts probably would have been led by the

---

11. *See* Mirkin, *supra* note 1, at 61.

12. George Washington's Circular Letter to the States (June 8, 1783), *reprinted in* COLONIES TO NATION, 1763–1789: A DOCUMENTARY HISTORY OF THE AMERICAN REVOLUTION 436, 443 (Jack P. Greene ed., 1967).

13. Letter to James Madison (Jan. 30, 1787), *in* 12 THE PAPERS OF THOMAS JEFFERSON, *supra* note 4, at 61, 92, *cited in* Mirkin, *supra* note 1, at 64, n.13.

14. Mirkin, *supra* note 1, at 66.

15. *Id.* at 63.

16. Letter to Edmund Randolph (Aug. 19, 1799), *reprinted in* THE WORKS OF THOMAS JEFFERSON IX 74 (Paul L. Ford ed., 1904–05) [hereinafter THE WORKS OF THOMAS JEFFERSON IX], *cited in* Mirkin, *supra* note 1, at 63.

17. *See* Mirkin, *supra* note 1, at 72, n.5 (explaining that most of Jefferson's famous revolutionary statements were made relatively early in his career in support of Shays' Rebellion). *See also* Jefferson's Letter to William Smith (Nov. 13, 1787), *in* 12 THE PAPERS OF THOMAS JEFFERSON, *supra* note 4, at 356.

18. *See* Mirkin, *supra* note 1, at 62.

natural aristocrats.[19] To resolve the tension between the right of resistance and the right to live in a safe, orderly system of government, Jefferson actually preferred the use of alternatives to revolution such as elections, constitutional amendments, threats of revolution, and partial rebellion.[20] Although Jefferson continued to talk in terms of real revolution, he actually used rebellion and the threat of revolution as a persuasive tool of reform.[21] Even though Jefferson incorporated civil disobedience into the constitutional structure, he actually relied far more on limited rebellions that are short and contained rather than on the checks and balances of the constitutional system for the preservation of minority rights.[22]

In the eighteenth century, the French Revolution and its aftermath persuaded Americans of the need to limit popular sovereignty to avoid the chaos and anarchy that consumed France. Everyone in the United States knew that after the French Revolution, France "groaned under the tyranny of the mob";[23] government became anarchy, and violence replaced law and order.[24] The French drafted, ratified, and then abrogated constitutions with alarming frequency.[25] They formed illegal assemblies that usurped the powers of existing French legislatures.[26] The Americans looked at France and feared that popular sovereignty unbridled in the United States could lead to a similar state of chaos. The leaders in the United States sought to establish a balance between the right to dissent and the need to maintain a stable government. The right to revolution and rebellion became obsolete in this climate, and the right to resistance needed careful limitations.

B. Tensions Between Rights of Resistance and National Security and the Origins of a Constitutional Protection of Resistance

After the Revolutionary War, American leaders sought to dampen the "spirit of resistance" by drafting and ratifying a new constitution that created a stronger national government with the power to suppress unlawful resistance.[27] Article IV, Section 4 of the new constitution granted the national government the power to protect the states "against domestic violence."[28] This power was used against the

19. *Id.* at 68.

20. *Id.* at 63.

21. *Id.* at 70.

22. *Id.*

23. Francis Bowen, The Recent Contest in Rhode Island 64 (1844).

24. Caleb C. Smith, Speech on the Memorial of the Democratic Members of the Legislature of Rhode Island 9 (Washington, 1844).

25. Bowen, *supra* note 23, at 64.

26. *Id.*

27. Thompson, *supra* note 5, at 393.

28. U.S. Const. art. IV, § 4. However, the U.S. Constitution also provides U.S. citizens with the right to criticize, to protest, and to peaceably assemble, and the states must respect

states to suppress uprisings in Pennsylvania in 1794 and 1799 when federal troops were sent in to stop the Whiskey Rebellion[29] and the Fries Rebellion.[30]

A few of the Founding Fathers believed there was a need to defend the spirit of resistance, even in the new republic. Thomas Jefferson wrote that the "spirit of resistance" was "so valuable on certain occasions, that I wish it to be always kept alive."[31] This spirit of resistance survived after the Revolution in the form of popular sovereignty, which gave the people a direct role in their government by allowing them to monitor their rulers and investigate abuses.[32] Defenders of popular sovereignty and the right of resistance pointed to the Declaration of Independence that they reasoned granted the people the right "to alter or abolish" their government whenever they deemed it expedient.[33] They argued the Declaration of Independence empowered the people to exercise the right of resistance without the consent of their current government.

Espousing what would be termed today a theory of constitutional interpretation known as *original understanding* (sometimes referred to as *original intent*), defenders of popular sovereignty in the eighteenth century based their belief in the constitutional right of resistance on historical evidence. They argued that the manner in which the U.S. Constitution of 1787 was drafted and ratified confirmed their belief that it is constitutionally legal for the people to abolish their existing government and build a new one. Instead of merely revising the Articles of Confederation (which was the original plan), the framers proceeded to set up an entirely "new system of government."[34] Those who drafted the Constitution of 1787 defied the instructions of Congress and the amendment provisions in the Articles of Confederation themselves that allowed for amendments only by unanimous consent of all states. Thus, popular sovereigntists reasoned that the "irregular and unauthorized" manner in which the Constitution was drafted and

---

these rights and refrain from punishing the citizens from exercising them. If necessary, the state is required to send out state troopers or police to protect a mass march of people who are protesting against the state itself. This occurred in Selma, Alabama. *See* ABE FORTAS, CONCERNING DISSENT AND CIVIL DISOBEDIENCE 44 (1968).

29. *See* THOMAS P. SLAUGHTER, THE WHISKEY REBELLION: FRONTIER EPILOGUE TO THE AMERICAN REVOLUTION (1986); THE WHISKEY REBELLION PAST AND PRESENT PERSPECTIVES (Steven R. Boyd ed., 1985).

30. *See* WILLIAM W.H. DAVIS, THE FRIES REBELLION, 1798–99 (1969).

31. Letter from Thomas Jefferson to Abigail Adams (Feb. 22, 1787), *reprinted in* 12 THE PAPERS OF THOMAS JEFFERSON, *supra* note 4, at 174.

32. *See* Thompson, *supra* note 5, at 407–08 for a discussion of Dorr's Rebellion, the Dorrites' view of popular sovereignty, and the right of resistance in the United States in the eighteenth century.

33. *Id.* at 410.

34. Majority Report, *reprinted in* Letter from John Whipple to John Tyler, Apr. 9, 1842, in Interference of the Executive in the Affairs of Rhode Island, H.R. REP., NO. 546, 28TH CONG., at 39 (1844).

ratified justified their continued right of resistance.[35] Thus, the U.S. Constitution of 1787 was in itself an act of civil disobedience because the framers did not comply with the onerous amendment procedures of the Articles of Confederation and the requirements of the Continental Congress.

Consistent with the original intent theory, Professor Saul Cornell argues that the dissenters or anti-federalists are the founders of a long and powerful dissenting tradition in American politics, with anti-federalist ideas being at the center of American constitutionalism.[36] Professor Paul Finkelman defines *anti-federalism* as a belief in limited government, a weak national leader, and great deference to Congress as representing the "states" through the Senate.[37] Dissenting minorities, such as birth control advocates, abolitionists, persecuted religious minorities, and civil rights advocates such as the Reverend Martin Luther King, Jr. have turned to the Constitution for protection.[38] Rather than denouncing the Constitution, the most oppressed minorities in America have embraced it.[39] Finkelman persuasively shows that the Confederation embraced much of the spirit and philosophy of the anti-federalists because it was a state-centered nation that stressed limited national powers. Finkelman also argues that the Articles of Confederation resembled the Constitution of 1787 as amended by the Bill of Rights.[40] The Confederation embodied anti-federalist ideas such as rotation in office, limited government, and states' rights, while it simultaneously (and inconsistently) attempted to create a modern national state.[41] This inconsistency reflects the duality of civil disobedience itself which at once protects the right of dissent and threatens the right to live in an ordered society under the principle of the rule of law.

To protect the stability of government, the U.S. Constitution and state constitutions limited popular sovereignty by setting up a judicial and legislative process to effectively object to law and policy. Conservatives like John Calhoun argued:

> It would be the death-blow of constitutional democracy, to admit the right of the numerical majority, to alter or abolish constitutions at pleasure, regardless

---

35. Thompson, *supra* note 5, at 411.

36. *See* Paul Finkelman, *Turning Losers into Winners: What Can We Learn, if Anything, From the Antifederalists?* 79 TEX. L. REV. 849 (Mar. 2001), reviewing SAUL CORNELL, THE OTHER FOUNDERS: ANTIFEDERALISM AND THE DISSENTING TRADITION IN AMERICA (1999).

37. Finkelman, *supra* note 36, at 853. Finkelman believes that the anti-federalists, known as the "loyal opposition," were "people with little faith, limited vision and to a great extent, horrifying notions of how society ought to work and government ought to operate." *Id.* at 856.

38. *Id.* at 892.

39. *Id.* at 893.

40. *Id.*

41. *Id.* at 894.

> of the consent of the Government, or the forms prescribed for their amendment. It would be to admit that it had the right to set aside, at pleasure, that which was intended to restrain it, and which would make it just no restraint at all.[42]

A constitution can be changed in two ways: (1) by complying with the amendment procedures in the constitution, or, if there is no amendment provision, (2) by obtaining the consent of the existing government. Daniel Webster said that by adopting a constitution, "the people agreed to set bounds to their own power."[43] Therefore, the state constitutions and the U.S. Constitution limit the right of resistance. U.S. Supreme Court Justice Taney clearly stated "the right of revolution" which requires "a change by force," "is nowhere sanctioned . . . in the Constitution of the United States. . . ."[44]

In light of this historical and cultural context of the use of civil disobedience and the right of resistance, Part II will examine different definitions proposed for the term *civil disobedience* in an attempt to uncover its deep structures. Part III will examine the inherent duality of the term *civil disobedience* and the impact of that duality on legal protection for civil disobedients. Part IV will examine arguments for and against the use of civil disobedience to protect minority rights in American society. Part V will examine whether the U.S. Constitution protects the act of civil disobedience under the First Amendment rights to protest, dissent, peaceably assemble, and the most precious of all constitutional guarantees, free speech.

II. THE DEEP STRUCTURE OF CIVIL DISOBEDIENCE

Let us begin by decoding the term *civil disobedience* and its hidden meanings. Civil disobedience is a nonviolent act of breaking the law openly and publicly, without harming others, which is accompanied by a willingness to accept punishment.[45] The term is built on an oxymoron that reflects the positive and negative aspects of the concept. Strict law and order proponents take the view that the term *civil disobedience* is "semantically inaccurate"[46] because disobedience cannot be civil (i.e., acceptable in a civilized society), stating: "In democratic societies any violation of the law is an uncivil act."[47] Opponents of civil disobedience claim

---

42. Thompson, *supra* note 5, at 424.

43. *See* The Rhode Island Question: Arguments of Messrs. Whipple and Webster in the Case of Martin Luther Plaintiff in Error, Versus Luther M. Borden and Others 1, 40 (Charles Burnett ed., 1848).

44. Luther v. Borden, 48 U.S. (7 How.) 1, 25 (1849).

45. William Sloane Coffin, Jr. & Morris I. Leibman, Civil Disobedience; Aid or Hindrance to Justice? 14 (1972).

46. *Id.* at 13.

47. *Id.* at 12.

that civil disobedients actually flaunt their lack of civility. In other words, civil disobedience is about disobeying the law, and disobeying the law simply cannot be deemed "civil" in a society that values order and stability.

But civil disobedience is more than disobeying the law—it is a means by which the disobedient can accomplish a higher moral or political purpose. This purpose may be the accomplishment of necessary legislative enactment or reform. Civil disobedience is about disobeying man-made laws that the disobedient believes are unjust[48] or unconstitutional. Civil disobedients disobey invalid law in order to obey a higher law. Martin Luther King believed that people have a moral duty to disobey unjust law,[49] which King defined by using the words of St. Thomas Aquinas, who extolled the virtues of civil disobedients: "An unjust law is a human law that is not rooted in eternal and natural law." King not only justified the illegal acts of civil disobedience but raised civil disobedients to the level of near-sainthood:

> I submit that an individual who breaks a law that conscience tells him is unjust, and who willingly accepts the penalty of imprisonment in order to arouse the conscience of the community over its injustice, is in reality expressing the highest respect for law.[50]

Civil disobedients are not just lawbreakers. Some of our greatest heroes violated the laws: Socrates, Thoreau, Gandhi, and King. Some of our finest leaders, such as George Washington, Benjamin Franklin, Alexander Hamilton, Thomas Jefferson, and Samuel Adams, were civil disobedients who were deemed to be traitors by some and patriots by others.[51] U.S. Supreme Court Justice Abe Fortas said that civil disobedience is an act of courage, even though each of us is subject to the law and each of us is duty-bound to obey it:

> But if I had lived in Germany in Hitler's days, I hope I would have refused to wear an armband, to Heil Hitler, to submit to genocide . . . If I had been a Negro living in Birmingham or Little Rock or Plaquemines Parish, Louisiana, I hope I would have disobeyed the state laws that said that I might not enter the public waiting room in the bus station reserved for 'Whites' . . . I hope I

48. Martin Luther King, Jr., *Letter from Birmingham Jail, in* THE AUTOBIOGRAPHY OF MARTIN LUTHER KING, JR. 187 (Clayborne Carson ed., 1998) (1963). Also published in Martin Luther King, Jr., *Letter from Birmingham Jail, in* WHY CAN'T WE WAIT? 84–85 (1963) (explaining why civil disobedience is more effective than waiting for Congress to pass new laws). *See also* Susan Tiefenbrun, *Semiotics and Martin Luther King's* Letter From Birmingham Jail, 4 CARDOZO STUD. L. & LITERATURE 255 (1992) and its revised version in Chapter 6 of this book.

49. *See* Tiefenbrun, *supra* note 48, at 274.

50. *See* King *supra* note 48, at 193 (citing St. Thomas Aquinas).

51. COFFIN & LEIBMAN, *supra* note 45, at 2.

would have had the courage to disobey, although the segregation ordinances were presumably law until they were declared unconstitutional.[52]

The term *civil disobedience* has a fixed composite structure that requires the adjective *civil* to be linked to the term *disobedience.* The word *civil* is a necessary element in the concept and reflects the duality inherent in the act of civil disobedience. What is so "civil" about "civil disobedience"? The word *civil* conjures up notions of *civility* and *civilization,* both of which lend a positive connotation to the otherwise unacceptable act of disobeying the law in a society that believes in the rule of law. Civil disobedience is a deliberate but nonviolent act of lawbreaking designed to call attention to a particular law or set of laws of questionable legitimacy or morality. Civil disobedience is thought to be a morally justifiable violation of the law,[53] an act of obedience to natural law. Civil disobedience is conduct that is distinguishable from ordinary disobedience and from crime itself—that is why it is called "civil." Civil disobedience, as with social protest, serves the law's need for growth and reform.[54]

The positive connotations of the act of civil disobedience are reflected in the connotations rather than the denotations of the term *civil.* The first meaning of *civil* refers to that which relates to the state or to its citizenry, such as *civil rights,* or that which relates to private rights and remedies sought via lawsuits (as distinct from criminal proceedings)[55] such as *civil litigation.* The term *civil* also refers to any of the modern legal systems derived from Roman law, such as that of France or Louisiana's civil law jurisdiction derived from the Napoleonic Code. But the term *civil* also relates to the concept of *civility*: politeness, behavior characterized by civilized society, and the civilized way of dealing with other human beings. Ironically, civility is the antithesis of anarchy, lawlessness, or chaos, the very thing those engaging in civil disobedience have been accused of producing.[56] The relationship of the term *civil* to *civility* adds a positive connotation to the otherwise negative concept of civil disobedience that is grounded in an impermissible violation of the law.

There are two kinds of civil disobedience. One is protest in the form of a refusal to obey a law the disobedient seeks to have overturned. This form of civil

52. *See* FORTAS, *supra* note 28, at 18.

53. *See* COFFIN & LEIBMAN, *supra* note 45, at 12.

54. Archibald Cox, *Civil Rights, the Stimulus of Protest,* 40 N.Y. STATE B.J. 161, 169 (1968).

55. BLACK'S LAW DICTIONARY 238 (7th ed. 1999).

56. *See* COFFIN & LEIBMAN, *supra* note 45, at 23: "These doctrines of civil disobedience have been eroding our civilization in recent years. In action they have led to what I call brinkmanship. In other words, they have encouraged people to express discontent—with the system, with the laws, with government officials and policies, and with ideas—by organizing mass groups that create the potential for violence and law-breaking. This severely strains the necessary function of social order almost to the breaking point."

disobedience (which is what Martin Luther King practiced) is protest against the law itself. The other form of civil disobedience is the violation of laws that the protester does not challenge because of their own terms or effect. In other words, the laws are not the subject of attack in this form of civil disobedience; instead, dissenters violate the laws to turn attention to a greater cause such as freedom from oppression and the right to self-determination. Mahatma Gandhi practiced this type of civil disobedience.[57]

III. CIVIL DISOBEDIENCE AND TERRORISM

The term *civil disobedience,* just like the currently popular term *terrorism,*[58] has been misapplied in recent years.[59] Civil disobedience is not an effort to overthrow the government. Civil disobedience is a person's refusal to obey a law which that person believes to be unconstitutional or immoral. Civil disobedience is also not the use of violence to compel the government to grant autonomy to a specific group. That is rebellion or revolution, whose aim is to seek change by destroying the system. In contrast, King and other civil disobedients sought reform within the established order.[60] Violation of the law is a necessary part of civil disobedience to publicize the protest and to bring pressure on the public or the government to accomplish purposes that may have nothing to do with the law that is breached.[61]

Civil disobedience is clearly not terrorism, although there are certain similarities between the two concepts. Both are associated with anarchy and chaos. Both are about protest. Terrorists and civil disobedients both have an overarching cause (political, military, religious, ethnic, ideological, etc.) that they want to publicize by their symbolic acts. Terrorist acts are always intentional and always associated with violence and harm to innocent civilians. Civil disobedience is also an intentional act, but not necessarily violent, and rarely (if ever) intentionally harmful to innocent civilians. The main difference between terrorists (who are sometimes viewed as heroes) and civil disobedients (who are also sometimes viewed as heroes) is that terrorists intend to cause fear in order to coerce or intimidate an enemy. Civil disobedience does not work on the principle of fear. The main structural element of civil disobedience is resistance against a law that is conceived of as an unjust law.

---

57. FORTAS, *supra* note 28, at 63.

58. *See* Susan Tiefenbrun, *A Semiotic Approach to a Legal Definition of Terrorism, supra* Chapter 3 of this book.

59. FORTAS, *supra* note 28, at 59.

60. *Id.* at 60.

61. *Id.* at 61.

A. The Duality of Civil Disobedience

Martin Luther King's definition of civil disobedience clearly reflects the duality inherent in the term. King advocated both obedience and disobedience of the law. He implored his followers to obey just laws, but encouraged them to engage in open, public, nonviolent direct action in violation of unjust laws that are out of harmony with what he called the "moral laws of the universe."[62] Understanding the publicity value of incarceration, King fully expected to be punished for the unlawful act of civil disobedience: "One who breaks an unjust law must do so openly, lovingly, and with a willingness to accept the penalty."[63]

Like Martin Luther King, U.S. Supreme Court Justice Abe Fortas defined civil disobedience as the violation of a law that is believed to be immoral or unconstitutional.[64] Justice Fortas and Reverend King were both opposed to violence, and both sought legislative reform within the established order.[65] Susan B. Anthony, the legendary American suffragette, is a perfect example of this form of civil disobedience. She committed voter fraud twice and willingly refused bail in order to go to jail simply to have her day in court to challenge women's right to vote.[66] Ironically, Anthony's own lawyer deprived her of her right of appeal to the U.S. Supreme Court on a petition for habeas corpus because (against her wishes) he posted a bond, thereby liberating her from prison.[67]

Her case is one of the most egregious examples of due process violations in history. At trial, her case was decided not by a jury, but by a judge. She was denied the right to speak during the trial because as a woman, she was declared by the judge to be "incompetent" to testify on her own behalf.[68] The judge ultimately decided by directed verdict in her criminal trial (a violation of due process) that she was guilty of illegal voting. He fined her $100 but refused to give her a jail sentence because he did not want her to become a martyr for the cause of women's right to vote.[69] This refusal to incarcerate Anthony reflects the importance of punishment in civil disobedience and why it is necessary to accept punishment in order to achieve results.

Gandhi defined civil disobedience more broadly than King. Gandhi's civil disobedience has two different forms: (1) King's form of civil disobedience, which is nonviolent disobedience of unjust laws in order to reform the law, and (2) disobedience of the law not to protest the law, but purely as a symbolic

---

62. *See* King, *supra* note 48, at 193.

63. *Id.* at 194.

64. *See* FORTAS, *supra* note 28, at 59.

65. *Id.* at 60.

66. Adam Winkler, *A Revolution Too Soon: Woman Suffragists and the "Living Constitution,"* 76 N.Y.U. L. REV. 1456, 1507 (2001).

67. *Id.* at 1507.

68. *Id.* at 1508.

69. *Id.* at 1513.

gesture of revolt against a corrupt or tyrannical State.[70] Gandhi was a great proponent of violating laws to publicize a protest and bring pressure on the public or the government to accomplish purposes that had little to do with the law being breached.[71]

John Rawls defined civil disobedience as acts that are "public, non-violent,[72] conscientious yet political. . . done with the aim of bringing about a change in the law or policies of government."[73] The key elements missing in Rawls' definition are the word *illegal* and the expectation by those who engage in civil disobedience to be punished for their illegal act. Rawls defined three conditions that a movement must meet to practice civil disobedience in a reasonably just society. The first is to determine whether the object of protest is appropriate for civil disobedience.[74] The second is to prove that the political process failed, even though "normal appeals to the political majority have already been made in good faith."[75] The third condition arises when the natural duty of justice requires a certain restraint.[76] Society can absorb only so much civil disobedience, or serious disorder could follow and disrupt "the efficacy of the just constitution."[77] Rawls assumes that civil disobedience has a limit because if it goes too far, it may lead to a breakdown in the respect for law. Thus, for Rawls as well as for Justice Fortas, there is a need to balance a person's constitutional right to protest with the person's duty of civility in society, which prohibits the use of violence even to accomplish a just purpose.[78]

Thus, an act of civil disobedience must be nonviolent, open and visible, illegal, and performed for a moral purpose to protest an unjust law or to object to

---

70. MAHATMA GANDHI, NON-VIOLENT RESISTANCE 175 (1961).

71. *See* FORTAS, *supra* note 28, at 61 (discussing Gandhi's form of protest, which is not directed to an unjust law but to a government policy).

72. LAWRENCE R. VELVEL, UNDECLARED WAR AND CIVIL DISOBEDIENCE: THE AMERICAN SYSTEM IN CRISIS 191 (1970) (claiming that violence is necessary in order to bring about change because people do not listen to reasonable arguments); *cf.* FORTAS, *supra* note 28, at 80 (1968) (claiming that violence "is never defensible . . . where there [are] alternative methods of winning the minds of others to one's cause and securing changes in the government or its policies").

73. JOHN RAWLS, A THEORY OF JUSTICE 365 (1971).

74. *Id.* at 371–73.

75. *Id.* at 373.

76. *Id.*

77. *Id.* at 374.

78. *See* Roger Higgins, *Vittitow v. City of Upper Arlington: As Mixed Questions of Law and Fact, Should Ordinances and Injunctions be Reviewed under the Madsen and Frisby Standards of Review by Using a De Novo Standard or a "Clearly Erroneous" Standard*, Note, 33 SAN DIEGO L. R. 453, 492 (Winter 1996) (discussing the court's review for content-neutral limits to methods of protest in abortion clinic cases).

the status quo and with the expectation of punishment.[79] Within the confines of this definition, we may ask why anyone would choose civil disobedience over other permissible forms of reform, and whether the U.S. Constitution protects civil disobedience as a form of dissent or protest. In view of the definition proposed, it is clear civil disobedience is more than mere dissent or protest, both of which are constitutionally permissible. Civil disobedience is an illegal form of protest, a kind of dissent that is probably not protected by the constitutional right of dissent or the right to assemble peaceably. Moreover, civil disobedience involving unlawful acts is a form of expressive speech or conduct that is probably not protected by the First Amendment right of free speech.[80] Even though King, one of the great proponents of civil disobedience in the United States, believed that the U.S. Constitution was on his side,[81] it is my contention that the Constitution cannot protect civil disobedience. To do so would undermine the very force of this particular speech act. Civil disobedience is by its very nature designed to draw attention to the moral or political cause the disobedient is proposing to reform.

IV. ARGUMENTS FOR AND AGAINST CIVIL DISOBEDIENCE

Civil disobedience is an oxymoron that reflects a basic duality inherent in its meaning. Civil disobedience falls somewhere on the continuum between blind obedience to the law, the right to resistance, and total revolution. The concept is confusing, and like the term *terrorism*, civil disobedience has no universally accepted definition.[82] Some consider civil disobedience to be a permissible form of dissent, protest, speech or expressive conduct: a last ditch effort to be used when the courts and Congress have failed to reform unjust law or to create necessary legal protections for minorities. Others consider civil disobedience to be impermissible lawlessness—the road to anarchy—and even if the conduct is nonviolent and done for a moral purpose, civil disobedience is per se illegal in a society built on the principles of the rule of law.

---

79. *See* Susan Tiefenbrun, *On Civil Disobedience, Jurisprudence, Feminism and the Law in the Antigones of Sophocles and Anouilh*, 11 Cardozo Stud. L. & Literature 35, 36 (Summer 1999), and as revised here in Chapter 7.

80. Leslie Gielow Jacobs, *Applying Penalty Enhancements to Civil Disobedience: Clarifying the Free Speech Clause Model to Bring the Social Value of Political Protest into the Balance*, 59 Ohio St. L.J. 185, 197 (1998) (discussing civil disobedience as expressive conduct not currently protected by the free speech clause of the U.S. Constitution).

81. Coffin & Leibman, *supra* note 45, at 5 (". . . the Supreme Court decided that it was not King but the segregationists he opposed who were civilly disobedient").

82. Mark Edward DeForrest, *Civil Disobedience: Its Nature and Role in the American Legal Landscape*, 33 Gonz. L. Rev. 653, 654 (1997/1998).

A. Arguments For Civil Disobedience

Proponents of civil disobedience claim it is an alternative means to accomplish a valid purpose in society and should be protected as political speech under the First Amendment.[83] John Rawls compares civil disobedience to public speech.[84] But to adduce a free speech argument[85] for civil disobedience, we must determine how far the protection of free speech really goes and whether the form of illegal protest in question is like other protected forms of communication (i.e., gestures, symbolic responses, and other nonverbal acts protected under the First Amendment). Carl Cohen claims that open and uninhibited political criticism is of such fundamental importance in a democracy that such conduct will be protected even when it may appear otherwise rightly unlawful.[86] Martha Minow argues persuasively that the legal system itself *needs* people willing to break the law for political reasons: "The legitimacy of the system itself requires confrontation with disobedience defended by individuals who view compliance as immoral or by individuals seeking to persuade lawful officials to change."[87] Ronald Dworkin refers to civil disobedience as "*justifiable* disobedience"[88] because the conduct is morally motivated. Henry David Thoreau, in his famous essay on *Civil Disobedience*, reminds his readers that all men have the right of revolution, the right to rebel, and the right to refuse allegiance to and to resist the government, when its tyranny or its inefficiency are great and unendurable.[89] Thoreau goes on to say that men who blindly obey the law are "not as men mainly, but as machines."[90] He advocates breaking the law rather than waiting for the slow process of the majority to alter unjust laws.[91]

King, in his famous *Letter from Birmingham Jail*,written while he was in prison for violating a permit to parade and demonstrate, adopts many of Thoreau's radical theories. King refuses to wait any longer for the constitutional and God-given

---

83. *See* Jacobs, *supra* note 80, at 197.

84. *See* Rawls, *supra* note 73, at 365.

85. *See infra*, text accompanying notes 118–32 for a discussion of the constitutionality of civil disobedience as a form of free speech.

86. Carl Cohen, Civil Disobedience: Conscience, Tactics, and the Law 179 (1971) (citing New York Times Co. v. Sullivan, 376 U.S. 254 (1964), protecting the "proud national commitment to the principle that debate on public issues should be uninhibited, robust, and wide open, and that it may well include vehement, caustic, and sometimes unpleasantly sharp attacks on government and public officials").

87. Martha Minow, *Breaking the Law: Lawyers and Clients in Struggles for Social Change*, 52 Harvard L. Rev. 723, 741 (1991).

88. Ronald Dworkin, Taking Rights Seriously 206 (1977).

89. *See* Thoreau, *supra* note 2, at 227.

90. *Id.* at 226.

91. *Id.* at 231. *See* King, *supra* note 48, at 192 ("We have waited for more than 340 years for our constitutional and God-given rights").

rights of Blacks, and he espouses his own form of legal relativism.[92] King goes so far as to say that one has a moral *duty* to disobey unjust laws that are man-made.[93] King's moral argument reflects the legal reasoning of the Nuremberg Tribunal and the London Agreement of August 8, 1945, creating the International Military Tribunal that conducted trials of Nazis. The London Agreement and the Nuremberg trials established the principle that an individual is legally and personally responsible for carrying out unjust laws, even if the individual claims to have merely obeyed superior orders.[94] King claims all people have a moral and a legal obligation to obey just laws, but they have an equally important moral obligation to disobey unjust laws in order to obey a higher, natural, or divine law whose authority preempts man-made laws.[95]

Those who argue that civil disobedience is protected or should be protected by the Constitution find the origins of this argument in conflict-of-law theory. Civil disobedients are torn between obedience to man-made law and to a higher natural law. This argument has deep roots in the history of Western thought: Cicero, Aquinas, Grotius, Locke—even Jefferson who inscribed these words on the Great Seal of the United States: "Rebellion against tyrants is obedience to God."[96] St. Thomas Aquinas declared that "human law does not bind a man in conscience, and if it conflicts with the higher law, human law should not be obeyed."[97] Aquinas is claiming that natural law preempts man-made law. The difficulty inherent in the conflict-of-law argument is the vagueness of natural law and the impossibility to codify it or to determine what it requires or prohibits; therefore, natural law is inapplicable to concrete cases.[98]

---

92. *See* King, *supra* note 48, at 193 ("You express a great deal of anxiety over our willingness to break laws . . . How can you advocate breaking some laws and obeying others? The answer lies in the fact that there are two types of laws: just and unjust. I would be the first to advocate obeying just laws").

93. *Id.* at 193–94. "One has not only a legal but a moral responsibility to obey just laws. Conversely, one has a moral responsibility to disobey unjust laws. I would agree with St. Augustine that 'an unjust law is no law at all.'" *Id.* at 193. "Of course, there is nothing new about this kind of civil disobedience . . . It was practiced superbly by the early Christians, who were willing to face hungry lions and the excruciating pain of chopping blocks rather than submit to certain unjust laws of the Roman Empire . . . In our own nation, the Boston Tea Party represented a massive act of civil disobedience." *Id.* at 194.

94. *See* Fortas, *supra* note 28, at 111.

95. King, *supra* note 48, at 193.

96. *See* Heinrich Rommen, The Natural Law: A Study in Legal and Social History and Philosophy (Thomas R. Hanley trans., 1947), discussing Thomistic philosophy. *See also* Tiefenbrun, *supra* note 79, at notes 33–37 and *infra* Chapter 7 of this book.

97. *See generally* Rommen, *supra* note 96.

98. Tiefenbrun, *supra* note 79, at notes 33–37 and *infra* Chapter 7 of this book.

B. Arguments Against Civil Disobedience

There is much opposition to civil disobedience. For the past two thousand years, philosophers have asked themselves whether people have an obligation to obey an unjust law. Scholars have grounded an obligation to obey unjust laws in six different legal theories:[99] (1) the duty to obey the law out of gratitude to an existing legal system (i.e., Socrates and Plato's *Crito*); (2) the duty to obey the law because of the individual's contractual agreement or consent to obey (i.e., John Locke and Jean-Jacques Rousseau); (3) the duty to obey because of the negative consequences of disobedience; (4) the duty to obey out of fairness; (5) the duty to obey in order to support just institutions (i.e., H.L.A. Hart and John Rawls), and (6) the duty to obey in order to support the community (i.e., Ronald Dworkin).[100]

Proponents of the argument to obey unjust laws out of a debt of gratitude to our legal system have met with three oppositions. First, citizens of the State arguably receive benefits involuntarily, and therefore they do not need to show gratitude to the State by obeying unjust laws. Second, obedience to the law does not necessarily represent the only appropriate way in which to express gratitude to the law. Third, a benefactor must operate from altruistic motives to deserve the beneficiary's gratitude—and the State is not necessarily altruistic.[101]

Proponents of the argument to obey unjust laws out of implied consent to obey the law have been challenged on the theory that citizens did not knowingly "agree" to obey the laws of their community. We cannot infer consent to obey the laws of a place just from continued residence in that location.[102]

Theorists also criticize the argument that it is necessary to obey unjust laws because to do otherwise would have negative consequences. Undesirable consequences do not flow from every act of disobedience; thus, the argument from negative consequences is insufficient to justify a general obligation to obey.[103] The negative consequence theory is even more fallacious when applied to obedience to "bad laws." A bad law might be the very cause of the negative consequences rather than the act of disobedience of the law.

Critics of the duty to obey unjust law based on a fairness theory argue that fairness does not supply a ground for an obligation to obey the law.[104] Rawls argues that an individual's duty to support just institutions requires that individuals "comply with and . . . do their share in just institutions.[105] Opponents argue that

---

99. *See* Teresa M. Bruce, *Neither Liberty Nor Justice: Anti-Gay Initiatives, Political Participation, and the Rule of Law*, Note, 5 CORNELL J.L. & PUB. POL'Y 431, 479–94 (Spring 1996), discussing the six legal theories requiring one to obey unjust laws.

100. *Id.* at 480.

101. *Id.* at 482.

102. *Id.* at 486–87.

103. *Id.* at 487.

104. *Id.* at 489.

105. RAWLS, *supra* note 73, at 114.

individuals have difficulty determining when institutions apply to them. Moreover, a "natural duty" to support institutions does not tie political obligations to the particular community to which individuals have an obligation to belong.[106]

Professor Ronald Dworkin argues that the obligations attaching to familial relationships and friendships do not arise from free choice. The obligation to obey the law derives from the same source as do communal obligations. Dworkin, like Rawls, believes that individuals have natural duties towards justice that override any communal obligation in contravention to justice.

Another argument based on the Machievellian principle that laudable ends do not justify purely illegal means is often used by law-and-order supporters who refuse to consider the benign motivation of civil disobedients. They argue that legitimizing civil disobedience is contrary to a system governed by respect for the rule of law. Erwin Griswold (cited by Dworkin) believes "it is of the essence of law that it is equally applied to all, that it binds all alike, irrespective of personal motive. For this reason, one who contemplates civil disobedience out of moral conviction should not be surprised and must not be bitter if a criminal conviction ensues . . . organized society cannot endure on any other basis."[107] Judge Robert H. Bork believes that civil disobedience is pure lawlessness,[108] political anarchy, and that "there is no reason for courts to protect any advocacy of law violation since that is merely advocacy of a piecemeal overthrow of the democratic system."[109] Critics of civil disobedience as a means of legal reform remind us that under the U.S. system, a person is entitled to challenge the validity of a law being applied against him by resisting its enforcement *in court* on a plea of invalidity, and that lawful resistance to law is a cornerstone of our liberties.[110] Civil disobedience should be only a last resort after negotiation, conciliation, the courts, and Congress have failed.[111]

V. CIVIL DISOBEDIENCE IS NOT PROTECTED BY THE CONSTITUTIONAL RIGHT TO DISSENT OR FREE SPEECH

A. Constitutional Right to Dissent

The First Amendment of the U.S. Constitution guarantees us the right to dissent, to protest, to assemble peaceably, to criticize a law or government, and to

106. Bruce, *supra* note 99, at 491.

107. DWORKIN, *supra* note 88, at 206.

108. ROBERT BORK, THE TEMPTING OF AMERICA: THE POLITICAL SEDUCTION OF THE LAW 334 (1990).

109. *Id.* at 335.

110. Harrison Tweed, Bernard G. Segal & Herbert L. Packer, *Civil Rights and Disobedience to Law*, *in* CIVIL DISOBEDIENCE: THEORY AND PRACTICE 90, 92 (Hugo Adam Bedau, ed., 1969).

111. *Id.* at 97.

oppose a law. The more difficult question is *how* we may permissibly dissent if our first legal and moral imperative is to obey the law. Using means of opposition and dissent permissible under the U.S. system of law will not subject a dissenter to punishment by the State. The right to dissent may be exercised by the use of written and spoken words and by acts or conduct such as picketing, "peaceable" mass assembly, sit-ins[112] and demonstrations (which are referred to as "symbolic speech"). The basic means of permissible protest under the U.S. system is the right to vote, the right to organize, and the right to elect new officials to enact and administer the law.[113] Burning the American flag has been defended as a permissible form of protest and was protected as symbolic speech;[114] however, burning a draft card was found not to be protected because it interfered with the record-keeping function of the U.S. government.[115]

There are occasions when a person may feel morally justified in resorting to impermissible methods of dissent, such as a direct disobedience of a law. The use of impermissible means of dissent is an act of civil disobedience that is done intentionally and for moral purposes, and the disobedient (believing there is no other alternative to accomplish the moral aim) expects to be punished for the unlawful act, irrespective of the noble motivation. U.S. Supreme Court Justice Abe Fortas insisted that a punishable offense will not—and should not—be excused unless the law which is violated (such as a law segregating a public library) is unconstitutional or invalid.[116] If the right to protest or to assemble peaceably is exercised for the purpose of violating valid laws that are reasonably designed to avoid interference with others, the Constitution's guarantees will not shield the protester.[117]

B. Constitutional Right to Free Speech

Breaking the law can be a forceful means of expression and can have effective social value if the violation ultimately accomplishes a reform of bad law. However, the free speech clause of the First Amendment does not protect this form of expressive conduct[118] even if breaking the law is done for a good purpose. The fact that a particular criminal's purpose in breaking the law is to publicize an injustice is no defense to prosecution,[119] and accepting the penalty is part of the dissident's speech. Thus, the U.S. Constitution does not protect civil disobedients from imposition of punishment for their crimes—and to do otherwise

112. Brown v. Louisiana, 383 U.S. 131 (1966). *See* FORTAS, *supra* note 28, at 30.
113. FORTAS, *supra* note 28, at 25.
114. Texas v. Johnson, 491 U.S. 397 (1989).
115. United States v. O'Brien, 391 U.S. 367 (1968).
116. *Id.* at 34.
117. *Id.*
118. *See generally* Jacobs, *supra* note 80.
119. *Id.* at 186.

would subvert the rule of law upon which the U.S. constitutional democracy is based.[120]

There are limitations on the right to free speech. For example, the State has been known to require a permit for mass meetings or demonstrations, or to prescribe reasonable regulations as to when and where to assemble a crowd. Justice Oliver Wendell Holmes made it clear that no one may falsely cry "Fire" in a crowded theater and cause a panic, even though that person may be motivated by good intentions. Good motives do not excuse action that will injure some or diminish the rights of others.[121]

Constitutional First Amendment theory divides protected speech into two categories: (1) speech or pure speech covering expressions through verbal or written words, and (2) conduct. The line between speech and conduct is sometimes hazy.[122] Conduct is either expressive (i.e., communicates a message and is understood by an audience) or non-expressive.[123] Another way to analyze free speech issues is not to classify different types of "speech" or "conduct," but to classify kinds of government restrictions on such speech or conduct. The question then becomes whether the government restriction is aimed at the expressive content of the behavior or whether the government restriction is content-neutral.

The Court will apply a three-pronged test to determine if government restrictions on expressive conduct are permissible: (1) whether the action is within the government's power, (2) whether the action serves an important or substantial governmental purpose, and (3) whether the incidental restriction of speech is no greater than necessary to serve the government's purpose. The inquiry is similar to the deferential rational basis standard.[124] If government action restricting speech is directed at the content of the message, then a strict scrutiny standard applies (unless the government is regulating speech on its own property that it has not opened for expression or the content of the speech falls within one of the categories that the Supreme Court has determined to be entirely unprotected or less protected than most speech).[125]

The U.S. government may suppress unprotected speech and less protected speech subject to a less rigorous balancing test because the Supreme Court has determined that the particular type of speech is of lesser social value than fully protected speech.[126] Only a compelling interest and "means narrowly tailored" to meet that interest will justify a content-based regulation of protected speech. Where a government action is content-neutral, regulating the time, place, or

---

120. *Id.* at 187.
121. FORTAS, *supra* note 28, at 28.
122. Jacobs, *supra* note 80, at 194.
123. *Id.* at 194–95.
124. *Id.* at 196–97.
125. *Id.* at 198.
126. *Id.*

manner of speech rather than its message, the analysis is a balancing test that weighs the legitimacy and importance of the government interest, the impact of the government action, the availability and adequacy of alternate means of speech, the traditions associated with the place of expression, and the affect of the regulation on discrete groups.[127]

Professor Leslie Jacobs applies the traditional free speech clause model to civil disobedience and concludes that civil disobedience is not protected by the U.S. Constitution, even though she recognizes its important social value.[128] Civil disobedience is *expression* conveyed by means of breaking the law, and its most fundamental message is the symbolic statement that comes from deliberately breaking the law. Thus, lawbreaking is *conduct* rather than pure speech. Under the Supreme Court's two-pronged test that looks to speaker intent and audience perception, civil disobedience should, by definition, be deemed *expressive conduct*. It is possible though that civil disobedience would be classified as per se non-expressive conduct because it produces noncommunicative harms that stem from the functional act of breaking the law. If this is true, the free speech clause inquiry would be over at this point. Even if the Court were willing to view civil disobedience as expressive conduct, the traditional free speech clause analysis would terminate almost as quickly. If the government's action is directed at the speech component of the conduct, the government's action becomes highly suspect. If government action is content-neutral, judicial deference would apply, and the action would be deemed valid according to an inquiry that is equivalent to rational basis scrutiny.

Professor Jacobs asserts that civil disobedience should not be judged according to the traditional free speech model summarized above. Moreover, Jacobs argues in favor of the adoption of a different free speech model that would include the public value of civil disobedience and the harms it necessarily causes.[129] Because civil disobedience is intentional lawbreaking done for the purpose of expression and under circumstances where it is likely to be understood, civil disobedience should be viewed as expressive conduct. However, as civil disobedience differs from the broad class of *lawbreaking* and also from[130] the other broad class of *expressive conduct*, Jacobs believes that civil disobedience requires a free speech analysis all its own. Nevertheless, Jacobs realizes that lawbreaking as a protected form of expression could lead to anarchy, and therefore she reasons that civil disobedience cannot be protected under the First Amendment. This reasoning brings to mind the example that we cannot conceive of political assassination as constitutionally protected expression. Moreover, the Supreme Court decided in 1993 that physical assault cannot be "expressive conduct

127. *Id.* at 200.
128. *Id.* at 202.
129. *Id.* at 218.
130. *Id.* at 231.

protected by the First Amendment."[131] Although Jacobs rightly concludes that civil disobedients should be subject to penalty, she argues persuasively that civil disobedients should not be subject to enhanced penalties.[132]

VI. CONCLUSION AND THE DELICATE BALANCE

This chapter has shown that the U.S. Constitution probably will not—and should not—protect nonviolent civil disobedience by exempting it from punishment because to do so would undermine respect for the rule of law and erode effectiveness of the very act of civil disobedience itself. Arguably, the Constitution may "permit" civil disobedience and offer some protection against excessive punishment, but the Constitution cannot exempt civil disobedients from reasonable punishment or penalties for disobeying the law. The Constitution might protect civil disobedients from excessive or enhanced penalty because of the expressive or even moral purpose of civil disobedience. Those who in good faith engage in civil disobedience as a form of protest with the aim of reforming what they consider to be unjust laws are caught in the tension between the right of resistance and the right to live in a safe, orderly system of government. The Constitution certainly will not protect civil disobedience coupled with violence. The individual's constitutional rights to free speech, to protest, and to dissent must be balanced delicately with the right to live in an ordered society.

Supreme Court Justice Abe Fortas explained that the Constitution seeks to accommodate two conflicting values, each of which is fundamental: (1) the need for the right to speak freely, to protest effectively, to organize and to demonstrate; and (2) the need to maintain order so that other people's rights and the peace and security of the State will not be impaired.[133] To strike the proper balance between these two competing principles, the courts will decide whether a particular form of protest or resistance to the law is within the confines of the First Amendment or whether the protesters have overstepped the broad limits in which constitutional protection is guaranteed. If the dissenting, protesting, picketing, or staging "freedom walks" or mass demonstrations are peaceable, and if the protesters comply with reasonable regulations designed to protect the general public without substantially interfering with effective protest, then the Constitution will protect this form of expressive speech.[134] Moreover, the State is obligated constitutionally to protect protestors who march peaceably as in the famous Selma march.[135] Many of us stood by speechless as Neo-Nazis marched in Skokie with

131. Wisconsin v. Mitchell, 508 U.S. 476, 484 (1993).
132. Jacobs, *supra* note 80, at 233.
133. Fortas, *supra* note 28, at 36.
134. *Id.* at 37.
135. *Id.* at 44.

the constitutionally mandated protection afforded by the government under the First Amendment. But if any of these forms of dissent or protest are done with the intent to cause unlawful action (such as a riot or an assault upon others), or to cause injury to the property of others (such as a stampede for exits or the breaking of doors or windows), and if such unlawful action or injury occurs, the dissenter will not be protected by the Constitution.[136] The dissenter may be arrested, and if properly charged and convicted of violating a law, the dissenter will not be saved by the First Amendment. For civil disobedience to be an effective means of legislative reform, penalty must be a component of the free speech act and a necessary result of breaking the law, even if the purpose is noble and the ultimate consequences of the act are beneficial to society.

136. *Id.* at 38.

6. SEMIOTICS AND MARTIN LUTHER KING'S *LETTER FROM BIRMINGHAM JAIL*[*]

I. INTRODUCTION: *THE LETTER*

Many literary works have been written about legal issues as lofty as civil disobedience. The *Letter from Birmingham Jail* (*Letter*) by Martin Luther King, Jr.[1] is one of the classics in the literature of civil disobedience,[2] which belongs on the shelf next to Sophocles' *Antigone*, Henry David Thoreau's *Walden and Civil Disobedience*,[3] Gandhi's writings, and Jean Anouilh's *Antigone*. One of the many black men suffering in "the prison of segregation,"[4] King wrote the *Letter* from his prison cell on the margins of a newspaper. King was jailed on Good Friday, April 12, 1963, for failing to obtain a parade permit from the Birmingham city commission and for disobeying a court order forbidding civil rights leaders from taking part in or encouraging demonstrations.[5] What emerges from these scraps of paper is a

---

* This chapter first appeared as an article in 2 CARDOZO STUDIES IN LAW AND LITERATURE 255–87 (1992). It has been revised, updated, and adapted to the themes investigated in this book.

1. Martin Luther King, Jr., *Letter from Birmingham Jail, in* WHY WE CAN'T WAIT 77 (1963).

2. David Luban, *Legal Storytelling: Difference Made Legal: The Court and Dr. King*, 87 MICH. L. REV. 2 152, 2164 (1989).

3. Thoreau's views on civil disobedience and the existence of unjust laws are similar to those of King. *See* HENRY DAVID THOREAU, ON THE DUTY OF CIVIL DISOBEDIENCE 223 (1960) ("It is not desirable to cultivate a respect for the law, so much as for the right . . . Law never made men a whit more just"). Thoreau discusses unjust laws and King defines them. Thoreau says, "Unjust laws exist: shall we be content to obey them, or shall we endeavor to amend them, and obey them until we have succeeded, or shall we transgress them at once: men generally, under such a government as this, think that they ought to wait until they have persuaded the majority to alter them. They think that, if they should resist, the remedy would be worse than the evil. But it is the fault of the government itself that the remedy is worse than the evil. It makes it worse . . . If the injustice is part of the necessary friction of the machine of government, let it go, let it go." *Id.* at 228–29.

4. MARTIN LUTHER KING, JR., STRENGTH TO LOVE 83 (1981).

5. *See* Luban, *supra* note 2, at 2162 for a detailed analysis of the Supreme Court majority opinion in Walker v. City of Birmingham, 388 U.S. 307 (1967), sustaining King's conviction. Despite his failure to obtain a parade permit, and in defiance of the ex parte injunction from Alabama Circuit Court that Judge W. A. Jenkins, Jr. served on Thursday April 11, 1963 at 1:00 AM, King went ahead with his planned demonstration on Good Friday and was arrested. A second demonstration took place on Easter Sunday, with several demonstrators being arrested and found guilty of criminal contempt by Judge Jenkins.

literary, legal, and religious masterpiece, an apology for civil disobedience, via a letter written personally to the eight white moderate clergymen who attacked civil rights protesters publicly. The *Letter* ranks high among the masterpieces of prison literature, like the philosophy of Gramsci[6] and the poems of Verlaine. The *Letter* is a call to arms without violence, a plea for freedom, and a cry for communal brotherhood. But King's epistolary message comes in a strange envelope: a medium designed to shock and disturb its readers by creating a crisis in order to cause constructive tension. King's *Letter* stands the world on its head when in it he proclaims that man's failure to disobey an unjust law is as evil as his resisting justice.[7]

King's goal in the *Letter* is to create publicity, to cause a reaction, and to shock his white moderate readers out of the "dark dungeons of complacency to the bright hills of creative protest."[8] King uses the force of language to accomplish his goal. The philosophy of the *Letter* and its soul-stirring language lift the spirit, jostle the mind, and cause the reader to become a creative mediator as King wrestles with the question of man's obligation to obey unjust laws. The *Letter* is more than just a defense of nonviolent direct action—it is a debunking of the American dream of equality and freedom. Poetic, persuasive, and passionate, the *Letter* is designed to disturb its readers and to reverse their expectations by King's calculated use of contradiction.[9] "One who breaks an unjust law . . . is in reality expressing the highest respect for law."[10] At first blush this hyperbolic metaphor contradicts a generally accepted norm that laws must be obeyed. The affirmation reverses the reader's expectation and causes what King called a "constructive non-violent tension"[11] through creative wordplay.

These demonstrators, including King, were sentenced to five days in jail and a $50 fine. The Walker Court upheld this conviction. While King was in jail, eight white clergymen took out a full-page advertisement in the Birmingham News denouncing the demonstrators' actions. It was to this public denunciation that King responded from his prison cell.

6. Anthony Cook, *Beyond Critical Legal Studies: The Reconstructive Theology of Dr. Martin Luther King, Jr.*, 103 Harv. L. Rev. 985, 1013 (1990). Cook discusses Gramsci's conception of the organic intellectual that he claims provides a useful framework for understanding the thought of King. "Gramsci's organic intellectual struggles to transform those who are oppressed as a means of transforming the conditions under which they are oppressed." Antonio Gramsci, Selections from the Prison Notebooks of Antonio Gramsci 332–33 (Q. Hoare & G. Smith eds., 1971).

7. *See* King, Jr., *supra* note 1, at 86 ("One who breaks an unjust law . . . is in reality expressing the highest respect for law").

8. *Id.* at 95.

9. Douglas Sturm, *Crisis in the American Republic: The Legal and Political Significance of Martin Luther King's "Letter from a Birmingham Jail"*, 2 J. L. & Religion 309, 314 (1984) ("The letter, though addressed to a particular occasion, is thus an ideogram, revealing contradictory principles at the heart of the American social order").

10. *See* King, *supra* note 1, at 86.

11. *Id.* at 81.

King's wordplay is structured on the principles of similarity and difference. Stated simply, the message contained in the *Letter* is that racial difference is nothing more than similarity disguised. The *Letter* deconstructs[12] the myth that racial equality exists in America by first confirming the existence of racial differences, then rejecting the notion of "difference made legal," a concept King considered to be the basis of unjust laws.[13] King accomplished this deconstruction by playing a highly sophisticated structural and stylistic game of semiotics. As discussed in Chapter 2, semiotics is the aesthetic metalanguage that when applied to a literary text can penetrate the surface of its specialized discourse and uncover deeply embedded meanings. In the case before us today, the discourse to which we shall apply semiotic theory is the *Letter* by Martin Luther King, Jr., which has both literary and legal significance.

II. SEMIOTICS

A. Codes

In literary discourse, messages are often concealed in a coded form, embedded in a symbolic language containing the essence of a referent. In semiotic parlance, a *code* refers to words that belong to the same metaphoric or metonymic semantic field, with these words being related to each other either by contiguity or similarity.[14] For example, King's choice of the words *dark dungeons of complacency*[15]

---

12. *See* J.M. Balkin, *Deconstructive Practice and Legal Theory*, 96 YALE L.J. 743 (1987) for an excellent summary of Jacques Derrida's deconstructive theory, a list of Derrida's works, and application of this theory to the analysis of legal writing. *See also* a special issue of the *Cardozo Law Review* devoted to Derrida's theory and its application to the law. *Deconstruction and the Possibility of Justice*, 11 CARDOZO L. REV. 919 (1990). For a view radically opposed to deconstruction, *see* RICHARD POSNER, LAW AND LITERATURE: A MISUNDERSTOOD RELATION 211–16 (1988). Posner believes "the particulars of deconstruction have nothing to contribute to law." According to Posner and other adversaries of deconstructive theory, deconstruction invites political nihilism. *Cf.* Robert Weisberg, *The Law-Literature Enterprise*, 1 YALE J.L. & HUMAN. 1, 47 (1988). *See also* Peter Goodrich, *Rhetoric, Grammatology and the Hidden Injuries of Law*, 18 ECON. & SOC'Y 167 (1989), *reprinted in* PETER GOODRICH, LANGUAGES OF LAW: FROM LOGICS OF MEMORY TO NOMADIC MASKS 111–48 (1990).

13. *See* King, *supra* note 1, at 85 ("An unjust law is a code that a numerical or power majority group compels a minority group to obey but does not make binding on itself. This is *difference* made legal. By the same token, a just law is a code that a majority compels a minority to follow and that it is willing to follow itself. This is sameness made legal.").

14. *See* Susan Tiefenbrun, *Legal Semiotics*, 5 CARDOZO ARTS & ENT. L.J. 89 (1986) reviewing the history of semiotics as it developed in France and in the United States as well as the relationship of semiotics to other disciplines such as the law; *see supra* Chapter 2 of this book.

15. *See* King, *supra* note 1, at 95.

is an expressive metaphor based on color and relative height. This metaphor is related by similarity to several others in the *Letter*, as for example the "dark depths of prejudice"[16] and the "dark mountain of disappointment."[17] Structural semioticians[18] analyze these metaphors as variants of a basic pattern that is more or less concealed in the symbolic and literary representation.

Literary language is characterized by the high frequency of coded symbols, which attract the reader's[19] attention because the symbols emphasize form rather than content. The reader who sees the form (e.g., a metaphor, a metonymy, an understatement, etc.) may be a bit puzzled by its meaning, then become naturally moved to figure out the significance of the coded message. Readers of the *Letter* are immediately captured by its persuasive and poetic style. The style of the *Letter* is the symbolic *signifier* conveying messages or *signifieds* about legal issues of significance.

B. Decoding the Messages

How does the reader know when an important message is hidden between the lines? Issues having significance are signaled by repetition, emphatic language, and clustering of rhetorical tropes and figures such as metaphor, metonymy, comparison, antithesis, allusion, irony, and a myriad of literary conventions, all of which King used in his *Letter* and which are the author's vehicles for the communication of his messages. In other words, King's messages, which have legal significance, are transmitted indirectly through a literary and rhetorical communication system requiring *decoding* or interpretation to understand their significance. When the reader sees a cluster of rhetorical figures or literary devices in the *Letter*, she usually slows down the reading in an attempt to decipher the hidden meaning. In the language of communication theory, the reader attempts to perceive a set of equivalents existing between the symbolic system and the referential system. These equivalents or variants of a structure or pattern[20] constitute the textual material to be decoded. Once the reader has determined what the symbols actually refer to, then meaningful communication among the author, the reader, and the text takes place.

---

16. *Id.* at 81.

17. *Id.* at 97.

18. *See* BERNARD S. JACKSON, SEMIOTICS AND LEGAL THEORY 3 (1985), on the range of semiotic theories and the differences between Peircian (pragmatic) and Saussurian (structuralist) semiotics.

19. For a more detailed discussion of the nature of King's audience and the role of the reader, *see infra* text at Section III.

20. Legal semiotics and semiotics in general tend to focus on the study of recurrent patterns within a discourse. *See* Jeremy Paul, *The Politics of Legal Semiotics*, 69 TEX. L. REV. 1779, 1780 (1991).

C. Interpretation and Decoding

Most readers engage in this process of decoding without even knowing it. They become keenly aware of the process when they are confronted with a text that is hard to understand or interpret. How does a reader know his interpretation is valid? Because literary language is indirect and symbolic, it is conceivable that a string of symbolic words might have several different meanings or interpretations. In fact, the use of symbolic language encourages multiplicity of meaning. This is why law students are very quickly cautioned not to use "poetic" language in their briefs, but rather to develop what Roland Barthes referred to as a "degree zero" style, a "colourless writing . . . a neutral writing . . . which deliberately foregoes any elegance or ornament"[21] and which is clear, univalent, and not subject to varying interpretations. Stated differently, law students should develop a writing style that does not invite indeterminacy of interpretation or meaning.

Literary language may be interpretable, but there are limits to the interpretations possible. Just as the imposition of a code limits the entropy of a system (be it aesthetic, legal, or other), so the semantic context of a text limits and controls the interpretation of its coded message. Thus, the meaning of the literary text having legal significance is not entirely indeterminate.[22]

An aesthetic text, such as the *Letter*, conveys messages in a symbolic language. The text carries within it the seeds of its own constructive deconstruction by the reader. Intent on deciphering the hidden messages of the text, the reader engages in an analytical quest of decoding and creating meanings that may be unknown even to the author. The nature of this analytical quest is semiotics.[23]

Stated otherwise, decoding is a process semioticians use to penetrate the surface of a text and excavate meanings buried below the signs of its written language.[24] This process of uncovering meaning is the basis of semiotics and is best expressed by the equation *sign = signifier/signified*, where the line above the signified represents the surface of the text. One of the central principles of Ferdinand de Saussure's work in semiology[25] is that signs (words, legal concepts,

21. Roland Barthes, WRITING DEGREE ZERO AND ELEMENTS OF SEMIOLOGY 76–78 (A. Lavers & C. Smith trans., 1967).

22. *See* Charles Yablon, *The Indeterminacy of the Law: Critical Legal Studies and the Problem of Legal Explanation* 6 CARDOZO L. REV. 197 (1985).

23. Confusion surrounding the term *semiotics* is legendary. For Peirce, the term was *semiotic* in the singular; for Saussure it was *semiology*. Americans now use the term *semiotics* in the plural while the French have adopted the term *la sémiotique* in the singular. *See* Thomas Sebeok, *The Semiotic Web: A Chronicle of Prejudices*, 2 BULLETIN OF LITERARY SEMIOTICS 1, 8–15 (1976).

24. SUSAN TIEFENBRUN, SIGNS OF THE HIDDEN: SEMIOTIC STUDIES (1980) (an introduction to semiotic theory and its application to literary texts of the seventeenth century); *see also* SUSAN TIEFENBRUN, THE CLASSICAL SIGN (1984).

25. FERDINAND DE SAUSSURE, COURSE IN GENERAL LINGUISTICS (W. Baskin trans., 1959).

theories, etc.) derive their meaning from mutual relationships in a system of signification.[26] Decoding is the determination of the mutual relationship between signifier and signified. In this chapter, I shall engage in this process of decoding to tease out of the *Letter* King's stated and hidden messages about racial discrimination and civil disobedience. The goal is not only to uncover the legal issues in a literary text but to appreciate the artful and persuasive manner in which King communicated his messages.

III. ROLE OF THE READER

Who are King's readers? Initially the readers are eight white moderate clergymen of different religious backgrounds. Eventually through publicity, King's readership expanded to include the public at large and anyone concerned about human rights. King's language is imbued with religious imagery (mainly from the New Testament), and his *Letter* is an apology for the values of the Christian religion. Nevertheless, the *Letter* addresses Christians, Jews, and people of any faith because he firmly believed in the essential similarity of all human beings regardless of faith and color.

King's *Letter* is disturbing! He tries to shake middle class whites into the realization that blacks are victims of discrimination and racial inequality. But he launches his nonviolent attack on complacency persuasively through subtlety and the art of understatement.[27] King plays a clever game with his readers, the name of which I call *differentiation and equalization*. The game is based on the principles of similarity and difference. Although the game is subtle and enticing, it requires active participation by the readers. King initially sets up thematic oppositions based on the structure of difference, the logic of which the reader has no trouble understanding, but then he equalizes these oppositions and destroys them, much to the dismay of the reader.

For example, at the very beginning of the *Letter*, King addresses the reader's attention to the clergymen's claim that King is an "outsider" and does not belong in Birmingham, Alabama. First, King admits that he is an outsider, but he argues that he has the right to be in Birmingham because he was invited there and because he has organizational ties with the Southern Christian Leadership

---

26. *See* J.M. Balkin, *The Hohfeldian Approach to Law and Semiotics*, 44 U. Miami L. Rev. 1119, 1121 (1990).

27. *See, e.g.*, King, *supra* note 1, at 98. After vividly describing such brutal police tactics as "dogs sinking their teeth into unarmed, nonviolent Negroes" and the "ugly and inhumane treatment of Negroes here in the city jail" where the police "refuse to give us food because we wanted to sing our grace together," King then states ironically in a classical understatement: "I cannot join you in your praise of the Birmingham police department."

Conference whose affiliated organization is in Alabama.[28] Second, although King admits he is an "outsider," he claims that he belongs in Birmingham because injustice is there. Like the prophets of the eighth century and like St. Paul, King must leave home and respond to the call for aid.[29] Third, King claims that he is not really an "outsider" because all communities and states are interrelated. He says, "I cannot sit idly by in Atlanta and not be concerned about what happens in Birmingham. Injustice anywhere is a threat to justice everywhere."[30] Thus, King reverses his initial premise that he is an outsider and, through the force of language and the rhetorical figures of opposition ("justice," "injustice") and hyperbole ("anywhere," "everywhere"), he proves that the concept of an outsider does not exist. "Anyone who lives inside the United States can never be considered an outsider anywhere within its bounds."[31]

Another example of King's linguistic gymnastics and his depolarization of opposition is seen in his initial, understated claim that he is not an extremist. "You speak of our activity in Birmingham as extreme. At first I was rather disappointed that fellow clergymen would see my nonviolent efforts as those of an extremist."[32] King then affirms his opposition to extremism by contrasting himself to the extreme black nationalists. He then modifies his non-extremist position by stating that he is a mediator between the two forces of extremism and non-extremism. "I have tried to stand between these two forces, saying that we need emulate neither the 'do-nothingism' of the complacent nor the 'hatred and despair' of the black nationalist."[33] Finally, King reverses his initial claim of non-extremism, contradicts himself, and admits that he is an extremist like Christ ("the extremist for love");[34] like St. Paul ("the extremist for the Christian gospel");[35] and like Martin Luther, John Bunyan, Abraham Lincoln, and Thomas Jefferson. King identifies himself with Biblical figures (prophets such as Paul, Amos, Jesus, Shadrach, Meshach, and Abednego); with Christian dissidents (martyrs, Luther, Bunyan); with theological philosophers (Augustine, Aquinas, Buber, Tillich); with American egalitarians (Jefferson, Lincoln); and finally with the greatest of all civil disobedients, Socrates. He identifies himself with these unimpeachable figures whom he calls "extremists" to encourage the readers to see the similarity between these praiseworthy men and King himself.

The reader, caught in the middle of this depolarization process, is left with a sense of ambiguity and disturbance that causes her to read and reread the *Letter*

---

28. *Id.* at 78.
29. *Id.*
30. *Id.* at 79.
31. *Id.*
32. *Id.* at 91.
33. *Id.* at 90.
34. *Id.* at 92.
35. *Id.*

more deeply and more creatively in an attempt to make sense out of what appears to be nonsense or contradiction. The act of slowing down the reading process is the reader's attempt at uncovering "the meaning between the lines," as the saying usually goes, but which is more accurately described as "the meaning below the words" and "behind" the stylistic device of contradiction. Contradiction teases and tempts the reader into taking a closer look at what is really meant by the author. Like fine-tuning a microscope, this closer look has the beneficial and pleasurable effect of producing a discovery by the reader of the minute and often invisible secrets of the text.

But the reader's role in this game is assisted by the author. As do his readers who act as mediators reconciling the author's contradictory ideas in the *Letter*, King mediates somewhere between believing the illusory evidence of racial difference (which he presents and confirms), and believing the more convincing evidence of hidden human similarity that is synthesized in his philosophy of communal brotherhood. In short, King plays a sameness/difference game, and the reader's failure to participate in it will result in confusion and misreading.

Thus, there is active complicity among the author, the readers, and the text that results in an intellectually challenging game called reading and interpreting. The signal to start the game is located on the surface of the text, visible for all to see, but the target of the game is not always apparent; rather it is deeply embedded in a region somewhere between the signifier and the signified located in the mind of the reader. The reader's role in this game is to determine the relationship between the signifier and signified to identify and better understand the hidden meanings. The interplay of similarity and difference, triggered by the author King and actualized by the reader, results in the reader's ultimate sense of pleasure[36] that comes from his creative participation in the game. Like King, the reader is the mediator who teases meaning out of the linguistic fabric[37] of the *Letter*.

King actually encourages all men and women to engage in creative participation and protest.[38] Ironically, by enticing his readers into playing the game of reading and interpretation, King has momentarily transformed the readers of the literary *Letter* into the kind of creative participant he wishes the moderate whites to become. King's medium cleverly fulfills his message that all men are the same, interrelated, and connected in a "World House" of brotherhood.

---

36. Roland Barthes, Le Plaisir du Texte (1973).

37. *See* Balkin, *supra* note 12, at 743.

38. *E.g.*, "We must use time *creatively in* the knowledge that the time is always ripe to do right." *See* King, *supra* note 1, at 89. "Now is the time to make real the promise of democracy and transform our pending national elegy into a *creative* psalm of brotherhood." *Id.* at 90. "Perhaps the South, the nation and the world are in dire need of *creative* extremists." *Id.* at 92.

Echoing King's hope and faith in the ultimate success of the blacks,[39] the reader is hopeful by the end of the *Letter* and has shaken off all doubts and fears inspired by its ambiguities and by King's desperate cries for help. The reader is left with a deeper sense of satisfaction in the knowledge that King's alternations between despair and optimism are synthesized in his utopian vision of equality in brotherhood. The reader's interpretive role in the unraveling of King's network of Hegelian dialectics is an essential part of King's message, but it is a difficult role that is greatly enhanced by the magnifying lens of semiotics.

IV. GENRE OF THE *LETTER*

The *Letter* resembles a legal brief. King presents arguments convincingly for and against immediate nonviolent direct action to protest racial discrimination and enforce the right of equality. But unlike a good legal brief that is clear and persuasive, King's *Letter* is contradictory and ambiguous. This semantic and stylistic dissonance[40] (which is designed to wrench conservative white moderates out of their political and legal indifference) does not go unnoticed by the readers who are more than just the eight clergymen to whom the *Letter* is addressed.[41]

King's *Letter* is both personal and public. It is a personal letter written to only eight clergymen who criticized the civil rights protesters for causing trouble in Birmingham. However, the *Letter* is not unlike the Epistles of Paul, and we are reminded that Paul often used to write letters from jail.[42] The literary prototype of King's *Letter* is Paul's Epistle to the Galatians, which became public.[43] The *Letter* is also public in the tradition of Emile Zola's 1898 letter written to the president of France denouncing Dreyfus.[44]

---

39. *Id.* at 97 ("I have no despair about the future . . . We will reach the goal of freedom in Birmingham and all over the nation, because the goal of America is freedom").

40. *See* Cook, *supra* note 6, at 985 for a discussion of how King synthesized disparate strands of theological and political thought and created a prophetic vision of a reconstructed society.

41. *See supra* at Section III for a discussion of King's audience. *See* Keith D. Miller, VOICE OF DELIVERANCE: THE LANGUAGE OF MARTIN LUTHER KING, JR. AND ITS SOURCES OF LIBERATION 163 (1992). The *Letter* was King's response to eight moderate clergy, and it first appeared in *Christian Century*, *Liberation*, and *Christianity and Crisis*, three left-of-center journals and in pamphlets disseminated by the Fellowship of Reconciliation and another leftist, pacifist organization, the American Friends Service Committee. It appeared later in other liberal periodicals. Publication in the *New York Post* and in the *San Francisco Chronicle* further expanded King's readership.

42. *See* Miller, *supra* note 41, at 161.

43. *See infra* at Section V for a discussion of St. Paul's *Epistles to the Galatians.*

44. Haig Bosmajian, *The Letter from Birmingham Jail, in* MARTIN LUTHER KING JR., A PROFILE 128 (C. Eric Lincoln ed., 1970).

King's *Letter* can also be classified as a modern version of an oration from ancient Greece or Rome.[45] The *Letter* seems to follow the steps of a typical classical speech: introduction, proposition, division, confirmation, refutation, and peroration. King extends his arguments through short digressions and repetition, a standard classical strategy. King wrote the greater part of his argument in the form of a refutation.[46] Thus, the *Letter* constitutes the development of an extended refutation of the major and minor premises of the eight clergymen's implicit syllogisms.[47]

V. INTERTEXTUALITY AND THE *LETTER*: BIBLICAL ALLUSIONS

The *Letter* is deceptively simple and covers a complex system of intertextuality (textual references and allusions to other texts) whose meanings require the assistance of a learned and cultivated reader to unravel. King makes explicit Biblical allusions to the Apostle Paul, Amos, Jesus, Shadrach, Meshach, and Abednego, and implicit allusions to unnamed Biblical passages from the Book of Acts,[48] the Book of Amos,[49] St. Paul's Epistle to the Galatians,[50] the Sermon on the Mount,[51] and the Book of Daniel, all of which are designed to defend the principles of the Christian religion and to condemn white moderates and the inactive religious leadership of the Southern churches. Through these allusions King hopes to rekindle the spirit of the early authentic Church, the Church full of sacrifice and martyrdom, the "inner spiritual church, the church within the church . . . the true *ekklesia* and the hope of the world,"[52] the Church that is ready to fight and die for just causes, in contrast to the contemporary Southern white churches that are beautiful but ineffectual.

45. *See* Miller, *supra* note 41, at 167.

46. *See infra* at Sections VI–IX for an analysis of King's refutation.

47. *See* Miller, *supra* note 41, at 167.

48. "And a vision appeared to Paul in the night: a man of Macedonia was standing beseeching him and saying: Come over to Macedonia, and help us." (Acts 16:9).

49. "Let justice roll down like waters and righteousness like an ever-flowing stream." *See* King, *supra* note 1, at 92.

50. "I bear in my body the marks of the Lord Jesus." *Id.* at 92 quoting Galatians 6:17. This passage is a New Testament declaration that love and community stand above the law. *See* Luban, *supra* note 2, at 2196.

51. King quotes the "love your enemies" verse from the Sermon on the Mount. (Matthew 5:44): "The Sermon on the Mount radicalizes the message of love by extending it to those unlike oneself. This message is in consonance with King's rejection of difference and his proposal of universal community." *See* Luban, *supra* note 2, at 2197.

52. *See* King, *supra* note 1, at 96–97.

VI. BIBLICAL UNDERPINNINGS OF MARTIN LUTHER KING'S ANTI-LAW STANCE

Characteristic of King's duality, the *Letter* is both reverent and irreverent toward the law. The source of King's anti-law position is in the writings of St. Augustine,[53] St. Paul, Jesus Christ, and the natural law theory of St. Thomas Aquinas, whom King cites throughout the *Letter*.[54] King shared St. Augustine's view that unjust laws are not laws at all, and therefore, man may and should disobey them. The civil disobedient should welcome imprisonment as did the Christian martyrs who welcomed sacrifice.[55]

Despite the Biblical underpinnings of King's view on civil disobedience, the eight clergymen accused King of an inherent contradiction in his logic.[56] They could not reconcile King's own willingness to disobey an Alabama court order prohibiting demonstration and protest and his continued appeal to the whites to obey the Supreme Court's desegregation orders. King's views on civil disobedience emerge from his refutation of that accusation.

King's belief that love and community stand above the law are not unlike those of St. Paul expressed in the Epistle to the Galatians.[57] Community and brotherhood in faith were more important to Paul than fidelity to established law.[58] Paul's Epistle to the Galatians, which is the prototype of King's *Letter*, was taken from Christ's Sermon on the Mount, which rejected the Mosaic law.[59]

---

53. "I would agree with St. Augustine that 'an unjust law is no law at all.'" *Id.* at 84.

54. "To put it in the terms of St. Thomas Aquinas: An unjust law is a human law that is not rooted in eternal law and natural law." *Id.* at 85. *See* St. Thomas Aquinas, *The Summa Theologica, in* Great Books of the Western World 11, Part I, Second Part Q. 97, Art. 6 (Robert Maynard Hutchins ed., 1952). St. Thomas Aquinas grapples with the basic question of civil disobedience: "Whether he who is under a law may act beside the letter of the law?"

55. "There was a time when the church was very powerful—in the time when the early Christians rejoiced at being deemed worthy to suffer for what they believed." *See* King, *supra* note 1, at 96. "They have left their secure congregations and walked the streets of Albany, Georgia, with us. They have gone down the highways of the South on tortuous rides for freedom. Yes, they have gone to jail with us." *Id.* at 97.

56. "You express a great deal of anxiety over our willingness to break laws . . . One may well ask: "How can you advocate breaking some laws and obeying others?" *Id.* at 84.

57. "Christ redeemed us from the curse of the law. . . ." (Galatians 3:13). "Now before faith came, we were confined under the law, kept under restraint until faith should be revealed. So that the law was our custodian until Christ came, that we might be justified by faith. But now that faith has come, we are no longer under a custodian."(Galatians 3:23–25).

58. "We must obey God rather than men." (Acts 5:29).

59. "Christ redeemed us from the curse of the law . . . For the whole law is fulfilled in one word: You shall love your neighbor as yourself." (Galatians 3:13; 5:14).

Christ's anti-law positions are as ambivalent and contradictory as King's.[60] Just as Paul understood the Sermon on the Mount to be Christ's reevaluation and rejection of the Mosaic law, King's *Letter* is a reevaluation and rejection of the laws on racial discrimination. King's Biblical reference to Shadrach, Meshach, and Abednego creates an identity between the Alabama demonstrators' form of civil disobedience and "the refusal of Shadrach, Meshach and Abednego to obey the laws of Nebuchadnezzar, on the ground that a higher moral law was at stake."[61]

King states his views on law in a classically contradictory fashion, but his words are musical as they resonate with the wisdom of Christ, the anti-law theory of St. Paul, and the natural law theory of St. Thomas Aquinas: "One who breaks an unjust law must do so openly, lovingly, and with a willingness to accept the penalty. I submit that an individual who breaks a law that conscience tells him is unjust, and who willingly accepts the penalty of imprisonment in order to arouse the conscience of the community over its injustice, is in reality expressing the highest respect for law."[62]

VII. PLATO'S *ALLEGORY OF THE CAVE*

Besides King's biblical allusions, which bring credibility and validity to his controversial views on the law, King's *Letter* is full of literary and philosophical references to Sophocles, Socrates, Plato, and many others. Plato's *Allegory of the Cave*[63]

---

60. "Think not that I have come to abolish the law and the prophets; I have come not to abolish them but to fulfill them." (Matthew 5:17–18).

61. *See* King, *supra* note 1, at 86–87. *See* Luban, *supra* note 2, at 2199 for a detailed discussion of the biblical allusions in the *Letter* and the religious sources of King's anti-law position.

62. *See* King, *supra* note 1, at 86.

63. Plato, *Republic, in Great Dialogues of Plato* (W.H.D. Rouse trans. 1956). The *Allegory of the Cave* is in Book VII of Plato's *Republic.* Socrates tells the story of the cave that illustrates the escape of the philosopher from the fetters and darkness of the physical world of the senses to the freedom and dazzling radiance of the world of the mind (*Id.* at 122). However, the philosopher must eventually return to the cave to enlighten and set free those still imprisoned there. For Socrates the world of the senses, as expressed by man's existence in the cave, is constantly changing. The world of the mind is unchanging and is expressed by the light. King utilizes the metaphors of darkness, shadows, and a variant of these (clouds) to express his despair about persistent prejudice and the myth of equality. *E.g.*, "As in so many past experiences, our hopes had been blasted, and the *shadow* of deep disappointment settled upon us." *See* King, *supra* note 1, at 80. "Just as Socrates felt that it was necessary to create a tension in the mind so that individuals could rise from the bondage of myths and half-truths to the unfettered realm of creative analysis and objective appraisal, so must we see the need for nonviolent gadflies to create the kind of tension in society that will help men rise from the *dark* depths of prejudice and racism to the majestic heights of understanding and brotherhood." *Id.* at 81. ". . . Funtown is closed to colored

is a recurring leitmotif throughout the *Letter*. The "cave" is a metaphor of the very essence of semiotic theory, which seeks to find truth behind the shadows and demystifies hidden antinomies of language and thought. As did Plato, King believed that whatever is visible on the surface of things is only a shadow of the true reality, a mere representation of the truth hidden below. As with the semiotician, King's goal is to uncover hidden realities and to deconstruct myths that keep men complacent and uncommitted about the goals of racial equality.

King undertook this process of deconstruction by making use of a literary technique designed to create a mere illusion of difference: the myth. Once King establishes the myth of difference, he then destroys it by pointing out the inherent similarities in the opposed entities. To create the illusion of difference, King also resorts to comparisons, antitheses, contrasts, contradictions, and reversals of his point of view that all constitute the fabric of a complex network of binary oppositions. These illusions of difference are the equivalents of Plato's shadows on the walls of the cave. King gently and creatively equalizes and inevitably destroys these oppositions by creating yet another illusion of similarity through the use of similes, parallelisms, repetition, coupling, identities,[64] and a sophisticated system of intertextuality.

VIII. HISTORICAL AND LEGAL CONTEXT OF THE *LETTER*

The *Letter* was composed in April 1963, a turning point in the black struggle for racial equality.[65] To establish the immediate historical context of the *Letter*, let us go back only as far as 1948 when there was a strong civil rights platform in the Democratic convention echoing Truman's civil rights program begun in 1947.

---

children, and see ominous *clouds* of inferiority beginning to form in her little mental sky." *Id.* at 83. The *Allegory of the Cave* represents two states of mind: belief and illusion and the ascent of the mind from illusion to pure philosophy. Socrates refers to the difference between substance and shadow. Like the blacks who are imprisoned in racial segregation, the men in the cave have been prisoners there since they were children, "their legs and necks being so fastened that they can only look straight ahead of them and cannot turn their heads." PLATO, THE REPUBLIC 278 (H.D. Lee trans., 1955) ("A fire is burning behind and above the prisoners in the cave. A curtain wall and a road separates the prisoners from the fire. Prisoners see only shadows of the real objects outside the cave").

64. *See* Balkin, *supra* note 12, at 748 on the role of identity in Derridean deconstructive theory to reverse oppositional hierarchies. "Philosophers have regarded identity as a basic ground for metaphysical thought: Anything that exists is identical to itself. Difference is a derivative concept based upon identity . . . The deconstructionist wants to show that the notion of identity, which seems so basic, so 'present' actually depends upon the notion of difference."

65. For a historical and legal analysis of the period, *see* Randall Kennedy, *Martin Luther King's Constitution: A Legal History of the Montgomery Bus Boycott*, 98 YALE L.J. 999 (1989).

In 1954, the landmark case *Brown v. Board of Education*[66] overturned *Plessy v. Fergusson* (1896) that had established separate but equal public facilities. In 1955–56, the Montgomery Alabama bus boycotts protested inequality in transportation facilities, which were not protected under *Brown*. In 1957 and 1960, civil rights acts were passed. In 1960, the era of the sit-ins and freedom rides, and voter education programs began. The South was systematically failing to enforce the rights provided in *Brown* and various civil rights acts.

Protests continued, and King was arrested along with other demonstrators in April 1963 when he wrote the *Letter*. In August 1963, King marched on Washington in a plea for jobs and for freedom, and it is there that he delivered his famous "I Have a Dream" speech. In 1964, the comprehensive Civil Rights Act was passed, and in 1965 a Voting Rights Act was passed. The Selma March took place in 1965, and in 1968 another civil rights act was passed. However, King was assassinated on April 4, 1968 in a Memphis hotel.

Birmingham, Alabama was the seat of Southern racial discrimination in the 1960s. Eugene Bull Connor was the ominous political leader of Birmingham who perpetuated racial inequality. A group of whites campaigned to alter Birmingham's municipal government by abolishing the offices of three segregationist commissioners who ran the city, including Connor. Connor went to court to demand that he be allowed to finish his term; during the pending case, Birmingham was governed by two city governments.

The leaders of the Southern Christian Leadership Conference (SCLC) had been planning since January 1963 in the famous Project C to hold two demonstrations in Birmingham in 1963 that eventually led to King's arrest and incarceration.[67] Birmingham whites wanted the SCLC to cancel the Easter demonstrations to give the new government a chance to show what it could do in its support of racial equality. But the SCLC wanted to proceed with its demonstration as part of a concerted attack on segregation in Birmingham.[68]

A Birmingham city ordinance required demonstrators to obtain a parade permit from the city commission to protest or demonstrate. When on April 3, 1963, Mrs. Lola Hendricks (representing the demonstrators) approached the infamous Eugene Bull Connor to request a permit, Connor refused. He also refused a second request for a parade permit. Out of frustration and respect for their principles, the demonstrators proceeded to protest without a permit. It is important to note that Project C included plans for King to place himself in a position to be arrested on Good Friday, April 12, 1963.

---

66. 347 U.S. 483 (1954).

67. *See* Luban, *supra* note 2, at 2156 for an account of *Walker v. City of Birmingham*. King and other demonstrators were convicted of criminal contempt for violating an ex parte injunction.

68. *Id.* at 2162.

On April 10, Connor obtained an ex parte injunction from Alabama Circuit Court Judge W.A. Jenkins, Jr. that forbid civil rights leaders (including all the leaders of Project C) from taking part in or encouraging demonstrations. After the injunction was served at 1 a.m. on Thursday, the SCLC leadership debated how to respond. They felt that compliance with the injunction and delay in demonstrating would deflate the protest.[69]

King went ahead with the planned demonstration the following day, and was arrested and thrown into the Birmingham jail. A second demonstration took place on Easter Sunday, April 14, 1963. Subsequently, Judge Jenkins found several of the demonstrators guilty of criminal contempt and sentenced each of them including King to five days in jail and a $50 fine.[70]

While King was in jail, eight white clergymen, "liberals" who had publicly opposed Governor George Wallace's "Segregation Forever" speech, took out a full-page advertisement in the *Birmingham News* denouncing the demonstrators' actions. King responded to that denunciation by writing a *letter* on scraps of newspaper he found in his prison cell. When King was permitted visitors, he gave his manuscript to friends who typed it and returned it to him in jail for revisions. The reception of the *Letter* was initially cool, but later it was printed by the American Friends Service Committee and reprinted in numerous periodicals. It is considered by many today to be one of the most famous documents to emerge from the civil rights movement.

At the contempt hearing, the civil rights leaders averred that the parade permit ordinance and the ex parte injunction were unconstitutional. The judge refused to consider the issue because the demonstrators had never attempted to get the injunction dissolved. Later the U.S. Supreme Court agreed that the ordinance on which the injunction rested was unconstitutional.[71] But the Court in *Walker v. City of Birmingham* declined to overturn the demonstrators' convictions for criminal contempt, holding that even a constitutionally questionable court order must be obeyed. This decision is the so-called "Mine Workers Rule" derived from the 1947 case *United States v. United Mine Workers*.[72]

IX. NARRATIVE STRUCTURE OF THE *LETTER*

King's *Letter* is a prophetic appeal to the ideals of brotherhood, freedom for all, and equality for all, encoded alternately in secular and religious imagery. The *Letter* is also an apology for the values of the Christian religion.

---

69. *Id.* at 2163.

70. *See* A. Westin & B. Mahoney, The Trial of Martin Luther King (1974).

71. Shuttlesworth v. City of Birmingham, 394 U.S. 147 (1969).

72. 330 U.S. 258 (1947). *See* Luban, *supra* note 2, at 2164 for a discussion of this decision.

The *Letter* begins on an ironic note as King greets his "dear fellow clergymen"[73] with whom King (the clergyman) identifies, and from whom King (the prisoner and civil disobedient) wishes to disassociate himself. Throughout the *Letter*, King refutes specific allegations made against him by the clergymen. Towards the end of the *Letter*, King makes his own accusations against the clergymen and all indifferent white moderates. He then resumes his defensive, negative tone by refuting several other specific allegations.

King defends himself eloquently, persuasively, and above all reasonably against the following accusations published in a newspaper advertisement:

First, King and his fellow organizers are outside agitators who do not belong in Birmingham at all. King gives three reasons why he belongs in Birmingham.[74] He denies he is different from any other man, and he communicates his vision of a utopian world of human connectedness through two metaphoric codes that are quite familiar to semioticians: network and fabric. "We are caught in an inescapable *network* of mutuality, tied in a single *garment* of destiny"[75] (emphasis added). It is significant that King identifies with the prophet Paul "who left his little village of Tarsus and carried the gospel of Jesus Christ to the far corners of the Greco-Roman world . . . to respond to the Macedonian call for aid."[76] The prophet Paul and the Book of Acts reflect a utopian appeal to a world community that is not unlike King's own vision of a community united in peace and brotherhood. Like King, Paul tried to weld the people of many nations into a City of God.[77]

Second, to the charge that the demonstrations are "unwise and untimely", King retorts that the clergymen are simply blind to reality. They have only a superficial understanding of the black man's plight, and they are responsive only to the publicized and illusory effects of demonstration. They fail to see the conditions that brought about the need to protest.[78] King reviews Birmingham's long history of racism and the unfulfilled promises given to the members of the civil rights movement. He concludes that Blacks had no other alternative but to demonstrate at this time because the white power structure gave them no options. King further demonstrates the systematic steps (including information gathering, negotiation, self-purification, and direct action) taken by the civil rights movement to prepare itself for nonviolence.[79]

Third, the clergymen claim that the demonstrators have consistently preferred confrontation to negotiation. King rejoins that negotiation cannot take place

---

73. *See* King, *supra* note 1, at 77.
74. *See* analysis of these three reasons *supra* Section III.
75. *See* King, *supra* note 1, at 79.
76. *Id.* at 81–82.
77. *See* Luban, *supra* note 2, at 2194 for a discussion of St. Paul and the City of God.
78. *See* King, *supra* note 1, at 79.
79. *Id.* at 79–81.

until the white community perceives that there is a problem of racial inequality. The white community must be "forced to confront the issue."[80] King believed that negotiation would never take place unless the demonstrators forced it to happen by creating a "tension" producing a crisis in the community.[81] In short, King, like Socrates, wanted to create dramatic tension in order to bring men out of the darkness of the cave and into the light of truth. He wanted to force individuals to rise from the bondage of myth to the "unfettered realm of creative analysis," to "rise from the dark depths of prejudice" to the "majestic heights" of brotherhood.[82]

Fourth, the clergymen claim that the demonstrators should wait so as to give the new administration time to solve the problem of inequality in race relations.[83] King was a man of action and thought, and he knew that the legendary curative power of time was a myth.[84] In his *Letter,* King suggests that Boutwell and Connor are both segregationists dedicated to maintaining the status quo. King refuses to wait because "freedom is never voluntarily given by the oppressor; it must be demanded by the oppressed."[85]

At this point in the *Letter,* the reader is faced with a cluster of literary devices that appear in a highly emotional and moving passage describing the evils of segregation. Here King contrasts his own prophetic vision with the clergymen's blindness. The accelerating rhythm of the passage, its classical symmetry, use of vivid imagery and alliterations, and general musicality make it a soul-stirring example of King's literary talents:

> Perhaps it is easy for those who have never felt the stinging darts of segregation to say, "Wait." But when you have seen vicious mobs lynch your mothers and fathers at will and drown your sisters and brothers at whim; when you have seen hate-filled policemen curse, kick and even kill your black brothers and sisters; when you see the vast majority of your twenty million Negro brothers smothering in an airtight cage of poverty in the midst of an affluent society; when you suddenly find your tongue twisted and your speech stammering as you seek to explain to your six-year-old daughter why she can't go to the public amusement park that has just been advertised on television, and see tears welling up in her eyes when she is told that Funtown is closed to colored children, and see ominous clouds of inferiority beginning to form in her little mental sky, and see her beginning to distort her personality by developing an unconscious bitterness toward white people; when you have to

80. *Id.* at 81.
81. *Id.* at 81–82.
82. *Id.* at 81.
83. *Id.* at 82.
84. "I had also hoped that the white moderate would reject the myth concerning time in relation to the struggle for freedom." *Id.* at 89.
85. *Id.* at 82.

> concoct an answer for a five-year-old son who is asking: "Daddy, why do white people treat colored people so mean?"; when you take a cross-country drive and find it necessary to sleep night after night in the uncomfortable corners of your automobile because no motel will accept you; when you are humiliated day in and day out by nagging signs reading "white" and "colored"; when your first name becomes "nigger," your middle name becomes "boy" (however old you are) and your last name becomes "John," and your wife and mother are never given the respected title "Mrs"; when you are harried by day and haunted by night by the fact that you are a Negro, living constantly at tiptoe stance, never quite knowing what to expect next, and are plagued with inner fears and outer resentments; when you are forever fighting a degenerating sense of "nobodiness" then you will understand why we find it difficult to wait. There comes a time when the cup of endurance runs over, and men are no longer willing to be plunged into the abyss of despair.[86]

In this memorable passage, King plays with words. He deconstructs the conventional meaning of the term *wait* and supports his redefinition by citing the concurring view of a distinguished jurist: "For years now I have heard the word 'wait'! This 'Wait' has almost always meant 'Never.' We must come to see, with one of our distinguished jurists, that 'justice too long delayed is justice denied.'"[87] For King, change is inevitable, and therefore, patience is merely the postponement of the unavoidable. "Oppressed people cannot remain oppressed forever. The yearning for freedom eventually manifests itself, and that is what has happened to the American Negro."[88]

Fifth, the clergymen object to the civil rights movement because the protesters are willing to break laws. King's initial response is indirect and comes in the form of a rhetorical question: How can he request whites to comply with *Brown v. Board of Education* if he himself is suggesting the legitimacy of disobedience?[89] King's reply is an ironic response to the systematic disobedience by the Southern whites who from 1954 to 1963 refused to enforce *Brown*.

King defends the right to break the law. This defense is based on a series of distinctions drawn between just and unjust laws—distinctions that take their source from the natural law tradition. King espouses a radical view of civil disobedience.[90] Because man has a legal and moral duty to obey just laws, man has the right and the duty to disobey unjust laws.

In the second half of the *Letter*, King temporarily moves out of the refutation section and accuses the leaders of the church of shallowness, blindness, and lack

---

86. *Id.* at 83–84.
87. *Id.* at 83.
88. *Id.* at 91.
89. *Id.* at 84 ("How can you advocate breaking some laws and obeying others?").
90. *See infra* Section XII for a discussion of civil disobedience.

of understanding of the black man's plight.[91] Then he tones down his attack by referring to his deeply-felt emotion as "disappointment"[92] with the church itself, comparing its weakness and otherworldly brand of religion to the ancient and powerful church that transformed the mores of society by its sacrificial acts and direct responsiveness to real issues.[93] King encodes this comparison of the old and new church in an interesting metaphor. The new church is more like a thermometer that merely records "the ideas and principles of popular opinion" while the old church is like a "thermostat that transformed the mores of society."[94] King's condemnation of the powerlessness of the church is strident, personal, and even dangerous coming from the pen of a "minister of the gospel."[95] He predicts that the church will "lose its authenticity, forfeit the loyalty of millions, and be dismissed as an irrelevant social club with no meaning for the twentieth century."[96] There is no wonder that after such blasphemous accusations King felt the need to defend himself: "In deep disappointment I have wept over the laxity of the church. But be assured that my tears have been tears of love. There can be no deep disappointment where there is not deep love. Yes, I love the church."[97]

King's admitted disappointment in the church occasionally masks his anger and scorn that he translates into rhetorical questions dripping with irony and sarcasm: "I have traveled the length and breadth of Alabama, Mississippi and all the other southern states. . . . I have beheld the impressive outlines of her massive religious-education buildings. Over and over I have found myself asking: 'What kind of people worship here? Who is their God? Where were their voices when the lips of Governor Barnett dripped with words of interposition and nullification? Where were they when Governor Wallace gave a clarion call for defiance and hatred?'"[98]

King also accuses contemporary white moderates of being "archdefenders of the status quo,"[99] more devoted to law and order than to justice. Like Antigone who defies orders by burying her brother contrary to the authority of the King

---

91. "I had hoped that the white moderate would see this need. Perhaps I was too optimistic; perhaps I expected too much. I suppose I should have realized that few members of the oppressor race can understand the deep groans and passionate yearnings of the oppressed race, and still fewer have the vision to see that injustice must be rooted out by strong, persistent and determined action." *See* King, *supra* note 1, at 93.

92. *Id.*

93. *Id.* at 94–95.

94. *Id.* at 96.

95. *Id.*

96. *Id.*

97. *Id.*

98. *Id.*

99. *Id.*

of Thebes,[100] King also feels it necessary to upset the existing order and create chaos in order to bring about a sense of real community and brotherhood, a greater order, and a true justice.

King contrasts the notion of an illusive negative peace that exists in the South to the real positive peace he seeks to establish by creating constructive chaos. In the South, there is an obnoxious "negative peace," a myth, whereby the black passively accepts his "unjust plight."[101] King deconstructs this myth and advocates the creation of tension to bring about a positive peace "in which all men will respect the dignity and worth of the human personality."[102]

After this digression King then returns to the refutation of several other claims made by the clergymen:

Sixth, to the claim that the demonstrators' actions, though peaceful, must be condemned because they precipitate violence, King responds that the clergymen are confusing cause for effect and condemning the victim and not the criminal.[103]

Seventh, to the claim that King's activity is extreme, he responds by shaming the clergymen. He also points out the illogical connection between the terms *nonviolent* and *extreme.*[104] King follows a typical dialectical pattern in his refutation of the extremism allegation.[105]

Finally, King attacks the beautiful Southern white churches for their failure to embrace Christian principles and the cause of civil rights, which King calls a fundamental moral issue.[106] He argues that the church merely urges compliance with civil rights laws as a matter of prudence.[107] Embracing Emersonian principles of nonconformity, King bemoans the fact that the church is simply afraid to be different. "Far from being disturbed by the presence of the church, the power structure of the average community is consoled by the church's silent and often even vocal sanction of things as they are."[108]

King concludes his *Letter* by reversing his negative tone and affirming optimistically that blacks will eventually win. Here, King identifies the black man's plight with both the goals of our nation and the eternal will of God.[109]

---

100. *See* Chapter 7 of this book discussing Sophocles' *Antigone* and comparing it to Jean Anouilh's more modern *Antigone.*

101. *See* King, *supra* note 1, at 88.

102. *Id.*

103. *Id.*

104. *Id.* at 90.

105. *See* discussion of this dialectic in the section devoted to extremism *supra* Section III.

106. *See* King, *supra* note 1, at 93–98.

107. *Id.* at 94.

108. *Id.* at 96.

109. *Id.* at 98.

Before ending his *Letter*, King adds a short digression to humiliate the eight clergymen for having congratulated the Birmingham police on their so-called humane prevention of violence.[110] He resorts to a semiotic display of surface appearances and hidden realities when he declares the Birmingham police are publicly compliant, but privately brutal. The police bring out their dogs that sink "their teeth into unarmed, nonviolent Negroes,[111] and they commit unrelenting violence on innocent men, women, and children."[112]

King declares that the real heroes are not the policemen but the meek, the Rosa Parks, the James Merediths, the "old, the oppressed, battered Negro women, symbolized in a seventy-two year old woman in Montgomery, Alabama, who rose up with a sense of dignity, and with her people decided not to ride segregated buses, and who responded with ungrammatical profundity to one who inquired about her weariness: 'My feets is tired, but my soul is at rest.'"[113]

King ends the *Letter* politely and formally, with tongue in cheek, by wishing that the *Letter* "finds these clergymen strong in the Christian faith."[114]

X. THE NOTION OF DIFFERENCE AND "DIFFÉRANCE"

King's *Letter* is a demonstration of Jacques Derrida's notion of difference and deconstruction.[115] King sets up hierarchical oppositions based on a relationship of difference that he proceeds to cancel by the subsequent establishment of an identity between these opposing entities. Throughout the *Letter*, the reader will be confronted with variants of the following structural antinomies: friend/enemy, patience/impatience, clergymen/secular men, jail/freedom, waiting/action, reason/emotion, dark/light, outsider/insider, theory/practice, blindness/vision, separation/community, order/chaos, unjust laws/just laws, extremism/indifference, I/we, and cause/effect. All these antinomies are linked by the overriding theme of *difference*.

Like Derrida, King shows that racial difference is a derivative concept based upon the fundamental notion of man's identity to other men. "We are caught in an inescapable network of mutuality."[116] "Whatever affects one directly, affects all indirectly."[117] As Derrida put it, identity is only comprehensible in terms of difference, just as difference can only be understood in terms of identity because

110. *Id.* at 97.
111. *Id.*
112. *Id.*
113. *Id.* at 99.
114. *Id.* at 100.
115. *See* Cook, *supra* note 6, at 985 on deconstruction.
116. *See* King, *supra* note 1, at 78–79.
117. *Id.* at 79.

each is mutually dependent upon the other.[118] Both terms of the hierarchical opposition rely for their coherence on the differentiation between them. Thus, the relation between similarity and difference or between white and black is one of mutual dependence and difference or what Derrida calls *différance*. Derrida's term *différance* is actually a pun based upon the French word *différer*, which means both to differ and to defer. *Différance* simultaneously indicates that (1) the terms of an oppositional hierarchy are differentiated from each other. (2) each term in the hierarchy defers the other (in the sense of making the other term wait for the first), and (3) each term in the hierarchy defers to the other (in the sense of being fundamentally dependent upon the other).[119]

The best illustration of King's use of *différance* and deconstruction of accepted realities is his refutation of the allegation of extremism. King first sets up a thesis structured on negation and contrast: *Martin Luther King, Jr. is not an extremist. He is neither complacent nor violent.* "At first I was rather disappointed that fellow clergymen would see my nonviolent efforts as those of an extremist."[120] King then contrasts his nonviolent efforts to those of the complacent, "the demoralized Negroes and a few middle-class Negroes who profit from segregation, and are insensitive to problems of the masses . . . Negroes who, as a result of long years of oppression are so drained of self-respect and a sense of somebodiness that they have adjusted to segregation."[121] It is ironic and in perfect keeping with the Derridean notion of *différance*, which is dependent on identity, that King should here contrast himself to other black men. He then further differentiates himself from what he refers to as "the forces of bitterness and hatred, the Black nationalists, Elijah Muhammad's Muslim movement." "This movement is made up of people who have lost faith in America, who have absolutely repudiated Christianity, and who have concluded that the white man is an incorrigible devil."[122] It is also ironic and in perfect harmony with the Derridean notion of deconstruction that King later in the *Letter* identifies himself (by means of a simile) with the Black nationalists, and says that although he has not lost faith, his dreams, like those of the Black nationalists, have been shattered.[123]

King then draws a parallel between himself and the two opposed Black groups by identifying himself as a middle of the roader: "I stand in the middle of two opposing forces in the Negro community."[124] His is the way of God: "I am

---

118. *See* Balkin, *supra* note 12, at 748 for a discussion of this Derridean concept.
119. *Id.* at 751.
120. *See* King, *supra* note 1, at 90.
121. *Id.*
122. *Id.*
123. *Id.* at 94.
124. *Id.* at 90.

grateful to God that, through the influence of the Negro church, the way of nonviolence became an integral part of our struggle."[125]

King's antithesis, which follows directly from his thesis, is structured positively on a series of identities. He is like Jesus "an extremist for love."[126] Like Amos, King is an extremist for justice: "Let justice roll down like waters and righteousness like an ever-flowing stream."[127] Like Paul, he is an extremist for the Christian Gospel: "I bear in my body the marks of the Lord Jesus."[128] He is also like the extremist Martin Luther, who "cannot do otherwise"[129] and who inaugurated the Protestant reformation. He is like John Bunyan, who was jailed for his Puritan preaching and who vowed to "stay in jail to the end of my days before I make a butchery of my conscience."[130] He is an extremist like Abraham Lincoln, who said "this nation cannot survive half slave and half free."[131] He is an extremist like Thomas Jefferson, whose Declaration of Independence established the principle that "all men are created equal" as a self-evident truth. King likens himself to the three men on Calvary who were all crucified for the same crime of extremism, adding that "two were extremists for immorality, and thus fell below their environment. The other, Jesus Christ, was an extremist for love, truth and goodness, and thereby rose above his environment."[132] Thus, by a series of identities between King and respected religious and political heroes, King validates the necessity of extremism in the cause of racial equality.

King's synthesis is found in the proposal of a new form of extremist: the creative extremist with whom he identifies: "Perhaps the South, the nation and the world are in dire need of creative extremists."[133] Creative extremists create drama and the constructive tension necessary to bring about a "world house," a community of brotherhood, and a global mutual interdependence based on the recognition of man's fundamental similarity and difference.

XI. NATURAL LAW THEORY AND CIVIL DISOBEDIENCE

King is ambivalent about the law. Like St. Thomas Aquinas, he advocates a natural law legalism and considers obedience to God to be above obedience to the law. King sees no real contradiction in his own willingness to disobey a court order

125. *Id.* at 91.
126. *Id.* at 92.
127. *Id.*
128. *Id.*
129. *Id.*
130. *Id.*
131. *Id.*
132. *Id.*
133. *Id.*

while urging others to obey the ruling in *Brown v. Board of Education* because he believes in the existence of just and unjust laws and in man's duty to obey only just laws. He encodes his philosophy in religious and secular terminology. "One has not only a legal but a moral responsibility to obey just laws. Conversely, one has a moral responsibility to disobey unjust laws."[134] He radically rejects the validity of an unjust law by identifying with the respected religious figure of St. Augustine: "I would agree with St. Augustine that 'an unjust law is no law at all.'"[135]

King defines just and unjust laws by the use of several different metaphoric codes, including religious, psychological, and legal. Firstly, he offers the strictly theological explanation citing St. Thomas Aquinas, Martin Buber, and Paul Tillich: "A just law is a man-made code that squares with the moral law or the law of God. An unjust law is a code that is out of harmony with the moral law. To put it in the terms of St. Thomas Aquinas: An unjust law is a human law that is not rooted in eternal law and natural law."[136]

King further couches his theological definition of unjust and just laws in psychological terms derived from a theory of the personality: "Any law that uplifts human personality is just. Any law that degrades human personality is unjust. All segregation statutes are unjust because segregation distorts the soul and damages the personality. It gives the segregator a false sense of superiority and the segregated a false sense of inferiority."[137]

King returns to the theological definition of an unjust law by further describing segregation as a form of dehumanization, an objectification of the human being: "Segregation, to use the terminology of the Jewish philosopher, Martin Buber, substitutes an 'I-it' relationship for an 'I-thou' relationship and ends up relegating persons to the status of things. Hence segregation is not only politically, economically and sociologically unsound, it is morally wrong and sinful."[138]

King explains that segregation is sinful because it is a form of separation. "Paul Tillich has said that sin is separation. Is not segregation an existential expression of man's tragic separation, his awful estrangement, his terrible sinfulness? Thus, it is that I can urge men to obey the 1954 decision of the Supreme

---

134. *Id.* at 84.

135. *Id.*

136. *Id. See also,* MARTIN LUTHER KING, JR., *Love, Law, and Civil Disobedience, in* A TESTAMENT OF HOPE: THE ESSENTIAL WRITINGS OF MARTIN LUTHER KING, JR. 43, 49 (James M. Washington ed., 1986) (This essay contains a shorter version of the same definition of just and unjust laws proposed in the *Letter*).

137. *See* King, *supra* note 1, at 84.

138. *Id.* at 85.

Court, for it is morally right; and I can urge them to disobey segregation ordinances, for they are morally wrong."[139]

For King the eternal law and natural law will be fulfilled when sinful separation of human beings in the act of segregation finally ends. King sees the future in a communitarianism, a "World House" of brothers united in peace and equality.

King then offers a purely secular argument for civil disobedience based on his distinction between an unjust and just law and the notion of fairness. King defines an *unjust law* as "difference made legal." "An unjust law is a code that a numerical or powerful majority group compels a minority group to obey but does not make binding on itself. This is difference made legal. By the same token, a just law is a code that a majority compels a minority to follow that it is willing to follow itself. This is sameness made legal. . . ."[140] King's notion of justice is inseparable from the concept of evenhandedness and is reminiscent of the theory of Hart and Rawls.[141]

King links injustice to values, democratic process, and voting practices: "A law is unjust if it is inflicted on a minority that, as a result of being denied the right to vote, had no part in enacting or devising the law . . . Can any law enacted under such circumstances be considered democratically structured?"[142]

King further refines his definition of an unjust law by using strictly legal language: "Sometimes a law is just on its face and unjust in its application. For instance, I have been arrested on a charge of parading without a permit. Now there is nothing wrong in having an ordinance which requires a permit for a parade. But such an ordinance becomes unjust when it is used to maintain segregation and to deny citizens the First Amendment privilege of peaceful assembly and protest."[143]

King's view of natural law as "sameness made legal" is similar to the fair play concept elaborated by Hart and Rawls,[144] in which man must obey the law only if the law is a cooperative enterprise requiring widespread compliance to achieve its beneficial aims. An unfair law is one that is not cooperative and not generally beneficial. This is what King called "difference made legal." King's *Letter* not only establishes the right of civil disobedience, but a moral duty to disobey unjust laws. This is based on King's acceptance of St. Augustine's view that "an unjust law is no law at all."

---

139. *Id.*

140. *Id.*

141. *See* discussion of Rawls and Hart *infra*, at note 144.

142. *See* King, *supra* note 1, at 173.

143. *Id.* at 85–86.

144. Rawls, *Legal Obligation and the Duty of Fair Play, in* LAW AND PHILOSOPHY 9–10 (S. Hood ed., 1964). H.L.A. Hart, *Are There Any Natural Rights,* 64 PHILADELPHIA REV. 175, 185 (1955). *See also* Luban's discussion *supra* note 2, at 2207–09 of Socrates' contradictory views of civil disobedience in the *Apology* and the *Crito.*

To persuade his readers of the wisdom of this radical point of view that denies the legality of an unjust law and asserts a duty for its disobedience, King resorts to yet another identification with a philosopher of unimpeachable integrity. He compares himself to Socrates, the patron saint of civil disobedience.[145] King points out the similarity between his own actions and those of his fellow demonstrators in Birmingham, then their similarity to those of Socrates who "felt that it was necessary to create a tension in the mind so that individuals could rise from the bondage of myths and half-truths to the unfettered realm of creative analysis and objective appraisal."[146] King calls the Birmingham demonstrators "nonviolent gadflies," which is the same description Socrates used for himself in the *Apology*. King again alludes to Socrates when he points out the illogical reasoning of the clergymen to condemn the demonstrators for provoking violence by their protest. "Isn't [condemning the Birmingham demonstrators for provoking violence] like condemning Socrates because his unswerving commitment to truth and his philosophical inquiries precipitated the act by the misguided populace in which they made him drink hemlock?"[147] King reminds us that Socrates' conscientious disobedience of the order to stop teaching protected academic freedom for all.[148]

Thus, King goes beyond the establishment of a right of civil disobedience—he refers to it as a duty. As Anthony Cook put it, "King balanced pragmatic and revolutionary Christianity, as well as rights and duties. King's prophetic Christianity recognized the importance of both rights and duty as a practical matter. Rights were prerequisites to survival; nonviolent civil disobedience was the heart of duty. Duty was consistent with rights because through civil disobedience one could simultaneously demonstrate respect for the rule of law in preserving social order while opposing laws supportive of unjust social orders. Thus, King envisioned a rule of law rooted in experience and responsive to the conditions of oppression that denied the humanity of so many."[149]

XII. FOR AND AGAINST CIVIL DISOBEDIENCE: DWORKIN AND BORK

King's views on civil disobedience are not as clear-cut as I have made them sound. He encodes his point of view in contradictory language that states one

---

145. *See* Luban's discussion *supra* note 2, at 2207 of Socrates' contradictory views of civil disobedience in the *Apology* and the *Crito*.

146. *See* King, *supra* note 1, at 81.

147. *Id.* at 88–89.

148. *See* Richard Kraut, Socrates and the State (1984) for a distinction between Socratic conscientious disobedience and civil disobedience for expressive and political purposes.

149. *See* Cook, *supra* note 6, at 1037.

premise, cancels it, then accepts this premise, leaving the reader with the task of creating a synthesis that resolves the ambiguity.

This process of synthesis is similar to the German notion of *Aufhebung*, which involves adopting a statement and then subsequently cancelling and preserving the statement all in one. The notion of *Aufhebung* is very dear to the deconstructionists and constitutes a procedure frequently adopted by King. For example, King elaborates a theory on just and unjust laws in answer to the question "How can you advocate breaking some laws and obeying others?"[150] He states categorically and unequivocably that people must obey just laws and disobey unjust laws: People have not only a "legal but a moral responsibility to obey just laws. Conversely, one has a moral responsibility to disobey unjust laws."[151] But then two pages later he contradicts that statement: "In no sense do I advocate evading or defying the law, as would the rabid segregationists. That would lead to anarchy."[152]

This facet of King's point of view on civil disobedience is similar to the conservative view espoused by Robert H. Bork in *The Tempting of America*. Bork cites and comments upon King and his *Letter*. Bork believes that civil disobedience is lawlessness. He states that King rarely "advocated lawbreaking except in an effort to challenge the constitutionality of the law. When he himself violated a law, he accepted the punishment that ensued. . . ."[153] "There is surely no reason to think it is proper to punish those who violate the law but improper to punish the person who persuades them to do so."[154] Bork goes on to suggest "that there is no reason for courts to protect any advocacy of law violation since that is merely advocacy of a piecemeal overthrow of the democratic system."[155] For Bork, civil disobedience is tantamount to political anarchy, and King very briefly espouses this radical position only to reject it defiantly in one of his stunning reversals.

King more than advocates breaking an unjust law; he establishes a duty to disobey unjust laws. King's view of civil disobedience includes penalty, but penalty for King does not mean punishment. King considers penalty not as a punishment for the civil disobedient, but as an educative experience for the majority. Penalty has the purpose of arousing the conscience of the community to the injustices of racial discrimination. Like Gandhi, King actually believed in

---

150. *See* King, *supra* note 1, at 84.

151. *Id.*

152. *Id.* at 86. *See* King's original discussion of this issue in *Love, Law and Civil Disobedience, in* A TESTAMENT OF HOPE: THE ESSENTIAL WRITINGS OF MARTIN LUTHER KING, JR., *supra* note 136, at 49, a speech he gave in 1961 and from which he rewrote and condensed his thoughts on civil disobedience in the *Letter*.

153. ROBERT BORK, THE TEMPTING OF AMERICA: THE POLITICAL SEDUCTION OF THE LAW 334 (1990).

154. *Id.*

155. *Id.* at 335.

the beneficial effects of imprisonment, which was a symbol of the desperate fight for justice. Imprisonment for King did not have the negative connotations traditionally associated with the referent of jail. In King's lexicon, imprisonment was not associated with evil, but with goodness, purity, and nobility. Thus, imprisonment came to mean its opposite in King's mind for he had undergone a revaluation and deconstruction of the very myth of this concept. "I submit that an individual who breaks a law that conscience tells him is unjust, and who willingly accepts the penalty of imprisonment in order to arouse the conscience of the community over its injustice, is in reality expressing the highest respect for law."[156]

He then cites Biblical examples of civil disobedients such as Shadrach, Meshach, and Abednego who disobeyed laws on the grounds that a higher moral law was at stake. He cites early Christian martyrs who were "willing to face hungry lions and the excruciating pain of chopping blocks rather than submit to certain unjust laws of the Roman Empire."[157] Finally he cites Socrates, deifying him forever in the minds of all law professors in American law schools: "To a degree, academic freedom is a reality today because Socrates practiced civil disobedience."[158] Unlike Jean Anouilh for whom the heroic act of Antigone's civil disobedience was fraught with despair and futility,[159] King had the sense of accomplishing a real purpose in the act of defying authority. He cites the Boston Tea Party, which represented a massive act of civil disobedience[160] and which was one of the early important steps in the establishment of freedom for all Americans.

King's notion of civil disobedience appears to be rooted in a curious theory of legal relativity in which one man's crime is another man's law. He further persuades his audience of the righteousness of the duty of civil disobedience to unjust laws by pointing to the example of Nazi Germany. "Everything Adolf Hitler did in Germany was 'legal' and everything the Hungarian freedom fighters did in Hungary was 'illegal.'"[161] "It was 'illegal' to aid and comfort a Jew in Hitler's Germany. Even so, I am sure that, had I lived in Germany at the time, I would have aided and comforted my Jewish brothers."[162]

156. *See* King, *supra* note 1, at 86.

157. *Id.* at 87.

158. *Id.*

159. *See* Chapter 7 of this book comparing Sophocles' *Antigone* to Jean Anoulh's *Antigone*. The latter's pessimism and despair reflects the desperation felt by all those in France and in Europe who were suffering during World War II from the German occupation and oppression.

160. *See* King, *supra* note 1, at 86.

161. *Id.*

162. *Id.*

King's point of view of civil disobedience, which the reader has to piece together by reconciling King's contradictory statements that constitute a rather typical reversal pattern, is a more radical view than Bork's and one closer to that proposed by Ronald Dworkin in *Taking Rights Seriously*:[163] "Some people reach this conclusion [that the government must prosecute the dissenters, and if they are convicted it must punish them] because they hold the mindless view that conscientious disobedience is the same as lawlessness. They think that the dissenters are anarchists who must be punished before their corruption spreads."[164] Dworkin recognizes that disobedience to the law may be morally justified. He objects to those who accept only the moral justification for civil disobedience but who reject a legal justification. "It is of the essence of law, said Erwin Griswold, that it is equally applied to all, that it binds all alike, irrespective of personal motive. For this reason, one who contemplates civil disobedience out of moral conviction should not be surprised and must not be bitter if a criminal conviction ensues . . . organized society can not endure on any other basis."[165]

Dworkin believes that we must take into consideration the motives of the dissenter. In addition, when the law is uncertain and a plausible case can be made on both sides of an issue, a citizen who follows his own judgment is not behaving unfairly. "The path of justice is in tolerance. The popular view that the law is the law and must always be enforced refuses to distinguish the man who acts on his own judgment of a doubtful law."[166] Dworkin holds the view that the government has a special responsibility to those who act on a reasonable judgment that a law is invalid.[167]

For Dworkin, leniency depends on whether the law in question rests on a moral right. The civil rights laws clearly "embody the view that Negroes, as individuals, have a right not to be segregated . . . If we take no action against the man who blocks the school house door, therefore, we violate the moral rights, confirmed by law, of the schoolgirl he blocks. The responsibility of leniency cannot go this far."[168] This view seems to be in sync with King's view on civil disobedience. Dworkin advocates allowing the greatest possible tolerance of conscientious dissent while minimizing its impact on policy.

Dworkin would advocate fulfilling a legal responsibility toward those who disobey laws out of conscience by not prosecuting them, but by changing laws or adjusting sentencing procedures to accommodate them. "The simple Draconian propositions, that crime must be punished, and that he who misjudges the law must take the consequences, have an extraordinary hold on the professional as

---

163. RONALD DWORKIN, TAKING RIGHTS SERIOUSLY 206 (1977).

164. *Id.*

165. *Id.*

166. *Id.* at 216.

167. *Id.* at 217.

168. *Id.* at 218.

well as the popular imagination. But the rule of law is more complex and more intelligent than that, and it is important that it survive."[169]

XIII. CONCLUSION

King was ahead of his time. His goal of a utopian community of brothers based on human dignity and respect was not fulfilled before his assassination and may never be. In his soul-stirring *Letter from Birmingham Jail,* King attempted to jolt the conservative White community out of its state of indifference to the obvious injustices suffered by Blacks. He deconstructed certain myths that drug people into complacency and corrupt society into the false belief in an illusory negative peace. He criticized conservative Christianity's preference for law and order over justice and freedom. Hopeful and optimistic, King replaced the conservative evangelical conception of a fundamentally evil human nature with the view of man as fundamentally good. King synthesized opposites and embraced a Christian existentialism that advocated individual nonviolent direct action and permitted a struggle for the goal of community. He believed that an alternative social order was both desirable and obtainable; he envisioned a community that respected the need for individual freedom, yet realized the need for a state that protected and legally promoted that freedom. He also had a firm belief in the essential similarity of all human beings who could be united in a world house of brotherhood through creative participation and protest.

King invites his readers to participate creatively in the unraveling of these messages hidden in the symbolic language of the *Letter*. The subtle complicity of the author, the readers, and the text that takes place during the act of reading and interpreting the *Letter* actually illustrates the interconnectedness of mankind. King encourages his readers to participate in a sameness/difference game that is based on the frequent use of identity and contradiction. In the course of playing this game, King's legal theories about civil disobedience and racial inequality (which are expressed throughout his earlier writings) are never more poetically and persuasively revealed to the readers than in the *Letter from Birmingham Jail.*

---

169. *Id.*

7. ON CIVIL DISOBEDIENCE, JURISPRUDENCE, FEMINISM, AND THE LAW IN THE *ANTIGONES* OF SOPHOCLES AND ANOUILH*

Antigone's star has shone brightly through
the millenia. The archetype for civil disobedience has
claimed a constellation of first magnitude emulators.
—*Robert M. Cover*1

I. INTRODUCTION

Antigone is one of the first great heroines of civil disobedience and the inspiration of resistance movements against tyranny.[2] This heroic woman is also the symbolic representation of the feminist. Feminism is the discourse of resistance against tyranny and the oppression of women.[3] By her civil disobedience and resistance to what she considers to be an unjust law, Antigone is the prototype of the Other.

The myth, the character, and the play *Antigone* have inspired more than one hundred recreations and interpretations[4] by writers of stature and prominence in the legal and literary communities. Scholars of law, literature, and feminism continue to analyze the play to better understand its jurisprudential

---

* A very small section of this chapter first appeared as an article in 11 Cardozo Stud. L. & Literature 35 (Summer 1999). It has been completely revised, updated, and adapted to the themes of this book. A paper on *Antigone* was presented at Cardozo Law School on April 18, 1999 for a Conference on Theatre of Justice and Fictions of Law. I wish to extend my deepest appreciation to my research assistant, Annie Ugurlayan, for her assistance with the preparation of the original article, and to Michelle Hoskinson for her assistance with the revision of this chapter.

1. Robert M. Cover, Justice Accused: Antislavery and the Judicial Process 1 (1975).

2. Lloyd Weinreb, Natural Law and Justice 21(1987).

3. Definition provided publicly at the annual meeting of the American Society of International Law held in Washington on March 24, 1999 by the well-known feminist and activist Professor Annie Snitow of the New School for Social Research.

4. George Steiner, Antigones 121 (1984).

underpinnings[5] and, in particular, the difference between natural law and legal positivism as well as the effectiveness of civil disobedience for legal reform. Thoreau, noting that people live with "too passive a regard for the moral laws," cited Antigone as a stirring example of civil disobedience.[6] By comparing Sophocles' *Antigone,*[7] written in Athens in fifth century B.C., and Jean Anouilh's *Antigone,*[8] written and performed in France in 1944 during the tyranny of the German Occupation, this chapter will focus on the connection between civil disobedience, jurisprudence, and feminism in ancient and modern comparative legal systems as viewed from a postmodernist[9] perspective.

In Sophocles' *Antigone,* civil disobedience is represented by the tension between two different characters, Antigone and Creon. The most dramatic form of tension in the play is Antigone's act of civil disobedience that effectively causes legal reform in Thebes. Despite the obvious similarities between Antigone and Creon, Sophocles stresses the differences between their opposing jurisprudential positions on natural law and legal positivism. Sophocles espouses the argument that illegal protest can accomplish legal reform, but Jean Anouilh does not appear to agree. In Sophocles' *Antigone,* the mind-set of the ruler and the hegemonic political system that produced an unjust law are ultimately reformed by virtue of the insight that tragedy naturally produces.[10] Creon is eventually enlightened by Antigone's nonviolent protest, and his new understanding has the positive effect of suggesting a move away from a hegemonic to a pluralistic conception of the law. In contrast to the Sophoclean tragedy, Anouilh's melodrama does not propose civil disobedience as an effective force for legal or political reform. The two plays are in fact very different in form and substance. In this chapter I shall try to tease out the underlying causes for Anouilh's radical change from his Sophoclean source.

---

5. *See* Robin West, *Jurisprudence and Gender, in* FEMINIST LEGAL THEORY: FOUNDATIONS 75, 86–87 (D. Kelly Weisberg ed., 1993), especially her argument that modern jurisprudence is "masculine" and the rule of law neither recognizes nor values intimacy nor individuation, which is what women long for.

6. HENRY DAVID THOREAU, CIVIL DISOBEDIENCE 232 (1960) (1849), *cited in* Louis Rene Beres, *The Oslo Agreements in International Law, Natural Law, and World Politics,* 14 ARIZ. J. INT'L & COMP. L. 715, 728 (1997).

7. THE COMPLETE GREEK TRAGEDIES: SOPHOCLES I: OEDIPUS THE KING, OEDIPUS AT COLONUS, ANTIGONE 162–209 (D. Grene & R. Lattimore eds., E. Wyckoff trans., 1954).

8. JEAN ANOUILH, ANTIGONE (D. Grossvogel ed., 1959).

9. For a discussion of the difficulty in defining the term *postmodernism, see* Dennis Patterson's *Introduction* to POSTMODERNISM AND LAW XI (Dennis Patterson ed., 1994).

10. Postmodernist thought is based on arguments for pluralism and for a cultural turning away from hegemonic to pluralistic conceptions of justice, politics, ethics, and aesthetics. *See* Peter Murphy, *Postmodern Perspectives and Justice, in* POSTMODERNISM AND LAW, *supra* note 9, at 125.

II. WHAT IS CIVIL DISOBEDIENCE?

A. The Purpose of Civil Disobedience

Throughout history civil disobedience has played an important role in political, social, and cultural debates.[11] There is no doubt that civil disobedience has been instrumental in changing the conventional laws of society,[12] and Sophocles' *Antigone* underlines that message quite dramatically in a classical style of writing. According to Ronald Dworkin, civil disobedience has "a legitimate if informal place in the political culture of our community."[13] In the past, civil disobedience was practiced effectively by such leading national and international figures as Henry David Thoreau,[14] Mohatma Gandhi,[15] Susan B. Anthony,[16] and Martin Luther King, Jr.[17] Civil disobedience continues to be practiced today. For example, just a few years ago the Reverend Al Sharpton, Kweisi Mfume (the then-president of the National Association for the Advancement of Colored People), and many people in New York City were arrested for protesting the shooting death of an unarmed African immigrant, Amadou Diallo, by four white New York City police officers.[18]

B. Is Civil Disobedience Merely Protest?

Despite its historical acceptance, civil disobedience is nonetheless an illegal form of protest. Like terrorism, civil disobedience is a confusing concept with no universally accepted definition.[19] John Rawls defined *civil disobedience* as acts that are "public, nonviolent, conscientious yet political . . . done with the aim of

---

11. Mark Edward DeForrest, *Civil Disobedience: Its Nature and Role in the American Legal Landscape*, 33 Gonzaga L. Rev. 653 (1997–98).

12. Bruce Ledewitz, *Civil Disobedience, Injunctions, and the First Amendment*, 19 Hofstra L. Rev. 67, 80 (1990).

13. Ronald Dworkin, A Matter of Principle 105 (1985).

14. *See generally* Henry David Thoreau, Civil Disobedience, *supra* note 6.

15. Mohandas K. Gandhi, *Gandhi: A Plea for the Severest Penalty Upon Conviction of Sedition*, *cited in* Stephen J. McEwen, Jr., *The Defense of Justification and Its Use by the Protestor: A Focus on Pennsylvania*, 91 Dick. L. Rev. 1, 9–10 (1986).

16. Susan B. Anthony, *Statement to the Court* (1873), *reprinted in* David R. Weber, Civil Disobedience in America 185–88 (1978).

17. Martin Luther King, Jr., *Letter from Birmingham Jail*, *in* Why We Can't Wait 77 (1963). *See* Susan Tiefenbrun, *Semiotics and Martin Luther King's "Letter from Birmingham Jail"*, 4 Cardozo Stud. L. & Literature 255 (1992) and its revised version *supra* Chapter 6 of this book.

18. Dan Barry, *Daily Protesters in Handcuffs Keep Focus on Diallo Killing*, N.Y. Times, Mar. 19, 1999, at 1 (reporting a demonstration that began on March 10, 1999 in New York City).

19. *See* DeForrest, *supra* note 11, at 654.

bringing about a change in the law or policies of government."[20] Mere dissent,[21] protest, or disobedience of the law is not enough to qualify as civil disobedience. Several elements have been generally recognized as necessary for a particular act of protest to qualify as civil disobedience.[22] The act must be nonviolent, open and visible, illegal,[23] performed for a moral purpose to protest an unjust law or to object to the status quo,[24] and performed with the expectation by the actor that the illegal act will result in punishment.[25] These are the structural elements of the definition of civil disobedience.

C. Arguments Against Civil Disobedience

Persuasive arguments against civil disobedience as a means of effectively correcting the legal system have been presented on numerous occasions whenever protest movements start to organize.[26] The arguments are as follows: (l) Civil disobedience is an illegal act and, therefore, shows contempt for the law. If allowed to continue, civil disobedience will undermine the legal system; (2) The purpose of civil disobedience is to satisfy selfish interests, and the act cannot be morally justified; (3) Civil disobedients are anarchists who take the law into their own hands; (4) Civil disobedients show disrespect for the law by their unlawful acts and bring society near social chaos in the name of defending a vague and nebulous "natural" or higher law; (5) Civil disobedience is self-defeating because even if its objectives are worthy, the deliberate unlawfulness it requires creates resentment in the minds of legislators and the general public; (6) Lawlessness is not justified if lawful ways to correct the situation are still available; and (7) Civil disobedience is not justified because it subverts the democratic process. These arguments, which are easily refuted by systematic application of the definition of civil disobedience proposed above, are articulated literarily in the *Antigones* of Sophocles and Jean Anouilh by Creon who is staunchly opposed to civil disobedience.

D. Arguments For Civil Disobedience

Arguments in favor of civil disobedience are imprudent to propose because this line of reasoning would be tantamount to justifying every act of civil

---

20. John Rawls, A Theory of Justice 365 (1971).

21. *See* Abe Fortas, Concerning Dissent and Civil Disobedience (1968) for a distinction between legal dissent and illegal civil disobedience.

22. DeForrest, *supra* note 11, at 655.

23. Carl Cohen, Civil Disobedience: Conscience, Tactics, and the Law 4 (1971) ("An act of civil disobedience is an act that breaks the law").

24. DeForrest, *supra* note 11, at 656.

25. *See generally, id., et passim.*

26. *See* Cohen, *supra* note 23, at 129–72.

disobedience.[27] Each act of civil disobedience is committed in response to a particular law, and each act is undertaken in a particular social context that must be taken into consideration before it can be determined whether that particular act of civil disobedience can be justified. Although civil disobedience is distinguishable from revolution and from the desire to overthrow the Constitution or the existing system of laws, it necessarily involves an illegal act and, therefore, cannot be given a legal justification.[28]

The legal system cannot support arguments for civil disobedience except in the unusual cases of grossly immoral tyranny producing cruel and oppressive laws, such as the racial laws passed in Nuremberg, Germany or in Vichy, France.[29] Some argue that civil disobedience is justified by the principles developed at the Nuremberg Tribunals in 1945, which ultimately determined that the individual German officers, not the German government, must be held responsible for their acts.[30] The Nuremberg Tribunals made it clear that individuals could not justifiably claim they were merely obeying the law when their acts, in compliance with evil and oppressive laws, resulted in cruel and inhuman treatment of prisoners and civilians during World War II. On these grounds some persons—notably some Americans during the war in Vietnam—refused to obey certain apparently lawful orders that would have resulted in cruelty to civilians. In fact, those who failed to disobey the orders that were likely to produce cruel and inhuman treatment of civilians or war prisoners were convicted for the unlawful acts they committed during the My Lai massacre.[31] Nuremberg, then, justifies military disobedience for wrongs that are blatant and horrific, but it is debatable whether Nuremberg justifies civil disobedience for laws whose compliance might result in humanly intolerable pain and suffering.[32] Applying the Nuremberg principles to *Antigone,* we should ask if Creon's decree prohibiting the burial of the dead rises to the level of a law so pernicious that compliance with it would result in intolerable human pain and suffering, thereby justifying Antigone's act of civil disobedience and the tragic effects which her act ultimately caused.

---

27. *Id.* at 93.

28. *Id.* at 94.

29. *See id.* at 102. *See also* TELFORD TAYLOR, THE ANATOMY OF THE NUREMBERG TRIALS (1992). For a discussion of the Nuremberg trials in the context of ethical considerations, *see* Annas & Grodin, *Medical Ethics and Human Rights: Legacies of Nuremberg, in* WAR CRIMES AND WAR CRIMES TRIBUNALS: PAST, PRESENT, AND FUTURE 111 (L. Friedman & S. Tiefenbrun eds., 1999). *See also* RICHARD WEISBERG, VICHY LAW AND THE HOLOCAUST IN FRANCE (1996).

30. *See* Cohen, *supra* note 23, at 198.

31. Jeannine D'Avanzo, Note, *Accountability for the My Lai Massacre, in* WAR CRIMES AND WAR CRIMES TRIBUNALS: PAST, PRESENT, AND FUTURE, *supra* note 29, at 287.

32. *See* Cohen, *supra* note 23, at 200–10 for the analysis of the defense of civil disobedience and the Nuremberg judgments.

Arguably, the Nuremberg principles are not applicable to acts of civil disobedience that are customarily undertaken in response to local ordinances. Civil disobedience is more typically committed in democratic societies rather than in totalitarian regimes, even though tyrannical leaders in totalitarian regimes often promulgate oppressive laws. Civil disobedience is simply not tolerated under tyranny, as is clearly expressed by Creon's immediate and cruel punishment of Antigone. In fact, one of the features of civil disobedience is that it is a by-product of democratic government that tolerates dissent and welcomes legal protest. But civil disobedience is illegal protest. Therefore, since justification for the concept of civil disobedience cannot be found in the legal system per se, defense of civil disobedience must come from outside the legal system.

E. Civil Disobedience and a Conflict-of-Law Argument

Civil disobedients may attempt to justify their acts on the basis of a conflict of laws argument, claiming a moral obligation to perform the illegal acts or, as Antigone claimed, an obligation to obey a higher, natural, or divine law whose authority preempts man-made laws. Thus, the civil disobedient recognizes a conflict between a man-made law and a "higher" law, referred to by names such as "natural law," "moral law," "unwritten law," "God's law," etc. This line of reasoning has deep roots in the history of Western thought[33] and is shared by Cicero, Aquinas, Grotius, Locke, and even Thomas Jefferson who inscribed on the Great Seal of the United States: "Rebellion against tyrants is obedience to God." St. Thomas Aquinas declared that "human law does not bind a man in conscience, and if it conflicts with the higher law, human law should not be obeyed."[34] In his *Letter from Birmingham Jail*, Martin Luther King wrote that "an unjust law is a code that is out of harmony with the moral law."[35] King made frequent references in that *Letter* to a conflict between moral law (or natural law) and man-made law. King believed moral law preempted human law and justified his act of civil disobedience in order to protest and draw attention to a bad man-made law.

The difficulty inherent in the conflict of laws argument that civil disobedience is obedience to a higher law stems from the vagueness of natural law. It is impossible to codify natural law or to determine with any degree of reliability what that law actually commands or forbids. As it is difficult to determine if these higher laws are part of a legal system at all, it is also difficult to determine how they would even apply to concrete cases.[36] Some argue that the legal system itself needs people who are willing to break the law for political reasons.

---

33. *See infra* text accompanying notes 48–101 for a discussion of the history of natural law.

34. *See infra* ROMMEN, at note 92 discussing Thomistic philosophy. *See infra* text accompanying notes 88–97 for a discussion of the legal theory of St. Thomas Aquinas.

35. KING, *supra* note 17, at 84–85.

36. *See* Cohen, *supra* note 23, at 114.

"The legitimacy of the system itself requires confrontation with disobedience defended by individuals who view compliance as immoral or by individuals seeking to persuade lawful officials to change."[37]

F. Civil Disobedience and a Free Speech Argument

Some may attempt to adduce a free-speech argument that civil disobedience is a form of protected political speech.[38] John Rawls compared civil disobedience to public speech.[39] The issue in such an argument is to determine how far the protection of free speech really goes and whether the form of illegal protest in question is like other protected forms of communication: gestures, symbolic responses, certain conventional patterns of conduct and other nonverbal acts that are protected under the First Amendment of the U.S. Constitution. Open and uninhibited political criticism is of such fundamental importance in a democracy that conduct that falls into this category will be protected even when it may appear to fall also into categories otherwise rightly unlawful.[40]

G. Civil Disobedience and Postmodernism

The practice of civil disobedience is both an ancient and modern form of illegal dissent that reflects the essence of postmodernist thought. The postmodern perspective in critical legal studies began to make its presence felt in the academic community in the early 1990s and has been identified as incorporating hermeneutics,[41] post-structuralism, deconstruction, and semiotics.[42] Postmodernists question many of the key concepts incorporated in formal law, which they identify with manipulation and control.

Civil disobedients and postmodernists both seek reform. The perpetration of an illegal act by a civil disobedient is designed not to destroy the social order, but

---

37. Martha Minow, *Breaking the Law: Lawyers and Clients in Struggles for Social Change*, 52 HARV. L. REV. 723, 741 (1991).

38. Leslie Gielow Jacobs, *Applying Penalty Enhancements to Civil Disobedience: Clarifying the Free Speech Clause Model to Bring the Social Value of Political Protest into the Balance*, 59 OHIO ST. L.J. 185, 197 (1998) (discussing civil disobedience as expressive conduct).

39. JOHN RAWLS, A THEORY OF JUSTICE, *supra* note 20, at 366.

40. Cohen, *supra* note 23, at 179, citing New York Times Co. v. Sullivan, 376 U.S. 254 (1964) (protecting the "proud national commitment to the principle that debate on public issues should be uninhibited, robust, and wide open, and that it may well include vehement, caustic, and sometimes unpleasantly sharp attacks on government and public officials").

41. Dennis Schmidt, *Can Law Survive? On Incommensurability and the Idea of Law*, 26 U. TOL. L. REV. 147 (1994), an interesting article on hermeneutic theory, postmodernist theory, and the separation of law and justice. He cites William Gaddis, "Justice–you want justice? You get justice in the next world. In this world you have the law."

42. Dragan Milovanovic, *The Postmodernist Turn: Lacan, Psychoanalytic Semiotics, and the Construction of Subjectivity in Law*, 8 EMORY INT'L L. REV. 67 (1994).

to reform it by challenging a particular law or action promulgated by the government.[43] "The motivation of civil disobedience is the dissonance caused by an alleged injustice, and the goal is justice . . ."[44] not anarchy or revolution. Like the postmodernist, the civil disobedient intends to debunk certain premises of the legal system and to call into question the bases of certain laws that offend human dignity.[45]

Despite their mutually moral intentions, both postmodernists and civil disobedients are perceived by some as dangerous anarchists whose shared goal is to undermine the legitimacy of the legal system. The argument against civil disobedience is that nonviolent protest may lead to violence and revolution, which the State has a legitimate right to prevent.[46] In Sophocles' tragedy, Creon vigorously opposes Antigone's act of defiance because it threatens to decenter the order and destabilize the discipline required to preserve the State. Therefore, for civil disobedience to be effective, it must be predominantly nonviolent.[47]

III. CIVIL DISOBEDIENCE AND JURISPRUDENCE

The question that both Sophocles and Anouilh ask literarily but answer very differently is whether civil disobedience is truly effective in changing an unjust law and in reforming the legal system that created it. To answer this question, we must posit the existence of an objective moral standard beyond or implicit in the man-made laws. This objective moral standard, which is referred to in different ways as natural law, divine law, the law of God, revelation, or universal law, is often compared and contrasted to human law, which is otherwise referred to as legal positivism.

A. Natural Law versus Legal Positivism: What is Natural Law?

Natural law, like civil disobedience or terrorism, is a concept that is difficult to define. Blackstone defined natural law as "the eternal, immutable laws of good and evil, to which the creator himself in all his dispensations conforms; and which he has enabled human reason to discover so far as they are necessary for

---

43. Richard A. Vachon, *The Relevance of St. Thomas More,* 13 CATH. LAW. 145, 147 (1967).

44. Paul J. Weber, *Toward a Theory of Civil Disobedience,* 13 CATH. LAW. 198, 202 (1967).

45. "An unjust law is a human law that is not rooted in eternal law and natural law . . . Any law that uplifts human personality is just. Any law that degrades human personality is unjust." KING, *supra* note 17, at 84.

46. Weber, *supra* note 44, at 201–02.

47. DeForrest, *supra* note 11, at 657.

the conduct of human actions."[48] According to John Locke in his second treatise,[49] natural law is understood to be the law of reason. It is the eternal, immutable, universal law which is in opposition to the relative "positive, existing law"[50] that varies according to time and place. Natural law is based upon unchanging fundamental principles that provide norms for justice. Our revolutionary Declaration of Independence, unlike our Constitution, is permeated with natural law concepts that deny the validity of the British law of its time.[51] The Declaration of Independence distinguishes true "law" from the commands of the existing sovereign or of the existing State and defines the former as a transcendent quality that can only be freed by revolutionary action.[52]

Natural law is often contrasted to legal positivism. Since the fundamental credo of legal positivism is that "no law can be unjust,"[53] many legal scholars (notably the utilitarians such as Jeremy Bentham and John Austin) draw attention to an inherent and disturbing separation between law and morality in legal positivism. Positivists perceive the law as a command of the sovereign requiring obedience to what law "is" and not necessarily to what law "ought" to be.[54]

B. History of Natural Law: Homer and Ancient Greece

The philosophical conception of the natural law made its first appearance in a literary form in the Homeric epics[55] in Western culture among the ancient

---

48. William Blackstone, Commentaries on the Laws of England 62, bk IV, ch. V (adapted by Robert Malcolm Kerr, 1962), *cited in* Louis Rene Beres, *Opposing the "Peace Process": Israel, Civil Disobedience and the Principle of a Higher Law,* 13 Ariz. J. Int'l. & Comp. L. 117 (1996).

49. *See* John Locke, Two Treatises of Government 123 (T.I. Cook ed., 1947).

50. Ernst Bloch, Natural Law and Human Dignity XIV (Dennis J. Schmidt trans., 1986).

51. J. Ely, Democracy and Distrust: A Theory of Judicial Review 49 (1980).

52. *See* West, *supra* note 5, at 162: "As narrative, the [Declaration of Independence] tells the romantic story of the 'birth of a hero', a tumultuous ending and a new apocalyptic beginning. The American Rule of Law is the hero that triumphs over English monarchic authority."

53. Bloch, *supra* note 50, at xiv, citing Hobbes' remark in Leviathan.

54. *See* H.L.A. Hart, *Positivism and the Separation of Law and Morals,* 71, 4 Harv. L. Rev. 593, 617 (2/1958). "Thus, the insistence on the separation of law as it is from law as it ought to be powerfully contributed to horrors." Hart explains how Nazis exploited subservience to mere law, that is, law as law (*Gesetz als Gesetz*) and the failure of the German legal profession to protest against the injustice they were required to perpetrate in the name of law. *See also* Kelsen, General Theory of Law and State 58–61, 143–44 (1945) for an elaboration of pure formalism and legal positivism which extols the virtues of law as a science.

55. Weinreb, *supra* note 2, at 16.

Greeks[56] before the fifth century B.C. The relationships in Homer between human and divine agency, the interventions of the gods, and the will of Zeus have been the subject of endless scholarly debates through the ages.[57] The classical example of the conflict between natural law and human law was written in fifth century B.C. by Sophocles in the tragedy *Antigone,*[58] which reflects debates that were very much in the air in Greece at that time.

The Greeks distinguished two conceptions of natural law. One espouses the basic doctrine of a state of nature and the State as a social unit resting upon a free contract, which is arbitrary, artificial, and determined by utility.[59] The other Greek conception of natural law is grounded in metaphysics. According to that view, natural law is a mythical state of nature that existed before laws were created and is intricately connected to the notion of God as supreme lawgiver.

C. Natural Law at the Time of Heraclitus, Plato, and Aristotle

Both of these conceptions of natural law were dominant in the Greek era of the first Sophists and at the time of Heraclitus.[60] Heraclitean dicta, which appeared around 500 B.C., entered into later Stoic philosophy and offered the proposal of one universal and rational law: "For all human laws are nourished by one, which is divine. For it governs as far as it will, and is sufficient for all, and more than enough."[61] Building upon Plato's theory of Ideas, which sought to elevate "nature" from the sphere of contingent facts to the realm of immutable Forms, Aristotle advanced the concept of "natural justice" in his *Ethics*. Aristotle quoted Antigone arguing that "an unjust law is not a law."[62] For centuries Aristotle passed as the "father of natural law," and St. Thomas repeatedly appealed to Aristotle as the Philosopher, par excellence.[63] But Aristotle had as little to say about the content

---

56. HEINRICH A. ROMMEN, THE NATURAL LAW; A STUDY IN LEGAL AND SOCIAL HISTORY AND PHILOSOPHY 5 (Thomas R. Hanley trans., 1947).

57. *See* WEINREB, *supra* note 2, at 17.

58. *See id.* at 21 for an analysis of Sophocles' *Antigone* as an example of civil disobedience to the law of the State and as an example of the conflict between obedience to the law of the State and to another, higher obligation. "Antigone is represented as the first great heroine of civil resistance, almost the leader or inspirator of a resistance movement against tyranny." *Id.*

59. ROMMEN, *supra* note 56, at 5.

60. *Id.*

61. *See* THE PRESOCRATICS, 75 Section 81, Fragment No. DK 22B114 (Philip Wheelwright ed., 1960), *cited in* Beres, *supra* note 48, at 120.

62. *See* Beres, *supra* note 48, at 212.

63. ROMMEN, *supra* note 56, at 16.

of natural law as Plato,[64] who defined the law as the "discovery of true reality."[65] It was not Aristotle or Plato but rather the Sophists (the revolutionaries of ancient Greece) who, like today's postmodernists, made many reform proposals and placed demands on the natural law.

D. Legal Positivism and Natural Law under the Sophists and the Birth of Athenian Democracy

In an era in which laws were considered the pride of the citizens of the Greek *polis*, the Sophists were considered foreigners, rationalistic revolutionaries, and enemies of the law.[66] Sophocles' *Antigone* reflects these radical Sophists' views. Sophocles wrote *Antigone* in the midst of a rapidly changing world in 440 B.C., and his play mirrors the transition between the old and the new world in Greece.[67] Sophocles elucidated the idea of true law as an act of discovery challenging the superiority of human rulemaking.[68]

The birth of Athenian democracy in the fifth century B.C. created a demand for a new education system—and the professional educators were the Sophists. They asked the proverbial questions: Is morality merely convention—*nomos*—or is there a higher sanction to be found in nature—*physis*? *Nomos* is the establishment of the rule of law and the product of the fifth and sixth century B.C. *Nomos* became the laws, the codified customs of the State, and the rules created for rational and prudent State regulation. *Physis* and *nomos*, nature and convention, were the pillars of a great debate at that time, and one which continues today. Sophists brought out a sharp contrast between the prevailing order of the city-state and the natural law, as they preached it.

Sophists ridiculed Socrates who looked upon the laws of Athens as purely and simply just.[69] Sophists contrasted what they considered to be naturally right with what is legally right, believing that the unwritten laws were eternal, unalterable, and emanating from a higher source than the changing decrees of men.[70]

---

64. *See* WEINREB, *supra* note 2, at 31–35 for a discussion of the role of Plato and Aristotle in the development of a natural law theory.

65. *See* West, *supra* note 5, at 152, at n.22 ("The natural law tradition begins with Plato, who defines law as the 'discovery of true reality.' Plato, *Meno*, at 73rd (M. Brown ed. 1971). Other natural lawyers have claimed that law must, in order to qualify as true 'law' accord with moral norms derived from God's law (Augustine), human nature (Aquinas), rights (Dworkin), procedural fairness (Fuller), generality (Wechsler), neutrality (Ackerman), the human good (Finnis), or the community good (Aquinas and Aristotle) . . .").

66. ROMMEN, *supra* note 56, at 7.

67. Andrea L. Timoll, *Antigone, Irigaray, and the Archetypical Problematic: The Classical Opposition of Human and Divine Law*, 19 QUEENS L.J. 583, 589 (1994).

68. *See* Beres, *supra* note 48, at 117–27 (1996) for a detailed discussion of the history and development of natural law.

69. ROMMEN, *supra* note 56, at 8.

70. *Id.* at 9.

Antigone's objection to Creon's decree seems to reflect the Sophists' adherence to natural law. Originally, the Sophists established an opposition between *physis* and *nomos*,[71] but later the Sophists sharpened the distinction between man-made laws (*thesis*) and natural laws (*physis*). The Sophists established the principle that there is a unity between what is right and what is the highest expression of nature.[72] *Physis* or natural law was defined as the constant value in the changes of human laws.[73] Soon *nomos* became equated with the law of the universe, and *physis* became a synonym for *nomos*.[74]

Pericles believed that laws held a city together and that the individual and the *polis* will be destroyed if this union is broken. To enforce the rule of law, Pericles espoused legal, rule-based formalism for the Athenian city-state. This view constitutes a shift from a communally based conception of the State to one that gives primacy to the individual. In Periclean Athens, the customary principle of the collective health of the community (*physis*) was replaced by laws based on the paradigm of individuality.[75] At this point in time, legal rule formalism was the State-sanctioned code of conduct, like the decree espoused in *Antigone* by Creon. Customs, such as the burial of the dead, were not codified into the rules and regulations of the city-state. The prevailing laws were internal rationalizations or systemizations of the dominant principles of the Athenian city-state.

During the transition from the ancient world to democracy, a competition developed between the varying forms of newly established man-made laws (such as Creon's decree) and the preexisting customary practices (such as Antigone's burial of Polyneices) that evolved from *physis* or nature. The conflict between new laws and preexisting customs is represented in the bitter opposition between Creon and Antigone, with the aim of Sophocles' literary representation being to determine the supremacy of divine law/*physis* over human law/*nomos*.

E. Sophocles, the Sophists, and Natural Law

In fifth-century B.C. Athens, the marginalization of natural law was expressed in edicts or decrees criminalizing behavior that complied with natural law. Thus, State law became legal, natural law became illegal, and those faithful to natural law became outlaws. Antigone's defiance of Creon's decree represents an example of this new form of criminal deviance. Sophocles' tragedy does not conclude that either natural law (the right of the family) or human law (the right of the State) is supreme. The fact that the play has elicited more than one hundred different interpretations since its performance in ancient Greece is a sign of Sophoclean ambiguity and the author's muted refusal to advocate for one or the

71. Bloch, *supra* note 50, at 10–11.
72. *Id.* at xiv.
73. *Id.* at 11.
74. *Id.* at 13.
75. *See* Timoll, *supra* note 67, at 589–90.

other forms of legal system. Antigone and Creon both come to realize that rigid adherence to either system of law has led them to err. Sophocles' ambiguity marks an interesting impasse in the jurisprudential debate and invites scholars to consider a more balanced view of law that encompasses features of both natural and human law.[76] What is clear from the Sophoclean tragedy is that civil disobedience does produce positive effects for legal and political reform. In Greek tragedy, the central conflict in which one protagonist is pitted against the other reflects the basically contradictory nature of law itself which was said to be incommensurate with justice or morality.[77]

F. Stoics, Natural Law, and Rome

The Stoics, whose legal philosophy arose on the threshold of the Greek and Roman worlds, viewed nature itself as the supreme legislator in the moral order.[78] They applied Platonic and Aristotelian thought and defined the emerging *cosmopolis* as one in which humankind, through its divinely granted capacity to reason, can commune with the gods. Although Stoicism was founded in Greece as a school of philosophy by Zeno (340–265 B.C.), Stoicism ultimately came to fruition in Rome in the imperial age in 106–43 B.C. with the advent of Cicero, who interpreted and transmitted the Stoic doctrine of natural law.[79] Cicero's writings in *De Republica* contain the first clear statements of natural law as a distinct philosophical doctrine.[80] Cicero said, "True law is right reason, harmonious with nature, diffused among all, constant, eternal; a law which calls to duty by its commands and restrains from evil by its prohibitions . . . It is sacred obligation not to attempt to legislate in contradiction to this law; . . . Nor is it one law at Rome and another at Athens; one now and another at a later time; but one eternal and unchangeable law binding all nations through all time."[81]

Cicero was the great popularizer of natural law, and Stoicism greatly influenced the various schools of Roman jurisprudence that adopted Stoic natural law traditions.[82] Two pillars support the true Stoic doctrine of natural law: the concept of common notions, *koinai ennoiai*, and the postulate of a life in harmony with nature, *homologoumenos te physei zen*.[83] Man has an inborn notion of

---

76. *Id.* at 593.

77. *Id.* at 152 ("Since the tragic poets present a view of law as divided in itself and as never fully positioned to be commensurate with justice, they expose the institutions as a fiction rather than a simple unconflicted act of reason").

78. *See* Beres, *supra* note 48, at 121.

79. Robert N. Wilkin, *Cicero and the Law of Nature, in* ORIGINS OF THE NATURAL LAW TRADITION 1 (R. Wilkin et al. eds., 1954).

80. WEINREB, *supra* note 2, at 39.

81. CICERO, DE REPUBLICA, *cited in* ALEXANDER P. D'ENTREVES, THE NOTION OF THE STATE 24 (1967).

82. ROMMEN, *supra* note 56, at 21.

83. BLOCH, *supra* note 50, at 14.

right and wrong, and law in its very essence rests not upon the arbitrary will of a ruler such as Creon or Hitler, or upon the decree of a multitude, but upon nature and upon innate ideas. Obedience to the eternal law in a life lived according to reason and embraced with religious fervor is the ethical principle of Stoicism,[84] which prepared the way for Christianity.

G. Christianity, St. Augustine, and Natural Law

When Christian faith entered into the ancient world, the Christian philosophers adopted the Stoic natural law traditions. St. Augustine, writing at the beginning of the fifth century A.D. (430 A.D.), reaffirmed the principle that temporal law must conform to the unchangeable eternal law. St. Augustine believed that the substantial ideas were the thoughts of God and His eternal law.[85] Augustine identified the course of all global problems in the human potential for evil, attributing the trials of humankind to the taint of original sin. St. Thomas Aquinas recalled St. Augustine as saying, "There is no law unless it be just. So the validity of law depends upon its justice. But in human affairs a thing is said to be just when it accords a right with the rule of reason: and as we have already seen, the first rule of reason is the Natural Law. Thus, all humanly enacted laws are in accord with reason to the extent that they derive from the Natural Law. And if a human law is at variance in any particular with the Natural Law, it is no longer legal, but rather a corruption of law."[86]

H. Scholasticism, Thomas Aquinas, and Natural Law

As Scholasticism reached its peak in the Middle Ages, the natural law doctrine attained its most masterly expression, especially in the writings of St. Thomas Aquinas[87] who identified four kinds of law: eternal law, natural law, human law, and divine law. Aquinas believed that eternal law was clearly the core form of law from which all other forms derive.[88] According to Aquinas, natural law is not a set of rules but an inclination, a way man participates in eternal law.[89] Natural law needs discovery of self-evident truths.[90] To go against natural law is to go against the human good, and according to Aquinas, "civil laws, which are not

---

84. ROMMEN, *supra* note 56, at 22.

85. *Id.* at 38.

86. *See* SUMMA THEOLOGICA, 1A 2AE, 95, 2, *cited in* D'ENTREVES, *supra* note 81, at 42–43.

87. THOMAS AQUINAS, SUMMA THEOLOGIAE (Institute of Medieval Studies, Latin text, 1941). *See* THOMAS AQUINAS (Fathers of the English Dominican Province trans., 1947), reprinted by Christian Classics 1981.

88. *See* PAMELA M. HALL, NARRATIVE AND THE NATURAL LAW: AN INTERPRETATION OF THOMISTIC ETHICS 27 (1994).

89. *Id.* at 28.

90. *Id.* at 37.

ordered to the human good, are more like 'violence rather than laws.'"[91] Aquinas also believed that positive law must not conflict with natural law, and "so far as it is in conflict with the natural law and with the unchangeable norms, positive law is not law at all and cannot bind man in conscience."[92] This principle is the bedrock of justification for civil disobedience.

Some scholars believe that natural law is knowable to the unassisted human mind which is not illumined by divine revelation.[93] Natural law is simply a set of exceptionless rules prescribing or constraining action.[94] Others contend that as divine law completes natural law according to Thomas Aquinas, natural law is practically inseparable from theology which is based on belief in biblical revelation.[95] This connection between natural law and divine revelation renders questionable the efficacy of natural law as a standard for a legal system.[96]

I. Grotius, the Father of Natural Law

Despite the long history of natural law that goes back to the Greeks, some believe that the doctrine of natural law began with the Dutch scholar Hugo Grotius (1583–1645), often called the "Father of Natural Law."[97] Grotius marked the transition from a metaphysical conception of natural law to a more rationalist one. In the seventeenth and eighteenth centuries, Grotius strengthened the idea of a universally valid natural law transcending in obligation all human law, including the law of the sovereign State.[98] Unlike Machiavelli and Hobbes, Grotius did not reduce law to the will of the prince or of the State. He understood that human edicts must be derived from the overriding totality of natural imperatives. Grotius rejected "raison d'état" as a just cause for war. Thus, he did not agree with Creon, who reduced law to the will of the State.

J. Hobbes, Locke, and Jean-Jacques Rousseau on Natural Law

In contrast to Grotius, Thomas Hobbes (1588–1679) denied natural law. Like the Epicureans before him, Hobbes pictured the state of nature as a lawless condition of war, a conflict of all against all, of chaos.[99] Hobbes saw natural law as

---

91. Summa Theologica, 1A 2AE, Q. 96, A 4, resp, *supra* note 87 and *cited in* Hall, *supra* note 88, at 41.

92. *See* Rommen, *supra* note 56, at 55.

93. Leo Strauss, Natural Right and History 163 (1950).

94. E.A. Goerner, *On Thomistic Natural Law: The Bad Man's View of Thomistic Natural Right*, 7 Political Theory 101–22 (1979).

95. *See* Hall, *supra* note 88, at 3.

96. *Id.*

97. Rommen, *supra* note 56, at 70.

98. *See* Beres, *supra* note 48, at 124 (discussing Grotius).

99. Thomas Hobbes, Leviathan, or the Matter, Forme & Power of a Commonwealth, Ecclesiastical and Civil (A.R. Waller ed., 1904), *cited in* Rommen, *supra*, note 56, at 83. Hobbes said, "In the state of nature, there exist only lawless

the basis for the institution of positive law which, once instituted, would make natural law disappear. John Locke (1632–1704) was as individualistic in his social philosophy as Hobbes, but Locke saw the state of nature as idyllic and espoused the idea of natural law in order to establish the inalienable rights of the individual. Like Locke, Jean-Jacques Rousseau (1712–78) stood almost diametrically opposed to Hobbes and to Hobbes' conception of the natural law. Rousseau preached a state of nature that resembled "the biblical paradise."[100]

K. Immanuel Kant and the Age of Natural Law

In the eighteenth century, a new era arose called the age of natural law that was dominated by the philosophy of Immanuel Kant (1724–1804), who exhibited the individualist natural law in its highest form. During this period a newer natural law developed that was distinguishable from the natural law of the Scholastics. This newer natural law had three distinct features: the predominance of the doctrine of the state of nature as the proper place to find the natural law; the nominalist attitude that espoused the belief in the separation of eternal law and natural law, of God's essence and existence, of morality and law; and the doctrine of the autonomy of human reason.

L. Critics of Natural Law

Although natural law enjoyed a long reign, attacks upon it were launched mainly from two camps: the sceptics and the agnostics such as David Hume and the utilitarians such as Jeremy Bentham (1748–1832) and their disciples. Criticism of natural law also came from leaders of the romantic movement who were basically antirationalist and antirevolutionary. Common to both groups was a basic distrust of the power of human reason to govern man.

M. The Rise of Legal Positivism

In reaction to this skepticism, legal positivism soon supplanted natural law as the dominant philosophy of law. Rejecting the natural law as to its form and content, legal positivism claims that the natural law doctrine is vague, threatens legal security, and substitutes subjective opinions for fixed objective norms. Positivism regards the natural law as a non-law.[101]

When the horrific crimes of the Nazi regime were revealed and punished by the rule of law at the Nuremberg trials, the weaknesses of the legal positivist system of law were also exposed, which resulted in a revival of natural law theory.[102] This

---

individuals, in whom is found no natural tendency to live in society; and man's life is 'solitary, poore, nasty, brutish, and short.'" HOBBES, LEVIATHAN, Part I. Chap. 13.

100. ROMMEN, *supra* note 56, at 91.

101. *Id.* at 247.

102. David Luban et al., *Moral Responsibility in the Age of Bureaucracy*, 90 MICH. L. REV. 2348, 2351 (1992).

revival is seen especially in the work of Germain Grisez and John Finnis.[103] The Nuremberg Tribunal left its legacy in the Nuremberg Charter, specifically Article 8,[104] which provided justification for military disobedience: "The fact that the defendant acted pursuant to an order of this government or of a superior shall not free him from responsiblity." Article 8 is a rejection of the positivist excuse for atrocious official acts that were said to be licensed by German law.[105]

N. Positive Law

It is widely accepted that natural law is difficult to codify, and too general, too diffuse, and too inchoate to be, by itself, a wholly adequate standard for a legal system.[106] As Justice Oliver Wendell Holmes put it, "The jurists who believe in natural law seem to me to be in that naive state of mind that accepts what has been familiar and accepted by them and their neighbors as something that must be accepted by all men everywhere."[107] Legal positivism offers codified rules and claims to be a science of the law[108] that supplants the vague principles of natural law. Hans Kelsen objected to natural law because he considered it to be politically motivated.[109] In its place, he advocated legal positivism as an apolitical pure theory of law. Positive law is a regulating, schematizing, and generalizing reality that produces interconnection, security, safety, and predictability among men.[110] By bringing uniformity to human behavior, legal positivism safeguards the individual's security. Despite its advantages over natural law, positivism does impose itself in a compelling way, and natural law advocates are cautious about its obligatory and coercive power.[111]

---

103. *See* RUSSELL HITTINGER, A CRITIQUE OF THE NEW NATURAL LAW THEORY 5 (1987) (discussing JOHN FINNIS, NATURAL LAW AND NATURAL RIGHTS (1980) and Germain Grisez' works including *Kant and Aquinas: Ethical Theory*, 21 THOMIST 44–78 (1958)).

104. 1 TRIAL OF THE MAJOR WAR CRIMINALS BEFORE THE INTERNATIONAL MILITARY TRIBUNAL 12 (1947), available at http://www.loc.gov/rr/frd/military_law/pdf/NT_Vol_1.pdf.

105. Luban et al., *supra* note 102, at 2351.

106. HALL, *supra* note 88, at 46.

107. Oliver Wendell Holmes, *Natural Law*, 32 HARV. L. REV. 40, 40-41 (1918).

108. Hans Kelsen, *Was ist die Reine Rechtslehre?*, *in* DEMOKRATIE UND RECHTSSTAAT. FESTGABE ZUM 60.GEBURTSTAG VON ZACCARIA GIACOMETTI 145, 153 (1953) ("As a science of positive law, it is a doctrine of actual rights, of rights and duties as they have actually been created by custom, legislation and the administration of justice and are at work in social reality, regardless of whether such positive law is considered good or bad, just or unjust, from any value-standpoint, that is, from any political standpoint.").

109. *See* WILLIAM A. LUIJPEN, PHENOMENOLOGY OF NATURAL LAW 22–23 (1967) for a discussion of Kelsen's theories and objections to natural law, which he saw as politically motivated and based on subjective value judgments.

110. *Id.* at 13.

111. *Id.* at 12.

According to Robin West, the broad appeal of legal positivism as a jurisprudential method is based on its separation of law and morality.[112] As Jeremy Bentham, Oliver Wendell Holmes, the legal realists, and more recently the critical legal scholars have reiterated, "A realistic insistence on the separation of what 'is' from what 'ought to be' is essential to meaningful progress toward fulfilling our dreams. The positivist separation of law and morality—of what is from what ought to be and what could be—is indeed a prerequisite of legal reform, whether that reform be radical, liberal, individualist, or communitarian."[113]

Ironically, the very same separation of law and morality and the identification of right with the legal order (which positivists see as its advantage over natural law) constitute the source of arguments against legal positivism.[114] To make justice rule in a purely legal positivist system, power is required and often exalted not for its own sake, but as the only and last means to prevent chaos.[115] This view is clearly expressed in Sophocles' *Antigone* and espoused by Creon, the tyrant who passes an offensive decree merely to affirm his authority in his newly established reign, which by its rigidity and brutality foreshadows a reign of terror.

H.L.A. Hart presented a more balanced view of positivism than the pure legal positivism of Kelsen and others. He cautioned the legal community about the possibility that a system of legal positivism might create morally evil laws that would result in the duty to disobey them. "If laws reach a certain degree of iniquity, then there would be a plain moral obligation to resist them and to withhold obedience."[116] Pure legal positivism would deny the right to civil disobedience.

Scholars such as Martha Nussbaum argue strongly for a more balanced system of law, and they oppose a mere rule-based standard. Nussbaum adopts practical wisdom as an alternative to any set of rule-governed precepts and prohibitions.[117] Opponents of positivism argue that its laws are man-made and changeable whereas natural law (which is universal, eternal, immutable, and stable) is a means of holding together the social order.[118] This argument of stability will be proposed by Antigone when she attempts to defend her illegal act in defiance of Creon's man-made law. Creon also makes the very same argument of

---

112. *See* West, *supra* note 5, at 182.

113. *Id.*

114. *See* Luijpen, *supra* note 109, at 28–35, for arguments against legal positivism.

115. *Id.* at 209.

116. H.L.A. Hart, *supra* note 54, at 617.

117. *See generally* Martha Craven Nussbaum, *Practical Syllogisms and Practical Science, in* Aristotle's 'De Motu Animalium' (1978); Martha Craven Nussbaum, *The Discernment of Perception: An Aristotelian Conception of Private and Public Rationality, in* Proceedings of the Boston Area Colloquium in Ancient Philosophy 151–201 (J. Cleary ed., 1985); Martha Craven Nussbaum, The Fragility of Goodness: Luck and Ethics in Greek Tragedy and Philosophy (1986).

118. Hall, *supra* note 88, at 14.

stability in his defense of man-made laws that he believes must be obeyed if the State is to survive.

Nussbaum's more balanced view of the law is in consonance with Sophocles' view. In his depiction of Antigone and Creon as both dogmatic in their adherence to either natural or made-made laws, Sophocles seems to adopt the view that a legal system should be a more flexible synthesis of both natural law and legal positivism. Nussbaum argues that Greek tragedy is about conflict resolution in a world that is full of change and that is not governed by reason alone.[119] She demonstrates that both Creon and Antigone provide solutions to conflict resolution that are inadequate and oversimplified. Creon's solution is to adopt pure legal positivism, and he advocates the primacy of civic duty and unflinching obedience to man-made laws. Antigone's solution is to adopt natural law, and she advocates duty to family, blood ties, and the eternal law of the gods of the underworld. The conflict between Antigone and Creon is not just between natural law and legal positivism, but between higher law and human law, between nature and civilization, between emotion and reason, and between woman and man.[120] According to Nussbaum, both Antigone's and Creon's solutions for conflict resolution are too radical, and she argues for a more balanced view, like the one proposed by Hegel,[121] whose incisive reading of Sophocles' *Antigone* constitutes the traditional interpretation of the play adopted by many literary critics and law scholars including Richard Posner.[122]

IV. HEGEL'S READING OF SOPHOCLES' *ANTIGONE*

Hegel's favorite Greek drama was *Antigone*, and he saw in Antigone's defiance of the king's commands a quality basic to the Hellenic ethical ideal. According to Hegel, Antigone obeys a higher order, even if it means losing her own life. Her obedience to one legal order means disobedience to another legal order, the one established by the State that issues the decree she violates. Whether or not

---

119. Nussbaum, The Fragility of Goodness, *supra* note 117, at 51–79.

120. *See* Timoll, *supra* note 67, at 599–611 for a very interesting discussion of Irigaray's views on Hegel's interpretation of *Antigone*, the dialectic of sexual difference established in the play, and a feminine critique of the play.

121. G.W.F. Hegel's interpretation of Sophocles' *Antigone* is found in Hegel, Phenomenology of Spirit (A.V. Miller trans., 1977), chap.6, sec. A; and Hegel, Aesthetics: Lectures on Fine Art I, 221 (T.M. Knox trans., 1975). *See* David A. Reidy, *Antigone, Hegel & The Law: An Essay*, 19 Legal Studies Forum 239 (1995) for an interesting analysis of Hegel's interpretation of the play. *Cf.* Elizabeth Villers Gemmette, *Antigone, Creon, and Captain Vere: A Response to David A. Reidy*, 19 Legal Studies Forum 273 (1995).

122. Richard A. Posner, Law and Literature: A Misunderstood Relation 111–12 (1988).

Antigone "chooses" of her own free will to violate the natural law or she is actually fated to commit this transgression by virtue of her tragic family ties, the fact is that she violates a law and will be punished. However, at the same time Antigone disobeys one law, she also dutifully obeys "the immutable laws of Heaven" that "were not born today nor yesterday; they die not; and none knoweth whence they sprang."[123]

Antigone's conflict is not easy to resolve. The law she feels compelled to obey is a good law, not an unjust law, unlike the SS officers who felt compelled to obey patently racist laws that resulted in human suffering on a grand scale. Creon's law is an unjust law that is self-serving, but it is not one that will result in human suffering on a grand scale. Creon represents the other side of Hellenic ethical consciousness, which is duty to State authority. Thus, according to Hegel, Creon and Antigone both epitomize essentially ethical values.

A brief analysis of the Hegelian interpretation[124] of Sophocles' *Antigone* establishes the dialectical oppositions supporting arguments for and against civil disobedience. These arguments are at the heart of this controversial play. Sophocles' ambiguity and the many questions left unanswered in the Greek tragedy invite interpretation and explain why more than one hundred *Antigones* have been produced in translation, revision, and recreation since Sophocles first wrote his personal interpretation of the myth in the fifth century B.C.[125]

Hegel, who greatly admired both the play and the character Antigone, saw this drama as the struggle between human and divine law in the early *polis*. The conflict is represented in a paradigmatic form called tragedy, which Hegel believed to be a genre that would evoke enlightenment and positive knowledge on the part of the tragic hero. The inevitable failure to honor both human and divine laws in this tragedy results in a fateful suffering by both Creon and Antigone. This suffering is intended to produce awareness of the need for a new kind of wisdom based on synthesis. Hegel saw this new wisdom as the unity of natural law and legal positivism, which are fundamentally in opposition to each other.

A. Hegel and the Plot of *Antigone*

The play begins at a very dramatic moment: the day after the seige of Thebes that was brought about by Polyneices, Antigone's brother, and one of the two sons of the fated former king, Oedipus. The battle resulted in the death of both brothers, Eteocles and Polyneices, and the rise to power of a new king of Thebes.

---

123. J. GLENN GRAY, HEGEL AND GREEK THOUGHT 55 (1941), citing F. Storr's translation of *Antigone*.

124. *See* Cynthia Willett, *Hegel, Antigone, and the Possibility of Ecstatic Dialogue*, 14 PHILOSOPHY AND LITERATURE 268 (1990), for an analysis of the Hegelian interpretation of Sophocles' *Antigone*.

125. STEINER, *supra* note 4, at 121.

Creon, Antigone's uncle and the new king of Thebes, orders Polyneices, the traitor, to remain unburied in Thebes. While it was legal for Creon to forbid burial in the city that the traitor betrayed, it was not legal for Creon to forbid family members to bury their dead outside of Thebes.[126] Creon justifies his harsh decree on the need to preserve the authority of the State and the sanctity of its laws. His decree is also a show of force for a newly crowned king. Creon proclaims that any violation of the foundational and final laws of the *polis* can bring death and destruction to the State. He believes his decree is justified because the city possesses the authority to withhold burial from a traitor. The penalty for disobedience of Creon's decree is stoning to death.

Antigone claims an obligation to bury her brother based on divine law to which the netherworld gods demand absolute obedience. As Polyneices' sister, she cannot resist this demand for obedience based on kinship, blood ties, and an ethical bond. Antigone defies Creon's decree and twice goes out to bury her brother, without the help of her sister, Ismene, who does not think women should defy men in the *polis.*

Hegel points out that neither Antigone nor Creon ever sees the other's point of view, with both characters demonstrating a basic one-sidedness. In the course of the play, each character comes to know that the other is partially right and partially wrong, and each acknowledges his/her own guilt. After her incarceration by Creon in an underground cave and just before her suicide by hanging, Antigone acknowledges that her great suffering proves her error. But the main epiphany comes to Creon after suffering the tragic loss of his son, Haemon, and the death of his grief-stricken wife, Eurydice. Unlike the typical unswerving classical hero, Creon listens to the message of the Chorus and Tiresias; he realizes his mistakes; and he changes. The foreshadowing of this change is seen in Creon's early commutation of Antigone's sentence from stoning to imprisonment in an underground tomb where she can "pray to Death for life." Creon realizes his mistake is in not respecting customary laws and in excluding laws of the old tradition where the dead are buried in the earth: "I've come to fear it's best to hold the laws of old tradition to the end of life" (1112–13).[127] Having learned the error of his ways and the unjustness of his laws, Creon finally admits guilt and decides, too late, to free Antigone and to change the law. Even though Creon is one of the few who remains alive at the end of the play, his life ends

---

126. WEINREB, *supra* note 2, at 271–72 (1987). Thebans did not permit the burial of the enemy dead, and this was a common theme in Greek literature (Aeschyles, *Seven Against Thebes*, Euripedes, *The Suppliant Women*. Polyneices was a traitor, and the law of Athens prohibited the burial of traitors in Attica. But even traitors were not denied burial altogether. *See* Robert Coleman, *The Role of the Chorus in Sophocles'* Antigone, 198 PROCEEDINGS OF THE CAMBRIDGE PHILOLOGICAL SOCIETY 7–8 (1972), *cited in* WEINREB, *id.* at 272.

127. All references from Sophocles' *Antigone* are from the David Grene and Richmond Lattimore edition, *supra* note 7. Verses will be cited in the body of the chapter.

tragically, as he is reduced to "nothing more than nothing now" (1320), walking alone in Thebes. At the end of the play, Creon is a wailing wreck of a man stripped of dignity and longing for death.

V. ANTIGONE AND FEMINISM

Although Hegel was a statist who believed in preserving the *polis*, he nevertheless extolled the virtues of the heroine Antigone, calling her the "noblest of figures that ever appeared on earth." Hegel believed that Antigone's act of defiance was an ethical one (*Sittlichkeit*)[128] based not on personal desire but on a belief that she had a higher duty to bury her brother who was of her own blood. Hegel saw the play as representing the conflict between Antigone's obedience to the private imperatives of kinship (which Hegel reminds us is the domain relegated to *women*) and Creon's obedience to the public loyalties of the State (which is traditionally the domain of *men*).

Hegel's condescending opinion of women[129] results in his relegating women to family matters and men to more important political matters in a discriminatory system based on gender difference. Sophocles shared Hegel's view of gender difference and politics, but Jean Anouilh apparently did not. Anouilh contrasted more distinctly than Sophocles two different types of women (Antigone and Ismene) and transformed Antigone into a more masculine female with nontraditional qualities of inner beauty based on heroic and virtuous deeds that were nonetheless futile. Anouilh's recreation of Antigone established the foundation for a new doctrine of feminist esthetics.

Although Hegel admired Antigone and her devotion to natural law, he clearly preferred Creon and his loyalty to legal positivism and to civic duty of the *polis*. Hegel reflected his preference for Creon when he said that Antigone's loyalty is to "inferior" authorities, to natural law, and to the "underworld gods of Hades . . . the inner gods of feeling, love and kinship, not the daylight gods of free, and self-conscious, social and political life."[130]

Antigone's fascination with death and the underworld has been misinterpreted by many critics. Her attachment to the gods of Hades and the underworld is not at all due to her "love" of Polyneices, or her "death wish," but rather constitutes the symbolic and literary representation of her reverence for the immutable and eternal natural law, which is associated logically with everlasting death rather than with fleeting and temporal life.

128. *See* Gerhard Joseph, *The Antigone as Cultural Touchstone: Mathew Arnold, Hegel, G. Eliot, V. Woolf and Margaret Drapple*, 6 PMLA 22, 23 (1981).

129. *See* Allen W. Wood, Hegel's Ethical Thought 244–246 (1990), for Hegel's views on man and woman.

130. Joseph, *supra* note 128 at 32, *citing* Hegel, Aesthetics, I, 464.

Like Hegel, who believed that both Creon and Antigone held ethical but inadequate views of the law, the Chorus, the Messenger, and the Seer, Tiresias, all point out that both Creon and Antigone fail to judge with wisdom. According to Hegel, this play is about the conflict between basic aspects of ethical consciousness, between two laws each of which is universal but incomplete in itself, and each law is in conflict with the other. Creon's law embodies the human law of the *polis* and is represented by the *male,* the rational, the voice of reason. Haemon shares a belief in his father's man-made law. Haemon's diplomatic appeal to his father is an appeal to reason, not to sentiment, and it is for this reason that Haemon never once mentions his heartfelt passion for Antigone. Antigone's law is divine law, which is associated with emotion, not reason, and by extension Antigone herself becomes the symbol of emotion. Thus, the entire domain of *womanhood* represented by Antigone becomes intricately allied with emotion rather than rationality.

According to Luce Irigaray,[131] a French feminist scholar, Creon's human laws deny blood ties of matrilineal society and denigrate the significance of birth, thereby advocating patriarchal dominance and the degradation of women. Irigaray believes that Hegel perpetuated the classical devaluation of women represented by the views of Creon, who so much feared losing to a woman.[132] Creon said, "So I must guard the men who yield to order, not let myself be beaten by a woman . . . I won't be called weaker than womankind." (677–80) In Creon's patriarchal world women are associated with disorder, madness, and chaos, and they must be punished: "I am no man and she [is] the man instead if she can have this conquest without pain." (484–85). Antigone is a challenge to Creon's self image as a man: "No woman rules me while I live." (527) Creon'[s worst fear is that his son "is firmly on the woman's side" (740), and he accuses Haemon of becoming "a woman's slave" (755). Antigone's sister, Ismene, fears the male-dominated universe, recognizes her female inferiority, and refuses to challenge the laws and authority of the male leader by engaging in civil disobedience:

> And now look at the two of us alone.
> We'll perish terribly if we force law
> and try to cross the royal vote and power.
> We must remember that we two are women
> so not to fight with men.

As a result of Hegel's designation of women as keepers of the private sphere, women were relegated to an unrecognized, invisible status, which is the primary source of their gender discrimination.[133]

---

131. Luce Irigaray, Speculum of the Other Woman (Gillian Gill trans., 1985).

132. *See* Timoll, *supra* note 67, at 607 for a discussion of the degradation of women in Hegel and by Creon in Sophocles' *Antigone.*

133. *Id.* at 583.

A. Sophocles' *Antigone* and Feminism

Law and gender are clearly allied in the idiom of Sophocles. The law Antigone advocates is embodied in the universal and eternal law of the family that according to Creon and Hegel is represented by the female. Antigone acts publicly to honor divine law and suffers human, not divine, punishment. Her fate simultaneously affirms the claims of divine law and the authority of human law. Creon refuses to recognize the legitimacy of family law, preferring to establish the authority of human law, his law, which is the law of men. As a result, Creon is punished by the gods, not by humans. His fate affirms both the claims of human law and the authority of divine law. The judgment called for by the Chorus, the Messenger, and the Seer is governed by male-dominated reason and articulates the synthesis of divine and human law.

B. Anouilh's *Antigone* and Feminism

Unlike Sophocles, Anouilh in his theatre of revolt criticizes Creon's disrespect for women by depicting a Creon who is utterly indifferent to human suffering, inappropriately holding a five o'clock cabinet meeting as soon as he learns of his wife's tragic suicide. Anouilh parodies gender discrimination.

VI. CIVIL DISOBEDIENCE IN SOPHOCLES' *ANTIGONE*

In Sophocles' *Antigone*, civil disobedience is represented by the tension between two different characters (Creon and Antigone) who are the pillars of multiple bipolar oppositions established in the play: man/woman; old/young/; public need/private vision; the living/the dead; human law/divine law; temporal/eternal; Olympian gods/chthonic gods; manipulative rationality/emotionality; patriarchal lineage/matrilinear kinship, etc. These oppositions reflect tensions in the law and in the society of Athens in fifth century B.C. The most dramatic form of tension is Antigone's act of civil disobedience.

Antigone is a true civil disobedient who espouses a belief in natural law; the importance of private, family ties; and the efficacy of resistance against man-made laws that are unjust. Her action in defiance of Creon's decree prohibiting the burial of her brother is nonviolent, public, and committed for the moral purpose of protesting Creon's unjust law. Antigone willingly accepts her cruel punishment, which is to be buried alive in a cave with only enough food to prolong her agony. Like the true tragic heroine she is, Antigone's act is fated, doomed, and less intentional than we assume. Antigone fears dying "with a lack of grace" (97), and like all tragic heroines, her goal is to die with honor. Her act of civil disobedience accords her that honor.

In a sense, Creon is also a civil disobedient who violates natural law requiring burial of the dead. Charles Maurras called Creon "a rebel" and saw Creon, not Antigone, as the main protagonist in the play: "The rebel against civil law and order is not Antigone. It is Creon. Creon has against him the gods of religion, the fundamental laws of the *polis*, and the feelings of the living *polis*. What Sophocles sets out to show is the punishment of the tyrant who has sought to free himself from divine laws."[134]

Creon stands for the principles of law and order, allegiance to the public order and to the State, and the superiority of men over women in a universe governed by gender difference. However, Creon is not a true civil disobedient because he *is* the law. Although Creon's decree is public and visible, the motive for Creon's act is neither ethical nor generalizable, but rather stubbornly personal. Creon professes a firm belief in the need for power (". . . now it comes that I hold all the power and the royal throne") (172–73) to maintain discipline and to enforce obedience to law and order in a stable *polis* ("There is no greater wrong than disobedience. This ruins cities, this tears down our homes, this breaks the battle-front in panic-rout. If men live decently it is because discipline saves their very lives for them.") (672–77). In fifth century B.C., loyalty to the *polis* was not just an abstract cause—it was a necessity. Wars between one city-state and another were the normal condition. Defeat in a war meant enslavement for the people. The only way to preserve individual freedom was by the constant efforts and sacrifice of the citizen body as a whole.[135] Moreover, Creon does not expect punishment for his act, which is the sine qua non of civil disobedience. Therefore, Creon is not a true example of civil disobedience.

Notwithstanding the sincerity of Creon's belief in discipline to keep the ship of State upright, afloat, and "sailing straight" (189), we cannot help fearing Creon's intransigence, and the emergence of the Leviathan of State power encroaching on individual liberty. Although Pericles gloried in the individual liberty that Athens gave its citizens, he also reminded the people that the *polis* is more important than the individual.[136] Creon's form of government requires power and results in the rise of dictatorship; Creon's rule includes tyranny, oppression, paranoia, and intimidation of innocent victims falsely accused of conspiring against the government Decree: ("These are the people—oh it's clear to me—who have bribed these men and brought about the deed.") (294–96) and ("I charge Ismene too"). This decree flies in the face of custom and natural law, and it is less an expression of Creon's political philosophy and more a show of his force and fearlessness ("For I believe that who controls the State and does not hold to the best plans of all, but locks his tongue up through some kind of fear, that he is worst of all who are or were.") (179–181). His decree is a display of

134. Charles Maurras, Antigone Vierge-Mere de L'Ordre (1948), *cited in* Steiner, *supra* note 4, at 187.

135. Bernard Knox, The Heroic Temper: Studies in Sophoclean Tragedy 85 (1963).

136. *Id.* at 86.

raison d'état, the willful establishment of his absolute authority in a new legal order that must rule by example and by the unfair victimization of scapegoats.

Antigone's act of civil disobedience has both positive and negative effects. Her illegal act of protest is necessary, though she is doomed by her tragic fate that is linked to her family ties with Oedipus. Antigone's act, perpetrated not by freedom of choice but by force of fate, causes tragedy for Creon and his family. Nevertheless, her act of civil disobedience proves to be effective in changing the mind-set of the tyrant and the hegemonic political system that produced the unjust law. Through his tragic suffering, Creon is enlightened by the actions of Antigone, and his insight has a direct effect on reforming the flawed legal system.

Robin West reminds us that Antigone does not commit the act for the purpose of reforming the legal system. According to West, Antigone's motivation for civil disobedience is merely to follow her tragic fate. "Unlike the romantic, the classical tragedian perceives her illegal conduct not as a freely chosen means of dramatizing and ultimately correcting a flawed legal order, but as the sole moral alternative; for her, there is no truly human choice. The tragedian is not engaging in a free political act, thereby affirming the reformed future of the flawed system within which the act occurs. She is engaging in a necessary moral, human act and thereby affirming a higher morality and her own obedience to it."[137] Although I agree with West, I believe it is important to recognize that the byproduct of Antigone's action is legal reform. To insist too strongly on Antigone's lack of freedom is to nullify the very act of Antigone's civil disobedience, which is defined as an action committed for the moral purpose of upholding a belief in a higher good.

A. Similarities between Antigone and Creon

Many readers of *Antigone* have observed the profound similarities between Creon and Antigone. Creon seems at first to be the hero of the play.[138] "Creon is a commensurate counterpoise to Antigone, each reads himself in the other, and the language of the play points to this fatal symmetry."[139] The parallel between Antigone and Creon reflects the basic nature of classical symmetry and mirrors the underlying message of balance that is proposed by Sophocles as a preferable legal philosophy. Antigone's treatment of her sister, Ismene, is analogous to Creon's treatment both of his son, Haemon, and of Antigone. Neither Creon nor Antigone is flexible. Both are dogmatic in their respective beliefs in either human law or divine law, and Sophocles' message is a plea for synthesis, moderation, and unity of the two types of law into a more balanced system. That balance is represented literarily by the proposed marriage between Haemon, Creon's son,

137. West, *supra* note 5, at 201.

138. Knox, *supra* note 135, at 67.

139. Steiner, *supra* note 4, at 184.

and Antigone, a marriage that is never consummated de facto but is consummated symbolically by their mutual suicides in the dark cave. Haemon urges his father to be flexible, like "a tree that bends and survives the torrent" (712–18), like the natural world which is the paradigm for yielding to change and time. Creon and Antigone each represents, respectively, "the laws of the earth" and "the oath-bound justice of the gods" (365–75). By the constant juxtaposition of Antigone and Creon, like a symphony of similarity and difference, Sophocles achieves a "dialectic of kindred opposites"[140] and an understated plea for balance in the legal system.

Both Creon and Antigone are avid supporters of human and natural law, respectively; both are in protest of one or the other type of law; both are in a deadlocked conflict of values.[141] Neither is supported in his or her views by their respective family members, Haemon and Ismene. Both will ultimately come to realize their flaws through the tragic suffering their protest necessarily causes them. However, in the end only Creon will change his plan, pardon Antigone, and revoke his "royal law" (382) that ultimately causes his destruction, pollutes the city, offends the gods of the underworld, and reduces man to beasts.

By his decree, which denies the customary rituals of purification, burial, and sacrifice to Polyneices, Creon causes pollution in the *polis*. Creon is like Oedipus, a ruler charged with removing a pollution of which he is in fact the cause. Not only does Creon discount the possibility that the unburied corpse may spread pollution, but he uses a legalistic expedient to avoid the further pollution of the *polis* that killing Antigone would entail. He immures her with just enough food "to eat as clears the city from the guilt of death" (776). Creon's tyrannical rule, prophetic of the Nazi regime and of all totalitarian regimes to come, is characterized by the systematic use of scapegoating that informs the action of the whole play. Antigone serves in part as a human sacrifice who would cleanse the city of its polluted past.[142]

Creon is the aggressive, manipulative rationalist represented in the memorable first stasimon, the Ode to Man (332–75), which paints a radiant image of human intelligence and highlights the achievements of civilization. Man's invention of the law is seen in this Ode as the ultimate civilizing agent of the city:

> When he honors the laws of the land and the gods
> sworn right
> high indeed is his city (369–70)

---

140. *Id.* at 185.

141. CHARLES SEGAL, TRAGEDY AND CIVILIZATION: AN INTERPRETATION OF SOPHOCLES 157 (1981).

142. *Id.* at 174–75.

Creon embodies reason and the view of secular rationalism espoused by the Sophists during their Enlightenment.[143] He identifies the law (*nomos*) with his decrees and with his own personal voice, which is represented stylistically by the predominance of the first person singular ("I") in his speeches on political philosophy (184, 111, 173, 178). Despite Creon's identification with reason and the Rule of Law, his justice (*dike*) becomes less impartial, more personal, and more emotional as his rigidity and stubbornness get the best of him (400, 1059). In Creon's conception of the Rule of Law, the earth is an extension of the laws of the State, the "earth of the fatherland" (199, 110, 113). Normally in Greek tragedy justice belongs to the realm of the Olympian gods, the lofty throne of Dike (853–55), but Creon encounters another kind of justice, the "law" of the gods of the lower world, the Erinys (613–14), and he has to yield in fear to these established laws (1113–14).

B. Greek Terms for the Law

Several Greek terms related to *law* appear in the Sophoclean tragedy and are intertwined with hard to grasp concepts of the supernatural. The terms *right, justice,* and *law* occur with frequency in *Antigone* and need some explanation. *Right* refers to individual rights as well as the right order of things. *Justice* is represented by *Dike,* a fierce virginal woman on a funeral urn who is an intimate of Hades and concerned with the just treatment of the dead. *Law* is a more secular term, but not unrelated to the divine. *Nomos* means "institution," "custom," "universal norm," and the laws of the State. Antigone's *nomos* is personal, familial, emanating from the gods, and eternal (450, 519, 905–08, 913–14). Creon's *nomos* is secular and civic, demanding absolute obedience and discipline in order to preserve the State (175–191).

C. Antigone versus Creon or the War of the Laws: The Ancients versus the Moderns

Antigone and Creon represent the war of the Ancients and the Moderns in fifth-century Athens that was a city in transition and bent on establishing democracy. The central dispute in Sophocles' play is between the "archaic, familial usage and codes of sentiment,"[144] represented by Antigone, and the "new public rationality of the Periclean moment,"[145] represented by Creon. Ironically, the youthful Antigone represents the views of the Ancients, who revered the eternal gods, blood ties, family bonds, and natural law. She represents emotion and nature, the "mother bird" lamenting her empty nest (423–25), the hunted animal (433), Niobe, who clings like close winding ivy on a rock (826–27). Antigone's justice is associated with the universal, the immutable, the gods below (94, 451, 459–60),

---

143. *Id.* at 152.
144. Steiner, *supra* note 4, at 182.
145. *Id.* at 182.

death, and Hades. When asked by Creon why she dares disobey his law, Antigone responds in a famous speech describing the "unwritten laws" and the elements of the natural law she passionately defends:

> For me it was not Zeus who made that order.
> Nor did that Justice who lives with the gods below
> mark out such laws to hold among mankind.
> Nor did I think your orders were so strong
> that you, a mortal man, could over-run
> the gods' unwritten and unfailing laws.
> Not now, nor yesterday's they always live,
> and no one knows their origin in time. (450–57)

Creon is older than Antigone, but he represents the Moderns in a characteristically ironic idiom that identifies Sophocles' particular style. Creon shows admiration for Zeus (487, 1040–41) and Olympian justice that presides over the civic order. Creon mocks Antigone's "reverence of Hades" (777, 780), and Antigone, who rejects Olympian justice, is referred to scornfully as the "bride of Hades," the "bride of death." Creon resides comfortably with the Olympian gods, whereas Antigone is associated with the chthonic deities of the underworld. Creon rejects Antigone's belief in the sanctity of blood ties, kinship, and family bonds (38, 45–46, 80–81, 466–68, 511) that Antigone defends by reveling in the glory of burying her brother in defiance of Creon's decree (502).

D. The Role of Greek Tragedy in Debating the Law

Greek tragedy dramatized the dissonance between State law (which was public) and divine law (which protected the intimate private life of the family). In ancient Athens, tragedy mirrored the dialectic of public and private law, which became intricately associated with gender difference. The female was identified with the family and with blood ties whereas the male was associated with the demands of civic duty. For Athenians, the performance of tragedies such as Sophocles' *Antigone* was not a matter of entertainment or mere aesthetic enjoyment. Tragedy provided an arena for the serious examination of contemporary legal and political issues that were the subject of live debate in the recently formed Athenian democracy. New notions of crime and punishment and criminal procedure developed in democratic Athens. Divine justice was no longer considered the sole authority of the law. The emerging democratic community became the new grounds of the legal system.[146] Thus, the debate between natural and human law was the central axis around which many of the most significant works of Greek tragedy turned, reflecting the preoccupations of the day.

146. Schmidt, *supra* note 41, at 147.

E. Greek History, the Law, and Sophocles' *Antigone*

The juxtaposition of Antigone and Creon, the Ancients and the Moderns, reflects developments in Greek history at the time Sophocles was writing his tragedy. Antigone's definition of kinship is *homos planchmos sebein* ("reverence for those of the same womb") (511). Her definition of kinship reaches deeply into the conflict of values in fifth-century Greece during the establishment of Athenian democracy which depended on breaking down the power of the clan and rejecting blood ties. In earlier times, the tie of blood relationships was stronger even than the *polis*. This view, based on the continued use of power, was a threat to the establishment of democracy in a new Athens. The substitution of the *deme* for the clan meant the transition from a principle of kinship to that of locality. Thus, Athens was no longer a federation of kindreds after the reforms of Cleisthenes.[147] In Greek history, political reformers in Athens viewed old loyalties to family as a threat to the new democratic institutions. Primitive justice of the old family organization was personal justice administered for revenge by the murdered man's family. This old system of personal justice was supplanted by the creation of a new system of justice in which the State assumed the responsibility of the blood relative.[148]

Antigone is a Greek citizen and a woman in defiance of the *polis* (79, 90), in disrespect of the leader, and in devotion to a blood relative. Creon is a Greek ruler and a man who proclaims the right of the *polis* to demand loyalty of its citizens to the State, even if this right means betrayal of the age-old, sacred duty to bury a blood relative.[149]

Ismene, Antigone's own sister, recognizes Antigone's claim of the validity of blood relationships and defies the *polis* to protect that claim. Ismene's position is explained in two ways: She lacks courage. She also represents the Greeks of fifth-century Athens who considered Polyneices' treachery as the most heinous crime imaginable and worthy of the most savage punishment.[150]

The distinction between paternal and maternal lineage was a live issue for audiences of mid-fifth century Athens, and Creon stands for patriarchal lineage and authority (639–47, 635), a position that works well with his antifeminine and anti-maternal attitude (569). There is no doubt Creon is concerned with family, which is shown in his love for his son, Haemon, but he undervalues the blood ties that Antigone overvalues. Antigone's punishment is to be thrown in a cave. The dark forces it contains is a place of tragic isolation that resolves the tension between her devotion to her loved ones and her death-bent heroism.[151]

---

147. *Id.* at 76.
148. *Id.* at 77.
149. *Id.* at 79.
150. *Id.* at 84.
151. SEGAL, *supra* note 141, at 183.

Thus, neither Creon nor Antigone embodies a law or a system of justice that is fully satisfactory as a civilizing principle.[152]

VII. CIVIL DISOBEDIENCE AND JEAN ANOUILH'S *ANTIGONE*: A PARODY

We think of Jean Anouilh as a playwright of rebellion. Yet, this keen observer of the world around him was actually first a law student who enrolled at the University of Paris and spent eighteen months in law school before he took up writing as a career.[153] His fascination with the law and jurisprudence is clearly reflected in his admiration of Sophocles' play *Antigone*. However, after reading Jean Anouilh's *Antigone*, we are immediately struck by its difference from the Sophoclean tragedy. Anouilh himself said: "Sophocles' *Antigone*, which I read and reread and knew by heart forever, was a sudden shock for me during the war . . . and I rewrote it in my way, with the resonance of the tragedy we were living."[154]

Jean Anouilh's *Antigone*, which is based on—but very different from—Sophocles' Greek tragedy, reflects the horrific events of the second World War, the pervasiveness of existentialist philosophy, and its expression in a theatre of revolt in the medium of the absurd. Anouilh's *Antigone* is a play-within-a-play, written in a more modern, more colloquial, less laconic style than Sophocles' tragedy. It was performed first in 1944 in German-occupied France and many times thereafter during the Occupation. From 1939–45, the progress of the theatre was completely disrupted by the war, which shattered civilized life throughout the world. Nevertheless, under the German Occupation the French stage was somehow kept alive.[155] The French theatre of this period was marked by revivals of classical works, and Anouilh's play is a recreation of Sophocles' classical tragedy.

Sophocles' *Antigone* is a dark tragedy with no comic relief,[156] and it contains, in a disguised and literary form, a surprisingly optimistic message about the effectiveness of civil disobedience for legal reform. Although Anouilh's play is melodramatic with several light passages added for comic relief (such as the colorful conversations of Creon's guards), Anouilh's message about the effectiveness of civil disobedience is pessimistic, negative, and representative of the tone

152. *Id.* at 169.

153. B.A. Lenski, Jean Anouilh: Stages in Rebellion 2–3 (1975).

154. Jean Anouilh, *Oedipe ou le Roi Boiteux* (Paris: La Table Ronde, 1986), *cited in* Andrew Hunwick, *Tragédie et Dramaturgie: Les Ambiguités dans l'Antigone d'Anouilh*, 96 Revue D'Histoire Litteraire de la France 290–312, (1996).

155. Allarkyce Nicoll, World Drama from Aeschylus to Anouilh 897 (n.d).

156. "Humor is unknown to Greek tragedy." *See* Marc Eli Blanchard, *The Reverse View: Greece and Greek Myths in Modern French Theater*, 29 Modern Drama 41, 42 (1986).

of the theatre of the absurd that was prevalent at the time this play was performed.

Anouilh knew Sophoclean dramaturgy, even admitted knowing *Antigone* by heart, but his play is dramatically different in form, content, and language from Sophocles' play. Anouilh's literary changes are significant and reflect the nature of parody that attacks vice and folly by satire and irony in order to mask the author's subversive message. When Anouilh's protagonist, Antigone, momentarily assumes the lyric tone of the Greek theatre and cries out: "O tombeau! O lit nuptial! O ma demeure souterraine . . . ," this rich heroic language draws the reader's attention to Anouilh's different portrayal of the well-known Sophoclean classical tragedy. His use of heroic language, which every French reader identifies with the beginning of a classical *stance* containing all the poetic power that anaphora and evocation possess, is out of place when it appears in a comic scene of a modern drama. This heroic verse, like a parody of classical poetry, is pronounced inappropriately when a guard complains to his prisoner, Antigone, about the mundane concerns of his rank, advancement, and salary. In Anouilh's *Antigone*, mediocrity is represented by the guards Jonas, Boudousse, and Durand. It is absurd for Antigone to be uttering these heroic lines to such lowly characters.[157] In contrast to Anouilh's contextual mediocrity, Sophocles placed this heightened, noble, and heroic discourse in the heroine's last moments of life, in the dark cave where she languishes briefly with the hope that she will join her loved one in Hades: "O tomb, O marriage-chamber, hollowed out house that will watch forever, where I go." (891)

By its difference, Anouilh's recreation of Sophocles' *Antigone* rejects the very myth of Antigone on which the Greek tragedy was built. Anouilh's melodrama also rejects the genre of tragedy and produces instead a metatragedy that lacks conventional Aristotelian drama and tension. The typical audience involvement associated with Sophoclean tragedy, like the jury in a trial, is supplanted by the Prologue's and the Chorus' direct address to the audience at the beginning of the play. In Anouilh, the Prologue and Chorus are mere actors in a play, and Anouilh's *Antigone* is a play about a play.[158] Anouilh is a French postmodernist who debunks the tragic heroine, calls into question tragedy itself, and raises serious doubts about the effectiveness of civil disobedience.[159] He recreates the Antigone of Sophocles in very different terms not of the heroic, but of the absurd.

---

157. LENSKI, *supra* note 153, at 35.

158. Lewis W. Leadbeater, *Senecan Elements in Anouilh's* Antigone, 7 CLASSICAL AND MODERN LITERATURE: A QUARTERLY 63, 65 (1987).

159. Gary S. Meltzer, *Subversive Comedy in the Antigones of Sophocles and Anouilh*, 12 CLASSICAL AND MODERN LITERATURE: A QUARTERLY 343, 345 (1992): "Anouilh's use of comic relief is to call into question the dignity of his heroine and the meaning of her tragic gesture."

Anouilh's radical change from the original Sophoclean source play is troublesome. We are tempted to ask why Anouilh even bothered to rewrite Sophocles' *Antigone* in his own idiom if he disagreed with Sophocles' basic premise about the effectiveness of civil disobedience. This kind of literary disparity invites the reader to think about the effects of the political and cultural context on the author who had to contend with the German censors in order to produce his play.

Structurally, Anouilh adds new characters to the myth of Antigone. By juxtaposition to Puff the dog and to the nurse, Anouilh's Antigone appears to be even younger,[160] more family-oriented, more maternal,[161] more protective of her sister and brother, and more human than Sophocles' tragic heroine. Anouilh's Antigone is also more vulnerable, weaker, and more self-doubting. At one point, Anouilh's Antigone even renounces her decision to protest the king's decree by covering the body of her brother. Anouilh's Antigone is not a philsopher[162] bent on proving the superiority of divine law over human law. Rather she is an impassioned, youthful, maternal protectrice who must, by her act of defiance, simply protect her dead brother.[163]

A. The Nature of Parody in Anouilh's *Antigone*

The difficulty we face in determining the real motivation behind Antigone's act of civil disobedience in Anouilh's *Antigone* (whether her act is based on personal desire or on a more universal ethical principle) stems from the form of the play, which is a parody of civil disobedience and of Sophoclean tragedy. Parody is a means by which the author can hide his true feelings and the object of his attack. Couching the hidden message in the form of parody is Anouilh's defense against the censors.

To parody a play, the author must change the original source discretely but effectively so as to mask the author's real message and create ambiguity and doubt in the reader's mind. Anouilh makes sharp as well as discrete changes from the original. For example, he omits certain characters such as Tiresias, the Seer, who represents the people's opinions. In Anouilh's play, the Creon–Antigone agon is the central experience on which the playwright focuses the reader's attention by tightening the plot and omitting the character Tiresias.

---

160. Pol Vandromme, Jean Anouilh, Un Auteur et ses Personnages 95 (La Table Ronde, 1965) ("Le charme d'Antigone, dans la pièce d'Anouilh, c'est le charme de l'enfance." "Antigone's charm in Anouilh's play is the charm of youth.") (translation by Tiefenbrun).

161. *Id.* at 97 (" . . . il y a chez Antigone une aspiration invincible à la maternité." "Antigone has an invincible aspiration of being maternal") (translation by Tiefenbrun).

162. *Cf.* Lenski, *supra* note 153, at 43 ("Antigone's and Joan's rebellions are based on exalted heroic will rather than private feelings.").

163. Vandromme, *supra* note 160, at 98–99.

Anouilh also adds new scenes, such as the romantic ball, Antigone's arrest, a love scene between Antigone and Haemon, and Antigone's dictation to the guard of a farewell letter to her betrothed Haemon. In the Sophoclean tragedy, the poignant scene between Haemon and Creon is brief and pits an excessively obedient, admiring, immensely diplomatic son against his autocratic father, the king of Thebes, who cannot bear the thought of his son being reduced to the low level of womanhood. In Anouilh's play, the scene between Creon and Haemon is longer, presenting the picture of a more rebellious young Haemon who is desperately in love with Antigone and deeply disappointed in his father whom he sees (for the first time) as an unyielding tyrant.

Anouilh revives Sophocles' guards and rewrites them into a new symbol of "numbing conformity and moral apathy."[164] Anouilh's guards represent the indifferent political henchmen who are employed by the tyrant who resorts to power to enforce the letter of the law. Anouilh's guards are smug, self-righteous, and unfailingly tranquil as they arrest Antigone.[165] Jonas, Creon's scapegoat, is a reluctant spokesman, cringing, sweating, and stammering as he fearfully approaches Creon the tyrant. The guards play a more significant role in the plot of Anouilh's play, and their comic depiction makes it difficult but not impossible to identify their indifference and brutality with the excessively "civilized" Nazi SS officers who were carrying out Hitler's political philosophy with savage brutality and impunity within the German political and legal system. Anouilh's guards represent blind obedience to duty, obsession with honors and promotion, lack of imagination, and absence of any sense of culpability. They are oblivious to tragic suffering.[166] In Anouilh's *Antigone*, Jonas, the guard, needs to consider his "own safety" (439–40) before anything else. He is a comic character like Falstaff, a caricature who is sympathetic to Antigone's plight but afraid to speak up in her defense (504–05).[167] In the arrest scene Anouilh reveals the darker side of the guards' unthinking obedience, conformity, and allegiance to the *status quo*. The guards accuse Antigone of being a prostitute, an exhibitionist, and a madwoman, and they insult her, comparing her to an animal or a demon. The guards marginalize Antigone, reducing her to the status of the perverted, criminal, female Other.[168] In Anouilh's play, it is not Creon but the guards who represent evil, the creatures of the herd, the ultimate survivors, and the "tranquil inheritors of the earth."

Although parody has universal appeal, it is often a temporal, political response to a particular event. Thus, it is very tempting to interpret Anouilh's play as a dramatization of France's political problems of the 1940s. The pragmatic

---

164. Meltzer, *supra* note 159, at 330.
165. *Id.* at 353.
166. *Id.* at 358.
167. *Id.* at 349.
168. *Id.* at 354.

collaborationist policies of the Vichy regime are exemplified in Creon, who can be contrasted to the idealistic intransigence of De Gaulle's Free French forces and the Resistance movement, which are embodied in Antigone.[169] Rather than reduce the universal quality of Anouilh's play by this local interpretation, it seems more useful to consider the role contemporary political irony and satire play in the author's attempt to escape censorship. Anouilh encoded his politically subversive message in the form of parody to speak indirectly and thereby to disguise his personal attack on the vices and follies of totalitarian regimes. The writer, then, is a variant of the civil disobedient who unwilling to accept punishment seeks protection in literary disguise. Anouilh understood that the tyrant, too, masks his own obsession with power by calling this evil a civilizing principle of the Rule of Law.

Parody, like law, engages in the play of similarity and difference. Despite their obvious differences, Antigone and the guards have certain similarities. Both Jonas and Antigone are scapegoats for Creon, but Jonas fears execution and Antigone does not. The guard is lowborn, and his colloquial speech, strewn with French slang, is distinctly different from Antigone's noble status and discourse. While the guard fears death, Antigone seems to "yearn for death." The guard's intervention offers an ironic counterpoint to the tragic action "which reveals the folly behind Creon's reasoning and the sense behind Antigone's apparent folly."[170] Thus, by juxtaposing the guards with Antigone and by comparing Anouilh's and Sophocles' plays, the reader may gain insight into Anouilh's hidden message about the role of civil disobedience in achieving legal reform.

B. Anouilh and Existentialism

Like Sophocles' main character, Antigone, Anouilh's Antigone is a rebel. But Anouilh's Antigone is in existential revolt.[171] This female rebel is a Neo-Romantic raging against existence, ashamed of being human, and revolted by the body itself. One of the strongest identifying features of the existential drama is its attitude toward the flesh.[172] Polyneices' rotting carcass is the symbol of existential rot that is the microcosm of the world in 1944. Antigone's own body approaches this dark view of the world. In Anouilh's play, Antigone is dark, skinny, and not physically "beautiful" in the traditional sense. According to Anouilh, Antigone's beauty comes from within, by virtue of her deed, which is seen as nonetheless absurd in this theatre of the absurd. Antigone's link to her fated father, Oedipus, is stressed throughout Anouilh's play, and her stubborn pride (seen by Creon as insubordination and insolence) is explained by her fate and her relation to Oedipus: "la fille d'Oedipe."

---

169. Christopher Smith, Jean Anouilh, Life, Work, and Criticism 24 (1985).
170. Meltzer, *supra* note 159, at 351.
171. Robert Brustein, The Theatre of Revolt 27 (1962).
172. *Id.* at 28.

In contrast to the not-so-beautiful Antigone is Ismene, to whom Haemon is initially but not ultimately attracted during the newly created ball scene. Ismene is depicted as the woman of sensuous beauty incarnate, but a woman who (in contrast to her rebellious sister) is unwilling to do an insubordinate act even if its purpose is to protest an unjust law. Ismene plays a more important role in Anouilh's play than in Sophocles' tragedy. In drawing the reader's attention to the competition between the two sisters, Anouilh reinforces the view that Antigone's act of civil disobedience is undertaken for reasons of personal desire and not for adherence to a philosophical belief in the moral exigencies of natural law.

Nevertheless, the motivation of Antigone's act is not based on a mediocre personal desire for her own happiness. Antigone in fact spurns the "happiness" sought by Ismene and Creon, and she considers the quest for happiness as immeasurably inferior to the satisfaction she will gain from being true to herself. The motivation of Antigone's act is based on a refusal to compromise,[173] and in that refusal she sees herself as different from Ismene, from Creon, and from the guards—all survivors who compromise. Antigone, like no one else in the play, is the Other, the one who is unwilling to compromise her principles.[174] The compromisers in Anouilh's theatre are those who say "Yes," those who are governed by self-interest in the political kitchen in which compromisers are cast as chief cooks. Their existence is threatened by the insolent people who, like Antigone, say "No" to that which they believe to be unfair or unjust. The more autocratic the regime, the more frequent are accusations of insolence and insubordination.

Anouilh adds small but significant details to clarify interpretive gaps left open by Sophocles, such as the role of the gods in the mysterious second attempt to bury Polyneices. By adding a small but significant detail of Polyneices' shovel, Anouilh makes it clear that Antigone alone performed that second act of civil disobedience.

A parody is always based on a source that the parodist must change just enough to maintain the similarity but establish the difference between the two literary works. One of the most important differences between Sophocles' and Anouilh's *Antigone* is the character portrayal of Creon. Anouilh paints the picture of a new Creon, a leader in an ambiguous role, a leader without freedom in a State governed by the Rule of Law. Creon both obeys and disobeys certain laws, and the social order based on the Rule of Law he describes in the "ship of state" speech is a dehumanizing regime. Creon's view of the world is utterly meaningless; he denies his own edict; his vision of the world is one of chaos that can only be saved (but is actually perpetuated) by absolute authority. But in Anouilh's

---

173. *See* LENSKI, *supra* note 153, at 37 for a discussion of the theme of compromise in Anouilh's theatre.

174. SMITH, *supra* note 169, at 26.

parody, Creon does not like power, which is an indignity that overwhelms him. Creon's regime, which is supposed to be one of Reason, is based instead on absurdity, meaninglessness, and deceit. The putrid carcass, which Creon's edict causes to rot, symbolizes Creon's absurd universe in which law does not equate with justice.[175]

In Anouilh's play, Creon is more human; he complains that he has a hard job and feels sorry for himself because he often has to do what he does not want to do. He is also a man willing to make special deals with Antigone, willing to forgive and forget, if only she would agree to save the leader's face. It appears that the only reason Creon kills Antigone is to save his image of absolute authority. Anouilh's Creon is totally lacking in dignity and adherence to a particular philosophy. He mocks "natural law" unabashedly, calling it "absurd" (72). This charged and politically motivated adjective reminds the reader that Anouilh's play is the product of an existentialist era and was written and performed in the tradition of the theatre of the absurd.

Creon is a practical man, and the only reason he has been kind to Eteocles is that he needs to create a hero (89) for his people. Anouilh's Creon is a far cry from Sophocles' committed leader who stands firmly for the principles of human law and the sanctity of the *polis*. Anouilh's Creon actually considers himself to be like Antigone and ironically calls himself "a young Antigone at 20" (91). Creon's lack of self-awareness is at the heart of the play's irony. He is fundamentally quite different from the passionate and sensitive Antigone, as his shocking reaction to his own wife's death is one of cold indifference. He anachronistically, inappropriately (and therefore comically) holds a 5 o'clock cabinet meeting (122) right after learning of Eurydice's tragic suicide. Unlike Sophocles' Creon, Anouilh's Creon never gains insight into the unjustness of his totalitarian regime, never changes the unjust law he decrees, and never learns about himself from Antigone's act of civil disobedience. Creon remains Creon and carries on business as usual until the end of the play.

In Anouilh's parody, it is Antigone and not Creon who admits that she has erred when she apologizes for her verbal and physical acts of defiance (the constant recurrence of the exclamation "Non" and her burial of Polyneices). "I'm sorry," she says. In Anouilh's play, it is not Creon who is enlightened but Antigone, who in the end realizes how much damage she has caused by her act of civil disobedience. In his remarks on the tragic futility of events in Belfast, Dr. Conor Cruise O'Brien stressed the evil effects of civil disobedience and cited Antigone as a perfect example of this dangerous practice: "The act of non-violent civil disobedience, whereby Antigone sets out to inter Polyneices, breeds utmost violence: it brings on her own suicide, Haeman's attempt to slay his father and

---

175. Ruban Hewitson, *Anouilh's* Antigone*: A Coherent Structure,* 17 AUSTRALIAN J. OF FRENCH STUDIES 167, 177 (1980).

his suicide, the suicide of Eurydice, and the devastation of Creon's personal existence and political authority . . . a stiff price for that handful of dust on Polyneices."[176] Thus, Anouilh's pessimistic message about the ineffectiveness of civil disobedience is entirely different from Sophocles' more optimistic view. In Anouilh's *Antigone,* Creon wins and turns the world of civil disobedience topsy-turvy!

Anouilh's pessimistic view of the absurd world is reminiscent of the existentialist philosophy, which Anouilh adopted in his own plays several years before Sartre.[177] Anouilh's allegiance to existentialist philosophy helps to explain why Antigone must perform her "absurd" act, even if by this act she accomplishes nothing to change the hegemonic political and unjust legal system. Antigone acts not from a desire to satisfy the divine law for she feels it is meaningless. Hers is an inner compulsion, a desire to be true to herself. The only way Antigone can be true to herself is by refusing the compromise of life represented by the policy of Creon. Antigone's absurd act is a symbol of her liberty.[178] In compliance with existentialist doctrine, Antigone must perform the futile act, like Sisyphus, in order to live with dignity and self-worth and to die with honor.

VIII. CONCLUSION

Anouilh's play is a parody of classical Greek tragedy, of civil disobedience and its effectveness, and of absolute rule. Although Anouilh's drama[179] is less weighty than Sophocles' classical tragedy, Anouilh's absurdist view[180] is nonetheless more negative with respect to the effectiveness of civil disobedience to reform the legal system. Anouilh's *Antigone* is encoded in an existentialist discourse representative of the particular moment in legal and political history in which the play was written and performed. Anouilh's play also reflects the indomitable presence of the German censors whom he cleverly escaped by disguising his subversive message in the cloak of parody. Sophocles accomplished the same task of hiding his true beliefs behind a mask of irony and ambiguity. Anouilh's ironic depiction

---

176. STEINER, *supra* note 4, at 190, citing Dr. Conor Cruise O'Brien's lecture in Belfast in 1968, *reprinted in* THE LISTENER (BBC Publications, London, Oct. 1968).

177. SERGE RADINE, ANOUILH, LENORMAN, SALACROU: TROIS DRAMATURGES A LARECHERCHE DE LEUR VERITE 27 (Edition des Trois Collines 1951).

178. LEONARD CABELL PRONKO, THE WORLD OF JEAN ANOUILH 204 (1968). This book contains a very interesting comparison of Sophocles' and Anouilh's *Antigone. Id.* at 200–07.

179. Philip Thody refuses to classify Anouilh's play as a tragedy, and many literary critics have discussed the question of its classification as tragedy or melodrama. *See* Hunwick, *supra* note 154, at 291–93.

180. Hunwick, *supra* note 154, at 291: "The greatness of the Greek tragedy is reduced in Anouilh to a ('tragedy of the absurd'").

of an ineffectual civil disobedient and a flexible but strong leader managed to please and pass the censors so they would let the play go on.

Many have criticized Anouilh's negativity and radically different portrayal of the character of Antigone, whom Sophocles painted as a tragic heroine. Critics claim that Anouilh invalidated the myth of Antigone by marginalizing her and calling her names: "un sale caractère." Some say Anouilh substituted a "hysterical adolescent" for a Greek tragic heroine.[181] Anouilh's Antigone persists in an "absurd and vain revolt, even though she has a choice."[182] Anouilh's Antigone is not tragic at all. Her act is absurd and committed not in the name of personal happiness, but for questionable motivations associated with egotism and individualism. Antigone is a mere actress playing the role of the tragic heroine and reducing the heroine's heavy responsibility to an absurd self-involved search for self-worth.

Although these critical views have validity, they do not take into account the repressive political context in which Anouilh's play was written and the liberating influence of parody on the writer's freedom of speech. Anouilh's intentional and literary distortion of the original Greek myth and his parody of Sophocles' tragedy enable the writer to escape censorship and allow the public to revisit recurrent jurisprudential debates of legal positivism and natural law in the light of the tragic events of the first half of the twentieth century that unfortunately appear to be recurring despite the legacy of Nuremburg. By this recreation of the classical Greek tragedy, the modern play allows the public to rethink the underlying issues of civil disobedience and its ability to reform the law and influence changes in a legal system that is intricately connected to its political environment.

---

181. Philip Thody, *cited in* Hunwick, *id.* at 309.

182. Hunwick, *id.* at 296.

PART D

WOMEN'S HUMAN RIGHTS

8. THE SEMIOTICS OF WOMEN'S HUMAN RIGHTS IN IRAN*

I. INTRODUCTION

The status of women's human rights in Iran today is a complex issue mired in contradiction and paradox, not unlike the Iranian society itself. The Iranian language reflects this paradox because words reportedly have double meanings that produce vagueness and intentional ambiguity, resulting in misunderstandings for some and advantages for others engaged in the fine art of hiding what they really mean to say. This linguistic deception is not unusual especially for Iranian women who must behave one way publicly and another privately, even though society, in the Islamist State, has been forced to adopt a universalist moral code that proclaims against relativist ethics.

Human rights abuses are prevalent in Iran today, with women suffering the most from this deplorable condition. The following serious human rights abuses exist in Iran and detrimentally impact women: summary executions; disappearances; widespread use of torture and other degrading treatment including rape; severe punishments like stoning to death and public flogging; harsh prison conditions; arbitrary arrests and detention; and prolonged and incommunicado detention; impunity of government officials accused of misconduct in judicial proceedings; influence of conservative government clerics' in the judiciary preventing citizens from receiving due process or fair trials; governmental restriction of the freedom of religion; flagrant discrimination against religious minorities, particularly Baha'is and Jews; governmental control over the selection of candidates for elections; governmental restriction of the work of human rights groups in Iran; domestic and public violence against women; increase in women and children runaways, prostitution and sex trafficking; and increased poverty in Iran where 29 percent of the families below the poverty line consist of single mothers.

Women's human rights and the role of women in Iranian society are tied up in a thick web of historical, political, cultural, economic, social, and legal factors, all of which work together in an intricate contextual system like a structural puzzle whose parts or elements can be identified and analyzed. Each of these

---

* This chapter appeared as an article in 23 CONN. J. INT'L L. (2007); it has been revised and updated.

elements is itself a sign system with complex underlying mechanisms. Each sign system plays a significant role in the development and continuation of human rights abuses of women in Iran. Classical structural analysis provides insights into surface and deep meanings. Semiotic analysis, by which we study signs of women's human rights abuses, will reveal hidden, deeper structures that may be unknown even to the women themselves.

This semiotic study will examine various types of coded sign systems that, when decoded contextually and from the point of view of cultural peculiarities known to Iranians, reveal hidden realities about women's human rights in Iran. The analysis will attempt to determine how and the extent to which basic human rights are being denied to women in Iran today and whether there is hope for more justice and gender equality in Iran in the future.

Part I of this chapter will examine the historic and political contexts of women's human rights in Iran. Part II will look at the sign system of wearing women's Islamic garb known as the *hejab* or veil in an attempt to uncover the meaning of the many different messages this speech act conveys. I will discuss the significance of the French headscarf case and the Turkish headscarf case decided finally in the European Court of Human Rights. That court based its almost unanimous decision denying the right to wear a headscarf in public schools and universities on pure semiotics.

Part III will investigate cultural manifestations of women's human rights abuses in Iran through a study of the memoirs and films of four Iranian women. I will look at the best-selling memoir of Azar Nafisi, *Reading Lolita in Tehran*, written by an Iranian woman who is a literature professor. The second memoir is *Iran Awakening*, written by Shirin Ebadi, a Nobel Peace Prize winner and former Iranian female judge, who is currently a lawyer and women's rights activist working within the Iranian system to change it. The powerful documentary film, *Divorce Iranian Style*, sheds light on the institution of marriage in Iran and the deficiencies of its family laws and legal system, especially for women seeking a divorce. I will also look at the contrapuntal view of two Iranian women, one modern and one forced to be traditional, as represented in the very successful film *Two Women* directed by the Iranian feminist filmmaker, Tahmineh Milani. The juxtaposition of these two women represents the contradictions and paradoxes in Iranian society.

Part IV will investigate the Iranian family laws as a sign system that reflects the culture in Iran and conditions the status of women's rights today in that country. I will also discuss the inadequacies of the Iranian legal system that is caught up in a difficult relationship with Islam and the differing views of Koranic interpretation, some of which negatively impact women. Part V will examine some of the international human rights laws and instruments that protect gender equality. Finally, this study will conclude by looking at the future of women's rights in Iran.

II. HISTORY OF WOMEN'S RIGHTS IN IRAN

A. Iran and Its Invasion by Foreigners

Despite a constant tension between tradition and modernity in Iran, modern-day Iran actually began in the early nineteenth century[1] by exposure to a wide range of new and Western ideas. At that time, it was quite fashionable for rich young Iranian men to be educated in Europe, especially France. Iranians were also exposed to Western ideas by reading translations of European literary and political works. Moreover, after Iran's defeat in two wars with Russia, many European diplomats, merchants, and military advisors came to Iran and influenced the people by their very presence.[2]

But the presence of these foreigners also made Iranians suspicious. Many claimed that Britain and Russia had imperialistic interests in Iran. When foreigners sold their industrial and commercial concessions to the debt-ridden Iranian government,[3] this economic trade was interpreted by the religious classes as Iran's willingness to sell out the country and Islam to the West. Reza Shah's infatuation with Western traditions and modernity (which he imposed tyrannically on Iranians) was the start of a movement that resulted in the Constitutional Revolution of 1905–11 in Iran. The aim of this revolution was to limit the despotism of the Shah through the establishment of a constitution, an elected legislature, and an independent judiciary.[4] Ironically, these were the same goals of the critical revolutionary movement that took place in Iran in the 1970s, a revolution that would change the face of Iran forever and have serious consequences for women's rights and gender equality.

From 1911 to 1921, Iran was occupied by foreigners,[5] and the country experienced disorder and insurgency until Reza Shah Pahlavi, a westernizing secular nationalist and an army colonel, successfully carried out a coup d'état against the Iranian constitutional government.[6] Once Reza Shah Pahlavi came to power,

---

1. *See* ZIBA MIR-HOSSEINI & RICHARD TAPPER, ISLAM AND DEMOCRACY IN IRAN: ESHKEVARI AND THE QUEST FOR REFORM 11–18 (2006) (discussing the history and development of "modern" Iran from the nineteenth century to postrevolutionary Iran).

2. *Id.* at 11.

3. *Id.* at 12.

4. *Id.*

5. *See* JANET AFARY & KEVIN B. ANDERSON, FOUCAULT AND THE IRANIAN REVOLUTION: GENDER AND THE SEDUCTIONS OF ISLAMISM 106 (2005). Iran's history and the development of forced dress for women is very much a reaction to the presence of foreign powers in Iran and the desire to retain Iranian and Muslim identity. The 1979 Revolution was also an attempt to free Iran from foreign or Western influences imposed on them by the Shah. "Iran was freeing itself from a foreign yoke, he said (Khomeini 1999, 6:15)." *Id.*

6. *See* ELAINE SCIOLINO, PERSIAN MIRRORS: THE ELUSIVE FACE OF IRAN 371–78 (2000) (providing a time line of events leading up to the Iranian Revolution of 1979). *See also*

he immediately formed a strong military, centralized bureaucracy, secular judiciary, and secular educational system that appealed to the constitutionalists. His reforms were popular, but the constitution itself was largely ignored, and dissent was ruthlessly suppressed[7] during his repressive reign. Reza Shah Pahlavi's obsession with modernity reduced the religious clerics to silence, and they were labeled "fanatical reactionaries."[8]

During World War II, British and Soviet forces occupied Iran in 1941. Reza Shah was forced to abdicate in favor of his son Mohammad Reza. In April 1951, a reformist Mohammed Mossadegh was appointed Prime Minister of Iran, but when he decided to nationalize the British-dominated oil industry, the British (with the help of the American Central Intelligence Agency) carried out a coup d'état to oust Mossadegh and restore the Shah to power.[9] Thus, Mohammad Reza Shah resumed his reign with the support of the United States. The Shah's continued suppression of dissent and parliamentary activity in Iran were wrongs that Iranians blame heavily on the United States. The Shah further alienated much of the country by allowing a massive increase of Western (primarily American) influence in Iran after 1953.[10] In an effort to win popular support, in 1962 the Shah instituted his "White Revolution" that included land reform and voting rights for women. However, very soon thereafter, Ayatollah Khomeini came into the limelight, publicly denouncing the Shah for his reforms as undermining of Islam, for his attacks on the clergy, and for his dependence on foreigners. Khomeini was arrested in 1963 and ultimately was exiled to Turkey and later Najaf, where he remained until 1978, one year before the Revolution.

B. The Iranian Revolution Against "Westoxication"

The Iranian Revolution was a mobilization of the people against the tyranny of the monarchy[11] and the Shah's infatuation with Western and American customs and values (i.e., "Westoxication") that allegedly robbed Iranians of their own identity. The West's lack of sensitivity to cultural difference and the subtle humiliation of Iranians who many called primitive and backward[12] no doubt exacerbated the

---

Jahangir Amuzegar, The Dynamics of the Iranian Revolution: The Pahlavis' Triumph and Tragedy (1991) (discussing an in-depth view of postrevolutionary Iran and the compatibility of Islam and democracy); *see also* Mir-Hosseini & Tapper, *supra* note 1, at 11–18.

7. Mir-Hosseini & Tapper, *supra* note 1, at 13.

8. *Id.*

9. Sciolino, *supra* note 6, at 371.

10. Mir-Hosseini & Tapper, *supra* note 1, at 14.

11. *See* Azar Nafisi, Reading Lolita in Tehran 86 (2004).

12. Betty Mahmoody & William Hoffer, Not Without My Daughter (1987). This superb novel was made into an equally moving film about an Iranian man who left Iran at the start of the 1979 Revolution and received his medical training and degree in the United States, where he lived for twenty years and married an American woman with

revolutionaries' suspicions about the foreigners and the West. Opposition to the Shah came from many factions: the leftists, the religious people, and clerics, and the nationalists. The leftists included the *Tudeh* who were linked to the USSR, the Marxist *Fedayan-e Khalq*, and the Islamic-socialist *Mojahedine-e Khalq*[13] as well as the intellectuals, all of whom were opposed to the widespread corruption and oppression of the Shah's regime. Religious opposition to the Shah included a number of Islamic associations composed of professionals, students, and intellectuals who all helped forge more modern ideas about Islam and a new Islamic discourse. The nationalists, leftists, and religious revolutionary forces all sought the same goals: to reject the autocratic Pahlavi monarchy, the inequalities in society, and the overwhelming influence of the United States in Iran.[14] "The Revolution of 1979 was supposed to empower and embolden the oppressed masses and make them independent of the capitalist foreigners."[15] Furthermore, the Revolution "was supposed to disinfect the country of 'Westoxication'."[16]

C. The Role of Women in the Revolution

Proponents of gender equality and equal rights for women in Iran come from diverse social strata: leftist secularists, pro-monarchists, and Islamic feminists.[17]

---

whom he had a lovely daughter. Troubled by the prejudice against Iranians around him in the hospital and fraught with guilt about his failure to support Iran in its revolutionary years, he dupes his wife and child into returning to postrevolutionary Iran. Immediately upon arrival into Iran, Betty Mahmoody's husband shockingly transforms into someone she cannot even recognize. He asks her to wear the *chador* and scarf, which for all Iranians is a symbol of respect, national identity, and religious adherence to Islamic values. Very soon thereafter he starts to beat her and terrorize his daughter. The wife and child are held hostage by the troubled Iranian husband and his rural, very religious, and fanatical Iranian family who claim to be descendants of Mohammed. This family clearly hates Americans and the corrupt ways of the West. The husband *was* outraged in America by his colleagues' slurs about Iran's backwardness and primitive traditions, and he is equally outraged now back in Iran by his wife's similar accusations. He is angry at the United States for its support of Iraq during the Iran–Iraq War. As his wife tries desperately to escape from his clutches and the Iranian enslavement to which she has been subjected, he holds her forcibly captive inside the home and threatens to kill her and indoctrinate his child into Islam, which he calls "the greatest gift I can give my child."

13. The Iranian government has outlawed the *Mojahedine-e Khalq Organization*. Prison officials in Iran have threatened to execute a young sympathizer of this group who has been denied access to a lawyer. Valiollah Feyz Mahdavi's trial "did not meet international standards for a fair trial." *See* Human Rights Watch, *Iran: Political Prisoner at Risk of Execution*, Mar. 16, 2006, http://hrw.org/english/docs/2006/03/15/iran12998.htm.

14. Mir-Hosseini & Tapper, *supra* note 1, at 15.

15. Sciolino, *supra* note 6, at 13.

16. *Id.*

17. *See* Louise Halper, *Law and Women's Agency in Post-Revolutionary Iran*, 28 Harv. J.L. & Gender 85, 103 (2005). Professor Halper's article is one of the best on the subject of

The 1979 Revolution was a popular movement also composed of many different factions, all opposed to the repressive monarchy, and all determined to create a new order that would give greater rights to women.[18]

In the early days of the Revolution, Khomeini desperately needed the popular support of the Iranian women to help him overthrow Reza Shah's regime. To achieve his goal, Khomeini promised more rights and freedom for all women in a new form of government that would be an Islamist democratic theocracy.[19] At that time many secular women such as Azar Nafisi, who supported a revolution that would provide further rights to all citizens and equality for women, were not supportive of an Islamic or religious State. But these secular women were not prepared to counter the mass support given by religious women for Khomeini and for the Islamists during the Revolution.[20]

Although many secular women protested the idea of the formation of a theocracy, they were outnumbered by the religious women who believed an Islamic nation would rescue them from oppression.[21] Khomeini established the Islamic State by betraying many of his only moderate supporters and by eliminating his enemies. In fact, once the Revolution occurred, Khomeini and his supporters consolidated their power by eliminating the opposition, destroying the leftist forces, purging the unsupportive religious leaders, and dividing the secular intellectuals by gender.[22] The age-old tactic of divide and conquer worked brilliantly in Khomeini's favor, allowing him to eradicate several facets of opposition at once.[23] Needless to say that Khomeini's promises of freedom and equality to women were not completely fulfilled, and he perpetrated what could be called one of the greatest frauds in the history of women's human rights.

After the Revolution, Khomeini's social and legal policies towards women became stricter and more repressive as he consolidated his political power. For example, soon after his Islamic regime became firmly entrenched, he declared the Family Protection Law[24] *un-Islamic*. This law was instituted by the Shah in 1967 to give greater rights to women in the area of marriage, divorce, and child custody. Women judges such as Shirin Ebadi were forced to resign their positions[25] and veiling became mandatory. Khomeini's pronouncements

---

women's rights in Iran, and I am deeply indebted to her for her encouragement and impeccable scholarship.

18. *See id.* at 105.

19. *See id.* at 108.

20. *See id.* at 107.

21. *See id.*

22. *See id.* at 109.

23. *See id.*

24. Shirin Ebadi, Iran Awakening: A Memoir of Revolution and Hope 52 (2006).

25. *See id.* at 48.

forced secular women in government and in other high-level positions to resign or be fired.[26]

Ironically, the imposition of the veil under Khomeini's regime has taken on a different meaning, and has actually led to greater freedom for traditional, religious women who were now able to participate in the public sphere for the first time in many years.[27] Under Khomeini and in the Islamist Republic, the State guarantees that the public sphere is a safe place for Muslim women to be seen precisely because the State mandates religiously appropriate behavior by both sexes and strict adherence to the dress code by women. In accordance with the strict interpretation of the Koran, women must be covered up so as not to tempt men to behave indecently. In Iran's postrevolutionary, highly regulated society, many traditional Muslim women who were formerly isolated in the privacy of their home actually experienced more opportunities and greater freedom to participate in education, politics, health, and many other fields.[28] Nevertheless, forced veiling had an equal but opposite effect of alienating and isolating secular women, even those who had supported some form of revolution and who opposed the Shah.[29]

D. Religious and Secular Women in Iran After the Revolution

To gain the support of women before and during the Revolution, Khomeini made many pro-feminist promises to guarantee greater support of women's rights and freedoms.[30] Once the Revolution ended, Islamic women expected those promises to be fulfilled.[31] Khomeini did provide rural women with a university education and added more women in Parliament.[32] In the absence of secular feminists within the new government, religious women were soon appointed to positions dealing with women's affairs, and they actually became influential in the government's new policies towards women.[33] But the religious women in government helped foster anti-secular policies towards women, which was interpreted by the outside world as antifeminist behavior.[34]

The division between religious and secular women in postrevolutionary Iran became more pronounced in the early days of the Khomeini regime, where only Islamic feminists had a real voice in government while secular women such as

26. *See* Halper, *supra* note 17, at 123.
27. *See id.* at 124.
28. *See id.* at 124–25.
29. *See id.* at 125.
30. *See id.* at 108.
31. *See id.* at 117.
32. *See id.* at 108.
33. *See id.* at 110.
34. *See id.* at 111.

Azar Nafisi were marginalized.[35] The policies of the new regime seemed contradictory and lacked cohesion with respect to women. On the one hand, the government required women to wear the veil, eliminated secular women from government and academic posts, and imposed strict *Shari'a* law on most private matters affecting women and the family.[36] On the other hand, the government claimed to advocate for women's rights, gave all women the right to a public education, maintained women's suffrage, encouraged political activity in support of the government, and took a relatively moderate stance on family law issues.[37]

E. Women, War, and Feminist Activism in Postrevolutionary Iran

In the new Iran, "approaches to women's issues were divergent, even contradictory."[38] For example, soon after the Khomeini regime took power, Iran went to war with Iraq,[39]an event that gave women inordinate power in Iran while Khomeini continued to create laws and policies that would marginalize them and render them dependent on men in a patriarchal society.

In Europe during World Wars I and II, women gained power because they were left alone to run the family while the men fought the wars. Similarly, the Iran–Iraq War gave more rights to Iranian women than did any other event.[40] During that war, the strategy of the Iranian government was to outnumber the Iraqi forces. This approach took men out of the home onto the battlefield where dramatic numbers of injuries and fatalities in turn affected the gender balance of Iranian society.[41] Women became indispensable during the war, and they were forced to take over a large percentage of the workforce.[42] Women had to help maintain the war effort, and for the first time they became the heads of their own households in the absence of a male presence.[43]

To retain the political support of these women, the Khomeini government implemented some policies and human rights laws that were favorable to women, such as child custody laws for war orphans and widows, employment benefits for women, education for women, and many other benefits.[44] During the ten-year period of the Iran–Iraq War, women in Iran became accustomed to mobilizing for greater rights and achieving them. This pattern of feminist activism in Iran during the war period established a natural cycle in which

---

35. *See id.* at 110.
36. *See id.*
37. *See id.*
38. *Id.*
39. *See* Nafisi, *supra* note 11, at 157.
40. *See* Halper, *supra* note 17, at 115.
41. *See id.*
42. *See id.* at 115–16.
43. *See id.* at 114–15.
44. *See id.* at 114–16.

Iranian women were able to ask for and actually receive more rights without establishing a formal feminist movement. Thus, the mechanisms for Islamist feminism were firmly established during the Iran–Iraq War.[45] Arguably, the mobilization of women for greater women's rights established a kind of underground resistance movement initially led by the Islamist feminists and then continued by secular women in the 1990s.[46] In 2006, Shirin Ebadi actually spoke of a "feminist movement" in Iran, but she hastened to add that it was a movement without a leader or home office, purposely designed that way to avoid endangering any one woman.[47]

F. Foucault on the Global Impact of the Iranian Revolution

The Iranian Revolution was not any ordinary kind of revolution. Michel Foucault, a famous French philosopher, called it:

> . . . a new type of revolutionary movement . . . an 'Islamic' movement [that] can set the entire region afire, overturn the most unstable regimes, and disturb the most solid ones. Islam—which is not simply a religion, but an entire way of life, an adherence to a history and a civilization—has a good chance to become a gigantic powder keg, at the level of hundreds of millions of men.[48]

Michel Foucault's prescient remarks made on February 13, 1979[49] imply that the Iranian Revolution would have an impact far beyond Iran's borders due to the global influence of Islam.

Unfortunately, after the Revolution Foucault remained silent regarding human rights violations and feminist protests in Iran and abroad against Khomeini's order that women re-veil.[50] Foucault's deafening silence about women's human rights abuses in particular is the reason his writing was attacked by feminist, leftist, and liberal intellectuals[51] who were no longer in center stage after the Revolution. By late February 1979, the real power in Iran was in the hands of the Revolutionary Council, a small and secretive group of clerics hovering around Khomeini who were responsible for summary executions, public whippings for alcohol consumption,[52] and other infractions such as mal-veiling.

---

45. *See id.* at 117.

46. *See id.* at 119.

47. Shirin Ebadi, Lecture at the Univ. of San Diego Joan B. Kroc Inst. for Peace & Justice Distinguished Lecture Series, "Iran Awakening: Human Rights, Women and Islam" 16 (Sept. 7, 2006), http://peace.sandiego.edu/events/DLS/PDF/IPJBookEbadi.pdf.

48. Afary & Anderson, *supra* note 5, at 107.

49. *Id.*

50. *Id.* at 108.

51. *Id.*

52. *Id.* at 109.

Foucault actually traveled to Iran, met with Khomeini, and celebrated the Iranian Revolution.[53] He was initially impressed with the principles and concerns of the revolutionaries in Iran in 1979,[54] but was called upon to admit that his support for the Khomeini regime was an error.[55] Foucault considered the Iranian Revolution comparable to previous anticolonial struggles, referring to the United States and other Western backers of the repressive Shah as imperialists.[56]

For Foucault, the Iranian Revolution was typical of the contradictions in Iranian society in general.[57] The Iranian Revolution was greater and deeper than a pure manifestation of Iranian "nationalism" because the Revolution also involved a xenophobic revolt against modernism, against the West, against all foreigners, and against Jews.[58] Foucault identified a deep-seated anti-Semitism[59] in Iran around the time of the Revolution: "There were demonstrations, verbal at least, of virulent anti-Semitism. There were demonstrations of xenophobia, and not only against the Americans, but also against foreign workers who had come to work in Iran."[60] Later Foucault criticized the Islamist Republic for its unfair trials[61] and summary executions that the regime tried to justify as an attempt to purify the country of its Westernized corruption. For Foucault, the Iranian Revolution was a revolution unlike any other, and it was ". . . outside the Western paradigm of revolution . . . perhaps even outside history itself. . . ."[62]

---

53. *See id.* at 118.

54. *Id.*

55. *Id.* at 119–20.

56. *Id.* at 123.

57. *Id.*

58. *See id.* at 124–25.

59. *See* U.S. Department of State, Country Reports on Human Rights Practices, Bureau of Democracy, Human Rights, and Labor, *Iran* (March 4, 2002), http://www.state.gov/g/drl/rls/hrrpt/2001/nea/8251.htm (discussing the reported persistence of anti-Semitism in Iran).

> Estimates of the size of the Iranian Jewish community vary from 25,000 to 30,000. These figures represent a substantial reduction from the estimated 75,000 to 80,000 Jews who resided in the country prior to the 1979 revolution. While Jews are a recognized religious minority, allegations of official discrimination are frequent. The Government's anti-Israel policies, coupled with a perception among radicalized Muslim elements in Iran that Jewish citizens support Zionism and the State of Israel, create a threatening atmosphere for the small Jewish community. . . . an increase in anti-Semitic propaganda . . . education of Jewish children has become more difficult in recent years . . . Jews were gradually dismissed from most government positions after 1979.

Id.

60. Afary & Anderson, *supra* note 5, at 124.

61. *See id.* at 129.

62. *Id.* at 131.

G. The Birth of the New Islamist Republic

On January 16, 1979, the Shah left Iran never to return again, and Ayatollah Khomeini came into power triumphantly on February 1, 1979. Khomeini immediately appointed a provisional government whose members included moderate nonclerical Islamists and nationalists who all wanted a secular democratic republic. But Khomeini's clerical followers, who were populist Islamic radicals, were intent on establishing an Islamic State governed by Islamic law called *Shari'a*.[63] Religious hardliners soon took control of the government. On March 30, 1979, a referendum approved the formation of an Islamic Republic claiming to be a democratic theocracy.

H. The New Iranian Constitution and the New Structure of Government

On December 2, 1979, a referendum approved a constitution that was, at best, a compromise document composed of a mixture of democratic and theocratic principles. On the one hand, the Iranian Constitution recognizes the right of the people to choose who will govern them and the right to establish democratic and legislative institutions such as the parliament and the president, both of whom are elected by direct popular vote.[64] On the other hand, the Iranian Constitution subordinates the people's will to the rule of the clerics through the institutions of the all powerful *Velayat-e faghih* (rule of the Islamic jurist)[65] or Leadership (*rahbari*)[66] of the Revolution and the infamous Guardian Council (*shura-ye negahban*).[67] The Guardian Council is composed of twelve members, six of whom are appointed by the Supreme Leader of the Revolution. The other six are nominated by the head of the judiciary and approved by Parliament for a six-year tenure.[68] The Guardian Council acts as an "Upper House" endowed with veto powers to strike down any law passed by Parliament that does not conform to *Shari'a* law and the Iranian Constitution. Because the Guardian Council interprets the Iranian Constitution,[69] whatever civil, political, social, economic, or cultural human rights that are legislated in favor of women must ultimately come under the judicial review of the Guardian Council.

---

63. *See* Halper, *supra* note 17, at 114–15.

64. AFARY & ANDERSON, *supra* note 5, at 17–18.

65. GISBERT H. FLANZ, CONSTITUTIONS OF THE COUNTRIES OF THE WORLD: ISLAMIC REPUBLIC OF IRAN 52, art. 91 (Albert P. Blaustein & Gisbert H. Flanz eds., 1992) [hereinafter Constitution of the Islamic Republic of Iran].

66. *Id.* at 61, art. 110 (providing the duties for the leader of the Revolution).

67. *Id.* at 52, art. 91.

68. *See id.* at 52–55, art. 91–99 (discussing the scope of the powers of the Guardian Council).

69. MIR-HOSSEINI & TAPPER, *supra* note 1, at 18.

I. Women's Protest After the Revolution in March 1979: Signs of a Feminist Movement

In the early months of 1979, religious extremists implemented the first "Reign of Terror"[70] imposing hard-line interpretations of Islamic law that resulted in many summary executions of military officers of the previous regime, members of the Shah's court, and capitalists who were killed because they had waged "war against God."[71] Prostitutes, adulterers, and homosexuals were also executed summarily because they allegedly committed the crime of "corruption on earth."[72]

On March 8, 1979, Khomeini gave his "infamous order compelling women to wear the *chador*."[73] Hundreds of Iranian feminists on their way that day to Tehran University for the International Women's Day demonstration reacted with "bitter derision to this news."[74] At that demonstration, Iranian women activists and male supporters protested in Tehran and Qom against this transformative order for women to re-veil themselves in the traditional *chador* normally worn only by highly religious women.[75] The demonstration continued for five days and attracted tens of thousands in Tehran. Some leftist men formed a symbolic and protective circle around the women to fight off armed attackers from a newly formed group, the Hezbollah,[76] or Party of God. The Hezbollah chanted, "You will cover yourselves or be beaten," and they threw stones, knives and even bullets at the women protestors.[77] The *Komiteh*, a "shadowy political and police force that was controlled by Khomeini and other mullahs" also harassed and detained women activists.[78]

On March 10, 1979, many thousands marched for women's rights, and fifteen thousand women held a sit-in at the Ministry of Justice. Protesters presented an eight-point proposal to the government calling for freedom for all regardless of gender, color, race, language, and opinion. They demanded free choice concerning dress, freedom of expression, and the removal of "all inequalities between men and women in national law."[79] By March 12, 1979, the women's demonstrations

---

70. *See* Chapter 3 of this book proposing a Semiotic definition of *terrorism*.

71. *Id.* at 16.

72. *Id.*

73. Afary & Anderson, *supra* note 5, at 112.

74. *Id.* at 112–13.

75. *Id.* at 111.

76. *See* Michael Slackman, *Mideast Conflict a Setback for Iran Reform Movement*, N.Y. Times, Aug. 1, 2006, at A9. This article shows a provocative picture of a large crowd of aggressive Iranian women with fists clenched and dressed in the *chador* and veil, wearing ammunition to symbolize that they are suicide bombers. These Iranian women are clearly in support of Hezbollah and in opposition to Israel.

77. Afary & Anderson, *supra* note 5, at 111.

78. *Id.* at 112.

79. *Id.* at 113.

had spread to numerous cities around the country,[80] but that was the last big feminist demonstration in Iran, and soon after the women's movement called off its public demonstrations, largely because of pressures from leftist groups such as the *Fedayeen*, which was the most influential group on the campus of Tehran University.[81] The *Fedayeen* wanted above all to avoid a new civil war or possible foreign intervention in Iran.[82]

But support for the women demonstrators and activists continued internationally. Simone de Beauvoir called a press conference in Paris on March 19, 1979 to announce that an international delegation of feminist activists and intellectuals was going to Iran to gather information.[83] Although Simone de Beauvoir ultimately did not go to Iran for health reasons, she made a public statement of solidarity for the Iranian women's movement.[84] Kate Millet, a world-renowned feminist, actually went to the women's demonstrations, but she was expelled by the new regime for "provocations against the Islamic Revolution."[85] Millet also held a press conference at Orly airport in Paris saying, "The Iranian women are marvelous human beings" who are "armed with great courage" in spite of the repressive nature of the new regime.[86]

J. Religious Despotism in the Name of Democracy

After the 1979 Revolution and "in a violent return swing of the pendulum, religious despotism had ousted both secularism and democracy"[87] in Iran. Between June 1981 and May 1982, a second Reign of Terror took place in Iran, with many people being executed or imprisoned so that the Islamic State and clerical government could be firmly secured.[88]

Iran today calls itself a democratic theocracy, and its Constitution attests to its democratic intentions.[89] But a careful look at the structure of the government set up in the Iranian Constitution reveals some of the flaws in its democratic intentions—flaws that negatively impact the human rights protections theoretically available to women. For example, the Iranian Constitution names the Leader for life, and the Assembly of Experts eventually chooses his successor and even supervises his activities. However, in practice the Assembly of Experts and the Guardian Council form a kind of closed system that gives the Leader

80. *Id.*
81. *Id.*
82. *See id.*
83. *Id.* at 114
84. *Id.*
85. *Id.* at 115.
86. *Id.*
87. MIR-HOSSEINI & TAPPER, *supra* note 1, at 17.
88. *Id.*
89. *See id.* at 17–18.

unlimited power. He alone makes appointments to the Guardian Council and to the Assembly of Experts. In this way, Ayatollah Khomeini and his successors can control both the legislative and executive branches of government . . . hardly a Western notion of democracy at all.

K. Public/Private Split in Iranian Society

The religious clerics have enormous power in Iran, and they have "long since regulated Iran's cultural life, banning discotheques, nightclubs, bars, alcohol, coed sports, satellite dishes, gambling, and many kinds of music."[90] Women's social life in Iran is very restricted because they are relegated to the inside private arena of the home and dependent on their male protectors to provide a social life. Social relationships between men and woman are not permitted in public. This segregation forces people to act one way in public and another in private. As a result of the segregation of the sexes and an atmosphere of pervasive repression, Iran has seen a rise in prostitution,[91] which is illegal in Iran, and the trafficking of women,[92] which is a contemporary form of slavery.

---

90. SCIOLINO, *supra* note 6, at 2.

91. *See* PROSTITUTION BEHIND THE VEIL (Cosmo Film Doc ApS 2005).

92. The 2006 Trafficking in Persons Report (TIP Report) places Iran in Tier 3 for its poor record on human trafficking. DEP'T OF STATE, TRAFFICKING IN PERSONS REPORT 142 (2006), http://www.state.gov/documents/organization/66086.pdf.

> Iran is a source, transit and destination country for women and girls trafficked for the purposes of sexual exploitation and involuntary servitude . . . [Iranian] women and girls are trafficked to Pakistan, Turkey, the Gulf, and Europe for sexual exploitation . . . Afghan women and girls are trafficked [into Iran] . . . for forced marriages and sexual exploitation. Similarly, women and children are trafficked internally [in Iran] for the purposes of forced marriage, sexual exploitation, and involuntary servitude . . . Iranian authorities punish victims of trafficking with beatings, imprisonment, and execution.

Id. Addressing this injustice should be a primary objective for the Iranian Government. One author notes that in Iran for twenty-five years, the ruling mullahs have enforced humiliating and sadistic rules and punishments on women and girls, enslaving them in a gender apartheid system of segregation, forced veiling, second-class status, lashing, and stoning to death . . . The number of Iranian women and girls who are deported from Persian Gulf countries indicates the magnitude of the trade. Donna Hughes, *Sex Slave Jihad*, FRONTPAGE MAG., Jan. 27, 2004, http://www.frontpagemag.com/Articles/Printable.asp?ID-11791. *See also*, Susan W. Tiefenbrun, *Updating the Domestic and International Impact of the U.S. Victims of Trafficking Protection Act of 2000: Does Law Deter Crime?*, 382 CASE W. RES. J. INT'L. L. 249 (2007); Susan Tiefenbrun, *Copyright Infringement, Sex Trafficking, and Defamation in the Fictional Life of a Geisha*, 10 MICH. J. GENDER & L. 327 (2004); Susan Tiefenbrun, *The Saga of Susannah: A U.S. Remedy for Sex Trafficking in Women: The Victims of Trafficking and Violence Protection Act of 2000*, 2002 UTAH L. REV. 107 (2002); Susan W. Tiefenbrun, *Sex Sells But Drugs Don't Talk: Trafficking of Women Sex Workers and an Economic Solution*, 24 T. JEFFERSON L. REV. 161 (2002).

Hypocrisy and deception abound within this public/private split that characterizes Iranian postrevolutionary society. In public, uniformity, anonymity, and conformity reign supreme; they are accomplished by strict laws regulating women's dress code. In public, all women must conform to State rules requiring them to cover their hair completely and be devoid of any makeup or other adornment. The only individuality women have in public is the special way they intricately knot the headscarf under their chin as well as a restricted number of options they have in their choice of clothing. Even though uniformity and the invisibility of women are intended by the rules of mandatory covering, women can actually gain some identity by choosing from a range[93] of head covers that they are required to wear in public. Some women prefer simply a pastel-colored kerchief or scarf (*roosari*) covering only their hair or a more user-friendly *maqnaeh,* which is a tube of cloth that the women put over their head, around their face and over their shoulders.[94] A woman can even wear a bright blue *manto* or a red or yellow *maqnaeh,* evidencing more official tolerance to variation in *hejab.*[95] Many women wear a full-length black overcoat and head covering called a *chador* that covers them from their head to their ankles (supposedly worn by women holding official government positions).[96] Some women cover not only their head but also their face with a black veil so that only a small slit reveals their eyes. More informally, some women wear a coat over trousers with a head covering that is either a scarf or the *maqnaeh.*[97]

Even though adornment in public is strictly forbidden by law, various kinds of adornment actually accompany the *hejab,* such as a gold scarf holder that helps create a decorative bow under the chin or a frilled scarf worn under the *chador* to create a bit of color along the top of the woman's face.[98] Moreover, there are variations even within the black *chador* motif. The *chador* can be made of either light or heavy fabric with a pattern woven into it or a shimmery fabric that can catch the light as the woman wears it.[99] This is the very small range of dress code options within which all women in Iran, both Muslims and non-Muslims, can fulfill a basic need for self-expression and individuality by their choice of clothing worn in public.

In private, women enthusiastically seek out the latest fashion and variety in dress wear. Women, "even some of its most religious women—adorn themselves with makeup and jewelry behind high walls, then cover themselves in black on

93. *See* Halper, *supra* note 17, at 120–29 (providing a detailed discussion of the *hejab* and the range of dress wear).

94. *See id.* at 126.

95. *See id.*

96. *Id.*

97. *Id.*

98. *Id.*

99. *Id.*

the streets and struggle for their rights in the most creative and persistent ways."[100] Thus, the public/private split in Iranian society caused in part by the strictly enforced dress code results in contradictory behavior, if not hypocrisy.

L. The Quiet Revolt of Women[101]

People frequently ask, "Why don't the Iranian women revolt against the denial of their rights?" The answer is that they do, but the revolt is quiet to avoid harsh reprisals against them and their family. "[I]ranian women, whether they wear black *chadors* or Western dress topped with a small kerchief,"[102] are being denied their rights, and they are quietly engaged in "a sustained and creative ideological war"[103] against the State's denial of these fundamental human rights.

With this kind of passive aggression and resistance against authority, women in Iran have made some gains in the area of human rights.[104] For example, during the Iran–Iraq War, women pressured Parliament to change the custody laws relating to children of a war casualty.[105] Muslim women outside Iran, especially in France, are also waging a quiet revolution.[106]

M. Signs of the Denial of Women's Rights in Iran

Even though women have made some human rights gains, they are still discriminated against, repressed, and oppressed in Iran. For example, blood money—compensation for the victim of a crime—received by a man is double that of the sum received by a woman.[107] Moreover:

> [W]omen do not serve as judges or religious leaders. Adultery is still punishable by stoning to death. Polygamy is legal. In a divorce, fathers control custody of sons over the age of two and daughters over the age of seven. A girl can be tried for a crime as an adult at the age of nine (a boy at fifteen) . . . [G]irls are allowed to be married at nine . . . Women inherit only half of what men do. Men can divorce their wives at will, but women need to prove that

---

100. Sciolino, *supra* note 6, at 6.

101. *See* Massoume Price, *A Brief History of Women's Movements in Iran: 1850–2000*, http://www.payvand.com/women (last visited Aug. 24, 2007) (providing a brief overview of the basic information about the Iranian women's movement over the last two centuries).

102. Sciolino, *supra* note 6, at 113.

103. *Id.*

104. *See infra* notes 113–120 and accompanying text (providing a more in-depth analysis of the gains made in Iran to protect women's human rights).

105. Sciolino, *supra* note 6, at 115.

106. *See* Marlise Simons, *Muslim Women in Europe Claim Rights and Keep Faith*, N.Y. Times, Dec. 29, 2005, at A3.

107. Ziba Mir-Hosseini, Islam and Gender: The Religious Debate in Contemporary Iran 61 (1999).

> their spouse is insane, impotent, violent, or unable to support the family. A woman needs her husband's permission to start a business and sometimes even to get a job.
>
> Married women cannot get passports or leave the country without the written permission of their husband . . . Rape is more often than not blamed on the woman. A woman's testimony in court has half the weight of a man's. Women can be arrested for jogging or bicycling or swimming in sexually integrated places, and for exposing their heads and necks and the curves of their bodies in public. Women are not even allowed to share the same physical space with men of the same profession.[108]

Marriage in Iran[109] "is not a contract between equals but an acquisition of property"[110] by the male of the female. The standard marriage contract gives women rights on paper that are difficult to enforce in the Iranian family court, which is a "hothouse of double standards and male vengeance."[111] Wife beating in Iran is tolerated and quite common, but generally denied.[112]

The persistence of this long list of violations of women's fundamental human rights in postrevolutionary Iran is troubling but slightly balanced by some small and unexpected developments in women's rights.

N. Some Unexpected Developments in Women's Rights

Women in Iran today are no longer excluded from public life and politics, and their participation has in fact increased in some noted areas due to rather than in spite of the compulsory wearing of the veil or *hejab*.[113] As of 1996, over 33 percent of university students were female, including 49 percent in medicine.[114] By 2006, the statistics improved markedly, and Shirin Ebadi and others reported that over 65 percent of the university students in Iran were female.[115] In some

---

108. Sciolino, *supra* note 6, at 115.

109. For a more in-depth analysis of marriage laws and the marriage contract, see *infra* text accompanying notes 391–445.

110. Sciolino, *supra* note 6, at 121.

111. *Id.* at 124. For an in-depth view of the Iranian family court and the quagmire women face when they seek to be divorced from their abusive or neglectful husband, see the documentary Divorce Iranian Style (20th Century Vixen 1998), described at http://www.wmm.com/filmcatalog/pages/c454.shtml and analyzed in this chapter.

112. *See* Sciolino, *supra* note 6, at 123 ("Some people said there is no such thing as wife abuse. Others admitted these things happen but said it's better not to talk about them.").

113. *See* Mir-Hosseini, *supra* note 107, at 7.

114. *Id.* at n.13.

115. Shirin Ebadi Lecture, *supra* note 47, at 34.

subjects, up to 70 percent of Iran's university students are women.[116] Women are now permitted to study mining and agriculture and to serve as judges.[117]

Many advances in family law have taken place as well. For example, the Family Protection Law of 1967, which curtailed men's rights to arbitrary divorce, was dismantled and its courts were abolished[118] because that law was declared by Khomeini to be in contradiction with the *Shari'a* law. But amendments to Divorce Regulations enacted in 1992 effectively reinstated the rejected elements of the Family Protection Law.[119] This study will examine some of the new Iranian legislation[120] that provides more rights to women.

III. SEMIOTICS OF *HEJAB*, THE VEIL, AND WOMEN'S DRESS CODE

A. Regulated Dress Code as a Denial of Freedom of Speech

In the brief history and development of the Islamic Republic of Iran from the nineteenth century until today, we can see a consistent quest for more "opportunities and freedom"[121] for all Iranians. But Iranian women have borne the brunt of a predominately patriarchic and repressive regime that intentionally discriminates against women and denies them basic human rights. One of the most visible signs of the denial of freedom is the Islamic State's control of women's dress. Shirin Ebadi calls the imposed *hejab* "a symbol of [women's] broader lack of rights."[122] In fact, the way a woman dresses is one of the key signs of her freedom and one of the key issues in women's rights in Iran today.[123] The right to wear what one wants to wear in the public arena is the right to be seen as an individual, to make a statement about one's own essence, and to express one's own unique form of speech—and this right should not be restricted unreasonably or selectively.

The dress code is a difficult rule to implement legally and socially because its regulation is tantamount to denying a person the right to freedom of speech. To enforce the rule that women must dress in a manner that comports with Islamic

---

116. *See* Xin Li, *Iranian Regime Erases Progress on Women's Rights,* WASH. TIMES, Mar. 8, 2006 ("Up to 70% of university students in Iran are female, said Swannee Hunt, director of the Women and Public Policy Program at Harvard University's Kennedy School of Government."). *See also* Frances Harrison, *Women Graduates Challenge Iran,* BBC NEWS, http://news.bbc.co.uk/2/hi/middle_east/5359672.stm.

117. MIR-HOSSEINI, *supra* note 107, at 8.

118. *Id.*

119. *Id.*

120. For an analysis of some of Iran's domestic laws affecting women's human rights, see *infra* Section IV and text accompanying notes 391–445.

121. NAFISI, *supra* note 11, at 261.

122. EBADI, *supra* note 24, at 72.

123. *See* SCIOLINO, *supra* note 6, at 132.

principles, the Iranian government has resorted to nothing less than terrorism.[124] The government puts up warning signs everywhere in public areas stating that "bad-*hejab* (badly covered) women will not be served."[125] All women, even foreigners who are not Muslims, must wear the *hejab* in Iran. The morality police (men and women) circulate in cars and stop women on the street whom they claim are not properly veiled in order to humiliate, frighten, terrorize, and arrest them on a daily basis.

B. History of the Veil

1. To Wear or Not to Wear the Veil: Freedom of Choice Wearing a head covering known as the *hejab* (also referred to as the "veil") was practiced long before the Islamic Republic came into existence. Veiling probably existed among the Zoroastrians. The practice of wearing an all-enveloping Islamic veil began in the sixteenth century, although it was not black and its style varied by region.[126] Wearing of the all-black floor-length *chador* seen today in Iran and other Muslim countries probably began in the eighteenth century.[127] But then the *chador* was worn only by a minority of wealthy women who lived in cities and at court.[128] These women took up veiling and secluded themselves from public view. Some view the veil as highly "erotic,"[129] which is borne out by the many artistic representations of veiled, seductive women who cover not only their hair but their face. Others view the veil as a sign of religious observance, respect, and purity.

In the countryside, women have always worn veils, including lively scarves with veils over them, wrapping and gathering them at their waists to free up their arms and make the garments less cumbersome.[130] The *chador*, though, is a very bulky and uncomfortable garment that limits women's physical freedom. "It gets caught in escalators. It drags along the ground collecting dust. It makes it hard to climb stairs. It is hot in summer."[131] It is very difficult to wear.[132] The *chador* does not have a zipper, and in order to keep it closed, women have to hold it tightly at the neck, incapacitating one of their hands. Thus, the *chador* or long black zipless overcoat is another way in which women are rendered more dependent on men if not physically weakened and powerless.

2. "Do Not Wear the Veil": No Freedom of Choice The denial of the freedom to choose whether to wear the veil dates back to Reza Shah, when he began his

124. For a discussion of the elements of terrorism, *see* Chapter 3 of this book.
125. *Id.*
126. *Id.* at 133.
127. *Id.*
128. *See id.*
129. *Id.* at 138.
130. *Id.* at 133.
131. *Id.* at 138.
132. *Id.* at 140.

well-intentioned policy of modernizing Iran in 1929. When he forced women to take off the veil, they protested. Ironically, in a tectonic reversal, the same policy denying women the freedom to choose their own dress code was continued by Khomeini and his successors who now force all women to cover their hair and wear the veil. Thus, women protested vigorously when the Shah refused to let them wear the veil, and they also protested when Khomeini forced them to wear the veil. The protest was clearly about freedom of choice.

More specifically, in the interests of modernity, Reza Shah ordered all men to dress in European styles and then ordered *kashf-e hejab*, the forced unveiling of women "which led to rioting that was harshly repressed."[133] In 1935, Reza Shah actually issued an edict declaring the wearing of traditional dress by both women and men an offense punishable by a prison term.[134] The army and police enforced the rule by tearing *chadors* off women and handing out free Western-style suits to men.[135] Reza Shah also banned men from wearing turbans and forbade beards, even for clerics.[136] The Shah told all Iranian women to "cast their veils" which he referred to as a ". . . symbol of injustice and shame. . . ."[137] Many women objected to Reza Shah's edict and refused to leave their homes, either because they did not want to be seen bareheaded in public or just to protest the decree that restricted their freedom of choice. However, others found the decree liberating.

3. "Wear the Veil": No Freedom of Choice Similar to the public outcry against Reza Shah's limitations on women's freedom of choice in dress code, when Khomeini ordered all women to wear the veil in March 1979, women protested against the order, and men joined in by hurling stones, bottles, and insults. Khomeini called the *chador* that covers the whole body except the woman's face "the flag of the revolution."[138] Thus, the veil was a negative sign for Reza Shah (who saw it as a symbol of injustice, backwardness, and shame) and a positive sign for Khomeini (who raised the veil to the level of a forceful political symbol). By the beginning of 1982, three years after the Revolution, all women were forced to cover up in the public arena.[139]

C. Sign System of Wearing the Veil

1. Veil is a Sign of Virtue and Honor Wearing or not wearing the veil is a delicate and difficult issue that is tied up in a complex network of signs and symbols having both positive and negative connotations. For Iranian women, the veil represents many different things. It is a positive symbol designating the cultural

---

133. Halper, *supra* note 17, at 121.
134. SCIOLINO, *supra* note 6, at 133.
135. *Id.*
136. *Id.*
137. *Id.* at 133.
138. *Id.* at 134.
139. *Id.*

and religious "source of protection, respect, and virtue."[140] The importance of this symbol of virtue has been underestimated. The family honor in Iran rests on the virtue of women.[141] Thus, an unveiled daughter can signify dishonor to the father and the whole family.

2. Veil is a Sign of Muslim Identity The veil is also a positive sign signifying Muslim identity, which by extension can be interpreted to convey the message of the wearer's opposition to Western civilization. This threatening signification formed the basis of a legal argument in the courts of France, Germany, Turkey, and even the European Court of Human Rights. These courts all upheld the State's right to ban wearing the veil in public schools. This is known as the famous and controversial "headscarf case."[142]

3. Veil is a Sign of Power over Women The veil is also a negative symbol of the Islamic Republic's power over women.[143] By refusing to wear the veil, the woman may not only be signifying a lower degree of her religious conviction, but also her political distance from the legal decrees and policies of the State. Thus, refusing to wear the veil may be interpreted by the State as her refusing to adopt a Muslim identity and maybe even her affiliating with what is considered the "evil" West by the Iranian clerics and the State.

4. Veil is a Sign of Woman's Political Engagement and Jihad Women wearing the *chador* and the veil can be expressing their belief in *jihad*,[144] or the holy struggle to spread the faith and to defend the Muslim community. Teaching the faith or spreading the word through an exemplary life is a form of *jihad*. Unfortunately, *jihad* has become synonymous in the Western mind with acts of terrorism carried out by extremist Islamic groups,[145] by women soldiers,[146] and by women suicide bombers. *Jihad* is an obligation on all Muslims, but women can perform it by merely obeying their husband and wearing traditional garb. Thus, in this strange phenomenon called sign systems, wearing the *hejab* and covering the face and head with a veil can be construed in a multiplicity of ways as a sign of a woman's docile obedience to her husband, her aggressivity, her anti-West sentiment, or her active revolt against corruption. *Hejab* then is a contradictory "signifier of resistance"[147] and nonresistance.

---

140. SCIOLINO, *supra* note 6, at 133.

141. EBADI, *supra* note 24, at 114.

142. *See infra* text accompanying notes 187–209.

143. SCIOLINO, *supra* note 6, at 132.

144. *See* GERALDINE BROOKS, NINE PARTS OF DESIRE: THE HIDDEN WORLD OF ISLAMIC WOMEN 108–09 (1995).

145. *See id.* at 109.

146. *See* THE NAT'L COUNCIL OF RESISTANCE OF IRAN FOREIGN AFFAIRS COMM., *Women in the Resistance*, *in* WOMEN, ISLAM & EQUALITY 57 (1995), http://www.iran-e-zad.org/english/book_on_women/wi&e.pdf.

147. Halper, *supra* note 17, at 121.

5. Veil is a Polyvalent Symbol of Imprisonment and Liberation[148] The *hejab* is a polyvalent symbol that sends ambiguous and paradoxical messages because of the multiplicity of meanings associated with wearing the veil, the headscarf, and the *chador*. Depending upon the context, the *chador* and scarf can signify both a woman's imprisonment by tradition into the privacy of the home as well as her liberation into the more modern public arena.

For many women, wearing Islamic dress is now their welcomed entry into public spaces, a tool to be used to their advantage, and a liberating vehicle.[149] The veil is a garment that sends a double message to the world. The woman wearing the veil hides herself in anonymity and conformity, depicting herself by her outer garb as one of the masses of the many "shrouded wives and mothers."[150] She protects herself in this cloak by becoming just another passive, docile, and religious woman like any other. Paradoxically, however, the veil also represents her as a politically engaged person, a "warrior of Islam,"[151] giving her freedom to move about in society and feel powerful through political engagement.

Thus, wearing the veil is a paradoxical sign. The veil signifies both purity and political power and provides the woman with more social freedom while limiting her physical movement inside the cumbersome garment that she is forced to wear publicly. Wearing the veil is like ". . . a code that allows anyone and everyone to vent their private aspirations, fears, dreams, and nightmares. An emblem now of progress, then of backwardness, a badge now of nationalism, then of domination, a symbol of purity, then of corruption, the veil has accommodated itself to a puzzling diversity of personal and political ideologies."[152]

D. Veiling as a Form of Humiliation

The Iranian State has tried to justify its abusive power to regulate women's dress code by explaining to women that the headscarf and veil are actually a form of women's liberation. Wearing the veil permits women to appear in public in accordance with the rules laid out in the Koran. The veil covers a woman's body and thereby prevents women from tempting men and corrupting morality. In this way, *hejab* provides women with a lever of power.

---

148. *See* MARJANE SATRAPI, PERSEPOLIS 2 (2004). Satrapi makes fun of the view that wearing the veil is a form of liberation.

149. *See* SCIOLINO, *supra* note 6, at 134–35.

150. *Id.* at 136.

151. *Id.*

152. *Id.* at 134–35 (punctuation omitted) (quoting FARZANEH MILANI, VEILS AND WORDS: THE EMERGING VOICES OF IRANIAN WOMEN WRITERS (1992)).

But wearing the veil is also a means of humiliating women.[153] Humiliation is carried out by the "lower-class morals police"[154] (men and women) against higher-class Westernized women, who are accused unjustly of being "loose" women[155] simply because they choose not to follow the rules of the Koran to the letter and prefer to adopt their own dress code. Moreover, not wearing the veil could be interpreted for women as an act of political treason as the veil can signify a refusal of Western traditions.

E. Veiling and the Koran: A Matter of Interpretation

Although the veil is considered "the most distinctive emblem of Islam," forcing Muslim women to wear the veil, surprisingly, it does not appear anywhere in the Koran.[156] The tradition of women's "veiling and seclusion (known together as [*hejab*]) was introduced into Arabia long before Mohammed, primarily through Arab contacts with Syria and Iran, where the [*hejab*] was a sign of [upperclass] social status."[157] The "verse of [hejab]" first appeared in 627 C.E. and was addressed to Mohammed's wives.[158] The "veil was neither compulsory nor . . . widely adopted until [many] generations after Mohammed's death, when a large body of male scriptural and legal scholars began using their religious and political authority to regain the dominance they had lost in society as a result of the Prophet's egalitarian reforms."[159]

The Koran says, "Say to the believing women that they should lower their gaze and guard their modesty . . . They should draw their veils over their bosoms and not display their ornaments."[160] This rule, which is interpreted strictly to require all women to appear in public in Islamic dress, was also written into Iran's penal code under Khomeini. But many of the more moderate clerics and secularists claim "the Koranic verse that defines [the dress code] is subject to interpretation."[161] In fact, Monir Gorji, a woman preacher and activist for the Revolution and the only woman on the Constitutional Council, started to write Koranic exegesis in the late 1980s "in order to show that the Koran does not sanction the restrictions imposed on women by orthodox interpretations of

---

153. *See id.* at 142–43.

154. *Id. See also* EBADI, *supra* note 24, at 96 ("The *komiteh*, or morality police, harassed all Iranians—Muslims as well as Iranian Christians and Jews, old people as well as the young—but they preyed upon women with a special enthusiasm.").

155. SCIOLINO, *supra* note 6, at 143.

156. REZA ASLAN, NO GOD BUT GOD: THE ORIGINS, EVOLUTION, AND FUTURE OF ISLAM 65 (2005).

157. *Id.* at 65.

158. *Id.* ("Believers . . . when you ask something from the Prophet's wives, do so from behind a [*hejab*]. This will assure the purity of your hearts. . ..").

159. *Id.* at 66.

160. SCIOLINO, *supra* note 6, at 132.

161. *Id.* at 133.

the [*Shari'a*]."[162] But by making the dress code enforceable under criminal law, the Iranian government has removed the flexibility and denied the freedom that interpretation permits.

F. Women's Reaction to the Regulation of Their Dress Code

How have women reacted in the past to the regulation of their dress code? During the Revolution of 1979, women were permitted to go bareheaded in Iran and were promised increased freedom.[163] But one month after the Revolution, Khomeini ordered all women to wear Islamic dress.[164] Women felt betrayed, especially in view of Khomeini's promises to them and the significant role Iranian women played in his rise to power. Thousands of women marched and protested the mandatory veiling.[165] The American feminist Kate Millet showed up at the protest march, branding Khomeini a "male chauvinist" and marching with Iranian women.[166] When Millet was expelled,[167] that expulsion made waves among feminists the world over.

Similarly, when Reza Shah forced women to unveil, women objected to the denial of their right to dress as they please or as their religion requires. Wearing the veil later became permissible once again under Mohammed Reza, but ironically *hejab* then took on a decidedly political character and signified anti-Shah sentiments.[168] Women wore the veil to make a political statement against the tyranny of the monarchy. They remembered that during Reza Shah's modernization campaign, police began to forcibly unveil women in the streets,[169] not unlike the more recent "morality squads" of the postrevolutionary Islamic regime that would enforce mandatory veiling by corporal punishment in the streets.[170] The paradox here is that veiling is enforced in Iran today to purify the people from the corruption of capitalism and the West, yet stories abound about the

---

162. MIR-HOSSEINI, *supra* note 107, at 84. Mir-Hosseini's very scholarly and illuminating work uncovers the range of Koranic interpretations that are possible. She interviews clerics to analyze in depth the exegesis of many conservative and moderate clerics. For scholars of women's rights in Iran and the notions of gender that inform Islamic jurisprudence, this work is indispensable. She finds three main notions of gender and interpretation: an insistence on "traditional" patriarchal interpretations of the Koran based on "complementarity" and "inequality" of the sexes; an attempt to introduce "balance" into traditional interpretations; and finally a radical rethinking of the jurisprudential constructions of gender.

163. Sciolino, *supra* note 6, at 134.

164. *Id.*

165. *See id.*

166. *Id.*

167. *Id.*

168. Halper, *supra* note 17, at 121.

169. *Id.*

170. *Id.* at 123; *see, e.g.*, NAFISI, *supra* note 11, at 167.

corruption among security police who harass women for bad veiling and who steal their purses.[171]

Under the reign of Reza Shah, the issue of veiling led to undemocratic class distinctions and social unrest. A dichotomy existed between upper-class women, whose families wanted to curry favor with the modern Shah by agreeing to unveil, and the middle- and lower-class women (primarily in the countryside) who were forced to isolate themselves in order to wear the veil and maintain their religious observances.[172] Nevertheless, Reza Shah often supported further advancement in equality for women.[173] He tried to implement democracy under his rule, but his version of democracy was imperfect because only the secular, upper-class women in urban areas had access to public education, career opportunities, and political participation. Democracy under Reza Shah was imperfect because at this time "traditional" women living in rural areas were deprived of the right to work and to manage their own finances, and they were forced into seclusion in their own homes, far from public life.[174] Thus, the so-called democratic but heavy-handed reforms of Reza Shah that were administered harshly and selectively actually resulted in further repression and limitation of the rights of rural women in Iran.[175] Therein lay the roots of the Shah's downfall. Khomeini promised to right the wrongs the Shah inflicted upon women, but he betrayed the very women who put him into power. When Khomeini reintroduced *Shari'a* law, women's rights in Iran suffered a severe setback.

G. Veiling as a Form of Segregation

Wearing the *chador* and veil distinguishes women from men and, in that sense, isolates women. Mandatory segregation of men and women in Iran is actually regulated by law, but in practice it is rather complicated, confusing, and contradictory. For example, men and women are legally segregated in government offices, but not in the elevators leading up to the offices. When Ahmadinejad, the current President of Iran, was mayor of Tehran, he enforced separate male/female elevators in public buildings, canceled concerts, and reinforced wearing the full *chador*.[176] Men and women are still required by law to use separate entrances at airports, but they sit together on domestic flights. Prayer is always segregated in mosques.[177] Buses are segregated, and women must ride in the back, but taxis are not segregated.[178] Public toilets are integrated.[179] There is a ban on men and women shaking hands in order to implement the defined distance

171. *See* Sciolino, *supra* note 6, at 145.
172. *See* Halper, *supra* note 17, at 122.
173. *See id.*
174. *See id.*
175. *See id.*
176. Sciolino, *supra* note 6, at 367.
177. *See, e.g.*, Mir-Hosseini, *supra* note 107, at 79.
178. Sciolino, *supra* note 6, at 147.
179. *Id.* at 147.

allowed between men and women.[180] Accordingly, segregation of men and women in Iran is highly inconsistent.

H. Meaning of Resistance to Veiling

The *hejab* is undeniably a symbol of the will of the Islamic State, with women's quiet but courageous resistance to this kind of repression being barely visible, yet everywhere in everyday life in Iran. "[T]here is no consensus among Iranian women on *hejab* . . . enforcement of it can be empowering to women."[181] "Although it undoubtedly restricts some, it emancipates others by legitimizing their presence in public, which is still a male domain" in Iran.[182] "Many women in Iran today owe their education, their jobs, their economic autonomy, and their public persona, to *compulsory hejab*."[183] Nevertheless, many women try to resist compulsory veiling. When Shirin Ebadi accepted the Nobel Peace Prize in 2003, she wore Western garb and no headscarf. In a recent interview, I asked Shirin Ebadi whether the State as well as Iranian women at large objected to her choice of dress on that public occasion that was televised internationally.[184] She answered that women applauded her decision to choose Western garb, even though the State objected.[185] When I asked her if it is true that most women in Iran today would prefer to dress in Western garb, she said incontrovertibly, "It's true."[186]

I. Laws Outside Iran Banning the Veil in Public Schools: The Headscarf Case in France, in Turkey, and in the European Court of Human Rights[187]

The forced wearing of the headscarf is a very controversial legal and political issue that has risen to the level of domestic and international courts not

---

180. *See, e.g.*, Sciolino, *supra* note 6, at 148. In the movie, *Not Without My Daughter*, Betty's "liberator" is an Iranian "modern" secular man, who helps her escape captivity, but who flinches, nevertheless, when she shakes his hand at their first meeting. *See* Not Without my Daughter (Pathé Entertainment 1991).

181. Mir-Hosseini, Islam & Gender, *supra* note 107, at 278.

182. *Id.*

183. *Id.*

184. Shirin Ebadi Lecture, *supra* note 47, at 19.

185. *Id.*

186. *Id.*

187. *See* Olivier Dutheillet de Lamothe, "The French Headscarf Case: Why Girls Cannot Legally Wear Headscarves in French Public Schools" (July 10, 2006) (unpublished, on file with author, Susan Tiefenbrun). Olivier Dutheillet de Lamothe is a judge of the Constitutional Council of France. The unpublished paper was delivered on July 10, 2006 at the University of Nice School of Law International Conference on Women's Rights, sponsored by the Hofstra Law School International Law Summer Program in France. Much of the information contained in this section of the chapter is derived from his paper. I am deeply indebted to Judge Dutheillet de Lamothe for his incisive and sensitive analysis of the cultural dilemma on which this case is based. It is purely a matter of the interpretation of the sign system of the headscarf, which, as we have shown, involves an analysis of the historical, political, cultural, and legal contexts in which the sign appears.

only in France, but in Germany, Turkey, and the European Court of Human Rights (ECHR).

The French headscarf case has lasted more than a decade and has resulted in the passing of a law banning the headscarf in public schools, the legal reasoning of which is based on adherence to a sacred French principle of secularism (laicity) or the separation of religion and State.

The headscarf controversy in France erupted in October 1989 when the principal of a majority-Muslim middle school in the Parisian suburb of Creil suspended three Muslim girls because they wore their headscarves in the classroom of a public school. The Minister of Education, Lionel Jospin, referred the matter to the Conseil d'Etat, France's highest Administrative Court, for a legal opinion. The Conseil d'Etat ruled on November 27, 1989 that wearing religious garb in a school "is not in itself incompatible with the principle of secularism" but must not "constitute an act of pressure, provocation, proselytism or propaganda" that "impinges on the freedom of the other students or impedes the school's educational mission." Here the ruling has a double edge that reflects the principle of secularism in France requiring the public schools to respect the free expression of religion while also imposing limitations on that principle. Thus, the ruling of the Conseil d'Etat seems to be in favor of the girls and the right to wear a headscarf in public schools. However, the ruling places the implementation of limiting conditions in the hands of the individual school principals who must determine whether to ban the headscarf on a case-by-case basis. This determination is naturally based on the principal's interpretation of the significance of the person's act of wearing the headscarf.

The reaction to the ruling of the French Conseil d'Etat is quite interesting. In 1994, commentators began to report an increased number of girls wearing the headscarf. Because of the favorable rulings by the Conseil d'Etat in 1989, 1992, and 1999, what was once just a handful had grown to 700 students who wore the veil in public schools. In those rulings students in 41 of the 49 cases were given the right to wear the headscarf in French public schools. In 2003, the last year before implementation of the French law banning the headscarf, 1500 girls wore the headscarf out of ten million students. This large number reflects the intense pressure being put on principals to rule in favor of the free expression of religion and the wearing of the scarf in French public schools.

Political pressure against the headscarf began to mount because of this large increase in girls wearing the headscarf in French public schools. President Chirac appointed a commission in 2003 (headed by a conservative politician, Bernard Stasi) to examine the issue of secularism and the headscarf. On December 11, 2003, the Stasi Commission composed of politicians, scholars and other people unanimously recommended a ban on wearing the headscarf.

The Stasi Commission voted to ban the headscarf for many reasons. One justification was the liberation that such a prohibition would provide to the many girls who testified they were being pressured by their parents to wear the headscarf against their will. Other reasons for the ban are bound up in the political significance of the headscarf in France. Some argued the headscarf is a symbol of political passion felt by North African immigrants against native French people who feared the rise of fundamentalist Islam in France. The French are afraid that fundamentalism will infiltrate French political and social life. In fact, the headscarf was interpreted to be a clear sign by the girl wearing the scarf that she rejected the process of integration into French society. The Stasi Commission saw the headscarf, then, as a political threat. The French are very insistent on the importance of assimilation of immigrants into French mainstream culture. In fact, a new law was passed on June 27, 2008 denying French citizenship to a Moroccan woman simply because she chose to wear a *burqa,* which the French court deemed to be a symbol of her failure to show enough "assimilation."[188]

The French Parliament voted unanimously on March 15, 2004 to enact a short bill stipulating the following: "In public schools, the wearing of symbols of clothing by which the students *conspicuously* manifest a religious appearance is forbidden."[189] The interpretation of this law is troublesome for several reasons. What is a "conspicuous" religious symbol? Is it "conspicuous" to wear a big cross, a large Jewish star, a bright colored yarmulke, a black turban, clicking worry beads, etc.? How big does the symbol have to be before it becomes "conspicuous?" These questions of interpretation of the law trouble many jurists.

More bothersome, of course, is the law's arguably flagrant violation of the freedoms of speech and of religious expression. The French justify banning this form of symbolic speech because it is tantamount to a political threat, arguably like yelling "fire" in a crowded movie theater, which is impermissible speech under American law. The issue here is the interpretation of the symbol of the headscarf as a political threat. This interpretation is deeply bound up in a contextual matrix of French history, French culture, and the rise of a huge immigrant population in France—and with that, the rise of anti-West sentiment and current events in France and in other parts of the world related to terrorist threats.

Justification of the French legal ban on wearing a headscarf in public schools is virtually inconceivable to an American jurist and to American citizens for whom the principle of freedom of speech is a basic constitutional right. This right to free speech is so fundamental that American law permits the outrageous act of burning of the American flag[190] on the theory that this is a permissible yet reprehensible expression of free speech.

Moreover, the French ban on wearing the headscarf seems destined to cause more immigrant students to move out of the public schools in France and into

---

188. Décisions du Conseil d'Etat. Section du Contentieux, 2ème et 7ème sous-sections réunies. Séance du 26 mai 2008. Lecture du 27 juin 2008. No. 286798, cited in Robert O. Paxton, *Can You Really Become French, in* THE NEW YORK REVIEW OF BOOKS, April 9, 2009, Vol. LVI, No. 6, at 53, note 6.

189. Emphasis added.

190. Texas v. Johnson, 491 U.S. 397, 399 (1989).

the social isolation of private schools or to become influenced by some dangerous *imams* in *madrassas* or schools that reportedly harbor intense anti-West sentiments. The ban denying the right to young girls to manifest the expression of their religion could result in the erosion of a much-needed policy of integration of immigrants into French society.

It is true that most Americans cannot understand or justify this ban because it flies in the face of the First Amendment of our Constitution. Freedom of speech is America's most precious freedom. However, Americans must understand that the most precious legal principle in France is secularism and the separation of Church and State. In France, secularism is the dominant ideology of the French Republic that was founded in defiance of the Church and the monarchy. In the United States, the Establishment Clause, free exercise of religion, and freedom of speech were written early (1791) into the Bill of Rights of the U.S. Constitution. In contrast, in France the freedom of speech and the free exercise of religion were established much later by the French Parliament in 1905. Thus, to understand the French interpretation of the headscarf, we must consider the historical and cultural context of secularism in France.

The United States and France have very different attitudes toward immigrants. The United States is founded on the principle of a heterogeneous society or melting pot whereas France lays claims to a more homogeneous society. The United States was founded on the labors of the many immigrants who came in waves throughout its history. Generally speaking, the United States is very respectful and not fearful of the different faiths of its many immigrants.

Despite the arguments raised against the ban and the fears of its impact on French society, the implementation of the French ban on wearing a headscarf in public schools has been rather smooth. There are fewer headscarves in schools in France today because of the ban. In 2003, 1500 girls wore the headscarf, but in 2004, only 600 continued to wear it in areas with a higher number of Muslims in the community (e.g., Montpellier, Strasbourg, Lille, Creteil). Predictably, 143 girls left the public school either on their own recognizance or after being expelled for wearing the scarf and violating the ban. Three of the 47 students expelled were excluded for wearing a Sikh turban. When 28 immigrant families referred the expulsion decisions to the French courts, the referrals were all rejected.

1. Leyla Sahin v. Turkey (European Court of Human Rights) Even though the ban on wearing the headscarf in France seems inconceivable to the American jurist, a similar case was referred by a Turkish woman to the European Court of Human Rights. That Court, which is an international court whose final decision preempts State court decisions in Europe, expressly recognized the necessity to leave to the national authorities of each individual State "a margin of appreciation" to decide on cases involving the wearing of religious symbols in teaching institutions.

Leyla Sahin, a Turkish citizen, originally lodged a complaint with the European Commission of Human Rights under Article 25 of the European Convention for the Protection of Human Rights and Fundamental Freedom (ECHR)[191] against the Republic of Turkey for denying her the right to wear the Islamic headscarf in an institution of higher education in Turkey. The application was transmitted to the European Court of Human Rights on November 1, 1998, and the Court ultimately rendered a judgment based on an almost unanimous vote. On November 10, 2005, the European Court of Human Rights ruled to leave this decision up to the individual States because rules on the subject of the wearing of religious garb vary from one country to another depending on national traditions.

The Turkish law of 1998 banned the wearing of headscarves (and for men, beards) in universities. Leyla Sahin, a Turkish medical student, was refused admission to a neurology lecture on June 10, 1998 and to a written examination on oncology earlier because she wore her headscarf.

The European Court of Human Rights argued that the wearing of the headscarf is "a symbol of a political Islam."[192] The Court's interpretation of the act of wearing a headscarf is filtered by political conditions in Turkey at the time of this case. Turkey's attachment to democratic values was being threatened by "accession to power on June 28, 1996 of a coalition government comprising the Islamist [*Refah Partisi*], which was viewed as a "genuine threat to republican values and civil peace."[193] The European Court of Human Rights inferred that wearing the scarf was also a symbol of women's lack of equality in Turkey.[194]

Ultimately, the European Court of Human Rights declared the ban on wearing the headscarf in Turkish universities was not a violation of Article 9 of the ECHR.[195] The European Court of Human Rights claimed that there is no uniform European conception of the requirements of "the protection of the rights of others" and of "public order."[196] Therefore, whether the act of wearing the headscarf rises to the level of a political symbol or a political threat is up to the State to decide.[197] Accordingly, in *Leyla Sahin v. Turkey (European Court of Human Rights, 2004)*, the highest court of human rights voted 16:1 in favor of giving the State discretion to declare a ban on wearing the headscarf in public universities.[198] This decision, together with the French ban of March 15, 2004 in primary and secondary schools, leaves the issue of the woman's right to wear the

---

191. [European] Convention for the Protection of Human Rights and Fundamental Freedoms, Nov. 4, 1950, 4.XI Eur. Ct. H.R. 1950 [hereinafter ECHR].

192. Sahin v. Turkey, 44 Eur. Ct. H.R. 44754, para. 35 (2005).

193. *Id.*

194. *See id.* at para. 11 (Tulkens, J., dissenting).

195. *Id.* at para. 123.

196. *Id.* at para. 70.

197. *Id.* at para. 115.

198. *Id.* at para. 3.

headscarf in all public schools including universities up to the determination of the State.

2. The Meaning of Dissent in the Headscarf Case The one dissenting opinion in the European Court of Human Rights headscarf case by Judge Tulkens is very revealing. Judge Tulkens does agree strongly with the majority that the right to freedom of religion guaranteed by Article 9 of the ECHR is a "precious asset" not only for believers, but for atheists, agnostics, skeptics, and the unconcerned.[199] He also agrees that in "democratic societies, in which several religions co-exist, it may be necessary to place restrictions on freedom to manifest one's religion in order to reconcile the interests of the various groups and ensure that everyone's beliefs are respected."[200] Finally, he agrees that compromise is necessary in a pluralistic democratic society based on tolerance.[201]

Admittedly, this ban on wearing the Islamic headscarf on university premises is a clear interference with the right under Article 9 of the ECHR to manifest one's religion, but it is an interference that has a legitimate aim—"the protection of the rights and freedom of others and of public order."[202] To determine whether this interference is "necessary in a democratic society," the Court must be convinced the interference is "appropriate," that it is "the least restrictive [measure]," and that the "measure was proportionate."[203]

In this case, the reasons for imposing the ban on wearing the headscarf were based on two arguments: secularism and equality.[204] Judge Tulkens finds it inconsistent, if not paradoxical, that "manifesting one's religion by peacefully wearing a headscarf may be prohibited whereas, in the same context, remarks which could be construed as incitement to religious hatred are covered by freedom of expression."[205] The Court's decision is based on "the threat posed by 'extremist political movements' seeking to 'impose on society as a whole their religious symbols and conception of a society founded on religious precepts' which, in the Court's view, serves to justify the regulations in issue, which constitute 'a measure intended to (. . .) to preserve pluralism in the university.'"[206]

The judge agrees on the need to prevent radical Islamism, but he objects to the Court's reasoning because in his view, merely wearing the headscarf cannot be automatically associated with fundamentalism.[207] "[I]t is vital to distinguish

199. *Id.* at para. 1 (Tulkens, J., dissenting).
200. *Id.*
201. *Id.*
202. *Id.* at para. 2 (Tulkens, J., dissenting).
203. *Id.*
204. *Id.* at para. 4 (Tulkens, J., dissenting).
205. *Id.* at para. 9 (Tulkens, J., dissenting).
206. *Id.* at para. 10 (Tulkens, J., dissenting).
207. *Id.*

between those who wear the headscarf and 'extremists' who seek to impose the headscarf as they do other religious symbols.[208] "Not all women who wear the headscarf are fundamentalists. . ..."[209]

Judge Tulkens' dissent and the decision itself are based on semiotics. For this judge, the act of wearing a headscarf does not necessarily signify fundamentalist affiliation and anti-West sentiments that threaten the Western world. However, for a grand majority of the judges on the European Court of Human Rights, the French Courts, and the Turkish Courts, the headscarf did have this threatening signification that warranted the ban on the freedom of speech and the freedom to manifest one's religion.

IV. SIGNS OF WOMEN'S RIGHTS IN IRAN AS REPRESENTED IN THE HUMANITIES

The content of literature, film, and the law often reflect prevailing social, political, and economic conditions. Authors and filmmakers use mediated forms of communication to convey personal messages to readers and viewers about the need for social change. Legislators write laws, and lawyers and judges interpret and carry them out in order to change injustices in society. These vehicles of communication—literature, film, and the law—are sign systems reflecting infrastructural conditions that can and do affect women's rights to equality and justice. Important information about society, its traditions, and sometimes its hidden policies perpetuated by government can be conveyed most effectively through mediated signs. Messages are not conveyed by words alone. As the proverbial statement "a picture is worth a thousand words" suggests, communication happens by transmission of information through signs and symbols—and this is the essence of the semiotic system.[210] A writer speaks sometimes directly to her readers through words and sometimes indirectly through tropes and literary figures that need interpretation to uncover the meanings hidden in analogies. The filmmaker communicates messages through the immediacy of pictures that create an aura of authenticity and drama.

This study will look at four artistic works written or directed by four Iranian women all of whom portray the state of women's human rights in

208. *Id.*

209. *Id.*

210. *See* Susan Tiefenbrun, *Legal Semiotics*, 5 CARDOZO ARTS & ENT. L.J. 89 (1986) (discussing the history and development of semiotics and its application to the field of law) and its revised version in Chapter 2 of this book.I have written extensively on the application of semiotics to the law. *See, e.g.*, Susan Tiefenbrun, *A Semiotic Approach to a Legal Definition of Terrorism*, 9 ISLA. J. INT'L & COMP.L. 357 (2003), as revised in Chapter 3 of this book.

postrevolutionary Iran. The first is a memoir of an Iranian woman who is no longer living in Iran. *Reading Lolita in Tehran* was written by Azar Nafisi, a literature professor who chose to withdraw from the public arena in postrevolutionary Iran in order to immerse herself in the world of the imagination and in the privacy of her home (with a few of her favorite students, mostly women, who read, interpret, and discuss great books of primarily Western literature). Nafisi's decision to withdraw into the world of interpretation is her form of passive resistance to the violation of women's rights occurring in postrevolutionary Iran. She actively resisted against oppression when she wrote her own memoir after she left Iran. The book became an instant best seller not only because of its treasures of valuable information about Iranian society, but its beautiful, learned and literary style that appeals especially to experienced readers of Western literature.

The second book is also a memoir of an Iranian woman who lived through the 1979 Revolution and who still continues to fight within the legal system for human rights, women's rights, and rights of Iranian political prisoners. [211] Shirin Ebadi's *Iran Awakening* recounts the life of one Iranian woman who, like all women, assumes many roles—wife, mother, female judge (removed from the bench simply because she is a woman living in a patriarchal society), activist lawyer for women's human rights, and the 2003 Nobel Peace Prize winner. Although Shirin Ebadi can now become a judge again in Iran, she prefers to remain a human rights defense attorney to help more effectively in the advancement of women's rights. Her book is provocative and political; a form of active revolt by a woman who chooses to remain in Iran. Thus, Nafisi and Ebadi both represent two different styles of resistance and two legitimate forms of engagement.

The third work is a documentary film, *Divorce Iranian Style*, codirected by a woman, Ziba Mir-Hosseini, "who is a feminist, an Iranian, and a Muslim,"[212] with an independent British filmmaker, Kim Longinotto. The film was inspired by Mir-Hosseini's book *Marriage on Trial*, based on her ethnographic research on Islamic family law.[213] The film focuses on four women who come to court to divorce their husband, obtain their rightful marriage gift, teach their husband a lesson, or regain custody of their daughters who were taken away legally by their

---

211. *See also* Christopher De Bellaigue, In The Rose Garden Of The Martyrs: A Memoir Of Iran (2004). Christopher de Bellaigue was born in London and spent the past decade in the Middle East; he lives now in Tehran. He writes from personal experience about the mullahs, artists, traders, mystics, academics, and all who were revolutionaries in Iran.

212. Ziba Mir-Hosseini, *Negotiating the Politics of Gender in Iran: An Ethnography of a Documentary, in* The New Iranian Cinema: Politics, Representation and Identity 167, 196 (Richard Tapper ed., 2002).

213. *Id.* at 167.

husband as a result of a divorce initiated by the wife.[214] This film paints a vivid picture of the deficiencies of the Iranian family laws and the family court system, its bureaucracy, its patriarchy, and its lack of fairness to women.

Mir-Hosseini is a social anthropologist who collected case studies of marriage and divorce to report on the conflicts and contradictions between marriage as represented in the law and marriage as it exists in reality.[215] She put the results of her case studies into a creative documentary film that reveals many subtleties of the legal system in Iran. Due to strict censorship policies, the film has not been publicly screened in Iran, even though the codirectors successfully obtained a "permit to film by Khatami's reformist government."[216] Nevertheless, although the film was not shown in Iran, it is known and has been seen by those who regularly attend film festivals abroad and by ordinary people who heard reports of it on the "BBC and [on] Voice of America Persian-language programs, both of which have many listeners in Iran."[217] Most film critics (both Iranian and foreign) were enthusiastic about the film that apparently "helped to humanize Iranians, who have been demonized in the West since the Revolution."[218]

In order to contrast Mir-Hosseini's very accurate and at times humorous picture of the grim state of women's rights in Iran and the unfairness of its family laws, I will also look briefly at another very important film depicting two different kinds of women in Iran today. *Two Women*, directed by an Iranian feminist filmmaker Tahmineh Milani, portrays a woman who is actually a symbol of the modern Iranian woman. She is married and happily protected and supported psychologically by her husband who miraculously shares in the household chores. But the film also portrays the tragic transformation of another woman who was once young, beautiful, modern, and intellectually curious. Because of her father, she is forced to leave the university, marry a man she despises, and become a more traditional woman in Iran. She is enslaved in a loveless marriage with an abusive husband who imprisons her into the deepest interiors of his household. This movie "attracted more viewers and sparked more reaction than any other [film] in recent memory,"[219] and its filmmaker is one of the few women in Iran today who admits to being a "feminist."

Let us now look more deeply into these four different representations of women's human rights abuses in the humanities.

---

214. *See id.*

215. *See* Ziba Mir-Hosseini, *Tamkin: Stories from a Family Court in Iran, in* Everday Life in the Muslim Middle East 136, 137–50 (Donna Lee Brown & Evelyn A. Early eds., 2d ed. 2002).

216. Mir-Hosseini, *supra* note 212, at 192.

217. *Id.*

218. *Id.*

219. Sciolino, *supra* note 6, at 265.

A. Azar Nafisi: *Reading Lolita in Tehran*

> No amount of political correctness can make us empathize with a child left orphaned in Darfur or a woman taken to a football stadium in Kabul and shot to death because she is improperly dressed. Only curiosity about the fate of others, the ability to put ourselves in their shoes, and the will to enter their world through the magic of imagination, creates this shock of recognition. Without this empathy there can be no genuine dialogue, and we as individuals and nations will remain isolated and alien, segregated and fragmented.[220]

Reading Lolita in Tehran is a compelling narrative of a woman's struggle to protect her individuality and satisfy her passion for experiencing life through literature in postrevolutionary Iran. As the State continued to blur the distinction between the personal and the political, Azar Nafisi fought in her own way to separate the two through the use of creative imagination.[221]After being expelled from one university for refusing to wear the veil, Nafisi was forced to resign from another because of her "controversial" subject matter and teaching habits.[222] She then secretly formed a book group with some of her best female students and one male student who were also passionate about reading Western literature.[223] For two years, "her girls" identified their own struggles, hardships, losses, and political disappointments with those of the characters in the books they read, discussed, and interpreted together. In postrevolutionary Iran, these female readers yearned for personal freedom. They do experience freedom and agency vicariously in the act of reading and interpreting literature, but they are forced to do so in the secrecy of their teacher's home.

In its very poetic, personal, learned, and literary style, *Reading Lolita in Tehran* illustrates the contradictions about women in Iranian society and the human

---

220. Azar Nafisi, *Mysterious Connections that Link Us Together*, National Public Radio Morning Edition, July 18, 2005, http://www.npr.org/templates/story/story.php?storyId=4753976.

221. *See* NAFISI, *supra* note 11, at 273.

222. *See id.* at 10.

223. Even though Nafisi's book is very popular in the United States and Europe, she has been criticized severely by some commentators. They accuse her of not treating the very rich Persian literature she studied as a child and mastered as a student of world literature. Nafisi's choice of Western literature is viewed (perhaps too harshly) as a "sign" of her political affiliation with the West and her abandonment of the Iranian cause. She is even linked by some of her critics with the "neo-conservatives" simply because Bernard Lewis admires her book. Some attack her, no doubt, out of sheer jealousy because she has a comfortable teaching position at a prestigious university in the United States. *See* Hamid Dabashi, *Native Informers and the Making of the American Empire*, http://weekly.ahram.org.eg/2006/797/special.htm (providing a scathing review of Nafisi's book). *See infra* text accompanying notes 325–330 for an analysis of his negative critical commentary on Nafisi's work, which, in itself, is a sign that begs interpretation and decoding.

rights abuses they have had to endure since the Revolution. The women in Nafisi's reading group relate how they have witnessed or personally experienced arbitrary arrests, torture, summary executions without trials, restricted movement within Iran and across borders, degrading body searches, forced religion and religious expression, employment discrimination, limitations on the enjoyment of cultural life, unequal gender treatment by the legal system (especially Iranian family law regarding divorce and child custody), and restrictions on women's freedoms of assembly and expression, all of which are violations of basic human rights protected under customary international law and international human rights treaties and instruments that Iran has signed and ratified.

1. Narrative Structure of *Reading Lolita in Tehran* Azar Nafisi is a scholar and a reader of Western literature who identifies certain periods of her own life with various literary works[224] she has taught in Iranian universities. In a first-person narrative that creates a sense of authenticity and intimacy with her reader, Nafisi's memoir takes the reader on a personal journey into her own life through various works of fiction that reveal many of the hidden facets of the legal, social, and political realities the narrator has experienced as an academic in the Islamic Republic of Iran.[225] Nafisi juxtaposes the reality of the world of literary fiction and the seeming unreality of life in a changing Iran.[226] The act of reading and interpreting literature is an escape from an unstable and harsh reality. It is "our moment of pause, our link to that other world of 'tenderness, brightness and beauty.'"[227] "Only eventually, we were compelled to return."[228]

Nafisi shares her private thoughts, hopes, and fears with her students and eventually her readers.[229] Like Baudelaire, who spoke directly to his readers with whom he identified lovingly (and whom he also rejected harshly in an ironic ambivalence)—"Hypocrite lecteur, –mon semblable, –mon frère,"[230]—Nafisi, too, expresses her frustrations with a passive society that tolerates the political and social changes in Iran that detrimentally and unjustly affect her role as a professional woman.[231]

While working as a professor of literature in the Islamic Republic of Iran, Nafisi admits to despising the indifference of her colleagues and students to the transformations happening in Iran that greatly jeopardize the well-being of women. She is disgusted with the mindless bureaucracy in the university where less time is spent on intellectual matters than on what she considers formalistic

224. *See* Nafisi, *supra* note 11, at 170–71.

225. *See id.* at 168–69.

226. *See id.* at 6.

227. *Id.* at 57.

228. *Id.*

229. *See id.* at 6.

230. Charles Baudelaire, Les Fleurs du Mal 184 (Richard Howard trans., 1982).

231. *See* Nafisi, *supra* note 11, at 169.

trivia.[232] At one point, Khomeini even closed all the universities for several years to weed out his opponents and implement cultural changes. The increasing gap between the public and private life in Iran caused Nafisi to give up her tenured job and choose her private life over the public one.[233] She actually gives up her teaching career, which is a form of protest, and invests her efforts in a less visible form of political engagement by teaching only a few handpicked students whom she chooses to see in her home.[234] Despite the regime's everlasting goal of blurring the distinction between the public and the private life (a problem that is endemic to the erosion of women's rights in general),[235] Nafisi refuses to be completely controlled by the government and secludes herself in her books, her family, her few friends, and her girls—her only links to the outside world.[236]

2. Concept of Literature as a Reflection of Reality in *Reading Lolita* Nafisi focuses on the receivers of the hidden messages contained in books. Her memoir begins with a detailed description of her girls who read and discuss Nabokov's *Lolita*, a highly controversial book that titillates its readers by the daring treatment of such taboo subjects as incest and child molestation. Nafisi encourages the girls to use their imagination while reading and interpreting to rise above and beyond the closure and indignities they suffer every day as women in Iran. She also encourages her girls to see in *Lolita* the representation of what the Ayatollah and the Islamists really are. They are men who like Humbert actually fear giving women freedom, so they force them to "become the figment of someone else's dreams."[237] There is no doubt that Nafisi has always loved literature, but ironically it is the new Islamic Republic and its oppressiveness that gives her greater appreciation for these books and the freedom of thought and expression she finds within them through interpretation. [238]

Literature for Nafisi is a means of opening up a closed, suffocating world imposed on her by the new regime in postrevolutionary Iran. She adopts an elegant and authorial tone in contrast to the cacophony of this chaotic era[239] full of contradiction and paradox where women are given an education only to be forced to remain inside and isolated in the home. Nafisi examines and even dares to criticize this new and dehumanizing regime through the distancing elements of literature and the adoption of an academic and intellectual perspective.[240]

---

232. *See id.* at 151.

233. *See id.* at 29.

234. *See id.* at 3.

235. *See* Hilary Charlesworth & Christine Chinkin, *The Gender of Jus Cogens, in* International Human Rights in Context 173, 175 (Henry J. Steiner & Philip Alston eds., 2000).

236. *See* Nafisi, *supra* note 11, at 47.

237. *Id.* at 28.

238. *See id.* at 47.

239. *See id.* at 274.

240. *See id.* at 9.

By focusing attention on the literary words of Western authors, she exposes the complex methods and rationales of the postrevolutionary Iranian government. She asks her students to consider "how these great works of imagination [can] help us in our present trapped situation as women . . . [to] find a link between the open spaces the novels provided and the closed ones we [a]re confined to."[241]

3. Themes in *Lolita*: Women's Loss of Agency, Individuality, and Freedom In *Lolita*,[242] Nafisi's girls see parallels between their own vulnerability and the life of Lolita, a very young girl who is systematically but subtly reduced by the power of her own stepfather. Shockingly, Humbert has sex with his young adopted daughter, forcing her to become his mistress and to live according to his rules. Like the men in the new regime, Nafisi claims that Humbert controls every aspect of Lolita's life;[243] he cares nothing for her happiness or well-being and shifts the blame for any wrongdoing on his part to her.[244] Just like Lolita, who lost her freedom to the lustful demands of Humbert, the women in Iran have lost their sense of self.[245] The days following the Revolution did not lead to the kind of freedom the Iranian women who supported the Revolution were promised.[246] Instead, women were told how to dress and what to think as they were cut off from the outside "polluted" world.[247] Like Lolita, every aspect of the Iranian woman's life was controlled by the regime.[248] Like Lolita, Iranian women were gradually subsumed under the misogynistic rules of the regime.

However, unlike Lolita, Iranian women were made anonymous, invisible, indistinguishable, and any trace of personhood, femininity or individuality was erased and replaced by "black-scarved, timid faces"[249] that float about two by two like nameless masses of black-cloaked matter. Conformity is enforced by the media in Iran which controls women's behavior in society. Subtle forms of indoctrination, threats, and warnings are everywhere; posters shout at the women from the walls of the school corridors and streets, warning them against indecency or revolt.[250] Thus, reading *Lolita* is a lesson in the manipulation of women by controlling men who are supported by the patriarchal society.

4. Themes in *The Great Gatsby*: Women in a Black-and-White Ethos After *Lolita*, the girls read F. Scott Fitzgerald's *The Great Gatsby*, [251] and with this book, Nafisi transports her readers back to the early days of the Revolution and her

---

241. *Id.* at 19.
242. VLADIMIR NABOKOV, LOLITA (1955).
243. *See* NAFISI, *supra* note 11, at 33.
244. *See id.* at 42.
245. *See id.* at 38.
246. *See* Halper, *supra* note 17, at 107.
247. *See id.* at 106–12.
248. *See id.* at 106.
249. NAFISI, *supra* note 11, at 6.
250. *See id.* at 26–27.
251. F. SCOTT FITZGERALD, THE GREAT GATSBY (Charles Scribner's Sons, 1996) (1925).

teaching career.[252] The ambiguous morality and values of *Gatsby* were difficult for many of her now-indoctrinated students to grasp.[253] Her students were now living in the days of black and white morality touted by the emerging leadership of the Islamic Republic of Iran.[254] Nick, the protagonist of *Gatsby*, is not altogether good, and the other characters also commit major sins such as adultery, decadence, and indecency.[255] Students reacted to the potentially negative impact this kind of literature could have on society and on their own value system.

Like Plato who wanted to throw out the poets from the Republic, and the Soviet Communists who rigidly censored their writers and philosophers, the Khomeini regime also struggled with the concept of the role of writers and artists in an Islamist State. The Ayatollah proposed that writers espouse only the ideals of the regime, a similar policy of strict censorship that was implemented quite effectively for eighty years in Communist Russia.[256] Censorship in the Soviet Union ultimately forced the artists to go underground to develop a rich and penetrating literature.

Nafisi's students struggled with the allegorical implications of the novel.[257] Several of the religious students in the class vehemently objected to reading *Gatsby*,[258] claiming the novel's characters promoted ambiguous and immoral values as qualities that should be emulated by the readers.[259] Nafisi countered this objection by stating that a novel is not meant to be a parallel to, or an "allegory" of, real life, either in the West or in Iran.[260] A novel is meant to be:

> . . . the sensual experience of another world. If you don't enter that world, hold your breath with the characters and become involved in their destiny, you won't be able to empathize, and empathy is at the heart of the novel. This is how you read a novel: you inhale the experience.[261]

According to Nafisi, great novels are supposed "to make you feel like a stranger in your own home. [They make us] . . . question what we [take] for granted. . . . [and question] traditions and expectations when they [seem] too immutable."[262]

Despite the advice of the teacher, as the class reads *Gatsby* and fails to understand the concept of "experiencing"' the novel, one of the more radical Muslim students, Mr. Nyazi, claims that the book "poison[s]" the "minds" of the students,

---

252. *See* NAFISI, *supra* note 11, at 92.
253. *See id.* at 108.
254. *See id.* at 109.
255. *See id.* at 126.
256. *See id.* at 124.
257. *See id.* at 127.
258. *See id.* at 120.
259. *See id.*
260. *Id.* at 111.
261. *Id.*
262. *Id.* at 94.

and makes them susceptible to follow the immoral example set by the *Gatsby* characters.[263] Reading this book, he fears, would make them prone to forget the high-minded ideals of the Revolution.[264]

In those days of frequent public prosecutions and executions in Iran, Nafisi herself decides to place *Gatsby*, the book, on trial.[265] Mr. Nyazi would be the prosecutor, Nafisi would actually be the defendant (i.e., the book), a female student would be the defense attorney, and a male student would be the judge in this mock trial.[266] On the day of the trial, Mr. Nyazi sets forth his scathing allegations against "every page" of the novel, which he claims is full of the ideals of the West that comprise a sinister assault or rape of their culture.[267] Nyazi's accusations that reflect his fear of losing his own Iranian identity to the hegemony of the West are the prelude to Iran's current fears of "Westoxication" and to young Iranian children being taught in school to say "Death to America."[268] Nyazi concludes that Gatsby deserved to die for his actions, as does the whole American society for pursuing such a decadent and immoral dream.[269] Here Nafisi seems to foresee the Jihadist discourse that would develop in recent years.

Zarrin, the defense attorney, holds a more liberal position on freedom of speech, stating that to reject a book based on the "morality" and behavior of its characters is to oversimplify the novel and to completely miss the point.[270] The revolutionaries in Iran and Fitzgerald's characters have in common an obsessive pursuit of dreams. [271] When this obsession for revolution takes over reality, and the pursuit of an impossible dream becomes a mania of the masses, any means necessary to accomplish the dream becomes acceptable, even violence.[272] Just as Gatsby's dreams were lost in the façade of his reality,[273] the dreams of the revolutionaries are lost among the thousands of murdered youths—ghosts of their own ideals.[274]

5. Henry James' Novels: Existential Courage of Conviction Even If It Means Inevitable Defeat Nafisi points out that the days of the Iran–Iraq War left the

---

263. *Id.* at 120.

264. *See id.*

265. *Id.*

266. *Id.* at 121.

267. *Id.* at 126.

268. *See, e.g.*, Sciolino, *supra* note 6, at 3 ("On the day of the government rally, I watched from a street corner as thousands of angry bearded men and black-clad women screamed 'Death to America' and punched the air with their fists. The student unrest had to be blamed on somebody, so why not the United States?").

269. Nafisi, *supra* note 11, at 127.

270. *Id.* at 132.

271. *Id.* at 144.

272. *Id.*

273. *See id.*

274. *See id.* at 153.

citizens of both countries in a state of financial, structural, emotional, and intellectual ruin.[275] The government of Iran was forced to maintain strict control over its citizens in order to pursue the war.[276] Nafisi discusses the details of these repressive days in Iran through the lens of different works by Henry James.[277]

In the years following the Revolution, Nafisi observed her students gradually becoming acculturated into blind acceptance of the mandates of the regime.[278] They were told what to think, how to act, what to wear, and how to live.[279] Their personal narratives had been confiscated by the government, leaving them with no hope to think and form opinions for themselves.[280] Dissent was rarely an option for students or women after the Revolution, and when a dissenting voice rose up, this revolt was met with grave consequences, even death.[281] Nafisi paints a rather grim picture of women in postrevolutionary Iran who are reduced to subservience and silence. There is little evidence of women in revolt in Nafisi's book. Nevertheless, women did make some progress during this wartime period in achieving certain rights that they demanded and received because women were Khomeini's much-needed constituency. Shirin Ebadi, Ziba Mir-Hosseini, and others report the existence of an emerging feminist movement, feminist protest marches, and an attempt to make change for women by women in Iran.

As if attempting to encourage a nascent feminist movement in this oppressive environment, Nafisi introduces such courageous Jamesian characters as Daisy from *Daisy Miller* and Catherine from *Washington Square*. Once again, Nafisi's postrevolutionary students are unsure of what to think of the ambiguously immoral protagonists in Jamesian novels[282] because they have been indoctrinated into an absolutist system of morality. Nafisi wants her girls to see and understand the courage of the Jamesian characters that face up to unpleasant circumstances without wavering, even if they encounter bad consequences. Nafisi also wants her students to see the value of courage, which is the quality that makes these characters so admirable.[283] Even if they do not gain happiness in their existential effort, they do gain "self-respect."[284]

During wartime, basic human rights such as freedom of speech are sometimes denied in the name of national security. During the Iran–Iraq War, critics of the Iranian government or its policies were deemed "Iraqi-inspired and

275. *See id.* at 239.
276. *See id.* at 158–59.
277. *See id.* at 186–90.
278. *See id.* at 199–200.
279. *See id.* at 288.
280. *See id.* at 221.
281. *See id.* at 275–76.
282. *Id.* at 196.
283. *See id.* at 224–25.
284. *Id.* at 225.

dangerous to national security" and doomed to severe consequences.[285] Intellectuals were reduced to silence or forced to become either revolutionaries or hermits, such as Nafisi's "magician" and her friend Mina, who were compelled to retire from public life and seclude themselves with their books and their "dashed dreams."[286] The regime turned people into "perfectly equipped failure[s]," who had to sacrifice their public lives for their sense of integrity.[287] Although tempted to retire into seclusion as many of her academic friends had done to preserve their idealism, Nafisi is persuaded to return to teaching for the sake of her students—in order to teach them to think and to feel,[288] and to live the existential life of courageous action in the face of inevitable defeat.

Nafisi reads Henry James to find courage in her changing world of utter absurdity. "[T]he most courageous characters [in James' works] are those with imagination" and empathy.[289] Merely to exist, to live only as the regime insisted they must, is not enough for Nafisi.[290] She wants her students to think, to feel, to experience a full life outside of what the government tells them life was supposed to mean.[291] As James writes in *The Ambassadors*, "Live all you can; it's a mistake not to. It doesn't so much matter what you do in particular so long as you have your life . . . Live, live!"[292] James also writes in a letter to a friend,

> Feel, feel, I say—feel for all you're worth, and even if it half kills you, for that is the only way to live, especially to live at this terrible pressure, and the only way to honour and celebrate these admirable beings who are our pride and our inspiration.[293]

Nafisi adopts the philosophy of her existential brothers such as Camus and Sartre. By living life fully and trying to fight the impossible battle (like Sisyphus who was forced to roll the big rock up a hill only to see it roll down again every day of his life), any and all attempts to fight against the absurd make life worth living, even though defeat may be inevitable. The women in postrevolutionary Iran must fight against tyranny and oppression even though they may lose the battle. Life in this misogynistic regime is not worth living without trying. By engaging in imagination, feelings, and thought about the great books, Nafisi's girls could thwart any attempt the government made "to eliminat[e] the personal [and the] private."[294]

---

285. *Id.* at 158.
286. *Id.* at 204.
287. *Id.* at 202.
288. *Id.* at 215.
289. *Id.* at 249.
290. *See id.* at 215.
291. *See id.*
292. *Id.* at 247.
293. *Id.* at 215.
294. *Id.* at 237.

6. Jane Austen's Works: Freedom from Women's Human Rights Abuses Through the works of the great ironist, Jane Austen, Nafisi sheds light on basic women's rights issues in Iran such as systematic abuse of children and forced marriages. "[I]t's a truth universally acknowledged that a Muslim man, regardless of his fortune, must be in want of a nine-year-old virgin wife."[295] To Nafisi and her girls, the concepts of arranged marriages,[296] family courts that frequently side with men,[297] and harsh parental control over daughters seem to be outdated ideas from the days of Jane Austen.[298] But these traditions were all brought back and imposed upon women in modern-day Iran with the advent of the Islamic Republic[299] and the establishment of *Shari'a* law.

Austen's works revolve around the search for individual freedom by her heroines who struggle against overbearing parents, societal pressure to marry a "suitable" man, monetary pressures, and the desire by women to find true love and happiness in their own lives.[300] Like the women in postrevolutionary Iran who were subjected to the chaos of ten years of war, the women in the world in which Jane Austen lived were caught up in the Napoleonic wars.[301] Like Nafisi, who some blame for not being politically engaged because she uses books as a mere form of escape from reality, Jane Austen went even farther and refused to address the war or become involved in the politics of her time.[302] Instead, she "created her own independent world" of characters from her imagination, thereby allowing herself through fiction to escape from the society in which she lived.[303] This was Austen's form of engagement, her own form of revolt. Like Austin, Nafisi and her girls refuse to give up their imagination or their right to pursue personal happiness.[304] This refusal is a form of resistance against oppression because it alters the regime's ability to control them or to make them conform to the fantasy world of moral perfection that it had created.[305]

Nafisi admittedly was tempted to blame all of the problems faced by her girls on the Islamic Republic.[306] For example, it would be easy to claim that Sanaz was jilted by her fiancé because the regime had forced her to become the kind of

295. *Id.* at 260.
296. *Id.* at 258.
297. *Id.* at 273.
298. *Id.* at 258.
299. *Id.*
300. *See id.* at 262.
301. *Id.* at 282.
302. *See id.*
303. *Id.*
304. *See, e.g., id.* at 283–84 (describing female experiences with marriage through one special character's excitement at the prospect of marriage).
305. *See id.* at 282.
306. *Id.* at 278.

woman that he was no longer interested in marrying.[307] Similarly, it would be easy to claim that Azin was a victim of her abusive husband and a family court system prejudiced against women.[308] It would be easy to claim the incredibly intelligent and talented Mahshid could not advance in her job simply because her fundamentalist employer was suspicious of her political past.[309] The girls searched for happiness, fulfillment, and love in a new world in which sex or any form of intimacy with a man is evil.[310] In Iran, women are marginalized and mistrusted, and at times "don't know what it means to love."[311] The girls learn that the cruelties and misogyny they experience around them these days are not just due to the brainwashing and extreme cruelties of the new regime. Sadly, they learn that male misogyny is deeply engrained and commonplace in Iran, even prevalent in the mentality of the ordinary people who have been indoctrinated by the regime.[312]

According to Nafisi, the new government seeks obedience through uniformity and dehumanizing conformity. Thus, the true evil of the Islamic Republic is its blindness to the individuality of its citizens. Iran for Nafisi is like the blind film censor, "imposing [its] visions and desires on others."[313] "How does the soul survive? is the essential question. And the response is: through love and imagination."[314]

Nafisi tries to show that using one's imagination through a study of great works is a form of political engagement and a legitimate form of revolt against conformity and dehumanization. It is not without good reason that Nafisi quotes one of her favorite authors, Saul Bellow, who valorizes the political power of words and the use of poetic language in times of crisis:

> Perhaps to remain a poet in such circumstances . . . is also to *reach the heart of politics*. The human feelings, human experiences, the human form and face, recover their proper place—the foreground.[315]

7. Literary Critics on *Reading Lolita in Tehran*

a. Positive Assessments of the Book as Signs of Women's Human Rights Struggle. Reading Lolita has been at the top of the bestseller lists and a favorite among American book clubs.[316] Nafisi has also received high praise from

---

307. *See id.* at 279–80.
308. *See id.* at 272–73.
309. *Id.* at 270.
310. *See id.* at 302.
311. *Id.* at 323.
312. *See id.* at 315.
313. *Id.*
314. *Id.*
315. *Id.* (emphasis added).
316. *See, e.g., Paperback Bestsellers: Paperback Nonfiction*, N.Y. Times Book Rev., Aug. 6, 2006, at 24.

literary critics.[317] But what does this generally positive assessment of the book actually signify? No doubt readers appreciate the beauty of her style, the contagious excitement Nafisi finds in uncovering different interpretations of works in the canon of Western literature, and the activism she encourages through the interpretive process.

But many critics are stumped by the genre of this text: is it an autobiography, a literary critique, or a political commentary?[318] In truth, it is all of these, which explains its broad appeal. Although most Americans, especially women, cannot really identify personally with the abuses Nafisi or her girls endured, Nafisi urges each reader to use his imagination and to empathize with Nafisi's longing to be free from the restrictions of a theocracy under the totalitarian Islamic Republic of Iran. Nafisi's work reveals the various devastating effects of human rights violations on women from different social strata in Iran and on readers from outside the regime.

Susan Sontag (a well-respected writer, philosopher, and literary critic) enjoyed Nafisi's book. In her critical review of it, Sontag recognizes that teaching, reading, writing, and interpreting books do play an active role in the revolt against tyranny and oppression of women. Sontag writes:

> I was enthralled and moved by Azar Nafisi's account of how she defied, and helped others to defy, radical Islam's war against women. Her memoir contains important and properly complex reflections about the ravages of theocracy, about thoughtfulness, and about the ordeals of freedom—as well as a stirring account of the pleasures and deepening of consciousness that result from an encounter with great literature and with an inspired teacher.[319]

Mona Simpson in *Atlantic Monthly* writes:

> There are certain books . . . [that] carry inside their covers the heat and struggle of a life's central choice being made and the price being paid, while the writer tells us about other matters, and leaves behind a path of sadness and sparkling loss. *Reading Lolita in Tehran* is such a book.[320]

317. *See, e.g.*, Michiko Kakutani, *Books of The Times; Book Study as Insubordination Under the Mullahs*, N.Y. TIMES, Apr. 15, 2003, at E6.

318. *See* Margaret Atwood, *A Book Lover's Tale: A Literary Life Raft on Iran's Fundamentalist Sea*, AMNESTY MAG. (Fall 2003), http://www.amnestyusa.org/amnestynow/lolita.html.

319. NAFISI, *supra* note 11, at iii.

320. Mona Simpson, *Book Group in Chadors*, ATLANTIC MONTHLY, June 2003, http://www.theatlantic.com/doc/200306/simpson.

In an Amnesty International review, Margaret Atwood recognizes the tyranny of the Islamic regime in Iran and the effect this governmental regulation has on women who virtually become invisible to the public eye:

> *Reading Lolita* provides us with a chilling account of what it feels like to live under such conditions: the heaviness, the constant weighing down—which is what we mean by "oppression" —and at the same time a lightness, a sense of unreality—They can't be doing this!—and a feeling that one is becoming both invisible and fictional. Nafisi's reading group paid so much attention to Nabokov partly . . . because they saw, in the fate of the defenseless Lolita at the hands of Humbert, their own position reflected. Lolita was turned into a fantasy object, just as every woman in Iran had become a fantasy object for the regime—a regime that wanted to censor all narratives but its own. . . .[321]

Reading, writing, and discussing literature and its multiple interpretations are acts of escape and liberation that explain the attraction of this incredibly popular memoir: "*Reading Lolita in Tehran* is both a fascinating account at how [Azar Nafisi] arrived at th[e] belief [in freedom of imagination], and a stunning vindication of it."[322]

b. Negative Assessments of Reading Lolita: Signs of Women's Human Rights Abuses in Iran. The negative assessments of Nafisi's book are signs of underlying issues in women's rights abuses and are elements of the semiotic system. I have been told by several women in Iran[323] that *Reading Lolita* is not a popular book there. Critics attack the book for its failure to recognize the value of Persian literature and Nafisi's unwarranted emphasis on Western classics in an era when "postcolonial, black and Third World feminists, scholars and activists [have] finally succeeded to introduce a modicum of attention to world literatures."[324] They criticize the book because Nafisi herself came from a socially privileged class and is a secular woman, not a practicing devout Muslim. Without being a human rights activist or lawyer herself (such as Shirin Ebadi), Nafisi does reveal serious women's human rights violations in Iran such as forced marriage (including the very young age of women forced to marry), divorce inequities, loss of professorial academic freedom, purges, censorship, limited or lost access to many books, and show trials of professors and others who opposed the regime.

Some critics point to historic and cultural errors in the book such as the claim there were Communists in Iran in the middle of 1979. Apparently, most if not all

---

321. Atwood, *supra* note 318.

322. *Id.*

323. *See* Anicee Van Engeland, "Iranian People's Criticism of Azar Nafisi's *Reading Lolita*" (Aug. 9, 2006) (unpublished, on file with author, Susan Tiefenbrun) (Fr.). Much of this subsection comes from this excellent unpublished essay.

324. Hamid Dabashi, *Native Informers and the Making of the American Empire*, AL-AHRAM WEEKLY, June 1–7, 2006, http://weekly.ahram.org.eg/2006/797/special.htm.

Communists were virtually eradicated by Khomeini. Similarly, some object to Nafisi's claim that the marriage age for women is nine, despite marriages of young women in Iran at the age of nine being a rare phenomenon today, as is stoning. Nafisi attacks forced marriage as an unwanted cultural phenomenon, and yet historically, after the war many women actually desired to have an arranged marriage. Some claim that Nafisi's insistence on the rapes of virgins in prisons is pure rumor and myth.

Nafisi is accused of seeing Iran through the eyes of an upper-class privileged person who does not live in reality. Possibly some of these critics may be jealous and have a political predisposition against a very successful Nafisi who now lives comfortably and freely in the United States. To them, her book represents what the wearing of Western garb symbolizes to Iranian traditionalists: a rejection of Iranian/Muslim identity and a preference for Western civilization and its alleged corruption.

Hamid Dabashi published a very negative critique of Nafisi's book in *Al-Ahram Weekly*.[325] In a highly politicized and polemical discourse pitching East against West, Dabashi states that Nafisi's book has achieved three objectives: "(l) systematically and unfailingly denigrating an entire culture of revolutionary resistance to a history of savage colonialism; (2) doing so by blatantly advancing the presumed cultural foregrounding of *a predatory empire* and (3) while at the very same time catering to the most retrograde and reactionary forces within the United States, waging an all out war against a pride of place by various immigrant communities and racialised minorities seeking curricular recognition on university campuses and in the American society at large."[326]

The language of this reviewer's scathing critique of Nafisi's book reveals a clear political agenda. His vitriolic anti-Americanism blurs his objectivity and prevents him from analyzing and interpreting the book for what the words actually say and mean. He prefers to use hyperbolic language, exaggerations, and generalizations to persuade his readers, couching his commentary in politically coded phrases such as "US imperial designs" and "an American empire". He accuses Nafisi and her book of being "partially responsible for cultivating the US (and by extension the global) public opinion against Iran," He demonizes Nafisi and the book's "unfailing hatred of everything Iranian—from its literary masterpieces to its ordinary people."[327] He is outraged simply because Bernard Lewis endorses the book, and he resorts to calling Lewis bad names ("the most wicked ideologue of the US war on Muslims").[328] Although admitting that oppression of women exists under Muslim laws, he accuses Nafisi of denigrating Iranian and Islamic literary cultures and feminist movements, claiming a "collective

325. *See* Dabashi, *supra* note 324.
326. *Id.* (emphasis added).
327. *Id.*
328. *Id.*

amnesia of historical facts surrounding successive US imperial moves for global domination. . . ."[329] The author of this review actually admits to linking Azar Nafisi with the "US leaders of the neo-conservative movement" and claims that Nafisi engages in "a systematic deprecation of Iranian culture, and by extension local and regional cultures of actual or potential resistance to the US empire, glorifying instead a canonized inner sanctum for an iconic celebration of "Western literature". . . placing her squarely at the service of the predatory US empire." [330] This review continuously spews venom at Nafisi and the United States by referring to the United States more than several times as a "predatory empire."

I understand that for some, this type of negative criticism may be an understandable expression of sensitivity to a perceived disregard for Persian culture and literature in a time when upheaval and fragmentation have been particularly acute. Nevertheless, literary critical responses that are fraught with political prejudices have limited value. This brand of literary criticism is disreputable because it is blinded by cultural hatred and corrupted by a political agenda and an outdated 1980s' disdain of the Western literary canon and the "Euro-centricity of the literary imagination." It also fails both to illuminate the text and by its subjectivity and prejudices, to understand the multiplicity of hidden meanings that only an objective analysis of the words, the signs, and the symbols of the text itself can reveal.

This kind of critical commentary could be construed as a metaphor of the compulsory *hejab* itself. Just as Dabashi misreads Nafisi and misinterprets her messages because the reader/reviewer is himself blinded by a fanatical political agenda, the Islamic State justifies its strict regulation of women's garb on grounds of religious conservative traditionalism, and even more suspiciously, if not paradoxically, on grounds of women's liberation. This kind of critical commentary and governmental justification is a cover-up and a covert attempt to proselytize more important political goals. To the Islamic rulers the *hejab* is a symbol of the rejection of Western hegemony and Western civilization as well as a valorization of Muslim identity. The fact that only women are required to be bearers of this symbol of identity is unfair, just as Dabashi's commentary is unfair.

B. Shirin Ebadi's, *Iran Awakening*: A Lawyer's Look at Women's Human Rights in Iran

Shirin Ebadi is an Iranian woman who never left Iran and has no intentions of leaving. She recounts her personal life story in a memoir that, like Azar Nafisi's book, reveals the personal plight of a professional woman in postrevolutionary Iran. Nafisi's writing style reflects her immersion in literature and scholarship

---

329. *Id.*
330. *Id.*

while Shirin Ebadi writes with the clear and persuasive skills of a lawyer. Both are Iranian women who recognize the need to provide more opportunities and equal rights for women in Iran, but Nafisi left Iran early in her life and was educated in Switzerland, while Ebadi remained in Iran to fight for equal rights and fairness from within the system. Nafisi drinks endless cups of coffee (the proverbial Western European and American drink), and Ebadi drinks endless cups of tea (the Eastern and Iranian drink). This preference is an important sign that points to a significant difference in the perspectives of both women writers.

Ebadi is a woman, like all women, who must juggle many responsible roles in life. She was the first female judge in the Iranian high court and was forced to resign simply because she is a woman. She is now a lawyer, writer, human rights activist, devoted daughter, mother of two beloved daughters, wife, and courageous dissident. Ebadi was arrested and jailed; she eventually won the Nobel Peace Prize in 2003. Like Nafisi, she supported the Revolution at first, but later felt betrayed by it:

> I felt that I too had won, alongside this victorious revolution. It took scarcely a month for me to realize that, in fact, I had willingly and enthusiastically participated in my own demise. I was a woman, and this revolution's victory demanded my defeat.[331]

After the Revolution, "public space . . . became fraught with uncertainty. [Women] simply did not know where, at what hour, and under what pretext you might be harassed, and often the confrontations with the *komiteh* [morality police] turned alarming."[332] After the Revolution Ebadi herself was arrested and imprisoned in Evin where "[w]omen who are arrested . . . after dark are typically prostitutes"[333] and where prison conditions are appalling.[334] Like Nafisi, and despite her humiliation and fears, Ebadi writes about her prison experience in a very poetic style, revealing her deeply emotional state of mind and her profound understanding of the power of literature as a vehicle of liberation and escape:

> Ten more days in prison. Ten more days of clanking breakfast trays, of sullen guards smoking and despising me for a oneness that required the supervision of their four. Ten more days of trying to imagine the gentle, rocky slope of the Alborz Mountains behind Evin, where my poet friend Simin Behbahani and I hiked each week, talking languorously while we scaled the mountain, as teenagers scampered past us with their boom boxes and jaunty bandannas . . . Simin and I are kindred spirits, and many of the themes of her

---

331. Ebadi, *supra* note 24, at 38.

332. *Id.* at 103.

333. *Id.* at 164.

334. *See id.* ("The best cell was covered in filth, and the sink had no running water. Dirt and rust rimmed the metal toilet in the corner."). *See also id.* at 168 ("Torture there was rampant.").

> poetry—women's suffering, the celebration of their rights and existence—inspire my own work. I tried to force more hours to pass by remembering lines of her *ghazals*. The images came, of monsters soaring the sky in trails of smoke, of plundered mermaids. [335]

The Khomeini regime understood the power of literature and systematically arrested and tortured writers in Iran.[336] Ebadi sadly recognizes that there is no freedom for writers, journalists, or activists in Iran.[337]

Shirin Ebadi has been harassed and has experienced several assassination attempts[338] and the constant humiliation of her family in order to pursue her dream of a democratic Iran. On the day she came to San Diego to deliver her speech at the Kroc Peace and Justice Center, I had the privilege of interviewing her personally. She admitted in a taped interview that just before her departure to the United States, she received a threatening letter from the Iranian government telling her not to pursue her political agenda.

Ebadi understands that the "headscarf" has many meanings. She admits that "[t]he headscarf 'invitation' was the first warning that this revolution might eat its sisters, which was what women called one another while agitating for the Shah's overthrow."[339] Like Nafisi, Ebadi felt betrayed by the revolutionaries who believed that "[i]n their hierarchy of priorities, women's rights would forever come last. It was simply never the right time to defend women's rights."[340]

Between the lines of her book, Ebadi reveals her incredible courage, determination, modesty, and delightful sense of humor in the midst of a rather grim picture of Iran today. She never gives up hope, even though she recognizes the failure of the Iranian judicial system that lacks accountability, shows unfair preference for men,[341] and suffers from "rampant impunity, disregard for fundamental constitutional rights, manipulation of the law to promote a political agenda, systematic use of torture, and above all, abuse of judicial powers to repress peaceful expressions of dissent and criticism."[342] Ebadi is chronicler, a

---

335. *Id.* at 171–72.

336. *See, e.g., id.* at 177 (mentioning the case of the young poet Ezzat Ebrahimnezhad who was shot by paramilitaries).

337. *See id.* at 189.

338. *See id.* at xv (referring to a "transcript of a conversation between a government minister and a members of the death squad," Ebadi writes: "I blinked once, but it stared back at me from the page: 'The next person to be killed is Shirin Ebadi.' Me.").

339. *Id.* at 39.

340. *Id.* at 56.

341. *See id.* at 51 ("The drafters of the penal code had apparently consulted the seventh century for legal advice. The laws, in short, turned the clock back fourteen hundred years, to the early days of Islam's spread, the days when stoning women for adultery and chopping off the hands of thieves were considered appropriate sentences.").

342. Hadi Ghaemi, Op-Ed., *For Iran, the Man is the Message*, INT'L HERALD TRIB., June 30, 2006, at 6.

troubadour who sings to women and the world about critical current events that are bound to become legends. She writes articles in magazines[343] and books that become best sellers to let women in Iran know that their legal system discriminates again them and that women have an "inferior status in the [Iranian] penal code."[344] For example, in a vivid and gripping style she writes that there is a "section of the [penal] code devoted to blood money, *diyeh*, [which] holds that if a man suffers an injury that damages his testicles, he is entitled to compensation equal to a woman's life."[345] In questioning the significance of the language of these provisions, Ebadi asks "Is this really how the Islamic Republic regards its women?"[346] This language in the penal code is a sign of discrimination against women and the cultural devaluing of women in Iran.

Ebadi does recognize that the Islamic State has educated women from the provinces for the first time, but this right to education has resulted in major tension within families. Legal rights cannot be implemented effectively if the culture of society has not yet caught up with the intent of the legislation. Ebadi recounts a story in which an Iranian father refused to send his daughter to school, even though men and women were segregated at the universities, because he felt the need to defend her virtue and, thereby, his own honor.[347] This hypothetical is represented most vividly in the movie *Two Women* where one father yanks his brilliant daughter out of the university simply because he learns she is being stalked by a man on a bicycle.

Even though there have been more women in universities in Iran than men,[348] laws affecting women are discriminatory and inadequate. Marriage laws in Iran allow the man to remain a "person" while the woman becomes "chattel."[349] The man has a right to divorce the woman at whim, take custody of the children[350] (even if the father abuses the child), and acquire three wives who live together with the first wife.[351] Ebadi recognizes that one of the most serious problems in Iran is the inadequacy of the laws themselves[352] and the failure to enforce protective women's rights laws.

---

343. *See* EBADI, *supra* note 24, at 117.

344. *Id.*

345. *Id.*

346. *Id.*

347. *See id.* at 106–07.

348. *See id.* at 107.

349. *Id.* at 53.

350. *Id.* at 123.

351. *Id.* at 53.

352. *See id.* at 111 ("I had to choose cases, I realized, that illustrated the tragic repercussions of the theocracy's legal discrimination against women. I could recite a litany of objectionable laws—a woman's life is worth half as much as a man's, child custody after infancy goes automatically to the father . . . To attract people's attention, to solicit their

1. The Power of Interpretation Ebadi's hope for the future of Iran lies in the power of interpretation. She recognizes the need to adopt a more dynamic interpretation of the Koran in order to protect and provide equal rights for women. She believes "a basic right for women could be guaranteed within an Islamic framework of governance, provided those in government were inclined to interpret the faith in the spirit of equality."[353]

Ebadi reminds us that:

> In Islam, there exists a tradition of intellectual interpretation and innovation known as *ijtihad*, practiced by jurists and clerics over the centuries to debate the meaning of Koranic teachings as well as their application to modern ideas and situations. Sunni Islam effectively closed the door to *ijtihad* several centuries back, but in Shia Islam, the process and spirit of *ijtihad* thrive. *Ijtihad* is central to Islamic law, because [*Shari'a*] is more a set of principles than a codified set of rules.[354]

Ijtihad "imposes flexibility on Islamic law and creates an exciting space for adapting Islamic values and traditions to [women's] lives in the modern world."[355] But *ijtihad* can be burdensome because it lets clerics and jurists debate and interpret the Koranic teachings for an endless period of time. "An interpretation of Islam" must be "in harmony with equality and democracy." [356]

2. The Power of Words Shirin Ebadi believes in the power of the written word and its ability to free women from tyranny in Iran.

> [T]he written word is the most powerful tool we have to protect ourselves, both from the tyrants of the day and from our own traditions. Whether it is the storyteller of the legend Scheherazade, staving off beheading by spinning a thousand and one tales, feminist poets of the last century who challenged the culture's perception of women through verse, or lawyers like me, who defend the powerless in courts, Iranian women have for centuries relied on words to transform reality.[357]

3. Americans Must Keep Out of Iran and Its Fight for Women's Human Rights Ebadi firmly believes that change for Iranian women is possible, but it must come peacefully from within the system[358] with no help from foreign

---

sympathies and convince them that these laws were not simply unfair but actively pathological, I had to tell stories.").

353. *Id.* at 190–91.

354. *Id.* at 191.

355. *Id.*

356. *Id.*

357. *Id.* at 209.

358. *Id.* at 204.

countries.[359] There are signs of a feminist movement now in Iran, whereas during the 1990s women were "not yet organized" in a feminist movement, although they were working to change women's rights in the Islamist State of Iran.[360] The conditions for women in Iran are deplorable. Many women commit suicide, or become suicide bombers, preferring to die as martyrs rather than live lives of contradiction and paradox in a community that does not treat them fairly or equally. "The suicide rate among women rose after the Islamic Revolution, commonly taking the form of self-immolation. This tragic exhibitionism . . . is women's way of forcing their community to confront the cruelty of their oppression."[361] Today Iran has the third highest rate of self-immolation after India.[362] Suicide and self-immolations are signs of women's oppression. Protest and revolt are met with harsh responses. Any attempt to protest by the great number of unhappy young people in Iran or by the highly educated women in universities is crushed with typical brutality, especially if America supports the protest.[363] "Public American support for any pro-democracy phenomenon in Iran, whether from an individual or a trend or a demonstration, always provoked the Islamic system's ire and generally resulted in an even harsher crackdown."[364]

Ebadi abhors Iran's "patriarchy" and speaks out vocally against the oppression of the conservative rulers who have stripped women of their basic human rights and their political and social freedom. She clearly advocates sovereignty for Iran and a "hands off foreign policy" for America vis-à-vis Iran.[365] She admits her anger at the United States and its CIA for assisting in the removal of Mossadegh, whom she greatly admired.[366] In her moving speech at the Kroc Peace and Justice

359. Ziba Mir-Hosseini, *Muslim Women's Quest for Equality: Between Islamic Law and Feminism*, 32 CRITICAL INQUIRY 629, 645 (2006) (describing Mir-Hosseini's views shared by many feminists that the United States should not involve itself in Iran's internal problems, "especially in the context of the neo-imperialist war on terror, which many Muslims perceive to be directed against them once again. Such a perception—whether justified or not—not only puts them on the defensive and makes them more likely to cling to religious tradition; it also erodes the credibility and moral high ground of secular and Western discourses.").

360. EBADI, *supra* note 24, at 125.

361. *Id.* at 109.

362. These statistics were reported on the radio station KPBR, a San Diego public radio, at 7:00 a.m. Pacific Time on January 10, 2007.

363. EBADI, *supra* note 24, at 195.

364. *Id.*

365. *See* Shirin Ebadi Lecture, *supra* note 47, at 14.

366. *See id.* at 5 ("It was a profoundly humiliating moment for Iranians, who watched the United States intervene in their politics as if their country were some annexed backwater, its leader to be installed or deposed at the whim of an American president and his CIA advisors.").

Center in San Diego on September 7, 2006, she implored the United States to keep out of Iran. "We will not allow Iran to turn into another Iraq," she said.[367]

4. Iran's Esthetic of Death Ebadi describes her modest beginnings in a Tehran family that had no power to put her in high places.[368] She had to build her own career by herself, using her own determination, intelligence and hard work.[369] She believed in the ideals of the 1979 Revolution and was as disillusioned as Nafisi with the direction that Iran has since taken under the hard-line clerics and their strict interpretation of the Koran.[370] After the Revolution and during the Iran–Iraqi War, Ebadi spoke of the number of "secret show trials" and public executions,[371] arrests, and tortures in prison.[372] Ebadi and women in general felt betrayed by Khomeini but also by the West because of its support for Saddam and Iraq.[373] But she concedes that "[i]f we admitted to ourselves that the revolution had been betrayed, we would surely lose the war."[374] Iran's Revolution and the Iran–Iraq War produced a frightening "cult of martyrdom . . . that glorified human sacrifice in the name of Islam."[375] The "engorged enthusiasm for martyrdom and the aesthetic of death"[376] that Ebadi and all the women around her observed in Iran did not feel alien or excessive to them because "everything—public space, rituals, résumés, newspapers, television—became dominated by death, mourning and grief."[377]

5. Patriarchy in Iran and Male-Child Preference Women's role in Iranian society is conditioned by a widespread cultural preference for male children. This preference is one of the main causes of the establishment and continuation of a troublesome patriarchy in Iran as well as the persistence of women's low self-esteem and their social and economic dependence on males for survival. Ebadi understands that in Iran, male children are preferred, even though in her own family she was lucky enough to be treated as equal to her brother.[378]

---

367. *Id.*at 39.

368. *See id.* at 14.

369. *See id.*

370. *See id.*

371. Ebadi, *supra* note 24, at 59.

372. *Id.* at 69.

373. *Id.* at 61 ("Freshly wounded by a violent revolution, we put aside our grievances and betrayal. Those images marching across the television every night inflamed our nationalism. My heart cracked for our young men, setting out for Saddam's killing fields with their shoddy weapons, no match for a dictator armed with the latest from the West's arms boutiques.").

374. *Id.* at 60.

375. *Id.* at 61.

376. *Id.* at 62.

377. *Id.*

378. *Id.* at 11. *See* Chapter 9 and the cultural preference for male children in China that has resulted in an increase in trafficking of women and a serious decrease in the number of women in China due to female infanticide among other causes.

> In most Iranian households, male children enjoyed an exalted status, spoiled and cosseted by a coterie of aunt and female relatives. They often felt themselves the center of the family's orbit . . . As children grew older, the boys' privileges—from running about the neighborhood to consorting with a range of friends—expanded, while the girls' contracted, to ensure that they remain *najeeb*, honorable and well-bred. In Iranian culture, it was considered natural for fathers to love their sons more; the sons are the repository for the family's future ambitions; affection for a son was an investment.[379]

Ebadi admits that her own upbringing spared her "from the low self-esteem and learned dependence that [she] observed in women reared in more traditional homes."[380]

Ebadi's book breathes life into the cult of death that permeates the Iranian society today, and she brings a message of hope for women in her belief in the power of words and the liberating effects of interpretation and the message of semiotics.

C. Ziba Mir-Hosseini's Documentary Film, *Divorce Iranian Style*[381]

Women in Iran today revolt against oppression through the medium of art. Despite Iran's policy of censorship, filmmakers, journalists, and writers abound in Iran. Artists attempt to reveal the injustices imposed upon women in Iran in the name of religious tradition. For instance, Ziba Mir-Hosseini's extraordinary film addresses the inadequacy of the Iranian legal system, especially its family court and divorce laws. Mir-Hosseini is an Iranian woman, an independent consultant, and a researcher and writer on Middle Eastern issues, specializing in gender, family relations, Islamic law, and development. She is a social anthropologist who earned her PhD in social anthropology from the University of Cambridge. She lives in Britain and has held numerous prestigious research and visiting fellowships and professorships in the United States. She was herself twice divorced and understands profoundly divorce proceedings in Iran. She also codirected an important documentary film that illuminates the vagaries of the Iranian system of divorce, the Iranian family court, and the way the legal system and culture in Iran affect women's rights.

Divorce Iranian Style was produced with the cooperation of the Ministries of Justice and of Islamic Guidance in Iran. It provides a clear picture of the bureaucracy of the legal system, the litany of allegedly "lost files" in the court, the mean-spirited nature of the male judges and the female clerks of the court, and the male-driven nature of the judicial system where judges are predisposed not to

---

379. *Id.*

380. *Id.* at 12.

381. *See* DIVORCE IRANIAN STYLE, *supra* note 111. The statement in this section, which refers to the movie, is supported by the author's review of the movie.

grant a divorce to the woman. The few female clerks in the courts are deeply indoctrinated in the patriarchal system that openly favors men. The whole judicial system in Iran is highly politicized, and there is no guarantee of due process or judicial independence.

Mir-Hosseini's film takes place in a tiny, overcrowded and messy Tehran courtroom presided over by a judge wearing a white turban. The goal of the judge is to persuade couples in dispute to save the marriage because in the eyes of God, divorce is shameful and abominable. Women come into this court to plead for a divorce using every form of persuasion available from yelling, screaming, threatening, and deceiving to smiling, flirting, and being charming or applying logic, reason, and legal argument, but all to no avail. One woman tries to convince the prejudiced judge that her husband is mad and abusive: "This man has made my life hell," and she claims he refuses to let her answer the phone even if it rings a hundred times. The judge's response to this testimony is to tell the woman to go back home and make herself more beautiful for her husband so she can get from him what she wants and needs.

Another woman who at age fourteen was forced by her family to marry a man she did not love, seeks a divorce and her $10,000 *mehriyeh* (a kind of dowry or marriage gift given by the husband to the wife and pledged at the time of marriage in case of divorce) on the theory that her virginity was taken from her and that she has the legal right to the marriage gift. After she goes to court, she also argues her case before a group of family members in a kind of arbitration setting in the living room of a relative, surrounded by her uncles who serve as mediators. Even though she was attempting to claim her legal right to the *mehriyeh*, the husband and his family object to the materialistic way the woman and her family perceive of the marriage. "Her family is treating it like a business deal." In Iran, the marriage gift rarely is given to the woman by the man in a divorce, even though women have a legal right to the marriage gift. Instead it is used as a bargaining chip to get a divorce.

Another woman, who courageously initiated a divorce and married another man whom she loved, is ordered by the court to give custody of her beloved four-year-old daughter to her first husband, who already had custody of their eleven-year-old daughter. Apparently, the father does not care at all about providing an education for his daughters. But in Iran, when a woman wants to divorce her husband, custody for the children automatically reverts to the father. This is a harsh impediment to divorce.[382] This woman sobs and pleads for the mercy of the court, but the unsympathetic female clerk of the court whispers, "She's ruined her children's lives just for lust . . . lust, lust, lust." The judge is equally

382. *See* MAHMOODY & HOFFER, *supra* note 12 (describing how Betty Mahomoody refused to get a divorce in Iran from an abusive husband because she knew it would mean having to give up her daughter, whom the father was indoctrinating with force into the Muslim religion).

unsympathetic with the despondent woman's pleas: "You remarried, and when you remarry you lose the child."

1. Reactions to the Film as a Sign of the State of Women's Rights in Iran Iranians abroad (primarily educated and sophisticated diaspora Iranians) objected to the film, claiming it did not represent the reality of women's lives in Iran. They argued the film gave foreigners a "distorted and wrong image of Iranian culture and society."[383] These Iranians abroad as well as officials in Iran were shocked to see illiterate and uneducated women portrayed on screen because this "shattered the picture of Iranian culture that they were trying to build in their host communities."[384] In other words, the film went against the party line. Islamic officials claimed the film undermined the image of the strong Iranian family (which is the basis of the Islamic system) by showing women trying to get out of bad marriages.[385] Both these criticisms, one sociological and the other political, are characteristic of the sensitivities of Iranian society today. Iranian critics of the film believe the film judges them too harshly. [386] They believe the West cannot accept the powerful role religion plays in Iranian society today and in its legal system, which the West believes should be independent.[387]

Hosseini's film, *Divorce Iranian Style*, illustrates the difficult relationship that exists between Islam, gender, and democracy—a subject about which Mir-Hosseini has written several very important articles and books.[388] Mir-Hosseini is one of the most reliable sources for providing consistently in-depth analyses of this highly complex issue. She is no longer living in Iran.

D. The Cinematographic Representation of the Modern Iranian Woman in a Traditional Society: *Two Women*[389]

The feminist film *Two Women* tells the story of two very different types of women, Fereshteh and Roya, who represent tradition and modernity in Iran today. At the outset, the two had much in common: as friends in college in Tehran, both were

---

383. Mir-Hosseini, *supra* note 212, at 197.

384. *Id.*

385. *Id.*

386. *See id.*

387. *See id.*

388. *See, e.g.*, ZIBA MIR-HOSSEINI, MARRIAGE ON TRIAL: A STUDY OF ISLAMIC FAMILY LAW: IRAN AND MOROCCO COMPARED (1993); MIR-HOSSEINI, *supra* note 107; MIR-HOSSEINI & TAPPER, supra note 1; Ziba Mir-Hosseini, *Women and Politics in Post-Khomeini Iran: Divorce, Veiling and Feminist Voices, in* WOMEN AND POLITICS IN THE THIRD WORLD (H. Afshar ed., 1996); Ziba Mir-Hosseini, *Powers and Limits of Negotiations: Women's Strategies in Marriage and Divorce, in* STRATEGIES DES FEMMES EN IRAN (Nouchine Yavari-d'Hellencourt ed., 1997).

389. TWO WOMEN (1999). *See also* Jasmine Darznik, *Free Bird: Tahmineh Milani's "Two Women"*, The Iranian (Aug. 8, 2000), http://www.iranian.com/JasminDarznik/2000/August/Women/ (last visited Dec. 5, 2007).

very happy, bright, intellectually engaged women who believed in their own futures. Fereshteh was an exceptionally brilliant math student who loved college until one day she started to be stalked by a man on a motorcycle who refused to give up. He followed her for many days, and Fereshteh was very frightened. This incident caused her father to send her back home to Isfahan. Her father then forced Fereshteh to marry a man she did not love. Her husband soon transforms himself from a kind, caring person into a cruel, controlling tyrant, not unlike the husband in *Not Without My Daughter*, who also changed from a kind, loving Iranian husband and father (when they were living in the United States) into a wife beater in Iran. Fereshteh's husband reneges on his promise to allow her to finish her education. Instead he forbids her from reading books, denies her the right to use the telephone by locking it, and becomes paranoid, accusing her of having a lover. This loveless marriage and sequestration transform the once beautiful and vibrant Fereshteh into a pale, lifeless being whose appearance scares even her best friend, Roya, who luckily married an emancipated husband.

Roya's husband allows her to work in a high-level management position. She drives a car, wears Western garb with a headscarf only, and juggles many roles like most Western women do in society. She is a happy woman who represents if not the modern Iranian woman living in Iran today, then perhaps the image of what modern women in Iran could be like.

When the enslaved Fereshteh tries to get a divorce on the grounds that her husband "humiliates" her, the judge declares her grounds insufficient. Despondent and hopeless, she retires to her prison-like life in the home with no connections to the outside world. But she is amazingly liberated by the very same stalker who threatened her in college and caused her downfall. The stalker kills her terrible husband, leaving Fereshteh "like a free bird" without "wings to fly." Now newly emancipated, she contemplates going back to school and work, but she is overwhelmed by her liberation.

"[W]omen in the audience cheered and clapped[, and] *Two Women* became the biggest box office hit in Iranian history."[390] This reaction is a clear sign of women's hope for equality in the future.

What went wrong for all these women represented in these four literary and cinematographic works? The answer can be found by looking closely at the inadequacy of Iranian domestic laws and the lack of enforcement of women's human rights despite those rights being protected by international laws and treaties to which Iran is either a signatory or subject to their provisions by customary international law. I shall now examine the history and development of Iranian family laws and later the international instruments that should theoretically protect women's rights in Iran if the political will to enforce them is developed.

---

390. Sciolino, *supra* note 6, at 265.

V. IRANIAN FAMILY LAWS: THEN AND NOW

Iranian family law in postrevolutionary Iran is based on *Shari'a* law, as interpreted according to the Ja'fari school of *Shi'a* law.[391] *Shari'a* law is not very favorable to women. The implementation of *Shari'a* law is arguably one of the causes for the establishment of gender inequality leading to a "gender apartheid"[392] in Iran. Family law in Iran has changed several times, once under the Pahlavi monarchy in 1925 and again in 1979 under the Islamic Republic. According to Donna Hughes, "[n]ew laws strengthening gender apartheid and repression of women are not a thing of the past."[393] Even under Khatami's reformist regime in 1997, new restrictive laws and policies were enacted in order to segregate women and men in the fields of medicine and healthcare.[394] Until the 1930s, the *Shi'a* clergy performed marriages and divorces in *Shari'a* courts that had jurisdiction in all family matters. Under Reza Shah's reign there was a move to create a more centralized judicial system based on a Western model, establishing new courts and laws reminiscent of European legal concepts and codes. A Civil Code was enacted between 1927 and 1935.[395] However, Iranian Civil Code (ICC) Articles 1034–1206 on marriage, divorce, family affairs, and children "retain the patriarchal bias of the *Shari'a*."[396] In ICC Article 1129, an attempt was made to extend the grounds upon which a woman could obtain a judicial divorce to include the husband's refusal or his inability to provide for her, his refusal to perform his sexual duties, his mistreatment of her, and his affliction with a disease that could harm her life (Article 1130).[397] The Civil Code departed from *Shari'a* law by prohibiting the marriage of girls under thirteen in Article 1041.[398]

The 1931 Marriage Law consisting of twenty articles and two notes reduced the administrative and judicial functions of the clergy.[399] The Iranian Marriage Law also established financial penalties and a prison term for anyone involved in the marriage of girls under thirteen (Article 3). ICC Articles 4 and 8–17 provide

---

391. *See* Ziba Mir-Hosseini, *Family Law in Modern Persia*, 9 ENCYCLOPEDIA IRANICA 192–96 (1999).

392. *See generally* Donna Hughes, *Women and Reform in Iran* (Feb. 2000), http://www.uri.edu/artsci/wms/hughes/reform.htm.

393. *Id.*

394. *See id.*

395. Mir-Hosseini, *supra* note 391, at 192.

396. *Id. See* Qanun-i Madani [Civil Code] Tehran 1314 [1935], articles 1034–1206 (Iran), *translated* in Iran Human Rights Documentation Center, http://www.iranhrdc.org/english/pdfs/Codes/TheCivilCode.pdf (last visited Dec. 5, 2007) [hereinafter Iranian Civil Code].

397. *Id.*

398. *Id.*

399. *Id.*

the wife with a right to maintenance and the right to initiate divorce proceedings in a civil court.[400]

In 1967, a big change in family law occurred when the Iranian Family Protection Law was enacted.[401] This law, which prohibited men from having a right to an automatic divorce and prohibited polygamy, was written into the Civil Code as well.[402] The Family Protection Law set up new court procedures for family disputes.[403] Divorcing couples were required to appear in courts presided over by civil judges, some of whom were women.[404] If both parties did not agree to a divorce, the court could issue a certificate evidencing "Impossibility of Reconciliation."[405] Men and women could appoint arbitrators to try to bring about reconciliation, but the final decision rested with the court (Articles 6–13).[406] The Family Protection Law included many other provisions favorable to women's rights to a divorce in Iran.[407]

In 1975, the Family Protection Law was amended, and the minimum age for marriage was increased from fifteen to eighteen for females and from eighteen to twenty for males.[408] The new law also provided more rights to women seeking a divorce and child custody.[409] However, many clergy opposed this law, viewing it as the destruction of Muslim values and the dissolution of the entire Iranian family structure.[410] "Ayatollah Khomeini denounced it [the Family Protection Law (FPL)] as contrary to Islam, declaring divorces issued under the FPL to be void"[411] retroactively.

Khomeini and the Islamic Republic reinstated strict *Shari'a* law and special civil courts presided over by religious judges who were "free" from the Civil Procedure Code.[412] During this period, Khomeini instituted certain contradictory policies resulting in the reduction in restrictions imposed on men's rights to divorce and polygamy and the increase in compensation to women who are harmed by divorce and polygamy.[413] The Council of Guardians was now required to revise any laws found to be in contradiction with *Shari'a* law.[414] Thus, for

---

400. *Id.*
401. *Id.*
402. *Id.*
403. *Id.*
404. *Id.*
405. *Id.*
406. *Id.*
407. *See id.* (providing an in-depth analysis of Iranian Family Law).
408. *Id.*
409. *Id.*
410. *Id.*
411. *Id.* at 194.
412. *Id.*
413. *Id.*
414. *Id.*

example, Article 1041, which formerly set a minimum age for marriage at thirteen for females and fifteen for males, was amended in 1982 to prohibit marriage prior to the age of nine for girls and fifteen for boys.[415] Legalizing marriage for nine-year-old girls is a serious step backwards for women's human rights because these young girls are generally forced into marriage by their parents.[416] Incidentally, Article 3 of the 1931 Marriage Law makes it illegal and punishable by six months to two years imprisonment to marry a girl under thirteen.[417] Similarly contradictory rules exist in Iran for polygamy.

Temporary marriage (*sigheh*, a custom that allows a married man to have sex with another woman by temporarily "marrying" her and unmarrying her after the sex is completed) is recognized as a valid marriage under the Iranian Civil Code, but the 1931 Marriage Laws are silent as to the legality of this temporary marriage.[418] After 1979, special civil courts heard disputes involving temporary marriages and even authorized their registration, thus giving legal status to the temporary marriage and the legitimization of extramarital sex.[419]

Women's custody rights were also curtailed in 1979. The Iranian Civil Code gives a mother the right to the custody of her daughter only until the age of seven and to the custody of her son only until the age of two (Article 1169).[420] In the case of the husband's death, a woman naturally acquires custody of her children (Article 1170), but loses custody if she remarries (Article 1171), in which case the child is then raised by the child's paternal grandfather (Article 1180).[421] Mothers of martyrs have the right to receive their deceased husband's salary and to keep custody of their children under a new legislation that was passed on 6 Mordad 1365 (Islamic year). [422]

In 1982, new stipulations were added to the marriage contract entitling a woman to claim half the wealth acquired by her husband during the marriage (provided she does not initiate the divorce) and enabling women to seek a judicial divorce without the signature of their husband.[423] Article 1130 of the Civil Code was amended in 1982 to give judges the power to grant or withhold a divorce requested by a woman.[424] Article 1130 was again amended in 2002 to empower a judge to issue a divorce when a woman establishes that the continuation

415. *Id.*
416. *Id.*
417. *Id.*
418. *Id.*
419. *Id.*
420. *Id.*
421. *Id.*
422. *Id.*
423. *Id.*
424. *Id.*

of the marriage would entail intolerable suffering or hardship.[425] The enforcement of Islamic jurisprudence rules (*figh*) in Iran since the 1979 Revolution resulted in these two favorable amendments to Article 1130 of the Civil Code; however, there are serious gaps between legal theory and social practice in Islamic law as enforced in Iran.[426] These gaps have "made the unequal construction of gender relations a site of contestation."[427]

In 1992, Amendments to Divorce Regulation (ADR) were passed to reinstate some of the elements of the Family Protection Law's divorce provisions that were rejected earlier.[428] ADR "requires all divorcing couples . . . to go through a process of arbitration," and if the arbiters fail to reconcile the couple, then "the court allows the man to effect and register a divorce . . . after he has paid his wife" what she has a legal right to receive.[429] ADR note 6 "enables the court to place a monetary value on women's housework and to force the husband to pay her 'wages in kind' for her work done during her marriage" (provided that the wife does not initiate the divorce and provided that the divorce is not caused by any fault of hers).[430] Thus, if the woman decides to divorce her husband, she loses her right to the housework wages.[431] If wages for housework are not possible, the husband must provide the wife with a marriage gift, "the amount [of which is] to be decided by the court" on the basis of the husband's financial need.[432]

A new Law of Formation of General Courts, enacted in June 1994, was designed to bring about a restructuring of the courts in Iran.[433] Mir Hosseini predicted that the Special Civil Courts governing family law matters would disappear. [434] In the future family disputes would appear in General Courts presided over by either a *mojtahed* or a civil judge who has jurisdiction over all penal and family law cases.[435] Currently, the political regime in power is very repressive, and women's rights in Iranian courts have taken a turn for the worst.

A. Concept of Marriage in Iran: The Marriage Contract

Marriage in Iran is a contract regulated by a code of law that is deeply rooted in religious precepts and based on a "patriarchal ethos."[436] The three elements of an

---

425. Ziba Mir-Hosseini, *When a Woman's Hurt Becomes an Injury: "Hardship" as Grounds for Divorce in Iran*, 5 HAWAA 111 (2007).

426. *Id.*

427. *Id.*

428. Mir-Hosseini, *supra* note 391, at 196.

429. *Id.*

430. *Id.*

431. *Id.*

432. *Id.*

433. *Id.*

434. *Id.*

435. *Id.*

436. *See* Mir-Hosseini, *supra* note 215, at 137–38.

Iranian marriage contract constitute (1) the offer of marriage made by the woman or her guardian, (2) the acceptance by the man, and (3) the payment of a dower (*mahr*) called the "marriage gift," which is "money or any valuable [item] that the husband pays or pledges to pay the wife on consummation of the marriage."[437] Polygamy is a man's legal right to marry more than one woman.[438] Therefore, one man can enter into more than one marriage at a time, "up to four permanent unions and as many temporary ones as he desires or can afford," by virtue of the "temporary marriage" (*mut'a*).[439]

The marriage contract sets forth certain rights and duties for the man and for the woman, such as *tamkin* (sexual submission, obedience) and *nafaqa* (maintenance).[440] The husband has the right to demand the woman's sexual submission because this is the wife's duty.[441] The husband must provide shelter, food, and clothing, and the wife has a right to this maintenance.[442] According to the Iranian marriage contract, a wife possesses nothing more than her marriage gift and her own personal wealth.[443] Only the husband has the unilateral right to terminate the contract, which he can do without any grounds and without the wife's consent or even her presence.[444] The inherently patriarchal discrimination and the lack of equality established by this contract are vividly portrayed in *Divorce Iranian Style*, a film that illuminates the vagaries of Iranian family law[445] and the procedural difficulties of divorce cases initiated by women in Iran.

> A large majority of divorce cases initiated by women never reach a decision [because] they are [either] abandoned after two or three hearings [or the] couple succeed[s] in reaching an out-of-court agreement or they give up [because of] the futility of their efforts. More than 70 percent of all divorces registered in any given year in Tehran are . . . by mutual consent . . . [involving] the wife waiving her claim to *mahr* [the marriage gift] in exchange for the husband's consent [to divorce].[446]

The marriage gift is, thus, a bargaining chip used by women to get the husband to consent to the divorce.

---

437. *Id.* at 137.

438. *Id.* (citing SHAHLA HAERI, LAW OF DESIRE: TEMPORARY MARRIAGE IN IRAN 50 (1989)).

439. *Id.*

440. *Id.*

441. *Id.*

442. *Id.*

443. *See id.*

444. *See id.*

445. DIVORCE IRANIAN STYLE, *supra* note 111; *see also* SCIOLINO, *supra* note 6, at 264 ("'In our country, the problem is the law,' Hashemi says. 'All the judges are men, and they don't understand the problems of women.'").

446. Mir-Hosseini, *supra* note 215, at 149.

VI. INTERNATIONAL HUMAN RIGHTS LAWS PROTECTING WOMEN'S RIGHTS AND THEIR REPRESENTATION IN THE HUMANITIES

"Respect for basic human rights in Iran, especially freedom of expression and opinion, deteriorated considerably in 2005."[447] Human Rights Watch reports routine use by the government of torture, ill treatment in detention, and prolonged solitary confinement where the judiciary commits serious human rights violations.[448] Abuses are perpetrated by parallel institutions such as paramilitary groups, plainclothes men, and intelligence services that attack protestors.[449] Iran has signed and is bound by certain international human rights treaties that, if enforced, would provide protection against these abuses and give women the justice and equality they deserve.

A. The Convention on the Elimination of All Forms of Discrimination Against Women (CEDAW)

The Convention on the Elimination of All Forms of Discrimination Against Women (CEDAW) was adopted in 1979 by the U.N. General Assembly; it is considered to be the international bill of rights for women.[450] This comprehensive treaty codifies human rights as they specifically apply to women and girls. It defines discrimination against women and sets up a program for nations to eradicate discrimination domestically. As there are currently 183 State parties to the Convention, and the treaty has been in existence for more than twenty-seven years, arguably the provisions of CEDAW can be considered "customary international law" and applicable to even non-signatory States.[451] Iran, along with the United States, has not signed CEDAW.

CEDAW provides the foundation for achieving equality for women publicly, politically, and privately.[452] It protects equality in voting, education, health, employment, access to the legal system, nationality, and many other fundamental freedoms. Although Iran's parliament approved CEDAW in August 2003, the

---

447. Human Rights Watch, Essential Background: Overview of Human Rights in Iran (Dec. 31, 2005), http://hrw.org/english/docs/2006/01/18/iran12214.htm (last visited Sept. 25, 2007).

448. *Id.*

449. *Id.*

450. U.N. Convention on the Elimination of All Forms of Discrimination Against Women, Dec. 18, 1979, 1249 U.N.T.S. 14 [hereinafter CEDAW], http://www.un.org/womenwatch/daw/cedaw/index.html.

451. *See* Henry J. Steiner & Phillip Alston, International Human Rights in Context: Law, Politics, Morals 69, 72 (2d ed., 2000) ("Customary law refers to conduct, or the conscious abstention from certain conduct, of states that becomes in some measure a part of international legal order" (inferring that CEDAW is accepted as customary law because more than 140 states have adopted it since its inception)).

452. *See* CEDAW, *supra* note 450.

hard-line clerics in the Guardian Council ultimately refused to sign the treaty, stating that it went against Islamic law and was unconstitutional.[453] Nevertheless, because CEDAW has risen to the level of customary international law, Iran may not take any action inconsistent with it.[454]

Article 2 of CEDAW requires States to implement policies of equality between men and women within their national constitutions and legal systems.[455] All forms of discrimination against women are forbidden, whether by public or private entities, and "penal provisions which constitute discrimination against women" must be repealed.[456] Discrimination against women exists on many levels of the public and private sphere in Iran.[457] Women are not given as many rights as men,[458] and they are under the constant domination and control by their husbands or fathers.[459] Women in Iran cannot travel without their husbands' permission[460] and must sit in the back of gender-segregated buses.[461] A woman's testimony in court is worth only half as much as a man's,[462] and judges frequently give preference to men in domestic matters even if the man has a history of domestic violence.[463] Women are punished more severely than men in criminal matters—such as stoning women for adultery as they are buried from the neck down, while men are buried from the waist down, thus arguably giving men a greater opportunity for escape.[464] Women are rarely given the promotions they deserve; even when they work tirelessly, and women cannot reach their full potential[465] in a stultifying, patriarchal system that looks down on working women. For example, the Islamic Republic applies "blood money" (compensation to the victim) in criminal cases, and the family of a victim of homicide or manslaughter has the right to choose between legal punishment or

453. Nazila Fathi, *Iran's Hard-Liners Reject Reform Bills Approved by Parliament*, N.Y. Times, Aug. 14, 2003, at A11; *see also* CEDAW, *supra* note 450 (showing that Iran has not adopted CEDAW—Country Reports section).

454. *See* Steiner & Alston, *supra* note 451.

455. CEDAW, *supra* note 450, at 16.

456. *Id.*

457. *See* Nafisi, *supra* note 11, at 261.

458. *Id.*

459. *See* Hughes, *supra* note 392; *see also* Brooks, *supra* note 144, at 106 (using the main character in that chapter as an example of the extraordinary amount of control that a man in Iran has over his wife's life).

460. *See* Nafisi, *supra* note 11, at 286. ("Azin had applied for a visa to Canada, but even if her application was accepted, she couldn't leave the country without her husband's permission.").

461. *Id.* at 27.

462. *Id.* at 261.

463. *Id.* at 273.

464. Brooks, *supra* note 144, at 46.

465. *See* Ebadi, *supra* note 24, at. 75.

blood money.[466] Under the Iranian Code, the worth of a woman's life equals half of a man's.[467] In one case, a judge ruled that the blood money for two men was worth more than the life of the murdered nine-year-old girl, and the judge demanded that her family pay thousands of dollars to finance the execution of the male criminals, thus unjustly punishing the victim's family.[468]

States are obligated by Article 5 of CEDAW "to modify the social and cultural patterns of conduct of men and women" in order to eliminate the idea that women are inferior to men or that men are their superiors.[469] In Iran, women are blamed for their beauty and sexuality and forced to bear the responsibility of a man's lustful looks, thoughts, or behavior.[470] To "protect" the men after the Revolution, women were forced to veil themselves,[471] and they could not even maintain eye contact with a man.[472] After the Revolution women could not sing publicly because a woman's voice is considered provocative.[473] Because "family honor rests on the virtue of women," the shame of a woman's rape could only be erased by execution of the perpetrator, for which the family of the woman would have to pay "blood money."[474]

Article 7 of CEDAW requires that women have equal access to voting rights and to run for election for public office.[475] CEDAW also requires that women participate equally "in the formulation of public office" and "perform all public functions at all levels of government."[476] Although women in Iran are allowed to vote, there are severe restrictions upon women who run for public office, and only approximately 4 percent of seats in Parliament are held by women.[477] Women in Iran who held ministerial positions at the time of the Revolution were stoned to death (e.g., the Minister of Education) or forced into exile (e.g., the Minister of Women's Affairs).[478] Female members of Parliament are segregated and forced to work in an empty room behind a curtain, without chairs, a table, or even office equipment to make their attempts to legislate any easier.[479]

---

466. *Id.* at 113–14.

467. *Id.* at 114.

468. *Id.*

469. CEDAW, *supra* note 450, at art. 5.

470. *See* NAFISI, *supra* note 11, at 27.

471. *See id.* at 152.

472. *See id.* at 183.

473. NAFISI, *supra* note 11, at 108; EBADI, *supra* note 24, at 181.

474. EBADI, *supra* note 24, at 114.

475. CEDAW, *supra* note 450, at art. 7.

476. *Id.*

477. U.N. DEVELOPMENT PROGRAMME, *Human Development Report 2005*, 304 (2005), http://hdr.undp.org/en/media/hdr05_complete.pdf [hereinafter UNDP].

478. NAFISI, *supra* note 11, at 262.

479. EBADI, *supra* note 24, at 185–86.

Female government employees are regarded as a "nuisance," especially those who are vocal about their oppression.[480]

In Article 9 of CEDAW, women are assured their right "to acquire, change or retain their nationality."[481] A woman's nationality is protected because marriage does not "change the nationality of the wife, render her stateless or force upon her the nationality of the husband," and women shall be granted "equal rights with men with respect to the nationality of their children."[482] In Iran, women must convert to Islam in order to marry an Iranian.[483] Any children born to a non-Iranian mother and an Iranian father are considered Iranian, and the father has complete control over his wife and children.[484] Fathers and husbands even have the ability to notify the government and forbid their wives from leaving the country.[485]

Article 10 of CEDAW requires States to "take all appropriate measures to eliminate discrimination against women in order to ensure to them equal rights with men in the field of education. . . ."[486] Education of women is one of the areas that has been gradually improving in Iran.[487] Immediately after the Revolution, some women were refused tenure,[488] forced out of universities, and fired from teaching positions because of their refusal to wear the veil and conform to Khomeini's "ideal of . . . a Muslim woman teacher."[489] University faculty and students were expelled, jailed, and purged for a variety of offenses, from being "too Western in . . . attitude"[490] to being "an enemy of God"[491] and for "using obscene language in class."[492] Nafisi's university did not allow women to enter through the main university entrance, so they had to use a separate door to the side.[493] It "segregate[d] men and women in classes"[494] and even segregated them in the cafeteria.[495] Professors extolled the differences between virtuous Muslim girls and promiscuous Christian girls,[496] and the faculty were summoned to

480. *Id.* at 73.
481. CEDAW, *supra* note 450, at art. 9.
482. *Id.*
483. Brooks, *supra* note 144, at 92.
484. *See id.* at 106; *see* Nafisi, *supra* note 11, at 286.
485. *See* Nafisi, *supra* note 11, at 286.
486. CEDAW, *supra* note 450, at art. 10.
487. Halper, *supra* note 17, at 90.
488. *See* Nafisi¸ *supra* note 11, at 10.
489. *Id.* at 165.
490. *Id.* at 118.
491. *Id.* at 119.
492. *Id.* at 117.
493. *See id.* at 29.
494. *Id.* at 9.
495. Ebadi, *supra* note 24, at 106.
496. *See* Nafisi¸ *supra* note 11, at 30.

endless meetings and debates over "women's rights" and the government's "war against women."[497]

Women were also forbidden to have certain careers or study in certain technical and experimental fields.[498] Other fields were restricted for women because of quotas ranging from 20–50 percent.[499] Women were not allowed to receive scholarships for study-abroad programs without the permission of their husbands or fathers.[500] Schools below the university level were segregated by gender.[501]

However, in the years following the Revolution, many changes occurred in the area of education for women.[502] Religious women were able to attend universities once they became "protected" by the veil.[503] Because of increased gender segregation in Iran, more female teachers, doctors, and social workers were needed.[504] As the restrictions on women's study of science and technical subjects were lifted, the percentage of female university students also dramatically increased.[505] There was also a drive to improve the literacy rates of women in rural areas,[506] which cut the illiteracy rate of women from 60 percent in 1980 to 30 percent in 2005.[507] Although these numbers are far from perfect, they do show an improving trend in the government's commitment to the education of women in Iran after the Revolution.

The right to equal employment rights guaranteed in Article 11 of CEDAW[508] is another area of fluctuation within the political tide of Iran's government.[509] After the Revolution, the government initially encouraged women to stay inside the home and refrain from working.[510] However, during the Iran–Iraq War, working conditions for mothers improved significantly, such as the addition of daycares to workplaces and the availability of better benefits for women.[511] Once the war ended and the government began to rebuild its economy with greater global involvement, the need for women in the workplace continued.[512]

---

497. *Id.* at 111.
498. Halper, *supra* note 17, at 106.
499. *Id.* at 106; *see* EBADI, *supra* note 24, at 108.
500. Halper, *supra* note 17, at 88.
501. *Id.* at 106.
502. *Id.* at 116.
503. *See id.* at 124; EBADI, *supra* note 24, at 106.
504. Halper, *supra* note 17, at 116.
505. *Id.* at 116.
506. *Id.* at 113; EBADI, *supra* note 24, at 106.
507. UNDP, *supra* note 477, at 228, 308.
508. CEDAW, *supra* note 450, at art. 11.
509. *See* NAFISI, *supra* note 11, at 275.
510. Halper, *supra* note 17, at 116.
511. *Id.*
512. *Id.* at 117.

In Iran today, improvements in the area of women's salary need to be made as half of the women in Iran contribute to the family income; yet a woman typically earns less than a third of a man's salary.[513] With the increase in educational opportunities for women, many more have earned university and graduate degrees, but the professional market has been unable to keep up.[514] The few jobs available usually go to men, and "[t]hough educated women outnumber educated men, the rate of women's unemployment is three times higher."[515]

Article 13(c) of CEDAW requires that women have the "the right to participate in recreational activities, sports[516] and all aspects of cultural life."[517] But after the Revolution, sports became segregated by gender,[518] and women's teams received far less funding, training, or quality coaching.[519] Attendance at women's games or sporting events is limited to women only, so that they may participate without wearing the *hejab*.[520] Recently, President Ahmadinejad made a surprising move towards allowing women to attend soccer games with men, but he was overruled by the Supreme Leader Ayatollah Khameini.[521] Women's participation in the arts was also severely curtailed after the Revolution.[522] Ballet and dancing were forbidden, and eventually, women singers were banned "because a woman's voice, like her hair, was sexually provocative and should be kept hidden."[523]

Equality with men before the law is guaranteed to women in Article 15 of CEDAW.[524] One of the first decisions of the new Islamic Republic, before even establishing a constitution or electing a parliament, was to abolish the Family Protection Law that guaranteed women equal rights in marriage, divorce, and child custody issues.[525] By abolishing this law, the drafters of the postrevolutionary penal code "turned the clock back fourteen hundred years" and imposed laws highly discriminatory towards women.[526] For example, a woman may not travel

513. UNDP, supra note 477, at 312.

514. Ebadi, *supra* note 24, at 108.

515. *Id.*

516. *See* Brooks, *supra* note 144, at 201–13 (discussing Iranian women in sports in pre- and postrevolutionary Iran).

517. CEDAW, *supra* note 450, at art. 13(c). *See also* Brooks, *supra* note 144, at 201–13 (discussing Iranian women in sports in pre- and postrevolutionary Iran).

518. Halper, *supra* note 17, at 106.

519. *See* Jenny Steel, *Sports and the Scarf*, BBC News, Dec. 9, 2005, http://news.bbc.co.uk/go/pr/fr/-/2/hi/middle_east/4511680.stm (last visited Oct. 1, 2007).

520. *See* id.

521. *Iran Women Sports Ruling Vetoed*, BBC News, May 8, 2006, http://newsvote.bbc.co.uk/mpapps/pagetools/print/news.bbc.co.uk/2/hi/middel_east/4751033.stm (last visited Oct. 1, 2007).

522. Nafisi, *supra* note 11, at 108.

523. *Id.*; Ebadi, *supra* note 24, at 181.

524. CEDAW, *supra* note 450, at art. 15.

525. Nafisi, *supra* note 11, at 261.

526. Ebadi, *supra* note 24, at 51.

outside the country without the permission of her husband, and the husband may notify the government not to allow his wife to leave.[527] A "woman [must] ask her husband's permission for divorce."[528] In some cases, physical and mental abuse of women is not considered sufficient grounds for a divorce, and the judge might even blame the woman for her husband's beatings.[529] In Iran, alimony is not given to women, and child custody is usually awarded to the father,[530] even if the father is "guilty of horrific abuse" of the child.[531] Women are given harsher sentences in criminal matters[532] and their testimony is worth only half that of a man's.[533]

Finally, Article 16(f) of CEDAW gives women "[t]he same rights and responsibilities with regard to guardianship, wardship, trusteeship and adoption of children."[534] However, when Khomeini declared that the Family Protection Law was un-Islamic, this decision quickly set a patriarchal precedent affirming that men and paternal family members would be given preference in child custody matters.[535] If divorced, women are allowed to retain guardianship of male children but only until the male child reaches the age of two and until the female child reaches the age of seven.[536] Although the proactive demands of women during the Iran–Iraq War gave widows more physical custody over their children, guardianship is still technically held by paternal family members.[537] Women need the permission of their husbands to travel even just overnight with their children,[538] and parenting duties are heavily unequal, with the mother shouldering most of the responsibility.[539]

B. International Covenant on Civil and Political Rights (ICCPR)

The International Covenant on Civil and Political Rights (ICCPR)[540] is one of two major international human rights treaties that guarantee the rights of every individual to civil and political freedoms. The ICCPR codifies the first-generation

527. Nafisi, *supra* note 11, at 286.
528. Ebadi, *supra* note 24, at 51.
529. Nafisi, *supra* note 11, at 273.
530. *Id.* at 286; Ebadi, *supra* note 24, at 111.
531. Ebadi, *supra* note 24, at 123.
532. Nafisi, *supra* note 11, at 261.
533. *Id.*; Ebadi, *supra* note 24, at 51.
534. CEDAW, *supra* note 450, at art. 16(f).
535. Nafisi, *supra* note 11, at 286; Ebadi, *supra* note 24, at 53.
536. Halper, *supra* note 17, at 95.
537. *Id.* at 115.
538. Ebadi, *supra* note 24, at 100.
539. *Id.* at 153.
540. International Covenant on Civil and Political Rights, G.A. Res. 2200A (XXI), U.N. Doc. A/6316 (Dec. 16, 1966), http://www.unhchr.ch/html/menu3/b/a_ccpr.htm [hereinafter ICCPR].

civil and political rights delineated in the Universal Declaration of Human Rights (UDHR),[541]such as freedom of speech, the right to due process and a fair trial, and freedom of religion. Iran signed the ICCPR in 1968 and ratified it without reservations in 1975. Although there was a regime change in Iran in 1979, State parties are still obligated to respect their international treaty obligations.

Ayatollah Khomeini faced criticism from many international human rights groups because of the large number of summary executions that followed the Revolution.[542] Khomeini's response was heartless and indicates a flagrant disrespect of traditional notions of human rights:

> Criminals should not be tried. The trial of a criminal is against human rights. Human rights demand that we should have killed them in the first place when it became known that they were criminals. . . . They criticize us because we are executing the brutes.[543]

In direct violation of the right to life guaranteed by Article 6 of the ICCPR, executions became the rule rather than the exception in postrevolutionary Iran.[544]

Dynamic interpretation of the Koran is the key to providing women with civil and political rights as well as human rights under Islam. Although these and other human rights of all persons men and women alike are often violated under a totalitarian regime such as the Islamic Republic of Iran, women's basic civil and political rights are particularly implicated in Iran because of the strict Islamist regulations set by the clerics.[545] They interpret the Koran more narrowly than the feminists such as Shirin Ebadi would like.[546] For Ebadi, Islam and women's rights are compatible as long as the Koran is interpreted in a manner to favor women.[547]

Fundamentalists apply a literal interpretation of the Koran, resulting in harsh sentences such as stoning being the punishment for adultery and prostitution.[548] Unfair show trials for suspected criminals are quite common.[549] For example, one woman was charged with "corruption on earth," "sexual offenses," and "violation of decency and morality," but her only real "crime" was her position under the Shah as the former Minister of Education. She was placed in a sack and

---

541. Universal Declaration of Human Rights, G.A. Res. 217A, U.N. Doc. A/810 (Dec. 12, 1948), http://www.unhchr.ch/udhr/lang/eng.htm [hereinafter UDHR].

542. Nafisi, *supra* note 11, at 96.

543. *Id.*

544. Ebadi, *supra* note 24, at 140–41.

545. Nafisi, *supra* note 11, at 108.

546. Ebadi, *supra* note 24, at 122.

547. *Id.* at 187–88; *see also* Abdullah Ahmed An-Na'im, *Human Rights in the Muslim World*, *in* International Human Rights in Context 396 (Henry J. Steiner & Philip Alston eds., 2000).

548. Nafisi, *supra* note 11, at 261.

549. *Id.* at 101; Ebadi, *supra* note 24, at 59.

either stoned or shot to death.[550] One official, whose only crime was to name his dogs after two clerics as an insult to them, was ordered to die.[551] So-called "enem[ies] of God" were murdered daily, whether former ministers and educators, prostitutes, leftist revolutionaries,[552] or women of amazing beauty.[553]

In Iran, several sources report that Iranian girls believed to be virgins and convicted of a crime were often "married" off to prison guards who would rape them before executing them to deprive the girls of eternal bliss in heaven, confident that if the girls died as virgins they would go to heaven.[554] Khomeini issued a *fatwa* sanctioning the rape of girls before their execution and another *fatwa* permitting the execution of pregnant women.[555] Minors were not exempt from this series of murders, and many teenagers and young children were killed without mercy or even a trial.[556] During the Iran–Iraq War, boys under the age of thirteen were abducted off the streets and sent off to war to die in the minefields (although these boys died as martyrs, and their families boasted of their martyrdom with pride in a prevailing new cult of death). Iran became bloodthirsty, publishing the names, pictures, and crimes of those executed in the paper on a daily basis.[557] Rather than protests calling for an end to the killings, there were increasing demands and slogans calling "for more blood."[558] A female photojournalist, Zahra Kazemi, was imprisoned and tortured for taking pictures and defying a prison guard.[559] Her injuries from the torture and the beatings were so severe that she died only a few weeks after her imprisonment.[560]

Article 7 of the ICCPR forbids degrading treatment or punishment.[561] Like the villainous Humbert in Nabokov's *Lolita*, who regulated every step of Lolita's young life,[562] Ayatollah Khomeini forced women with threats of punishment and humiliation to live as he envisioned them: as ideal Muslim women.[563] Failure to adhere to this vision with improper dress length, scarf thickness, wearing of nail

---

550. Nafisi, *supra* note 11, at 112–13.
551. *Id.* at 137.
552. *Id.* at 119.
553. *Id.* at 212.
554. *Id.* at 212; Ebadi, *supra* note 24, at 91.
555. The Nat'l Council of Resistance of Iran Foreign Affairs Comm., *Islam: Beacon of Women's Emancipation, in* Women, Islam & Equality 37 (1995), http://www.iran-e-azad.org/english/book_on_women/wi&e.pdf.
556. Nafisi, *supra* note 11, at 191.
557. *Id.* at 102.
558. *Id.* at 100.
559. Ebadi, *supra* note 24, at 196.
560. *Id.* at 196–97.
561. ICCPR, *supra* note 540, at art. 7.
562. Nafisi, *supra* note 11, at 49.
563. *Id.* at 165.

polish, makeup,[564] or even pink socks[565] subjected women to violent inspections, molestations,[566] detainment, or public lashing.[567] When one girl was found in mixed company, she and the other girls were arrested for infractions on matters of morality and subjected to two brutal virginity tests, forced to sign confessions at a "trial", and sentenced to twenty-five lashes.[568]

The arbitrary nature of these arrests and the severe punishments meted out for minor infractions allegedly committed by women cannot remain unnoticed. For example, one girl traveling with her fiancé and two male companions was arbitrarily detained by the morality police, tried, and sentenced to forty lashes; however, the punishment was given instead to her fiancé (who committed no crime or infraction at all) as there was no woman present to mete out her punishment.[569] Propoganda admonishing women to adhere to this vision of Khomeini's morality adorned the streets. In this repressive climate, women were reduced to "ethereal being[s] drifting soundlessly down the street."[570]

Arbitrary arrests and detentions are prohibited by Article 9 of the ICCPR.[571] However, during the days of the Revolution, many were unfairly arrested by the government simply for belonging to certain political groups,[572] speaking out or writing against the government,[573] or traveling with a man who was not a relative.[574] People were arrested just because the Revolutionary Guards had a search warrant, and even though they found no evidence of illegal activities, they could not let the warrant "go to waste."[575] The "frightening, thuggish"[576] morality police in later years roamed the city of Tehran in white jeeps, jailing any woman they found for showing hair from underneath their scarves, wearing improper robes,[577] and wearing makeup or even slippers.[578] A few of Nafisi's girls were imprisoned for several years after the Revolution because of their "political

564. *Id.* at 29; Ebadi, *supra* note 24, at 180.
565. Nafisi, *supra* note 11 at 76.
566. *Id.* at 168.
567. Ebadi, *supra* note 24, at 180.
568. Nafisi, *supra* note 11, at 73.
569. Ebadi, *supra* note 24, at 98–99.
570. Nafisi, *supra* note 11, at 168.
571. ICCPR, *supra* note 540, at art. 9.
572. Nafisi, *supra* note 11, at 31; Ebadi, *supra* note 24, at 67.
573. Nafisi, *supra* note 11, at 116.
574. Ebadi, *supra* note 24, at 98.
575. Nafisi, *supra* note 11, at 72–73.
576. Ebadi, *supra* note 24, at 102.
577. Nafisi, *supra* note 11, at 275; Ebadi, *supra* note 24, at 102–03.
578. Ebadi, *supra* note 24, at 102–03.

activities"; they reported being grateful they were the lucky ones who were not executed.[579]

Article 12(2) of the ICCPR states that "everyone shall be free to leave any country, including his own."[580] Women in Iran do not have this basic human right. When one of Nafisi's girls struggled with a bad marriage, she applied for a visa to Canada, "but even if her application was accepted, she couldn't leave the country without her husband's permission."[581] A husband could also forbid his wife from leaving the country by refusing to sign the papers that would allow her to travel.[582] Women who were granted scholarships to study abroad were also not allowed to leave the country without being accompanied by their father or husband.[583]

Article 18 of the ICCPR guarantees that "[e]veryone shall have the right to freedom of thought, conscience and religion."[584] When the Revolution ended, the Islamic forces took power and made everyone wear a religious façade, regardless of their religious beliefs.[585] Women were forced to wear *hejab*, whether or not they were practicing Muslims.[586]

> [Once] the mullahs ruled the land, religion was used as an instrument of power, an ideology. It was this ideological approach to faith that differentiated those in power from millions of ordinary citizens, believers like Mahshid, Manna and Yassi, who found the Islamic Republic their worst enemy.[587]

In addition to forced religious garb, Iranian women were also required to support the war against Iraq. Iranians were forbidden to protest the war or to show grief when loved ones were killed or a neighbor's house was bombed.[588] Censorship was then and is now everywhere in Iran. Nafisi reports that "certain books had been banned as morally harmful"[589] or "politically objectionable."[590]

---

579. NAFISI, *supra* note 11, at 323 ("There, in jail, I like the rest of them thought we would be killed and that would be the end.").

580. ICCPR, *supra* note 540, at art. 12(2).

581. NAFISI, *supra* note 11, at 286.

582. *Id.*; BROOKS, *supra* note 144, at 106.

583. *See* Halper, *supra* note 17, at 88.

584. ICCPR, *supra* note 540, at art. 18(1).

585. EBADI, *supra* note 24, at 40. *See* NAFISI, *supra* note 11, at 112 (discussing the reimposition of the veiling of women signifying the "victory of the Islamic aspect of the revolution").

586. NAFISI *supra* note 11, at 152; *see* EBADI, *supra* note 24, at 72.

587. NAFISI, *supra* note 11, at 273.

588. *Id.* at 211.

589. *Id.* at 108.

590. EBADI, *supra* note 24, at 66.

"Fires were set to publishing houses and bookstores for disseminating immoral works of fiction."[591]

Iran's xenophobia spread from inside Iran to the rest of the world. In Iran, discriminatory treatment of religious minorities, such as Bahias and Armenians, is pervasive. Minorities face constant threats, and they can not even be buried in the same graveyard as Muslims.[592] Anti-semitism also abounds in Iran, with the recent case of thirteen Iranian Jews accused and convicted unjustly for their alleged spying and affiliation with Israel arousing suspicion and controversy worldwide.

According to Article 19 of the ICCPR, "[e]veryone shall have the right to hold opinions without interference" and "have the right to freedom of expression . . . orally, in writing or in print, in the form of art, or through any other media of his choice."[593] Yet protestors during the Revolution were often beaten or arrested for passing out leaflets.[594] Any critics of the new regime or of its laws were deemed "enemies," "against Islam," and "counterrevolutionar[ies]"; these victims of oppression "faced, often as not, the firing squad."[595] Secular women who initially refused to wear the veil were fired from their positions[596] and then pushed out because of their ideological beliefs and expressed opinions.[597] Today all women in Iran must wear at least the headscarf, if not the *chador*.

In particular, the Iranian postrevolutionary regime understood the power of the word. Those who did not support the war and wrote or even spoke about it were considered unpatriotic and faced severe consequences.[598] As in the repressive Soviet regime, the Iranian government actually killed writers and poets such as Ahmad Mir Alai and Jahangir Tafazoli.[599] The government made attempts to kill any intellectual who did not support the Islamic regime.[600] On a manhunt, the Islamic Republic began searching for writers, poets, and intellectuals, sending death squads to assassinate them one by one.[601] Some were detained, tortured, and imprisoned for several years[602] while many others died under mysterious circumstances[603] or were even blatantly murdered.[604] "Reporters were

591. Nafisi, *supra* note 11, at 136.
592. *Id.* at 230.
593. ICCPR, *supra* note 540, at art. 19.
594. Nafisi, *supra* note 11,at 191.
595. Ebadi, *supra* note 24, at 52.
596. Nafisi, *supra* note 11, at 152–53.
597. *Id.*
598. *Id.* at 158–59.
599. *Id.* at 310.
600. *Id.*, at 308; Ebadi, *supra* note 24, at 128–29.
601. *See* Ebadi, *supra* note 24, at 129–32.
602. *Id.* at 134–35.
603. *See id.* at 132.
604. *Id.* at 137.

jailed, magazines and newspapers closed and some of our best classical poets, like Rumi and Omar Khayyam, were censored or banned."[605]

In Article 21 of the ICCPR, "the right of peaceful assembly shall be recognized."[606] After the Revolution, the ability for writers and intellectuals to meet in public or in private was drastically curtailed by the government.[607] Unmarried men and women were not allowed to be alone together, so dating couples often "borrow[ed] a young niece or nephew on their evenings out, to appear as a family and pass through checkpoints unmolested."[608] "Young people risked being intercepted by the morality police simply for venturing into the mountains together for a hike."[609] Nafisi herself was forced to cut short her meetings with her "magician" during police raids of a public café.[610] Even Nafisi's class with her girls had to remain a secret.[611]

Article 23 of the ICCPR refers to marriage and family rights, declaring that "no marriage shall be entered into without the free and full consent of the intending spouses."[612] Once the Islamic Regime took power, Khomeini lowered the acceptable age of marriage from eighteen to nine,[613] which increased the number of forced marriages in postrevolutionary Iran. While women of Nafisi's age had been able to choose a spouse for love, the women students in her class now had little choice, and their younger sisters would have even less.[614] Fathers often selected a husband for their daughters, confining them to perpetual domestic life rather than letting them pursue their education.[615] Marriage became more of a family agreement with the parents making the important decisions, rather than a decision of the intended bride and groom. Women can also not easily obtain a divorce by initiating the procedures in a family law court. One woman was so miserable in her marriage that when her husband would not grant her a divorce, she "doused herself with gasoline and lit herself ablaze."[616] Self-immolation by women in Iran is a much too common occurrence, a sign of the hopelessness of women in search of basic human rights that are provided by international treaties, but unavailable to them because of failed enforcement by the Iranian State.

---

605. NAFISI, *supra* note 11, at 136.
606. ICCPR, *supra* note 540, at art. 21.
607. NAFISI, *supra* note 11, at 309; EBADI, *supra* note 24, at 130.
608. EBADI, *supra* note 24, at 96.
609. *See id.* at 180.
610. NAFISI, *supra* note 11, at 312–13.
611. *Id.* at 3.
612. ICCPR, *supra* note 540, at art. 23.
613. NAFISI, *supra* note 11, at 261.
614. *Id.* at 259.
615. EBADI, *supra* note 24, at 106–07.
616. *Id.* at 108–09.

Finally, according to Article 26 of the ICCPR, "all persons are equal before the law and are entitled without any discrimination to the equal protection of the law."[617] As noted above, women "under law, [a]re considered to have half the worth of men,"[618] and they are often treated unfairly by family court judges.[619] Women, including Shirin Ebadi, were removed from their positions of power as judges[620] and from ministerial positions merely because they are women.[621] Women are also treated far more harshly by the criminal system than are men accused of committing the same crimes.[622] After the Revolution, as women became more aware of their rights and also of their oppression, the suicide rate of women rose, "commonly taking the form of self-immolation."[623]

C. International Covenant of Economic, Social, and Cultural Rights (ICESCR)

The International Covenant on Economic, Social and Cultural Rights[624] (ICESCR) is the second of the two major international human rights treaties that embodies many of the principles found in the Universal Declaration of Human Rights.[625] The ICESCR sets forth the second-generation economic, social, and cultural rights, such as the right to work, the right to social welfare programs, and the right to take part in the cultural life of the country.[626] Iran signed the ICESCR in 1968 and ratified it without reservations in 1975. Thus, Iran may not take any actions inconsistent with the object and purpose of the ICESCR.[627]

State parties to the ICESCR must "guarantee that the rights enunciated in the present Covenant will be exercised without discrimination of any kind as to race, colour, *sex*, language, religion, political or other opinion, national or social origin, property, birth or other status."[628] In Iran, preferential treatment of men begins at an early age. Men and boys "enjoy an exalted status" in the household and they

---

617. ICCPR, *supra* note 540, at art. 26.

618. Nafisi, *supra* note 11, at 261.

619. *Id.* at 273.

620. Ebadi, *supra* note 24, at 48.

621. Nafisi, *supra* note 11, at 261–62.

622. *Id.* at 261.

623. Ebadi, *supra* note 24, at 109.

624. *See, e.g.*, International Covenant on Economic, Social and Cultural Rights, G.A. Res. 2200 (XXI) U.N. Doc. (Dec. 16, 1966) http://www.unhchr.ch/html/menu3/b/a_cescr.htm [hereinafter ICESCR].

625. *See, e.g.*, UDHR, *supra* note 541.

626. *See generally* Barbara Stark, *The "Other" Half of the International Bill of Rights as a Postmodern Feminist Text, in* The American Society of International Law, Reconceiving Reality: Women and International Law 19, 21 (1993).

627. Vienna Convention on the Law of Treaties, 1155 U.N.T.S. 331, 8 I.L.M. 679, U.N. Doc. A/CONF. 39/29 (May 23, 1969).

628. ICESCR, *supra* note 624, at art. 2 (emphasis added).

remain at "the center of the family's orbit."[629] As children grow older, the rights of boys expand "while the girls' contract[ed]."[630] Men have relative autonomy in Iranian society while women are given fewer rights than men,[631] and women are considered inferior to men in the workplace.[632] Women in Iran may only travel with their husband's permission.[633] Judges often treat men with preference in domestic matters, even if the men have a past record of domestic violence.[634] In addition, women are punished more severely than men in criminal matters and crimes such as "adultery and prostitution [which are] punished by stoning to death."[635]

Article 3 of the ICESCR requires that "States . . . undertake to ensure the equal right of men *and women* to the enjoyment of all . . . social and cultural rights. . . ."[636] After the Revolution, women's participation in the arts was severely restricted.[637] In a country where the people love Persian poetry and music, it is amazing that dancing and singing were gradually eliminated altogether.[638] Women now are still unable to participate in sports or even to be spectators at men's events.[639] At a music concert, the management admonished the crowd that "if anyone acted in an un-Islamic manner, he or she would be kicked out. He went on to instruct women to observe the proper rules and regulations regarding the use of the veil."[640] Women may not socialize with men in public, and they are not permitted to sit in the same classrooms with men;[641] "even the lunch tables in the [university] cafeteria were segregated."[642] Article 7 of the ICESCR addresses "the right of everyone to the enjoyment of just and favorable conditions of work."[643] ICESCR Section (a)(i) of Article 7 further provides that all workers are entitled to "[f]air wages and equal remuneration for work of equal value without distinction of any kind, in particular women being guaranteed conditions of work not inferior to those enjoyed by men."[644] ICESCR Section (c) of Article 7 guarantees "equal opportunity for everyone to be promoted in his employment

---

629. Ebadi, *supra* note 24, at 11.
630. *Id.* at 11.
631. Nafisi, *supra* note 11, at 261.
632. *Id.* at 261; Ebadi, *supra* note 24, at 75.
633. *See* Nafisi, *supra* note 11, at 286.
634. *Id.* at 273; Ebadi, *supra* note 24, at 123.
635. Nafisi, *supra* note 11, at 261.
636. ICESCR, *supra* note 624, at art. 3 (emphasis added).
637. *See, e.g.*, Nafisi, *supra* note 11, at 108.
638. *Id.*; Ebadi, *supra* note 24, at 181.
639. *Iran Women*, *supra* note 521.
640. Nafisi, *supra* note 11, at 300.
641. Ebadi, *supra* note 24, at 106.
642. *Id.*
643. ICESCR, *supra* note 624, at art. 7.
644. *Id.* at art. 7(a)(i).

to an appropriate higher level, subject to no considerations other than those of seniority and competence."[645] During the Iran–Iraq War, women worked for free, but now women in Iran are demanding pay to cover the rising cost of living.[646] After the Revolution, women were forced out of positions of prominence within the government, such as judges[647] and cabinet ministers,[648] and they were reduced to accepting only administrative and clerical positions.[649] Women were then and are now still denied "promotion[s] and permanence" at work because of their past political affiliations[650] or simply because they are women.[651] "[M]ale superiors will not look [women] in the eye,"[652] and they "reward . . . [women's] exceptional work with something akin to envy."[653]

VII. CONCLUSION

There is no doubt that without the popular support of the women in Iran, Ayatollah Khomeini would never have succeeded in leading the Revolution.[654] Disgusted by the Shah's excesses, repression, compromises, and conformity to the ideals of the West (all of which seemed contrary to the moral values of Islam), various political forces in Iran struggled to bring about a revolution that would bring the Iranian society back to its traditional values.[655] In the early days of the Revolution, it was not clear whether the leftist movement or the Islamic movement would take control, but the Islamists (with the support of the U.S. government) gradually eliminated any opposition from the left, the intellectuals, or secular voices within the government structures.[656]

Khomeini continued to listen to the demands of his women constituents whose rights were being paradoxically expanded on certain levels and drastically reduced on other levels. The state of women's human rights in Iran is represented effectively in the humanities. Women writers such as Azar Nafisi and Shirin Ebadi both fight for women's rights, one from outside and the other from inside Iran. This is true as well for the filmmakers Ziba Mir-Hosseini and

645. *Id.* at art. 7(c).

646. Roksana Bahramitash, *Revolution, Islamization, and Women's Employment in Iran*, 9 Brown J. World Affairs 235 (2002).

647. Ebadi, *supra* note 24, at 48.

648. Nafisi, *supra* note 11, at 262.

649. *See* Ebadi, *supra* note 24, at 48.

650. Nafisi, *supra* note 11, at 270.

651. *See* Ebadi, *supra* note 24, at. 75.

652. Nafisi, *supra* note 11, at 328.

653. *Id.* at 288.

654. Halper, *supra* note 17, at 105.

655. *Id.* at 104.

656. *Id.* at 109.

Tahmineh Milani, both of whom directed and produced feminist films that shed light on the deplorable conditions of women in Iran today.

In her book, Shirin Ebadi engages in active and public protest while Azar Nafisi's memoir uses a more passive, private form of resistance. Ebadi writes in a direct, legal, personal, and even passionate style that persuades and excites the reader to respond. Nafisi transmits messages through a more indirect, highly imaginative, learned, and poetic prose that transports the reader into a state of heightened awareness. Through the power of the written word and the persuasion of visual images on screen, these four Iranian women depict changes developing in the life of Iranian women both after the Revolution and now. These changes are reflected in and caused by domestic and international laws and their enforcement. These four women's artistic representations similarly reflect the paradoxes in Iran's totalitarian theocracy that claims to be a democracy.

The status of women's human rights in Iranian society is conditioned by contradictions in the legal and political system of this totalitarian theocracy. Paradoxically, women's rights in Iran today are simultaneously both expanding and diminishing. These two faces of Iranian society are represented brilliantly by the feminist cinematographer Tahmineh Milani in her film, *Two Women*, that portrays a modern woman in Iran who may be more symbolic than actual. Ziba Mir-Hosseini's documentary film, *Divorce Iranian Style*, reveals the weaknesses in the Iranian family court system and its domestic laws and procedures that discriminate against women. Only a dynamic interpretation[657] of the Koran together with radical transformations of the Iranian legal system and its procedures—and a systematic attempt to enforce the international treaties to which Iran is bound by ratification or by customary international law—can provide hope for women's equality.

If justice and equality are intrinsic values in Islam and the *Shari'a*, why are justice and equality not reflected in the Iranian family laws that treat women as second-class citizens, put women under men's domination, strictly regulate gender relations, and treat the rights of men and women unfairly? [658] Despite the movement backwards since 1979 particularly with regard to the enactment of family laws that discriminate against women in Iran, there is intense social pressure in Iran to change these laws and customs. Demographic developments in Iran constitute hope for the protection of human rights for women. Seventy percent of the population in Iran is below the age of thirty, and the young people in Iran want more freedom. There are twenty-two million students in Iran, and 70 percent of university students are women. Educated Iranian women who cannot find expression for their learning and young Iranian people who are

657. " . . . *Shari'a* is not inherently inimical to women's rights . . . the question of who gets to interpret *Shari'a* is critical." Isobel Coleman, *Women, Islam, and the New Iraq*, 85 Foreign Aff. 24, 26 (2006).

658. Mir-Hosseini, *supra* note 359, at 629.

frustrated by oppression make a volatile combination poised for transformation, if not revolution! In 2009, the Iranian people's opposition to the fraudulent re-election of Ahmadinejad and the murder of a high profile woman (who symbolized emancipation in a repressive regime) fell short of developing into a revolution.

The burgeoning feminist movement in Iran wants more rights for women and more protective laws. Ideally, this feminist movement should be engaged more systematically in demanding the enforcement of the international human rights treaties to which Iran is a signatory. The populist movement in Iran wants to separate religion and the State, which could result in a diminution of the appreciation of *Shari'a* law and its application in private family matters directly affecting women. The development of a new gender discourse and the rise of a popular reformist movement in Iran are positive signs of the emergence of more equality for women within an Islamic framework.

In the 1990s, feminist readings of Islam were tolerated as the process of the Islamization of Iran continued to take place. Although the ruling clerics continue to validate a patriarchal interpretation of the Koran and its translation into the laws of the Iranian courts, there is movement in Iran to consider the legitimacy of a more dynamic interpretation of the Koran that would extend more protection to women and expand their rights through the laws. While Khomeini's office restored the *Shari'a* in order to "protect the family" and to realize women's "high status" in Islam, women are treated as second-class citizens in the law, in the society, and in the family structure that is decidedly patriarchal in Iran. Women cannot understand why husbands can divorce them automatically without even first securing their consent. Iranian women are justified in asking, "Is this what the *Shari'a* says? . . . Is this how Islam honors women? Is this the justice of Islam?"[659] Rather than "producing the intended . . . marital harmony or a generation of docile wives," the return to *Shari'a* in 1979 "further exposed and accentuated the gap between the patriarchal assumptions [about] marriage . . . [and the kind of] egalitarian marriage lived and experienced by most people today."[660]

There is hope for women's human rights in Iran. Change will likely happen because of the emergence of a "sustained, indigenous feminism." The rise of an activist feminist movement in Iran has been delayed for many reasons other than the obvious fear of repression and reprisals. Women in Islam and in Iran are the symbols of cultural authenticity, the carriers of a religious tradition and a way of life. Thus, any form of dissent by women could be construed as a betrayal of their Muslim and/or Iranian identity,[661] and protest could, by extension, be construed as treasonous and pro-Western. Because of compulsory *hejab* and the

---

659. *Id.* at 635.
660. *Id.* at 636.
661. *Id.* at 639.

multiplicity of meanings underlying women's dress, women in Iran have to choose between their Muslim identity and their new gender awareness.[662] This is a hard and dangerous choice that is unfairly imposed on women alone.

Islamic feminists are now engaged in finding the sources for so-called Islamic traditions that discriminate against them and force women to wear clothing that is cumbersome and renders them all the more dependent on men. Many studies show that men's unilateral rights to divorce and polygamy were not textually granted to them by the Koran or by God, but were instead given to men by Muslim male jurists.[663] Iranian feminists[664] who are now focusing attention on Koranic interpretation (*tafsir*) have successfully uncovered the Koran's egalitarian message.[665] If continued, this belief in the power of interpretation is the clearest sign of hope for equality of women in Iran. The work of the Islamic feminists[666] should be examined in this light. By both uncovering a hidden history[667]and rereading textual sources, women will come to see that there are two opposing views of Islam. One view is absolutist and legalistically inflexible with regard to the acceptance of modernity. The other view is pluralistic and tolerant, especially of equality between men and women. The new emphasis on interpretation of the original sacred texts will reveal that the inequalities embedded in Iranian law are not the manifestations of a divine will written into the Koran. Iranian jurisprudence is not the product of an inseparable bond between religion and the State. Iranian jurisprudence is not the product of a primitive, backward social system. The law and its system are human constructions that

---

662. *Id.*

663. *Id.* at 642.

664. *See id.*, at n.22 for a list of works showing how the Koran and Islam's sacred texts have been tainted by "the ideologies of their interpreters." *See generally*, Azizah Al-Hibri, *Islam, Law, and Custom: Redefining Muslim Women's Rights*, 12 AM. U. J. INT'L L. & POL'Y, 1–44 (1997); Kecia Ali, *Progressive Muslims and Islamic Jurisprudence: The Necessity for Critical Engagement with Marriage and Divorce Law, in* PROGRESSIVE MUSLIMS 163, 163–89 (Omid Safi ed., 2003); ASGHAR ALI ENGINEER, THE RIGHTS OF WOMEN IN ISLAM (1992); Farid Esack, *Islam and Gender Justice: Beyond Simplistic Apologia, in* WHAT MEN OWE TO WOMEN: MEN'S VOICES FROM WORLD RELIGIONS 187, 187–210 (John C. Rianes & Daniel C Maguire eds., 2001); HAIFAA JAWAD, THE RIGHTS OF WOMEN IN ISLAM: AN AUTHENTIC APPROACH (1998), Ziba Mir-Hosseini, *The Construction of Gender in Islamic Legal Thought and Strategies for Reform*, 1 HAWWA 1, 1–18 (2003); *and* Amira El-Azhary Sonbol, *Rethinking Women and Islam, in* DAUGHTERS OF ABRAHAM: FEMINIST THOUGHT IN JUDAISM, CHRISTIANITY, AND ISLAM 108, 108–46 (Yvonne Yazbeck Haddad & John L. Esposito eds., 2001). *See also* Mir-Hosseini, *supra* note 359, at n.19 (providing a list of literature on Islamic feminism and its politics).

665. Mir-Hosseini, *supra* note 359, at 642.

666. To some the term *Islamic feminism* is an oxymoron. *See* Nayereh Tohidi, *Islamic Feminism:Perils and Promises*, 16 MEWS REVIEW 1 (2001), http://www.amews.org/review/reviewarticles/tohidi.htm.

667. *See* Mir-Hosseini, *supra* note 359, at 642.

reflect political and ideological agendas of the controlling class. When Khomeini called back *Shari'a* law in Iran, this came with a forceful attempt "to impose anachronistic jurisprudential constructions of gender relations"[668] upon Iranian society whose women, unfortunately, suffer the most in the name of the preservation of tradition and national identity.

Why should women's equality depend upon ideological influences and patriarchal beliefs that filter people's personal and politically charged interpretations of sacred texts? Rigid originalist interpretations put Islam and women's rights into a closed, static, and inflexible legal system that breeds unfairness to women, gender inequality, and unhealthy social relationships between men and women. To open this closure and liberate women in Iran, the feminists must overcome specious dichotomies[669] (established for self-serving reasons by men) between Islam and feminism, tradition and modernity, the quest for protection of Iranian national/religious identity and the fear of equality that comes from integration and exposure to cultural difference in the course of international relations. Women's liberation from human rights abuse in Iran is an issue deeply entrenched in semiotics and a serious matter of interpretation.

668. *Id.* at 644.

669. *See* Abdullahi An-Na'im, *The Dichotomy Between Religious and Secular Discourse in Islamic Societies, in* FAITH AND FREEDOM: WOMEN'S HUMAN RIGHTS IN THE MUSLIM WORLD 51, 51–60 (Mahnaz Afkhami ed., 1995).

9. GENDERCIDE AND THE CULTURAL CONTEXT OF SEX TRAFFICKING IN CHINA*

When a son is born,
Let him sleep on the bed,
Clothe him with fine clothes,
And give him jade to play with.
How lordly his cry is!
May he grow up to wear crimson
And be the lord of the clan and the tribe.
When a daughter is born,
Let her sleep on the ground,
Wrap her in common wrappings,
And give her broken tiles for playthings.
May she have no faults, no merits of her own,
May she well attend to food and wine,
And bring no discredit to her parents.
—Book of Songs (800–600 B.C.)[1]

I. INTRODUCTION

A. Background of China's Demographic Crisis

China is experiencing a demographic crisis that arguably rises to the level of gendercide.[2] Women in China are bought and sold, murdered, and made to disappear to comply with a governmental policy that coincides with the cultural phenomenon of male-child preference. In 1979, the Chinese government instituted a One-Child Policy to control the enormous population expansion.[3] To comply with the One-Child Policy and ensure that the family has a coveted boy child, millions of people in China have committed sex-selective abortions,

---

* This chapter was written by me with the collaboration of my research assistant Christie Edwards. It was published as an article in 32 FORDHAM INT'L L.J. 731–779 (2009). I have revised, updated, and expanded it to include an analysis of the literary work by Lisa See, SNOW FLOWER AND THE SECRET FAN (2005).

1. *See* ELISABETH J. CROLL, FEMINISM AND SOCIALISM IN CHINA 23 (1978).

2. *See generally* Eric Baculinao, *NBC: China Begins to Face Sex-Ratio Imbalance*, MSNBC.COM, Sept. 14, 2004, http://www.msnbc.msn.com/id/5953508 (last visited Jan. 21, 2009).

3. *See* Michael Bristow, *Has China's One-Child Policy Worked?* BBC NEWS, Sept. 20, 2007, http://news.bbc.co.uk/2/hi/asia-pacific/7000931.stm.

infanticide of their own baby girls, non-registration of the first or second infant in the family, and abandonment or sale of their own girl children. Demographers estimate that there are between fifty and one hundred million missing women in China.[4] In answer to the resulting scarcity of women, gangs, "specialist households," and "specialist villages" have been working in an organized chain to kidnap and sell women in China.[5]

Several factors work interdependently to cause a serious shortage of women in China. Women are disappearing because of the social pressures of male-child preference, the zealous enforcement of the One-Child Policy by local government authorities, and the murderous responses to this policy undertaken by millions of ordinary people in China who are desperate to have a son. The 2000 official Chinese census reported there were 117 boys born for every 100 girls, compared to the global average of 105 or 106 boys to every 100 girls.[6] This disparity may be linked to the practice of aborting female fetuses and killing female babies. The scarcity of women has produced a gender imbalance and an increase in prostitution and human trafficking in China.[7]

Trafficking in China has many forms: the purchase of women for brides, the abduction and/or purchase of a male son, or the sale of unwanted female children. Men, primarily in rural China, are desperately seeking a bride in a country where women are in short supply. These men will resort to purchasing a trafficked woman for marriage. Couples seeking a male child will sell, drown, or even murder their girl child in order to make room for the purchase of a trafficked baby boy. Young adult women and infants are bought and sold like cargo in China. Human trafficking in China is a lucrative international business that is expanding due to several factors: the aggressive implementation of the One-Child Policy, the faulty legal system, and the blind adherence to long-standing cultural traditions that devalue women. In China, Communist Party directives overshadow the legislative and judicial process. The primacy of governmental

---

4. *See* World Health Organization [WHO], WHO Regional Office for the Western Pacific, *Women's Health in a Social Context in the Western Pacific Region* 27 (1997) [hereinafter Women's Health]; *see generally* Calum MacLeod, *Life Begins Again for Chinese Girl Sold as Slave at 12*, THE INDEPENDENT, May 17, 2000, at 14, http://find articles.com/p/articles/mi_qn4158/is_20000517/ai_n14313948.

5. *See* Hong Ju et al., *Female Criminal Victimization and Criminal Justice Response in China*, 46 BRIT. J. CRIMINOLOGY 859, 861 (2006). China's longtime preference for boy babies has recently fueled a serious problem of the abduction of boy babies, especially in rural China. *See e.g.* Andrew Jacobs, *Rural China's Hunger for Sons Fuels Traffic in Abducted Boys*, N.Y. TIMES (Apr. 5, 2009), at 1 and 8.

6. *See* Celia W. Dugger, *The World; Modern Asia's Anomaly: The Girls Who Don't Get Born*, N.Y. TIMES, May 6, 2001, at 44, http://query.nytimes.com/gst/full page.html?res=9902EEDC1 138F935A35756C0A9679C8B63.

7. *See* Nicole M. Skalla, *China's One-Child Policy: Illegal Children and the Family Planning Law*, 30 BROOK. J. INT'L. L. 329 (2004).

policy results in the laws that theoretically protect women and female children in China being ineffective.[8]

B. Chinese Culture

Women's inferiority is deeply ingrained in the Chinese culture as reflected in the *Five Classics*, a canonical literary text ascribed to Confucius. The Confucian view of woman is clearly stated:

> The female was inferior by nature, she was dark as the moon and changeable as water, jealous, narrow-minded and insinuating. She was indiscreet, unintelligent, and dominated by emotion. Her beauty was a snare for the unwary male, the ruination of states.[9]

In Chinese culture, girls typically marry into the husband's family, leave home, and take care of their husband's parents. China's feudal tradition continuously subjected women to subordination by their father, husband, and even their son due to a patriarchal and patrilineal system. In addition, according to the rules of primogeniture, only the first male born traditionally inherited the parents' fortune. Moreover, only boys can continue the patrilineal family line. Thus, girl babies are considered financial burdens because they are unavailable to take care of their elderly parents who, upon retirement, do not receive enough money from the inadequate social services system in China. If only one child is allowed, the general consensus in China is that it had better be a boy!

Between 1949 and 1978, the Communist rule under Mao Zedong temporarily tried to relieve the subjugation of women by giving them the legal right to vote, education, employment, and marriage and inheritance rights. Prostitution was eradicated completely during this period.[10] Nevertheless, the economic reforms set in place later by Deng Xiaoping in 1978 brought significant transformations in Chinese society and a setback to women's equality. With the transition from a planned economy under Communism to a free market one in 1979, China saw the reemergence of prostitution and the abduction of women for the sex trade and for marriage.[11] Trafficking of women became rampant as Chinese society moved forward toward a free market system. This transition also promoted wider differences between urban and rural societies. Ironically, although the economic reform produced greater wealth for China, it also produced greater discriminatory treatment

---

8. *See* Xiaorong Li, *License to Coerce: Violence Against Women, State Responsibility, and Legal Failures in China's Family Planning Program*, 8 Yale J.L. & Feminism 145, 183–84 (1996).

9. *See* Richard W. Guisso, *Thunder Over the Lake: The Five Classics and the Perception of Women in Early China*, *in* Women in China: Current Directions in Historical Scholarship 59 (Richard W. Guisso & Stanley Johannesen eds., 1981).

10. *See* Hong Ju *et. al.*, *supra* note 5, at 859.

11. *See id.*

of women, which continues today especially in the rural parts of China where tradition and cultural values remain the same as they have been for centuries.[12]

C. Trafficking in China

Trafficking of women in China is a serious human rights violation. Domestic trafficking is "the most significant problem in China,"[13] and an estimated 10,000 to 20,000 victims are trafficked internally each year.[14] From 1991 to 1996, police freed 88,000 kidnapped women and arrested 143,000 people for engaging in the slave trade.[15] From 2001 to 2003, China's police freed more than 42,000 kidnapped women and children.[16] How many more women in China today remain enslaved in brothels and forced marriages is difficult to determine because of the unsavory nature of the crime and the lack of transparency in China.

China is designated as a source, transit, and destination country for women and children trafficked for the purpose of sexual exploitation and forced labor.[17] Trafficking occurs mainly within China's borders, but Chinese citizens are also trafficked out of China into Africa, Asia, Europe, Latin America, the Middle East, and North America.[18] Poor and desperate Chinese women are lured abroad with false promises of legitimate work only to be forced into prostitution and commercial sexual exploitation. They are trafficked typically into Japan, Malaysia, Thailand, and Taiwan. Foreign women and children are trafficked into China from Burma, Mongolia, North Korea, Russia, and Vietnam for purposes of forced labor, marriage, and prostitution.[19]

Experts believe that China's One-Child Policy has resulted in a male–female birth ratio imbalance, and the scarcity of women has contributed mightily to the increase in trafficking of women for brides.[20] The government of China is making efforts to comply with minimum standards for the elimination of trafficking, but it fails to adequately punish traffickers or protect Chinese and foreign victims of

---

12. *See id. See also* Jacobs, *supra* note 5: "The centuries-old tradition of cherishing boys—and a custom that dictates that a married woman moves in with her husband's family—is reinforced by a modern reality: Without a real social safety net in China, many parents fear they will be left to fend for themselves in old age." *Id.*

13. *See* U.S. DEP'T OF STATE, TRAFFICKING IN PERSONS REPORT 80 (2007), http://www.state.gov/documents/organization/82902.pdf [hereinafter TIP REPORT 2007].

14. *See id.*

15. *See* Chen Yiyung, *Trying to Stand on Two Feet*, NEWSWEEK, June 29, 1998, at 48, http://www.newsweek.com/id/92948/page/1.

16. *See id.*

17. *See* U.S. DEP'T OF STATE, TRAFFICKING IN PERSONS REPORT 91 (2008), http://www.state.gov/documents/organization/105501.pdf [hereinafter TIP REPORT 2008].

18. *See id.*

19. *See id.* at 92.

20. *See id.*

trafficking.[21] China still continues to treat trafficking victims as criminals and regularly deports North Korean trafficked women back to horrendous conditions in their home country.[22] In December 2007, China released a National Action Plan to Combat Trafficking, but the government has not allocated enough funds to implement the plan.[23]

D. Definitions of Trafficking

Trafficking in women and children is viewed as an illegal form of international trade that is associated with forced prostitution. Trafficking is the "trade of women for the purpose of prostitution."[24] Each year, more than 2.4 million victims of sex trafficking are bought and sold for the purpose of sexual exploitation.[25] Trafficking typically involves the transportation of a woman across an international border,[26] but it is not smuggling, which is a different crime. Human trafficking involves movement of people with force, fraud, or deception in order to have them engage in exploitative, slave-like labor. Forced labor is also a form of trafficking and is a significant problem in China.

Although there is no consensus among scholars or governments on the definition of trafficking, in 1995 the U.N. General Assembly defined trafficking broadly in this way:

> [T]he illicit and clandestine movement of persons across national and international borders, largely from developing countries and some countries with economies in transition, with the end goal of forcing women and girl children into sexually or economically oppressive and exploitative situations for the profit of recruiters, traffickers and crime syndicates, as well as other illegal activities related to trafficking, such as forced domestic labor, false marriages, clandestine employment and false adoption.[27]

The United Nations Protocol to Prevent, Suppress and Punish Trafficking in Persons, Especially Women and Children, Supplementing the United Nations Convention Against Transnational Organized Crime ("Palermo Protocol")

---

21. *See id.*

22. *See id.*

23. *See id.*

24. *See* Roelof Haveman, *Traffic in Persons as a Problem, in* COMBATING TRAFFIC IN PERSONS 137–39 (Marieke Klap et al. eds., 1995).

25. U.N. INT'L LABOR ORG., A GLOBAL ALLIANCE AGAINST FORCED LABOUR 10 (2005), http://www.ilo.org/dyn/declaris/DECLARATIONWEB. DOWNLOAD_BLOB?Var_DocumentID=5059.

26. *See* TIP REPORT 2008, *supra* note 17, at 7.

27. The Secretary General, *Report of the Secretary-General on Traffic of Women and Girls*, ¶ 8, G.A. Res 49/166, U.N. Doc. A/50/369 (Aug. 24, 1995).

defines *trafficking in persons* as a form of slavery, forced labor, and forced prostitution:

> [T]he recruitment, transportation, transfer, harbouring or receipt of persons, by means of the threat or use of force or other forms of coercion, of abduction, of fraud, of deception, of the abuse of power or of a position of vulnerability or of the giving or receiving of payments or benefits to achieve the consent of a person having control over another person, for the purpose of exploitation. Exploitation shall include, at a minimum, the exploitation of the prostitution of others or other forms of sexual exploitation, forced labour or services, slavery or practices similar to slavery, servitude or the removal of organs.[28]

The U.S. Trafficking Victims Protection Act of 2000 (TVPA) distinguishes between sex trafficking and "severe forms of trafficking in persons."[29] Severe forms of trafficking, which provide victims when rescued with enhanced benefits, include trafficking a minor or trafficking a person with forced violence:

> (A) sex trafficking in which a commercial sex act is induced by force, fraud, or coercion, or in which the person induced to perform such act has not attained 18 years of age; or
> (B) the recruitment, harboring, transportation, provision, or obtaining of a person for labor or services, through the use of force, fraud, or coercion for the purpose of subjection to involuntary servitude, peonage, debt bondage, or slavery.[30]

Sex trafficking is defined as: "the recruitment, harboring, transportation, provision, or obtaining of a person for the purpose of a commercial sex act."[31] By contrast, China's definition of trafficking does not include acts of forced labor, debt bondage, coercion, or involuntary servitude, or offenses committed against male victims.[32]

Trafficking involves the forced movement of human beings from poor source countries through transition countries into relatively rich destination countries, such as the United States, Western Europe, North America, Australia, China,

---

28. Protocol to Prevent, Suppress and Punish Trafficking in Persons, Especially Women and Children, Supplementing the United Nations Convention Against Transnational Organized Crime, art. 3(a), Dec. 12, 2000, G.A. Res. 55/25, U.N. Doc. A/55/ 383 (2000) [hereinafter Palermo Protocol].

29. Trafficking Victims Protection Act of 2000, 22 U.S.C. §§ 7101 (b) (19), 7101–12 (2000) [hereinafter TVPA].

30. *Id.* § 7102(8).

31. *Id.* § 7102(9).

32. *See* TIP Report 2008, *supra* note 17, at 93.

and Japan.[33] Globalization, the advancement of technology, and the expansion of Internet use increase people's access to remote parts of the world and facilitate trafficking. The ease with which traffickers can transport their victims across international borders through modern technology also increases the incidences of trafficking.[34]

According to the International Organization of Migration, trafficking follows migration routes. Women move because of poverty, economic disparity among nations, general lack of economic opportunities for women (especially in poor or transition countries), and the cultural and political marginalization of women in source countries.[35] The World Bank has encouraged the promotion of tourism as a development strategy, but tourism has also contributed to the rise in trafficked women for prostitution.[36] Women from developing countries are highly susceptible to traffickers who falsely promise them high paying jobs or advantageous marriages in developed countries.[37] These women are duped and ultimately sold to brothel owners or to men who buy them as wives or concubines for the purpose of slave labor and exploitation.[38]

Sex trafficking laws around the world are either weak or nonexistent; those that do exist are either not enforced or often enforced to the detriment of the victim rather than the perpetrator.[39] For example, China has a trafficking law, but it is not well enforced.[40] In addition, national laws that prohibit prostitution often discourage victims from seeking help from the authorities who might either throw the trafficking victims in jail for engaging in illegal prostitution or deport them to their home countries where they would be forced to live as social outcasts in horrific conditions.[41] Even legalized prostitution facilitates trafficking because the trafficked woman forced to engage in sex work against her will cannot be distinguished from the voluntary prostitute.

Because the criminal penalties for trafficking in women are typically very light and the economic benefits of trafficking are very great, international crime

---

33. *See* Susan Tiefenbrun, *The Saga of Susannah—A U.S. Remedy for Sex Trafficking in Women: The Victims of Trafficking and Violence Protection Act of 2000*, 2002 UTAH L. REV. 107, 131–32 (2002); *see also* Radhika Coomaraswamy & Lisa M. Kois, *Violence Against Women*, *in* 1 WOMEN AND INTERNATIONAL HUMAN RIGHTS LAW 177, 203 (Kelly D. Askin & Dorean M. Koenig eds., 1999).

34. Coomaraswamy & Kois, *supra* note 33, at 202.

35. *See* INTERNATIONAL ORGANIZATION FOR MIGRATION, TRAFFICKING OF WOMEN TO COUNTRIES OF THE EUROPEAN UNION: CHARACTERISTICS, TRENDS & POLICY ISSUES 6 (1996).

36. *See* Coomaraswamy & Kois, *supra* note 33, at 202.

37. *See id.* at 203.

38. *See id.*

39. *See* Tiefenbrun, *supra* note 33, at 114.

40. *See* TIP REPORT 2008, *supra* note 17, at 93.

41. *See* Tiefenbrun, *supra* note 33, at 113–14.

syndicates are drawn to the sex trade industry.[42] Sex trafficking is the third most lucrative international crime after the traffic of arms and drugs.[43] The economic advantages of human trafficking make it difficult to eradicate.

This chapter will address sex trafficking in China and the root causes of this human rights violation and international crime that has developed from the strict enforcement of a governmental One-Child Policy and the cultural phenomenon of male-child preference. The disappearance of women in China due to the One-Child Policy and the male-child preference is referred to as *gendercide*, or the systematic destruction of a group (women) based on their gender. The chapter is organized in six parts. Part II will examine the laws protecting women in China from trafficking; Part III will discuss specific problems related to sex trafficking in China; Part IV will unearth the root causes of sex trafficking in China based on the One-Child Policy and the increasing scarcity of women; Part V will address the changing role of women in Chinese society and the need for cultural reform; and Part VI will offer policy suggestions to combat the growth of sex trafficking in China and to encourage the Chinese government to protect the lives and rights of women. Part VII will discuss the literary representation of the human rights violations of women in China as expressed in Lisa See's beautiful novel *Snow Flower and the Secret Fan*. Part VIII will offer some suggestions to help eliminate the trafficking of women in China.

II. LAWS PROTECTING WOMEN IN CHINA FROM TRAFFICKING

A. International Instruments Regulating Trafficking

There are many international instruments regulating trafficking because it is both a human rights violation and an international crime.[44] Trafficking is at the crossroads of slavery, forced prostitution, torture, and forced labor. Therefore, the aim to eliminate human trafficking benefits from legislation prohibiting these other crimes and human rights violations. Trafficking also involves the illegal sale of children including their use as soldiers.[45] Some of the international instruments that protect trafficking victims include the International Agreement for the Suppression of the White Slave Traffic (1904);[46] the International

42. *See id.* at 114, 132.

43. *See id.* at 137.

44. *See generally* Susan Tiefenbrun, *Sex Sells but Drugs Don't Talk: Trafficking of Women Sex Workers and an Economic Solution*, 24 T. Jefferson L. Rev. 161 (2002).

45. *See generally* Susan Tiefenbrun, *Child Soldiers, Slavery and the Trafficking of Children*, 31 Fordham Int'l L.J. 415 (2008) and its revision in chapter 10 of this book.

46. International Agreement for the Suppression of the White Slave Traffic, May 18, 1904, 2 U.S.T. 1997, T.I.A.S. No. 2332, 30 U.N.T.S. 23.

Convention for the Suppression of Traffic in Women and Children (1921);[47] the Convention to Suppress the Slave Trade and Slavery (1926);[48] the Forced Labor Convention (1930);[49] the International Convention for the Suppression of the Traffic in Women of Full Age (1933);[50] the U.N. Charter (1945);[51] the Universal Declaration of Human Rights (1948);[52] the Geneva Convention for the Suppression of the Traffic of Persons and the Exploitation of the Prostitution of Others (1950);[53] the Supplementary Convention on the Abolition of Slavery, the Slave Trade, and Institutions and Practices Similar to Slavery (1957);[54] the International Covenant on Civil and Political Rights (1966);[55] the Convention on the Elimination of All Forms of Discrimination Against Women (1979);[56] the Convention Against Torture and Other Forms of Cruel, Inhuman or Degrading Treatment or Punishment (1984);[57] the Convention on the Rights of the Child (1989);[58] the Convention Against Transnational Organized Crime: Protocol to Prevent, Suppress and Punish Trafficking in Persons, Especially Women and Children;[59] the Protocol Against Smuggling of Migrants by Land, Sea and Air (2000);[60] and the Optional Protocols to the Convention on the Rights of the Child

---

47. International Convention for the Suppression of Traffic in Women and Children, Sept. 30, 1921, 9 L.N.T.S. 415.

48. Convention to Suppress the Slave Trade and Slavery, Sept. 25, 1926, 46 Stat. 2183, 60 L.N.T.S. 253.

49. Forced Labor Convention, June 29, 1930, 39 U.N.T.S. 55.

50. International Convention for the Suppression of the Traffic in Women of Full Age, Oct. 11, 1933, 150 L.N.T.S. 431.

51. U.N. Charter, June 26, 1945, 59 Stat. 1931, T.S. No. 933.

52. Universal Declaration of Human Rights, Dec. 10, 1948, G.A. Res. 217(III), U.N. GAOR, 3d Sess., Supp. No. 13, U.N. Doc. A/810.

53. Convention for the Suppression of the Traffic in Persons and of the Exploitation of the Prostitution of Others, Mar. 21, 1950, 96 U.N.T.S. 271.

54. Supplementary Convention on the Abolition of Slavery, the Slave Trade and Institutions and Practices Similar to Slavery, Apr. 30, 1957, 266 U.N.T.S. 3.

55. International Covenant on Civil and Political Rights, Dec. 19, 1966, G.A. Res. 2200A, U.N. GAOR, 21st Sess., Supp. No. 16, 999 U.N.T.S. 171, U.N. Doc. A/6316.

56. Convention on the Elimination of All Forms of Discrimination Against Women, Dec. 18, 1979, G.A. Res. 34/180, 34 U.N. GAOR, Supp. (No. 46), U.N. Doc A/34/46 (1979) [hereinafter CEDAW].

57. Convention Against Torture and Other Forms of Cruel, Inhuman or Degrading Treatment or Punishment, Dec. 10, 1984, G.A. Res. 39/46, Annex, U.N. Doc. A/ Res/39/46/ Annex (1984) [hereinafter CAT].

58. Convention on the Rights of the Child, Nov. 20, 1989, G.A. Res. 44/25, annex, U.N. GAOR, 44th Sess., Supp. No. 49, U.N. Doc. A/RES/44/25 (1989) [hereinafter CRC].

59. Palermo Protocol, *supra* note 28.

60. Protocol Against the Smuggling of Migrants by Land, Sea and Air, Supplementing the United Nations Convention Against Transnational Organized Crime, Nov. 15, 2000, U.N. GAOR, 55th Sess., Annex 3, U.N. Doc. A/55/383 (2000).

on the Involvement of Children in Armed Conflicts and on the Sale of Children, Child Prostitution and Child Pornography (2000).[61]

China is not a signatory to the International Covenant on Civil and Political Rights or the International Covenant on Economic, Social and Cultural Rights, which, along with the Universal Declaration of Human Rights, comprise the "International Bill of Rights." However, China has ratified CEDAW, which grants positive and negative reproductive rights to women.[62] Article 16 of CEDAW provides:

> States Parties shall take all appropriate measures to . . . ensure, on a basis of equality of men and women . . . the same rights to decide freely and responsibly on the number and spacing of their children and to have access to the information, education and means to enable them to exercise these rights.[63]

The strict regulation of women's reproduction choices through compulsory birth control measures and limited forms of contraceptives deny Chinese women the freedom to make their own reproductive decisions.[64] In addition to the severe lack of quality reproductive care in rural areas, access to information and education about contraceptives in China is also extremely limited.[65] Thus, the restrictive birth planning regulations under the Chinese One-Child Policy violate Chinese women's reproductive rights under CEDAW.

China also signed the Convention against Torture and Other Forms of Cruel, Inhuman or Degrading Treatment or Punishment (CAT)[66] and the Convention on the Rights of the Child (CRC).[67] These treaties give China international

---

61. Optional Protocols to the Convention on the Rights of the Child on the Involvement of Children in Armed Conflicts and on the Sale of Children, Child Prostitution and Child Pornography, May 25, 2000, G.A. Res. 54/263, Annexes I & II, U.N. GAOR, 54th Sess., Supp. No. 49, U.N. Doc. A/54/49 (2000).

62. *See generally* CEDAW, *supra* note 56. China ratified it on Nov. 4, 1980. *See* Office of the U.N. High Commissioner for Human Rights, Convention on the Elimination of All Forms of Discrimination against Women, New York, Dec. 18, 1979, http://www2.ohchr.org/english/bodies/ratification/8.htm (last visited Nov. 22, 2008).

63. *See* CEDAW, *supra* note 56, art. 161(1)(e).

64. *See* Li, *supra* note 8, at 184.

65. *See id.*

66. *See generally* CAT, *supra* note 57. China ratified the Convention Against Torture and Other Cruel, Inhuman or Degrading Treatment or Punishment (CAT) on Oct. 4, 1988. *See* Office of the U.N. High Commissioner for Human Rights, Convention Against Torture and Other Cruel, Inhuman or Degrading Treatment or Punishment, New York, Dec. 10, 1984, http://www2.ohchr.org/english/bodies/ratification/9.htm.

67. *See generally* CRC, *supra* note 58. China ratified the Convention on the Rights of the Child (CRC) on Mar. 2, 1992. *See* Office of the U.N. High Commissioner for Human Rights, Convention on the Rights of the Child, New York, Nov. 20, 1989, http://www2.ohchr.org/english/bodies/ratification/11.htm.

obligations to protect women and children from trafficking, slavery, torture, and other forms of cruel, inhumane, or degrading treatment.[68] Thus, international treaties protecting the traffic of women are abundant, but trafficking still exists and thrives. Clearly, the fault lies in the lack of enforcement of these treaties to which China and other nations assisting China in its traffic of women are in serious noncompliance.

B. Chinese Trafficking Law

In addition to China's marriage, family planning, and inheritance laws, which do theoretically protect women and children, China has enacted several laws that specifically address trafficking, kidnapping, and sexual exploitation of women and children. In 1991, the National People's Congress Standing Committee criminalized the purchase of women by enacting a "Decision Relating to the Severe Punishment of Criminal Elements Who Abduct and Kidnap Women and Children" ("the Decision"), making the abduction and the sale of women and children separate offenses.[69] Prior to the promulgation of this Decision, many traffickers who sold women that others had kidnapped were released by the courts.[70] Now both the kidnapper and seller can be prosecuted under this Decision. The use of force to prevent the rescue of trafficked women was also specifically criminalized.[71]

In 1992, the Law on the Protection of Women's Rights and Interests (LPWRI)[72] was passed, which was the first basic law to protect women's rights and interests in China.[73] The LPWRI prohibits kidnapping, trafficking, and buying women, though it fails to prescribe any specific penalties for these offenses.[74] The LPWRI

68. *See generally* CAT, *supra* note 57; CRC, *supra* note 58.

69. *See* Decision of the Standing Committee of the National People's Congress Regarding the Severe Punishment of Criminals who Abduct and Traffic in or Kidnap Women or Children, Sects. 1(2), 1(6) (promulgated Sept. 4, 1991, effective Sept. 4, 1991) http://www.asianlii.org/cn/legis/cen/laws/dotscotnpcrtspocwaatiokwocv 1424/.

70. Human Rights in China, *Caught Between Tradition and the State: Violations of the Human Rights of Chinese Women*, 17 WOMEN'S RTS. L. REP. 285, 290 (1996).

71. *See id.*

72. Law Protecting Women's Rights and Interests (promulgated by Order No. 58 of the President of the People's Republic of China on Apr. 3, 1992, effective Oct. 1, 1992), http://www.unescap.org/esid/psis/population/database/poplaws/ law_china/ch_record002.htm [hereinafter LPWRI]; *see also* Maternal and Infant Health Care Law (promulgated by Order No. 33 of the President of the P.R.C. on Oct. 27, 1994, effective June 1, 1995), http://www.unescap.org/esid/psis/population/database/poplaws/law_china/ch_record006.htm [hereinafter MIHCL].

73. *See* U.N. Gen. Assembly, *Report of the Committee on the Elimination of Discrimination Against Women*, Sect. 272, U.N. Doc. A/54/38 Rev. 1 (Aug. 20, 1999) [hereinafter CEDAW Report].

74. *See* LPWRI, *supra* note 72, art. 36.

also fails to provide a definition of discrimination against women.[75] However, those who buy abducted women and force them to have sex may be tried for the crime of rape under the Chinese Criminal Code.[76] Other types of violence against abducted women are subject to penalties under the Chinese Criminal Code.[77] The rights of women in Hong Kong are protected by the Sex Discrimination Ordinance (1995) and the Family Status Ordinance (1997).[78]

Article 236 of the Chinese Criminal Code provides a three-to-ten year sentence for rape, while those who sexually exploit girls under the age of fourteen can receive a sentence of life imprisonment or the death penalty.[79] Article 240 prohibits abducting and trafficking a woman or child and specifies a five-to-ten year sentence for this crime.[80] A ten year-to-lifetime sentence or the death penalty may be imposed on those who abduct and traffic a woman or child, rape or prostitute a woman, steal an infant for the purpose of selling the victim, or sell the victim outside of China.[81] Purchasing an abducted woman or child carries a punishment of up to three years, although the punishment can be combined with other provisions in instances of rape or other crimes to give the perpetrator a longer sentence.[82] However, China's Criminal Code does not prohibit commercial sexual exploitation involving coercion or fraud, nor does it prohibit all forms of trafficking, such as debt bondage.[83] Chinese law enforcement efforts to arrest and prosecute perpetrators of these crimes are seriously lacking, and China does not even report statistics on prosecutions, convictions, or sentences for these crimes.[84]

The Fourth World Conference on Women was held in Beijing, China in September 1995, where the Beijing Declaration and Platform for Action were adopted.[85] Subsequently, China made some efforts to implement the Beijing Declaration and Platform for Action and to advance the goals of equality,

---

75. *See* CEDAW Report, *supra* note 73, Sect. 283.

76. *See* Criminal Law, arts. 236, 241 (P.R.C.) (adopted by the Second Sess. of the Fifth Nat'l People's Cong. on July 1, 1979 and revised at the Fifth Sess. of the Eighth Nat'l People's Cong. on Mar. 14, 1997), http://www.com-law.net/findlaw/ crime/criminallaw1.html (last visited Nov. 23, 2008) [hereinafter Criminal Law].

77. *See* Human Rights in China, *supra* note 70, at 290.

78. *See* CEDAW Report, *supra* note 73, ¶ 260.

79. *See* Criminal Law, *supra* note 76, art. 236.

80. *See id.* art. 240.

81. *See id.*

82. *See id.* art. 241.

83. *See* TIP Report 2007, *supra* note 13, at 80.

84. *See* TIP Report 2008, *supra* note 17, at 93.

85. *See generally* U.N. Division for the Advancement of Women, Fourth World Conference on Women, Beijing, China, (Sept. 1995), http://www.un.org/womenwatch/daw/beijing/.

development, and peace for Chinese women.[86] The Program for the Development of the Chinese Women ("the Program") was also created to "promote the progress and development of Chinese women" by the All-China Women's Federation ("Women's Federation") in 1995.[87] The Program aimed to improve the status and equality of women in China by establishing agencies to increase women's political and decision-making power, guarantee labor rights for women, develop education rights and opportunities for women, improve women's health and rights within the family, contain violence against women and the criminal acts of abducting and prostituting women, and give aid to poverty-stricken women in rural areas.[88] China renewed the Program in 2001 to further promote the full participation of women in economic and social development and to achieve greater equality for women in China.[89] The Committee on the Elimination of Discrimination Against Women lauded this Program for its achievements "in ensuring social and economic rights for hundreds of millions of people" in China.[90] If this Program were properly enforced, the plight of trafficked women and children in China would be greatly improved.

The Law on the Protection of Minors, adopted in 1991, was revised in 2006 and became effective in June 2007.[91] This law specifically prohibits the trafficking, kidnapping, and sexual exploitation of minors.[92] The chairman of the Standing Committee of the National People's Congress has "urged tighter supervision on the implementation of the law," and warns that inspection teams will be visiting several provinces in the summer of 2008 to investigate compliance.[93]

In December 2007, the Chinese government established a new Office for Preventing and Combating Crimes of Trafficking in Women and Children.[94] At that time, China also released its much-anticipated National Action Plan to Combat Trafficking, but "there are no plans for resources to be allocated to local

86. *See* CEDAW Report, *supra* note 73, Sect. 275.

87. *See* The Program for the Development of the Chinese Women (1995–2000), para. 1 (promulgated by the All-China Women's Federation 1995), http://www.unescap.org/esid/psis/population/database/poplaws/law_china/ch_record016.htm.

88. *See generally id.*

89. *See* The Program for the Development of the Chinese Women (2001–10) (promulgated by the All-China Women's Federation 1995), http://www.womenofchina.cn/Policies_Laws/Policies/1458.jsp.

90. *See* CEDAW Report, *supra* note 73, Sect. 273.

91. *See* Law on the Protection of Minors (P.R.C.) (adopted by the Standing Comm. Nat'l People's Cong., Sept. 4, 1991, revised Dec. 29, 2006, effective June 1, 2007), http://www.npc.gov.cn/englishnpc/Law/2007-12/12/content_1383869.htm.

92. *See id.* art. 41.

93. *See* Embassy of the People's Republic of China in the United States of America, *China's Top Legislator Urges Better Protection of Minors*, June 2, 2008, http://www.china-embassy.org/eng/xw/t443171.htm.

94. *See* TIP Report 2008, *supra* note 17, at 92.

and provincial governments for the implementation of the plan. Additionally, the action plan covers only sex trafficking of females, and does not address labor trafficking or male victims of sex trafficking."[95]

C. U.S. Trafficking Laws

The Trafficking Victims Protection Act of 2000[96] (TVPA) is the U.S. law with an international prong that is designed to combat human trafficking by punishing traffickers, protecting victims, and preventing trafficking.[97] On October 28, 2000, President Bill Clinton signed the TVPA to provide an international solution to an international crime.[98] This law severely punishes sex trafficking as if it were a crime as serious as rape with a sentence of twenty years to life imprisonment.[99] The TVPA has been hailed as the "most significant human rights legislation of [the 106th U.S.] Congress."[100] It provides desirable financial assistance, benefits, protection, services, and education to victims of trafficking both in the United States and abroad, as well as the right to permanent residency in the United States and a work permit if the trafficked victim cooperates in the prosecution of her trafficker[s].[101] The TVPA establishes the very real threat of prosecution and severe punishment for sex traffickers.[102] Since the passage of the TVPA in 2000, the U.S. government has spent over 528 million dollars in programmatic assistance abroad to help foreign governments and organizations eliminate trafficking.[103] The United States has been the catalyst for international cooperation on anti-trafficking efforts. President George W. Bush issued the first National

---

95. *Id.*

96. TVPA, *supra* note 29.

97. *See generally id.*

98. *See generally Clinton to Sign Bill to Help Battered Women*, CNN.com, http://archives.cnn.com/2000/ALLPOLITICS/stories/10/28/clinton.radio.ap/index.html (last visited Nov. 20, 2008). *See also* Susan Tiefenbrun, *William J. Clinton's Legacy to Women's Rights*, Symposium Issue, 12 CARDOZO J. LAW & GENDER 858 (Summer 2006).

99. *See* Trafficking with Respect to Peonage, Slavery, Involuntary Servitude or Forced Labor, 18 U.S.C. § 1590 (2000).

100. *See* Press Release, Eric Hotmire, *Senate Passes Brownback, Wellstone Trafficking Victims Protection Act* (July 27, 2000), http://brownback.senate.gov/pressapp/record.cfm?id=175961&&year=2000&; *see generally* TVPA, *supra* note 29. President Clinton stated that the TVPA of 2000 was "the most significant step we've ever taken to secure the health and safety of women at home and around the world." Deb Riechmann, *Clinton Signs Law to Combat Violence*, DAYTON DAILY NEWS, Oct. 29, 2000, at 3A.

101. *See generally* TVPA, *supra* note 29.

102. *See id.* §§ 111–12.

103. *See* TIP REPORT 2008, *supra* note 17, at 2.

Security Presidential Directive on Trafficking[104] and called for more countries to join the United States in the fight to eliminate sex trafficking.[105] In a bipartisan commitment to the eradication of trafficking and the protection of trafficked victims, President George W. Bush and the Republican-led Congresses signed the Trafficking Victims Protection Reauthorization Acts (TVPRA) in 2003 and 2005.[106] Bush also signed the Prosecutorial Remedies and Other Tools to end the Exploitation of Children Today Act ("PROTECT Act") of 2003, which is designed to protect children from sexual predators.[107] The PROTECT Act has extraterritorial reach, and any U.S. citizen who engages in sex with a minor overseas, even in a country where this act is legal, will be investigated, prosecuted, and convicted.[108] The 2007 TVPRA was passed by the House of Representatives on December 4, 2007 but was not passed by the Senate before the end of the session. The TVPRA of 2008 was passed by both Houses and enacted on December 23, 2008.[109] The frequent reauthorization of the TVPA demonstrates the U.S. government's firm commitment to the eradication of human trafficking.

In addition to providing protection for victims, prosecution for perpetrators, and prevention of the crime of trafficking, the TVPA also intends to "encourage foreign governments to take effective actions to counter all forms of trafficking in persons" by enacting or amending sex trafficking legislation.[110] The TVPA seeks to strengthen enforcement policies and coordinate international anti-trafficking efforts through the publication of the annual Trafficking in Persons Report ("TIP Report") by the U.S. Department of State.[111] The first TIP Report,

---

104. *See* Press Release, Office of the Press Sec'y, *Trafficking in Persons National Security Presidential Directive* (Feb. 24, 2003), http://www.whitehouse.gov/news/releases/2003/02/20030225.html; *see also* Paula J. Dobriansky, Under Sec'y of State for Global Affairs, U.S. Dep't of State, Remarks to Conference to Stop Child Trafficking: Modern-Day Slavery (June 3, 2003), http://www.usis.it/file2003_06/alia/A3060506.htm.

105. *See* George W. Bush, President Bush Addresses United Nations General Assembly (Sept. 23, 2003), http://www.whitehouse.gov/news/releases/2003/09/200309 23-4.html.

106. *See generally* Trafficking Victims Protection Reauthorization Act of 2003, 22 U.S.C. § 7101 (2003); Trafficking Victims Protection Reauthorization Act of 2005, 22 U.S.C. § 7101 (2005).

107. *See generally* Prosecutorial Remedies and Other Tools to End the Exploitation of Children Today Act of 2003, 18 U.S.C. § 1 (2003).

108. *See generally id.*

109. *See* William Wilberforce Trafficking Victims Protection Reauthorization Act of 2007, H.R. No. 3887, *available at* http://thomas.loc.gov/cgi-bin/bdquery/z?d110:H.R. 3887. *See* William Wilberforce Trafficking Victims Protection Reauthorization Act of 2008, PUB. L. no. 110-457, 122 Stat. 5044

110. *See* TIP REPORT 2008, *supra* note 17, at 5.

111. *See id.*

published in July 2001, reported on the trafficking status of eighty-two countries in the world.[112]

The TIP Report divides countries into three tiers based on the individual government's efforts to combat trafficking within the country.[113] Countries placed on Tier 1 have to meet the minimum standards set forth in Section 108(a) of the TVPA, which are: (1) the government must prohibit and punish severe forms of trafficking in persons; (2) the punishment must be commensurate with that for grave crimes such as forcible sexual assault or rape; (3) the punishment must be sufficiently stringent to deter the crime and to reflect its heinous nature; and (4) the government must make serious and sustained efforts to eliminate severe forms of trafficking in persons.[114] Governments can demonstrate "serious and sustained efforts" to combat trafficking by investigating and prosecuting traffickers, protecting victims and encouraging them to help in the prosecution of the traffickers, starting education programs to alert potential victims about the dangers of trafficking, extraditing traffickers at the request of other countries, monitoring immigration, and investigating public officials who may be complicit in the trafficking process.[115]

Countries are placed on Tier 2 if they do not fully comply with the minimum standards of the TVPA, but are nevertheless making significant efforts to bring themselves into compliance by committing to take additional future steps over the next year.[116] Tier 2 countries often do not have anti-trafficking legislation or specific criminal punishments for the crime of trafficking, but are making serious and sustained efforts to enact legislation to address the problem of trafficking.[117] In 2003, the TVPA also created the Tier 2 Watch List to monitor countries in danger of falling into Tier 3.[118] A Tier 2 country can be placed on the Tier 2 Watch List if the country has a significant number of trafficking victims or the number of victims is significantly increasing and the country fails to provide evidence of increasing efforts to combat trafficking and complicity by public officials.[119]

Countries are placed on Tier 3 if they do not comply with the minimum standards of the TVPA and are not making significant efforts to become compliant by enacting or enforcing trafficking laws.[120] Countries placed on Tier 3 may be

---

112. *See id.* at 1.

113. *See* U.S. Dep't of State, Trafficking in Persons Report 4–5 (2001), http://www.state.gov/documents/organization/4107.pdf [hereinafter TIP REPORT 2001].

114. *See* TIP Report 2008, *supra* note 17, at 284.

115. *See id.* at 284–85.

116. *See id.* at 12.

117. *See id.* at 284.

118. *See id.* at 13.

119. *See id.* at 12–13.

120. *See id.* at 12.

subject to sanctions by the U.S. Government,[121] which may withhold non-humanitarian, non-trade related assistance, and the United States may register its opposition to international assistance from financial institutions such as the World Bank or the International Monetary Fund.[122] Many of the worst offenders on Tier 3 fear that sanctions and the stigma of being placed on that tier might negatively affect their international trade, tourism, and international aid, and they have asked the United States for assistance to move up.[123]

As stated above, China fell from Tier 2 to the Tier 2 Watch List in 2005 for its failure to comply with the minimum standards of the TVPA.[124] China was on Tier 2 in 2001 while Hong Kong was on Tier 1.[125] China was on Tier 2 in 2002 because it did not meet minimum standards, although China maintains a database of abducted and rescued people and a DNA database to facilitate the return of abducted children to their families.[126] China was on Tier 2 again in 2003, and the PRC continued its public awareness campaigns against trafficking of women and children. In 2003, women were reintegrated into their communities through resettlement centers offering legal, medical, and psychological help.[127]

China was on Tier 2 again in 2004, and the TIP Report mentioned China's 1992 Law Protecting Women's Rights and Interests that specifically outlaws trafficking or kidnapping of women, as well as China's Criminal Code, which imposes the death penalty for traffickers who coerce girls under fourteen into prostitution.[128] In 2005, China moved down to the Tier 2 Watch List due to its "failure to provide evidence of increasing efforts to combat trafficking, specifically its inadequate protection for trafficking victims, specifically foreign women and P.R.C. women identified from Taiwan."[129] The Chinese government also did not take measures to protect foreign women who were trafficked for commercial sexual exploitation and forced marriages with Chinese men.[130]

In 2006, China again was placed on the Tier 2 Watch List, even though China's Women's Federation reportedly provided some assistance to trafficked

---

121. *See id.* at 13–15.
122. *See id.* at 15.
123. *See id.* at 18.
124. *See id.* at 93.
125. *See* TIP Report 2001, *supra* note 113, at 20, 37.
126. *See* U.S. Dep't of State, Trafficking in Persons Report 39 (2002), http://www.state.gov/documents/organization/10815.pdf [hereinafter TIP Report 2002].
127. *See* U.S. Dep't of State, Trafficking in Persons Report 47 (2003), http://www.state.gov/documents/organization/21555.pdf [hereinafter TIP Report 2003].
128. *See* U.S. Dep't of State, Trafficking in Persons Report 92 (2004), http://www.state.gov/documents/organization/34158.pdf [hereinafter TIP Report 2004].
129. *See* U.S. Dep't of State, Trafficking in Persons Report 83 (2005), http://www.state.gov/documents/organization/47255.pdf [hereinafter TIP Report 2005].
130. *See id.* at 84.

women.[131] In 2007, China stayed on the Tier 2 Watch List because protection services were reportedly "inadequate,"[132] and China still had not adopted its draft National Action Plan to Combat Trafficking. China has still not ratified the Palermo Protocol.[133] In the TIP Reports 2008 and 2009, China remains on the Tier 2 Watch List for the fifth consecutive year. The TIP Report 2008 specifically refers to an increase in trafficking due to the need for "women for brides" and cites forced labor as a continuing source of serious trafficking.[134] The Report specifically mentions corrupt local officials who are complicit in the trafficking of women.[135] However, in 2008, the National Action Plan to Combat Trafficking was finally released.[136] China has made some progress in the protection of trafficked victims, but there are not enough shelters to take care of these women.[137]

Although new laws designed to combat trafficking in China have been enacted, there is a serious lack of enforcement in the most vulnerable areas.[138] In addition, most of the Chinese laws that pertain to underlying crimes and elements that lead to trafficking (such as kidnapping, infanticide, child abandonment, sex selective abortions, and patriarchal inheritance) are rarely enforced.[139]

III. SEX TRAFFICKING IN CHINA

A. Domestic Trafficking of Women Within China

According to the 2008 U.S. State Department Trafficking in Persons (TIP) Report, China remains "a source, transit, and destination country for men, women and children trafficked for the purposes of sexual exploitation and forced labor."[140] After spending four years on Tier 2[141] of the TIP rankings from 2001 to 2004, China was dropped to the Tier 2 Watch List in 2005, where it has remained up to the present due to its noncompliance "with the minimum standards for the elimination of trafficking. . . ."[142] Some of the factors impeding progress in China's anti-trafficking efforts include "tight controls over civil organizations,

---

131. *See* U.S. DEP'T OF STATE, TRAFFICKING IN PERSONS REPORT 92 (2006), http://www.state.gov/documents/organization/66086.pdf [hereinafter TIP REPORT 2006].

132. *See* TIP REPORT 2007, *supra* note 13, at 81.

133. *See* TIP REPORT 2008, *supra* note 17, at 94. *See also* TIP REPORT 2009, at www.state.gov/g/tip. at p. 22.

134. *See id.* at 92.

135. *See id.*

136. *See id.*

137. *See id.* at 93.

138. *See id.*

139. *See id.* at 93–94.

140. *See id.* at 91.

141. *See id.* at 93.

142. *See id.* at 92.

and the government's systematic lack of transparency," as well as its failure to "address labor trafficking or male victims of sex trafficking."[143]

Because of the scarcity of women in China due to the impact of the One-Child Policy and the force of the male-child preference, domestic trafficking is one of the leading problems in China today. In 2007, the TIP Report stated there are "an estimated minimum of 10,000 to 20,000 victims trafficked internally per year."[144] The profit earned in human trafficking in China is more than US$7 billion annually, more than arms trafficking or drug trafficking.[145] International organizations state that 90 percent of the trafficking victims are women and children from the Anhui, Guizhou, Henan, Hunan, Sichuan, and Yunnan Provinces who are sent to wealthier provinces in the east and trafficked primarily for sexual exploitation.[146]

The abducted women are usually between the ages of thirteen and twenty-four.[147] While many women are sold into forced and exploitative prostitution, most are purchased as brides in rural parts of China.[148] As the number of available women decreases and the number of peasant families moving to urban areas for jobs increases, peasant men look to traffickers to supply them with a wife.[149] Some say it is economically cheaper to purchase a wife than to pay for a wedding and dowry gifts.[150] Local villagers often sympathize with the husband whose bride tries to escape, and villagers sometimes will return the purchased wife to her husband even if she complains of abuse.[151]

B. International Trafficking Into and Outside of China

International trafficking of Chinese citizens to Africa, Asia, Europe, Latin America, the Middle East, and North America is increasing.[152] Many poor Chinese women are duped by false promises of legitimate jobs in Taiwan, Thailand, Malaysia, and Japan, only to be sold into prostitution upon their

---

143. *See id. See also* Jacobs, *supra* note 5, at 8: "The reluctance of the [Chinese] police to investigate such cases [of child abduction]" is a serious problem in China. China claims the problem of trafficking and stolen children is "exaggerated." *Id.* The persistence of old Chinese government practices (including false reporting of statistics and strong oppression of the people by "public criticism," "education," and force or violence producing fear) reminds us of the State-sponsored terrorism under Mao's leadership. *See* Jonathan Mirsky, *The China We Don't Know, in* N.Y. Review of Books (Feb. 26, 2009), vol. LVI, No. 3, at 38.

144. *See* TIP Report 2007, *supra* note 13, at 80.

145. *See* Hong Ju *et al.*, *supra* note 5, at 863.

146. *See* TIP Report 2007, *supra* note 13, at 80.

147. *See* MacLeod, *supra* note 4, at 14.

148. *See id.*

149. *See id.*

150. *See id.* para. 6.

151. *See id.* para. 1.

152. *See* TIP Report 2008, *supra* note 17, at 91.

arrival.[153] Although trafficking remains illegal in China, this crime is inadequately enforced, especially in the vulnerable southern provinces near Thailand and Taiwan.[154] In relation to the number of women and children trafficked in China, there are relatively few investigations of trafficking and even fewer trials or convictions.[155] In 2006 in Anhui Province, one of the major sources of trafficking victims, only six traffickers were reported convicted and sentenced to life imprisonment.[156] In 2007, China did not report any countrywide conviction records for trafficking.[157]

In 2007, the Chinese government "reported investigating 2,375 cases of trafficking of women and children . . ., which is significantly lower than the 3,371 cases it cited in 2006."[158] These figures are likely based on China's definition of the term *trafficking*, which "does not include acts of forced labor, debt bondage, coercion, or involuntary servitude, or offenses committed against male victims."[159] Although China "sustained its record of criminal law enforcement against traffickers," the U.S. Department of State reports that these government statistics are difficult to verify.[160] Finally, in 2007, "Chinese law enforcement authorities arrested and punished some traffickers involved in forced labor practices and commercial sexual exploitation, but did not provide data on prosecutions, convictions, or sentences."[161] The lack of transparency in the Chinese judicial system exacerbates the problem of data verification.

Trafficking is not limited to women and children, but also includes infant girls.[162] In poor rural districts of China, the preference for male children is high, and family planning rules are strictly enforced. The One-Child Policy limits the number of children that women may bear, and many women prefer to sell their infant daughter for relatively large sums of money in order to try again for a son.[163] Many women are afraid of the social stigma as well as large fines and penalties imposed on them for violating the one-child limit.[164] While many families are willing to pay the fines if a son is born, most "would never pay that kind

---

153. *See id.* at 91–92.

154. *See* TIP REPORT 2007, *supra* note 13, at 81.

155. *See* TIP REPORT 2008, *supra* note 17, at 92.

156. *See* TIP REPORT 2007, *supra* note 13, at 80–81.

157. *See* TIP REPORT 2008, *supra* note 17, at 93.

158. *Id.* at 93.

159. *Id.*

160. *See id.* at 92.

161. *Id.* at 93

162. *See* Elisabeth Rosenthal, *Bias for Boys Leads to Sale of Baby Girls in China*, N.Y. TIMES, July 20, 2003, at 16,

http://query.nytimes.com/gst/fullpage.html?res=9E06EEDB1E3CF933A15754C0A9659C8B63&sec&spon&pagewanted=1.

163. *See id.*

164. *See id.*

of fine for a daughter."[165] The trafficked infant girls are often sold to childless urban parents or rural farmers who desire a girl to help with the housework. Some girls in China are even raised to be child brides for farmers in remote villages.[166]

C. Complicity of Corrupt Local Officials

One of the big issues facing the Chinese government's efforts to combat trafficking is "the significant level of corruption and complicity in trafficking by some local government officials."[167] In many cases, corrupt local officials participate in the sexual exploitation of women, making it difficult to combat the trafficking industry on a national level.[168] Many of these officials do not view trafficking as a serious crime and do not take steps to prevent it.[169] At times, officials even accept bribes to overlook trafficking.[170]

Slave labor is a variant of trafficking. In May and June 2007, several cases of slave labor in brick kilns in China's Henan and Shanxi Provinces were discovered. Over one thousand farmers, teenagers, and children were confined, subjected to physical abuse, and forced to work without pay for their labor.[171] The brick kiln operators claim to have paid off local officials to turn a blind eye to the slave labor and sweatshop conditions.[172] There are unconfirmed press reports that some local officers have resold rescued children to similarly abusive factories in other districts.[173] According to the latest 2008 TIP Report, "[t]he Chinese government has not demonstrated concerted efforts to investigate, prosecute, and punish government officials for complicity in trafficking."[174] In addition, "Chinese law does not prohibit commercial sexual exploitation involving coercion or fraud, nor does it prohibit all forms of trafficking."[175] Chinese law recognizes only abduction as constituting a means of trafficking, not other forms of coercion.[176] Finally, Chinese law specifies only a three-year sentence for purchasers of women and children—and this light sentence is rarely implemented.[177]

---

165. *See id.*
166. *See id.*
167. *See* TIP REPORT 2008, *supra* note 17, 92.
168. *See id.*; *see also* CEDAW Report, *supra* note 73, ¶ 291–92.
169. *See* Human Rights in China, *supra* note 70, at 290.
170. *See id.*
171. *See* TIP REPORT 2008, *supra* note 17, at 93.
172. *See id.*
173. *See id.*
174. *Id.*
175. *See id.*
176. *See id.*
177. *See* Criminal Law, *supra* note 76, art. 241; MacLeod, *supra* note 4, at 14.

D. Criminalization Of and Reprisal Against Trafficking Victims

One main obstacle to the eradication of trafficking in China is the criminalization and punishment of the victims rather than the traffickers.[178] Prostitution is illegal in China, and authorities often falsely or mistakenly accuse trafficked women of engaging in this crime.[179] Authorities fail to distinguish between a trafficked woman who was forced into prostitution and a voluntary prostitute. China arrests trafficked women for prostitution and does not refer them to organizations providing services.[180] In other words, China treats the victims of trafficking as mere criminals.[181] "Victims are sometimes punished for unlawful acts that were committed as a direct result of their being trafficked—such as violations of prostitution or immigration/emigration controls."[182]

In the southern border provinces, local authorities rely heavily upon nongovernmental organizations to identify trafficking victims and to provide victim protection services because the local governments there lack significant resources and are severely underfunded.[183] Many trafficking victims are returned home without any rehabilitation.[184] Foreign trafficking victims are forcibly evicted from China and sent back to their home countries where they often face punishment and rejection.[185] North Korean trafficking victims are treated solely as illegal economic migrants, and a few hundred of them are deported each month to North Korea where they may face severe penalties.[186] Some Chinese trafficking victims also face punishments in the form of fines for leaving China without proper authorization, even if they were coerced to leave by authorities.[187] China clearly continues to punish the victims of trafficking.

Trafficked women face discrimination from their own families and communities upon their release and return home.[188] Families feel that the trafficking victim has caused them shame and "a loss of face" by having sex with her purchaser, even if she was forced to do so.[189] A commonplace view in China is that the woman is at fault for being trafficked.[190] Moreover, people believe that a woman's virtue is the property of the man; if a woman's virtue is "used"' by

178. *See* TIP REPORT 2008, *supra* note 17, at 93.
179. *See id.*
180. *See id.*
181. *See id.*
182. *Id.* at 92.
183. *See id.* at 93.
184. *See id.*
185. *See id.*
186. *See id.* at 93–94.
187. *See id.* at 93.
188. *See* Human Rights in China, *supra* note 70, at 291.
189. *See id.*
190. *See id.*

another, it loses its value.[191] These beliefs are a sign of the pervasiveness of feudal attitudes deeply entrenched within the Chinese culture.[192]

IV. ROOT CAUSES OF TRAFFICKING

A. One-Child Policy

During the period of the Great Leap Forward and the Cultural Revolution, which were designed to spur on China's industrial growth and eradicate political enemies, Mao also encouraged population growth and accepted the idea of an unbridled population increase.[193] However, in the 1970s, a "population crisis" developed, and demographers reported that the continuing population growth of the country would hinder the developing economic progress of China.[194] The population overgrowth was touted as the cause of "many of the world's ills—including poverty, hunger, health problems, housing shortages, transportation problems, illiteracy, lack of education, unemployment, overcrowding, resource depletion, soil erosion, and environmental degradation."[195] China has about a fifth of the world's population but only about 7 percent of the world's arable land.[196] There is no question China has an exponential population growth, which, if unchecked, will have serious consequences. But for the governments of developing nations, a population crisis "has the added virtue of putting the blame for socioeconomic problems on the reproductive habits of the people rather than on defective political leadership or misconceived politics."[197]

In 1970, the "Wan-Xi-Shao" or "Later-Longer-Fewer" (later marriages, longer spacing between children, and fewer births) family planning program began to show a decrease in Chinese fertility rates.[198] In 1979, the One-Child Policy was launched.[199] This policy was outlined in countless Communist Party directives with hopes that growth would be slowed and population would be 1.2 billion by

191. *See id.*

192. *See id.*

193. *See* JOHN S. AIRD, SLAUGHTER OF THE INNOCENT: COERCIVE BIRTH CONTROL IN CHINA 20–28 (1990).

194. *See id.* at 6–7.

195. *Id.* at 7.

196. Farhana Haque Rahman, International Fund for Agricultural Development, *The Status of Rural Women in China* 82 (1995).

197. AIRD, *supra* note 193, at 8.

198. *See* JAMES Z. LEE & WANG FENG, ONE QUARTER OF HUMANITY: MALTHUSIAN MYTHOLOGY AND CHINESE REALITIES, 1700-2000, at 93 (1999); CECELIA NATHANSEN MILWERTZ, ACCEPTING POPULATION CONTROL: URBAN CHINESE WOMEN AND THE ONE-CHILD FAMILY POLICY 49 (1997).

199. *See* LEE & FENG, *supra* note 198, at 94.

2000 rather than the projected 1.4 billion.[200] At first, only three children or more were prohibited, but the policy was revised after only a few years to forbid couples from having more than one child.[201] Vice Premier Deng Xiaoping declared, "In order to reduce the population, use whatever means you must, but do it! With the support of the Party Central Committee, you will have nothing to fear."[202] In 1980, The Chinese Marriage Law was enacted requiring family planning for all married couples and prescribing age restrictions for marriage.[203] For example, according to this law, women cannot marry before they are twenty, and men cannot marry before the age of twenty-two.[204] Late marriage and late childbirth are strongly encouraged.[205] The 1982 Chinese Constitution also required all Chinese citizens to practice family planning.[206]

The One-Child Policy is not outlined in a single national law: it is a policy that has been strictly and even coercively enforced throughout the country since 1979 to limit couples as to the time and manner of conception.[207] The 1982 Constitution stipulates that the absolute leadership of the Central Communist Party is one of the four cardinal principles that govern China.[208] Therefore, adherence to Communist Party directives is equivalent or superior to codified legislation.[209] As one scholar states, "[t] he leadership of the Communist Party, the guidance of Marxism–Leninism and Mao Zedong thought, the preservation of socialism, and the continuation of the proletarian dictatorship are commonly known as the four cardinal principles of the [Chinese] [C]onstitution."[210] Individual rights are thus subordinate to the State's interest.[211] Although women and children are

---

200. *See* Penny Kane & Ching Y. Choi, *China's One Child Family Policy*, 319 Brit. Med. J. 992 (1999).

201. *See id.*

202. Steven W. Mosher, A Mother's Ordeal: One Woman's Fight Against China's One Child Policy 274 (1993).

203. Marriage Law (promulgated by Order No. 9 of the Chairman of the Standing Comm. Nat'l People's Cong., Sept. 10, 1980, effective Jan. 1, 1981), http://www.unescap.org/esid/psis/population/database/poplaws/law_china/ch_record003. htm [hereinafter Marriage Law].

204. *Id.*

205. *Id.*

206. Xian Fa art. 25 (1982) (P.R.C.), http://english.people.com/cn/constitution/constitution.html [hereinafter Chinese Constitution].

207. Li, *supra* note 8, at 151–59.

208. The Preamble to the 1982 Constitution states, "Under the leadership of the Communist Party of China and the guidance of Marxism-Leninism and Mao Zedong Thought, the Chinese people of all nationalities will continue to adhere to the people's democratic dictatorship. . .." Chinese Constitution, *supra* note 206, pmbl. ¶ 3.

209. *Id.*

210. Li, *supra* note 8, at 151 n.21.

211. *Id.* at 152.

given some rights under the LPWRI[212] and the Maternal and Infant Health Care Law (MIHCL),[213] the family planning policies of the State necessarily infringe on the reproductive rights of all Chinese women.

In China, family planning is a revolutionary motto that takes hold of the people by subtle forms of brainwashing. Family planning directives are pervasive and have "almost replaced revolutionary rhetoric in contemporary media" as evidenced by the following statement:

> Advertisements, billboards, blackboards, books, cartoons, cassettes, CDs, comics, movies, news, paintings, plays, poems, posters, radio, songs, television, videos, VCDs, even web sites, numerous speeches, and, of course, endless group meetings are devoted to the exhortation to have only one child.[214]

Family planning is a basic part of everyone's sex education beginning in grade school.[215] It is continued during premarital counseling, and it is widespread in the popular culture.[216] Chinese citizens all receive an ideological education to ensure their awareness of and adherence to all the One-Child Policy requirements.[217] They are instructed in the significance of the population policy and its relationship to China's overall economic development.[218] The sacrifice of having only one child in the Chinese culture is routinely glorified as obedience to duty and an expression of the love of one's country.[219] Those who exceed the family planning limits are publicly vilified as "irresponsible free-riders."[220] However, one Chinese Minister of Agriculture called the idea of persuading peasants to adhere to family planning standards "an illusion."[221] He stated, "Only coercive measures can be effective in alleviating the problems caused by [the] population explosion . . . From the perspective of future generations . . . temporary coercion is actually a philanthropic and wise policy."[222] Thus, force and various forms of intrusive persuasion are used to implement the One-Child Policy.

1. Chinese Birth-Planning Workers or Agent Informants Approximately fifteen million Chinese women have volunteered to become government agents in order to implement and enforce the One-Child Policy through the Women's

212. LPWRI, *supra* note 72; Li, *supra* note 8, at 152.
213. MIHCL, *supra* note 72; Li, *supra* note 8, at 152.
214. LEE & FENG, *supra* note 198, at 134.
215. *Id.*
216. *Id.*
217. *Id.*
218. MILWERTZ, *supra* note 198, at 75.
219. LEE & FENG, *supra* note 198, at 134.
220. *Id.*
221. AIRD, *supra* note 193, at 83.
222. *Id.*

Federation.[223] The basis of the One-Child Policy is a system of government quotas granting permission to bear children, government regulations of birth control methods and menses cycles, and intense ideological peer pressure to conform to Communist ideals based on a theory of the sacrifice of the individual for the good of the country.[224] Every woman is "continuously and closely monitored by both her street committee and work unit."[225] Under the One-Child Policy, all women in China are forced to use the same form of birth control, and "[b]irth control pills or [surgically implanted] intrauterine devices ("IUDs") are the preferred methods" of contraception.[226] IUDs are inserted into women who have not yet received their quota permission to have a child as well as women who have had their first child and before the child passes the age of high mortality.[227] Women who have had a child are often pressured into signing a "One-Child Agreement" with the government and to undergo sterilization through tubal ligation.[228] While the One-Child Policy does not specify whether males or females should undergo the sterilization process, it is exceptionally rare for a man in China to have a vasectomy.[229] There is an underlying stigma associated with the loss of a man's virility after a vasectomy, and this stigma exists throughout Chinese culture, which accounts for increased female sterilizations.[230]

2. Forced Abortions The coercive tactics of the Chinese officials are not limited to just enforcing strict contraceptive requirements. Chinese officials also force abortions upon women who have conceived outside of the quota system.[231] Although official government policy states that participation in family planning must be voluntary and that coercion is forbidden, actual practice within the country is in direct contrast to the government policy.[232] A radio broadcast in 1986 declared:

> Regarding pregnancies not covered by the plan, it is necessary to conduct education by persuasion and take remedial measures to terminate the pregnancies. If education by persuasion has no effect, those concerned can be fined and subjected to administrative discipline.[233]

223. Milwertz, *supra* note 198, at 95; Mosher, *supra* note 202, at 117.
224. Mosher, *supra* note 202, at 267; Lee & Feng, *supra* note 198, at 135.
225. Milwertz, *supra* note 198, at 106.
226. Mosher, *supra* note 202, at 147.
227. Milwertz, *supra* note 198, at 107.
228. Mosher, *supra* note 202, at 199.
229. *Id.*
230. *Id.*
231. *Id.* at 250.
232. Aird, *supra* note 193, at 30.
233. *Id.* at 102.

Women who are illegally pregnant are typically subjected to weeks of high-pressure tactics by members of the Women's Federation and Communist Party leaders using threats, financial pressure, and public family planning "study sessions."[234] Women are actually escorted by officials to abortion clinics to ensure that they go through with the abortion procedure.[235] To avoid the coercive tactics of the government officials seeking to abort an over-quota child, some mothers choose "childbirth on the run."[236] These women flee their city or village where their pregnancy would be monitored to go to the home of a distant friend or relative who can keep the birth a secret.[237] On occasion, such women are caught and forced into a late-term abortion and forcibly "sterilized at the same time."[238]

Due to the strict monitoring efforts by the Women's Federation and population control officials, illegal pregnancies are often detected in the early stages, and mothers are encouraged to take immediate "remedial measures."[239] "Remedial measures" is a common Chinese euphemism for mandatory abortions.[240] "Technical services" is a different term referring to birth control surgeries such as IUD insertions, sterilizations, and abortions.[241] Suction abortions can be performed in the first few months of pregnancy. However, Chinese doctors have also used far more inhumane methods to abort babies, such as inducing premature labor and "inject[ing] pure formaldehyde into the fetal brain through the fontanel, or soft spot" before the baby comes through the birth canal; doctors have also been known to "reach in with forceps [to] crush the baby's skull."[242]

3. Forced Sterilizations For women in China who are caught giving birth to over-quota children, forced sterilizations in addition to abortions are required.[243] At the height of the coercive population planning campaigns, "sterilization presently emerged as the principal 'technical measure'" to control the population growth.[244] The number of sterilizations exploded between 1970 and 1985.[245] In the 1970s, the number of sterilizations typically ranged between two and three million, compared to over sixteen million sterilizations reportedly performed in 1983.[246] During many of the "propaganda month" campaigns, extreme efforts

234. *Id.* at 17; Mosher, *supra* note 202, at 267–68.

235. Aird, *supra* note 193, at 17.

236. Mosher, *supra* note 202, at 280.

237. *Id.*; Aird, *supra* note 193, at 17.

238. Mosher, *supra* note 202, at 285.

239. *Id.* at 252.

240. Aird, *supra* note 193, at 12.

241. *Id.*

242. Mosher, *supra* note 202, at 255.

243. Kay Johnson et al., *Infant Abandonment and Adoption in China*, 24 Population & Dev. Rev. 469, 477–78 (1998).

244. Aird, *supra* note 193, at 33.

245. *Id.* at 40.

246. *Id.*

were made to ensure that a "spouse of every couple with two or more children was sterilized."[247] Mass mobilizations and extreme physical coercion were initiated at the hands of the birth planning cadres.[248] One newspaper stated, "[w]e should implement thoroughly our policy on sterilization in those areas and resort to remedial measures when dealing with pregnancies that do not comply with planning."[249] One woman who chose "childbirth on the run" to carry her third pregnancy to full term was immediately arrested by birth planning authorities after her return home, "taken under guard to commune medical clinic [and] . . . given a tubal ligation the same day."[250]

4. Carrot and Stick Coercion for Compliance A strong sense of egalitarianism in family planning has produced a highly effective atmosphere of public intimidation in order to implement population controls.[251] Punitive coercive measures for disobedience of the One-Child Policy also exist and are used to implement the policy.[252] State officials at all levels are responsible for their own compliance and for the compliance of all those under their jurisdiction.[253] Failing to meet the birth quota limits in an official's jurisdiction can result in the official's demotion or even dismissal.[254] Therefore, officials use any means possible to enforce the family planning program to ensure the success of their own careers.[255] Although the government policy officially disallows coercion, the authorities use a very narrow definition of *coercion*, referring only "to overt physical coercion and the use of administrative commands without accompanying propaganda."[256]

Chinese authorities presume that a majority of the population will conform to the birth-planning regulations as a result of a pervasive and persuasive ideological education that begins for all Chinese citizens at a very early age.[257] Not only are couples that do not comply subjected to increasing economic penalties, but the birth planning workers and fellow employees of State-run agencies are also subject to fines or loss of yearly bonuses.[258] Thus, strong group pressure to comply with family-planning measures ensures compliance by most couples to the One-Child Policy.[259]

---

247. *Id.* at 100.
248. *Id.* at 17.
249. *Id.* at 44.
250. MOSHER, *supra* note 202, at 243.
251. LEE & FENG, *supra* note 198, at 134.
252. *Id.* at 135.
253. *Id.* at 132.
254. *Id.*
255. *Id.*
256. AIRD, *supra* note 193, at 16.
257. MILWERTZ, *supra* note 198, at 88.
258. *Id.* at 89.
259. *Id.* at 90.

Far more extreme measures have also been reported to retaliate against families with over-quota births or even those who simply refuse to sign the One-Child Agreement.[260] These people are denied food, given less drinking water and electricity,[261] forced to see their homes destroyed, refused shelter because their friends are forbidden to help them, fired from jobs, fined up to several times their annual salaries, and denied the right to register their child's birth.[262] A child who is not registered cannot receive health-care or education services.[263] In 1995, in a village called Xiaoxi, a man named Huang Fuqu along with his wife and children, was ordered out of his house, which was then blown up with dynamite by government officials.[264] On a nearby wall, the officials painted a warning: "Those who do not obey the family planning police will be those who lose their fortunes."[265] In 1996, in the town of Shenzhen, 906 families were given fifteen days to leave because they had produced too many children.[266] Government officials confiscated their residence permits, revoked their licenses to work, and ordered the housing department not to rent them houses or shops.[267]

By contrast, parents who comply with the One-Child Policy are rewarded with economic incentives. They receive a "signing bonus" after they sign the "One-Child Agreement."[268] Parents receive monthly health-care cash payments until their child turns fourteen, milk subsidies for young children, child-care subsidies, and priority in free health-care and education.[269]

5. Scarcity of Women Since the inception of the One-Child Policy in 1979, population statisticians estimate that millions of infant girls are missing from projected birth rates.[270] In September 1997, the World Health Organization's Regional Committee for the Western Pacific released a report stating that "more than 50 million women are 'missing' in China, victims of female feticide,[271] selective malnourishment of girls, lack of investment in women's health and

---

260. Trent Wade Moore, *Fertility in China 1982–1990: Gender Equality As A Complement to Wealth Flows Theory*, 17 Population & Dev. Rev. 197, 198 (1998).

261. Aird, *supra* note 193, at 16.

262. Report on Implementation of CEDAW in the People's Republic of China 74 (Human Rights in China 1998), http://www.hrichina.org/fs/download-ables/reports/cedaw_98.pdf?revisionid=1_4195 [hereinafter Report on Implementation of CEDAW]

263. *Id.*

264. Patrick E. Tyler, *Birth Control in China: Coercion and Evasion*, N.Y. Times, June 25, 1995, at 1.

265. *Id.*

266. Graham Hutchings, *Chinese Town Expels 906 Families for Over-Breeding*, The Telegraph, Dec. 4, 1996.

267. *Id.*

268. Milwertz, *supra* note 198, at 91.

269. *Id.*

270. Women's Health, *supra* note 4, at 27.

271. This term refers to the killing of the girl fetus.

various forms of violence."[272] Other reports project even higher estimates of missing women—up to 100 million.[273] In the latest census in China in 2000, 117 boys were born for every 100 girls compared to the global average of 105 or 106 boys to every 100 girls.[274] In some rural areas, the imbalance is even higher—130 boys to 100 girls.[275] Approximately 15 percent of the girls missing are due to "excess female mortality" stemming from sex-selective abortions, abandonment, neglect, and female infanticide.[276]

a. Abandonment of Infant Girls. One of the major sources of gendercide and the decimation of the female population in China is the abandonment of infant girls. The strict birth planning controls of the 1980s revitalized the problems of abandonment and infanticide of female children.[277] There is a long-standing "tradition" of "throwing away" very young children in the Hubei province.[278] In a Chinese/American study that examined parents who abandoned babies and those who adopted them, the majority of children whom parents admitted to abandoning were first or second-born daughters.[279] Many hoped that by abandoning their newborn daughter, they would be permitted to try again for a son.[280] Child abandonment, particularly of girls and children with disabilities, is a huge problem throughout China in both rural and urban areas.[281] Many parents leave their children close to their homes to ensure that the babies are found, such as on well-traveled roads, on doorsteps, or at orphanages.[282] Other parents travel great distances to abandon their girl baby in a crowded public place, such as railways or bus stations.[283] One official in the district of Shenyang stated, "[e]very year, no fewer than 20 abandoned baby girls are found in dustbins and corners."[284]

---

272. Women's Health, *supra* note 4, at 27.

273. MacLeod, *supra* note 4, at 14.

274. Dugger, *supra* note 6, at 44.

275. Justin McCurry & Rebecca Allison, *40 Million Bachelors and No Women . . . The Birth of a New Problem for China*, THE GUARDIAN, Mar. 9, 2004, at 3.

276. Susan Greenhalgh, *Fresh Winds in Beijing: Chinese Feminists Speak Out on the One-Child Policy and Women's Lives*, 26 Signs: J. WOMEN CULTURE & SOC'Y 847, 872 (2001).

277. Johnson et al., *supra* note 243, at 472.

278. Kay Johnson, *The Politics of the Revival of Infant Abandonment in China, with Special Reference to Hunan*, 22 POPULATION & DEV. REV. 77, 78 (1996).

279. Johnson et al., *supra* note 243, at 475.

280. *Id.* at 476.

281. HUMAN RIGHTS WATCH, DEATH BY DEFAULT: A POLICY OF FATAL NEGLECT IN CHINA'S STATE ORPHANAGES 132 (1996).

282. Johnson et al. *supra* note 243, at 479.

283. *Id.* at 478.

284. REPORT ON IMPLEMENTATION OF CEDAW, *supra* note 262, at 83.

Over 95 percent of babies in State-run orphanages are healthy baby girls.[285] However, due to the poor conditions of the orphanages, a high percentage of the baby girls die within months.[286] In the Shanghai Children's Welfare Institute, the most prominent orphanage in China, the rate of deaths after admission was a staggering 77.6 percent in 1991, with an increase in 1992 for the months reported.[287] In 1995, Human Rights Watch published "Death by Default," a report that chronicled the horrifying conditions of Chinese orphanages, including a "waiting for death room" where undesired infant girls were left to starve to death or die from neglect.[288] A British documentary entitled "The Dying Room" chronicled many orphanages where baby girls sit on bamboo benches in the middle of a courtyard with their wrists and ankles tied to the armrests and legs of the bench, rocking listlessly back and forth.[289] Baby girls suffered from liver failure, vitamin deficiency, disease, and sheer neglect, dying in large numbers after their arrival at the orphanages.[290]

According to the Marriage Law of 1980 and the omnibus Law Protecting the Rights and Interests of Women and Children (LPWRI),[291] child abandonment is illegal but has become endemic in Chinese society since the promulgation of the One-Child Policy nearly thirty years ago.[292] Parents who have abandoned their children are subject to fines, sanctions, and even forced sterilizations.[293] Even though the laws make child abandonment illegal, there are few provisions for the prosecution of parents who abandon their children.[294] Even as the number of abandoned children has increased since the late 1980s, there are only a few, rare cases of successful prosecution and sentencing of these parents.[295] Child abandonment is generally considered to be within the purview of the birth-planning authorities who levy fines on parents for exceeding birth-quota limits. However, these punishments are not considered civil or criminal offenses for endangering or violating the rights of the child.[296] China ratified the Convention on the Rights

285. Brian Woods, The Dying Room (Lauderdale Productions 1995), http://www.channel14.com/fourdocs/archive/the_dying_room_player.html [hereinafter *The Dying Room*].

286. Johnson et al., *supra* note 243, at 469.

287. Human Rights Watch, *supra* note 281, at 135–36.

288. *Id.* at 126.

289. *See generally* The Dying Room, *supra* note 285.

290. *Id.*

291. Marriage Law, *supra* note 203; LPWRI, *supra* note 72.

292. *Id.*

293. *Id.* at 478.

294. *Id.* at 479.

295. Johnson, *supra* note 278, at 84.

296. Johnson et al., *supra* note 243, at 480.

of the Child on April 1, 1992.[297] In its initial report to the Committee on the Rights of the Child, China stated that it would only consider the abandonment of children a crime "where the circumstances are grave enough."[298]

In the rural Yunnan province, rather than merely abandoning their babies, many women sell their newborns on the black market to smugglers. They resell the babies to wealthier or childless parents in eastern China who need an extra set of hands to work on farms or who do not want to wait through China's endless adoption system.[299] The mothers who sell their daughters do so for many reasons: the fear of exceeding the limits set forth in the One-Child Policy, their hope to have a male child in a future pregnancy, or their need for extra money to pay off their debts.[300] Highly coveted male babies are also sold if the mother has exceeded the One-Child Policy or wants to make extra money.[301]

The Adoption Law of China[302] requires adoptive parents to be childless and over the age of thirty.[303] Childless adoptive parents who do not meet the age requirement are not usually subjected to fines. Nevertheless, many people report that they cannot in fact register their adoption or obtain a proper household registration until they reach age thirty.[304] This delay subjects the child to an unregistered status, which deprives the child of benefits and human and civil rights protections.[305] Adoption of abandoned babies also carries risks for the adoptive parents who have other children. These adoptive parents are subjected to steep fines and even sterilizations because the Adoption Law requires the adoptive parent to have no other children.[306] A few families were even forced to give up their adoptive children to a State-run orphanage, where, paradoxically, the State incurred the cost of raising the child until another adoptive family could be found.[307]

---

297. U.N. Comm. on the Rights of the Child, *Initial Reports of States Parties Due in 1994: China*, ¶ 100, U.N. Doc. CRC/C/11/Add.7 (Aug. 1, 1995), http://www.unhchr.ch/tbs/doc.nsf/(Symbol)/CRC.C.11.Add.7.En?

298. *Id.*

299. Hannah Beech Xicheng, *China's Infant Cash Crop*, TIME PACIFIC, Jan. 29, 2001, at 38, http://www.time.com/time/pacific/magazine/20010129/china.html.

300. *Id.*

301. *Id.*

302. Adoption Law (adopted by the Standing Comm. Nat'l People's Cong., Dec. 29, 1991, revised Nov. 4, 1998), http://www.unescap.org/esid/psis/ population/database/poplaws/law_china/ch_record008.htm.

303. Johnson et al., *supra* note 243, at 482.

304. *Id.* at 492.

305. *Id.* at 482.

306. *Id.* at 491–92.

307. *Id.* at 492.

b. Infanticide. Infanticide has been practiced in China since the early part of the first millennium by all classes of society.[308] Although male infants also suffered from infanticide, the majority of victims have been female infants due to the traditional Chinese preference for male children to carry on the bloodline and for ancestor worship.[309] Infanticide has even been sanctioned at times in religious practice.[310] Throughout Chinese history, the practice of female infanticide was caused by changes in the economy, the high cost of living, and the scarcity of food.[311] Historically, infanticide was not considered immoral. In some areas, up to half of all infants were killed by their parents.[312] In sixteenth and seventeenth century Chinese Buddhist culture, parents were ordered not to kill their babies, but this injunction was placed alongside orders not to leap over food served on the floor, not to step over a person lying on a floor mat, and not to spit at a shooting star or point at a rainbow.[313] Today, infanticide is generally considered immoral in China and also illegal under Chinese law.[314]

Yet despite its illegality, female infanticide has increased dramatically since the One-Child Policy was put into practice in 1979. Infanticide can be committed by parents who want to have a son in the future and at birth by doctors in hospitals because the babies are unauthorized.[315] Several sources report the practice of female infanticide by obstetricians who administer injections to women giving birth in order to cause stillbirths or delivery of nonviable babies.[316] In 1983, it was reported from Guangzhou that doctors were being required to kill babies to ensure that any infant born without a permission slip from the mother's employer was not allowed to leave the hospital alive.[317] The doctors were allowed to use any method to kill the babies, even strangulation.[318] In 1989, another report was uncovered disclosing infants being killed by having gauze stuffed into their mouth and being given alcohol or ether injections.[319] In rural clinics,

308. LEE & FENG, *supra* note 198, at 47.

309. *Id.*

310. VALERIE M. HUDSON & ANDREA M. DEN BOER, BARE BRANCHES: SECURITY IMPLICATIONS OF ASIA'S SURPLUS MALE POPULATION 14 (2004).

311. Johnson *et al.*, *supra* note 243, at 472.

312. LEE & FENG, *supra* note 198, at 47.

313. HUDSON & DEN BOER, *supra* note 310, at 13.

314. LEE & FENG, *supra* note 198, at 61.

315. Coercive Population Control in China: Evidence of Forced Abortion and Forced Sterilization: Hearing Before the Subcomm. on Int'l Relations House of Representatives, 107th Cong. 16 (2001) (testimony of Stephen Mosher, President, Population Research Institute), http://commdocs.house.gov/committees/intlrel/hfa75 761.000/hfa75761_0f.htm.

316. MOSHER, *supra* note 202, at 255.

317. AIRD, *supra* note 193, at 91.

318. *Id.*

319. *Id.* at 92.

there are reports that babies were "thrown into boiling water and scalded to death or placed in airtight jars and smothered."[320]

Reports of prosecutions for infanticide are extremely rare because no enforcement mechanism exists for the relevant laws prohibiting infanticide.[321] Under Chinese law, the government typically fails to act unless the victim presses charges.[322] Because the victims here are infants, it is unlikely that charges could be brought, especially if the perpetrators are the infant's parents. Family-planning measures take precedence over individual rights. This protection typically exempts physicians from prosecution for infanticide because they are deemed to be carrying out the State's birth-rate goals.[323]

c. Sex-Selective Abortions. In addition to the abortions required by the family planning officials for over-quota pregnancies, many women choose to have sex-selective abortions after determining the sex of the baby through ultrasound.[324] Population expert Professor Chu Junhong states: "Prenatal sex selection was probably the primary cause, if not the sole cause, for the continuous rise of the sex ratio at birth."[325] The popularity of sex-selective abortions has grown with the increase of technology and the accessibility of mobile ultrasound machines.[326] Illegal scanning and backstreet hospitals can provide a sex scan for as little as fifty dollars.[327] The strong preference for male children has increased the use of ultrasound machines.[328] Although it has been forbidden by law since 1998 for ultrasound technicians or doctors to reveal the sex of the fetus,[329] many doctors will perform this service for a small fee or as a favor to friends and family.[330] Enforcement of the laws prohibiting the use of sonograms for sex selection is practically nonexistent, and law enforcement agents seem to be unable or unwilling to implement them.[331] Several factors contribute to the lack of enforcement, including widespread participation by the medical community, strict birth

---

320. Mosher, *supra* note 202, at 255.

321. LPWRI, *supra* note 72; Criminal Law, *supra* note 76, art. 241.

322. Li, *supra* note 8, at 167.

323. *Id.* at 169.

324. Milwertz, *supra* note 198, at 61.

325. Baculinao, *supra* note 2, para. 16.

326. Milwertz, *supra* note 198, at 60.

327. Baculinao, *supra* note 2, para. 15.

328. Milwertz, *supra* note 198, at 61.

329. *Id.*; Regulation on Prohibiting Fetal Sex Identification and Selective Termination of Pregnancy for Non-Medical Reasons (adopted by the Standing Comm. Nat'l People's Cong., Nov. 21, 1998),

http://www.unescap.org/esid/psis/population/database/poplaws/law_china/ch_record021.htm.

330. Li, *supra* note 8, at 170.

331. *Id.*

control measures, and the strong desire by couples for a son.[332] In a 2008 study by Professor Wei Xing Zhu, Professor Li Lu, and Therese Hesketh published in the *British Medical Journal*, these doctors concluded: "Sex selective abortion accounts for almost all the excess males. One particular variant of the one=child policy, which allows a second child if the first is a girl, leads to the highest sex ratios."[333]

d. Non-Registration of Children at Birth. Article 2 of the Maternal and Infant Health Care Law[334] declares: "The State shall develop the maternal and infant health care undertakings and provide necessary conditions and material aids so as to ensure that mothers and infants receive medical and health care services."[335] This law endeavors to provide increased rights to mothers and their children, but it only applies to sanctioned births within the strict family-planning guidelines.[336] Parents who give birth to an over-quota child and parents who adopt an abandoned child will often avoid registering the birth of the child to avoid steep fines or the risk of losing the child.[337] Many of the "missing women" in China and the unbalanced sex-ratios stem from underreporting or non-registration of female births.[338] Underreported births are tied to female abandonment or infanticide, and the non-registration of female children leads to fewer resources and fewer educational opportunities for these women as they grow older.[339]

Many provincial family-planning regulations punish parents with over-quota births by imposing stiff financial penalties.[340] Moreover, over-quota children are not entitled to State subsidies and are deprived of admission to public education and access to public health care.[341] Couples that have over-quota children also

---

332. *Id.*

333. Wei Xing Zhu, Li Lu & Therese Hesketh, *China's Excess Males, Sex Selective Abortion, and One Child Policy: Analysis of Data from 2005 National Intercensus Survey*, 338 BRIT. MED. J. 1211 (2008).

334. MIHCL, *supra* note 72.

335. *Id.*

336. Li, *supra* note 8, at 171.

337. Johnson et al., *supra* note 243, at 492–93.

338. MILWERTZ, *supra* note 198, at 60.

339. *Id.*

340. Li, *supra* note 8, at 157.

341. Tianjin Shi Jihua Shengyu Tiaoli [Tianjin Family Planning Regulations] art. 22 1111 1, 25, 27, 28 (adopted by the Standing Comm. Tianjin People's Cong., Nov. 2, 1988), 1989 Zhongguo Falu Nianjin [Law Year Book of China] 341; Shangdong Sheng Jihua Shengyu Tiaoli [Shandong Family Planning Regulations] arts. 29, 32, (adopted by the Standing Comm. Shandong People's Cong., July 20, 1988), 1989 Zhongguo Falu Nianjin [Law Year Book of China] 419; Anhui Sheng Jihua Shenyu Tiaoli [Anhui Family Planning Regulations], (adopted by the Standing Comm. Anhui People's Cong., Oct. 31, 1988), art. 22, 1989 Zhongguo Falu Nianjin [Law Year Book of China] 397, 399, *cited in* Li, *supra* note 8, at 157.

invalidate the benefits of their first child.[342] These parents are even required to pay back the benefits the first child received, and they also face large fines.[343] They are at risk for salary reductions or loss of their jobs.[344] These penalties also apply to parents who illegally adopt abandoned children.[345] In effect, the government punishes over-quota children for being born by withdrawing their entitlement (and that of their siblings) to basic services.[346]

B. Recent Changes to the One-Child Policy

In light of the growing scarcity of women in China and the surge in trafficking of baby girls, in 2004 the Chinese government "diversified" its birth control policy.[347] According to Population Vice-Minister Zhao Baige, one child is allowed in China's cities, two in the rural regions, and three in the ethnic regions.[348] China also began a "Girl Care Project" to encourage the birth of girls by cracking down on sex-selective abortions, female infanticide, and abandonment by rewarding families who give birth to girls.[349] Preferential treatment in housing, healthcare, and employment is now given to families with only daughters, as well as financial incentives and pensions.[350] In some provinces, school fees for girls have been reduced or eliminated, and propaganda banners advocate that preferring

---

342. Hebei Sheng Jihua Shengyu Tiaoli [Hebei Family Planning Regulations] art. 24 (adopted by the Standing Comm. Hebei People's Cong., Mar. 14, 1989), 1990 Zhongguo Falu Nianjin [Law Year Book of China] 422; Heilongjiang Sheng Jihua Shengyu Tiaoli [Heilongjiang Family Planning Regulations], art. 29 11 4 (adopted by the Standing Comm. Heilongjiang People's Cong., Dec. 13, 1989), in 1990 Zhongguo Falu Nianjin [Law Year Book of China] 457, *cited in* Li, *supra* note 8, at 157.

343. *Id.*

344. Heilongjiang Sheng Jihua Shengyu Tiaoli [Heilongjiang Family Planning Regulations], art. 29 11 2 (adopted by the Standing Comm. Heilongjiang People's Cong., Dec. 13, 1989), 1990 Zhongguo Falu Nianjin [Law Year Book of China] 457; Tianjin Shi Jihua Shengyu Tiaoli [Tianjin Family Planning Regulations] art. 22 1111 1, 25, 27, 28 (adopted by the Standing Comm. Tianjin People's Cong., Nov. 2, 1988), 1989 Zhongguo Falu Nianjin [Law Year Book of China] 341, *cited in* Li, *supra* note 8, at 157.

345. Hebei Sheng Jihua Shengyu Tiaoli [Hebei Family Planning Regulations] art. 24 (adopted by the Standing Comm. Hebei People's Cong., Mar. 14, 1989), 1990 Zhongguo Falu Nianjin [Law Year Book of China] 422; Heilongjiang Sheng Jihua Shengyu Tiaoli [Heilongjiang Family Planning Regulations], art. 29 ¶ 4 (adopted by the Standing Comm. Heilongjiang People's Cong., December 13, 1989), 1990 Zhongguo Falu Nianjin [Law Year Book of China] 457, *cited in* Li, *supra* note 8, at 157.

346. Li, *supra* note 8, at 157.

347. *See generally*, Baculinao, *supra* note 2.

348. *Id.*

349. *Id.*

350. Lesley Stahl, *China: Too Many Men, Lesley Stahl Reports on the Country's Unique Population Problem*, CBS NEWS, April 16, 2006,
http://www.cbsnews.com/stories/2006/04/13/60minutes/main1496589.shtml.

boys over girls is "old thinking."[351] Recently, reports have circulated in China about a new policy allowing two children to be born in a family in which both the husband and the wife were themselves only children.[352]

V. CHANGING ROLE OF WOMEN IN CHINESE SOCIETY

A. Low Image of Women in Chinese Society: Confucius

One of the fundamental teachings of Confucius found in his "Five Classics" is that an essential difference between men and women must be upheld to preserve the cosmic order.[353] Women are inferior to men because of their tempermental personalities and limited intellectual abilities.[354] Confucius emphasized the need for women to be quiet, obedient, neat, chaste, and hard-working within the home, all of which furthered their seclusion and isolation.[355] For centuries, Chinese women's feet were bound for aesthetic reasons that also rendered them crippled and dependent on men. Chinese women became increasingly viewed in society as a mere commodity as they cost their parents money in the form of a dowry, even though the girl children ultimately move out to live with the husband's family.[356]

B. Historical Patriarchy: Women as a Commodity

> *Daughters are like water that splashes out of the family and cannot be gotten back after marriage.*
> *—Traditional Chinese saying*

A strong preference for sons in China that has existed since the second and third millennia B.C. can be traced to the custom of ancestor worship.[357] This practice was reinforced by a strong patrilineal system that systematically discriminated against daughters.[358] Sons are responsible for caring for their parents' spirits in

---

351. *Id.*

352. *Official: Single-Child Parents in China Can Have Second Child*, Xinhua (Beijing), July 10, 2007, http://news.xinhuanet.com/english/2007-07/10/content_6356302.htm.

353. Guisso, *supra* note 9, at 48; *see also* CHINA'S STOLEN CHILDREN (HBO Documentary Films 2008), which provides a vivid example of the hardships that the One-Child Policy wields on Chinese families and on women in particular. The documentary confirms the human rights violations of women in China, the persistent discrimination against women, and the low opinion that many Chinese people have of women in Chinese society.

354. LIN YUTANG, MY COUNTRY AND MY PEOPLE 154 (1935).

355. *Id.* at 153.

356. HUDSON & Den Boer, *supra* note 310, at 135.

357. LEE & FENG, *supra* note 198, at 47.

358. *Id.*

the afterlife "so they do not wander for eternity as hungry ghosts."[359] Only sons could sacrifice to the family spirits or carry on the family name.[360] Daughters marry out of the family, are required to have a large dowry supplied by their father, but must support and take care of their husbands' parents.[361] In Chinese history, women were never full members of the family they were born into or the family they married into, and they could not inherit property.[362]

In the southeast of China, daughters are referred to as "goods on which one loses one's capital" as it costs money to raise a daughter, only to hand her over to her husband's family.[363] "The triple threat of patrilocality, male-oriented food provision systems, and the dowry" has made "female infanticide . . . a rational choice" in Chinese culture.[364] Today, there is no significant social security system in China, so sons are expected to take care of their parents financially in their old age.[365] Most men have higher earning power than women because the pay scale for men versus women remains unequal.[366] Couples prefer to have a son who can better afford to take care of them as well as extended family members in later life.[367]

In rural areas of China, women are held responsible for the sex of their children, and instances of physical assault, persistent abuse, violent beatings, and even murder have been documented for women who give birth to girls.[368] Decisions regarding fertility and childbearing still largely remain in the realm of the husband's family rather than this decision being up to the woman and her husband.[369] Mothers who give birth to sons receive a higher quality of medical care and better nutrition, and they are expected to perform less housework.[370] Male babies also receive better food, finer clothing, and more expensive gifts at traditional ceremonies, emphasizing the greater hopes parents have for male children.[371]

One of the goals of the Chinese Communist Revolution of 1949 was to achieve equality, including gender equality, by granting equal economic, social, and cultural rights to men and women.[372] Under the slogan, "Women hold up half the

---

359. Dugger, *supra* note 6.

360. Lee & Feng, *supra* note 198, at 47.

361. *Id.* at 60; Johnson et al., *supra* note 243, at 475.

362. Milwertz, *supra* note 198, at 46.

363. Hudson & den Boer, *supra* note 310, at 17.

364. *Id.* at 11.

365. Johnson et al., *supra* note 243, at 475.

366. Milwertz, *supra* note 198, at 155.

367. B.G. Rosenberg & Qicheng Jing, *A Revolution in Family Life: The Political and Social Structural Impact of China's One-Child Policy*, 52 J. Soc. Issues 51, 56 (1996).

368. Milwertz, *supra* note 198, at 16

369. *Id.* at 80.

370. Women's Health, *supra* note 4, at 29.

371. *Id.* at 29.

372. Hudson & den Boer, *supra* note 310, at 148.

sky," the new government led by Mao Zedong attempted to provide equal access to education and jobs for men and women.[373] Mao also tried to give women more domestic rights, marriage rights, and inheritance rights.[374] Yet despite the reforms under Mao, women were often placed in menial positions and paid far less than a man for similar work.[375] During the period of decentralization, privatization, and economic efficiency in the 1980s under the leadership of Deng Xiaoping, a huge number of government positions held by women were the first to be cut.[376]

Although women in China have increasingly entered the workforce, their identity is still strongly tied to their role as a wife and mother. Women are expected to maintain the household as well as work outside the home.[377] "A virtuous wife and good mother [is] . . . first of all defined in relation to how a woman minds her home, her husband, and her child."[378] Women also consistently receive lower wages then men even when their labor is the same.[379] A common saying in China is that a "fine worker who neglects her husband and beats her children is a bad woman. A fine worker who neglects his wife and beats his children is a fine worker."[380]

In 1996, it was reported that women make up the majority of the workers laid off or unemployed, and men are commonly preferred for hiring and promotion.[381] Women also work in more dangerous and untenable working conditions, exposed to toxins and accident-prone factories.[382] Female migrant workers face the harshest working conditions. They are prone to exploitation and abuse from employers because of their economic desperation and generally submissive natures.[383] Protection for pregnant female migrant workers is usually nonexistent and contributes to a high level of gynecological disorders.[384] Sexual harassment in the workplace is a common phenomenon, and many women report that the degree and frequency of harassment has risen.[385]

---

373. Emily Honig & Gail Hershatter, Personal Voices: Chinese Women in the 1980s 24 (1988).

374. *Id.* at 148–49.

375. *Id.* at 150.

376. Honig & Hershatter, *supra* note 373, at 250.

377. *Id.* at 255; Milwertz, *supra* note 198, at 154.

378. Milwertz, *supra* note 198, at 167.

379. *Id.* at 155.

380. Margery Wolf, Revolution Postponed 182 (1985).

381. Human Rights in China, *supra* note 70, at 299.

382. *Id.*

383. *Id.* at 300.

384. *Id.* at 301.

385. *Id.*

C. Impact on Men of Shortage of Women

The Chinese vernacular for young adult males who will never marry is *guang gun-er*, or "bare branches"—those who will never marry because they cannot find spouses.[386] Scholars across a wide array of social sciences (including anthropology, biology, criminology, psychology, organization behavior, and sociology) agree that large numbers of bare branches lead to increased instability, violence, and a potential threat to Chinese society.[387] Bare branches tend to share similar characteristics: they belong primarily to the lowest socioeconomic class; they are likely to be underemployed or unemployed; they are typically transient with few ties to the communities where they work; and they live with other bare branches, creating a distinctive bachelor subculture.[388]

In a speech on the demographic crisis in China, Li Weixiong, an advisor to China's political consultative conference on population issues, states "[s] uch serious gender disproportion poses a major threat to the healthy, harmonious and sustainable growth of the nation's population and would trigger such crimes and social problems as abduction of women and prostitution."[389] An official magazine entitled *Theory and Time* published in Shenyang predicts that the disproportionate gender balance will lead to "a large army of bachelors composed of 90 million men" as well as a severe breakdown in social order and the abduction and sale of women.[390] Other scholars agree that as Chinese families consciously select male children over female children, there "will be a significant increase in societal, and possibly intersocietal, violence"[391]—a terrifying prospect for an elite governing class.[392]

In addition to the high probability of civil unrest, the consequences for women in high sex-ratio countries are dire and typically cause their already low societal status to decline further.[393] "[T]heir levels of literacy and labor-force participation are low," and "[t]heir suicide rate, relative to men's, is also high."[394] Women are also more likely to be kidnapped or sold.[395] "From 1991 through 1996, Chinese police freed 88,000 kidnapped women and children and arrested 143,000 people

---

386. Hudson & den Boer, *supra* note 310, at 187–88.

387. *Id.* at 20.

388. *Id.* at 188–90.

389. McCurry & Allison, *supra* note 275, at 3.

390. Graham Hutchings, *Female Infanticide 'Will Lead to Army of Bachelors,'* The Telegraph (London), Apr. 11, 1997, http://www.telegraph.co.uk/htmlContent.jhtml?html=/archive/1997/04/1 1/wchi1 1.html.

391. Hudson & den Boer, *supra* note 310, at 200.

392. Robert Wright, The Moral Animal: The New Science of Evolutionary Psychology 98–101 (1994).

393. Hudson & den Boer, *supra* note 310, at 202.

394. Scott J. South & Katherine Trent, *Sex Ratios and Women's Roles: A Cross-National Analysis*, 93 Am. J. Soc. 1096, 1112 (1988).

395. Yiyung, *supra* note 15, at 48.

for participating in the slave trade."[396] In a major campaign against human trafficking in 2000, police claim to have rescued 100,000 women and children in addition to breaking up kidnapping gangs.[397] These figures are viewed as conservative since law enforcement agencies face large obstacles when trying to enforce the kidnapping and slavery laws. Moreover, there is strong community support of men who buy kidnapped women.[398]

The black market trade in infants, especially girls, has increased dramatically due to the desire of some childless couples to have a daughter. The growing sex trade and the increased popularity of foreign adoptions has caused some orphanages to buy healthy children from parents or traffickers.[399] High sex-ratio societies usually have higher levels of prostitution.[400] During the 1990s, an increased number of brothels was reported, servicing mainly urban areas populated by unmarried migrant workers.[401]

VI. POLICY SUGGESTIONS TO COMBAT SEX TRAFFICKING IN CHINA

China must improve its trafficking record. To do so, it must provide adequate funding to local and regional governments to effectively implement the new National Action Plan to Combat Trafficking. The Chinese judiciary is currently under serious reform in order to build people's confidence in the legal system.[402] The judiciary must become and remain independent, and its officials must prosecute and severely punish sex traffickers as well as recruiters and employers of forced laborers. The government must provide meaningful protection to foreign and domestic victims of forced labor and sex trafficking, including formal victim identification, rehabilitation, and financial as well as psychological and medical services. The legal system must actively investigate, prosecute, and convict public officials who participate in or facilitate trafficking. Chinese trafficking laws need to be revised to criminalize all forms of labor that rise to the level of slavery. Laws must also be revised to criminalize sex trafficking effectively and in accordance with international standards. The Chinese government must conduct widespread

---

396. *Id.*

397. *China's Kidnap Victims Freed*, BBC NEWS, Sept. 16, 2000, http://news.bbc.co.uk/2/hi/asia-pacific/927309.stm.

398. Yiyung, *supra* note 15, at 48.

399. Beth Loyd, *China's Lost Children*, ABC NEWS, May 12, 2008, http://a.abcnews.com/International/story?id=4774224&page=1.

400. HUDONS & DEN BOER, *supra* note 310, at 205.

401. Vincent E. Gil et al., *Plum Blossoms and Pheasants: Prostitutes, Prostitution, and Social Control Measures in Contemporary China*, 38 INT'L J. OFFENDER THERAPY & COMP. CRIMINOLOGY 322–23 (1994).

402. *See generally* Congressional-Executive Commission on China 2005 Annual Report, http://www.cecc.gov/pages/annualRpt/annualRpt05/2005_5c_ judicial.php#2b.

public awareness campaigns through local nongovernmental organizations to inform the public of the dangers and risks of trafficking.[403]

In addition, China must provide foreign victims trafficked into China with legal alternatives to the current inhumane practice of deporting them to their own countries where they may face serious hardship or retribution upon reentry. China must adhere to its obligations under the 1951 Refugee Convention and its 1967 Protocol by not deporting North Korean women protected by these treaties. China must also cooperate with the United Nations Refugee Agency in the exercise of its functions.

The national laws of China that protect rights of women and children must be enforced. The health and reproductive rights found in the Law Protecting Women's Rights and Interests[404] and the Maternal and Infant Health Care Law[405] must not be subjugated to State policies that deny individual rights. China cannot allow coercive measures to force women to adhere to the One-Child Policy. Greater law enforcement measures must be taken against doctors and those individuals who murder and abandon their own infant daughters, as well as those who choose sex-selective abortions in order to have a male child. The State should actively prosecute these cases rather than rely on the families of the victims (who are often themselves the perpetrators) to press charges. Medical personnel who perform illegal ultrasound scans or infanticide must be held legally accountable.

Finally, the One-Child Policy must be drastically revised to comport with basic international human rights laws (such as CEDAW, CAT, and CRC) to which China is a signatory. The population growth can be checked by providing incentives to limit the number of children rather than by inflicting coercive or harsh tactics.

China must also begin to address effectively the long-standing cultural prejudices against women. Government practices that promote active discrimination against women in the country must be stopped. Although the inheritance laws in China state that males and females are equal in their right to inheritance, in practice women are rarely given a share of their parents' estate as they are considered part of their husband's family after marriage.[406]

If strict enforcement of the existing laws in China were a government priority, women in China could be given equality in their inheritance rights. They should have wage parity and job opportunities so that men and women alike are able to sufficiently care for their parents in later years. Substantial pension

---

403. *See* TIP REPORT 2008, *supra* note 17, at 92.

404. LPWRI, *supra* note 72.

405. MIHCL, *supra* note 72.

406. Law of Succession (promulgated by Order No. 24 of the President of the People's Republic of China, Apr. 10, 1985, effective Oct. 1, 1985), http://www.unescap.org/esid/psis/population/database/poplaws/law_china/ch_record004.htm.

systems or retirement plans should also be established for people in rural as well as urban areas in China to alleviate the elderly's high level of economic dependence upon their children for financial security in agricultural communities. Finally, China must address the illiteracy rate of over 100 million women by abolishing school fees that exclude rural girls from the right to education.[407] Textbooks in China must be revised to eliminate gender stereotypes. The implementation of these measures could pave the way toward cultural reform in China. The revision of the One-Child Policy, the eradication of male preference, and the elimination of discrimination against women in Chinese society will reduce trafficking in women.

VII. LISA SEE, *SNOW FLOWER AND THE SECRET FAN*

A. Women's Life in China in the Nineteenth Century

Lisa See has written a beautiful novel that takes the reader back in time to nineteenth century China when wives and daughters were forced to obey[408] and to endure the excruciating pain of footbinding.[409] Women then lived in almost total seclusion in the private area of the house known as the women's quarters upstairs.[410] To survive this isolation and inhumanity perpetrated upon an entire gender, women in a remote Hunan county developed their own secret language called *nu shu* ("women's writing"), which was their own coded form of communication and expression of rebellion,[411] if not empowerment. Some girls in this remote and secluded male-dominated society were lucky enough to be paired by their parents to another similarly situated little girl (*laotong* or "old same"). The two little girls would remain emotionally tied all their lives, painting letters to each other in coded communication on silk fans, embroidering secret messages on handkerchiefs, and writing stories for each other in order to survive in their utter loneliness and hopeless existence. This secret coded language was their only source of pleasure and communication with the outside world.

---

407. CEDAW Report, *supra* note 73, ¶ 257.

408. Lisa See, Snow Flower and the Secret Fan, A Novel 24 (2005) ("I always understood that two Confucian ideas ruled our lives. The first was the Three Obediences: "when a girl, obey your father; when a wife, obey your husband; when a widow, obey your son.").

409. *Id.* at 28 ("Mama yanked me out of the chair. The word *pain* does not begin to describe the feeling. My toes were locked under my feet so that my body weight fell entirely on the top of those appendages. I tried to balance backward on my heels. When Mama saw this, she hit me. "Walk!" I did the best I could. As I shuffled toward the window, Mama reached down and pulled Third Sister to her feet, dragged her to Elder Sister, and said, "Take her back and forth across the room ten times.").

410. *Id.* at 4 ("I have spent my life in upstairs women's rooms.").

411. *Id.* at 4 ("My only rebellion came in the form of *nu shu*, our women's secret writing.").

Lily is the narrator of this very sad and realistic story about her life with her dear friend Snow Flower whom she has known since the age of seven. Snow Flower is the unlucky girl who marries a brutal man (the "butcher"). Snow Flower commits the ultimate sin of giving birth to a girl child. Her husband continues to beat her senselessly throughout their horrible marriage simply because she fails to conceive a male child.[412] Lily, on the other hand, marries a kind man and has a better life. The whole novel rests on the antithesis between Lily's good life with a kind husband and Snow Flower's horrid life with a cruel husband.

The story begins when Snow Flower writes a secret poem for Lily in *nu shu* on a silk fan that seals their deep female friendship for life. Lily describes in vivid detail the torturous process of footbinding that she and all the girls in her family and all the girls in China were forced to endure. Footbinding was done for esthetic reasons, to please men so as to attract the best husband possible. Footbinding involved breaking the bones of the little girl's feet, folding the toes towards the heel, and being forced by beatings and threats to walk on these crippled feet even though the pain was excruciating.[413] One of Lily's sisters actually died from "the pus, blood and infection caused by this long-standing custom and dangerous procedure."[414]

---

412. *Id.* at 207 ("He proceeded to beat her so badly that she miscarried in a violent gush of black blood that stained the icy slopes throughout our campsite. She was not very far along, so we never found a fetus, but the butcher was convinced that he'd rid the world of another girl. 'There is nothing so evil as a woman's heart,' he recited again and again, as though none of us had heard that saying before . . . When I look back, I think it was a miracle that Snow Flower survived those last two weeks in the mountains as she passively accepted beating after beating. Her body weakened from the loss of blood from the miscarriage. Her body bruised and tore from the daily punishment her husband rained down on her.").

413. *Id.* at 30 ("One day, as I made one of my trips across the room, I heard something crack. One of my toes had broken. I thought the sound was something internal to my own body, but it was so sharp that everyone in the women's chamber heard it. My mother's eyes zeroed in on me. 'Move! Progress is finally being made!' Walking, my whole body trembled. By nightfall the eight toes that needed to break had broken, but I was still made to walk. I felt my broken toes under the weight of every step I took, for they were loose in my shoes. The freshly created space where once there had been a joint was now a gelatinous infinity of torture.").

414. *Id.* at 31. "Mama began to unwrap the bindings. A disgusting odor infused the room. Aunt gagged. Although it was snowing, Elder Sister tore away the rice paper that covered the windows to give the stench an exit. Finally, Third Sister's feet were fully exposed. The pus was dark green and the blood had coagulated into brownish, putrid mud. Third Sister was brought to a sitting position and her unbound feet set into a steaming bowl of water. She was so far away in her mind that she did not cry out . . . She died four days later, enduring more suffering and pain than was fair for such a short life." *Id.* at 33.

Matchmaking and early arranged marriages[415] were the custom in China in the nineteenth century, and this custom continues even today in other modern nations such as India. Lily writes that in China women were considered "worthless branches on the family tree . . . [a] drain [on] the family resources" because the father must provide a dowry for a daughter even though he reaps no real "benefit" because the married daughter must by custom leave to remain under the sometimes tyrannical rule of her husband's family. "We are raised by one family for another," says Lily.[416] It seems that women in China were fated to lead a bad life. "But this is how it is for women. You can't avoid your fate. It is predestined."[417]

Lily explains that women in Chinese society are "seen as completely useless . . . a burden" to their families, forced to marry "into new families; go to our husbands sight unseen, do bed business with them as total strangers, and submit to the demands of our mothers-in-law. If [women] are lucky, we have sons and secure our positions in our husband's homes. If not, we are faced with the scorn of our mothers-in-law, the ridicule of our husband's concubines, and the disappointed faces of our daughters." [418]

Women are raised to be silent and obedient. The woman's subservience to a man, her enslavement to her father and husband, and her imprisonment in isolated quarters of the house continues throughout her life in the many roles she is forced to play in Chinese society. Women are born for one purpose: to give birth to a son. "My husband says it is better to have a dog than a daughter."[419] When Snow Flower gives birth to a dead baby girl, she writes a letter to her dear friend Lily that reveals the depths of women's plight in China:

> "Lily,
>
> My daughter was born dead. She left without planting roots, so she knew nothing of the sorrows of life. I held her feet in my hands. They would never know the agony of footbinding. I touched her eyes. They would never know the sadness of leaving her natal home, of seeing her mother for the last time, of saying goodbye to a dead child. I put my fingers over her heart. It would never know pain, sorrow, loneliness, shame. I think of her in the afterworld. Is my mother with her? I don't know either of their fates . . . I cannot stop thinking about my dead baby girl.
>
> Snow Flower[420]

---

415. *Id.* at 41. Girls as young as eight or nine in China were matched up by a matchmaker for marriage.

416. *Id.* at 59.

417. *Id.* at 78.

418. *Id.* at 127.

419. *Id.* at 163.

420. *Id.* at 165–66.

Lily tells us that stillbirths were common in China, but they were considered dreadful only if the baby was a son.[421] The duty of all women then was to keep trying to give birth to sons.[422] Snow Flower miscarried four daughters; she says, "If I had carried all my children to term, I would have four daughters—a disaster."[423] Only sons in China were entitled to an education, not daughters.[424] The isolation of girls into the private sector further guaranteed their ignorance.[425] A woman's worth was measured by her husband's status, and once her husband died, the widow had nothing more to do but contemplate suicide.[426] Lily sums up the sad life of women in China, a cultural slice of life that gives us a window into the root causes of trafficking in modern-day China:

> If it is perfectly acceptable for a widow to disfigure herself or commit suicide to save face for her husband's family, why should a mother not be moved to extreme action by the loss of a child or children? We are their caretakers. We love them. We nurse them when they are sick. In the case of sons, we prepare them to take their first steps into the men's realm. In the case of daughters, we bind their feet, teach them our secret writing, and train them to be good wives, daughter-in-laws, and mothers, so they will fit into the upstairs chambers of their new homes. But no woman should live longer than her children. It is against the law of nature. If she does, why wouldn't she wish to leap from a cliff, hang from a branch, or swallow lye?[427]

Wife abuse may have been common in nineteenth-century China, and Snow Flower exemplifies the despondent, beaten, starved, and abused wife who was subject to the constant brutality of her husband.[428] Snowflower's only source of joy was the coded language with which she used to communicate to her spiritual sister, Lily. By decoding the letters and placing them in the context of the Chinese culture, we can better understand how and why the trafficking of women in China today has developed into such a big business despite the serious human rights violations perpetrated on defenseless little girls and undervalued women.

421. *Id.* at 166.
422. *Id.*
423. *Id.* at 185.
424. *Id.* at 169.
425. *Id.* at 174.
426. *Id.* at 175.
427. *Id.* at 210.
428. *Id.*

VIII. CONCLUSION

Failures in China's One-Child Policy, the inadequate enforcement of Chinese laws protecting women, and the longstanding cultural preference for males have led to discrimination against women and an increase in forced prostitution and trafficking in China. Millions of women are missing in China because of female child abandonment and infanticide. The scarcity of women has resulted in a major increase in the trafficking and sale of foreign women into China. As China shifted from a planned economy to a market economy in 1979, the price of women in China increased in accordance with the market economy principle of supply and demand. The One-Child Policy has caused women to become a high-cost commodity.

To reverse the deleterious effects of the One-Child Policy and its commodification of women, the Chinese government must make a commitment to implement laws and policies that can reverse long-standing cultural trends and combat discriminatory traditions against women. Civil rights laws enacted in the United States in the 1960s have had a profoundly ameliorative affect on reducing discrimination against African-Americans in American society. There is no reason why the adoption and strict enforcement of Chinese civil rights and trafficking laws could not similarly result in profound cultural change and equality for women in a traditionally male-dominated society now in transition. Since 1979, China has instituted economic reform policies that miraculously work in harmony with a Communist political system. Now China needs to perform another miracle: the adoption of cultural reforms that produce gender parity and that stop the marginalization of women in Chinese society. Only then will the lucrative business of trafficking in women be reduced, if not eliminated entirely.

PART E

CHILDREN'S HUMAN RIGHTS

10. THE CULTURE OF VIOLENCE
Child Soldiers, Slavery, and the Trafficking of Children*

I. INTRODUCTION

A. Definitions

Children suffer so much in this culture of violence that characterizes the twenty-first century. Very young children are being forced to engage in armed conflict with or without their consent. The prevalent use of children in armed combat is nothing less than a contemporary manifestation of slavery. It is a form of human trafficking that is as serious and as lucrative as the international crimes of trafficking in weapons and drugs.[1] Trafficking is defined as the illegal trade of contraband goods, usually across borders, in order to make a profit.[2] Trafficking in persons, especially women and children, is the purchase and sale of human beings as cargo for the purpose of engaging in exploitative forms of labor such as sex work[3] or participation in armed conflict. Trafficking in children for their use on the battlefield is a human rights violation that rises to the level of slavery.[4]

---

* Parts of this study were presented at a Symposium on the Challenges of Children's Rights sponsored by the Center for Global Legal Studies at Thomas Jefferson School of Law in San Diego, CA. Professor Jonathan Todres and I were the co-organizers of the Symposium that took place on March 2, 2007 at Thomas Jefferson School of Law. A longer version of that presentation was published in 31 FORDHAM INT'L L.J. 416–486 (2008). That article has been expanded, updated, and revised for this book. I have done extensive research and writing in the field of human trafficking, sex trafficking of women, and the economic implications of women and children trafficked for sex work. I wish to thank Nichole Denton for her assistance with the research of the original published article on child soldiers. I also wish to thank June MacLeod, the librarian at the Thomas Jefferson School of Law, for her able assistance with the research of this study.

1. *See generally* Susan Tiefenbrun, *Sex Sells But Drugs Don't Talk: Trafficking of Women Sex Workers and an Economic Solution*, 24 T. JEFFERSON L. REV. 161 (2002).

2. *See* Sandrine Valentine, *Trafficking of Child Soldiers: Expanding the United Nations Convention on the Rights of the Child and Its Optional Protocol on the Involvement of Children in Armed Conflict*, 9 NEW ENG. J. INT'L & COMP. L. 109, 109 (2003); *see also* U.N. CHILDREN'S FUND (UNICEF), CHILD PROTECTION INFORMATION SHEETS 27 (2006), http://www.unicef.org/publications/files/Child_Protection_Information_Sheets.pdf.

3. *See* Tiefenbrun, *supra* note 1, at 167; *see also* Valentine, *supra* note 2, at 109.

4. *See* Victims of Trafficking and Violence Protection Act of 2000, 22 U.S.C. § 7105 (2000) [hereinafter TVPA], for the link between trafficking of persons and slavery. The Rome Statute that founded the International Criminal Court (ICC) also recognizes trafficking in persons as "enslavement" (Article 7), which is considered a "crime against humanity."

The United Nations Protocol to Prevent, Suppress and Punish Trafficking in Persons, Especially Women and Children, Supplementing the United Nations Convention Against Transnational Organized Crime ("Palermo Protocol")[5] defines trafficking as:

> [T]he recruitment, transportation, transfer, harboring or receipt of persons, by means of the threat or use of force or other forms of coercion, of abduction, of fraud, of deception, or the abuse of power or of a position of vulnerability or of the giving or receiving of payments or benefits to achieve the consent of a person having control over another person, for the purpose of exploitation.[6]

The recruitment of a child (i.e., a person under the age of eighteen) for the purpose of sexual exploitation or participation in armed conflict falls under the ambit of "trafficking in persons."[7]

The international definition of the trafficking of child soldiers involves three necessary elements: consent, exploitation, and movement within a country or across a border.[8] A child soldier is "trafficked" when there is forced recruitment or no genuine voluntary recruitment; when the recruitment is done without the informed consent of the person's parent or legal guardians; and when such

---

Rome Statute of the International Criminal Court, United Nations Diplomatic Conference of Plenipotentiaries on the Establishment of an International Criminal Court, Rome, Italy, June 15–16, 1998, U.N.Doc. A/CONF.183/9 (1998), art. 7 (entered into force July 1, 2002) [hereinafter Rome Statute]. On the issue of trafficking of persons as a contemporary form of slavery, *see generally* Susan Tiefenbrun, *The Cultural, Political, and Legal Climate Behind the Fight to Stop Trafficking in Women: William J. Clinton's Legacy to Women's Rights*, 12 CARDOZO J. L. & GENDER 855 (2006); Susan Tiefenbrun, *The Domestic and International Impact of the U.S. Victims of Trafficking Protection Act of 2000: Does Law Deter Crime?* 2 LOY. U. CHI. INT'L L. REV. 193 (2005), *reprinted and completely updated in* 38 CASE W. RES. J. INT'L L. 249 (2007); Susan Tiefenbrun, *Sex Slavery in the United States and Its Law to Stop It Here and Abroad*, 11 WM. & MARY J. WOMEN & L. 317 (2005); Susan Tiefenbrun, *Copyright Infringement, Sex Trafficking, and Defamation in the Fictional Life of a Geisha*, 10 MICH. J. GENDER & L. 327 (2004); Susan Tiefenbrun, *The Saga of Susannah: A U.S. Remedy for Sex Trafficking in Women: The Victims of Trafficking and Violence Protection Act of 2000*, 2001 UTAH L. REV. 107 (2002); Tiefenbrun, *Sex Sells*, *supra* note 1, at 161.

5. U.N. Protocol to Prevent, Suppress, and Punish Trafficking in Persons, Especially Women and Children, supplementing the United Nations Convention Against Transnational Organized Crime, G.A. Res. 55/25, Annex II, U.N. GAOR, 55th Sess., U.N. Doc. A/RES/55/25 (2001) [hereinafter Palermo Protocol].

6. *Id.* art. 3(a).

7. *Id.* art. 3(c). In the Palermo Protocol a "child" is any person under eighteen years of age. *Id.* art. 3(d). The definition of a child is controversial because the age that determines when a child becomes an adult differs in several international treaties.

8. *See* Valentine, *supra* note 2, at 116–19.

person was not fully informed of the duties involved in the military service.[9] Child soldiering is a form of child trafficking because the acts required of a child soldier are dangerous enough to interfere with a child's fundamental human right to education, health, and development.[10]

The abduction and employment of children as soldiers is a form of exploitative labor tantamount to slavery. Child soldiering is listed as "one of the worst forms of child labor" in the Convention Concerning the Prohibition and Immediate Action for the Elimination of the Worst Forms of Child Labour ("ILO Worst Forms of Child Labour Convention 182").[11] In the ILO Worst Forms of Child Labour Convention 182, child soldiering is included as a form of slavery on the same list as "all forms of slavery or practices similar to slavery, such as the sale and trafficking of children, debt bondage and serfdom and forced or compulsory labour, including forced or compulsory recruitment of children for use in armed conflict."[12]

The trafficking of child soldiers is directly connected to sexual violence and the sexual exploitation of children who are mainly, but not exclusively, young girls.[13] *Child sexual exploitation* is defined as a situation in which an individual takes "unfair advantage of some imbalance of power between themselves and another person under the age of eighteen in order to sexually use them."[14] The United Nations Children's Fund (UNICEF) draws attention to the economic benefits of child sexual exploitation when "a second party benefits, through making

---

9. *See* Optional Protocol to the Convention on the Rights of the Child on the Involvement of Children in Armed Conflict, G.A. Res. 54/263, Annex I, art. 3, U.N. GAOR, 54th Sess., Supp. No. 49, U.N. Doc. A/54/49 (2000) (entered into force Feb. 12, 2002) [hereinafter Children in Armed Conflict Protocol]; *see also* Jisha S. Vachachira, U.N. Reports, *Report 2002: Implementation of the Optional Protocol to the Convention on the Rights of the Child on the Involvement of Children in Armed Conflict*, 18 N.Y.L. SCH. J. HUM. RTS. 543 (2002).

10. *See generally* Rebecca Rios-Kohn, *The Convention on the Rights of the Child: Progress and Challenges*, 5 GEO. J. ON FIGHTING POVERTY 139 (1998).

11. Convention Concerning the Prohibition and Immediate Action for the Elimination of the Worst Forms of Child Labour (I.L.O. No. 182), arts. 1–3, June 17, 1999, 38 I.L.M. 1207, 1208 (1999) [hereinafter ILO Worst Forms of Child Labour Convention 182].

12. *See id.* art. 3; *see also* Recommendation Concerning the Prohibition and Immediate Action for the Elimination of the Worst Forms of Child Labour (Recommendation 190), art. 12(a), June 17, 1999, 38 I.L.M. 1211, 1213 http://www.ilo.org/public/english/standards/relm/ilc/ilc87/com-chir.htm [hereinafter ILO Recommendation 190].

13. *See* UZODINMA IWEALA, BEASTS OF NO NATION 83–85 (2005) (describing a young boy soldier who is sodomized and forced to engage in sex with his male commander on a regular basis).

14. Julia O'Connell Davidson, *The Sex Exploiter*, Second World Congress Against the Sexual Exploitation of Children 8, 8-9 (2001), http://www.csecworldcongress.org/PDF/en/Yokohama/Background_reading/Theme_papers/Theme%20paper%20The%20Sex%20Exploiter.pdf.

a profit or through a *quid pro quo*, through sexual activity involving a child."[15] The exploitation of child soldiers is typically accompanied by brutality and sexual violence. "Child soldiers serve within militaries and armed groups in which complete cooperation and obedience is demanded, in contexts where moral and legal safeguards against their abuse may have broken down. In this context sexual violence becomes sexual exploitation."[16]

Very often children are abducted from one place to another (from their home to a camp where they are trained and then to a field of combat where they kill).[17] But children do not have to actually cross a border to be trafficked. If they are moved within their own country and forced to engage in exploitative labor such as dangerous armed combat, this constitutes child trafficking.[18]

Thus, using children against their will to engage in armed combat involves human trafficking and unfair labor practices that rise to the level of child slavery. Slavery is one of the most heinous crimes imaginable, especially when it is inflicted on the most vulnerable victims—our children.

B. Extent of Child Soldiering Worldwide

Children who are on the move because they are displaced and impoverished by war or civil unrest are particularly vulnerable for abduction and forced child soldiering. In 2000, about thirteen million children were displaced as a result of warring conflicts.[19] During the civil war that lasted seventeen years in Sierra Leone, more than one million children were displaced, and twenty-five thousand children (some as young as six)[20] were abducted and forced to become members of armed groups.[21] The recruitment of children into armed conflict has claimed the lives of more than two million children, left more than six million children maimed or permanently disabled, caused one million children to be orphaned,

---

15. UNICEF, *supra* note 2, at 27.

16. Lisa Alfredson, Sexual Exploitation of Child Soldiers: An Exploration and Analysis of Global Dimensions and Trends 1 (2001), http://www.reliefweb.int/rw/lib.nsf/db900SID/LGEL-5RPBPA/$FILE/csusc-exploit.pdf?Open Element.

17. *See* Marsha L. Hackenberg, *Can the Optional Protocol for the Convention on the Rights of the Child Protect the Ugandan Child Soldier?*, 10 Ind. Int'l & Comp. L. Rev. 417, 426 (2000).

18. *See* Valentine, *supra* note 2, at 116–19.

19. *See generally* Colin MacMullin & Maryanne Loughry, *Investigating Psychosocial Adjustment of Former Child Soldiers in Sierra Leone and Uganda*, 17 J. Refugee Stud. 460 (2004).

20. *See* Payam Akhavan, *The Lord's Resistance Army Case: Uganda's Submission of First State Referral to the International Criminal Court*, 99 Am. J. Int'l L. 403, 407 (2005). *See generally* Nsongurua J. Udombana, *War Is Not Child's Play! International Law and the Prohibition of Children's Involvement in Armed Conflicts*, 20 Temp. Int'l & Comp. L.J. 57 (2006).

21. *See* MacMullin & Loughry, *supra* note 19, at 461.

afflicted ten million children with serious psychological trauma, and made twelve million children refugees.[22] Currently, over three hundred thousand children, most of them ranging in ages from eleven to fifteen, are serving as child soldiers in fifty countries in every region of the world.[23] With so many countries recruiting children by force, deception, and coercion to serve in armed conflicts, it is fair to say that children of today are "the world's most endangered species."[24]

Although the participation of children in armed conflict is not new—it occurred in World War II[25]—child soldiering today is a widespread phenomenon, prevalent particularly in developing countries where political, economic, and social instability are more commonplace and where approximately half the population are children.[26] Save the Children reported that hundreds of thousands of underage soldiers are currently being forced to fight around the world, despite guidelines set forth ten years ago in the Cape Town Principles[27] of 1997 that established eighteen as the minimum age for recruitment.[28] Children have served in government forces, paramilitaries, or in opposition forces in Colombia, Mexico, Peru, Turkey, Yugoslavia, Algeria, Angola, Burundi, Chad, Democratic Republic of Congo, Eritrea, Ethiopia, Rwanda, Sierra Leone, Somalia, Sudan, Uganda, Afghanistan, Iran, Iraq, Israel and the Occupied Territories, Lebanon, India, Indonesia, Myanmar, Nepal, Pakistan, the Philippines, Solomon Islands, Papua New Guinea, Sri Lanka, East Timor, Tajikistan, and Uzbekistan.[29] The use

---

22. *See* Udombana, *supra* note 20, at 67–68.

23. *See generally* Abigail Leibig, *Child Soldiers in Northern Uganda: Do Current Legal Frameworks Offer Sufficient Protection?*, 3 NW. U. J. INT'L HUM. RTS. 6 (2005).

24. Udombana, *supra* note 20, at 68.

25. *See* P.W. SINTER, CHILDREN AT WAR 14–15 (2005). "The Hitler Jugend were young boys who had received quasi-military training as part of a political program to maintain Nazi rule through indoctrination . . . Hitler's regime ordered these boys to fight as well . . . Lightly armed and mostly sent out in small ambush squads, scores of Hitler Jugend were killed in futile skirmishes, all occurring after the war had essentially been decided." *Id.*

26. *See* MacMullin & Loughry, *supra* note 19, at 460.

27. UNICEF, CAPE TOWN ANNOTATED PRINCIPLES AND BEST PRACTICE ON THE PREVENTION OF RECRUITMENT OF CHILDREN INTO THE ARMED FORCES AND DEMOBILIZATION AND SOCIAL REINTEGRATION OF CHILD SOLDIERS IN AFRICA (1997), http://iggi.unesco.or.kr/web/iggi_docs/02/952579100.pdf [hereinafter CAPE TOWN ANNOTATED PRINCIPLES].

28. *See* Nick Tattersall, *Child Soldiers Still Recruited 10 Years After Pact*, REUTERS, Feb. 5, 2007, http://www.reuters.com/article/homepageCrisis/idUSL05604214._CH_.2400.

29. *See* Human Rights Watch, *Where Child Soldiers Are Being Used*, http://www.hrw.org/campaigns/crp/where.htm (last visited Oct. 25, 2007).

of child soldiers is still occurring in the Western Hemisphere,[30] Europe,[31] Africa,[32] the Middle East, Central Asia,[33] and Asia.[34] Today fighting forces still recruit child soldiers in Afghanistan, Chad, Colombia, Democratic Republic of Congo, Ivory Coast, Myanmar, Nepal, the Philippines, Sri Lanka, Somalia, Sudan, and Uganda.[35] Graca Machel, the former first lady of Mozambique and the wife of Nelson Mandela who served as a special expert for the United Nations on the issue of child soldiers, wrote a ground-breaking report on child soldiering, summing up the extent of the use of child soldiers and its significance:

> These statistics are shocking enough, but more chilling is the conclusion to be drawn from them: more and more of the world is being sucked into a desolate moral vacuum. This is a space devoid of the most basic human values; a space in which children are slaughtered, raped, and maimed; a space in which children are exploited as soldiers; a space in which children are starved and exposed to extreme brutality. Such unregulated terror and violence

---

30. *See* SINTER, *supra* note 25, at 16.

> In the Americas since 1990, child soldiers have fought in Colombia, Ecuador, El Salvador, Guatemala, Mexico (in the Chiapas conflict), Nicaragua, Paraguay, and Peru. The most substantial numbers are in Colombia. There, more than eleven thousand children are being used as soldiers . . . one out of every four irregular combatants is underage . . . Child soldiers in Colombia are nicknamed "little bells" by the military that use them as expendable sentries and "little bees" by the FARC guerrillas, because they "sting" their enemies before they know they are under attack.

Id.

31. *See id.* at 18–19.

> On the European continent, children under eighteen years of age have served in both British government forces and their opposition in Northern Ireland and on all sides in the Bosnian conflict . . . It is in Turkey, though, where the most child soldiers in Europe are found, in the Kurdish Workers' Party ("PKK") . . . In 1998 it was reported that the PKK had three thousand underage children within its ranks, with the youngest reported PKK fighter being an armed seven-year-old. Ten percent of these were girls.

Id.

32. *See id.* at 19–21. Countries in Africa that employ child soldiers include Sierra Leone, Angola, Liberia, Uganda, Rwanda, Burundi, Kenya, Central African Republic, Tanzania, Congo-Brazzaville, Ivory Coast, Ethiopia, and Democratic Republic of the Congo. *See id.*

33. *See id.* at 21–22, 24. Today, children are fighting in Algeria, Azerbaijan, Egypt, Iran (even though it is against *Shari'a* law), Iraq, Lebanon, Sudan, Tajikistan, Yemen, including children younger than fifteen serving in a number of radical Islamic groups, and Palestine. Sudan has the largest use of child soldiers in the region, and as many as one hundred thousand children have served on both sides of the civil war. *See id.*

34. *See id.* at 26–27. The practice of using child soldiers is highly prevalent in Asia especially in Cambodia, East Timor, India, Indonesia, Laos, Myanmar, Nepal, Pakistan, Papua New Guinea, the Philippines, Sri Lanka, and the Solomon Islands. Myanmar alone has more than 75,000 child soldiers, one of the highest numbers of any country in the world, with some as young as eleven. *See id.* at 27.

35. *See* Tattersall, *supra* note 28, at 1.

> speak of deliberate victimization. There are few further depths to which humanity can sink.[36]

C. Abuses of Child Soldiers

Child soldiers are subjected daily to dehumanizing atrocities. They are often abducted from their own homes, tortured, indoctrinated with brutality, forced to become intoxicated with mind-altering drugs, threatened with death and/or dismemberment if they do not fight, forced to return to their own village to witness or participate in the death or disfigurement of their own family members, required to kill friends who do not obey the commanders, and made to watch the punishment of other child soldiers who attempt in vain to escape.Child soldiers are brainwashed thoroughly and brutally until their ethics and moral values become so distorted that they believe doing evil is good. One twelve-year-old child in Columbia described the leadership's obsession with the virtues of killing:

> If you join the paramilitaries [the AUC in Columbia,] your first duty is to kill. They tell you, "Here you are going to kill." From the very beginning, they teach you how to kill. I mean when you arrive at the camp, the first thing they do is kill a guy, and if you are a recruit they call you over to prick at him, to chop off his hands and arms.[37]

Brainwashing is accomplished by desensitizing children to the sight and commission of atrocities. Some children who try to escape are reportedly boiled alive, and the other child soldiers are then forced to eat the human flesh as part of their training.[38] Other child soldiers who manage to escape have reported that while they were at the training camp, they were forced to beat the dead body of a captured escapee and "smear themselves with his blood."[39] Rebels keep the children obedient through frequent beatings, threats of death, and threats of retaliation against the children's family members.[40]

---

36. Expert of the Secretary-General, Ms. Graca Machel, *Impact of Armed Conflict on Children*, ¶ 5, *delivered to the General Assembly*, U.N. Doc. A/5 1/306 (Aug. 26, 1996), [hereinafter Machel Report].

37. Human Rights Watch, You'll Learn Not to Cry: Child Combatants in Columbia 95 (2003), http://www.hrw.org/reports/2003/colombia0903/colombia0903.pdf.

38. *See Justice Versus Reconciliation: Hunting Uganda's Child-Killers*, Economist, May 7, 2005, at 41.

39. *See I Don't Know Why They Did It*, News 24 (S. Afr.), Oct. 6, 2005, http://www.news24.com/News24/Africa/Features/0,2-11-37_1719250,00.html.

40. *See* Human Rights Watch, The Scars of Death 37 (1997), http://www.hrw.org/reports97/uganda/.

Young girls are abducted as well; they make up 40 percent of the ranks of armed groups in some countries.[41] In El Salvador, Ethiopia, and Uganda, almost a third of the child soldiers are young girls,[42] who are raped, enslaved, given to military commanders as "wives," and victimized by sexual violence on a daily basis. Girl soldiers encounter serious abuse, including forced pregnancy. During the 1990s over eight hundred children were born to the Lords' Resistance Army (LRA) "wives" who were concentrated at Jabelein camp in southern Sudan.[43] Girl soldiers are often used as domestic servants and sex slaves during conflict, and when they become infected with HIV, they are usually not treated. These victimized girl soldiers require rehabilitation and special attention after their demobilization.[44]

These children who are trained to be fearless actually become dangerous killing machines. Anyone seeing them in action is naturally stunned into disbelief and is likely to wonder why these children kill, maim, and dismember their own friends and relatives. The answer is quite simple: child soldiers are pumped up on drugs to make them fearless.[45] These drugs are no doubt trafficked into the country for a hefty sum. Powerless and abandoned children are empowered with small, light weapons and indoctrinated with brutality into the virtues of committing wartime atrocities. These small weapons are trafficked into the country at a substantial cost. Young girls are also trafficked to service the commanders and even the boy child soldiers. The money earned from one form of trafficking typically supplies the goods and services of the other form of trafficking in a complex network that constitutes a lucrative industry run by international organized crime groups.

These children are victims of inhumane brainwashing and merciless combat training that makes them robotically obey orders to kill innocent victims just to stay alive. These children undergo a terrifying initiation that consists of killing or raping a close relative. They are forced to participate in acts of extreme violence and barbarity including beheadings, amputations, rape, and burning of people alive.[46] The Lord's Resistance Army (LRA) in Uganda initiates children into its gang by forcing them "to club, stamp or bite to death their friends and relatives,

---

41. *See* U.N. Office for the Coordination of Humanitarian Affairs, *AFRICA: Fighting for Children*, IRIN, Feb. 7, 2007, http://irinnews.org/report.aspx?reportid=70016 [hereinafter *AFRICA: Fighting for Children*].

42. *See* Leibig, *supra* note 23, at 6.

43. *See* Akhavan, *supra* note 20, at 408.

44. *See AFRICA: Fighting for Children, supra* note 41.

45. *See* Ishmael Beah, *The Making and Unmaking of a Child Soldier*, N.Y. TIMES MAG., Jan. 14, 2007, at 7 ("I smoked marijuana, ate and snorted cocaine and brown brown. That was all I did for a few days before we went back to the new base we had captured.").

46. *See* Akhavan, *supra* note 20, at 408; *see also* ISHMAEL BEAH, A LONG WAY GONE: MEMOIRS OF A BOY SOLDIER (2007); *Justice Versus Reconciliation: Hunting Uganda's Child-Killers, supra* note 38, at 41.

and then to lick their brains, drink their blood and even eat their boiled flesh."[47] The LRA slices off the lips and noses of children it suspects of disloyalty.[48] The children of Uganda are reportedly so frightened about being abducted and enslaved by the LRA that they do not sleep at home, preferring instead to become "night commuters"[49] who travel alone or in groups every night to "protected villages" where "they sleep on verandas, in bus parks, on church grounds" for safety.[50]

D. Organization of Chapter

Despite a proliferation of laws—international human rights treaties, conventions prohibiting slavery, labor laws, trafficking laws and laws of war that provide special protection for civilian children who are particularly vulnerable—the trafficking and use of children as soldiers is increasing! This study will examine the complex relationship of human trafficking, slavery, and child soldiering. Part II will examine the root causes of the development and expansion of the use of child soldiers. Part III will examine the international and domestic laws and instruments that attempt to protect against the use of children as soldiers. Part IV will examine some literary representations of the crime of child soldiering in order to raise awareness of the depths of this atrocity. Part V will conclude by offering practical suggestions and economic solutions to make these legal instruments more effective. Children are humanity's most valuable investment in the future, and it is the obligation of the adult world to protect them effectively.

II. THE ROOT CAUSES OF THE USE OF CHILD SOLDIERS

A. Voluntary and Forced Recruitment of Children

Children's recruitment in armed conflict is either by force (conscription) or voluntary (enlistment), even though voluntary recruitment is often coupled with hidden forms of coercion. Armed militia, police, or army cadres arbitrarily seize

---

47. *See Justice Versus Reconciliation: Hunting Uganda's Child-Killers, supra* note 38; *see also* Udombana, *supra* note 20, at 68.

48. *See Justice Versus Reconciliation: Hunting Uganda's Child-Killers, supra* note 38.

49. *See* Amnesty Int'l, *UGANDA: Child "Night Commuters"*, AI Index AFR 59/013/2005, Nov. 18, 2005, http://web.amnesty.org/library/print/ENGAFR590132005 ("We come to the shelter because I fear being abducted again. I was eight years old then. I do not want my brothers and sisters to be abducted as I was. We walk fast in the night to be here."); *see also* Amnesty Int'l, *UGANDA: Child "Night Commuters" Fear Abduction*, AI Index AFR 59/016/2005, Nov. 18, 2005, http://web.amnesty.org/library/print/ENGAFR590162005. ("Some walk for several kilometers, without the protection of adult family members . . . All risk harassment, physical abuse, sexual exploitation and rape on the way.").

50. Akhavan, *supra* note 20, at 409.

young recruits from the streets, schools, and orphanages.[51] Children forcibly recruited cannot exercise a choice or give their consent to serve in armed conflict. Nevertheless, consent is the key element required to determine whether the recruitment of children for armed conflict actually constitutes trafficking and not just the smuggling of migrants, in accordance with the definition of trafficking set forth in the Palermo Protocol.[52] If a child is voluntarily recruited and takes up arms "consensually," the child may not be protected under the trafficking statutes.

Various factors in a child's environment may cause her to join an armed group voluntarily. The child's parental and family background, peer groups, school, and religious community can strongly influence his decision to fight.[53] Poverty, ignorance, illiteracy, intellectual and developmental immaturity, and a lack of formal education prevent children from making an informed choice or even understanding why they are fighting.[54] Children without schooling are prone to recruitment, as were the many children in Sierra Leone who were without schooling for several years after 1997 when three hundred schools were closed due to damage or destruction.[55] Children often lack the capacity to determine their best interests, to form opinions, and to analyze competing ideologies.[56] This is why the element of *consent* required to determine whether or not a child is *trafficked* is complex and should not be determinative.

B. Why Children Become Soldiers

Several interrelated factors explain the underlying causes of the rise in the abduction and use of child soldiers. Social disruptions and governmental failures to protect children and adults have been attributed to globalization, to the increase in the number and length of wars, and to the spread of fatal diseases such as AIDS, all of which create familial and generational disconnections leaving many potential child recruits available for abduction. The social and psychological effects of war can create a need for children to join a group, especially one like an army that promises to provide relative security and stability, sense of power, and acceptance by peers and authority figures.

---

51. *See* Mike Wessells, *Child Soldiers: In Some Places, If You're as Tall as A Rifle, You're Old Enough to Carry One*, BULL. ATOM. SCI. Nov. 21, 1997, at 32.

52. *See* Palermo Protocol, *supra* note 5, art. 3(a); *see also* Valentine, *supra* note 2, at 117. *See infra* text accompanying notes 306–08 for discussion of "consent" in *Prosecutor v. Dyilo* (ICC, Jan. 29, 2007).

53. *See* Machel Report, *supra* note 36, at 36.

54. *See* Wessells, *supra* note 51, at 39; *see also* Tiffany A. Richards, *The War is Over But the Battle Has Just Begun: Enforcing A Child's Right to Education in the Wake of Armed Conflict*, 23 PENN ST. INT'L L. REV. 203, 205–06 (2004).

55. *See* Valentine, *supra* note 2, at 120.

56. *See* Udombana, *supra* note 20, at 63–64.

There are also purely military advantages of using children as soldiers in war. Technological improvements and the proliferation of thin, small, and lightweight weapons such as assault rifles, machine guns, pistols, and hand grenades have enabled child soldiers to engage effectively in warfare. The huge number of children available and the military successes of these child soldiers have accelerated the trend toward recruiting young soldiers.[57] The rise of a new type of armed warfare that is more brutal and lasts much longer than typical wars has encouraged military leaders to rationalize the forced recruitment and use of children as a low-cost military measure that enables them to mobilize and generate forces.[58]

C. Changes in Family and Ethical Values

A serious and pervasive change in family and ethical values is one of the most significant factors causing the rise in the use of child soldiers. In many countries, children are devalued in the family and in society at large. Children do not occupy the center of the life of the family. They do not represent a precious hope for the future. In some countries, children are considered less than human, expendable, and invisible, especially in the midst of an overwhelming cult of death and martyrdom that developed during the Iran–Iraq War and continues today in many parts of the world. The lack of respect and the marginalization of children are no doubt two of the most pernicious causes of the increased use of child soldiers. This perverse ethos that devalues and dehumanizes children will be particularly difficult to eradicate.

D. Globalization

Globalization involves travel, trade, and the displacement of families, all of which affect children.[59] Socioeconomic problems associated with globalization impact children because of their vulnerability and dependency on adults for survival. Despite the advancement of technology in the modern global community, today unprecedented numbers of children around the world are undereducated, malnourished, marginalized, and disaffected.[60] Desperate children who are excluded from the protection of their family for various reasons constitute an available pool of cheap labor for the traffic of weapons, drugs, and humans, which in that order are the three most serious and lucrative international crimes today. Each of these crimes is intricately involved in the abduction and exploitation of children in armed conflict. These crimes are very profitable, and money earned from one form of trafficking (e.g., weapons) helps finance the trafficking of the other (child soldiering). Trafficking is run by powerful international organized crime groups

57. *See* Valentine, *supra* note 2, at 119.
58. *See* Sinter, *supra* note 25, at 38.
59. *Id.* at 38–39.
60. *Id.* at 39.

that are in the trafficking business for reasons of pure profit.[61] Thus, the exploitation of the population of child soldiers drives a new "economy of war."[62]

E. AIDS and Orphans

The AIDS epidemic has created another available pool of orphans and abandoned children. Many children who have lost their parents and siblings due to the scourge of AIDS are especially susceptible to the lure of child soldiering.[63] Many orphans actually watched their parents die and were forced to fend for themselves at a very young age in an unusually dangerous environment. In this context, the structure of an army setting can provide orphans with the false sense of belonging to a community, an escape from loneliness, and the hope of more security and stability in a country at war.

F. Increase in the Use of Small Personal Weapons

Amidst the current dissolution of traditional notions of the family and the socioeconomic disconnections that wars invariably produce, people and especially children are scrambling for self-protection and a sense of security. For this reason there has been a proliferation in the sale of technologically advanced personal weaponry.[64] An estimated five hundred million small arms have been sold globally—one small weapon for every twelve persons.[65] The increased use of small personal weapons reflects the instability of the world and the development of a generalized sense of fear among people. The proliferation of small weapons also facilitates the expanded use of children in armed combat.

G. Changes in the Nature of Warfare

Conflicts around the globe are characterized not as temporary outbreaks of instability but as long, protracted states of mass violence and disorder.[66] Today's wars involve the organized and systematic use of mass violence and the blurring of distinctions between traditional conceptions of war, organized crime, and large-scale violations of human rights.[67] Vulnerable, abandoned, and orphan children are now more readily available and easily transformed into willing combatants. Because the leaders of combatants may not concern themselves with public

---

61. *See* Tiefenbrun, *The Saga of Susannah*, *supra* note 4, at 139.

62. *See* UNICEF, Children Affected by Armed Conflict: UNICEF Actions 3 (2002).

63. *See* Sinter, *supra* note 25, at 42.

64. *See id.* at 45.

65. *See* Charles Cobb, *Africa: Arms and Africa on UN Agenda This Week*, All Afr. (S. Afr.), July 9, 2001, http://allafrica.com/stories/200107090396.html.

66. *See* Sinter, *supra* note 25, at 52.

67. *See* Mary Kaldor, New and Old Wars: Organized Violence in a Global Era 1 (1999).

opinion, human rights, or decency,[68] they invariably seize upon impressionable and obedient young children as a cost-saving military measure. Thus, the doctrine of child soldiers and child exploitative employment in armed conflict is justified as a new and less expensive way of engaging in combat.[69]

Long wars lead to many casualties and cause shortages in manpower that some governments believe can be remedied by the involuntary recruitment of children. In Africa, conflicts are very long, and there is evidence of the extensive use of children in these conflicts to fill the ranks caused by adult casualties. For example, Sudan has been fighting a continuous civil war since 1956, with Darfur being the latest area of conflict rising to the level of genocide. Children were recruited during the Angolan conflict that lasted over thirty years. The use of children as soldiers enables wars to continue indefinitely. "War children have difficulty turning into peace children and this, itself, may contribute to prolonging conflicts and a serious erosion of local value systems."[70]

The use of child soldiers can change the very nature of the way wars are traditionally fought. Children are more likely to violate the rules of war due to their young age and diminished capacity to appreciate the consequences of their actions.[71] "The greater suggestibility of children and the degree to which they can be normalised (sic) into violence means that child soldiers are more likely to commit atrocities than adults."[72] In fact, the use of child soldiers may erode the applicability and effectiveness of well-established laws of war.

H. Military Reasons for the Use of Child Soldiers

Children are often recruited as soldiers for purely military reasons. The technological advances in weaponry and the prevalent use of small arms and light weapons facilitate the increasing use of child soldiers. Such weapons allow small children to shoot steady streams of bullets with the mere pull of the trigger. Presently, there is no universal treaty addressing the use of small arms and light weapons.[73] Children are recruited because they are small and can be used as guinea pigs by their leaders who force them to the front lines or to minefields ahead of older troops while their commanders stay behind.[74]

---

68. *See* SINTER, *supra* note 25, at 53.

69. *See id.*

70. *See* Udombana, *supra* note 20, at 71.

71. *See* FRANCOISE J. HAMPSON, UNIV. ESSEX CHILD AND ARMED CONFLICT UNIT, LEGAL PROTECTION AFFORDED TO CHILDREN UNDER INTERNATIONAL HUMANITARIAN LAW § 3 (1996), http://www.essex.ac.uk/armedcon/international/comment/Text/paper002.htm.

72. *See* RACHEL BRETT & MARGARET MCCALLIN, CHILDREN: THE INVISIBLE SOLDIERS 25 (Rädda Barnen ed., 1998).

73. *See* Udombana, *supra* note 20, at 66–67.

74. *See* Akhavan, *supra* note 20, at 408.

I. Social and Psychological Causes of the Use of Child Soldiers

Children may "volunteer" to go to war for many reasons. Some children have witnessed the brutal death of their own close family members, and they simply want revenge. Some have grown up in a chronic state of conflict in a country constantly at war, and they know no other way of life. They also may be influenced to fight out of a sense of loyalty to their community.[75] Finally, children who volunteer may do so out of fear of abduction and reprisals by the armed group just because they appear to be unwilling to fight for their country.

Children may seem to go to war "voluntarily" even though they may have actually been coerced and sold out to the armed group by their own poor and hungry parents.[76] Many of these parents do not understand the danger to which they are subjecting their children by making them join the army. Some parents may encourage their daughters to become soldiers if their marriage prospects are poor.[77]

In the chaotic environment of a country in armed conflict, children's survival skills instinctively start to work. They seek stability and three square meals a day. They may simply be making an "intuitive choice for the better of the bad alternatives."[78] Many of them are abandoned street children who crave physical protection and relief from abject poverty and loneliness. As with any normal child, a voluntary child soldier needs identification with a peer group. These powerless children search for acceptance, a sense of competence, and the sheer adventure associated with the glory and power of victory in armed conflict.[79] The United Nations Educational, Scientific and Cultural Organization (UNESCO) reports that "regardless of age, gender, or how they are recruited, child soldiers disproportionately come from the poor and marginalized segments of society, isolated rural areas, the conflict zones themselves, and from disrupted or non-existent family backgrounds."[80]

J. Economic Reasons for the Use of Child Soldiers

Sadly, children are recruited because they are perceived of as cheap labor and expendable. They are obedient, fast to indoctrinate and to control, physically vulnerable, and easily intimidated.[81] Young adolescents reportedly have a sense of their own omnipotence and "view themselves as invulnerable to harm

---

75. *See* Udombana, *supra* note 20, at 63.
76. *See id.* at 64.
77. *See id.*
78. *Id.*
79. *See id.*
80. *Id.*
81. *See id.* at 67.

and injury."[82] Thus, some believe it is arguably economically efficient to use children as soldiers.

These are some of the social, cultural, psychological, military, and economic root causes for the use of voluntary and forcibly conscripted child soldiers. Taking this larger context into consideration, the very concept of the "voluntary" recruitment of children into armed conflict is arguably discussable and clearly subject to interpretation. Children lack the capacity to determine their best interests, to form independent opinions, or to analyze competing ideologies.[83] We may legitimately question whether children living in a war-torn nation have the freedom of choice to go to war.[84] A culture of violence defines their childhood experiences, and the militarization of that culture may incite them to participate "voluntarily."[85] This complex issue of consent and the "voluntary" recruitment of child soldiers is crucial to the determination of whether child soldiers who are forced to fight out of fear for their lives should be held accountable in a court of law for the atrocities they commit.

K. Treatment of Child Soldiers as Criminals

Child soldiers who are coerced by the fear of death to commit atrocities are being arrested and convicted of war crimes.[86] These children are often treated as if they were adults simply because indoctrinated child soldiers do not look like children and have often committed atrocities together with adults.[87] For example, in January 1999, the Ugandan army executed five teenage boys between the ages of fourteen and seventeen suspected of being rebel soldiers, although such actions were not believed to be characteristic of the government forces.[88] In Colombia, child soldiers are not afforded special legal status or treatment.[89] In Rwanda, in 1999 the International Committee of the Red Cross reported that approximately 570 children under the age of fourteen were incarcerated on genocide-related charges and still remain in the prison system.[90] Yet in a leading neurology law

82. B.J. Sadock & V.A. Sadock, Kaplan & Sadock's Synopsis of Psychiatry 28 (9th ed. 2003).

83. *See* Amy Beth Abbott, *Child Soldiers—The Use of Children as Instruments of War*, 23 Suffolk Transnat'l L. Rev. 499, 517 (2000).

84. *See id.*

85. *See id.* at 517–18.

86. *See generally*, Manisuli Ssenyonjo, *Accountability of Non-State Actors in Uganda for War Crimes and Human Rights Violations: Between Amnesty and the International Criminal Court*, 10 J. Conflict & Security L. 405 (2005).

87. *See* Stephanie H. Bold, Note, *Searching for a Lost Childhood: Will the Special Court of Sierra Leone Find Justice for its Children?*, 18 Am. J. Int'l L. Rev. 537, 552 (2002).

88. *See* Valentine, *supra* note 2, at 128.

89. *See id.*

90. *See* U.S. Dep't of State, Bureau of Democracy, Human Rights, and Labor, Country Reports on Human Rights Practices: Rwanda (2000), http://www.state.

brief filed by the American Medical Association (AMA) and other groups, the AMA argued (and Justice Anthony Kennedy agreed) that "adolescent brains are not fully developed in the prefrontal regions, and adolescents are less able than adults to control their impulses and should not be held fully accountable for the immaturity of their neural anatomy."[91]

III. LAWS RELATING TO THE USE OF CHILD SOLDIERS

A. Introduction

The use and abduction of child soldiers is an international crime and a heinous human rights violation that is caught in the intersection of four different but related areas of the law: children's rights, slavery, human trafficking, and exploitative child labor. Child soldiers are protected under international human rights laws, international humanitarian laws (i.e., laws of war), international criminal laws, and international labor laws.[92]

The first international instrument to address specifically the legal rights of children was the United Nations Convention on the Rights of the Child (CRC)[93] enacted in 1989. The CRC was amended to include two Optional Protocols: the Optional Protocol to the Convention on the Rights of the Child on the Involvement of Children in Armed Conflict ("Children in Armed Conflict Protocol")[94] and the Optional Protocol on the Sale of Children, Child Prostitution, and Child Pornography ("Sale of Children Protocol").[95] The Children in Armed Conflict Protocol amends the CRC's minimum age for recruitment of persons into the armed forces from fifteen to eighteen years of age[96] on the theory that the CRC's age of fifteen as the standard for recruitment does not adequately protect children and in fact appears to have encouraged more recruitment, as evidenced by

---

gov/g/drl/rls/hrrpt/2000/af/index.cfm?docid=720; *see also* Judith Matloff, *Rwanda's Bind: Trying Children for Genocide*, Christian Science Monitor, Jan. 28, 1997.

91. Jeffrey Rosen, *The Brain on the Stand: How Neuroscience is Transforming the Legal System*, N.Y Times Mag., Mar. 11, 2007, at 48, 51.

92. See Udombana, *supra* note 20, at 70–90 for a complete analysis of the laws that cover child soldiering.

93. Convention on the Rights of the Child, 1577 U.N.T.S. 3 (entered into force Sept. 2, 1990) [hereinafter CRC].

94. Optional Protocol to the Convention on the Rights of the Child on the Involvement of Children in Armed Conflicts, G.A. Res. 54/263, Annex I, U.N. GAOR, 54th Sess., U.N. Doc. A/RES/54/263 (May 25, 2000) [hereinafter Children in Armed Conflict Protocol].

95. Optional Protocol to the Convention on the Rights of the Child on the Sale of Children, Child Prostitution, and Child Pornography, G.A. Res 54/263, U.N. GAOR, 54th Sess., Annex II, U.N. Doc. A/RES/54/263 (Jan. 18, 2002) [hereinafter Sale of Children Protocol].

96. *See* Children in Armed Conflict Protocol, *supra* note 94, art. 1.

the increasing number of child soldiers.[97] The Children in Armed Conflict Protocol also urges States Parties to take "all feasible measures to ensure that members of their armed forces who have not attained the age of 18 years do not take a direct part in hostilities."[98]

Before the adoption of the CRC and its subsequent two Protocols, many treaties were enacted to eradicate slavery, some of which specifically address the special needs of enslaved children. The international community has repeatedly condemned slavery and involuntary servitude. Community condemnations are manifested in the form of declarations, treaties, and United Nations resolutions and reports. They include, but are not limited to, the following legal instruments: the Universal Declaration of Human Rights of 1948,[99] whose nonbinding aspirations were given force in 1966 by the passage of the International Covenant on Civil and Political Rights[100] and the International Covenant on Economic, Social and Cultural Rights,[101] all of which condemn slavery. The 1904 International Agreement for the Suppression of the White Slave Traffic[102] was amended by the 1910 International Convention for the Suppression of White Slave Traffic,[103] which prohibits the trafficking of women for their use as sex slaves. International concern over the increased development of slave trafficking eventually resulted in the passage of the 1926 League of Nations Slavery Convention.[104] Due to the continued failed enforcement of these slavery conventions, the Supplementary Convention on the Abolition of Slavery, the Slave Trade and Institutions and Practices Similar to Slavery[105] was adopted in 1956 ("1956 U.N. Slavery Convention").

---

97. *See* Udombana, *supra* note 20, at 90.

98. Children in Armed Conflict Protocol, *supra* note 94, art. 1.

99. Universal Declaration of Human Rights, G.A. Res. 217A (III), at 71 U.N. GAOR, 3d Sess., 1st plen. mtg., U.N. Doc. A/810 (Dec. 12, 1948) [hereinafter Universal Declaration of Human Rights].

100. International Covenant on Civil and Political Rights, G.A. Res. 2200 (XXI), U.N. GAOR, 21st Sess., Supp. No 16, at 49, U.N. Doc. A/6316 (Dec. 16, 1966).

101. International Covenant on Economic, Social and Cultural Rights, G.A. Res. 2200 (XXI), U.N. GAOR, 21st Sess., Supp. No. 16, at 49, U.N. Doc. A/6316 (Dec. 16, 1966).

102. International Agreement for the Suppression of the White Slave Traffic, May 18, 1904, 35 Stat. 1979, 1 L.N.T.S. 83 [hereinafter 1904 Agreement] (commonly referred to as the Mann Act).

103. International Convention for the Suppression of White Slave Traffic, May 4, 1910, 2 U.S.T. 1997, 30 U.N.T.S. 23.

104. International Convention to Suppress the Slave Trade and Slavery, Sept. 24, 1926, 46 Stat. 2183 [hereinafter 1926 League of Nations Slavery Convention].

105. Supplementary Convention on the Abolition of Slavery, the Slave Trade, and Institution and Practices Similar to Slavery, Sept. 7, 1956, 18 U.S.T. 3201, 266 U.N.T.S. 3 [hereinafter 1956 U.N. Slavery Convention].

Earlier legal instruments such as the United Nations Charter of 1945,[106] the 1948 American Declaration on the Rights and Duties of Man,[107] and the Universal Declaration of Human Rights[108] enacted in 1948 all prohibit slavery. Other treaties purporting to eliminate slavery include the 1930 Convention Concerning Forced or Compulsory Labour, adopted by the General Conference of the International Labour Organization;[109] the 1957 Abolition of Forced Labour Convention;[110] the 1984 Convention Against Torture and Other Cruel, Inhuman or Degrading Treatment or Punishment;[111] the Final Report of the World Congress Against Sexual Exploitation of Children (Stockholm, 1996); the Convention on the Elimination of All Forms of Discrimination Against Women (CEDAW),[112] and the 2000 U.N. Convention Against Transnational Organized Crime and the Protocol to Prevent, Suppress, and Punish Trafficking in Persons, Especially Women and Children ("Palermo Protocol").[113]

Despite the profusion of declarations and treaties condemning slavery, this crime still exists today in the form of human trafficking and child soldiering. Laws protecting against child slavery have actually continued to increase because protection against slavery is included under the ambit of human trafficking laws and child sex tourism legislation. For example, the United States Victims of Trafficking Protection Act (TVPA)[114] was enacted in October 2000 to eliminate human trafficking, which is referred to as a form of slavery.[115]

---

106. See U.N. Charter.

107. American Declaration on the Rights and Duties of Man, O.A.S. Res., OEA/ Ser.L./ V/I.4 Rev. 9 (May 2, 1948).

108. Universal Declaration of Human Rights, *supra* note 99, at III.

109. Convention Concerning Forced or Compulsory Labour (ILO No. 29), June 28, 1930, 39 U.N.T.S. 55 (entered into force May 1, 1932).

110. Convention Concerning the Abolition of Forced Labour (ILO No. 105), June 25, 1957, 320 U.N.T.S. 291 (entered into force Jan. 17, 1959).

111. United Nations Convention Against Torture and Other Cruel, Inhuman or Degrading Treatment or Punishment, Dec. 10, 1984, 112 Stat. 2681, 1465 U.N.T.S. 85, 113.

112. Convention on the Elimination of All Forms of Discrimination Against Women ("CEDAW"), Dec. 18, 1979, 1249 U.N.T.S. 13.

113. Palermo Protocol, *supra* note 5. The Palermo Protocol was preceded by the 1949 U.N. Convention for the Suppression of the Traffic in Persons and the Exploitation of the Prostitution of Others (which made prostitution illegal regardless of any manifestation of consent by the person prostituted). Dec. 2, 1949, 96 U.N.T.S. 271, art. 3(a) (entered into force July 25, 2001).

114. TVPA, 22 U.S.C. § 7105 (2000). The TVPA has been reauthorized three times (in 2003, and 2005 and 2008). *See* e.g. Trafficking Victims Protection Reauthorization Act, Pub. L. No. 108-193 (codified as amended in scattered sections of the U.S.C. (2003)).

115. *See* Tiefenbrun, *The Domestic and International Impact of the U.S. Victims of Trafficking Protection Act of 2000*, *supra* note 4, for a detailed discussion of the international dimension of the TVPA and why trafficking is a contemporary form of slavery; *see also*

The goals of the TVPA are to prevent human trafficking, to protect trafficked women and children who should be treated as victims and not as criminals, and to punish the perpetrators with a severe criminal sentence of thirty years to life in jail. Recognizing that human trafficking is an international problem requiring an international solution, the TVPA requires the United States to provide financial and educational assistance worldwide to women and children who are in danger of being trafficked. Under the threat of non-humanitarian sanctions, the TVPA requires nations to draft trafficking laws that meet the minimum standards of protection against trafficking. Similarly, the U.S. Prosecutorial Remedies and Other Tools to End the Exploitation of Children Today Act of 2003 ["the PROTECT Act"][116] has extraterritorial effect and punishes U.S. citizens engaging in sex with minors in countries abroad where sex tourism might even be legal. The TVPA and the PROTECT Act protect children all over the world who are trafficked into slave-like conditions of forced labor, forced prostitution, or forced soldiering.

Most of the funds allocated for the TVPA and the PROTECT Act have been spent on prosecution of perpetrators. More emphasis should be placed on the prevention of trafficking while maintaining the legislative goals of victim protection and perpetrator punishment. Prevention of human trafficking, and especially the trafficking of children, must become the main focus. However, prevention of child trafficking requires worldwide consciousness-raising, the establishment of a political will to eliminate the crime, radical changes in current family value systems, and the eradication of poverty, which is at the root of the proliferation of armed conflicts that perpetuate child soldiering.

The increasing employment of children as soldiers is clearly a violation of international labor laws. The International Labour Organization (ILO) establishes and supervises the application of international labor standards, including standards for child labor. Child soldiering is identified as one of the worst crimes under the International Labour Organization Convention Concerning the Prohibition and Immediate Action for the Elimination of the Worst Forms of Child Labour Convention (No. 182), enacted in 1999,[117] and the recommended ILO Convention (No. 190).[118] The Minimum Age Convention of 1973[119] tried to eliminate child labor by requiring the completion of compulsory schooling and

---

Tiefenbrun, *Updating the Domestic and International Impact of the U.S. Victims of Trafficking Protection Act of 2000: Does Law Deter Crime?*, *supra* note 4.

116. Prosecutorial Remedies and Other Tools to End the Exploitation of Children Today (PROTECT) Act of 2003, Pub. L. No. 108-2 1, 117 Stat. 650 (codified as amended in scattered sections of the U.S.C. (2006)) [hereinafter PROTECT Act].

117. ILO Worst Forms of Child Labour Convention 182, *supra* note 11.

118. ILO Recommendation 190, *supra* note 12.

119. Convention Concerning Minimum Age for Admission to Employment art. 3, June 26, 1973, 1015 U.N.T.S. 297.

by setting the minimum age for child labor at fifteen. The ILO Worst Forms of Child Labour Convention 182 defines a child as a person under the age of eighteen and recognizes that forced labor (e.g., child soldiering) is a modern variant of slavery.[120]

B. International Legal Instruments that Specifically Protect Children

1. The Declaration of the Rights of the Child[121] Although the Declaration of the Rights of the Child was not a binding instrument, it established aspirational norms and set forth a code for the well-being of every child.[122] The Declaration provided, *inter alia*, that every child should be given opportunities and facilities (by law and by other means) to enable them to develop physically, mentally, morally, spiritually, and socially in a healthy and normal manner and in conditions of freedom and dignity.[123]

2. United Nations Convention on the Rights of the Child (CRC)[124] The CRC is the most universally accepted human rights instrument in history.[125] It has been ratified by every country in the world except the United States[126] and Somalia. By ratifying the CRC, States and their national governments express their agreement with the principles contained in the treaty and their commitment to protect children's rights by enacting measures to ensure these rights.[127]

The almost universal adoption of the CRC in 1989 is evidence of a profound shift in the world's thinking about children and their inalienable and definable rights.[128] The CRC specifically protects against child trafficking by asserting a child's right to protection from economic exploitation, child military recruitment,

---

120. ILO Worst Forms of Child Labour Convention 182, *supra* note 11, art. 3(a).

121. Declaration of the Rights of the Child, G.A. Res. 1386, U.N. GAOR, 14th Sess., Supp. No. 16, U.N. Doc. A/4354 (Nov. 20, 1959).

122. *See id.* at 19.

123. *See id.*; *see also* Udombana, *supra* note 20, at 79.

124. CRC, *supra* note 93.

125. *See* Rios-Kohn, *supra* note 10, at 140–41.

126. *See* Abbott, *supra* note 83, at 530 for some of the reasons why the United States refuses to ratify the CRC. According to Abbott, the United States is unwilling to change American policy. The United States recognizes that in order to sign the CRC, all fifty states must harmonize their laws relating to children. The United States opposes efforts to raise the minimum age of military recruitment from seventeen to eighteen because the United States now allows seventeen-year-olds to enlist. There are other serious reasons why the United States does not want to ratify the CRC, which it believes overly regulates parents, endorses abortion, denies parents their right to inculcate children with their religious beliefs, and other complex objections.

127. *See* CRC, *supra* note 93, art. 44, ¶ 1. "States Parties undertake to submit to the Committee, through the Secretary-General of the United Nations, reports on the measures they have adopted which give effect to the rights recognized herein and on the progress made on the enjoyment of those rights." *Id.*

128. *See* Udombana, *supra* note 20, at 79.

and participation in armed conflict.[129] The CRC sets the minimum age for military recruitment of children in armed conflict at age fifteen, and it asks States recruiting those under eighteen to give priority to the eldest.[130] In order to prevent child trafficking, Article 35 of the CRC requires States Parties to take all appropriate national, bilateral, and multilateral measures to prevent the abduction, sale, or trafficking of children for any purpose or in any form.[131] Article 32 refers indirectly to the forced recruitment of child soldiers by giving children the right to protection from economic exploitation and from performing any work that is likely to be hazardous or will interfere harmfully with a child's education; health; or physical, mental, spiritual, moral, or social development.[132] But if the child is not below the minimum age allowed for employment, any work that does not interfere with a child's rights to education and development is not necessarily deemed "harmful."[133]

The CRC has certain anomalies and contradictions. By using age fifteen as the threshold for its prohibition of recruitment and by precluding only direct participation in hostilities, only those children under the age of fifteen who are conscripted forcibly are protected, and only if they are placed in "direct" combat.[134] Given the problematic nature of informed consent in this context, children between the ages of fifteen and eighteen who appear to have voluntarily joined armed combat as child soldiers will not be protected. The CRC's Optional Protocol for Children in Armed Combat changed the minimum age for conscription to eighteen to address this problem.

The general failure to enforce the stipulations of the CRC has eroded the ideological shift that we have seen toward more universal recognition of children's rights. This ideological shift is evidenced by the almost unanimous adoption of the CRC treaty. However, failure to implement the CRC has resulted in the actual diminution of children's rights as manifested by an alarming increase in the use of child soldiers. For example, Article 32 of the CRC provides general protection for children from "any work that is likely to be hazardous or to interfere with the child's education."[135] Clearly, the participation of children between the ages of fifteen and eighteen in armed combat is, by its very nature, "hazardous" and thus constitutes a flagrant violation of Article 32 of the CRC. Moreover, the first part of Article 38 of the CRC provides: "States Parties undertake to respect and to ensure respect for the rules of international humanitarian law

129. *See* CRC, *supra* note 93, arts. 32 & 38.
130. *See id.* art. 18.
131. *See id.* art. 35; *see also id.* art. 19.
132. *See id.* art. 32.
133. *See* Valentine, *supra* note 2, at 113.
134. *See* Udombana, *supra* note 20, at 181.
135. CRC, *supra* note 93, art. 32(1).

applicable to them in armed conflicts which are relevant to the child."[136] In addition, specifically relating to child soldiers, Article 38 of the CRC declares: "States Parties should take all feasible measures to ensure that persons who have not attained the age of fifteen years do not take a direct part in hostilities."[137] Even though by 2000, 191 States had ratified the CRC and expressed agreement thereby with the terms of Article 38, child soldiering has increased exponentially. Although global treaty ratification signifies ideological agreement that persons under fifteen should not bear arms, perpetrate violence, or wear the uniform of any combative group in any form of political conflict in the world,[138] the reality on the ground is woefully far from this ideal.[139]

Even though the CRC recognizes a child's inherent right to life and creates the State's obligation to safeguard the survival and development of the child,[140] the CRC does not contain enforcement mechanisms, making its implementation dependent upon the domestic laws of each nation.[141] If the CRC is ever to move from a universal charter of idealism and aspiration to a working and implementable agreement, there must be an awareness of the contexts and horrific realities in which children come to fight[142]—often well below the age of fifteen. In an attempt to strengthen the CRC and to implement the aspirations of the Declaration of the Rights of the Child, two Optional Protocols have been added to the CRC.

3. Optional Protocol on the Involvement of Children in Armed Conflict ("Children in Armed Conflict Protocol")[143] The Children in Armed Conflict

136. *Id.* art. 38(1).

137. The United States allows seventeen-year-olds to enlist voluntarily in the American armed forces with parental permission, but bars them from combat training until they reach eighteen years of age. *See* Julie R. Hirschfeld, *United States Reluctant to Endorse Minimum Age for Military*, DETROIT NEWS, Jan. 21, 1998.

138. *See* Jo de Berry, *Child Soldiers and the Convention on the Rights of the Child*, 575 ANNALS 92, 93, (2001).

139. *See id.*

140. CRC, *supra* note 93, art. 39.

> 1.States parties undertake to respect and to ensure respect for rules of international humanitarian law applicable to them in armed conflicts which are relevant to the child. 2. States Parties shall take all feasible measures to ensure that persons who have not attained the age of fifteen years do not take a direct part in the hostilities. 3. States Parties shall refrain from recruiting any person who has not attained the age of fifteen years into their armed forces . . . States Parties shall take all feasible measures to ensure protection and care of children who are affected by an armed conflict.

Id.

141. *See* Abbott, *supra* note 83, at 524.

142. *See* de Berry, *supra* note 138, at 93.

143. Children in Armed Conflict Protocol, *supra* note 94.

Protocol[144] is the main international legal instrument that specifically addresses the use of children as soldiers, minimum age for compulsory recruitment, voluntary recruitment, and direct participation in hostilities. The United States signed it on July 5, 2000 and ratified it on December 23, 2002, subject to some reservations, understandings, and declarations. The Children in Armed Conflict Protocol raises the minimum age from fifteen (set forth earlier in the CRC) to eighteen for direct participation in hostilities, compulsory recruitment, and any recruitment by nongovernmental armed groups.[145] Article 3(3) of the Children in Armed Conflict Protocol obligates States to maintain safeguards with respect to voluntary recruitment by ensuring that such recruitment is genuinely voluntary, by requiring informed consent of the person's parents or legal guardians, by informing recruits of the duties involved in military service, and by requiring reliable proof of age prior to acceptance into military service.[146]

The Children in Armed Conflict Protocol requires States to take "all feasible measures" to ensure that members of their armed forces under the age of eighteen do not take a "direct part in hostilities."[147] Language of the Children in Armed Conflict Protocol is drawn from Article 38(2) of the CRC and from Article 77(2) of Geneva Protocol I,[148] both of which require States to take all "feasible measures" to ensure that children under the age of fifteen do not take a "direct part in hostilities."[149] The term *direct participation in hostilities* in the context of treaties relating to the law of armed conflict has been interpreted in the Rome Statute of the International Criminal Court[150] as covering "both direct participation

---

144. *See* Cris R. Revaz & Jonathan Todres, *The Optional Protocols to the Convention on the Rights of the Child and the Impact of U.S. Ratification*, *in* The U.N. Convention on the Rights of the Child 293 (2006).

145. Children in Armed Conflict Protocol, *supra* note 94, art 1. "States Parties shall take all feasible measures to ensure that members of their armed forces who have not attained the age of 18 years do not take a direct part in hostilities." *Id.*; *see* CRC, *supra* note 93, art. 4. "Armed groups distinct from the armed forces of a State should not, under any circumstances, recruit or use in hostilities persons under the age of 18 years." Children in Armed Conflict Protocol, *supra* note 94, art. 4(1); *see also* Michael J. Dennis, *Newly Adopted Protocols to the Convention on the Rights of the Child*, 94 Am. J. Int'l L. 789, 789 (2000).

146. Children in Armed Conflict Protocol, *supra* note 94, art. 3(3).

147. Dennis, *supra* note 145, at 789.

148. *See* Protocol Additional to the Geneva Conventions of 12 August 1949 and Relating to the Protection of Victims of International Armed Conflicts, *adopted* June 8, 1977, art. 48, 1125 U.N.T.S. 17512 [hereinafter Protocol I]; *see also* Protocol Additional to the Geneva Conventions of 12 August 1949, and Relating to the Protection of Victims of Non-International Armed Conflicts, *adopted* June 8, 1977, art. 13, § 2, 1125 U.N.T.S. 609 [hereinafter Protocol II].

149. *See* Working Group on Involvement of Children in Armed Conflict, *Report on Its First Session*, UN Doc. E/CN.4/1995/96, §§ 20–21; *see also* Second Session Report, §§ 27, 30 & 45.

150. Rome Statute, *supra* note 4.

in combat and also active participation in military activities linked to combat such as scouting, spying, sabotage, and the use of children as decoys, couriers or at military checkpoints."[151] For children to engage in "direct participation in combat," there has to be a direct causal relationship between the activity engaged in by the child soldier and the harm done to the enemy at the time and place where the activity takes place.[152] According to this standard, the Children in Armed Conflict Protocol does not prohibit indirect participation in hostilities or forward deployment.[153] Unfortunately, the legitimization of indirect participation in hostilities is a crack through which children trafficked for sexual exploitation or child soldiering may fall.

The Children in Armed Conflict Protocol sets the minimum age for compulsory recruitment at eighteen as distinguished from the age of voluntary recruitment.[154] The Children in Armed Conflict Protocol permits the voluntary recruitment of sixteen- to seventeen-year-olds, provided certain protections are put into place that safeguard their recruitment being truly voluntary. Thus, States that permit voluntary recruitment of children under the age of eighteen must maintain safeguards to ensure, as a minimum,:

> (a) Such recruitment is genuinely voluntary; (b) Such recruitment is done with the informed consent of the person's parents or legal guardians; (c) Such persons are fully informed of the duties involved in such military service; (d) Such persons provide reliable proof of age prior to acceptance into national military service.[155]

Children between the ages of fifteen and eighteen are not permitted to participate directly in the hostilities.[156]

The Children in Armed Conflict Protocol is not a perfect piece of legislation. It does not define a "child soldier"; it merely establishes legitimate parameters within which children can be used in government or nongovernment

---

151. *Id.*

152. *See* INT'L COMMITTEE OF THE RED CROSS (ICRC), COMMENTARY ON THE ADDITIONAL PROTOCOLS OF 8 JUNE 1977 TO THE GENEVA CONVENTIONS OF 12 AUGUST 1949, 516 (Yves Sandoz et al. eds., 1987) [hereinafter ICRC COMMENTARY]; *see also* ICRC, Statement on the Draft Convention on the Rights of the Child, UN Doc. E/CN.4/1987/WG.1/WP.4, at 2. "It can reasonably be inferred from the present Article 20 of the Draft Convention [ultimately Article 38] that indirect participation, for example gathering and transmitting military information, transporting weapons, munitions and other supplies is not affected by the provision." *Id.*

153. Dennis, *supra* note 145, at 789.

154. Children in Armed Conflict Protocol, *supra* note 94, arts. 2 & 3(1).

155. *Id.* art. 3(3).

156. *Id.*

armed forces.[157] Earlier in 1997, the Cape Town Principles[158] defined a child soldier as "any person under eighteen years of age who is part of any kind of regular or irregular armed force or armed group in any capacity, including but not limited to cooks, porters, messengers, and those accompanying such groups, other than purely as family members." The Cape Town Principles include girls recruited for sexual purposes and forced marriage.

In formulating a definition of a *child soldier*, there should be no confusion or identification of that term with the term *combatant*. In international humanitarian laws, the term *combatant* is frequently contrasted to the term *civilian*. Children who are either civilians or combatants have different rights to protection during armed conflict[159] under the international humanitarian laws. The problem is that a child soldier who is not in an official "army" and who is fighting nonconsensually is arguably neither a civilian nor a combatant and thus totally unprotected.

4. Optional Protocol on the Sale of Children, Prostitution, and Pornography ("Sale of Children Protocol")[160] The CRC protects against the illicit transfer of children abroad, their exploitation, and trafficking. Although the CRC is the main legislation regarding the protection of trafficked children, it has been poorly enforced and lacks effectiveness. In an effort to strengthen the CRC, the Protocol on the Sale of Children was adopted by the U.N. General Assembly on May 25, 2000,[161] and it came into force on January 18, 2002.[162] The United States signed it on July 5, 2000 and ratified it on December 23, 2002, subject to certain reservations, understandings, and declarations. It is the first international instrument to define the "'sale of children' as any act or transaction whereby a child is transferred by any person or group of persons to another for remuneration or any other consideration."[163] The Sale of Children Protocol is arguably applicable to the abduction and use of children as soldiers. It further defines child prostitution as "the use of a child in sexual activities for remuneration or any other form of consideration."[164] Girls abducted into the army are frequently forced into prostitution, sex slavery, and pregnancy. The Sale of Children Protocol was intended to provide the means for greater punishment of offenders through the use of cooperative law enforcement mechanisms.[165] For example, The Sale of Children

---

157. *See* Valentine, *supra* note 2, at 115.

158. *See* Cape Town Annotated Principles, *supra* note 27.

159. *See* ALFREDSON, *supra* note 16.

160. *See* Sale of Children Protocol, *supra* note 95.

161. Dennis, *supra* note 145, at 789.

162. One hundred and one instruments of ratification of the Optional Protocol on the Sale of Children were delivered to the Secretariat of the United Nations. The ratification list is available at http://www.ohchr.org/english/countries/ratification/11_c.htm#reservations (last visited Aug. 15, 2006).

163. Sale of Children Protocol, *supra* note 95, art. 2(a).

164. *Id.* art. 2(b).

165. *See* Dennis, *supra* note 145, at 789.

Protocol provides for broad jurisdiction, enabling the extradition of offenders to ensure prosecution regardless of where they are discovered.[166]

The Sale of Children Protocol also criminalizes any action relating to child prostitution.[167] Article 9 requires parties to strengthen existing laws or create new laws to protect child victims, particularly those who are most vulnerable to trafficking.[168] Articles 8 and 10 of The Sale of Children Protocol further encourage parties to take steps toward multilateral cooperation and to provide assistance to victims and their families.[169] But like many other international human rights agreements, The Sale of Children Protocol lacks the enforcement mechanism to ensure adherence to its provisions.[170]

C. International Humanitarian Laws and the Protection of Children

Current international humanitarian law (as defined in the four Geneva Conventions of 1949[171] and the two Additional Protocols of 1977)[172] provides standards for the treatment of persons including children who are members of the civilian population during a state of armed conflict or occupation. Most of the current armed conflicts today are "internal," whereas the Geneva Conventions regulate international conflicts. However, Article 3 common to the Geneva Conventions defines certain rules to be applied in armed conflicts of a non-international character, like a civil war. Protocol II also applies to all non-international armed conflicts taking place in a territory of a State Party between its armed forces and dissident armed forces.[173] The Additional Protocols of 1977 combine rules of war with rules protecting civilians, including children.

International humanitarian laws protect children in three ways. First, they recognize the need to provide children with *special* protection because children are persons of particular vulnerability, which is a norm of customary

---

166. *See id.*

167. *See id.* at 794.

168. *See* Sale of Children Protocol, *supra* note 95, art. 9.

169. *See id.* arts. 8 & 10.

170. *See id.* art. 15.

171. Geneva Convention for the Amelioration of the Conditions of the Wounded and Sick in Armed Forces in the Field, Aug. 12, 1949, 6 U.S.T. 3114, 75 U.N.T.S. 31 [hereinafter First Convention]; Geneva Convention for the Amelioration of the Condition of the Wounded, Sick and Shipwrecked Members of the Armed Forces at Sea, Aug. 12, 1949, 6 U.S. T. 3217, 75 U.N.T.S. 85 [hereinafter Second Convention]; Geneva Convention Relative to the Treatment of Prisoners of War, Aug. 12, 1949, 6 U.S.T. 3316, 75 U.N.T.S. 135 [hereinafter Third Convention]; Geneva Convention Relative to the Protection of Civilian Persons in Time of War, Aug. 12, 1949, 6 U.S.T. 3516, 75 U.N.T.S. 287 [hereinafter Fourth Convention].

172. *See generally* Protocol I, *supra* note 148; Protocol II, *supra* note 148.

173. Protocol II, *supra* note 148, art. 1.

international law.[174] Second, they question the use of children in military operations.[175] Third, they take into account children's immaturity if they commit offenses during armed conflicts.

International humanitarian law distinguishes between combatants and noncombatants.[176] Children who are civilians are protected against inhumane treatment and directed attacks during international and domestic armed conflicts under the international humanitarian laws.[177] Article 1 common to all Geneva Conventions affords children, as members of the civilian population, protection against inhumane treatment and directed attacks during armed conflicts, whether international or non-international. Article 3 of the Geneva Conventions protects persons "taking no active part in hostilities." Arguably, children used as soldiers are not protected under either Article 1 or Article 3 common to all the Geneva Conventions.

Protocols I and II of the Geneva Conventions provide children with special protection and preferential treatment during warfare.[178] Protocol I obligates States to prevent children under the age of fifteen from taking a direct part in international armed conflict, specifically in recruitment efforts, requiring the States to give priority to the eldest children when recruiting persons between the ages of fifteen and eighteen.[179] Protocol II specifically prohibits children in armed conflict under the age of fifteen from both direct and indirect participation in non-international conflicts.[180]

Article 24 of the Fourth Geneva Convention is devoted to children under the age of fifteen who are orphaned or separated from their families as a result of war. Article 51 of the Fourth Geneva Convention prohibits forced labor of children under the age of eight. The Fourth Geneva Convention also prohibits the use of the death penalty for persons younger than eighteen.

The international humanitarian laws also prohibit killing civilians for revenge. The Geneva Conventions prohibit murder, torture, mutilation, and any other form of brutality imposed by civilians or military representatives. All these international humanitarian legal protections for civilians, if implemented, should amply protect children from being abducted and mistreated during a war, but

---

174. *See* Udombana, *supra* note 20, at 75.

175. *Id.*

176. *See id.* at 74; *see also* Protocol I, *supra* note 148, art. 48. "In order to ensure respect for and protection of the civilian population and civilian objects, the Parties to the conflict shall at all times distinguish between the civilian population and combatants and between civilian objects and military objectives and accordingly shall direct their operations only against military objectives." *Id.*

177. *See* Abbott, *supra* note 83, at 520.

178. *See* Protocol I, *supra* note 148, art. 77; Protocol II, *supra* note 148, art. 4 (according children "special respect" and protections "against any form of indecent assault").

179. *See* Protocol I, *supra* note 148, art. 77; *see also* Protocol II, *supra* note 148, art. 4.

180. *See* Protocol II, *supra* note 148, art. 4.

they arguably will not cover children if they are deemed voluntary child soldiers or combatants. Thus, children taking part in hostilities lose the protective status of "civilians" and become legitimate military targets under the Geneva Conventions and the Additional Protocols.[181]

Notwithstanding the clarity of the laws of war inscribed in the Geneva Conventions and the Additional Protocols of 1977, participants in a majority of the internal conflicts today blatantly violate international humanitarian laws, especially Common Article 3 of the Geneva Conventions that mandates humane treatment of civilians, including children. The Geneva Conventions fall short of providing a precise definition of a "child,"[182] but they do establish fifteen as the age below which a child must enjoy some special protections. In contrast, the Convention on the Rights of the Child actually defines a child and commits States to respect and ensure the rights set forth in the Convention without any discrimination.[183] The African Charter on the Rights and Welfare of the Child[184] defines a *child* as "every human being below the age of 18 years."[185]

The continued use of child soldiers in so many countries today illustrates the failure by the international community to protect the world's children[186] or to implement and adhere to the principles inscribed in the international humanitarian laws. The laws of war and international humanitarian laws as implemented simply do not adequately protect children as civilians[187] and certainly do not adequately protect child soldiers.

D. Domestic and International Human Trafficking Laws

Child soldiers are children who are trafficked into exploitative and dangerous forms of work performed under slave-like conditions. Thus, the laws relating to human trafficking are applicable to the illegal abduction and forcible use of children as soldiers. The U.S. trafficking law, the TVPA,[188] considers children who are trafficked to be "victims of severe forms of trafficking"[189] and therefore eligible for "enhanced benefits." "Traffickers abuse virtually the entire spectrum of rights protected in the Universal Declaration of Human Rights."[190] Victims of

181. *See* Abbott, *supra* note 83, at 523.

182. *See* Udombana, *supra* note 20, at 73.

183. CRC, *supra* note 93, art. 2(1).

184. African Charter on the Rights and Welfare of the Child, July 11, 1990, OAU Doc. CAB/LEG/24.9/49 (entered into force Nov. 29, 1999).

185. *Id.* art. 2.

186. *See* Abbott, *supra* note 83, at 520.

187. *Id.* at 519–20.

188. TVPA, 22 U.S.C. § 7105 (2000). *See* Tiefenbrun, *Sex Slavery in the United States and the Law Enacted to Stop it Here and Abroad*, *supra* note 4 for a complete analysis of the TVPA and its provisions.

189. TVPA, 22 U.S.C. § 7105(b)(1)(C)(ii)(I).

190. Universal Declaration of Human Rights, *supra* note 99.

trafficking are denied the right to freedom of movement, freedom of association, and freedom to have and enjoy a childhood. Traffickers profit mightily from the arbitrary detention; enslavement; rape; and cruel, inhuman, and degrading treatment of children who are deprived of their dignity and equality. Traffickers view their victims as objects, "chattel to be bought and sold as needed."[191]

1. The United States Trafficking Victims Protection Act (TVPA)[192] In October 2000, Congress enacted the Trafficking Victims Protection Act to prevent trafficking, protect victims, and punish perpetrators of trafficking. The TVPA is narrower in scope than the U.N. Palermo Protocol that was passed in November 2000, just one month after the passage of the TVPA. Unlike the Palermo Protocol, the TVPA does not address trafficking for the purposes of exploitative labor, intercountry adoption, organ harvesting, or pornography.[193] The stated purpose of the TVPA is to combat trafficking in persons, which it recognizes to be nothing less than a modern manifestation of slavery[194]—one that disproportionately affects women and children. The TVPA prevents the transnational crime of trafficking from spreading by establishing and funding international programs to educate women and children about trafficking.[195] It also grants victims of trafficking permanent residency status and the right to work in the United States if they are willing to assist with the prosecution of their perpetrators.[196] However, the inadequate protection of these witnesses and the fear of retaliation against their families in their native countries remain challenges to the enforcement of the TVPA.[197]

The TVPA is by far the most comprehensive piece of legislation to address the global problem of trafficking in persons, including children. Children trafficked abroad or into the United States from abroad for the purpose of child soldiering are arguably protected under this statute. The Trafficking in Persons Report ("TIP Report") of 2006 specifically refers to child soldiering in Uganda as an

---

191. *The Global Problem of Trafficking in Persons: Breaking the Vicious Cycle on "Trafficking of Women and Children in the International Sex Trade": Hearing Before the H. Comm. on Int'l Relations*, 106th Cong. 2 (1999) (statement of Harold Koh, Assistant Secretary of State).

192. TVPA, 22 U.S.C. § 7105.

193. Stacey Mathews, *International Trafficking in Children: Will New U.S. Legislation Provide an Ending to the Story?* 27 Hous. J. Int'l L. 649 (2005).

194. *See id.* at 675.

195. TVPA § 102(a), 22 U.S.C. § 7101.

196. *See id.* § 107(c)(3), 22 U.S.C. § 7105.

197. *See Global Trends in Trafficking and the "Trafficking in Persons Report": Hearing Before the Int'l Relations Subcomm. On Int'l Terrorism, Nonproliferation and Human Rights*, 108th Cong. 44 (2003) [hereinafter Mattar Statement] (statement of Mohamed Y. Mattar, S.J.D., Co-director, The Prot. Project, Johns Hopkins Univ. School of Advanced Int'l Studies).

example of one form of human trafficking.[198] Although there is no significant incidence of child soldiering occurring in the United States,[199] the TVPA can help to educate parents in other countries about its dangers and serve as a good model statute for other nations where child soldiering is more prevalent. The TVPA expands U.S. involvement in prevention measures worldwide by increasing assistance and protection available to victims and by enhancing penalties for perpetrators. In other words, it takes the "three P approach"—prevention, protection, and prosecution—and adds the "three R approach"—rescue, rehabilitation, and reintegration—that have been advocated by human rights groups and legal scholars for the past decade.

An important feature of the TVPA is its mandate to compile and publish a yearly report to assess the efforts of governments in meeting minimum standards to eliminate trafficking.[200] This Trafficking in Persons Report (TIP Report) is a comprehensive collection of data on trafficking in countries worldwide. However, although former Secretary of State Colin Powell accurately described the TIP Report as a diplomatic tool to end modern day slavery, others see it as a form of U.S. hegemony and American imperialism designed to embarrass other nations.

The TIP Report includes a short narrative of each country describing the scope and severity of trafficking within that country; a brief discussion of the government's conformity with the requisite minimum standards; and a description of the country's attempts to prevent the offense, prosecute the offenders, and protect the victims involved in trafficking.[201] Governments that fully comply with the minimum standards set forth in the TVPA are placed in Tier One.[202] Governments that are not in full compliance, but are making significant efforts to comply are placed in Tier Two. In 2003, a new Tier Two Watchlist was added

---

198. DEP'T OF STATE, TRAFFICKING IN PERSONS REPORT 10 (2006), http://www.state.gov/documents/organization/66086.pdf [hereinafter 2006 TIP REPORT]; *see also* DEP'T OF STATE, TRAFFICKING IN PERSONS REPORT 7 (2003), http://www.state.gov/documents/organization/21555.pdf [hereinafter 2003 TIP REPORT]; DEP'T OF STATE, TRAFFICKING IN PERSONS REPORT 2 (2002), http://www.state.gov/documents/organization/10815.pdf, [hereinafter 2002 TIP REPORT]; DEP'T OF STATE, TRAFFICKING IN PERSONS REPORT 1 (2001), http://www.state.gov/ documents/organization/4107.pdf [hereinafter 2001 TIP REPORT]. *See generally* DEP'T OF STATE, TRAFFICKING IN PERSONS REPORT (2005), http://www.state.gov/ documents/organization/47255.pdf [hereinafter 2005 TIP REPORT]; DEP'T OF STATE, TRAFFICKING IN PERSONS REPORT (2004), http://www.state.gov/documents/organization/34158.pdf, [hereinafter 2004 TIP REPORT].

199. *See* Colonel Ann Wright, *Blood Diamonds and Blood Oil*, TRUTHOUT, Mar. 6, 2007 (discussing child and teen soldiers in the United States).

200. TVPA, 22 U.S.C. § 7107(b)(1).

201. *See* Tiefenbrun, *The Saga of Susannah*, *supra* note 4 for a complete overview of the TVPA, its organization and content.

202. TVPA, 22 U.S.C. § 7107(b)(1).

for countries that have a significant amount of trafficking but are making some efforts to comply.[203] Countries that do not fully comply with the minimum standards and are not making significant efforts to comply are placed in Tier Three. These countries are subject to the imposition by the United States of non-humanitarian sanctions and the withholding of non-trade related assistance.[204]

The TVPA puts political and economic pressure on countries through sanctions. Although sanctions can be used to modify a government's behavior to conform to U.S. and international law standards, sanctions can also harm women and children in poor countries. The president of the United States can waive the sanctions when necessary to avoid significantly adverse effects on vulnerable populations, including women and children.[205]

The TVPA allows victims of severe trafficking (i.e., trafficked children) to receive enhanced benefits and services from the United States.[206] Victims of severe forms of trafficking are defined as people held against their will "for labor or services, through the use of force, fraud, or coercion for the purpose of subjection to involuntary servitude, peonage, debt bondage, or slavery."[207] Children trafficked into the United States have the opportunity to obtain a T-visa permitting them to stay in the country at least through the duration of their captors' prosecution and perhaps even permanently, if they are willing to assist in the prosecution.[208]

Children who are trafficked are considered "victims of severe forms of trafficking" and as such are "not [to] be detained in facilities inappropriate to their status as crime victims."[209] Moreover, victims of severe forms of trafficking are eligible for assistance programs that provide such benefits as housing, living expenses, medical care, and other services to assist victims in becoming self-sufficient and safe from their perpetrators.[210] Before the passage of the TVPA, adequate protection services were not available to victims of trafficking. For example, a woman under the age of eighteen could be held in jail or prison prior to the trafficker's trial rather than being housed in a facility that could appropriately meet her needs. The refugee programs now available to victims provide an infrastructure for people who have suffered from persecution and torture. Often victims have been torn away from their families and from the culture familiar to

---

203. *Id.* § 7101(b)(1)(B). Note that the additional level in Tier Two, called the Tier Two Watchlist, is provided in the Victims of Trafficking Reauthorization Act of 2003, Pub. L. No. 108-193 Stat. 2875.

204. TVPA, 22 U.S.C. § 7107(b)(1)(C) & (d)(1).

205. *See generally* 2003 TIP REPORT, *supra* note 198.

206. TVPA, 22 U.S.C. § 7105(C) (1).

207. *Id.* 22 U.S.C. § 7102(8)(b).

208. *Id.* 22 U.S.C. § 7105(c)(3).

209. *Id.* 22 U.S.C. § 7105(c)(1)(A).

210. Mathews, *supra* note 193, at 685.

them. Enhanced assistance, intensive mental health counseling, and specialized foster care programs are offered to child victims of trafficking. All these and similar benefits could presumably apply to child soldiers who should be rehabilitated if and when they escape; however, child soldiers are sometimes treated with Western-style therapy that simply does not work for children from Africa, Asia, and other parts of the world.

The U.S. TVPA could serve as a model statute for the establishment of domestic laws in foreign lands against the abduction and use of child soldiers. It is the first U.S. law to penalize a range of serious offenses associated with the trafficking of children. The TVPA advances the prosecution of perpetrators of trafficking through increased punishments and the creation of new criminal offenses. Unfortunately, the TVPA lacks an enforcement arm to reach U.S. citizens engaging in sex acts with minors abroad. That is why President Bush passed the important PROTECT Act.[211]

2. Prosecutorial Remedies and Other Tools to End the Exploitation of Children Today (PROTECT) Act of 2003 ("U.S. PROTECT Act")[212] The U.S. PROTECT Act has extraterritorial reach and can target individuals—both U.S. citizens who commit sexual crimes against children abroad, and those who enter the United States to traffic children for sexual exploitation illegally. Any U.S. citizen aiding in the abduction of child soldiers for the purpose of performing sex acts could be subject to this Act. The PROTECT Act "comprehensively strengthens law enforcement's ability to prevent, investigate, prosecute and punish violent crimes committed against children."[213] Violent crimes are often committed against children by commanders of child soldiers. If U.S. citizens are in any way connected to this activity, they are subject to the PROTECT Act that increases penalties for sex crimes and crimes associated with the trafficking of children. It also modifies the burden of proof requirements for convictions.[214]

Harsh punishment applies to anyone who benefits financially from a child trafficking venture.[215] Penalties for the sexual exploitation of children by previous offenders have been increased as well.[216] For example, a person who was previously convicted of any offense relating to the sexual exploitation of children faces increased minimum and maximum sentences (from ten to twenty years

---

211. *See* PROTECT Act, (2003) Pub. L. No. 108-21.

212. *Id.*

213. Dep't of Justice, Fact Sheet: PROTECT Act (April 30, 2003), http://www. usdoj.gov/opa/pr/2003/April/03_ag_266.htm [hereinafter Fact Sheet: PROTECT Act].

214. World Vision, U.S. Congress Passed Sweeping Child Protection Legislation, http://www.worldvision.org/worldvision/wvususfo.nsf/stable/globalissues_childprotection_protectact?open&lid=protect_act_bkgrnd&lpos=day:txt:protect_act (last visited Oct. 24, 2007).

215. PROTECT Act, *supra* note 211,*Pub.* L. No. 108-21, § 103.

216. *Id.* §§ 103–04.

and from thirty to fifty years, respectively).[217] Another provision adds aiding and abetting liability such that anyone who, for financial gain, "arranges, induces, procures, or facilitates the travel of a person"—knowing that such a person's interstate or foreign travel is "for the purpose of engaging in illicit sexual conduct"—can be sentenced up to thirty years in prison.[218] Such a scenario could arise if a U.S. citizen aids and abets the trafficking of child soldiers. Previously, defendants charged with crimes against children were normally granted bail while awaiting trial. Now, the PROTECT Act models its bail determination rules after legislation used for deciding bail in drug, firearm, and violent crime cases.[219] The PROTECT Act attempts to fill certain gaps in the TVPA and thereby strengthen the U.S. government's ability to prosecute child trafficking offenders.[220] This statute could be used as a model statute for nations whose citizens engage in the recruitment and exploitation of child soldiers from other neighboring countries and who traffic them across a border to engage in direct or indirect hostilities in their own nation.

3. The U.N. Convention Against Organized Transnational Crime and Supplementary Protocol to Prevent, Suppress and Punish Trafficking in Persons, Especially Women and Children ("Palermo Protocol")[221] In December 2000, in Palermo, Italy, the U.N. General Assembly approved and signed the International Convention against Organized Transnational Crime ("Palermo Protocol") and its supplementary protocols on alien smuggling and trafficking in persons.[222] This international trafficking law closely resembles the TVPA and clearly links the crime of child trafficking to international organized crime. The Palermo Protocol defines an organized criminal group as "a structured group of three or more persons existing for a period of time and having the aim of committing a serious crime in order to, directly or indirectly, obtain a financial or other material benefit."[223] The need for the supplementary Protocol to Prevent, Suppress, and Punish Trafficking in Persons, Especially Women and Children came from the knowledge that well-established criminal organizations traffic women and children.[224] Clearly stated, the purpose of the Palermo Protocol is:

217. *Id.* § 103.

218. *Id.* § 105(d).

219. Fact Sheet: PROTECT Act, *supra* note 213. There is no statute of limitations in the PROTECT Act for crimes involving the abduction or physical or sexual abuse of a child.

220. PROTECT Act, *supra* note 211, Pub. L. 108-21, §§ 101–204.

221. Palermo Protocol, *supra* note 5.

222. Press Release, United Nations, More Than 120 Nations Sign New U.N. Convention on Transnational Organized Crime, As High-Level Meeting Concludes in Palermo, U.N. Doc. L/T/4359, Dec. 15, 2000 [hereinafter U.N. Press Release L/T/4359].

223. Palermo Protocol, *supra* note 5.

224. *See generally* Christopher Pilkerton, *Traffic Jam: Recommendations for Civil and Criminal Penalties to Curb the Recent Trafficking of Women From Post-Cold War Russia*, 6 MICH. J. GENDER & L. 221 (1999); Becki Young, *Trafficking of Humans Across United States*

a) To prevent and combat trafficking in persons, paying particular attention to the protection of women and children; and
b) To protect and assist the victims of such trafficking, with full respect for their human rights; and
c) To promote cooperation among States Parties in order to meet those objectives.[225]

The trafficking standards proposed by the Global Alliance against Trafficking Women just prior to the enactment of the Palermo Protocol include eight specific principles that the Palermo Protocol incorporates in its definition of trafficking:

1) Principle of Non-Discrimination: States shall not discriminate against trafficked persons in substantive or procedural law, policy or practice.
2) Safety and Fair Treatment: States shall recognize that trafficked persons are victims of serious human rights abuses, protect their rights notwithstanding any irregular immigration status, and protect them from reprisal and harm.
3) Access to Justice: The police, prosecutors and court shall ensure that their efforts to punish traffickers are implemented within a system that respects and safeguards the rights of the victims to privacy, dignity and safety. An adequate prosecution of traffickers includes prosecution where applicable, for rape, sexual and other forms of assault (including, without limitation, murder, forced pregnancies and abortions), kidnapping, torture, cruel, inhuman or degrading treatment, slavery or slavery-like practices, forced or compulsory labor, debt bondage, or forced marriage.[226]
4) Access to Private Actions and Reparations: States must ensure that trafficked persons have a legal right to seek reparations from traffickers as well as assistance in bringing such actions, if necessary.
5) Resident Status: States shall provide trafficked persons with temporary residence visas (including the right to work) during the pendency of any criminal, civil or other legal actions and shall provide trafficked persons with the right to seek asylum and to have the risk of retaliation considered in any deportation proceedings.[227]
6) Health and Other Services: States shall provide trafficked persons with adequate health and other social services during the period of temporary residence.

Borders: How United States Laws Can Be Used to Punish Traffickers and Protect Victims, 13 GEO. IMMIGR. L.J. 73 (1998).

225. Palermo Protocol, *supra* note 5, art. 2.

226. Girls who are abducted as child soldiers are frequently victims of rape, sexual assault, sex slavery, forced pregnancy, and marriage. They would be protected under this provision.

227. Child soldiers who return home are frequently rejected by their family and friends (if they are alive). They would be protected under this provision.

7) Repatriation and Reintegration: States shall ensure that trafficked persons are able to return home safely, if they so wish, and when they are able to do so.
8) State Cooperation: States must work cooperatively in order to ensure full implementation of these standards.[228]

4. **Palermo Protocol and Provisions Specifically for Trafficking in Children** Mary Robinson, the former U.N. High Commissioner for Human Rights, advocated that a separate section for children be added to the Palermo Protocol.[229] Such a section would help clarify the special problems and needs of children who are victims of trafficking. The Palermo Protocol does include a subsection that provides in particular that the recruitment, transportation, transfer, harboring, or receipt of a child for the purpose of exploitation shall be considered "trafficking in persons" even if this does not involve any of the means set forth in the aforementioned definition of trafficking in persons.[230] A separate section in the Palermo Protocol on trafficking and children not only highlights the special needs of children, but provides an important forum to advocate States' adoption of protections designed specifically for child victims of trafficking schemes.[231]

E. International Laws Relating to Slavery

The prohibition against slavery and the slave trade is a well-established rule of customary law that has been elevated to the status of *jus cogens* in international law.[232] State practice and *opinio juris* on the issue of slavery and the slave trade are

---

228. Trafficking Standards proposed by Global Alliance Against Traffic in Women, Human Rights Standards for the Treatment of Trafficked Persons, http://www. hrlawgroup.org/site/programs/traffic.html (last visited Oct. 24, 2007).

229. U.N. General Assembly, Ad Hoc Comm. on the Elaboration of a Convention Against Transnational Organized Crime, *Informal Note by the United Nations High Commissioner for Human Rights*, ¶ 13, U.N. Doc. A/AC.254/16 (June 28–July 9, 1999).

230. Palermo Protocol, *supra* note 5, art. 3(c).

231. Le Roy G. Potts, Jr., *Global Trafficking in Human Beings: Assessing the Success of the United Nations Protocol to Prevent Trafficking in Persons*, 35 GEO. WASH. INT'L. L. REV. 227, 246 (2003).

232. For a definition of *jus cogens*, see A. Yasmine Rassam, *Contemporary Forms of Slavery and the Evolution of the Prohibition of Slavery and the Slave Trade Under Customary International Law*, 39 VA. J. INT'L. L 303, 311 (1999). Certain customary international rules are elevated to the status of *jus cogens*—rules that cannot be set aside by treaty or acquiescence but only by the formation of a subsequent customary rule of contrary effect. The concept of *delicta juris gentium* or general wrongs against international society takes four forms:

> (1)breach of *jus cogens* or high illegality; (2) cases where international law recognizes general competence to exercise jurisdiction to apprehend, irrespective of nationality (like piracy); (3) acts that harm states indiscriminately (like nuclear testing); and

unequivocal—almost every State has prohibited institutionalized slavery and the slave trade. Nevertheless, human trafficking and the forced use of children as soldiers are contemporary forms of slavery that exist and that blatantly contradict State obligations set forth in international treaties outlawing slavery.

1. Slavery Convention of 1926[233] The 1926 Slavery Convention is the first important attempt made by the League of Nations to fight against slavery and the first international legal instrument to define slavery:

> (1) Slavery . . . [is] the status or condition of a person over whom any or all of the powers attaching to the right of ownership are exercised . . . (2) The slave trade includes all acts involved in the capture, acquisition or disposal of a person with intent to reduce him to slavery; all acts involved in the acquisition of a slave with a view to selling or exchanging him; all acts of disposal by sale or exchange of a slave acquired with a view to being sold or exchanged; and, in general, every act of trade or transport in slaves.[234]

2. U.N. Slavery Convention of 1956 Subsequently, the United Nations expanded the definition of slavery by adopting a new treaty supplementing the 1926 Convention on Slavery. The Supplementary Convention on the Abolition of Slavery, the Slave Trade and Institutions and Practices Similar to Slavery adopted

---

(4) acts infringing principles of law creating rights the beneficiaries of which do not have legal personality or means of protecting (*i.e.*, non-self-governing peoples).

See also IAN BROWNLIE, PRINCIPLES OF PUBLIC INTERNATIONAL LAW 3 (2d ed. 1979). *Jus cogens* is defined in Article 50 of the Vienna Convention on Treaties which states: "A treaty is void if it conflicts with a peremptory norm of general international law from which no derogation is permitted and which can be modified only by a subsequent norm of general international law having the same character." *See* Vienna Convention on the Law of Treaties, art. 50, opened for signature May 23, 1969, 1155 U.N.T.S. 331, 8 I.L.M. 679; *Draft Articles on the Law of Treaties*, [1966] II Y.B. Int'l L. Comm'n, 247–49, 261, 266, art. 50. Despite its universal acceptance, "more authority exists for the category of *jus cogens* than exists for its particular content." Specific human rights are often cited to as *jus cogens*—the least controversial examples being the prohibition of aggressive war, the law against genocide, and the rules prohibiting trade in slaves and slavery. For example, in the Barcelona Traction Case, the International Court of Justice recognized that *jus cogens* were obligations, *erga omnes*—owing to the entire legal community—and that they derive "from the principles and rules concerning the basic rights of the human person, including protection from slavery and racial discrimination." Barcelona Traction, 1970 I.C.J., at 32. The International Law Commission cites as an example of a violation of *jus cogens* "a treaty contemplating or conniving the commission of acts, such as trade in slaves, piracy, or genocide. The most well-established *jus cogens* as human rights are the prohibitions against slavery, genocide, torture and other cruel, inhuman and degrading treatment." OSCAR SCHACTER, INTERNATIONAL LAW IN THEORY AND PRACTICE 343 (1991).

233. *See* 1926 League of Nations Slavery Convention, *supra* note 104.

234. *See id.* art. 17.

in 1956[235] includes certain practices in the definition of slavery: debt bondage, serfdom, and any other institution or practice whereby a woman or a child may be transferred by a person to another. The abduction, transport, and forcible use of children as soldiers is arguably within this definition of slavery.

3. Working Group on Contemporary Forms of Slavery Although the Slavery Conventions of 1926 and 1956 outlaw slavery, they fail to create a permanent international body to evaluate and pursue information about governmental violations that are tantamount to slavery.[236] In place of a formal mechanism to monitor and implement States' obligations to abolish slavery, the Sub-Commission on the Prevention of Discrimination and the Protection of Minorities ("the Sub-Commission") created the Working Group on Contemporary Forms of Slavery ("the Working Group").[237] The Working Group reviews developments on contemporary forms of slavery at the annual session of the Sub-Commission.[238] In order to focus on specific issues pertinent to modern forms of slavery, the Working Group established the Special Rapporteur on the Sale of Children, Child Prostitution and Child Pornography and the Special Rapporteur on Violence Against Women.[239]

The United Nations Working Group consists of independent experts who study current problems regarding slavery and who make recommendations for future action. Its official mandate is to review developments in the field of slavery and the slave trade in all their variant forms of practices and manifestations (including the slavery-like practices of apartheid and colonialism, the traffic in persons, and the exploitation of the prostitution of others) as they are defined in the League of Nations Slavery Convention of 1926, the Supplementary Convention on the Abolition of Slavery of 1956, and the Convention for the Suppression of the Traffic in Persons and of the Exploitation of the Prostitution

235. *See* 1956 U.N. Slavery Convention, *supra* note 105.

236. For more detail, see United Nations Working Group on Contemporary Forms of Slavery, 24th Session Statement by David Weissbrodt on the Working Paper he prepared in association with Anti-Slavery International and Recommendations for the Working Group (June 1999), http://www.antislavery.org/archive/ submission/submission1999-02-Conven.htm.

237. In the early 1970s, the group was known as the "Working Group on Slavery." In 1989, it became "the Working Group on Contemporary Forms of Slavery." U.N. Econ. & Soc. Council [ECOSOC], Comm'n on Human Rights, *Report on the Forty-Fourth Session, Supp. No. 2*, at 102, U.N. Doc. E/CN.4/1988/88 (Feb. 1–Mar. 11, 1988).

238. *See* Richards, *supra* note 54, at 832.

239. *See* Bertrand Ramcharan, Acting High Comm'r for Human Rights, Opening Statement of the Twenty-Eighth Session of the Working Group on Contemporary Forms of Slavery (June 16, 2003), http://www.unhchr.ch/huricane/ huricane.nsf/0/CD157D7658 D8E0D6C1256D480025F878?opendocument.

of Others of 1949.[240] This list should also include the use of child soldiers as victims of slavery and exploitative labor. The U.N. Working Group is the primary body responsible for interpreting the slavery and trafficking conventions. Over the years, the Working Group has integrated a wide range of exploitative practices under its ambit such as sex tourism, sale of children, child prostitution, child pornography, exploitation of child labor, sexual mutilation of female children, and use of children in armed conflict.[241] Therefore, the practice of using child soldiers has been specifically linked to contemporary forms of slavery and trafficking studied by the U.N. Working Group.

Despite repeated requests from the Working Group and from the U.N. Secretary General, governments continually fail to provide information on measures taken to implement the relevant slavery and trafficking conventions and the Working Group's recommendations.[242] Moreover, the lack of mandatory government participation in the Working Group's process diminishes the force of its recommendations.[243]

F. International Labor Conventions and Child Soldiers

1. The Convention Concerning the Prohibition and Immediate Action for the Elimination of the Worst Forms of Child Labour ("ILO Worst Forms of Child Labour Convention 182")[244] The ILO Worst Forms of Child Labour Convention 182 includes the trafficking of children for their use as child soldiers within the definition of child slavery:

---

240. *See* Convention for the Suppression of the Traffic in Persons and of the Exploitation of the Prostitution of Others, G.A. Res. 317(IV), Supp. No.1, at 25, U.N. Doc. E/5544 (Dec. 2, 1949).

241. *See* Richards, *supra* note 54, at 832.

242. U.N. Comm'n on Human Rights, Sub-Comm'n on the Promotion and Protection of Human Rights, *Report of the Working Group on Contemporary Forms of Slavery, Sub-Commission Resolution 1999/17*, E/CN.4/SUB.2/RES/1999/17 (Aug. 26, 1999) [hereinafter *Report of the Working Group*], www.unhchr.ch/Huridocda/Huridoca.nsf/TestFrame/378b8b630886d40c802567ed005027a6?Opendocument.

243. *See* Richards, *supra* note 54, at 835.

244. ILO Worst Forms of Child Labour Convention 182, *supra* note 11. The General Conference of the International Labour Organization adopted the Convention in June 1999, and it entered into force on November 19, 2000, with 158 countries having ratified it. For a complete list of the States that ratified the ILO Worst Forms of Child Labour Convention 182, *see* http://www.ilocarib.org.tt/childlabour/c182.htm (last visited Oct. 24, 2007). Article 22 of the ILO Constitution states that:

> Each of the Members agrees to make an annual report to the International Labour Office on the measures which it has taken to give effect to the provisions of Conventions to which it is a party. These reports shall be made in such form and shall contain such particulars as the Governing Body may request.

Id.; *see also* ILO Recommendation 190, *supra* note 12.

> [A]ll forms of slavery or practices similar to slavery, such as the sale and trafficking of children, . . . including forced or compulsory recruitment of children for use in armed conflicts."[245]

The use of child soldiers is linked to human trafficking, child labor violations, and slavery. The definition of child soldiering in the ILO Worst Forms of Child Labour Convention 182 underscores the link between the trafficking of children and their abduction and illegal employment as child soldiers and slaves. Child soldiers, especially girls, often lead dual lives acting as combatants by day and sex slaves by night. Children are trafficked and used by other soldiers and commanders for sexual exploitation and as child soldiers for combat in direct hostilities.

According to the ILO, approximately 180 million working children between the ages of five and seventeen are engaged all over the world in the worst forms of child labor, as defined above in the ILO Worst Forms of Child Labour Convention 182.[246] Over eight million children are engaged in the so-called *unconditional worst forms of child labor*, including: "slavery, trafficking, and forced recruitment for use in armed conflicts."[247] However, this figure has to be treated with caution, considering the hidden and illegal nature of such activities.

Usually young boys are employed as messengers or spies because of their ability to penetrate enemy lines. Boy children may also be used as porters to carry provisions and munitions while engaging in direct hostilities. Girls are exploited as cooks and sexual slaves for soldiers, and they may be forced to engage in combat and in direct hostilities as well. These children are exposed to injuries and death. Even if they survive, they will forever bear the traces of the physical and psychological violence they suffered during their captivity. Girls who have been victimized by gender violence have difficulty reintegrating in society without special assistance.[248] The ILO finds an identity of circumstances for "the sale and trafficking of children, and forced or compulsory recruitment of children for use in armed conflicts" as well as "other forms of slavery." Thus, there is a direct link between child trafficking, child slavery, and child soldiers.

---

245. *See generally* ILO Worst Forms of Child Labour Convention 182, *supra* note 11.

246. *See generally* INTERNATIONAL LABOUR OFFICE, A FUTURE WITHOUT CHILD LABOUR (2002), http://www.ilo.org/wcmsp5/groups/public/-ed_norm/-declaration/documents/publication/kd00130.pdf.

247. *Id.* at 31–33.

248. For example, Special Rapporteur on Violence Against Women, Ms. Radhika Coomaraswamy states that "[c]orruption in the police seems to be a significant problem in all the countries of the region, especially in the area of trafficking." U.N. Econ. & Soc. Council [ECOSOC], Comm'n on Human Rights, *Integration of the Human Rights of Women and the Gender Perspective: Violence Against Women*, 4, U.N. Doc. E/CN.4/2001/ 73/Add.2. (Feb. 6, 2001).

2. U.S. Department of Labor Recommendation on Child Labour (190) The U.S. Department of Labor recommends the implementation of certain initiatives to stop the increase in the illegal use of child labor for the purposes of engaging in direct or indirect hostilities. To change this horrible trend, the Department recommends a "holistic" approach involving direct interventions, data collection, and partnerships.[249] Direct interventions should be done to raise awareness, monitor the workplace, create alternative income generation for families, create alternative production processes to make child labor unprofitable and unnecessary, and establish affordable and accessible education for children and families. Data collection establishes the basis for selecting and shaping the direct intervention. ILO-IPEC's Statistical Information and Monitoring Program on Child Labor (SIMPOC) has central statistical offices in several countries to conduct household surveys that yield national estimates on the number of working children.[250] Partnerships consist of working relationships between the ILO and governments, employers, and workers to incentivize the elimination of child labor and offer technical assistance to countries that do eliminate child labor as a national policy.[251]

Other strategies proposed to eliminate the worst forms of child labor including child soldiering are: legal, educational, market-based, rescue, rehabilitation, and reintegration. Any of these approaches requires a willingness and capacity of the society to find and help these children. The key to the implementation of these strategies is the identification of children in the worst forms of child labor, awareness raising of the society, and implementation of capacity-building measures.[252]

IV. LITERARY REPRESENTATIONS OF CHILD SOLDIERS

A. *Allah is Not Obliged* by Ahmadou Kourouma[253]

This short but powerful book about the life of a child soldier in Liberia and Sierra Leone won the two most prestigious literary awards in France: the Prix Renaudot

---

249. Elaine L. Chao, *U.S. Secretary of Labor, Faces of Change: Highlights of U.S. Department of Labor Efforts to Combat International Child Labor*, http://digitalcommons.ilr.cornell.edu/cgi/viewcontent.cgi?article=1148&context= key_workplace [hereinafter Faces of Change].

250. *Id.* at 3.

251. *Id.*

252. *See* Elaine L. Chao, U.S. Secretary of Labor, Advancing the Campaign Against Child labor, Volume II: Addressing the Worst Forms of Child Labor, U.S. Department of Labor, Bureau of International Labor Affairs 9 (2002), www.dol.gov/ILAB.

253. The French title of this book is *Allah n'est pas obligé* (Editions du Seuil, 2000), translated into English by Frank Wynne and published in London (William Heinemann, Random House Group Limited: London 2006) [hereinafter Allah is Not Obliged], available in French and English.

and the Prix Goncourt. The book is written by Ahmadou Kourouma, an African man who was born in the Ivory Coast in 1927, fought in the French colonial army in Indochina, and later studied science in France. Ahmadou Kourouma eventually returned to the Ivory Coast, worked in insurance, was put in jail because he opposed the regime, and spent many years in exile. He ended up becoming a playwright and the author of four novels before dying in 2004. Kourouma is recognized as one of the major figures of contemporary African literature.

Allah is Not Obliged is more than just a book about child soldiers—it is a tale about the utter despair of children victimized by decadence in Africa and the corruption of social values during endless and inhumane tribal warfare. Kourouma shocks his readers into seeing that even the most humane members of society can somehow lose their values and be capable of committing unspeakable atrocities. The brutality of a child soldier's life experience can make even innocent young children become professional killers. For example, at the end of the book the young narrator is saddened because he cannot ever become an evil "lycaeon" (as his mother and father are already both dead, he cannot personally kill them, which is the rite of passage to become a prestigious lycaeon). Kourama describes this serious ethical transformation of the innocent boy into an evil killing machine through the effective symbolic metaphor of the lycaeon:

> [L]ycaeons are wild dogs that hunt in packs. They gobble everything; mother, father, all and everything. When they finish sharing a victim, every lycaeon goes off to clean his self. If one comes back with blood on his fur, even one drop of blood, they think he is wounded and he's gobbled up by the others right there. That's what it is. Got it? They have no mercy. Your mother alive?[254]

The narrator adds that "[t]o be a brave young lycaeon of the revolution, you must first kill with your bare hands . . . one of your own parents."[255] Thus, Birahima, who grew up in a very religious home, has his ethics and social values totally transformed by the devastating experience of being a child soldier.

In the spirit of Voltaire and through the extensive use of irony and sarcasm Kourouma debunks the power of religion to purify man's soul.[256] He depicts the fate of a convent transformed into a brothel[257] for the carnal use of the commanders, describing Mother Superior Marie-Beatrice as "a saint who made love like every woman in the universe." Mother Superior Marie-Beatrice turns out to be one of the most superior fighters in this topsy-turvy world where good is evil and evil is good. Kourouma accuses the U.N. Peacekeepers of "slaughtering

254. *Id.* at 173.
255. *Id.* at 174.
256. *See id.* at 134.
257. *See id.* at 74.

innocent civilians and massacring people, all in the name of humanitarian peacekeeping."[258]

This sad but insightful tale is told by an innocent ten-year-old boy, Birahima, who is ceaselessly stunned by the horrors of war, sickened by the cruelty and barbarism[259] of his own people, and educated into the power structures and customs that fuel Africa's bitter tribal wars. For example, he stuns the readers by revealing Sierra Leone's leader of the Rebels, Foday Sankoh, and his unique solution to stop democratic elections that might vote him out:

> Someone with no arms couldn't vote. All Foday Sankoh had to do was cut off the arms of as many people, as many of the citizens of Sierra Leone as possible. Every Sierra Leone prisoner had his hands cut off before being sent back into the territory occupied by government forces. If a woman showed up with a baby on her back, the woman's hands were amputated and the baby's hands too . . . because they'll be voters some day.[260]

This is the kind of madness that Birahima witnessed as a child soldier and that ultimately transformed him into a killer.

Birahima grew up in the Ivory Coast in a matriarchal family with a crippled mother, a feisty grandmother, and an absentee father who traveled all the time. Birahima was a "fearless, blameless kid" who "slept anywhere [he] wanted and stole all kinds of stuff to eat."[261] He loved his long-suffering mother who was always crying because she, like her son, was a victim of a failed society caught up

---

258. *Id.* at 126; *see also id.* at 140–41. "The peacekeeping forces didn't keep the peace, they didn't take any unnecessary risks. They weren't bothered about details, they just fired shells at random, they fired shells at the people doing the attacking and at the people being attacked. They bombed every part of the town. . . ." *Id.*

259. *See id.* at 132–33.

> Prince Johnson . . . took Doe by the ear and sat him down. He cut off his ears, the right ear after the left . . . The more the blood flowed, the more Johnson laughed, the more delirious he became. Prince Johnson ordered that Samuel Doe's fingers be cut off, one by one, and with this torture victim squealing like a suckling calf, he had his tongue cut out. Through the torrent of blood, Johnson hacked at the arms, one after the other. When he tried to hack off the left arm, the victim had had enough: he gave up the ghost ("give up the ghost" means "die").

Later Kourouma narrates that Johnson ordered Samuel Doe's heart to be removed, and "one of the officers ate some human flesh to make himself look more cruel, more brutal, more barbarous and inhuman—real, genuine human flesh. Samuel Doe's heart was put to one side for the officer so he could make a delicious kebab out of it." *Id.* at 133.

260. *Id.* at 165.

261. *Id.* at 5.

in mystery, magic,[262] and superstition.[263] African society deprived her of her rights as a child and as a woman:[264] She was the victim of a forced and badly executed female genital circumcision[265] and sacrificial ceremony of excision where the most beautiful girl is killed by the djinn (magical creature) of the forest who keeps her as his sacrifice.[266] Birahima's mother also suffered from a festoring, painful ulcer on her amputated leg that was never treated properly[267] because she was a black African native who did not have the same privileges as the black African Americans. Birahima remembers that "sometimes, I'd fall on to Maman's ulcer and she'd howl with the pain. The ulcer would start bleeding. Maman would howl like a hyena with its paws caught in the teeth of a wolf trap."[268] Birahima's mother dies literally rotting to death, like the corrupt African society that will soon capture Birahima and force him into a child soldier's life of murder for murder's sake.

When both his father and mother die, Birahima leaves his native village in search of a faraway aunt, hoping to find a family and stability. Birahima and his friend Yacouba, the sorcerer, go off together on this thankless journey. They cross the border into Liberia and are soon captured by a rebel force. They are then recruited into military service as child soldiers where they learn to terrorize and murder civilians in Liberia and Sierra Leone. In these countries people are not protected by civil order, and these child soldiers have no choice but to struggle for survival.

---

262. *Id.* at 24. "My maman died because Allah wanted her back. The imam said that a devout Muslim isn't allowed to criticize Allah or say anything bad about him. Then he said that my mother didn't die of magic, she died of her ulcer." *Id.*

263. An example of this superstition is the belief that "[i]f you truly loved the Lord God and Jesus Christ, bullets wouldn't hit you; they'd kill other people instead, because it is God alone who kills the bad guys, the arseholes, the sinners and the damned." *Id.* at 70.

264. *See id.* at 26. "Everywhere in the world a woman isn't supposed to leave her husband's bed even if that husband curses her and punches her and threatens her. The woman is always wrong. That's what they call women's rights." "On account of women's rights, the two children were taken from their mother and given to their father." *Id.*

265. *See id.* at 11.

266. *See id.* at 14.

267. *See id.* at 17.

> The nurse said that what maman was suffering from was not a *toubab* disease, it was a Black Nigger African Native disease. A disease that the medicine and the science of the white man could not cure. "Only the grigris of an African healer can heal your wound. If the captain operates on your leg, you will die, absolutely die, you will die like a dog." Said the nurse who was also a major. The nurse was a Muslim and could not tell a lie.

Id.

268. *Id.* at 9.

One of the most vivid examples of why children become child soldiers is the story Birahima tells of a young boy named Kik whose village is attacked during the tribal wars:

> Kik ran into the forest. And the kids stayed in the forest all the time they could hear the gunfire from the village. Kik stayed in the forest. It was only the next morning when there was no more noise that the children dared to go back to their family huts. Kik went back to his family hut and found his father's throat cut, his brother's throat cut, his mother and his sister raped and their heads bashed in. All of his relatives, close and distant, dead. And when you've got no one left on earth, no father, no mother, no brother, no sister, and you're really young, just a little kid, living in some fucked-up barbaric country where everyone is cutting everyone's throat, what do you do? You become a child-soldier of course, a small-soldier, a child soldier so you can have lots to eat and cut some throats yourself, that's all your only option.[269]

The narrator describes how the children are captured and recruited:

> The kid, the child-soldier, who's about as tall as an officer's cane, chats to the guys on the motorbike protecting the convoy. They get to know each other a bit, laughing and joking as if they drank beer together every night. Then the kid whistles, then he whistles again. Then a four-by-four truck comes out of the forest all covered in camouflage leaves. A four-by-four full of kids, child-soldiers, small soldiers. Kids about this tall . . . as tall as an officer's cane.[270]

Kourouma also describes the significant role that girl child soldiers play in these tribal wars. "The funniest thing is that there's girls, genuine girls with real AK-47s showing off. But there aren't too many girls. Only the cruel ones: only the one's who'd stick a live bee right in your eye."[271] One of the cruelest girls becomes a general in the group of child soldiers.[272] Another commander girl soldier sexually violates a boy soldier in a surprising and ironic reversal of expectation.[273]

The book is a mixture of fact and fiction as the author tries to debunk traditional beliefs about African society through a blend of irony, sarcasm, humor,

---

269. *Id.* at 90.

270. *Id.* at 46.

271. *Id.* at 47.

272. *Id.* at 102. "General Onika was a small woman, lively as a nanny-goat whose kid has been taken from her. With her general's stripes and her AK-47, she ran the whole show." *Id.* "The son had married three wives and all three wives were commanders in charge of the three most important divisions: finance, prisons and child-soldiers." *Id.* at 103.

273. *Id.* at 104.

and vivid descriptions of atrocities. The author shocks the readers by making outrageous but ironic proclamations such as:

> Child-soldiers are the most famous celebrities of the late twentieth century, so whenever a child-soldier dies, we have to say a funeral oration. That means we have to recount how in this great big fucked-up world they came to be a child-soldier.[274]

The book appears to be factual because Kourouma provides detailed information about the life of child soldiers and the bestial conduct of corrupt criminal despots and warlords of various West African countries, such as Charles Taylor, Foday Sankoh, and Prince Johnson. Despite rumors about the good life of child soldiers,[275] Birahima is amazed that he is given only a gun, very little food, scant wages, and plenty of hash to fight in a civil war with other child and adult soldiers who are also constantly starving[276] and constantly pumped up on drugs. He refers to the child soldiers as "the drugged-up child-soldiers," "the child-soldiers [who] were fucked up on drugs."[277] The drugs make them strong and fearless: "We were dying to fight, we all felt as strong as bulls from all the hash. . . ."[278]

Birahima recounts what he sees in this chaotic world of war through the eyes of a naïve ten-year-old and in the fresh idiom of a child who is just learning French. Thus, with the use of four dictionaries, he writes in passable French mixed with *malinke* and pidgin English, giving parenthetical explanations of the most basic terms, as if he is speaking to an audience of children. The immediacy of Kourouma's style and language and the gripping details of his narration add authenticity to his depictions of death, torture, amputations, fear, superstition, and madness that surround him on this journey through the hell of war. When the book comes to an end, Birahima finally escapes and the tale is brought full circle to where it began, like the classical pattern of inevitable tragic repetition.

---

274. *Id.* at 83.

275. *See id.* at 37.

> He said they had tribal wars in Liberia, and street kids like me could be child-soldiers. Small soldiers had every-fucking-thing. They had AK-47s. AK-47s are Kalashnikov guns invented by the Russians so you can shoot and keep shooting and never stop. With the Ak-47s the small-soldiers got every-fucking-thing. They had money, they even had American dollars. They had shoes and stripes and radios and helmets and even cars that they call four-by-fours. I shouted *Walahe*! *Walahe*! I want to go to Liberia. Right now this minute. I want to be a child-soldier, a small soldier.

Id.

276. "With all the hash, we got hungrier and hungrier. Hash isn't good when you're hungry. So we ate all the fruit we could find and after that we ate roots and after that leaves. And even after all that Yacouba still said Allah in his infinite goodness never leaves empty a mouth he has created." *Id.* at 81–82.

277. *Id.* at 107.

278. *Id.* at 109.

B. *Beasts of No Nation* by Uzodinma Iweala[279]

> *All we are knowing is that, before the war we are children and now we are not.*[280]

Uzodinma Iweala's Harvard thesis developed into a very beautiful and informative work of fiction that effectively illustrates how child soldiers become trafficking victims.[281] *Beasts of No Nation* is a novel written in the urgency and immediacy of the present tense in order to highlight the severity of the related crimes of child abduction for the use of soldiering and child sex trafficking. Iweala's novel is a realistic slice of life that portrays in vivid pictures the human rights principles and laws relating to child enslavement via abduction, forced enlistment, and trafficking.

Beasts of No Nation paints a close-up portrait of a traumatized child soldier who was victimized, just like the three hundred thousand child soldiers today who are begging for help to escape from enslavement and the fear of death. These child victims and their parents or caretakers do not know that laws actually exist to protect children. Iweala portrays one of these desperate children, Agu, who tells his tragic tale in pidgin English bristling with repetition, adjectival verbs, metaphors, similes, and capitalized exclamations that reveal his youth and the depth and intensity of his pleas for help from the international community.

Agu is the precocious, gentle son of a village school teacher and a religious mother who is dragooned one day into the madness of a West African nation's civil war. Despite his youth, he is forced through rigorous indoctrination to shoulder a soldier's heavy burden. Agu is very soon molded into a hard fighting man by his demented guerrilla leader who forces him to witness his father's savage slaying. After his father's murder, Agu is left all alone in the world, and he is driven by an unrelenting need to belong to a group or a family. When he is captured and indoctrinated by the armed group, Agu soon becomes a killer, plagued by a muddled sense of revenge and guilt. He butchers a mother and her daughter when his ragtag unit raids a defenseless village. Starved for both food and affection, Agu is frequently sodomized by his Commandant and rewarded with extra food scraps and a dry place to sleep.[282]

---

279. IWEALA, *supra* note 13.

280. *Id.* at 36.

281. *See generally* Boris Kachka, *Young Gun*, NEW YORK, Nov. 28, 2005, at 41.

282. Jolisa Gracewood, *I am Hearing Screaming*, NZ LISTENER May 13–19, 2006, http://www.listener.co.n2/issue/203/artsbooks/6060/i_am_hearing_screaming.html.

The unnamed West African nation provides the setting for this unsettling story of the life of a child soldier.[283] Iweala's fiction represents the "countless victims whose names remain unknown." When asked by *New York Times* writer Boris Kachka, "Why fictionalize it at all?" Iweala responded, "In non-fiction there is still that distance: 'This is not happening to me' . . . but in fiction, it allows you to transport yourself in the way that nonfiction doesn't."[284] The reality is that *Beasts of No Nation* could be the life story of any child soldier in any country afflicted by hatred, mistrust, and civil war.[285]

The story grips the reader by its brutality and unremitting intensity. Iweala is a trafficked child who is deprived of the most basic human rights and prevented from "develop[ing] physically, mentally, morally, spiritually and socially in a healthy and normal manner and in conditions of freedom and dignity."[286] Through its impressionistic narration, the exotic singsong cadence of its style, and the narrator's peculiar use of tense,[287] the book enables its readers to observe with disbelief the human rights violations and horrifying experiences Agu is forced to endure: rape, denial of education, utter despair, development of his own desire for revenge, constant starvation, use of serious weaponry, exposure to and forced intake of drugs that make him fight fearlessly. His experience fosters self-hate, a lingering sense of hopelessness, and the impossibility of his escape from his dreadful captivity and enslavement.

1. Rape Agu participates in massacres and rapes of an ill-defined enemy. The International Criminal Tribunal of the Former Yugoslavia (ICTY) and the International Criminal Tribunal in Rwanda (ICTR)[288] have made major strides in deciding cases involving the systematic use of rape as a method of warfare. Rape is not only a war crime, but also a crime against humanity, a form of torture,[289] and a form of genocide. When rape is inflicted on or by children, it is even a more heinous crime. Agu rapes women indiscriminately, but he is himself

---

283. *See* Renee Graham, *In Beasts Lambs Are Forced to Lead the Slaughter*, Boston Globe, Dec. 5, 2005.

284. *See generally* Kachka, *supra* note 281.

285. *See generally* Graham, *supra* note 283.

286. Declaration of the Rights of the Child, *supra* note 121, princ. 2; *see also* CRC, *supra* note 93, art. 27.

287. *See generally* Iweala, *supra* note 13.

288. *See generally* Prosecutor v. Akayesu, Case No. ICTR 96-4-T, Judgment (Sept. 2, 1998).

289. Statute of the International Criminal Tribunal for the Former Yugoslavia ("ICTY"), art. 5(g), *reprinted in* 32 I.L.M. 1159, 1194 (1993) (noting that crimes against humanity include rape); *see* Janet Halley et al. *From the International to the Local in Feminist Legal Responses to Rape, Prostitution/Sex Work, and Sex Trafficking: Four Studies in Contemporary Governance Feminism*, 29 Harv. J.L. & Gender 335, 342–47 (2006) (discussing the role of ICTY and International Criminal Tribunal for Rwanda (ICTR) in developing law on rape and sexual violence of women).

made into a sex slave by the Commandant.[290] In this maddening world of tribal warfare, sexual violence is equated with manliness in the mind of the child soldiers, even though Agu is personally repelled by the act of having sex with his Commandant. Agu refers frequently to his penis as "my soldier."[291] When the Commandant sodomizes him, Agu is in pain and fear:

> He is telling me, take off your clothe(sic). I do not want to be taking off my clothe but I am not saying so because Commandant is powerful more than me and he is also sometimes giving me small favor like more food . . . But me, I am not struggling because I am knowing that he will be killing me if I am struggling and since I am not wanting to die, I just let him to be moving back and forward even though it is hurting me so much.[292]

2. Denial of Education Agu's life represents flagrant violations of CRC Article 32 that protects children from "any work that is likely to be hazardous or to interfere with the child's education."[293] Before Agu was abducted into the rebel army, he was like any typical little boy receiving a compulsory education in a small village schoolhouse. His abduction into armed combat deprived him of an education. Wars actually forced the schools to close in Uganda and in other African countries.[294]

> I am learning how to read very early in my life from my mother and my father . . . I was the smartest person in my class, so smart that the only thing I am having to learn is writing. . . . But these thing are before the war and I am only remembering them like dream.[295]

3. Helplessness and the Desire for Revenge of "Lost Children" Agu describes the state of helplessness and revenge experienced by children like himself who are victims of family massacres and who volunteer to become soldiers once they are abducted: "If you are staying with me, I will be taking care of you and we will be fighting the enemy that is taking your father . . . So I am joining. Just like that. I am soldier."[296]

Additionally, child soldiers who are survivors of family massacres experience "survivor's guilt," and are filled with anger and desire for revenge.[297] Iweala's responses to his own family massacre demonstrate the concept of "survivor's

290. *See* Iweala, *supra* note 13, at 84–85.
291. *Id.* at 95–96.
292. *Id.* at 83–85.
293. CRC, *supra* note 93, art. 32(1).
294. *See* Iweala, *supra* note 13, at 29.
295. *Id.* at 24–28.
296. *Id.* at 11.
297. Brett & McCallin, *supra* note 72, at 61–63.

guilt":[298] "Commandant is saying that she is enemy, she is stealing our food, and killing my family, because she is enemy . . . I am liking the sound of knife chopping KPWUDA KPWUDA on her head and how the blood is just splashing . . ."[299]

C. Soldiers But Not Real Soldiers: Prosecutor v. Thomas Lubanga Dyilo[300]

Children who are abducted by a group that engages in armed combat see themselves as "soldiers," but they also know that they are not "real soldiers" because they have no uniform.[301] In *Beasts of No Nation*, the narrator's fine distinction between soldiers and real soldiers refers to a very important and controversial legal issue regarding the nature of "national armed forces or groups" as set forth in the Rome Statute of the International Criminal Court (ICC).

The ICC Pretrial Chamber I (the "Chamber") decided this very question when it issued its decision on the confirmation of charges in the case of *Prosecutor v. Thomas Lubanga Dyilo*.[302] In that case, the Chamber confirmed that there were substantial grounds to believe that Lubanga (the President of the *Union des Patriotes Congolais* (UPC) and the Commander-in-Chief of its former military wing, the *Forces Patriotiques pour la Libération du Congo* (FPLC)) is responsible for committing war crimes in the Ituri region of the Democratic Republic of the Congo (DRC) in 2002 and 2003. The Chamber confirmed there was substantial evidence to believe that Lubanga was responsible, as co-perpetrator, for the conscription and enlistment of children under the age of fifteen years into the FPLC from the beginning of September 2002 to June 2, 2003 in violation of Articles 8(2)(b)(xxvi) and 25(3)(a) of the Rome Statute, and from June 2, 2003 to August 13, 2003 in violation of Articles 8(2)(e)(vii) and 25(3)(a).[303] The *Lubanga* case is only the second major international criminal proceeding to focus on the use of child soldiers, following the decision of the Special Court for Sierra Leone in the case of *Prosecutor v. Sam Hinga Norman* in 2004.[304]

---

298. *See* Gracewood, *supra* note 282.

299. Iweala, *supra* note 13, at 51.

300. Prosecutor v. Dyilo, Doc. No. ICC-01/04-01/06, Decision on Confirmation of Charges (Jan. 29, 2007). The charges of this important case in the International Criminal Court (ICC) will be discussed in this section of the paper, especially with regard to the distinction made between national armed forces and other paramilitary groups.

301. *See* Iweala, *supra* note 13, at 33–34.

302. Prosecutor v. Dyilo, *supra* note 300, Doc. No. ICC-01/04-01/06.

303. *See id.*; *see also* Jason Morgan-Foster, *ICC Confirms Charges Against DRC Militia Leader*, ASIL Insights, Mar. 9, 2007, http://asil.org/insights/2007/03/ insights070307.html.

304. Prosecutor v. Sam Hinga Norman, Case No. SCSL-2004-14-14-AR72 (E), Decision on Preliminary Motion Based on Lack of Jurisdiction (May 31, 2004). (Special Court of Sierra Leone).

The prosecutor in the *Lubanga* case, Luis Moreno-Ocampo, charged Lubanga under Articles 8(2)(e)(vii) and 25(3)(a) of the Rome Statute with the war crimes of (1) conscripting children into armed groups, (2) enlisting children into armed groups, and (3) using children to participate actively in hostilities.[305] Article 8(2)(e)(vii) provides that "conscripting or enlisting children under the age of fifteen years into the national armed forces or using them to participate actively in hostilities" during a non-international armed conflict constitutes a war crime. Article 25(3)(a) of the Rome Statute provides for individual criminal responsibility for anyone who "commits . . . a crime, whether as an individual, jointly with another or through another person, regardless of whether that other person is criminally responsible."

The Chamber concluded that between July 2002 and June 2, 2003 there existed in the Ituri region an international armed conflict, and between June 2, 2003 and August 13, 2003 there was a non-international armed conflict.

The Chamber then examined three material elements of the crime. It looked at the terms *conscription or enlistment*, and noted that these terms in the Rome Statute do not carry the same meaning as *recruiting*, which is the term used with respect to the prohibition against child soldiers in Article 77 of Additional Protocol I to the Geneva Conventions.[306] The Chamber further concluded that the terms *conscription* and *enlistment* are distinct from each other. Conscription is "forced recruitment" whereas enlistment is "voluntary recruitment." It is important to note that the Chamber concluded that "consent of the child" is not a valid defense to a charge of "conscription or enlistment." Hopefully, this decision will finally put to rest the problematic necessary element of consent with regard to the distinction between trafficking of persons and smuggling.

The Court then examined the phrase "using them to participate actively in hostilities" as distinguished from the controversial phrase "take a direct part in hostilities" found in Article 51(3) of Additional Protocol I of the Geneva Conventions.[307] The Chamber placed limits on this "participate actively" standard, holding that any activity that is "manifestly without connection to the hostilities" would not fall within the prohibition (e.g., food delivery, or "domestic help in an officer's married accommodation"). But acting as a bodyguard would fall within the "active participation" standard.[308] However, girl soldiers who are employed against their will as domestic help in the armed camp and forced into becoming the "wife" of a commander will no longer be protected under this finding.

---

305. *See generally* Prosecutor v. Dyilo, *supra* note 300, Document Containing the Charges (Aug. 28, 2006).

306. *See* Protocol I, *supra* note 148, art. 77(2).

307. *Id.* art. 51(3).

308. *See* Prosecutor v. Dyilo, *supra* note 300, at ¶¶ 261–63.

The Chamber then compared the language of Article 8(2)(b)(xxvi) with Article 8(2)(e) (vii), noting that Article 8(2)(b)(xxvi) of the Rome Statute regarding child conscription in international conflict uses the language "into the *national armed forces*" whereas Article 8(2)(e)(vii) of the Rome Statute (under which Lubanga was actually charged) uses the language "into *armed forces* or *groups*." The Chamber held that if the term *national* refers only to "governmental" that would contravene the very purpose of the Rome Statute, which is to make sure that "the most serious crimes of concern to the international community as a whole must not go unpunished." The Chamber concluded that the term *national armed forces* was not limited to the armed forces of a State.[309] Thus, the Rome Statute permits Lubanga to be prosecuted for conscripting or enlisting child soldiers into the FPLC, which is a nongovernmental force, during both the non-international and international phases of the conflict.

D. Child Soldiers: Civilians or Combatants

The distinction between *civilians* and *combatants* is related to the issue of whether a paramilitary or nonnational armed group is a real army and whether the persons serving in this armed group are real soldiers. According to the finding in *Prosecutor v. Thomas Lubanga Dyilo*, the leader of the Congolese militia can be prosecuted for conscripting or enlisting child soldiers into a nongovernmental force during both the non-international and international phases of the conflict. Does this hold true for the soldiers in this armed group? Is a child soldier a civilian or a combatant if he is not wearing a uniform and not working for State armed forces, but rather is acting against his will as a soldier in an armed group? The distinction between combatants and civilians is critical to the protection of the rights of a child soldier. Civilians and combatants are treated differently under the Geneva Conventions and under other laws of war. If Agu is a soldier, he is not a civilian. But if he is not a "real" soldier, does that mean he is eligible for civilian protection during wartime? Or worse, is he not protected under either category?

1. Starvation Children, particularly those orphaned or disconnected from civil society, often volunteer to join any group if they believe it is the only way to guarantee regular meals, clothing, or medical attention.[310] But Agu remains hungry most of the time that he is with the other child soldiers.[311] Iweala says, "On the ground he is writing HUNGRY and I am wanting to say to him I am hungry too. I am hungry too, but the word are not coming out of my mouth."[312]

2. Slavery The children who are abducted and used as child soldiers are abused badly and enslaved, especially because they are not permitted to leave or

---

309. *Id.* at ¶¶ 280–85.

310. SINTER, *supra* note 25, at 62.

311. IWEALA, *supra* note 13, at 117–18.

312. *See id.* at 37.

return home to the comforts of their family. Agu realizes very soon after he joins the ranks of the young soldiers that he is in fact a slave. He has a deep sense of despair knowing that he cannot escape his enslavement.[313]

3. Use of Weaponry Agu and the other child soldiers are powerless and alone. That is why they are especially impressed with the power of the small guns they are given.[314] The special names the child soldiers give themselves (such as "Rambo"),[315] the guns themselves, and the drugs[316] they are forced to take (appropriately called "gun juice") all give these young soldiers a false but effective sense of power.

Regrettably, there is presently no universal treaty addressing small arms and light weapons proliferation. Most of the laws that exist in this area are nation-specific and lack international coordination.[317] However, the ongoing elaboration of a draft Protocol on the Illicit Manufacturing, Circulation, and Proliferation of Small Arms and Light Weapons and Illicit Trafficking in Firearms, Ammunitions and Other Related Materials by the U.N. Group of Experts on Small Arms is a welcome development.[318]

Article 38 of the CRC states that persons under age fifteen[319] should not bear arms, perpetrate violence, or wear the uniform of any combative group in any form of political conflict in the world. Yet even though 191 States have ratified the CRC, many nations violate this provision and forcibly recruit children younger than fifteen.[320] "Commandant is saying that I am too small to be carrying gun because small person is not holding gun well and just bouncing up and down when they are shooting. Instead he is giving me knife."[321] Iweala shows, through a powerful child's-eye view, how disposable especially the smallest child is to the commanders of these armies of children: "[I]f I am throwing gun away, then Rambo will be throwing me away because gun is more important than me."[322]

---

313. *See id.* at 41–42.

314. *See id.* at 31.

315. *Id.* at 43.

316. Agu calls his drug "gun juice." *Id.* at 43–44.

317. *See* GRADUATE INST. INT'L STUDIES, SMALL ARMS SURVEY 2001: PROFILING THE PROBLEM 123–26 (2001) (outlining various national approaches to the problem of illegal arms transfers).

318. *See* Udombana, *supra* note 20, at 67. The Protocol relating to small arms traffic, when adopted, will supplement the Convention Against Transnational Organized Crime, signed at the High-Level Political Signing Conference in Palermo, Italy in Dec. 2000.

319. Note that the age is now eighteen, pursuant to the Children in Armed Conflict Protocol, *supra* note 94.

320. *See* CRC, *supra* note 93, art. 38.

321. IWEALA, *supra* note 13, at 43.

322. *Id.* at 129.

4. Exposure to and Forced Intake of Drugs Another human rights violation affecting child soldiers and trafficked children is the forced use of drugs to numb the experience of warfare. Drugs such as cocaine and marijuana are often given to child soldiers to alleviate their fears and enhance their capacity in battle.[323] However, the use of drugs destroys a child's ability to develop physically, mentally, morally, spiritually, and socially in a healthy and normal manner and in conditions of freedom and dignity.[324] "[E]verybody is getting gun juice. Everybody is always wanting gun juice because it is drug and making life easy easy."[325]

5. Fostering of Self-Hate In Iweala's novel gruesome depictions of random killings alternate with Agu's confused sense of guilt: "I am not bad boy. I am not bad boy. I am soldier and soldier is not bad if he is killing."[326] They feel guilty because they have survived and others are dead due to their inability to fight against the leader's commands. The children have lost their autonomy and self-control.

6. Autonomy "He (Commandant) is taking my hand and bringing it down so hard on top of the enemy's head. I am vomiting everywhere. I cannot be stopping myself."[327] Children recruited into war have no choice but to obey orders and commit atrocities or die themselves. The more people they kill, the better they are accepted by their commanders and peers:

> If they are ordering me KILL, I am killing, SHOOT, I am shooting, ENTER WOMAN, I am entering woman and not even saying anything even if I am not liking it. I am killing everybody, mother, father, grandmother, grandfather, soldier. It is all the same. It is not mattering who it is, just that they are dying.[328]

7. Inability to Escape Once abducted, children must comply with their captors or die.[329] The ultimate aim of the process is to foster a child's dependency on an armed organization and prevent escape.[330]

> I am not wanting to fight today because I am not liking the gun shooting and the knife chopping and the people running. I am not liking to hear people scream or to be looking at blood. So I am asking to myself, why am I fighting? Why can I not just be saying no? Then I am remembering how one boy is

---

323. *See* Machel Report, *supra* note 36, ¶ 47; *see also* David Ott, *Under Age and Under Arms*, HERLAD (Glasgow), Jan. 12, 1999, at 11 (revealing that leaders give children drugs to make them more efficient killers).

324. *See* Udombana, *supra* note 20, at 79.

325. IWEALA, *supra* note 13, at 43.

326. *Id.* at 22.

327. *Id.* at 21.

328. *Id.* at 135.

329. *See* SINTER, *supra* note 25, at 61.

330. *See id.* at 57.

> refusing to fight and Commander is just telling us to jump on his chest, so we are jumping on his chest until it is only blood that is coming out of his mouth.[331]

Agu represents children who are hopeless victims of war.[332] "Hope is dying, just burning up in the fire of bomb that is hitting truck."[333] The use and abduction of child soldiers is one of the most horrifying forms of child slavery and trafficking that must be stopped before we raise a whole generation of deprived and hate-filled children who populate the world and proliferate more conflict. Agu understands this when he says, "I am knowing I am no more child."[334]

V. CONCLUSION AND PROPOSALS FOR SOLUTIONS

A. So Many Laws

Despite a profusion of domestic and international laws that prohibit the use of child soldiers, this inhumane and widespread practice continues today and is likely to increase in the future due to the economics of war and a worldwide culture of violence. Considering that the use of child soldiers is "rooted in the endemic competition for economic resources"[335] and fueled by the huge profits from the traffic in drugs, weapons, and human beings, any proposal to eradicate child soldiering must necessarily involve economic solutions in order to effectuate real change in this hideous practice and to firmly reestablish traditional ethics relating to the protection and preservation of children's rights. Moreover, to eradicate the misuse of children as soldiers, we need to change cultural values. People must learn to see the value of children and the need to provide for their health and safety.

I would like to propose some solutions that might make the practice of using child soldiers more difficult and thus pave the way towards its eradication. Stated differently, I believe we need to destabilize the cost/benefit ratio and decrease the economic benefits of child trafficking by increasing the business costs and legal risks.

B. Prevention

The key to the elimination of child soldiering and trafficking is prevention, which can be accomplished by raising public awareness of the extent of this international crime and its impact on the society at large. Consciousness-raising can be

---

331. IWEALA, *supra* note 13, at 42.
332. *See* GRAHAM, *supra* note 283.
333. IWEALA, *supra* note 13, at 119.
334. *Id.* at 93.
335. Udombana, *supra* note 20, at 107.

done by education, effective use of the media, State support for NGOs, publicity about international conferences, and publications that disseminate information widely about the following issues: children's rights, recruitment guidelines,[336] new anti-trafficking and anti-child soldiering legislation, and dangers of child soldiering. States should publicize information widely through the media about children's rights and recruitment guidelines[337] to educate the public at large. Governments and people must be made aware of children's rights and the international agreements that protect children against their endangerment and enslavement as child soldiers. Education of the most vulnerable children such as refugees and street children must be made more available so that parents and children can avoid being duped into thinking the life of a child soldier provides security and stability.

Awareness about the use of child soldiers can be raised by holding and widely publishing international conferences on child soldiering such as the "Free Children from War" Conference that just took place in Paris on February 6, 2007.[338] African nations participating in that conference pledged to do their utmost to prevent children from being used as fighters, although the commitment is not legally binding. This conference was hosted by France and UNICEF and included delegates from nearly sixty nations, other U.N. agencies, and thirty nongovernnmental organizations, all of whom vowed "to spare no effort to put an end to the illegal use and recruitment of children by groups of armed forces."[339] This conference should have been picked up by the media, televised on C-SPAN, and covered by CNN International to disseminate the message that our children are in danger worldwide.

The international community must raise awareness worldwide of the extent and impact of the crime of child soldiering in order to create the political will to eradicate the crime and to shame government leaders into implementing legislative protection of children. The media can and should draw more attention to the plight of children in armed conflict. For example, in May 2001, sixty Angolan children were abducted by the National Union for the Total Independence of Angola (UNITA); the documentation available on these children (including their names, ages, and photographs) enabled UNICEF and the U.N. Humanitarian

---

336. For example, The Principles and Best Practices on the Prevention of Recruitment of Children into the Armed Forces and on Demobilization and Social Reintegration of Child Soldiers in Africa, adopted in Apr. 1997, provide a strategy to address the factors that contribute to the use of children as soldiers. *See generally* Cape Town Annotated Principles, *supra* note 27.

337. *Id.*

338. *See generally AFRICA: Fighting for Children, supra* note 41.

339. *Id.*

Coordinator in Angola to launch an international publicity campaign that prompted the release of children to a Catholic mission after twenty days.[340]

States must show support for nongovernmental organizations as well as for religious and community leaders who do work on the ground to educate the public. NGOs can change values and influence ethics by appealing to the people to adhere to local values and to customs that validate children and their basic human rights.[341] However, in the past many of the nongovernmental organizations, groups. and the international coalition[342] created to stop the use of child soldiers have been distracted or misdirected by anti-American sentiment that thwarts their mission.[343] The international community must put these distractions aside to help create the political will to eradicate child soldiering by shaming government leaders into implementing legislative protection of children.

C. Protection of Child Victims

To eliminate child soldiering, the global community must address the protection of the child victims by strengthening compliance and implementation[344] of international humanitarian laws, human rights norms, slavery conventions, trafficking conventions, international criminal laws, and fair labor laws applicable to children's rights and child soldiering. Implementation starts by abolishing the general perception of impunity for crimes related to child soldiering.[345] The Rome Statute of the International Criminal Court established child soldiering as a war crime in 2002. The international *ad hoc* tribunals and the permanent International Criminal Court should prosecute individuals and States Parties engaging in child soldiering and widely publicize the outcome of its cases. Foreign victims of child soldiering should be informed that they can also file lawsuits in the U.S. federal courts under the Alien Tort Claims Act.

---

340. *See* Amnesty Int'l, *Innocent Victims of Angola's Cruel War*, WIRE, Nov. 2001, http://web.amnesty.org/wire/November2001/Angola; *see also* Justin Pearce, *UNITA Attack East of Luanda*, BBC NEWS, May 22, 2001, http://news.bbc.co.uk/2/hi/ africa/1345364.stm.

341. *See* SINTER, *supra* note 25, at 146.

342. *See id.* at 148. "The Coalition to Stop the Use of Child Soldiers has wasted its political capital by engaging in a long-drawn-out public relations war with the U.S. and British governments." *Id.*

343. *Id.*

344. If a State is not a party to the relevant treaties protecting children, they may be obligated to enforce the provisions anyway because the provisions have become part of international custom. *See* Vienna Convention on the Law of Treaties, *supra* note 232, art. 38. "Nothing in articles 34 to 37 precludes a rule set forth in a treaty from becoming binding upon a third State as a customary rule of international law, recognized as such." *Id.*

345. "The referral of LRA leaders to the ICC by the Ugandan Government provided the first experiment of the ICC's ability to suppress impunity. In December 2003, the Ugandan Government referred the LRA atrocities committed in Northern Uganda to the ICC Prosecutor." Udombana, *supra* note 20, at 102.

To protect the child victims, the international community must support the availability of birth records. This would better document the age of children and avoid inadvertent underage recruitment.[346]

States should provide child victims of war with rescue missions, financial aid, health and psychological assistance, meaningful rehabilitation, and carefully planned reintegration programs so that abducted children can live again in the community that once welcomed them as children.

D. Economic Solutions

Shaming States and engaging in a universal moral outcry are necessary and helpful, but the most effective form of deterrence is linked to economic solutions affecting trade and international aid that do not negatively impact women and children. The international community should limit small arms trade to non-State actors and target trading partners of States engaging in child soldiering. States should withhold recognition and financial benefits to any groups that seize power through the use of child soldiers or to States that aid them.[347] States should reduce international aid and trade or implement divestiture policies in countries engaging in child soldiering. "International aid donors should make compliance with the CRC Protocol a condition for development assistance."[348]

U.N. Resolution 1612[349] requires States to monitor and report on the recruitment and use of child soldiers, and any State engaging in child soldiering could be subject to a ban on the export and supply of small arms, light weapons, and other military equipment. States should also develop a policy that targets the external support structures providing donations to the groups or States that engage in child soldiering. Any State engaging in human rights violations such as the use of child soldiers could be deprived of their Most Favored Nation status in the General Agreement on Tariffs and Trade and the World Trade Organization, pursuant to the Jackson–Vanick amendment. Other effective measures to eliminate child soldiering might include taking away seats at the United Nations for States engaging in or aiding and abetting this crime.

E. Prosecution of Perpetrators

The next step in the process of eliminating child soldiering is effective prosecution of the perpetrators. Governments should be held accountable for their deliberate decision to use children as human shields and combatants. States must establish and implement laws that criminalize perpetrators with a severe sentence of imprisonment for thirty or more years for anyone who employs child

346. *See* SINTER, *supra* note 25, at 146.

347. *See id.* at 160.

348. Udombana, *supra* note 20, at 105.

349. S.C. Res. 1612, ¶ 9, U.N. Doc. S/RES/1612 (July 26, 2005).

soldiers. This increased sentence would act as a deterrence measure and provide victims with a sense of justice and retribution. For example, on December 16, 2003, Uganda referred the situation concerning the Lord's Resistance Army to the prosecutor of the International Criminal Court.[350] The referral was an attempt by Uganda to engage an "otherwise aloof international community"[351] to stop this inhumane practice and to address the moral outrage of using children as soldiers. The prosecution of perpetrators of child soldiering with a severe sentence would increase the risk and thus the cost of engaging in the business of child soldiering.

Leaders may know that child soldiering is a war crime, but they seem to believe they will never be brought to justice because of a sense of "rampant impunity."[352] Criminalizing the practice could be accomplished by prosecuting former leaders of groups that use child soldiers in *ad hoc* international tribunals such as the war crimes tribunal in Sierra Leone or in the permanent International Criminal Court. Local communities should increase their level of financial support for the *ad hoc* tribunals that are plagued by fund limitations.

One of the problems associated with implementing accountability for atrocities associated with child soldiering is the possibility that child soldiers themselves will be prosecuted unfairly. The prospect of prosecuting children for war crimes is controversial. Sierra Leone seems to have found a good solution to this problem. The Statute of the Special Court of Sierra Leone does allow for the prosecution of children between the ages of fifteen and eighteen, but the prosecutor has not taken such action yet, focusing instead on the adult leaders.[353] Children implicated in these crimes are given hearings in special closed juvenile chambers so that their identity is not disclosed. Children are also given psychological counseling and other assistance. Moreover, children are not sentenced to prison with adult perpetrators, but rather are placed in special custody and rehabilitation/demobilization programs as well as foster care. This kind of response recognizes that child soldiering is a unique crime because perpetrators are often themselves the victims.[354]

In view of the uniqueness of the crime of child soldiering, the U.N. Security Council should consider establishing a new *ad hoc* tribunal specifically centered on the crime of child soldiering.[355] In addition, the rules of the ICC might be

---

350. *See* Akhavan, *supra* note 20, at 403.
351. *Id.*
352. SINTER, *supra* note 25, at 149.
353. *Id.* at 155.
354. *Id.*
355. *Id.* at 151.

modified to allow children to testify before the court[356] and thereby create a more accurate historical record that should be publicized widely.

Three years after the CRC Protocol on Children in Armed Combat entered into force, the U.N. Security Council expressed deep concern "over the lack of overall progress on the ground, where parties to conflict continue to violate with impunity the relevant provisions of applicable international law relating to the rights and protection of children in armed conflict."[357] The use of children as soldiers in armed combat is nothing less than a contemporary form of slavery that must be eradicated by carefully implemented measures to reestablish ethical norms that valorize children.

Hope is not dead in this campaign against the enslavement of child soldiers. Recently, fifty-eight countries and nongovernmental agencies signed a treaty to free current and potential child soldiers from peril.[358] On January 29, 2007, the International Criminal Court forged ahead with its first war crimes prosecution targeting the leader of the Congolese militia with charges of recruiting child soldiers. The act was declared a war crime when the International Criminal Court was established in 2002. Radhika Coomaraswamy, the U.N. envoy for children and armed conflict, stated "We've come a long way. Ten years ago this was an invisible issue."[359] Last summer groups in Burundi, Ivory Coast, Myanmar, the Democratic Republic of the Congo, Sudan, and Somalia were referred to the U.N. Security Council for possible sanctions related to their use of children as soldiers. Individual commanders are being held responsible for their war crimes.

But to do more to eradicate this crime, funds must be found and steps taken to restore normal life to the children victimized by this atrocity. Many of these children need rehabilitation and serious counseling in improved rehabilitation and transit centers.[360] Many of the escapees who return home are rejected by their own families (if they are still alive) and shunned by villagers who view them as killers. Changing community and family norms to safeguard the reintegration of these victims is no easy task and can only be done by a widespread information and education campaign—as well as a serious attempt to eradicate the poverty that is at the source of many of the armed conflicts producing and perpetuating the use of child soldiers as a military strategy. The fact is that children are devalued, viewed as expendable, and serve as a convenient natural resource

356. *Id.* at 153.

357. *See generally* S.C. Res. 1612, *supra* note 349.

358. *See* Ann O'Neil, *Stole Kids Turned Into Terrifying Killers*, CNN, Feb. 12, 2007, http://www.cnn.com/2007/WORLD/africa/02/12/child.soldiers/indes.html.

359. *Id.*

360. *See* Naomi Cahn, *Poor Children: Child "Witches" and Child Soldiers in Sub-Saharan Africa*, 3 Ohio St. J. Crim. L. 413, 442 (2006).

for economic efficiency during war. Public condemnation of this kind of perverse thinking and of the leaders who recruit children into armed combat can help to reduce future recruitment. Imposing sanctions on corporations that trade with leaders of groups who use children as soldiers is more effective than punishing women and children by imposing sanctions on the State as a whole. Without the moral outcry and the effective intervention of the international community, these children could become a lost generation of migratory professional killers who perpetuate conflict and war.

PART F

CULTURE AND SEMIOTICS

11. THE JAPANESE CULTURE, COPYRIGHT INFRINGEMENT, DEFAMATION, AND SEX TRAFFICKING

A Study of The Fictional Life of a Geisha*

Why, in the West, is politeness regarded with suspicion?
Why does courtesy pass for distance, if not, in fact, evasion or hypocrisy? Why is an "informal" relation (as we greedily say) more desirable than a coded one?
—Roland Barthes, *L'Empire des Signes (1970)*

I. INTRODUCTION

The geisha is a very vivid and significant part of the Japanese culture. Japanese people become quite passionate about defending the image and unraveling the real significance of the symbol of the geisha. Is the geisha an artisan[1] or a

* This chapter appeared as an article in the 10 MICH. J. GENDER & L. 327–400 (2004). The original article has been revised in part. I would like to thank Jane Connors for her assistance with the research and editing of this study as well as Dorothy Hampton, the librarian at Thomas Jefferson School of Law, without whose excellent research skills this study could not have been undertaken. I would also like to thank Professors Marybeth Herald, Maureen Markey, and Bryan Wildenthal for their insightful comments on earlier drafts of this study.

1. This chapter discusses the legal issues underlying Arthur Golden's depiction of the life of a geisha in his book, *Memoirs of a Geisha*. An actual geisha named Mineko Iwasaki provided Golden with information about the geisha life and tradition that Golden used to write his book. Four years after the publication of Golden's book in 1997, Mineko Iwasaki sued Golden for copyright infringement and defamation. Mineko Iwasaki actually wrote two books on the geisha tradition after the publication of Golden's book. In her books Mineko Iwasaki emphasizes that geishas are neither prostitutes nor whores but artists. "I wanted to stress the fact that geisha are consummate artists, fully committed to the highest standards of professionalism." MINEKO IWASAKI, GEISHA, A LIFE (2002) in "A Conversation with Mineko Iwasaki." In writing her books about the geisha life, Iwasaki presents a one-dimensional view of geishas as artists; in contrast, Arthur Golden's view of the geisha is multidimensional.

courtesan,[2] a prostitute[3] or a whore?[4] Since the 1700s, Western audiences have been fascinated by the geisha tradition that is alternately glorified by the Japanese society and outlawed by the Japanese legal system because it is considered by some to be a form of prostitution. The geisha is the only subculture in Japan that is ruled exclusively by women[5] who are permissibly present among men and who thereby manage to alter the social dynamic of male/female relationships in Japan.

Arthur Golden's *Memoirs of a Geisha*[6] captures the duality of the geisha who is both revered as an artist and reviled as a sex slave. At its worst, the geisha tradition involves force, fraud, deception, and the horrifying practice of selling one's own children into slavery for purposes of sexual exploitation. It is my contention

---

2. "The *okiya* owner is the *queen* of the realm, the *atotori* is the heir apparent, and the other members of the *okiya* are like the *royal court.*" IWASAKI, GEISHA, A LIFE, *supra* note 1, at 39. After Arthur Golden's *Memoirs of a Geisha* was published in 1997, Iwasaki, Golden's informant, wrote two of her own books about the life of the geisha, which she describes metaphorically as a life of royalty. *Id. at* 39. *See also* MINEKO IWASAKI, GEISHA OF GION (2002).

3. "I also hoped to dispel the myth, once and for all, that geisha are prostitutes." IWASAKI, *supra* note 1, at "A Conversation with Mineko Iwasaki." *See also*, LESLIE DOWNER, GEISHA: THE SECRET HISTORY OF A VANISHING WORLD (2001), arguing that geisha are not prostitutes. However, the history of the geisha has always been entangled with prostitution. This link of the geisha with prostitution can be traced back to the 10th century glamorous courtesans in the Heian period, who were the predecessors of the geisha. The word *geisha*, meaning "art person," entered the Japanese language in the 17th century. In modern times, geisha are sometimes thought of as prostitutes. The Japanese modern poet Hagiwara Sakutaro believes modern geisha are too much like prostitutes: "It's too bad if geisha are called high-class prostitutes, but that, in fact, is what they have become . . . the geisha of the past were more admirable than what we have now—they were not so quick to offer their bodies," *quoted in* LIZA DALBY, GEISHA 86 (1983).

4. *See generally* ARTHUR GOLDEN, MEMOIRS OF A GEISHA (1997). The term *whore* signifies a prostitute, but carries a more negative connotation than the term *prostitute.* In the novel, the geisha is sometimes glorified, but sometimes disparaged and referred to as resembling a prostitute. "Like prostitutes, their lower-class counterparts, geisha are often in the unusual position of knowing whether this or that public figure really does put his pants on one leg at a time like everyone else" *Id.* at 3. In the novel, the geisha is even referred to indirectly and more disparagingly as a "whore." For example, the translator's fictional name is "Jakob Haarhuis," which literally means "whorehouse" in Dutch." *Id.* at 4. The translator's name carries an ironic inference that the glorified and "royal" geisha is also associated with the image of the lowly whore who is paid for sexual services offered in a whorehouse, otherwise referred to in the novel as the geisha house or *okiya*. In Japanese a certain type of geisha exists that is actually named "whore": *joro* geisha. *See infra* note 71 for a discussion of the evolution of the term *geisha*.

5. Statement by Arthur Golden in an interview by Alec Foege Nacy Day, *Geisha Guy Arthur Golden Isn't Japanese*, PEOPLE MAGAZINE, Nov. 23, 1998, at 90–91.

6. *See generally* GOLDEN, *supra* note 4.

that the involuntary abduction of little girls into the geisha world is a variant of sex slavery. Recruitment of children for the purposes of sexual exploitation and slave labor cannot be justified by cultural relativism because slavery in any form is a universal crime that must be universally condemned. However, at its best, the geisha tradition is the bastion of Japanese culture, the symbol of the apogee of a nation, and the representation of Japan's most respected values—the search for beauty and the love of the arts. To ban the geisha would be to violate the soul of Japan.

The duality of the geisha, who is perceived as both artisan and courtesan, is a leitmotif in Arthur Golden's novel. *Memoirs of a Geisha* realistically reflects the Japanese society's ambivalence towards the geisha tradition. The evolution of Japanese laws on prostitution also mirrors this perceptual duality of the geisha tradition. From 1872 to 1958, Japanese laws alternately ban and permit prostitution and the sex work of the geisha. This legal evolution reflects the shifting sands of official Japanese morality that Golden, an American writer, is able to capture in his novel with the help of a Japanese informant who is one of Japan's most famous geishas.

In striving for historical accuracy and narrative verisimilitude, Golden obtains an intimate interview with a real geisha named Mineko Iwasaki.[7] He tapes their conversations for several ten-hour sessions over the course of two weeks from May 10, 1992 to May 23, 1992[8] before writing his novel about the geisha life in Japan in the 1930s. With the informant's consent, Golden transcribes Iwasaki's intimate first-person account of her life as a geisha in the 1970s. This account contains valuable secrets the informant reveals to Golden about the closed geisha society. Golden then uses Iwasaki's information as source material to write a fictional biography of a little girl named Chiyo who is sold by her own father at the age of nine into slavery, confinement, and debt bondage. As with many little girls in Japan who are abandoned and sold reluctantly into forced prostitution and slavery by their impoverished parents, Chiyo endures a harsh and sometimes cruel indoctrination into the geisha life and eventually becomes a famous

---

7. Mineko Iwasaki is not the real name of the geisha who agrees to be interviewed during several taped sessions with Golden. "Iwasaki" is actually the name of the geisha house that five-year-old Masako was sent to by her father to become the heir apparent of the geisha house. Iwasaki "is my professional name. I got it when I was five years old. It was given to me by the head of the family of women who raised me in the geisha tradition. The surname of the family is Iwasaki. I was legally adopted as the heir to the name and successor to ownership of the business and its holdings when I was ten years old." IWASAKI, GEISHA, A LIFE, *supra* note 1, at 2.

8. *See* Mineko Iwasaki vs. Arthur Golden, Random House, Inc. and Alfred A. Knopf, a division of Random House, Inc., Complaint filed in United States District Court, Southern District of New York, on April 23, 2001, at para.11 of Background [hereinafter "Iwasaki Complaint"].

geisha known as Nitta Sayuri. The essence of Golden's novel is the transformation of Chiyo into Nitta Sayuri.

In Golden's novel, Chiyo is magically changed from an abused little maid servant languishing in a geisha house into a glorified geisha. When she works in the infamous Gion district of Japan, Chiyo plays beautiful music on the shamisen and pleases rich and powerful business men with dance, artful conversation, and other charms. Chiyo receives money for her services, which she must surrender to the rigidly structured geisha house until she pays back her debt. Chiyo continues to live and work under these slave-like conditions of forced labor and debt bondage (which are thinly masked by the veneer of courtly manners and artistry) until she becomes rich and famous.

The fairy-tale quality of the novel, its unusual narrative style, and its poetic prose, created an instant literary success for Arthur Golden. However, four years after its publication in 1997, Iwasaki shocked the literary world by filing a lawsuit against Arthur Golden and his publishers claiming breach of a confidentiality agreement, quantum meruit, unjust enrichment, copyright infringement, defamation of character, misappropriation of property, and violation of her rights to privacy and publicity.

It seems that after she read the novel in Japanese translation, Iwasaki became outraged by the discrepancies she found between her own life and that of Golden's purportedly fictional geisha. She claimed that the book is an insult to Japanese culture. As a point of honor[9] and to get revenge, cultural clarity, or just to draw public attention to her own two books that she was writing about the geisha life, Iwasaki sued the author and his publishers in a New York court under Japanese law and New York law and asked for an accounting under the U.S. copyright laws.[10] In her complaint, Iwasaki alleged she was the coauthor of Golden's book and asked for "no less" than an "appropriate percentage" of what she believed was $10 million in sales for the novel.[11] Among the unusual aspects of Iwasaki's lawsuit was her claim of copyright infringement and defamation of character in a work of fiction and in the promotion of the book. Despite the existence of several defamation-in-fiction cases, Iwasaki's lawyer stated that there was no legal precedent for such a lawsuit; however, the lawyer claimed that

9. "If I don't sue, Arthur will have gotten away with insulting traditional Japanese culture. It is not only rude to me, but to all women. I don't want even a single copy to contain our names," she said. "We thought of asking that the books all be collected. It is not a matter of money. It is our honor," Iwasaki said in an interview with Gary Tegler, *"Memoirs of a Geisha" Muse Vents Spleen at Author*, THE JAPAN TIMES ONLINE, May 1, 2001, http://www.japantimes.co.jp/cgi-bin/20010501k3.htm.

10. U.S. Copyright Act of 1976, 17 U.S.C § 101 (1976).

11. Iwasaki Complaint, *supra* note 8, at para. 20.

Iwasaki had a very strong case.[12] Golden never responded to Iwasaki's complaint, and Iwasaki ultimately voluntarily dismissed the lawsuit in 2003.

Memoirs of a Geisha has sold and made millions for Arthur Golden since 1997. This is his first novel, and it has earned him worldwide acclaim. A beautiful, very successful feature film version of the book produced by Steven Spielberg and directed by Rob Marshall has earned enormous respect from the movie industry.[13] The book is translated into more than twenty languages.

This chapter tries to answer the following two questions about the cultural tradition of the geisha: first, is the geisha tradition (as described by Golden in his fictional biography) a variant of sex trafficking and sexual slavery, which despite possible cultural justifications should be abolished by law? Second, did Iwasaki's lawsuit have any legal merit? To answer these questions, this study will proceed in accordance with structuralist and post-structuralist literary critical methods by looking first at the *text* itself and then its *context, subtext,* and *post-text* to explain the plaintiff's *pre-text* for suing. I will analyze the narrative structures and style of the *text*; the legal and historic *context* of the novel; the legal issues hidden in the *subtext* (which include sex trafficking, feminist legal theory, and the role of cultural relativism as a justification for the geisha tradition); the *post-text* (which are the merits, if any, of Iwasaki's legal claims in the Complaint she filed four years after the publication of the fictional biography); and finally, the big issue, the *pre-text*, or why the real geisha sued Arthur Golden and his publishers.

II. TEXT

A. Structures of Voyeurism and Mirroring in *Memoirs of a Geisha*

The American author, Arthur Golden, is like a voyeur who hides behind two narrative masks (his Dutch translator, Haarhuis, and his Japanese narrator, Sayuri). Sayuri the narrator happens to be a female geisha. The translator and the narrator are both Golden's fictional creations. Another figure lurks in the shadows of the text—a real geisha, Iwasaki, who lives in Japan and provides

12. Mark Feeney, *Geisha Sues Golden Over 1997 Bestseller*, THE BOSTON GLOBE, Apr. 26, 2001 ("When asked, neither Weber nor Stuart Applebaum, spokesman for Random House Inc., which owns Knopf, could cite any precedent for such a case.").

13. Even before the movie came out, people in the movie industry were anxiously awaiting the film; *e.g.*, Cherry Norton, *Betrayal of a Geisha*, SUNDAY TIMES (London), Apr. 20, 2001, at 3G ("The story has proved so popular that it is in the process of being made into a . . . film [produced] by Steven Spielberg; some actors have already been cast and a crew has been scouting for locations in Kyoto."). *See also* THE EVENING STANDARD (London), April 25, 2001: "A Steven Spielberg film of the book is due to be released next year." Given the secrecy of the clients who service geishas in Japan, it is difficult to get permission to shoot scenes in the real Gion district. (*Memoirs of a Geisha* did become a film that won many awards for its cinematographic depiction of the geisha life).

Golden with information never before disclosed about the geisha world. Thus two fictional characters, the translator and the narrator, mirror two real people, the author and the real geisha. The reader plays the role of the grand voyeur who remains fascinated by the game of seductive unmasking that takes place during the act of reading.[14]

Reading this novel and contemplating the lawsuit that ensues is a complex but pleasurable experience enhanced by the juxtaposition of reality and fiction. The interplay of reality and fiction in the novel creates an effect of mirroring and causes the establishment of parallel tensions that produce symmetry and order in the mind of the reader. In this fictional biography, the narrator creates tension between herself and the translator by imposing certain conditions on the translator that he must fulfill in order for Sayuri to proceed with the narration of her secret life as a geisha. A similar tension is created in reality between Golden and Iwasaki, who also allegedly imposed certain conditions on Golden prior to the publication of his novel. The parallelism thus created in the fiction and in reality produces a pleasurable effect of symmetry the reader enjoys while reading the novel and while reading the publicity about the lawsuit.

In the novel, Sayuri agrees conditionally[15] to reveal secrets of the geisha life to the translator only if he agrees to publish the novel after her death. In a perfect parallelism, the real geisha mirrors the fictional geisha by allegedly agreeing conditionally[16] to disclose precious mysteries of the closed geisha world to the author, but only if Golden promises to keep Iwasaki's name confidential. The artistic quality of this novel is found in the subtle play of mirrors and voyeurism producing pleasurable tension in the mind of the reader in the course of the act

---

14. Roland Barthes was a famous French literary critic and semiotician who wrote about the Japanese culture in *l'Empire des Signes* (1970) and who elaborated a theory of reading texts based on a principle of eroticism in *Le Plaisir du texte* (1973). For Barthes, the very act of reading is an experience of erotic pleasure. Golden's use of voyeurism as a narrative structure enhances a tension sustained in the pleasurable act of reading. *See* Susan Tiefenbrun, *The Third Degree of Language: Mediation and Roland Barthes's Semiotic Production*, 34, 1/2 SEMIOTICA 34-1/2 at 143–66 (1981) for a survey of Roland Barthes' literary theories.

15. *See* GOLDEN, *supra* note 4, at 4 ("Though she was eager to have her biography recorded, Sayuri did insist upon several conditions. She wanted the manuscript published only after her death and the deaths of several men who had figured prominently in her life."). *See also id.*, *supra* note 4, at 2 ("One day I asked her if she would ever permit her story to be told. 'Well, Jakob-san, I might, if it's you who records it.' She told me.").

16. *See* Iwasaki Complaint, *supra* note 8, at para. 9 ("When Ms. Iwasaki first met Golden in 1992, she agreed to be interviewed about her geisha life, Gion, and her family's experiences there on certain express conditions. The first condition was complete anonymity for herself and her family. The second was total confidentiality regarding the personal stories and information she related from her life and career as well as her family's experiences.").

of reading and of contemplating the merits of the legal act inspired by the novel.

The play of mirrors and the act of voyeurism produce not only narrative tension, but beneficial confusion in the mind of the reader. This confusion is the basis of Iwasaki's lawsuit and her claims of copyright infringement, defamation of character, and violation of right to privacy and publicity relating to a work of fiction. The confusion between the author and his personae begins on the very first page. A fictional translator appears, calling himself a historian, scholar of Japan, and an academician,[17] which are the very same characteristics that coincidentally happen to describe the author, Arthur Golden. As the story unfolds, the translator, Jakob Haarhuis, sounds more and more like the author of the book. Haarhuis admits to having translated the narrator's special Kyoto dialect, but his translation is more like that of a skilled author, such as Golden. The so-called translation is in delicate and poetic English, flavored with exotic spices and imagery, which transports the readers to Japan in the 1930s. As a guarantee of the authenticity and accuracy worthy of an academician, the translator confesses that he also used the narrator's secretary to verify and transcribe Sayuri's first-person account of her intimate life as a geisha.

The parallel confusion between the real and the fictional geisha begins after the publication of the novel and the filing of the lawsuit by Iwasaki. The narrator in *Memoirs of a Geisha* is an elderly and famous[18] female geisha named Nitta Sayuri who (according to the translator) resided in New York for many years and who is now dead. But Sayuri is not Iwasaki, the real geisha, who decides to sue the author. Sayuri is a fictional narrator who (the translator tells us) came to the United States in 1956, which is the watershed year when prostitution became illegal in Japan. This is a legal fact that Golden, the historian, knew quite well. According to the narrator, in Sayuri's sunset years she lived in a suite in the Waldorf Towers in New York, and it was during this forty-year period that she agreed to describe the intimate details of her life as a geisha to Haarhuis, who captured it all on cassette.[19] In contrast, the real geisha Iwasaki actually stayed in Japan until her retirement from the geisha life at the age of twenty-nine, married a Japanese artist, and currently resides in a Kyoto suburb with her husband and children, where she permitted Golden to interview her for his

---

17. GOLDEN, *supra* note 4, at 1–2.

18. *See id.*, at 2. (The translator refers to a "lengthy" chapter about her "in the book *Glittering Jewels of Japan*, or in the various magazine articles about her that have appeared over the years."). The publicity about the narrator makes her a "public figure." Similarly, Iwasaki is a public figure in Japan, and the publicity surrounding Golden's *Memoirs of a Geisha* in the United States and Europe arguably make Iwasaki also a public figure in the United States, Europe, and Japan.

19. *Id.* at 2.

novel.[20] The similarities and differences between the real geisha and the fictional geisha, and between the narrator and the translator, are the bases of the lawsuit filed by Iwasaki against the author and his publishers for claims of copyright infringement, right of privacy, and defamation of character arising out of a work of fiction.

B. Voyeurism and Failure to Satisfy Conditions Precedent to Publication

The dispute between the real geisha and the author focuses on Golden's success or failure to satisfy certain conditions precedent to the publication of the novel. In her Complaint, Iwasaki alleges that she agreed to provide information to Golden on condition this information serve only as a "fact check"[21] to correct any errors in a book that Golden had already written about the geisha life. Golden did write two earlier drafts of a book about a geisha, both of which were in third-person narrative, but he abandoned these two drafts and adopted a first-person narrative style[22] after he heard Iwasaki's revealing personal account of her life as a geisha.[23]

Similarly, the fictional geisha also stipulates that she must first die as a condition precedent to the publication of Haarhuis' novel about her life as a geisha. Sayuri's death in the novel actually satisfies the condition precedent she had imposed on the translator.[24] But the real geisha claims Golden did not fulfill her first condition because he abandoned his earlier works and wrote an entirely new novel based on her information and her life story.

Iwasaki claims to have required the satisfaction of a second condition precedent to the publication of Golden's book. Because Golden failed to keep her name anonymous and all her personal information confidential, he did not satisfy the second condition precedent. Consistent with the voyeuristic structures of the novel and despite the force of Iwasaki's alleged conditions precedent, Arthur Golden brazenly writes Iwasaki's name clearly in the acknowledgment of the book, as if to lift the veil of the hidden geisha.[25] Writing Iwasaki's name in the

---

20. Iwasaki, *supra* note 1, at 294.

21. Iwasaki Complaint, *supra* note 8, a para. 10.

22. "And so I wrote this book twice in third person first, before I finally decided," Golden said in an Interview on *Good Morning America* (ABC television broadcast Jan. 24, 1999).

23. *See* Golden's statement in Day, *supra* note 5, at 91: "Mineko took my understanding of a geisha's daily existence and stood it on its head. I had to throw out my entire 800-page draft and start from scratch."

24. Golden, *supra* note 4, at 4.

25. "Although the character of Sayuri and her story are completely invented, the historical facts of a geisha's day-to-day life in the 1930s and 1940s are not. In the course of my extensive research I am indebted to one individual above all others. Mineko Iwasaki, one of Gion's top geisha in the 1960s and 1970s, who opened her Kyoto home to me during May 1992, and corrected my every misconception about the life of a geisha–even though

acknowledgment of the book is Golden's dramatic literary act, which Iwasaki perceives of as an illegal act, a breach of trust, and a breach of contract, which constitute the crux of some of the legal issues in the lawsuit. Golden's motivation for this act can easily be explained literarily as a manifestation of voyeurism, a narrative and stylistic structure the author uses throughout the novel to create artistic effects. This study will attempt to provide a legal analysis of the literary act that inspired and produced the lawsuit.

C. Play of Reality and Fiction Inside and Outside the Novel

Golden admits that Iwasaki is the source of his fictional geisha. There is no doubt that Golden used the real geisha's transcription as a launching pad for the creation of his own fictional character. But Golden then changed Iwasaki's words, selected only parts of her transcript, rearranged her thoughts and expressions into his own creation, and wrote with poetic license in his own idiom, as permitted by the First Amendment of the U.S. Constitution—and as required by the craft of fiction writing.

Golden adamantly insists the fictional geisha is entirely different from the real geisha, and this difference is essential to his defense against a claim of copyright infringement as well as defamation. Golden said, "Mineko would not recognize herself in Sayuri" because "they occupied different eras. Mineko reigned magnificent in Kyoto in the Sixties and Seventies, whereas Sayuri traveled to Kyoto from the fishing village where she was born in the early Thirties."[26] Iwasaki was a real geisha in the 1960s and 1970s. Sayuri represents the demimonde of the geisha tradition in Japan in the years 1930 to 1946. Despite these differences, Iwasaki bases her legal claims on the similarity of the two women and their geisha lives.

D. Motivation of Informants Inside and Outside the Novel

What are the underlying motives of the real and the fictional geishas who both violate a public trust[27] by revealing hidden secrets about the geisha tradition? Breaking with the geisha code of silence,[28] both the real and the fictional geishas shock the world by making personal statements that are memorialized on tapes and that expose the underbelly of a slowly disappearing Japanese geisha tradition.

---

everyone I knew who had lived in Kyoto, or who lived there still, told me never to expect such candor." GOLDEN, *supra* note 4, at 433.

26. Golden's statement in Interview with David Usborne, *The Real Geisha*, THE INDEPENDENT SUNDAY, Nov. 1, 1998, at WL 21741649 1998 (London Newspaper).

27. "[T]hese butterflies of the night regard their roles as a kind of public trust, but in any case, the geisha who violates that trust puts herself in an untenable position." GOLDEN, *supra* note 4, at 3.

28. "A geisha's unwritten code of honor theoretically prevents her from divulging what she overhears. . . ." DALBY, *supra* note 3, at 61.

According to Golden, Iwasaki actually met him in Kyoto where "over several days, she explained all there was to know about the life of a geisha, walked [Golden] around the Gion district and introduced him to others who had inhabited the same strange world."[29] In the novel Sayuri, too, reveals her secrets to the translator while they are both safely located in New York. The reasons Sayuri and Iwasaki both agree to reveal the secrets of the Japanese geisha tradition in violation of their public trust remains a mystery in the novel as well as in reality. If Iwasaki actually consented to have her secrets published in Golden's novel, then her claims of a breach of a verbal confidentiality agreement, defamation, and copyright infringement are baseless.

At the beginning of the novel, the translator questions Sayuri's motives for revealing secrets about her life as a geisha: "Why had she wanted to document her life?" 'What else do I have to do with my time these days?' she replied."As to whether or not her motives were really as simple as this, I leave the reader to decide."[30] Consistent with the narrative technique of mirroring and the sustained interplay of reality and fiction, Golden frequently questions Iwasaki's motives for revealing secrets about her life as a geisha in numerous interviews about his book.[31] In one of those interviews, Golden remarked, "While there was no shame to what she did while she was in the geisha life . . . in retirement, it is a past that carries some stigma."[32] Although it is still not clear to Golden what actually motivated Iwasaki to reveal her secrets to him, he insists that he and Iwasaki never entered into a confidentiality agreement,[33] and he disputes her claim to breach of contract, defamation, and copyright infringement. This study will analyze some of Iwasaki's reasons for revealing hidden secrets, for breaking the code of silence in the geisha world, and for deciding to sue Golden for writing the *Memoirs of a Geisha.*

E. Structure of Confession and Its Legal Consequences

Sayuri's accounting of her life as a geisha to the translator in Golden's novel falls in the category of very old and respected literary genre known as the *confession.*[34]

---

29. *See* Usborne, *supra* note 26.

30. GOLDEN, *supra* note 4, at 3–4.

31. Golden has given numerous interviews and public addresses in which he questions why Iwasaki decided to give him this information.

32. *See* Usborne, *supra* note 26.

33. "Denying there had been any confidentiality agreement, Golden states in an interview that Iwasaki had at one point asked him to set up a US publicity tour for her." *See* Feeney, *supra* note 12.

34. Confessional literature derives from a central ritual of the Christian faith and the confession of one's sins. The *Confessions of St. Augustine* (4th and 5th century A.D.) is the first example of confessional literature. But not all confessional literature is religious. Jean-Jacques Rousseau's *Confessions* (1781) reveal the author as he is, not as he ought to be. Chateaubriand's *Memoirs d'Outre Tombe* (1849), Dostoevsky's *Notes from the*

Confessional literature depends on secrecy, revelation, and voyeurism to capture and sustain the attention of the reader. Confessions imply the expiation of sins by the very act of narration, which is a catharsis for the narrator. By confessing, the narrator cleanses herself of past sins. Similarly, Iwasaki's decision to disclose intimate details of her life as a geisha to Golden may be her way of expiating her own deep-seated sense of sin. In interviews and in her own two books, Iwasaki repeatedly insists that she and all geishas are artists and not prostitutes. This insistence may be the speech act that evidences Iwasaki's underlying sense of guilt.

Iwasaki's own confession to Golden mirrors the confession of Sayuri in the novel. However, Iwasaki's accounting of her geisha life had dangerous consequences for her and for her family in Japan.[35] After the novel was published and the Japanese translation was distributed in Japan, the geishas were convinced that Iwasaki had betrayed them, broken the sacred geisha code of silence, and sullied the honor of the profession. The geishas of Japan cried out against Iwasaki, causing disgrace to herself, her children, and her family. Her sister geisha actually begged Iwasaki to commit hara-kiri.[36] Instead of suicide, Iwasaki decides to sue.

Arthur Golden is not a naïve author. He emanates from the savvy Sulzberger-Ochs family that for a century published the *New York Times*. Like the translator,

---

Underground (1864), Andre Gide's *L'Immoraliste* (1930), Saul Bellow's *Herzog* (1964), and Philip Roth's *Portnoy's Complaint* (1969) are the confessions of fictional narrators whose sins may or may not resemble those of the author or the real person from whose image the fictional character is created. Not all novels are strictly confessional, but just have confession scenes in them that have a similarly cathartic effect. For example, Madame de Lafayette's famous seventeenth-century French novel, *La Princesse de Clèves*, includes a very famous confession scene in which a dutiful wife, the Princess of Cleves, confesses to her husband that she loves Nemours. This confession sets up the typical love triangle that never comes to fruition because of the virtue and honor of the Princess who restrains her passion for Nemours. *See* SUSAN TIEFENBRUN, A STRUCTURAL STYLISTIC ANALYSIS OF *LA PRINCESSE DE CLEVES* (1976). The eroticism in *La Princesse de Clèves* is not unlike the erotic effects that *Memoirs of a Geisha* have on the reader, especially because of Golden's use of voyeurism, which is a device related to the structure of confession. The use of confession in Golden's *Memoirs* indirectly associates the narrator with her sinfulness that she is able to expiate by the narration itself.

35. The code of silence among geishas is designed to protect public figures who are the geishas' customers. "In 1989 the Japanese Prime Minister Sosuke Uno was forced to resign after only 69 days in power, after his former geisha lover broke her profession's code of silence and revealed their relationship." *See* Erling Hoh, *Memory and Desire*, FAR EASTERN ECON. REV. 46. 48 (Nov. 19, 1998).

36. "I thought about committing suicide when I realized what was in the book. But then I thought that if I kill myself, nobody will be there to tell the story," Iwasaki told Michael Sheridan in an Interview, *Geisha Who Inspired Novel Speaks Out Against Author*, THE TORONTO STAR, July 30, 2000, at F3.

Golden studied Japanese history and art at Harvard and Columbia. He spent fourteen months in Japan in the early 1980s. Prior to the post-text scandal that develops in Japan, Golden had immersed himself in the Japanese language and culture. He knew how difficult it would be to get a Japanese informant to reveal secrets about the geisha life, and he felt empowered by a clear expression of publication approval from the real geisha. It seems very unlikely that an author with a family history and real-life experience in the world of publication would knowingly violate an alleged confidentiality agreement and risk a suit for defamation, right to privacy, and copyright infringement.

F. Structure of Narrative Tension and *Memoirs* as a Genre

The author's ambivalence towards the geisha, whom he represents in the novel as both artisan and courtesan, reflects a cultural dialectic that has its roots in the history of Japanese society.[37] The tension Golden sustains artistically throughout the novel between the goodness and the badness of the geisha and of the whole geisha tradition is the source of Iwasaki's anger and, in part, the motivation for her filing a law suit against Golden.

The title of the novel crystallizes the sustained narrative tension. *Memoirs of a Geisha* contains the two poles of a dialectic that appear in myriad forms known as binary structures: fact/fiction; novel/reality; secrecy of geisha life/revelation in *Memoirs*; intimacy of *Memoirs*/opacity of Japanese society; politeness of geisha society/animosity of the geisha underworld; tradition/modernity; narrator/informant; translator/author; geisha/prostitute; and artisan/courtesan.

As the translator reminds us, memoirs are a narrative form that is not just a biography of one person, but tells the story of a whole world.[38] The term *memoirs* also signifies the disclosure of intimate secrets. Memoirs are a literary genre, a subset of confessional literature, which sets up the confessor's sin as a basic premise. The reader of *Memoirs of a Geisha* enjoys eavesdropping on the informed narrator-*cum*-confessor who reveals in her *Memoirs* some of the most hidden secrets about the mysterious, sinful yet sacred, and closed world *of a Geisha*.

G. Voyeurism, the Sex Trafficker, and Slavery in the Novel

The voyeuristic structure of the novel and its hidden messages about sex trafficking and slavery are recreated in miniature in a symbolic scene at the beginning of the novel. This scene illustrates the similarities of child abduction for purposes of sex trafficking and the recruitment of children for the geisha life. Chiyo's father has decided that his two daughters, little Chiyo and her sister, Satsu, should be adopted by Mr. Tanaka, the wealthy head of the Japanese Coastal

37. Downer, *supra* note 3, at 172: "Despite the many pious words which had been spoken and written to the contrary, there had always been gray areas where the geisha and prostitute worlds crossed . . . Geisha and prostitutes were part of the same community."

38. Golden, *supra* note 4, at 1.

Seafood Company. Mr. Tanaka is really a trafficker of geisha and prostitutes in disguise who works through fraud, force, and deception to bait his prey, two little girls, who will end up as slaves in a brothel and a geisha house.

Mr. Tanaka looks like any ordinary father. He has a daughter, Huniko, whom Chiyo meets on her first visit to his house. On that day Chiyo is treated royally by the Tanaka family, and she and her "adopted" sister Huniko play gleefully with each other all afternoon. In the evening, the two girls decide to spy on Mr. Tanaka from behind a little hole,[39] like the reader-voyeur who spies on the geishas through the eyes of the narrator. It is there that Chiyo gets her first glimpse of the flower and willow world[40] as she watches Mr. Tanaka engage in the nightly pleasures of a teahouse in Senzura. Little did the innocent Chiyo know that Mr. Tanaka's real idea of "adoption" was to buy her for a small sum from her father and then, without her consent and probably without her father's knowledge, sell her for a hefty sum to a geisha house in the Gion district of Kyoto. That hefty sum will be the start of Chiyo's ever-increasing debt to the geisha house that she must repay by servicing men.

Despite the shock and abuse Chiyo suffers at the hands of Mr. Tanaka and his agents, her attitude toward her trafficker is one of ambivalence, which is not uncommon among abused women. In Chiyo's wildest dreams, she could not have imagined that Mr. Tanaka, whom she considered her savior, would cause her to become a slave to men, to the geisha house, and especially to Hatsumomo, the most cruel and beautiful of all geishas. Upon meeting the pretty little Chiyo-chan for the first time, Hatsumomo becomes instantly jealous and refers to her disparagingly as "garbage."[41] Thereafter, Hatsumomo makes it her life's ambition to destroy Chiyo's chances of becoming a full-fledged geisha in the typically hierarchical and rigid social structure that exists in a geisha house.

Chiyo continues to have ambivalent thoughts about her trafficker during her bitter experiences of sex slavery, debt bondage, victimization, and marginalization caused by the heinous practice of trafficking and the nonconsensual sale of human beings for sexual exploitation. On the one hand, she thinks about Mr. Tanaka with affection because she perceives of him as her savior; on the other hand, however, she also thinks of him with hatred and disgust because he sold her into slavery. When she was still living at home, she claims to have had "fantasies of adoption"[42] by Mr. Tanaka. "But the truth is that the afternoon when I met Mr. Tanaka Ichiro really was the best and the worst of my life."[43] She expresses

39. *Id.* at 28.

40. *See* DALBY, *supra* note 3, at Preface (xiv) (discussing the "flower and willow world" which is the term given to the geisha society (i.e., *karyukai* in Japanese).

41. GOLDEN, *supra* note 4, at 37.

42. *Id.* at 20.

43. *Id.* at *7; see also id.* at 21: "Certainly it was true a part of me hoped desperately to be adopted by Mr. Tanaka after my mother died; but another part of me was very much afraid."

this ambivalence towards her trafficker at the beginning of the novel and repeats it again[44] later just before she falls in love with the ineffable Mr. Chairman, who is her Prince Charming, her "bodhisattva with a thousand arms who would help me."[45] Mr. Chairman becomes the savior that Mr. Tanaka never really was. Women who are poor and uneducated in Japan and in many countries around the world where sex trafficking is practiced often become dependent on men for survival.[46] Mr. Tanaka, Mr. Chairman, and the geisha lifestyle are various manifestations of that dependency created by bad economic conditions and deep-seated anti-feminist views about the value of women in a patriarchal society.

Mr. Tanaka is the prototype of the trafficker who works through fraud, coercion, and deception to snare innocent victims of poverty and ignorance into a life of sex slavery. He deceives Chiyo's father by claiming he will "adopt" Chiyo and her sister into his own family and give them both a better life than her own father could provide.[47] Tanaka uses the word *adoption* because in 1936 selling human beings was prohibited by edict and by the Emancipation of Prostitutes and Geisha Act of 1872,[48] but it was not illegal to adopt children. Like abused children who end up abusing their own children, Mr. Tanaka is recreating his only life by playing the role of trafficker. Tanaka was sold to a family when he was a young boy as a result of the early death of his mother and father.[49]

The sale of children in poor agricultural communities was part of the cultural tradition in Japan during the lean years, and this tradition still exists in many countries today. In Iwasaki's own biography, she reports that like her sister, she too was sold to a geisha house by her own father.[50] However, Iwasaki repeats a bit too often that she went to the geisha house consensually and by her own free will in order to save the honor of her impoverished family and to become the heir

---

44. *Id.* at 105.

45. *Id.* at 119.

46. *See* Golden's statement in Foege, *supra* note 5 ("Some geishas—a few still exist—accrue wealth and power by manipulating clients' affections.").

47. *See* GOLDEN, *supra* note 4, at 21 (Sayuri's father says, "I can't picture the girls living anywhere else." Mr. Tanaka responds, "I understand, but they'd be much better off, and so would you.").

48. Dajokan Cabinet Order No. 295 of Oct. 1872, and Notification No. 22 of the Ministry of Justice dated Oct. 9, 1982, *reprinted in,* MINISTRY OF JUSTICE, JAPAN, MATERIALS CONCERNING PROSTITUTION AND ITS CONTROL IN JAPAN 2–3 (1957) (called "Emancipation of Prostitutes and Geisha Act of 1872") [hereinafter "MINISTRY OF JUSTICE MATERIALS"].

49. GOLDEN, *supra* note 4, at 20.

50. IWASAKI, *supra* note 1 at 10 ("My father found positions for both Yaeko and Kikuko and was given contract money for their apprenticeships . . . my sisters were devastated at having to leave the safe haven of my grandparents' house. Yaeko never got over her feelings of being abandoned.").

apparent of the geisha house.[51] Iwasaki loves her father dearly, but it is clear to this reader that she also resents him deeply for abandoning her and for selling her to the geisha life. If we read between the lines of her romanticized biography, Iwasaki is arguably transferring her own hidden anger towards her father onto Golden whom she believes betrayed her confidence, much like her own father who abandoned and sold Iwasaki to a geisha house.

In Golden's novel, Mr. Tanaka works by deception to catch his bait, Chiyo and her sister, Satsu. He promises Chiyo that he will bring her back home after one night.[52] Once Chiyo and Satsu arrive in his big house in Senzuru, Mr. Tanaka feeds them well and provides entertainment. But by the end of the day, Chiyo and Satsu are caught off guard, forced to undress, brutally handled by Mrs. Fidget who tests their virginity with her own dirty fingers, and pinches them on the neck so hard that Chiyo "felt as if [she'd] fallen into a tub of creatures that were biting [her] everywhere."[53] The two girls are then driven off forcibly to Kyoto by a stranger, Mr. Bekku. On the train to Kyoto, Chiyo and Satsu are given no food to eat and are made to watch Mr. Bekku gulp down a lotus leaf of sweet rice.[54] Chiyo remarks,"I felt as sore as a rock must feel when the waterfall has pounded on it all day long."[55]

Like the typical sex slave trafficker that he is, Mr. Tanaka works with an agent, Mr. Bekku, and engages in fraudulent, deceptive, and coercive behavior to transport young women into a milieu of sexual exploitation for financial gain.[56] Mr. Tanaka is particularly cruel to Satsu, who is less beautiful than Chiyo, and who Tanaka sends to a brothel to lead the miserable life of a prostitute. Chiyo is beautiful enough to be sold to a geisha house *(okiya)* in Gion where she works her way up from a maid servant to become "one of the twenty greatest geisha in Gion's past."[57] From that fateful day when Chiyo leaves Mr. Tanaka's house to live in the *okiya* in Kyoto, she will continuously search for her sister, but never again be able to experience the tenderness of family love. She will be forced to pay back a constantly increasing debt to the geisha house for providing her with an

---

51. *Id.* at 25 ("My father assured me that we were just going for a visit and we could leave anytime that I wanted to."); *see also id.* at 28 ("If we get there and you don't like it, we can turn right around and come home, I promise."); *Id.* at 33 ("And your sister Tomiko has gone to the Iwasaki *okiya* to uphold our honor.").

52. GOLDEN, *supra* note 4, at 21.

53. *Id.* at 33.

54. *Id.* at 34.

55. *Id.*

56. *See* Susan Tiefenbrun, *The Saga of Susannah: A U.S. Remedy for Sex Trafficking in Women: The Victims of Trafficking and Violence Protection Act of 2000* 1,UTAH L. REV. 107, 120 (2002) [hereinafter "Tiefenbrun on Trafficking"] (discussing the common methods of sex trafficking).

57. GOLDEN, *supra* note 4, at 105.

education in the arts. This is known as debt bondage or the crime of peonage (a form of involuntary servitude), which is typically practiced by sex traffickers.

When Chiyo reaches the geisha house in Gion, her only source of kindness is doled out sparingly by the greedy "Mother" who manages the *okiya* and whose affection Chiyo describes as being "what a fish might feel for the fisherman who pulls the hook from its lips."[58] Chiyo soon learns the harsh reality: "My father sold me into slavery."[59] She pleads for help "to set me free" and to "free a little girl from slavery."[60] Her pleas fall on deaf ears, like many of the millions of women and children sold into sex slavery each year not only in Japan but all over the world.[61]

H. Style of the Novel, the Simile, and Its Relevance to Iwasaki's Legal Claims

The reader's awareness of a "style" and, thus, of an author in the novel supports the contention that this literary work, which is based on fact, is really pure fiction, and the characters in the book are merely inventions of the author. The very nature of literary creation is its balance of fact and fiction. To the extent an author manipulates the style of this fictionalized biography, the success of Iwasaki's defamation claim will, and should be, weakened in order to preserve poetic license, freedom of speech, and artistic creation. The author should be free to create without being in fear of legal consequences.

In a defamation-in-fiction claim, the plaintiff must show that the statements made in the book are false statements of *fact*, not opinion, and that these factual statements are "of and concerning" the plaintiff.[62] The merits of Iwasaki's claim to the defamation of her character are weakened by the constant reminder of a poetic style in Golden's novel. Style is the sign of fantasy, opinion, and fiction. Style evidences the author's choice to deviate from fact and reality for the purposes of creative expression. To win a defamation-in-fiction claim, Iwasaki has to prove that the main character is really her, not Sayuri, and that Golden is making false statements of fact about a real person (Iwasaki). But in *Memoirs of a Geisha*, Golden creates a totally new fictional character, different from Iwasaki, whom he names Sayuri. Despite certain similarities between Sayuri and Iwasaki, the

---

58. *Id.* at 49.

59. *Id.* at 82.

60. *Id.* at 101.

61. *See generally*, Tiefenbrun on Trafficking, *supra* note 56 (discussing the extent of the sex trafficking industry. More than two million women are trafficked around the world each year, and 50,000 of these women are trafficked into the United States where they are thrown forcibly into brothels to service as many as sixty men a day).

62. Frederick Schauer, *Liars, Novelists, and the Law of Defamation*, 51 BROOK. L. REV., 233, 236 (1985). *See* text accompanying notes 244–66 for a discussion of the difficulties of a defamation-in-fiction cause of action.

fictional character is separate and distinct from Iwasaki the plaintiff.[63] Iwasaki's defamation claim against Golden and his publisher is nothing more than a tug-of-war based on similarities and differences fought with freedom of speech banners flying high in the literary and legal backdrop.

Golden uses many stylistic devices to capture the specificity and otherness of the geisha world in Japan of the 1930s and 1940s—a world that is quite different from that of Iwasaki, who was a geisha in the 1960s and 1970s. There is a good reason why Golden uses the simile as one of his main stylistic devices: his aim in writing a fictionalized biography is to concretize the main character, to make her seem as real as possible and as similar to the kind of geisha who lived and worked in Japan in the 1930s and 1940s. The simile is the rhetorical figure that most effectively accomplishes this literary goal. When the reader sees a simile based on a clever comparison between two dissimilar entities, the reader is immediately reminded that hidden behind the narrative there is an author manipulating the comparison through the artful combination of words. The presence of the author is another subtle reminder that this biography of a geisha is pure fiction. Golden uses similes with abandon throughout the novel to create the effect of a prose poem. It is precisely because this fictional biography reads like poetry in prose that Iwasaki would have difficulty convincing a judge and a jury that this book is factual when it is clearly literary and fictional. Similes help establish a fairy-tale quality in the novel, which has been described by many as being a Cinderella story.[64] If it is the author who is manipulating the words, and if it is a fairy tale that he is creating, Iwasaki's legal claim to the defamation of her character is weak, and her claim to copyright infringement is baseless.

I. Duality and the Narrative Representation of the Geisha as a Prostitute

Duality is the overriding stylistic and structural device in the novel that the author employs in order to capture both the beauty and magic of the geisha fairy-tale world as well as the stark, dark reality of child abuse, sex slavery, and human cruelty that pervade the geisha underworld. In *Memoirs of a Geisha*, the exquisite delicateness of the geisha as artist coexists contrapuntally with the horrors of the helpless children abducted into a world of sexual exploitation represented by the

---

63. Dorothy Weber, Iwasaki's lawyer, said of the book that it is "so compelling, you really feel it is a true story, even though it is a novel." She said her client's position is that "the reason it is so compelling is that it is her story." Elizabeth Mehren, *Geisha Charges Writer's Fiction is Her Truth*, L.A. TIMES, Apr. 26, 2001, at E3.

64. *See* Joy Glassman's *Readers Praise "Fairy Tale" of Geisha's Life*, THE HARTFORD COURANT, June 22, 1998, at F1 (stating [Memoirs] "is a fairy tale, a 1930s Japanese 'Cinderella.'"). *See also* Gabriel Brownstein, *A Japanese Cinderella*, THE NEW LEADER, Nov. 3, 1997, at 18–19 ("His narrative is imposed on an exotic world rather than organic to it. In fact, it is a Cinderella story.").

courtesan or prostitute.[65] Golden crystallizes this ambivalence about the geisha in a poetic passage full of similes and an extended metaphor in which the geisha is depicted as a work of art emerging as a statue from the terrible coldness of a snow-covered garden:

> When I first learned the news of my family, it was as though I'd been covered over by a blanket of snow. But in time the terrible coldness had melted away to reveal a landscape I'd never seen before or even imagined. I don't know if this will make sense to you, but my mind on the eve of my debut was like a garden in which the flowers have only begun to poke their faces up through the soil, so that it is still impossible to tell how things will look. I was brimming with excitement; and in this garden of my mind stood a statue, precisely in the center. It was an image of the geisha I wanted to become.[66]

Golden's simultaneously negative and positive portrayal of the geisha as both artisan and prostitute is a leitmotif that establishes verisimilitude, creates narrative tension, and disturbs Iwasaki, the reader. She claims the author has dishonored her and her entire profession by putting too much emphasis on the sexual functions of the geisha. Iwasaki also claims Golden has misunderstood the real nature of the geisha, who is above all a highly trained artist, not a prostitute.[67] Outraged and insulted, she sues him for defamation of character.

In a defamation case, the defendant's defamatory statement may concern a group rather than an individual, but the statement will generally be defamatory as to the plaintiff only if the group is a relatively small one.[68] Iwasaki's defamation claim is weakened by the fictional quality of the biography, by the large size of the geisha group Iwasaki claims to represent, and by the difficulty she has in proving that the novel is "of and concerning" herself in view of the differences that exist between the real and the fictional geishas.

Golden's position is defended in that he emphasizes throughout the novel that there is a distinction between the geisha and the prostitute. The narrator discusses the etymology of the term *geisha,* which comes from the word *gei,* meaning "artist."[69] The narrator describes the difference between the costumes

---

65. *See* Hoh, *supra* note 35 ("In 1994 the Gion *maiko* (trainee) Kaori Takagi shocked the geisha world by suing her teahouse for physically abusing her—and then opening a geisha disco, DJ Palace, in Kyoto's upscale Gion district."); *see also* DALBY, *supra* note 3, at Preface (xix) (discussing this civil suit brought by a disgruntled Kyoto apprentice against the geisha house for exploitation).

66. GOLDEN, *supra* note 4, at 161.

67. *See* Tegler, *supra* note 9.

68. RESTATEMENT (SECOND) OF TORTS, §564A (1977). It is unlikely that the plaintiff could recover if the group were larger than twenty-five persons. Certainly, there are more than twenty-five geishas in Japan.

69. See GOLDEN, *supra* note 4, at 141. "But a geisha must study a great many arts besides shamisen. And in fact, the 'gei' of 'geisha' means 'arts,' so the word 'geisha' really means 'artisan' or 'artist.'"

of the geisha in contrast to the clothes of the prostitute. The *obi* (cumberbund) worn by the geisha is tied in the back rather than in the front where the prostitute ties her *obi* because, unlike the geisha, the prostitute has to take the sash on and off all night.[70] It is important to note that Chiyo's sister is sent to a brothel, not a geisha house, and the vivid contrast between the sisters' different ways of life is underlined in the novel. Golden also stresses the difference between the geisha and the prostitute in both his novel and in public interviews because he knows that in the mind of the reader, there is an association between the two terms that is borne out in the language,[71] in the history, and in the evolution of the laws of Japan.

J. Geisha and the Sex Act in the Novel

The link between the geisha and the prostitute is derived not only from language but from similarities in their geographic location and activities. These similarities have created a negative association of the geisha with the prostitute in the mind of the Japanese people. The geisha, who is respected as an artist, has always lived in the same neighborhood as the prostitute. The geisha frequently services the same clients as prostitutes. By virtue of this geographic propinquity, the immorality of the prostitute is transferred to or associated with the geisha. To reflect that duality, Golden provides numerous examples of the geisha's rigorous training as an artist, on the one hand, and also includes evidence of the geishas having sex[72] with their clients, on the other. For example, Golden adds a vivid yet

---

70. *See id.* at 83.

71. The word *geisha* has changed its meaning from the time it first appeared in the 1600s. The first geishas were men who entertained at parties where the prostitutes *(yujo)* entertained men. The male geisha were also called jesters *(hokan)* or drum bearers *(taikomochi)*. When in 1751 the first female drum bearer entered one of the parties, she was referred to as a *geiko*, which is the term used today in Kyoto to designate a geisha. It is the term used frequently in Golden's book. In the eighteenth century, geisha were purely entertainers referred to as *shiro* (white) geisha. There were many forms of entertainers at that time. One type was a *korobi* geisha who "tumbled" for guests at parties. The *kido* (gate) geisha were entertainers who stood at the entrance to carnivals, played the shamisen, and attracted business. The *joro* (whore) geishas were hired for their sexual skills. *See* Hoh, *supra* note 35. Dancing girls *(odoriko)* entertained in the feudal towns around 1770. They began to be called *machi* geishas or "town geishas." The town geishas were different from the geishas who appeared in the licensed quarters of the cities. *Machi* geishas were also referred to as *neko* or cat, which signifies by connotation the availability of their sexual services. Thus, a study of the evolution of the term *geisha* reveals linguistic and historical links with the term *prostitute*. *See* DALBY, *supra* note 3, at 56—57.

72. Commenting on the sexual activity of geisha in an interview with Miles O'Brien, Golden said, "Japanese men hire women to sit and kind of entertain them. That's really the role that geisha play. They're entertainers more than anything else. And, of course, sex does enter into it. Maybe you could say sex enters into most things, but it enters into this in a kind of borderline prostitution-like way, in the sense that a geisha can be available as

subtle detail about the rice paper used ostensibly for cleaning up the geisha and the client after sex:

> When I'd dressed that morning, I'd tucked several sheets of a very absorbent rice paper into the back of my obi. I hadn't expected to need it until afterward, when the Minister would want them for wiping himself off. . .."[73]

Sayuri admittedly has sex albeit reluctantly twice a week with the General, and she says these acts are "nothing more than an unpleasant twice-weekly routine."[74] Another example of Golden's indirect affirmation of the geisha's sexual activity is illustrated in the long account of the ritual of *mizuage*, an old tradition among young geishas known as deflowering, where a rich man such as Dr. Crab pays a good deal of money for the privilege of making the geisha lose her virginity.[75] Golden includes these and other details of the sexual activity of the geisha to reflect the duality of the term *geisha*, which connotes both artistic respectability and sexual immorality.

Iwasaki claims that most geishas do not engage in sexual activity.[76] Iwasaki assumes that Golden has associated her personally with illicit sex and with the deflowerment ceremony described in his novel. She claims the statements made in the novel are false and defamatory about her and about all geishas. But if geishas do not engage in any sexual activity, why was the traditional ceremony of deflowerment ever established? It is true that *mizuage*[77] no longer exists as a custom among geishas. The time gap between the events of the novel (which take place in the 1930s), and the reality of Iwasaki's own experiences when she rose to fame in the 1960s and 1970s may explain why she vehemently denies

a long-term kept mistress to a wealthy man for a significant sum of money. That's really mostly where it comes in." Interview by Miles O'Brien with Arthur Golden in *A Talk With Arthur Golden*, CNN.com Book News (Mar. 23, 1999), http://www.cnn.com/books/dialogue/9903/golden.interview/.

73. Golden, *supra* note 4, at 403.

74. *Id.* at 305.

75. *Id.* at 234.

76. In her own book, Iwasaki denies the sexual activity of the geisha: "And in the same way that a patron of the opera does not expect sexual favors from the diva, the Baron supported Yoneyu solely because of the artistic perfection that she embodied and the luster that she lent to his reputation." Iwasaki,, *supra* note 1, at 51–52. However, in an interview, Iwasaki does admit that some geishas did engage in prostitution: "Although some geisha quarters did engage in prostitution, most did not, and the perception that all geisha sleep with their clients is absolutely false. We are proud, accomplished women who have absolute rights over our own bodies." Tegler, *supra* note 9.

77. "Mineko Iwasaki, a former geisha girl, says she was most hurt by author Arthur Golden's claims that as a young girl, her virginity was 'auctioned to the highest bidder,'—which she says is false." Devlin Barret, *Geisha's Revenge—Sues Author of Book on Her Life*, The New York Post, Apr. 25, 2001, at 12.

ever having gone through such a ceremony. "The selling of her virginity, that rite of passage, did not happen," said Iwasaki's lawyer in an interview.[78]

Ironically, Iwasaki's Complaint is a result of Golden's successful craftsmanship as a fiction writer. The constant use of comic names that are plays on words (Mrs. Fidget, Dr. Crab) remind readers that this book is pure fiction. The male author hides so well behind his female narrator that the real geisha confuses her own identity with that of the narrator, even though they are two different people. Whenever the narrator draws attention to the immoral side of the fictional geisha, the real geisha is offended. Iwasaki's personal perception of the geisha is closer to that of the artisan, not the prostitute. The real geisha's protest is due to the author's artistic manipulation of a disturbing tension between the symbol of the geisha and the symbol of the prostitute. Decoding these symbols is a reflection of a historic and cultural contextual reality. Golden sustains that tension throughout the novel by his use of contrast, antithesis, metaphor, and simile as well as a panoply of rhetorical figures creating the pleasurable effect of ambivalence[79] about the geisha that unfortunately culminated in a lawsuit against him by the offended informant.

III. CONTEXT

A. Evolution of Japanese Laws on Prostitution and the Geisha

The duality between geisha and prostitute, artisan and courtesan, is reflected in the evolution of the laws passed in Japan[80] and in changes in the standards of morality in Japanese society from the early Heian period in 794 to 1195 until the twenty-first century.[81] In 1612, the Japanese feudal government considered a petition to build a red-light district in Edo, the capital of Japan; five years later the government granted its consent to regulate a licensed quarter called Yoshiwara

78. *Id.*

79. "The book is lies, all lies," the real geisha said in an interview given to London's *The Sunday Times.* "Golden has mixed up the well-respected and highly educated geisha profession with that of common prostitutes in order to 'spice up the story for Western audiences.' He has insulted all true geishas . . . There was no money put on virginity in my circles. The geisha world is not a place where you sell your body." Norton, *supra* note 13.

80. *See infra* text accompanying notes 81–104 (discussing the Japanese laws pertaining to the regulation of prostitutes, courtesans, and geisha).

81. *See* Downer, *supra* note 3, at 25–53 for a history and development of geisha and prostitution in Japan. *See also* Dalby, *supra* note 3.

in the city of Edo.[82] During the Edo period (1600–1867) prostitution was legal in Japan, but only if properly licensed and controlled.[83]

Under the Meiji regime in October 1872, the government announced a Proclamation for the Emancipation of Prostitutes and Geisha Act,[84] which required prostitutes to be licensed. However, geishas did not have to obtain such a license. As a result of the Emancipation of Prostitutes and Geisha Act, geishas were free to return to their parents' homes,[85] a reminder that the abduction of little girls into the geisha life was nothing less than slavery. Several years later, geishas were required to obtain a license to do their work as a geisha and a separate license to do prostitution, if they decided to engage in this activity to supplement their earnings.

In 1901, the government passed the Regulation for Control of Prostitutes,[86] attempting to limit prostitution to only those women officially registered with the government. In 1908, realizing the Regulation for Control of Prostitutes was not eliminating unregistered prostitution, the government passed the Ministry of Home Affairs Ordinance No.16.[87]

After World War II, many Japanese women became prostitutes to support themselves and their families. More than seventy thousand prostitutes catered to the U.S. military.[88] Prostitution was booming in Japan after the war, and the Japanese government debated how to alleviate the problem.[89] In 1946, the Japanese government promulgated Imperial Ordinance No.9[90] that punished persons who make women act as prostitutes. However, this law did not punish prostitutes or even ban prostitution because the Japanese view prostitutes as victims and do not believe they should be punished.[91] During this period, both the national and local Japanese governments continued to regulate prostitution

---

82. *See* Andrew Morrison, *Teen Prostitution in Japan: Regulation of Telephone Clubs*, 31 VAND. TRANSNAT'L 457,460 (1998). Morrison studies the evolution of Japanese laws on prostitution. *See generally* J. Mark Ramseyer, *Indentured Prostitution in Imperial Japan: Credible Commitments in the Sex Industry*, 7 J.L. ECON & ORG. 89 (1991).

83. DALBY, *supra* note 3, at 54.

84. Emancipation of Prostitutes and Geisha Act of 1872. *See* MINISTRY OF JUSTICE MATERIALS, *supra* note 48, at 2.

85. DALBY, *supra* note 3, at 65.

86. Regulation for Control of Prostitutes, *reprinted in* MINISTRY OF JUSTICE MATERIALS, *supra* note 48, at 4-7.

87. Ministry of Home Affairs Ordinance No. 16, *cited in* MINISTRY OF JUSTICE MATERIALS, *supra* note 48, at 7.

88. MINISTRY OF JUSTICE MATERIALS, *supra* note 48, at 8.

89. *Id.*

90. *Id.* at 19, Ordinance No. 9.

91. Morrison, *supra* note 82, at 467.

and passed related laws such as the Child Welfare Law,[92] the Labor Standard Law,[93] the Employment Security Law,[94] the Venereal Disease Prevention Law,[95] and the Enterprises Affecting Public Morals Law.[96] These laws indirectly restricted prostitution but only marginally affected geishas in Japan.

Despite the profusion of laws passed in 1947 and 1948 indirectly restricting prostitution and marginally affecting geishas in Japan, prostitution did not stop growing as an industry throughout the nation. Police had little interest in enforcing regulations, and brothel owners had significant legislative influence in their local areas.[97] Because of the ineffectiveness of Imperial Ordinance No. 9 and the complicity of national and local government officials in Japan who turned a blind eye to prostitution, Japan eventually passed the Anti-Prostitution Act of 1956,[98] which went into effect in 1958 and which banned prostitution. This law came about because of the influence of the occupation forces in Japan who drafted a new constitution giving women the right to vote and the right to be elected to public office. Women lobbied in Japan, and on May 24, 1956 the Japanese government enacted Law No. 118, The Prostitution Prevention Law[99] (otherwise referred to as Showa 33 or The Anti-Prostitution Act). This law significantly reduced the number of prostitutes, made *mizuage* or the practice of deflowerment of geishas illegal, and gave geishas more respectability.[100] However, the Anti-Prostitution Act of 1956 did not have any real impact on the great number

92. Child Welfare Law, No. 164 (1947) (making it illegal for a person to force a child under eighteen to engage in prostitution) *reprinted in* MINISTRY OF JUSTICE MATERIALS, *supra* note 48, at 48–49.

93. Labor Standard Law, No. 49 (1947) (stipulating that, unless permitted by law, no person shall obtain profit from the arrangement of the employment of others). *Id.* at 44–46.

94. The Employment Security Law, No.141 (1947) (providing criminal punishment for anyone conducting or engaging in the labor exchange labor recruitment or labor supply project for the intention of inducing workers to do works injurious to the public health or morals). *Id.* at 47–48.

95. Venereal Disease Prevention Law, No. 167 (1948) (punishing any sufferer from venereal disease liable to infect others, who has engaged in prostitution. Punishment is penal servitude not exceeding two years or a fine not exceeding 10,000 yen). *Id.* at 49–50.

96. "Fuzoku" Business Law, No 122 (1948) (law to control businesses that are likely to create a moral hazard). *Id.* at 51–53.

97. *See* Morrison, *supra* note 82, at 467.

98. Anti-Prostitution Law, No. 118 (1956), *reprinted in* MINISTRY OF JUSTICE MATERIALS, *supra* note 48 at 32–39.

99. *See* Morrison, *supra* note 82, at 471 (discussing the role of the female lobby in Japan). Women in Japan worked diligently to get the Anti-Prostitution Act of 1956 finally passed.

100. *See* DOWNER, *supra* note 3, at 173: "After the bill was passed, the geisha moved several steps closer toward respectability–though they never made it all the way; the ambivalence remains to this day."

of children being sold by their parents. As late as the mid-seventies, children from impoverished rural villages were still sold and used as maids in geisha houses.[101] Nevertheless, the law did help to change attitudes in Japan, and child abduction practices were being viewed as unacceptable.

After 1956, the watershed year for prostitution in Japan, geishas become even more clearly distinguished from prostitutes. Geishas are prohibited by the Anti-Prostitution Act of 1956 from accepting fees for sexual services. The institution of compulsory education up to the age of fifteen also impacted the geisha profession and meant that the training of geishas, which typically took several years and was very rigorous before the war, had to be seriously curtailed. However, despite the changes in behavior and attitudes brought about by the Anti-Prostitution Act of 1956, geishas continued to flourish. By the mid-1970s there were reportedly seventeen thousand geishas in Japan,[102] but today there are only a few real geishas in all of Japan. The postwar decades were a boom period for the geishas who serviced the rich and powerful industrialists and politicians in the teahouses of Shimbashi and Akasaka where discretion was guaranteed[103] by the geisha code of silence.

The decline of the geisha started in the 1970s after the oil crisis of 1973 and continued to decline during the rise of Japan's economy in the modern era. The Anti-Prostitution Act of 1956 clearly had a serious affect on the minds of the Japanese who began to see the geishas as rooted in old world traditions. Thus, in the course of the evolution of Japanese laws, geishas and prostitutes were banned, reallowed, emancipated and banned again, and both geishas and prostitutes had to find their way in the ebb and flow of official Japanese morality.

B. History of the Geisha Tradition

The geisha tradition arose out of a tension between two conflicting cultures: (1) the rigid strictures of Confucianism demanding order and absolute obedience to authority, and (2) the more flexible counterculture that was thriving in the walled cities of pleasure created entirely with government approval.[104] In the highly controlled Confucian society of seventeenth-century Japan, prostitution was tolerated but regulated.[105] In view of the widespread practice of arranged marriages in Japan, the Shogun recognized male society's need for sexual satisfaction. For this reason, Kyoto developed into a thriving center of prostitution. To reconcile

---

101. *Id.*

102. *Id.* at 174. The numbers of geisha were higher in the boom period of the 1920s, which is the period described in Golden's novel. Iwasaki was a geisha in a different boom period of post-war Japan in the mid-1970s.

103. *See id.* at 174–75.

104. *See id.* at 34–35.

105. *See* DALBY, *supra* note 3, at 54. *See also* Morrison, *supra* note 82 (discussing the history of prostitution in Japan and the laws enacted to prohibit this activity).

the conflicting needs of order and pleasure, the Shogun made prostitution legal, but he permitted the prostitutes to engage in sexual services only within the confines of the walled cities of pleasure where a true counterculture developed.[106] The geishas grew out of this Japanese counterculture where they flourished in the pleasure quarters. But it is from this early source and the geishas' connection with the counterculture that we can trace the dubiousness of the geishas' morality in the mind of the Japanese.

The inhabitants of the pleasure quarters of Shimbara were like caged birds, virtual slaves who were indentured to their brothel owners.[107] The indentured women in the pleasure cities of Kyoto came mostly from the lower classes. They were the beautiful children of poor agricultural families or debt-ridden townsfolk. The children were procured by pimps who scoured the countryside to find suitable young children for sex slavery. The pimps paid the parents for the child and resold the child to a brothel. As buying and selling of persons was illegal at this time, the procurers would bind the child with an employment contract for a fixed period of time, usually ten years.[108] For the poor parents in impoverished agricultural villages, sending their child off to the pleasure quarters was nothing out of the ordinary. The recruitment of children for sex slavery is still done to this day in Asia,[109] and a variant of this international crime is described in vivid detail in *Memoirs of a Geisha.*

In the seventeenth and eighteenth century, poor parents would attempt to justify the sale of their children by believing they were giving their daughters a better chance in life, an opportunity to go to Kyoto to eat fine food and wear beautiful clothes, and a chance to receive the luxury of an education in the arts. The child who was sold had absolutely no right to protest and was bound according to the Confucian code by filial duty to her father and to her family first before she could think of her own self. Girls sold to the pleasure quarters were considered virtuous and admirable for having sacrificed themselves for their family.[110]

In the seventeenth century, most children who were recruited against their will at the age of six or seven ended up living in the posh quarters of Shimabara but were considered the property of the brothel owner. Before they even arrived into the pleasure city, the children had already incurred an enormous debt for the privilege of being abducted! To repay this debt, they would have to work night and day as soon as they were old enough to fulfill the pleasures of men. This is

---

106. *See* Morrison, *supra* note 82, at 35.

107. *See* Dalby, *supra* note 3, at 57.

108. Downer, *supra* note 3, at 57.

109. *Id. See* Chapter 10 of this book for a discussion of the sale of children and women for sexual services in China.

110. *Id.*

the typical system of debt bondage normally associated with one of the most hideous of all crimes known as sex trafficking.[111]

In the sex entertainment system of the seventeenth century, Japanese courtesans and prostitutes were both slaves of debt, chattels to be bought and sold, and they did not own their own bodies. Courtesans and prostitutes were part of this floating underworld that continued into the eighteenth century and from which the geisha would ultimately appear in 1751. The entertainment system in Japan of the seventeenth century bears a striking similarity to the geisha world of the 1930s and 1940s described by Golden in his novel.

Unlike the courtesan who dressed flamboyantly, the geisha was regulated by official ordinances to dress in an understated, sophisticated manner. The geisha did not sell her body but only her arts. Soon geishas became known as women who had greater taste than the courtesans, who tied their *obi* in front while geishas tied theirs chastely at the back like ordinary townswomen.[112]

The question of the difference between the geisha and the prostitute has always been complicated, and Japan's feudal government made a considerable administrative effort to preserve a distinction between the two groups of women.[113] In 1779, geishas were recognized as practicing a distinct profession.[114] These female geishas descended from a long line of banished actresses and entertainers whom the Shogun refused to tolerate in the mid-seventeenth century.[115] "[A] registry office (*Kenban*) was set up to enforce rules of conduct for [the geishas]".[116] They were not permitted to sit next to prostitutes' (*yujos*) guests or associate with the prostitutes' business, establishing what seems to be a clear distinction between the geisha and the prostitute. When legal prostitution is abolished in 1956, the Anti-Prostitution Act did not apply to geishas.[117] The fact that many of the laws regulating prostitutes then and now in Japan do not apply to geishas is a sign that geishas are not prostitutes,[118] at least in the eyes of the law.

An open atmosphere of lasciviousness existed in the pleasure districts in the early nineteenth century that provoked the government in 1841 to pass a series

---

111. *See* Tiefenbrun on Trafficking, *supra* note 56. *See also* Nora Deimleitner, *Forced Prostitution: Naming an International Offense* 18 FORDHAM INT'L L.J. 163 (1994). For the development of sex trafficking as a lucrative industry, *see* Susan Tiefenbrun, *Sex Sells But Drugs Don't Talk: Trafficking of Women Sex Workers and An Economic Solution*, 24, 2 THOMAS JEFFERSON L. REV. 161 (Spring 2002). The traffic of women for sexual exploitation is the third most lucrative international crime after the traffic of weapons and of drugs.

112. DOWNER, *supra* note 3, at 80.

113. DALBY, *supra* note 3, at 57.

114. *Id.*

115. *See* DOWNER, *supra* note 3, at 49–50.

116. DALBY, *supra* note 3, at 57.

117. *See* DOWNER, *supra* note 3, at 49–50.

118. DALBY, *supra* note 3, at 57.

of edicts known as the Tempo Reforms to address public morality.[119] Several thousands of prostitutes and geishas were rounded up from the unlicensed districts and dumped into Yoshiwara. In contrast to the prostitutes, geishas were allowed to return to their work so long as they promised to restrict their activities to music and dance. Thus, for the first time the law of 1841 recognized the difference between geishas and prostitutes.[120]

The golden age of the geisha was in 1860. The fact is that Japan had a system of legalized prostitution at that time and until 1956 raised Victorian eyebrows and created doubts in the minds of the foreigners as to the degree of civilization of this nation.[121] And yet, looking at the Japanese-licensed quarters of the nineteenth century, we can see a type of civility and concern for cultural sophistication that matched only the salons of seventeenth-century France.

A major event occurred in 1872 that changed the course of the rise of geisha power and influence in Japan. In June 1872, a Peruvian ship, the *Maria Luz*, dropped anchor in Yokohama Harbor for repairs. The ship was carrying a cargo of 230 Chinese slaves. This incident created an international uproar, and the captain of the ship was arrested and tried. The slaves were finally declared free and sent back to Hong Kong. During this episode, the Peruvians let everyone know that the Japanese also trafficked in slaves—namely the women of Yoshiwara. This assertion was not exactly correct because the sale of human beings had been declared illegal as early as 1612[122] in Japan. To comply with this law, services by prostitutes and courtesans in Yoshiwara were referred to as "term employment."[123] Nevertheless, these women were not free to leave the employment area or to change jobs. The Meiji government, embarrassed about what the employment conditions of the geishas, prostitutes, and courtesans looked like to the Western powers, decided to make Japan appear as "civilized" as any other Western country. Therefore, "four months after the *Maria Luz* incident, the Meiji government passed the Emancipation of Prostitutes and Geisha Act of 1872, prohibiting the sale and trade of human beings."[124]

The Emancipation of Prostitutes and Geisha Act of 1872 recognized that "prostitutes and geisha have lost their human rights"[125] and should not be subject to the age-old practice of debt bondage. "Prostitutes and geisha . . . are treated no different from cows and horses. Human beings cannot logically demand

119. *Id.* at 60.

120. *See* DOWNER, *supra* note 3, at 42.

121. DALBY, *supra* note 3, at 63.

122. *See* DOWNER, *supra* note 3, at 107.

123. *Id.*

124. DOWNER, *supra* note 3, at 108.

125. Ministry of Home Affairs Ordinance No. 16, *supra* note 87, *cited in translation by* DOWNER, *supra* note 3, at 108.

payment of obligations from cows and horses. Therefore, the said prostitutes and geisha should not pay debts or the balance of installments."[126]

Because of the association of women with cows and horses, the Emancipation of Prostitutes and Geisha Act of 1872 ("the Act") is commonly referred to as the Cattle Release Act of 1872.[127] The most important provision of the Act includes the cancellation of all debts of geishas or prostitutes to their geisha houses and houses of prostitution.[128] But because geishas were not in the same state of bondage as many prostitutes, this law was less consequential to them.

Employment contracts for apprentices were limited to seven years and subject to renewal only by agreement of both parties. The city governments acquired the right to license and register any woman working as a geisha or prostitute. Thus, the geisha now had the official right to work, but she had to be licensed. Geishas who wanted to pursue their profession had to register in City Hall. After 1872, the prostitutes who actually wanted to continue their work could also obtain a license. Thus, the geisha who chose also to practice as a prostitute had to have two licenses, one for entertainment (*gei*) and one for the sale of sex.[129] The geisha continued to flourish despite the 1872 Cattle Release Act.

The link between prostitutes and geishas is reflected in the very name of the Emancipation of Prostitutes and Geisha Act of 1872. The word *emancipation* clearly identifies the practices of both prostitutes and geishas as forms of slavery. Even though the Emancipation of Prostitutes and Geisha Act of 1872 permitted prostitutes to work if they were licensed, the effect of the Act was devastating to the trade of the prostitute, but not to the geishas. In reality, this law was neither an Anti-Prostitution Act nor an Anti-Geisha Act, but merely created a highly regulated, government-controlled profession requiring licenses for both.

After 1872, geishas who had been forcibly recruited and abducted into the geisha houses were permitted to return home to their parents, but many did not want to do so. In contrast, many prostitutes did go home and brothels were forced to close. But brothels quickly reopened under the new name of "rental parlors."[130] Statistics support the dramatic effect that the Emancipation of Prostitutes and Geisha Act of 1872 had on prostitution and the opposite effect it had on geishas. For example, just prior to the enactment of the Act, there were 5,759 prostitutes and 280 geishas in seven licensed districts of Japan. After 1872, there were only 1,367 prostitutes, but the number of geishas in these same regions increased to 417,[131] further evincing the difference between geishas and

---

126. *Id., cited in translation by* Downer, *supra* note 3, at 150.

127. The Cattle Release Act is the popular term for the Emancipation of Prostitutes and Geisha Act of 1872. *See* Downer, *supra* note 3, at 108.

128. Dalby, *supra* note 3, at 65.

129. Downer, *supra* note 3, at 108.

130. *Id.*

131. *Id.*

prostitutes and the ineffectiveness of the Act to reduce or eliminate the geisha tradition.

In 1874, the local government responded to the geishas' desire to work by modifying the Emancipation of Prostitutes and Geisha Act of 1872. Geishas were clearly permitted to continue to work; however, a monthly tax was imposed on their wages. The wage tax on geishas was used for the financing of a Women's Handicraft Workshop[132] where geishas were taught practical skills such as spinning, weaving, reading, accounting, dancing, or music to enable them to find more respectable work. Classes in the handicraft workshop were compulsory, and if the geisha missed classes, she was not permitted to work as a geisha.[133] Seeking to become Westernized, the reformers of the new Meiji government instituted these compulsory workshops for geishas to rehabilitate them and force them to learn a decent and accepted skill. However, after attendance became optional, few if any geishas ever attended because conditions in the workshop resembled a sweatshop.[134] The government had substituted one form of slavery for another.

By the turn of the century, geishas had developed into political supporters and activists. In 1904, the Japanese declared war on Russia, and the geishas organized themselves into a National Conference of the Confederation of Geisha Houses to coordinate their war support activities.[135] The Confederation was a form of self-regulation that formalized rules of conduct for geishas and set a standard for the profession; by common consent, it had the power to enforce sanctions for transgressions. A charter with twelve articles was drawn up, and the board's approval was required for newly entering geishas. Any geisha found guilty of misconduct could be expelled by the board. Accordingly, the National Confederation of Geisha Houses was a professional guild organization, established to fix codes of conduct and standards for the profession.[136] However, the effectiveness of the Confederation began to decrease in the 1920s because of the increase in the numbers of geishas. In 1920, there were about ten thousand geishas, compared to 1905 when there were only 2300 in Tokyo.[137]

The rise of the geisha in the 1920s and 1930s continued until World War II, but some changes developed that affected geishas long before the attack on Pearl Harbor. Cafes with hostesses started to appear in prewar Japan. As the cafes grew in Japan, so did the number of hostesses who entertained and performed many of the same functions as the geisha. The growth of the café industry in prewar Japan challenged the geishas who could not find customers willing to pay

132. Dalby, *supra* note 3, at 65.

133. *Id.*

134. *Id.*

135. Dalby, *supra* note 3, at 70.

136. *Id.* at 71.

137. *Id.*

their hefty price. By 1934, there were over 100,000 café girls and reportedly only 72,000 geishas; in 1935, there were reportedly 74,200 geishas in all of Japan.[138]

At this point the geishas started to realize they had to rethink their image and their place in society. They were clearly not prostitutes, as the geishas were considered the "grand ladies of Tokyo and Kyoto."[139] They were also no longer part of the counterculture because they were the fashion plates of Japanese society. In the 1930s, the geishas began to question themselves, wondering if they should modernize, wear Western clothes, give up the sacred shamisen, learn the piano, or go to the university and become really educated to be able to keep up meaningful conversations with the rich and the powerful men they serviced. This is the prewar era in which Golden's Sayuri lived and worked as a geisha.

The war hit everyone very hard in Japan, and by 1944 the geishas had to stop working and leave the closed quarters. On March 4, 1944, all restaurants and teahouses were officially banned.[140] Geishas were not yet officially banned, but they were moving into other trades for want of clients.

At the close of the World War II, General Douglas MacArthur arrived in Japan with the American and other Allied occupation forces. The few women who remained in the cities (whether they were geishas, prostitutes, or simply destitute women and widows) managed to stay alive by sexually servicing the Allied forces army men. The Recreation and Amusement Association, set up to entertain the GIs in Japan, was coined "the world's biggest white-slave traffic combine."[141] General MacArthur was outraged by this dangerous and unhealthy trade. In 1946, he declared all brothels off-limits to GIs and issued a directive banning contractual prostitution. One year later in 1947, the Americans drafted an imperial edict[142] for the Japanese people outlawing all officially

138. In 1935 a book called *The Geisha Reader* was published in Tokyo; it reported there were 74,200 geisha of Japan in 1935. DALBY, *supra* note 3, at 82. Dalby reports that "in 1976 there were approximately seventeen thousand geisha in all of Japan." *Id.* Please note that the numbers of geishas, prostitutes, and courtesans cited by various authors vary and cannot possibly be accurate given the clandestine nature of the activities of these women. This is also true of the figures reported for trafficked women in various U.S. government reports. *See, e.g.*, Tiefenbrun, *supra* note 56, at 111, n.4. The statistics regarding geishas cited in this study may have been taken from various Japanese official consensus, but they are not reliable or even consistent.

139. DOWNER, *supra* note 3, at 194.

140. *Id.* at 201, citing a young Japanese writer Kafu Nagai (1879–1959) who reported that on March 4, 1944, "From tomorrow restaurants and tea houses are to be banned . . . Geishas have not yet been banned, but they appear to be moving into other trades for want of engagements. Without theaters and geishas, the music of Edo, based upon the shamisen, will perish." Kafu's *Diary*, vol. xxii, p. 317.

141. Downer, *supra* note 3, at 204.

142. Imperial Ordinance No. 9 (1947), MINISTRY OF JUSTICE MATERIALS, *supra* note 48, at 10. In January 1946, the Supreme Commander for the Allied Powers wrote a memorandum mandating that the Japanese government eliminate all laws and ordinances

sanctioned prostitution. But this law banning prostitution, like the Emancipation of Prostitutes and Geisha Act of 1872, punished aiders and abettors of prostitution, not the prostitutes themselves, and this law, like its predecessor, was unenforceable.[143]

It is important to note that geishas were excluded from the 1947 directive and the imperial edict banning prostitution. On occasion top American officers enjoyed geisha parties.[144] Basically, when prostitution was outlawed, the numbers of prostitutes declined; the working conditions also got much worse for both the prostitutes and the geishas because of the association of the two in the mind of the Japanese as well as the Americans occupying Japan at the time. Hostesses at bars, cabarets, and dance halls as well as whores, prostitutes and geishas were referred to disparagingly by the American GIs in Japan as "geisha gals."[145] This catch-all term for anyone of dubious morality was used widely during the post-war period in Japan and accounts for some of the reasons the geisha's reputation is fraught with contradiction.[146]

After the war and during the seven years in which the Americans and Allied forces occupied Japan, many cultural practices changed in Japanese society. World War II caused the geishas practically to disappear, and their buildup in numbers and prosperity was gradual. By 1947, there were 1,695 geishas in Tokyo and only 2,478 in all of Japan.[147]

---

permitting licensed prostitution and nullify all contracts that bound (either directly or indirectly), women to act as prostitutes. The Japanese government acted one year later by promulgating Imperial Ordinance No. 9 that punished persons who make women act as prostitutes. *See* M. Takeyasu, *Prostitution in Japan*, 5 Int'l Rev. Crim. Pol. 50, 51 (1954).

Imperial Ordinance No. 9, Article 1: "Any person who induces a woman to commit prostitution in an embarrassing way against her will, even if not by using violence or by intimidation, shall be sentenced to imprisonment with labour [sic] for not exceeding three years, or to a fine not exceeding 10,000 yen."

Imperial Ordinance No. 9, Article 2: "Any person who makes a contract and agreement of letting a woman commit prostitution shall be sentenced to imprisonment with labour [sic] for not exceeding one year, or to a fine not exceeding 5,000 yen."

Imperial Ordinance No. 9, Article 3: "Any person who attempts to commit crimes of the preceeding two articles shall be punished."

143. As a result of the ban on prostitution promulgated in Imperial Ordinance No. 9 of 1947, the government was no longer officially able to regulate the activities of the prostitutes. Prostitution became privatized and protected by international organized crime networks called the *yakuza* or members of the Japanese mafia. The *yakuza* protected the bordello owners and provided assurances by physical force that the women would not run off without repaying their debts to the illegal brothel owners. *See* Downer, *supra* note 3, at 206.

144. *Id.* at 207.

145. *Id.* at 206.

146. *Id.*

147. *Id.*, *citing* Dalby, *supra* note 3, at 182.

A new constitution was drafted in 1947[148] recognizing men and women as equal in politics, law, and education. This equality was utterly revolutionary for the Japanese society. Public kissing, for example, was introduced for the first time on stage and screen.[149] After the war, the geishas returned to Japan dressed in their usual exquisite kimonos signifying the return of old, traditional Japanese values.[150] The sight of a geisha must have pleased the Westernized Japanese who were quite fearful of losing their identity to the conquering foreigners.

The geisha world thrived until 1958 when the Anti-Prostitution Act of 1956 (also referred to as Showa 33)[151] was actually put into effect outlawing public solicitation and management of prostitutes. This Act officially ended licensed prostitution and many of the practices associated with prostitution and with the geisha tradition. For example, the Act outlawed *mirare*,[152] which was the practice of making four or five *maiko*, or geisha apprentices, appear at the teahouse for the sole purpose of "being seen" by the customer who would then choose one of the four with whom he would have sex.[153] In theory, the geisha had the right to refuse the customer, but in practice the *maiko* were too naive to say no. Showa 33 also outlawed the practice of "sleeping over."[154] Customers very much enjoyed sleeping next to several *maiko* and being surrounded by more than one woman in bed. But the rule in "sleeping over" was no touching.[155] Thus, the practices of *mirare* and "sleeping over," which were practiced with the geishas, did not actually involve forced sex but may have led to it. The Anti-Prostitution Act of 1956 also prohibited the deflowerment ceremony[156] (*mizuage*) and the horrifying practice of

---

148. Unsatisfied with the constitutional reforms of the Japanese government, General MacArthur had his staff draft a new constitution in February 1946. *See* EDWIN O. REISCHAUER, THE JAPANESE TODAY: CHANGE AND CONTINUITY 79 (1988), *cited in* Morrison, *supra* note 82, at n. 18.

149. DOWNER, *supra* note 3, at 208.

150. DALBY, *supra* note 3, at xiii: "Geisha are embedded in Japanese culture–Japanese regard them as 'more Japanese' than almost any other definable group." "Geisha remain standard-bearers of tradition." *Id.* at xviii. "[G]eisha are thought of as the epitome of Japanese Tradition [sic]." *Id.* at 20.

151. May 24, 1956 is the date the Diet enacted Law No. 118, the Prostitution Prevention Law [the Anti-Prostitution Act or Showa 33] *See* Morrison, *supra* note 82, at 471; THE ADMINISTRATION OF THE ANTI-PROSTITUTION LAW IN JAPAN 3 (1960). *See also* Anti-Prostitution Law, No. 118 (1956), *reprinted in* MINISTRY OF JUSTICE MATERIALS, *supra* note 48, at 32–39.

152. *See* DOWNER, *supra* note 3, at 230–33, for a discussion of the tradition of *mirare*.

153. *Id.* at 231.

154. *Id.* at 231–33, 136.

155. *Id.* at 232: "[M]en loved sleeping surrounded by beautiful young women."

156. *See* DALBY, *supra* note 3, at 109–11 (describing the formal ceremony of *mizuage* in which a man must swallow the yolks of eggs and rub the whites between the thighs of the virgin, repeating this act for seven days, as he moves closer and closer to the woman, until she loses her virginity).

debt bondage typically associated with slavery, sex trafficking, and the geisha tradition.

As a result of the serious constraints the Anti-Prostitution Act of 1956 placed on the fundamental practices of the geisha tradition, the geisha numbers slowly started to decline after the 1970s. By 1999, there were just 195 geishas and 55 *maiko* left, of whom 90 geishas and 22 *maiko* were in Gion. The geishas who continue the tradition today in Japan have a union to protect them.[157]

Laws passed in Japan after 1956 did affect the development of the geisha tradition. The fact that geishas were exempted from the Anti-Prostitution Act of 1956 gave them more respectability in Japanese society. Nevertheless, ambivalence towards the geisha remains in Japan to this day.[158] After 1956, the practice of child recruitment into prostitution and the life of the geisha still continued. As late as the mid-seventies, children from poor rural villages in Japan were sold by their parents only to end up as maidservants in geisha houses. This practice would change only when Japan started to experience great prosperity.[159]

History shows that the growth and decline of the geisha tradition in Japan has depended primarily on the state of the country's finances and secondarily on laws passed to regulate the profession. The laws banning prostitution and emancipating geishas only applied to pimps and were notoriously unenforceable. Under the reign of Emperor Hirohito from 1965–1975, Japan surged into the modern world financially and technologically. In this new age of modernity, the geisha continued to flourish. There were 17,000 geishas in Japan by the mid-1970s. However, the decline of the geisha began in 1973 around the time of the oil crisis. A new world of easy money, teenage prostitution,[160] host clubs, telephone clubs, and private golf clubs replaced the teahouses, and the geishas started to lose importance. When Japan's bubble economy was deflated in the 1990s, the population of geishas also drastically declined.

To many, the geisha is a very special symbol representing "the epitome of Japanese tradition."[161] Geishas are guardians of old world values that traditional Japanese hold sacred. Geishas remain the bearers of Japanese identity in a changing, integrating world. What is most sacred in the geisha tradition is their code of silence. It is generally accepted that only a low-grade geisha would talk about her experiences and break this code of silence.[162] The idiosyncrasies of the geisha world remained secret and impenetrable . . . until Iwasaki, one of the

---

157. Downer, *supra* note 3, at 171.

158. *Id.* at 211.

159. *Id.* at 211–12.

160. *See generally* Morrison, *supra* note 82 (discussing modern telephone clubs and the role they play in the increase in teenage prostitution in Japan).

161. Dalby, *supra* note 3, at 20.

162. Sayo Masuda, Autobiography of a Geisha (1957) was available in Japan despite the sacred code of silence among the geishas.

most prosperous and well known geishas of the 1960s and 1970s, curiously decided to divulge these precious secrets to Golden who recreated them in his fictional biography.

IV. SUBTEXT

A. Sex Trafficking, Slavery, and the Geisha

Is the recruitment of geishas a variant of sex trafficking and slavery that should be outlawed? In an official CIA Report,[163] the United States links trafficking with slavery, and defines it as "the recruitment, abduction, transport, harboring, transfer, sale, or receipt of persons within national or across international borders, through the use of fraud, coercion, force, or kidnapping, for the purposes of placing persons in situations of slavery-like conditions, forced labor, or services, domestic servitude, bonded sweatshop labor or other debt bondage."[164] The U.S. Victims of Trafficking and Violence Protection Act of 2000 (TVPA),[165] the sex trafficking laws of many other countries,[166] and international treaties[167] as well as the U.N. Protocol on Trafficking[168] clearly link sex trafficking with slavery.

---

163. Amy O'Neill Richard, Center for the Study of Intelligence, International Trafficking in Women to the United States; A Contemporary Manifestation of Slavery and Organized Crime (Apr. 2000), at v, http://www.cia.gov/csi/monograph/women/trafficking.pdf.

164. *Id.*

165. The Victims of Trafficking and Violence Protection Act of 2000, Pub. L. No. 106-386, 114 Stat. 1464 (codified as amended in various titles of U.S.C.) [hereinafter TVPA]. The definition in the TVPA is similar to that of trafficking in the Convention Against Transnational and Organized Crime: Protocol to Prevent, Suppress and Punish Trafficking in Persons, Especially Women and Children: and Protocol Against the Smuggling of Migrants by Land, Sea, and Air, G.A. Res. 25, U.N. GAOR, 55th Sess., U.N. Doc. A/RES/55/25 (2000), at Annex II, Art. 3 (a) [hereinafter "U.N. Protocol on Trafficking"]. The text of the Convention and U.N. Protocol may be obtained from the U.N. Office for Drug Control and Crime Prevention's web site (http:www.odccp.org/palermo). The texts of the Convention and the Protocols are annexed to the Draft Resolution contained in the November 2, 2000 Report by the Ad Hoc Committee (U.N. Doc. A/55/383) to the U.N. General Assembly.

166. *See generally* Susan Tiefenbrun, *Updating the Domestic and International Impact of the U.S. Victims of Trafficking Protection Act of 2000: Does Law Deter Crime?*, 38, 2 Case Western Reserve J. Int'l. 249–280 (2006–07) (discussing the different definitions of trafficking in other countries' anti-trafficking laws).

167. *See* Tiefenbrun, *supra* note 111, at Appendix I and II (listing international treaties prohibiting trafficking and linking trafficking with slavery).

168. U.N. Protocol on Trafficking, *supra* note 165, at Annex II, Art 3(a), defines trafficking as: "[T]he recruitment, transportation, transfer, harbouring [sic]or receipt of persons, by means of the threat or use of force or other forms of coercion, of abduction, of fraud,

The TVPA substantiates the link between sex trafficking and slavery and defines sex trafficking as the recruitment, harboring, transportation, provision or obtaining of a person for labor or services, through the use of force, fraud, or coercion for the purpose of subjection to involuntary servitude, peonage, debt bondage, or slavery.[169]

There is no doubt that in the eyes of domestic and international law, sex trafficking is a form of slavery. But is the recruitment of young girls into the life of a geisha also a form of sex trafficking? If it is, then the geishas tradition is similarly linked to slavery. Like Chiyo in Golden's novel who as a little girl was sold by her parents into a geisha house against her will, the recruitment by force or fraud of a young child to work as a geisha under slave-like conditions, with no right to leave until she pays back an ever-increasing debt that she incurred unwillingly and unknowingly, seems to fit the definitions of sex trafficking quite comfortably. Sex trafficking today is run by international crime organizations, and geisha houses in Japan are similarly protected by the *yakuza*.[170]

Every year more than two million[171] women around the world are bought and sold for the purpose of sexual exploitation. Women are trafficked by fraud and deception from relatively poor or war-torn regions of origin to relatively rich destinations. Although there are many different methods of trafficking, the common thread is that a woman is duped into believing she will find prosperity or simply a better life by taking a fraudulent offer from a trafficker in disguise. One of the worst case scenarios is the sale of a young, impoverished, and naive child to traffickers by her own parents for money.[172] This is precisely what happened to Chiyo in Golden's novel, which accurately reflects the social reality of Japan in 1930, but also casts a shadow on current practices of child abduction for sexual exploitation

---

of deception, of the abuse of power or of a position of vulnerability or of the giving or receiving of payments or benefits to achieve the consent of a person having control over another person, for the purpose of exploitation." *Id.* at Art. 3(a).

169. TVPA, *supra* note 165, at § 7102(8).

170. *See* text accompanying note 145 for a discussion of the privatization of geisha houses and their protection by the *yakuza*. *See also* Tiefenbrun on Trafficking, *supra* note 56, at 136–39 (discussing the role of international crime organizations in sex trafficking, and the linkage of other forms of trafficking (i.e., drugs and weapons) to sex trafficking).

171. Statistics are difficult to verify because of the secrecy of the activity. *See* Tiefenbrun, *supra* note 56, at 111, 126 (discussing the unreliability of statistics related to trafficking. Some sources have reported as many as four million women being trafficked each year, and these varying numbers appear in official U.S. government reports such as the Annual Trafficking in Persons Reports of 2001, 2002, and 2003). *See* Tiefenbrun, *supra* note 166 (discussing the statistics in these reports). *See also*, Becky Young, Note, *Trafficking of Humans across United States Borders: How United States Laws Can be Used to Punish Traffickers and Protect Victims*, 13 GEO. IMMIGR. L.J. 73 (Fall 1998)

172. *See* Sarah Shannon, *Prostitution and the Mafia: The Involvement of Organized Crime in the Global Sex Trade, in* ILLEGAL IMMIGRATION AND COMMERCIAL SEX: THE NEW SLAVE TRADE 119, 122 (Phil Williams ed., 1999).

in Japan and in other nations of the world. Chiyo and Satsu are victims of slavery, and Golden does not hesitate to use the word *slavery* several times in the novel when describing their plight. Whatever the motive and whatever the outcome, the practice of selling one's children for exploitation is intolerable and must be eradicated in Japan and elsewhere.

If trafficking is so widespread and if it is a variant of slavery, why have the laws of the nations not eradicated this universal crime? One reason is the difficulty of proving a case for trafficking. The element of *force* and the related concept of *consent* are necessary components to the definition of trafficking.[173] If the trafficker can present evidence that the woman consented to, or was not forced into, the act of prostitution or sex work of any kind, the victim may not be successful in proving that a crime of sex trafficking was actually committed. The insistence on proof of force and lack of consent has resulted in the failure to enforce many international conventions[174] protecting women against sex trafficking.

The use of force in sex trafficking can refer to either physical or psychological force that occurs when someone is held against her will. In the novel, Chiyo was unmistakably taken against her will to be a slave in a geisha house. She was a victim of both physical and psychological force each time she was beaten, pinched, threatened, humiliated, and disparaged by Mrs. Fidget, Mother, Auntie, Hatsumomo, and many others in the geisha house. There is no possibility for a viable claim that Chiyo actually consented to her sale and forced labor. In addition, Chiyo spends a good part of the novel trying to escape the geisha house. In her desperate attempt to find her sister, Chiyo even manages to fall off a roof and break her arm. She is beaten in the geisha house for this attempted escape.

Domestic laws in the United States and in other countries as well as international laws define sex trafficking as a form of slavery.[175] Sex trafficking has been referred to as "white slavery," and its prohibition resulted in the passage of the Mann Act in 1904 and many international treaties condemning trafficking as slavery.[176] Because U.S. law and international law both establish sex trafficking as

---

173. TVPA, *supra* note 165, at Section 7101(b). *See also The Sex Trade: Trafficking of Women and Children in Europe and the United States: Hearing Before the Comm'n On Security and Cooperation in Europe*, 106th Cong. 21 (1999) at 54, 55 (written submission of Dr. Laura J. Lederer, Director, The Protection Project) [hereinafter "Lederer Protection Project"].

174. *See* Tiefenbrun, *Sex Workers, supra* note 111, at App. I and App. II, at 187–90 (listing more than twenty international conventions to eradicate sex trafficking and other declarations; treaties; U.N. resolutions; and reports condemning slavery, violence against women, and other elements of trafficking).

175. *See* Tiefenbrun, *supra* note 56, at 144–55 (discussing the association of sex trafficking and slavery in domestic and international laws). *See also* Tiefenbrun, *supra* note 111, at 167 (discussing the definition of sex trafficking as slavery and the role of consent).

176. In the United States, trafficking-in-women cases have traditionally been prosecuted under Title 18 sections such as the Mann Act (§ 2421), involuntary servitude and slavery (§ 1581), and other related sections of the U.S. Criminal Code.

a form of slavery, consent should not be a probative issue in the requisite proof of sex trafficking since a person cannot legally consent to slavery. The recruitment of young women by force into the life of a geisha is a form of slavery, with or without the consent of the woman, especially if the geisha life contains involuntary confinement, violence, debt bondage, and forced labor without pay.

Multilateral treaties and customary international law[177] condemn slavery. Since its inception, the United Nations has always been committed to the abolition or elimination of slavery.[178] Yet despite a multitude of U.N. recommendations, decisions, and other pronouncements,[179] slavery is not dead, and the traffic and sale of human beings for sexual exploitation flourish in a lucrative sex trade industry. On November 14, 2000, the U.N. General Assembly adopted yet another anti-slavery convention, the U.N. Convention Against Transnational Organized Crime and the Protocol to Prevent, Suppress, and Punish Trafficking in Persons, Especially Women and Children [hereinafter "U.N. Protocol on Trafficking"].[180] In 2003, during his address to the United Nations President Bush asked each nation to join the United States in ratifying the U.N. Protocol on Trafficking and to cooperate with the United States in implementing its own multilateral effort (i.e., the TVPA) to eliminate sex trafficking, which he called "a modern-day form of slavery."[181]

The U.S. government is committed to the eradication of sex trafficking. In addition to the TVPA, which depends on the willingness of other nations to cooperate with the United States in a global effort to eliminate trafficking, the United States enacted another law, the PROTECT Act,[182] making it a crime for a U.S. citizen (or an alien admitted for permanent residence in the United States) to travel abroad for the purpose of engaging in illicit sexual conduct with another person.[183] Both of these U.S. laws may affect the geisha insofar as her recruitment and engagement in certain activities associated with the geisha tradition arguably constitute a form of sex trafficking. Under the TVPA, any nation failing to pass and make substantial efforts to enforce an adequate anti-trafficking law

---

177. A.Yasmine Rassam, *Contemporary Forms of Slavery and the Evolution of the Prohibition of Slavery and the Slave Trade Under Customary International Law*, 39 VA. J. INT'L. L. 303 (1999).

178. *Id.* at 304.

179. *See* Tiefenbrun, *supra* note 56 (discussing the international human rights laws and humanitarian rights laws that have been passed but not enforced with respect to the outlawing of sex trafficking).

180. U.N. Protocol on Trafficking, *supra* note 165.

181. Elisabeth Bumiller, *Bush Officials See Long Road to Resolution*, N.Y. TIMES, Sept. 25, 2003, at 2 (mentioning Bush's speech to the United Nations).

182. Prosecutorial Remedies and Tools Against the Exploitation of Children Today Act of 2003, Pub. Law 108–21, April 30, 2003, 117 Stat. 650 [hereinafter "The Protect Act"].

183. *Id.* at Section 105(b).

will be placed on a published list and can be subject to economic sanctions by the United States .

The PROTECT Act has a more direct extraterritorial reach than the TVPA. The PROTECT Act makes it possible to investigate, prosecute, and convict in the United States any person who engages in sex trafficking with a minor abroad (even if sex trafficking is legal in that country) or in the United States, and if convicted, that person may be fined or imprisoned for not more than thirty years (or both).[184] The PROTECT Act was passed to eliminate the abduction and involuntary involvement of children in the thriving sex tourism industry in Asia. If the recruitment of young girls by fraud and by force into the life of a geisha is sex trafficking, and if a U.S. citizen procures the services of a young geisha in Japan, that person is committing a crime under the PROTECT Act and can be brought before a court in the United States.

If what happened to Chiyo and Satsu in the novel is tantamount to slavery and sex trafficking, why does the international legal system allow the geisha tradition to continue? The answer can be found in the subtle but significant distinction between the geisha as artisan and the geisha as prostitute. If the geisha is viewed as nothing more than an artist who receives a privileged and courtly education in the arts, it is difficult to argue that she is enslaved and trafficked.

B. Feminist Legal Theory on Sex Trafficking

Feminist legal scholars writing about sex trafficking and forced prostitution typically fall into two distinct categories. One group of feminist scholars (referred to as neoabolitionists)[185] condemns both voluntary and involuntary prostitution on the theory that prostitution is never really entirely consensual and reduces all women to nothing more than pure sex objects.[186] They are against legalizing prostitution because this would justify the sexual exploitation of women. The Coalition Against Trafficking in Women is the organization that supports this position and is vigorously opposed to the legalization of prostitution. However, a second group of feminist scholars accepts the right of women to choose prostitution as a career and condemns sex trafficking only when the career choice is not

---

184. *Id.*

185. Kathleen Barry, Female Sexual Slavery (1979) and The Prostitution of Sexuality (1995). Barry is the founder of the Coalition Against Trafficking in Women and holds the neoabolitionist belief that all forms of prostitution, both consensual and nonconsensual, constitute violence against women and sexual exploitation as well as an institution that victimizes all women. *See also* Catharine MacKinnon, Toward a Feminist Theory of the State, 168 (1991) ("[P]rostitution may be legal or illegal, but so long as women are unequal to men and that inequality is sexualized, women will be bought and sold as prostitutes, and law will do nothing about it.").

186. Jo Doezema, *Loose Women or Lost Women? The Re-emergence of the Myth of White Slavery in Contemporary Discourses of Trafficking in Women*, 18 Gender Issues 23, 33 (2000).

voluntary or when the conditions imposed on the consensual prostitute are inhumane and unanticipated.[187] This group of feminist scholars clearly does not wish to place a value judgment on women who choose prostitution for their livelihood. The Global Alliance Against Trafficking in Women is the primary exponent of this feminist position.

Will legalizing prostitution in Japan aid in the eradication of sex trafficking and the recruitment of little children against their will to work as slaves in a geisha house? The history and development of Japanese laws on prostitution and the geishas do not support the effectiveness of legalizing prostitution, as this would only facilitate the recruitment of children for the geisha houses. When the Anti-Prostitution Act of 1956 was enforced in Japan in 1958, prostitution did decrease appreciably. However, the number of geishas did not decrease immediately after 1958 because the geishas were exempt from this law. In fact, the 1960s and 1970s were a heyday for geishas. The number of geishas started to decline only after Japan's economy started to boom and Japan had an interest in appearing modern to the Western world.

But should the evil practice of child abduction, which is an integral part of the geisha tradition, remain unpunished by law? The recruitment of children into the geisha life against their will and by abduction must be eradicated from this tradition by the force of law. The physical and psychological force used on geisha trainees must also be stopped by law. But that does not mean that the geisha tradition needs to be outlawed entirely; in fact, to do so would be a loss for Japan. Law is a reflection of society, and the aspects of the geisha tradition that involve forced prostitution, slavery, fraud, force and coercion must be condemned by law in order to change the mentality of the Japanese people. But this change in attitude toward the geisha tradition is already happening, but for cultural reasons, not moral or legal. In the past few years, the geisha tradition, including its cultural sophistication, fashionable trendsetting, and promotion of the arts, has seen a dramatic decline in Japan because of changes in the cultural tastes of the people who are affected by globalization and integration.

C. Cultural Relativism and the Geisha Tradition

Why should we as Western people sit in judgment of an age-old tradition that is considered the bastion of Japanese culture and tradition? To do so is a violation

---

187. *See* Tiefenbrun, *supra* note 56, at 123–24 (describing the feminist debate on sex trafficking and forced prostitution). Contrary to the position of the Global Alliance Against Trafficking in Women, Catherine MacKinnon and Andrea Dworkin maintain that "*all* prostitution is forced prostitution." *See* In Harms Way: The Pornography Civil Rights Hearings *supra* note 187, at 68 n. 23. (Catharine Mackinnon & Andrea Dworkin, eds., 2001),

of cultural relativism. Critical race theorists[188] have focused on the difficult question of determining when cultural relativism can justify egregious violations of human rights, such as stove burning, acid throwing, female genital mutilation, and female infanticide.[189] Western countries need to respect cultural norms practiced in other countries even if those norms differ from our own. But if sex trafficking and the practice of recruiting children for training as geishas are a variant of the slave trade, we cannot argue persuasively that the geisha is simply a cultural norm accepted in Japan that must be respected as such under the theory of cultural relativism.[190] Sex trafficking, like the slave trade, is a universal crime prohibited by the principle of *jus cogens* set forth in Articles 53 and 64 of the Vienna Convention on the Law of Treaties.[191] Recruiting children for labor in geisha houses simply cannot be excused by the argument of cultural relativism because, like female infanticide, it is a universal crime that must be universally condemned. Parents who sell their girl babies for money into the sex work industry—and traffickers like Mr.Tanaka who snare the poverty-stricken girls into a world of forced prostitution—are frowned upon in Japan. Child recruitment for forced sex work should not be viewed as a cultural practice but rather as a universal crime as heinous as the slave trade.

Changes in socioeconomic conditions in Japan have affected the root causes of sex trafficking, forced prostitution, and abduction of children for the geisha life. In the past, and sadly, in the present, young women are lured into sex trafficking and geisha work because they are victims of poverty, of the social practice that marginalizes women in Japan, of the failure to place a value on traditional women's work, and of the lack of real educational and employment opportunities for women. When Japan passed a law making education for all children compulsory, it put a severe damper on the indecent recruitment of young children into geisha work. The enactment of laws, the influence of foreign governments and practices, and the changes in the economy and infrastructure in Japan caused

188. *See e.g.* Hope Lewis, *Between* Irua *and "Female Genital Mutilation:" Feminist Human Rights Discourse and the Cultural Divide, in* CRITICAL RACE FEMINISM 361 (Adrien Katherine Wing ed., 1997).

189. Sharon K. Hom, *Female Infanticide in China, The Human Rights Specter and Thoughts Toward (An)other Vision, in* GLOBAL CRITICAL RACE FEMINISM: AN INTERNATIONAL READER 251 (Adrien Katherine Wing ed., 2000).

190. *See* Isabelle R. Gunning, *Arrogant Perception, World Traveling, and Multicultural Feminism: The Case of Female Genital Surgeries, in* GLOBAL CRITICAL RACE FEMINISM: AN INTERNATIONAL READER 352, 357 (Adrien Katherine Wing ed., 2000).

191. Vienna Convention on the Law of Treaties, *opened for signature,* May 23, 1969, 1155 U.N.T.S. 331, 344, art. 53 (defining *jus cogens* norms as principles "accepted and recognized by the international community of States as a whole as a norm from which no derogation is permitted and which can be modified only by a subsequent norm of general international law having the same character"). Sex trafficking is slavery and thus meets the *jus cogens* criteria. *See* Tiefenbrun, *supra* note 56, at 124–26.

the geisha tradition to change significantly since 1850. Some, like Iwasaki, fear it is disappearing entirely.

V. POST-TEXT: THE COMPLAINT IWASAKI V. ARTHUR GOLDEN AND PUBLISHERS

A. Plaintiff's Claims

On April 22, 2001, Mineko Iwasaki filed a Complaint against Arthur Golden, Random House, Inc., and Alfred A. Knopf, a division of Random House in the U.S. District Court of the Southern District of New York. The Complaint is an action for breach of contract, quantum meruit,[192] and unjust enrichment. Quantum meruit refers to "the reasonable value of services; damages awarded in an amount considered reasonable to compensate a person who has rendered services in a quasi-contractual relationship."[193] In addition, the Complaint alludes to viable claims of misappropriation of property (the name and likeness of a person), defamation of character, right to privacy and publicity, and copyright infringement under the laws of the State of New York and of Japan. The plaintiff asks for an accounting under U.S. copyright laws.[194] I shall now discuss the factual and legal basis of these claims and their merit.

1. Copyright Infringement and Common Law Copyright Plaintiff's claim of copyright infringement is based on the theory that she owns a common law copyright in her own personal account of her life, which Golden taped, transcribed, and allegedly misappropriated as source material for his novel. Plaintiff claims she is the sole owner of the copyrights in and to her personal history and family stories that she set forth in the tapes made by Golden during their interview sessions. According to Iwasaki, Golden wrongfully and without

---

192. Quantum meruit is derived from the Latin and means "as much as he has deserved." *See* Black's Law Dictionary (Bryan A. Garner, ed., 7th ed. 1999), at 1255 [hereinafter "Blacks Law Dictionary"].

193. *Id.* at 1255.

194. U.S. Copyright Act of 1976, 17 U.S.C. §§ 101–1332 (2000). Note that the jurisdiction of the New York court in the case against Golden and his publishers is predicated upon the existence of a federal question, the diversity of the parties, and a dispute arising between a U.S. citizen and a citizen of a foreign state, the dollar amount of the claim for damages which is greater than $75,000 and less than $10,000,000, and a copyright jurisdictional claim, as set forth in 28 U.S.C. §§ 1331, 1332(2), 1338 (a) (2000). The defendants reside or transact business in New York and in the Southern District which justifies the venue. The plaintiff, Mineko Iwasaki, resides in Kyoto, Japan and is a citizen and resident of Japan. The defendant, Arthur Golden, resides in Brookline, Massachusetts and transacts business in the Southern District of New York. The other two defendants, Random House, Inc. and Alfred A. Knopf, are New York corporations with their principal place of business in New York.

authorization reproduced Iwasaki's copyrighted materials in the book. Plaintiff claims she is the coauthor of the novel and should be compensated for her creative contribution. According to this theory, Golden merely put down on paper the actual words she gave him on tape and in transcription, and, therefore, she is the coauthor of the taped conversations that form the basis of the book. Plaintiff further claims that Golden licensed certain rights in the book to Alfred A. Knopf without her approval. As a result of the licensing, the defendants received over $10,000,000 (plaintiff seeks an accounting of the exact sum received by the defendants).

These facts form the basis of a claim for copyright infringement of Iwasaki's taped conversations presumably under the common law copyright doctrine.[195] Common law copyright is a property right that arises when the work is first created rather than when it is published. Under the U.S. Copyright Act of 1976, which went into effect on January 1, 1978, common law copyright was largely abolished for works created after the statute's effective date, but it still applies in a few areas, notably in a common law copyright received before January 1, 1978, which is entitled to protection.

Iwasaki will have difficulty proving that she has a common law copyright because she did not create the book. She will also have difficulty proving a legitimate copyright claim in the taped conversations unless she had initially or at some point designated to Golden which part of the total stream of the conversation is her own literary creation, as set forth in *Estate of Hemingway vs. Random House, Inc* ("*Hemingway*") in 1994.[196]

2. Misappropriation of Name and Likeness, Invasion of Privacy, and Publicity Plaintiff contends that she is a well-known and well-respected business person in Japan. Until her retirement in 1980, Iwasaki was one of the most famous geishas of Kyoto, and she worked in Gion, the most prestigious geisha district in Japan. These background facts in the Complaint contain the seeds of Plaintiff's claim that she is a public figure[197] in Japan and has a property right[198]

195. *See* BLACK'S LAW DICTIONARY, *supra* note 192, at 338.

196. 23 N.Y. 2d 341 (1968). *See infra* text accompanying notes 290–299 (discussing the *Estate of Hemingway v. Random House* case on the issue of common-law copyright claims in taped conversations resulting in a biography of Hemingway).

197. Iwasaki admits that she is well-known in Japan. But she is also arguably a "public figure" under U.S. law. A public figure is defined as a person who, by his accomplishments, fame, or mode of living, or by adopting a profession or calling that gives the public a legitimate interest in his doings, his affairs, and his character, has become a "public personage." Cason v. Baskin, 30 S.2d 635, 638 (Fla.1947). "Such public figures were held to have lost, to some extent at least, their right of privacy." WILLIAM L. PROSSER & W. PAGE KEETON, LAW OF TORTS 823 (1983).

198. RICHARD A. POSNER, ECONOMIC ANALYSIS OF LAW, Section 3.3, 43 (4th ed. 1992). Judge Posner discusses the tort of misappropriation as applied to celebrities. The question is whether there is anything unique about Iwasaki's name or likeness that creates value for

to her name and likeness. The law grants celebrities a property right to ration the use of their names to maximize their value over time.[199] However, a public figure's rights to privacy are diminished.[200] The basis of the Plaintiff's claim is that Golden misappropriated her famous name and likeness when he acknowledged her full name in the beginning of the book and on promotional tours and when he created a likeness of Iwasaki in the character of the narrator Sayuri.

The right of publicity arises out of the right of privacy. The tort of appropriation of a person's name or likeness for the defendant's pecuniary benefit or advantage is a form of invasion of privacy[201] and is based on a proprietary right.[202] In the Second Circuit,[203] an exclusive licensee of this "property" has also what has been called a "right of publicity."[204] The right of publicity is the right of every person to prevent the unauthorized, commercial use of his identity.[205] The right of publicity serves two primary purposes: to protect all persons from the anguish that may accompany the unwanted use of their identity, and to protect the property interest that persons (especially celebrities) have in their identities.[206]

In New York, as well as in many other states, plaintiffs have successfully recovered under a misappropriation theory when their name or picture or other likeness has been used without their consent for commercial purposes in order to advertise the defendant's product, to accompany an article being sold, to add luster to the name of a corporation, or for other business purposes.[207] But the unauthorized use by the defendant of the plaintiff's name and likeness is limited

---

Golden to appropriate. Her name and likeness may have value in Japan, but certainly not in the United States and Europe, at least when the book first came out in 1997. Golden should win summary judgment on this claim because of free speech and public domain defenses. *See* Matthews v. Wozencraft, 15 F. 3d 432 (5th Cir. 1994).

199. *Matthews*, *supra* note 198, at 438, n. 2. *See also* POSNER, *supra* note 198, at 43: "[C] reating a property right in such uses would not lead to any socially worthwhile investment but would simply enrich already wealthy celebrities. However, whatever information value a celebrity's endorsement has to consumers will be lost if every advertiser can use the celebrity's name and picture."

200. Samuel D. Warren & Louis D. Brandeis, *The Right to Privacy*, 4 HARV. L. REV. 193, 214–16 (1890).

201. PROSSER, *supra* note 197, at 804. *See also* RESTATEMENT (SECOND) OF TORTS § 652 C (1977) on right to privacy.

202. PROSSER, *supra* note 197, at 854.

203. Haelan Laboratories v. Topps Chewing Gum, Inc., 202 F.2d 866 (2d Cir.), *cert. denied* 346 U.S. 816 (1953)

204. Melville B. Nimmer, *The Right of Publicity*, 19 LAW & CON. PROB. 203 (1954).

205. PROSSER, *supra* note 197, at 807.

206. Bruce P. Keller, *The Right of Publicity: Past, Present and Future, in* PRACTICING LAW INSTITUTE COMMERCIAL LAW AND PRACTICE COURSE HANDBOOK SERIES, PLI 161 (Oct. 2000).

207. PROSSER, *supra* note 197, at 805.

only for advertising purposes or for "purposes of trade," otherwise referred to as "commercial purposes."[208]

If the misappropriation of the name or likeness occurs with respect to a public figure, the rights of privacy and publicity of that public person must be balanced with the demands of free speech. The standard set forth in *New York Times v. Sullivan*[209] requires proof that the use of a public figure's name in reporting is done with actual malice[210] and reckless disregard for the truth. Thus, assuming Iwasaki can prove she is famous in the United States as well as Japan, she would also have to prove that Golden used her famous name and likeness with reckless disregard for the truth and with malice in order to pirate her identity for some advantage of his own (as for example, to add luster to his novel because of the value of Iwasaki's name). Thus, the mere use of the plaintiff's name in the novel[211] is not enough to hold the defendant liable unless the defendant also made commercial use of the name and did so with malice.

3. Misappropriation in Fiction:*Matthews v. Wozencraft, Random House, Inc. et al.* William Prosser clearly indicates that a plaintiff will have difficulty in proving misappropriation in a work of fiction. "Nor is there any liability when the plaintiff's character, occupation, and the general outline of his career, with many real incidents in his life, are used as the basis for a figure in a novel who is still clearly a fictional one."[212] *Matthews v. Wozencraft.*[213] is the case on point that would work in Golden's defense against Iwasaki's claim of misappropriation of her name and likeness and her geisha life story in Golden's novel.

In *Matthews*, a former undercover narcotics officer[214] filed suit alleging breach of contract, misappropriation, and invasion of privacy against his former wife and the publisher of his wife's book (which happens to be Random House,[215] the

---

208. *Id.* at 805.

209. New York Times v. Sullivan, 376 U.S. 254 (1964). The Court in *Sullivan* announced the rule that a public figure can recover damages from a news organization for harms perpetrated by its reporting only by proving "actual malice," which requires that the statements were made with a reckless disregard for the truth. *Id.* at 279–80. If *Sullivan*, which refers to news reporting of public figures, also applies to works of fiction, Iwasaki would have to prove that Golden used her name with "actual malice."

210. *See also* Eastwood v. National Enquirer, Inc., 123 F.3d 1249 (1997). In the California Court of Appeals, Judge Kosinski held that actor Clint Eastwood could not recover costs because he did not show by clear and convincing evidence that an interview was printed with knowledge, that it was false, and that the newspaper had acted with actual malice.

211. *See* Maggio v. Charles Scribner's Sons, 205 Misc. 818, 130 N.Y.S. 2d 514 (1954); Harrison v. Smith, 20 L.T.R. 713 (1869); Swacker v. Wright, 277 N.Y.S. 296 (1935).

212. Prosser, *supra* note 197, at 806. *See also* Toscani v. Hersey, 271 App. Div. 445, 65 N.Y.S. 2d 814 (1946).

213. *Matthews*, 15 F.3d 432 (5th circuit 1994).

214. *Id.*

215. *Id.* at 436. Matthew's former wife, Wozencraft, sold her manuscript and the movie rights to Random House for one million dollars. Similary, Iwasaki decided to sue Golden

same publisher named as one of the defendants in Iwasaki's Complaint). Matthews claimed that when his former wife wrote a book about his life story, she was misappropriating his name and likeness and violating his right to privacy.[216] Furthermore, she was cashing in on the goodwill associated with the police officer's name.

Random House won this case because the Texas court held that a life story is not a "name or likeness" under Texas misappropriation law.[217] The Texas court also held that appropriation does not occur in a *fictionalized account* of a person's life under the "false light doctrine."[218] This holding is applicable to Iwasaki's case against Golden because the real geisha is claiming that the author misappropriated her information and painted her in a false light when he used her taped words, which she claims are protected by common law copyright.

On appeal from the U.S. District Court for the Eastern District of Texas, the *Matthews* court held that the author had created a fictionalized account of her husband's life, and she could not be held liable for misappropriation of a fictionalized biography.[219] The lower court held that the author of a novel falls under First Amendment protection, and is further protected by the *fair use* of information in the private domain.[220] Moreover, on appeal the *Matthews* court held that the book and its accompanying publicity[221] had converted the officer (about whose life the book was written) into a "public figure," and neither the book nor the movie held the officer in a false light or in an embarrassing way so as to constitute "actual malice."[222]

Like Iwasaki, who claims ownership rights to Golden's book, the plaintiff in *Matthews* also claimed that he had ownership rights in his former wife's fictionalized account of events surrounding his life.[223] Matthews also claimed that he received no compensation for his wife's use, portrayal, or promotion of his likeness in the book and in the movie.[224] The district court granted summary judgment against Matthews' appropriation claim because Texas law does not recognize a cause of action for appropriation of a life story, and even if it did,

---

when she learned about Steven Spielberg's intention to make a movie out of Golden's fictional biography. The large sums of money involved in the publication of the book and the prospects of the movie may have been some of the underlying motivations for Iwasaki's law suit.

216. *Id.* at 436.

217. *Id.* at 437.

218. *Id.* at 439.

219. *Id.* at 437.

220. *Id.* at 432.

221. *Id.* at 436.

222. *Id.* at 432, citing U.S. Const. amend. 1.

223. *Id.* at 441.

224. *Id.*

Texas law grants an exception for biographies and "fictionalized biographies."[225] Iwasaki's case against Golden and Random House also involves a "fictionalized biography," a claim of misappropriation of a public figure's name; thus if the case went to trial and the New York court had followed *Matthews*, the geisha could not succeed on the merits of her appropriation claim.

4. Breach of Contract Plaintiff claims that when she first met Golden in 1992, she agreed to be interviewed about her geisha life in Gion and her family's experiences only if Golden agreed to comply with certain express conditions. The first condition was complete anonymity for herself and her family. The second condition was total confidentiality regarding the personal stories and information she related to him about her life and career as well as her family's experiences. These facts form the basis of Iwasaki's claim for breach of contract. In May 1992, plaintiff alleges that she and Golden entered into an agreement whereby Golden agreed not to use the personal material supplied to him by plaintiff in her taped interviews and not to mention plaintiff's name in any publication by Golden. Plaintiff claims defendant breached the express terms of their oral confidentiality agreement by revealing and spotlighting her name in the acknowledgment of the book. This assertion, if true, would be difficult for Golden to defend against as he did place Iwasaki's name in the acknowledgment of the book and, therefore, could be held liable for breach of an oral agreement (notwithstanding the general difficulty to enforce[226] oral agreements). New York law on the enforceability of oral contracts is quite clear: "It is ordinarily unnecessary to allege whether a contract sued upon was oral or written.[227] However, an oral agreement "reached during negotiations will not be sufficient to defeat an action for breach of contract."[228] Moreover, the type of oral confidentiality agreement that Iwasaki alleges she and Golden entered into are not covered under the five classes of enforceable oral contracts listed in the U.S. Statute of Frauds.

Plaintiff claims that Golden represented to her that her collaboration in the book was only for the purpose of "fact checking" a certain novel that he had already written. Golden admits that he actually abandoned his earlier drafts and wrote an entirely new novel largely based on Iwasaki's testimony. This is the basis of plaintiff's claim that the author breached an alleged oral confidentiality agreement. However, even though there was an exchange of promises between Golden and Iwasaki, Golden could no doubt challenge the existence and enforceability of any

225. *Id.* at 437.

226. *See* E. ALLAN FARNSWORTH, CONTRACTS 4 (1982) (explaining enforceability of contracts and its relationship to consideration). "[T]he law of contracts is confined to promises that the law will *enforce.* It is therefore concerned primarily with *exchanges* because, as will be explained later, courts have generally been unwilling to enforce a promise unless the promisee has given the promisor something in return for it." *Id.*

227. Rubin v. Cohen, 129 A.D. 395, 113 N.Y.S. 843 (1908).

228. Namad v. Salomon, Inc., 74 N.Y. 2d 751, 753 (1989).

contract between Iwasaki and himself based on there being arguably no consideration,[229] no writing,[230] and no meeting of the minds[231] about conditions precedent[232] to the publication of the novel.

Pursuant to an alleged express verbal agreement between plaintiff and defendant, Iwasaki claims she permitted Golden to come to her home in Japan and to tape her recollections of Gion life for almost two weeks from May 10, 1992 through May 23, 1992. The interviews she accorded him averaged more than ten hours per day and involved more than one hundred hours of taping. Plaintiff claims unjust enrichment because she was never compensated for the time and work she contributed to the book whereas defendants have enjoyed substantial profits from its sale.

Plaintiff also alleges a claim for quantum meruit against the defendants for failure to compensate her for the fair value of her services to which she is justly entitled. She contends the defendants promoted and exploited the unprecedented access that she afforded Golden to the unknown world of the geisha and to Gion's history. Quantum meruit is a claim or right of action for the reasonable value of

---

229. *See* FARNSWORTH, *supra* note 226, at 20 (explaining the doctrine of consideration). "The doctrine of consideration took care of the bulk of economically vital commercial agreements, even if it afforded no ground for the enforceability of gratuitous promises, for which nothing was given in exchange . . . [T]he doctrine of consideration has been widely criticized." *Id.*

230. *Id.* at 369–70 ("It would be difficult to imagine a question more important to a person expecting to make agreements in an unfamiliar legal system than this: . . . when is a writing required to make an agreement enforceable? . . . [This question] is governed by the "statutes of frauds . . . In contrast to formal contracts, informal contracts might be oral. However, the trial of an action based on an oral contract raised problems.") (citations omitted).The five classes of enforceable oral contracts listed in the English Statute of Frauds (1677) [Stat.29 Car. 2, c.3] and the U.S. Statute of Frauds do not include the type of oral confidentiality agreement that Iwasaki alleges she and Golden entered into. *See id.* at 374; RESTATEMENT SECOND OF CONTRACTS, Section 110 (1981) (listing the six provisions of the English Statute of Frauds adopted in the United States).

231. "Actual assent to the agreement on the part of both parties was necessary; without it there could be no contract. As it was often expressed, there had to be a 'meeting of the minds.'" FARNSWORTH, *supra* note 226, at 113. Farnsworth calls the "meeting of the minds" a "much abused metaphor" and explains its derivation from the Latin *agregatio mentium* or a meeting of the minds. *See also* Farnsworth, *"Meaning" in the Law of Contracts*, 76 YALE L.J. 939, 943–44 (1967).

232. *See* FARNSWORTH, *supra* note 226, at 537–43 on conditions of a contract and conditions precedent: "According to the RESTATEMENT SECOND [Section 224] a condition is 'an event, not certain to occur, which must occur, unless occurrence is excused, before performance under a contract becomes due' . . . Almost any event may be a condition . . . [W]hat we have been calling a 'condition' has been called a 'condition precedent' . . . [T]he plaintiff ha[s] the burden of pleading and proof as to a condition precedent to the defendant's duty. . . ." (citations omitted).

services rendered.[233] At common law, quantum meruit was a count in an assumpsit action to recover payment for services rendered to another person. It is still used today as an equitable remedy to provide restitution for unjust enrichment. It is often pleaded as an alternative claim in a breach-of–contract case so that the plaintiff can recover even if the contract is voided.[234]

Given the lack of consideration, lack of a writing, and the arguable absence of a meeting of the minds between Golden and Iwasaki, Iwasaki's claim to the existence of a contract may be void, making her claim to quantum meruit all the more viable.

6. Defamation Plaintiff claims that Defendant breached his express promises to her and disparaged her reputation in the book and in his public promotions of the book. This statement is the basis of Iwasaki's claim against Golden for defamation.[235] Iwasaki alleges that Golden breached his promises by telling lies about her not only in the book, but in public interviews. For example, Golden stated during public promotions of the book that Iwasaki was sold into the geisha world as a child by her parents and that her virginity was auctioned to the highest bidder when she came out as a geisha. Plaintiff argues that these two statements are untrue and that Golden falsely represented these statements as facts.

Plaintiff further claims that Golden has defamed her and tarnished her reputation by citing her as his primary authority on geisha life and then *inaccurately* portraying many of the customs, ceremonies, and rituals in the book, thus making her look like an unreliable authority of the geisha tradition. As Iwasaki may have already been planning in 2001 to write two of her own books about the geisha life[236] that were actually published in 2002, her credibility as an authority

---

233. BLACKS LAW DICTIONARY, *supra* note 192, at 1255.

234. *See id. See also* FARNSWORTH, *supra* note 226, at 98–99 (distinguishing *quantum meruit* from *restitution*). "Since these claims [unjust enrichment for retaining a benefit without paying for it] for the redress of unjust enrichment did not fit comfortably into either the category of contract or that of tort, they came to be described as claims in *quasi-contract.* Some of them were originally characterized as being in *quantum meruit* (as much as he deserved), a form of action used for claims to payment for services. This procedural term has persisted and is sometimes used inexactly as a synonym for the more general term *quasi-contract,* which refers to any money claim for the redress of unjust enrichment. *Restitution* is a broader term, propagated by American scholars in this century to embrace all remedies having that function. . .," *Id.*

235. *See* RESTATEMENT SECOND OF TORTS, *supra* note 201, § 558 for a definition of defamation. *See also* PROSSER, *supra* note 197, at 739: "Defamation is rather that which tends to injure 'reputation' in the popular sense; to diminish the esteem, respect, goodwill or confidence in which the plaintiff is held, or to excite adverse, derogatory or unpleasant feelings or opinions against him." *Id.* at 739.

236. IWASAKI,, *supra* note 1; IWASAKI, *supra* note 2. Both books by Iwasaki were written with the collaboration of Rande Brown and published in 2002, one year after Iwasaki filed her Complaint.

on the geisha tradition was particularly valuable to her. These are the facts that constitute the basis of plaintiff's claim to the defamation of her character.

To establish a prima facie case for libel or slander (collectively known as defamation), the plaintiff must prove that a false and defamatory statement was made negligently (or, in certain circumstances, with actual malice), of and concerning the plaintiff, which resulted in a special harm of a pecuniary nature or loss of the plaintiff's reputation.[237] A defamatory statement must be based on false facts, not opinion. The publication of the defamatory statement must be a communication of that statement to a person other than the plaintiff. If the statement is made in reporting newsworthy events about a public figure, the plaintiff must prove actual malice, but otherwise, only negligence is required. A defamation claim can be actionable even if there is no existence of a "special harm."[238] Plaintiff will have difficulty proving defamation under New York law because this is a work of fiction, Iwasaki is arguably a public figure, and the author is protected by freedom of speech unless the plaintiff can prove actual malice. A Texas court refused to uphold a claim for defamation in a fictionalized biography of a person who became a public figure after the book was published and publicized.[239] Moreover, plaintiff provided Golden with written consent[240] for publicizing the book, knowing her name was in it. Consent is a bar to a claim of defamation.

Claims for defamation in a work of fiction rather than fact are very difficult to prove. When interviewed, the attorney for the plaintiff and the spokesman for Random House, Inc. could not cite any precedent for such a case,[241] even though there are several cases clearly on point for defamation in works of fiction.[242] This is truly an unusual case because normally the author indemnifies the publisher for claims of defamation, but in this case the publishers are "vigorously defending" Golden and his book[243] based on their firm belief that plaintiff's claims are baseless.

---

237. Restatement Second of Torts, *supra* note 201, at § 558.

238. *Id.*

239. *See supra* text accompanying footnotes 213–25 for a discussion of *Matthews, supra* note 198, and the doctrine of misappropriation of property and invasion of privacy and publicity in a work of fiction.

240. Consent is a complete defense to a claim of defamation. *See* Prosser, *supra* note 197, at 784 ("The general social policy of denying recovery for conduct to which the plaintiff has given his consent finds expression in an absolute immunity in cases where consent is given to defamation." "Where the plaintiff is uncertain as to just what will be said, but consents to publication which he has reason to believe may be defamatory, the defense would seem properly to be one of assumption of risk.") *Cf.* Chapman v. Ellesmere, 2 K.B. 431 (1932), cited in Prosser, *supra* note 197, at n.59.

241. Feeney, *supra* note 12.

242. *Matthews, supra* note 198.

243. Mehren, *supra* note 63.

7. Defamation-in-Fiction: Claims and Defenses Defamation-in-fiction is the publication of a false statement of fact, of and concerning the plaintiff, made with actual malice[244] or reckless disregard for the truth for a public figure or with negligence for any person, and which causes injury to the reputation of the plaintiff. It is particularly difficult to prove a defamation claim in a work of fiction[245] because fiction writers are presumably protected by the right of freedom of speech[246] and because the plaintiff has the burden of proving that the statements made in the work of fiction are actually factual and refer specifically to the plaintiff herself. The court's task in a defamation-in-fiction action entails a search for similarities and dissimilarities so as to determine whether a person who knew the plaintiff and who read the book could reasonably conclude the plaintiff was actually the fictional character.[247]

In a defamation-in-fiction case, the plaintiff must prove that the defamatory publication is *of and concerning* the plaintiff. In common law, the "of and concerning" element was referred to as the *colloquium* requirement of defamation.[248] To meet this burden, the plaintiff does not have to establish that everyone all over the world would understand the libelous or defamatory statement refers to the plaintiff; it is sufficient if those who knew the plaintiff can determine that she is the person referred to in the fiction.[249] Iwasaki believes everyone in Japan would identify her as the character in the fiction, and because of the notoriety she received subsequent to the novel's publication, it is arguable that everyone would recognize her in the fiction. Golden, however, adamantly maintains that Sayuri in the novel and Iwasaki are very different, and it is unlikely that anyone in Japan or elsewhere reading the book would confuse her with Sayuri.

The next big hurdle for the plaintiff in a defamation-in-fiction action is to rebut the presumption that all the material in a fictional work is untrue. In other words, the reader must be convinced the fiction is based on *fact*. In order for the reader to believe that the content of the novel is based on defamatory false facts, the presumption of invention in a work of fiction must be overcome.[250] Given the accepted fact that writers create their fictional works based on their own

---

244. *New York Times v. Sullivan*, *supra* note 209, at 279–80.

245. *See* Symposium Issue in 51 Brook. L. Rev. (1984–85), and especially Martin Garbus and Richard Kurnit, *Defamation in Fiction: Libel Claims Based on Fiction Should be Lightly Dismissed*, 51 Brook. L. Rev. 401 (1984–85).

246. Some scholars claim works of fiction are not covered under *New York Times v. Sullivan* so that writers of fiction are not protected by its high standard of fault. *See* Schauer, *supra* note 62, at 240 ("They assume that fiction is outside the paradigm of *New York Times* and *Gertz*.").

247. Springer v. Viking Press, 90 A.D. 2d 315, 319 457 N.Y.S. 2d 246 248 (1st Dept. 1982), aff'd., 60 N.Y.2d 916, 470 N.Y.S. 2d 579 (1983).

248. Schauer, *supra* note 62, at 236.

249. Fetler v. Houghton Mifflin Co., 364 F. 2d 650, 651 (2d Cir. 1966).

250. Welch v. Penguin Books USA, Inc., 1991 N.Y. Misc. Lexis 225, at 9.

experiences, it must be a requirement of an action for defamation in a work of fiction that the reader be totally convinced that the book in all its aspects as far as the plaintiff is concerned is not fiction at all.[251] Golden's presence in the book, his master craftsmanship, and his artistic rearrangement of plaintiff's statements into a work of poetic prose will make it difficult if not impossible for Iwasaki to prove this novel is fact and not fiction.

Defamation-in-fiction actions are difficult to win because they do not fit comfortably into defamation law. In a defamation-in-fiction case, the plaintiff must overcome the dichotomy between opinion and fact in a work of fiction. "[D]efamation law is predicated on two polar premises: first, *opinion* is protected under the first amendment [sic] because 'there is no such thing as a false idea;'[252] but second, 'there is no constitutional value in *false statements of fact*.'"[253] A work of fiction is not easily categorized either as opinion or as containing false statements of fact. Fiction contains many factual details, but by its very nature, works of fiction are not based solely on "statements of fact."[254] False statements of fact are unprotected. However, given the hybrid nature of works of fiction that are often based on truth but fashioned in fiction, a novel such as Golden's *Memoirs of a Geisha* does not fit easily into the requirement of proof of "falsity" in a defamation case.

Defamation law was first constitutionalized by the U.S. Supreme Court in *New York Times Co. v. Sullivan*.[255] This decision embodies "the central meaning of the First Amendment" and is "the best and most important [opinion] the Court has ever produced in the realm of freedom of speech."[256] If *New York Times v. Sullivan* is applicable to a work of fiction about a public figure, then Iwasaki's claim of defamation in fiction flies in the face of the writer's freedom of speech. Thus, if this case went to Court and Golden were found guilty of defamation in fiction, this would add to the small but significant increase in successful defamation-in-fiction litigation suits[257] and would have a chilling effect on the freedom

---

251. *Id.* at 9–10.

252. Gertz v. Robert Welch, Inc., 418 U.S. 323, 339–40 (1974).

253. *Id.* at 340.

254. Joel M. Gora, *Defamation in Fiction: Introduction: Literature, Life, and the Law*, 51 Brook. L. Rev. 225, 230 (1985). *See also* Milkovich v. Lorain Journal Co., 497 U.S. 1 (1990).

255. *New York Times v. Sullivan*, *supra* note 209, at 254.

256. *See* Harry Kalven, *The New York Times Case: A Note on "The Central Meaning of the First Amendment*, 1964 Sup.Ct.Rev. 191, 194".

257. Bindrim v. Mitchell, 92 Cal. App. 3d 61, 155 Cal. Rptr. 29, *cert denied*, 444 U.S. 984 (1979); Pring v. Penthouse Int'l, Ltd., 616 F.2d 438 (10th Cir. 1982) (reversing a $26.5 million jury verdict in "Miss Wyoming" defamation action against *Penthouse* magazine), *cert. denied*, 103 S. Ct. 3112 (1983); Geisler v. Petrocelli, 616 F.2d 636 (2d Cir. 1980) (finding that plaintiff's complaint, alleging libel and violations of privacy rights arising from publication of a novel about a transsexual tennis player, stated a valid cause of action).

of speech of writers. If Iwasaki succeeded in her defamation action, this could have seriously reduced the publication of traditional fiction, particularly the *roman à clef*, as well as newer forms of fiction such as the docudrama that are largely based on fact but placed within a framework of artistic fiction.[258]

The law continues to wrestle with the need to balance the writer's right to freedom of speech and the right of individuals allegedly harmed by fictional portrayals to protect themselves under defamation theory or alternative tort theories such as misappropriation. Modern libel and defamation law seeks to avoid self-censorship by writers and journalists fearing to be held strictly liable for factual errors. To protect against self-censorship, the U.S. Supreme Court requires that false statements by media defendants are actionable only if the statements are the product of actual malice (intentional or reckless disregard for the truth)[259] when the plaintiff is a "public official"[260] or "public figure"[261] or if the statements are the product of negligence when the plaintiff is a private individual.[262] Proof of actual malice is the safeguard of freedom of speech. However, in 1979 when the Supreme Court in *Bindrim v. Mitchell*[263] declined to review the judgment in favor of the plaintiff in a defamation-in-fiction litigation based on a nonfactual publication and an intentional or reckless disregard for the truth, a serious danger to literary freedom was established.[264]

If Iwasaki is deemed a "public figure," she would have to prove that Golden engaged in actual malice to harm her reputation and that he knew or should have known that what he published was false. Given the nature of the friendship between Golden and Iwasaki before the post-publication scandal developed, it seems unlikely that Iwasaki could prove either Golden's actual malice towards her or even his reckless disregard for the truth, especially in the light of Golden's family background and experience in newspaper publication. Moreover, the requirement of proof of actual malice for a public figure in a work of fiction would result in an absurdity because Golden is a writer of fiction who clearly knew that what he was publishing was fictional and therefore partially "false" in a literary but not entirely legal sense. Fiction involves the interplay of truth and falsity, reality and fantasy, and the application of the rules for actual malice to a fictional work may be problematical.

---

258. David A. Anderson, *Avoiding Defamation Problems in Fiction*, 51 BROOK. L. REV. 383, 393 nn. 56–57 (1985) (defining literary genres such as the *roman à clef* and the docudrama).

259. *Bindrim, supra* note 257, at 984. Note that Justices Brennan, Stewart, and Marshall dissented and voted to grant certiorari.

260. *New York Times v. Sullivan, supra* note 209, at 279–80.

261. Curtis Publishing Co. v. Butts, 388 U.S. 130, 155 (1967).

262. *Gertz, supra* note 252, at 347, n.10.

263. *Bindrim, supra* note 257.

264. *See* Gora, *supra* note 254, at 226.

8. Defamation-in-Fiction: Contradictions and Conundrums Defending a defamation-in-fiction action requires a plaintiff to contradict herself by asserting that the fictional character resembles her but is not like her at all. Thus, Iwasaki would have to prove that the fictional character, Sayuri, is both similar to, and different from herself. The plaintiff must assert simultaneously that the story or novel is "about" her based on similarities between Iwasaki and the fictional character. However, the plaintiff must also assert that the novel could not "be about" her because, in real life, she would never do the scandalous things ascribed to the fictional character.[265] Moreover, to prove she experienced harm to her reputation, she would have to prove that she is very different from the fictional character. Iwasaki would no doubt argue that she is a geisha artisan, not a courtesan or a prostitute like Sayuri. Thus, the plaintiff would have to prove similarities and differences and contradict herself in order to win her case.

Similarly, Golden would have to assert the absurd defense that he is a writer of fiction and did not knowingly, recklessly, or negligently make untruthful statements. This assertion is unthinkable for a writer of fiction. Therefore, bringing and defending such a defamation-in-fiction action requires "a kind of mutual doublethink."[266]

9. Damages As for damages, plaintiff makes an excessive and unreasonable request. She wants defendants to surrender *all* profits as a result of their infringing activities including the sale of all goods or services incorporating plaintiff's copyrighted materials.

---

265. Pring v. Penthouse Int'l, Inc., 695 F. 2d 438, 442-443 (10th Cir. 1982), *cert denied*, 103 S. Ct. 3112 (1983). In an earlier New York case, Geisler v. Petrocelli, 616 F. 2d 636 (2d Cir. 1980), the U.S. Court of Appeals for the Second Circuit held that a young woman, whose name was identical to the female transsexual heroine of a novel, could sue the book's author for defamation. The New York court in *Geisler* followed an earlier California defamation-in-fiction case, *Bindrim, supra* note 257, brought by a psychologist who conducted a nude group therapy session and successfully sued an author because the author had attended the session and thereafter wrote a novel that described a similar nude encounter session in an unflattering way. In *Pring*, the plaintiff obtained a $26,500,000 jury verdict in a defamation action against *Penthouse* magazine that portrayed her as a supposedly fictional baton-twirling Miss Wyoming engaging in fantastic sexual exploits during a pageant that was televised coast-to-coast. (*Pring*, 695 F.2d at 439). As a result of the outcome of the trial in *Pring* and the earlier holdings in *Geisler* and *Bindrim*, a "full blown first amendment problem" has emerged and authors' literary freedom is being infringed. However, the appellate court in *Pring* overturned the judgment by a narrow two-to-one vote on the ground that the story was too fantastic to have reasonably been taken as "true", 695 F.2d at 443). *See* Schauer, *supra* note 62, at 235–41; Gora, *supra* note 254, at 225–26.

266. *See* Gora, *supra* note 254, at 228.

B. Defendant's Response

The defendants never filed a Reply to the Complaint, which the plaintiff ultimately voluntarily dismissed on February 11, 2003. If Golden had filed a Reply, he would probably have argued the absence of a contract; the right to fair comment and free speech; the limitation of plaintiff's rights to privacy and publicity in a work of fiction; plaintiff's consent as a bar to her claims of right to privacy and publicity, as well as her claim of defamation; absence of a common law copyright claim based on the holding of *Hemingway*;[267] and the absence of a claim for quantum meruit or unjust enrichment.

1. Absence of a Contract In public interviews, Golden repeatedly and adamantly denies the existence of any agreement not to disclose Iwasaki's identity or to observe total confidentiality about her personal stories and her family's experiences. "There was no such agreement," he said.[268] Why would Golden have spent all those hours taping if he had agreed not to use the material in his book? Why would he, a man very familiar with the publishing world, so boldly place his source's real name in the acknowledgments of his own book if he had actually entered into a confidentiality agreement with her not to reveal it? The facts seem to support the contention that there is no written or verbal confidentiality agreement between Iwasaki and Golden.

The enforceability in the State of New York of an alleged oral confidentiality agreement by a plaintiff who (four years after the book was actually published), seeks astronomical amounts of compensation for services performed is, at best, questionable. Moreover, Iwasaki filed her Complaint on the eve of a Steven Spielberg movie of *Memoirs of a Geisha* and in anticipation of the publication of Iwasaki's own two novels about the geisha life. The timing of her Complaint undermines the legitimacy of her claims and the credibility of her testimony. The only explanation for the filing of this belated Complaint is that either she or Golden is lying about the existence of a confidentiality agreement. More probably there was a misunderstanding about what each party meant by confidentiality and trust. Given the disparity in the cultural backgrounds of the plaintiff and defendant, such a misunderstanding seems quite plausible. In any case, if there were an oral agreement not to divulge the plaintiff's identity, Golden is in breach of it.

Iwasaki claims that she began considering legal action in 1999 when the book was first translated into Japanese and after she read it for the first time. Apparently, Iwasaki believed she would be able to settle her differences with Golden without lawyers. This explanation is reasonable given the cultural pattern of the Japanese people to shy away from lawyers and courtrooms and to prefer mediation or conciliation as a form of dispute resolution. Other explanations for her delay are

267. Estate of Ernest Hemingway v. Random House, Inc., 23 N.Y. 2d 341 (1968).
268. Norton, *supra* note 13, at 15.

possible. Iwasaki probably had ulterior motives and second thoughts about the merits of suing Golden for breach of contract. Her ulterior motives could be based not only on greed and the desire for just compensation for her services, but also self-interest and the plan to bring publicity to her own forthcoming books via a lawsuit that would no doubt reach the press.

However, the most important reason for suing was her need to save face, which also is a culturally specific motivation. Many of Iwasaki's sister geishas in Japan were up in arms for breaking the geisha code of silence. Iwasaki must have reasoned that she could achieve her goal of saving face by attacking the book and its author publicly through a lawsuit. Her own legal claims of a breach of contract would reveal to the world that she had, indeed, respected the code of silence by insisting on confidentiality and anonymity. It was not she but the author who violated that code by breaching their agreement. This argument will probably fail because her own claim to coauthorship of the book militates against her need to distance herself from the assertions in the book.

2. Limited Rights to Privacy and Publicity in a Work of Fiction: Fair Comment and Free Speech Golden's main defense against Iwasaki's claims of a right to privacy and publicity[269] would have been that he wrote a work of fiction, specifically a fictionalized biography,[270] in which the main character is a literary creation. The book and its publicity (created largely by Iwasaki's filing of the Complaint) converted Iwasaki into a public figure.[271] In the eyes of the law, a public figure's right to privacy is significantly reduced.[272] Ironically, had Iwasaki

---

269. "The right to privacy and publicity are related. The right to privacy has been defined as the right of a person to be free from unwarranted publicity or the right to be protected against the commercial exploitation of one's personality without his written consent. The doctrine of privacy rests upon the proposition that an individual, as a private person, should be protected from unsought publicity." Rosenwasser v. Ogoglia (1916) 172 AD 107, 158 NYS 56; Joseph E. Conley et al., *Right of Privacy Defined*, NEW YORK JURISPRUDENCE §274; 44 N.Y. JUR. 2d (Defamation and Privacy Section) (2nd ed. 1994).

270. *See Matthews, supra* note 198, at 440 on the denial of a claim of a right to privacy in a fictionalized biography. *See also* Samuel D. Warren & Louis D. Brandeis, *The Right to Privacy,supra* note 200, at 214–15 ("To whatever degree and whatever connection a man's life ceases to be private before the publication under consideration has been made, to that extent the protection is withdrawn. . ..").

271. "The book and its accompanying publicity have converted Matthews into a public figure under *Gertz v. Robert Welch, Inc.*," 418 U.S. 323, 94 S. Ct. 2997, 41 L. Ed. 2d 789 (1974), cited in *Matthews, supra* note 198, at 440. "The same standards of constitutional protection apply to an invasion of privacy as to libel actions." Meeropol v. Nizer, 560 F. 2d 1061, 1067 (2d Cir. 1977), *cert denied*, 434 U.S. 1013, 98 S. Ct. 727, 54 L. Ed. 2d 756 (1978).

272. *See Matthews, supra* note 198, at 440–41, citing Douglass v. Hustler Magazine, Inc., 769 F.2d 1128, 1139 (7th Cir. 1985) ("Because all of the events were a part of the public domain, defendants were entitled to their fair use, including their narration in fictionalized form.").

filed suit immediately after the publication of the novel and before she became a public figure in the United States, she might have had a chance to win her invasion of privacy claim.

Golden would probably have argued that Iwasaki is not Sayuri. On many occasions, Golden has explained that he tried to make the novel look like it was the narrator's creation. "I was working very hard to make it look like I didn't really write this book, that it was just dictated by a geisha and that I wrote it down. And many people write me letters and say, 'Where–how can I get in touch with Sayuri?' The truth is, she doesn't exist. This character is entirely invented, and the woman that I interviewed wouldn't recognize herself, or really anything about herself, in this book."[273]

How wrong and yet how right Golden was when he said Iwasaki would not recognize herself in the character of Sayuri. Iwasaki does vigorously deny being like the person Golden wrote about in the book, even though in order to win her claim for defamation, Iwasaki must prove the book is about her."Everything is wrong," she said. "In the book, a geisha was beaten with a hanger and crippled. There is a very strict rule that '*maiko*' (apprentice geisha) and geisha should never be beaten."[274] Every time Golden paints a picture of the geisha that is not in accordance with Iwasaki's glorified perception of herself as a geisha/artist, she cannot help being offended. Iwasaki's flaw is her refusal to understand that the protagonist in this novel is an invented character drawn up by an author hiding in the background. "The book is fiction,"[275] Golden insists, and confesses that he made a lot of it up. "It's not about her," and Sayuri is not Iwasaki.[276]

If Iwasaki is not the character in the book, there can be no basis for her claim to a violation of her right to privacy because the statements in the novel are not about Iwasaki or her own life story.[277] Iwasaki's claim is something like the real person's reaction when she suspects she is the character in a *roman à clef.* [278] But this person has no basis for a claim of privacy or publicity because the character is fictional, not real, and the author is protected by his First Amendment right to freedom of speech.

Moreover, a qualified privilege has been developed at common law to cover what has been called *fair comment* on matters of public concern.[279] The U.S.

---

273. O'Brien, *supra* note 72.

274. Tegler, *supra* note 9.

275. *Id.*

276. Feeney, *supra* note 12 ("[T]he novel's protagonist, Nitta Sayuri, was not based on Iwasaki.").

277. *See Matthews*, *supra* note 198, at 432.

278. A *roman à clef* is a novel written with purportedly fictional characters but who are actually real people with fictional names. The public enjoyed trying to figure out who the actual people in the novel were in real life.

279. *See* Prosser, *supra* note 197, at 786.

Supreme Court has made this privilege a constitutional one under the First Amendment. It applies to invasions of the right of privacy as well defamation claims. Prior to 1964, cases dealing with both defamation and privacy made mention of the guarantee of freedom of speech contained in the First Amendment to the U.S. Constitution.[280]

3. Plaintiff's Consent is a Bar to Invasion of Privacy and Publicity Iwasaki's claim to a violation of her right to privacy and publicity[281] would probably have failed because of her own written consent to publicity. Golden has stated publicly that he has a fax from her proving that she actually asked him to set up a U.S. publicity tour for her.[282] Her desire to be recognized publicly and her claim to require a condition precedent of anonymity in the novel are contradictions of terms. Consent to publicity by the plaintiff in a claim of invasion of her right to privacy and publicity would result in the denial of her claims under New York law.

4. Plaintiff's Consent is a Bar to Defamation: Viability of Claim of Slander in New York Court Plaintiff's consent to publicity is a complete bar to a claim of defamation.[283] Iwasaki's vaguely alleged claim to defamation of her reputation based on Golden's references to the sexual activity of Sayuri would probably fail because of Iwasaki's own written consent[284] to the novel being publicized. Golden would have easily won against Iwasaki's claim of defamation in fiction because she consented to the publicity and converted herself into a public figure as a result of the self-imposed publicity. She also could not easily prove that the novel is "of and concerning" Iwasaki herself. In addition, Golden is protected by the most powerful of all constitutional rights, the right to free speech.

Notwithstanding the weakness of her defamation claim, Iwasaki could have alleged a viable claim of slander based on Golden's portrayal of the geisha, Sayuri, engaging in the sex act both in the novel and in his discussions during promotional tours of the book. The basis of Iwasaki's claim of slander would

---

280. *Id.* at 819.

281. "The right of publicity generally is defined as the right of every person to prevent the unauthorized commercial use of his or her identity. The right of publicity arose from the right of privacy and serves two primary purposes: (l) to protect all persons from the anguish that may accompany the unwanted use of their identity; and (2) to protect the property interest that persons, especially celebrities, have in their identities." *See* Keller, *supra* note 206, at 161.

282. Michael Ellison & Jonathan Watts, *Geisha Wants Cut of Golden's Goose,* THE GUARDIAN (LONDON), Apr. 26, 2001. ("The Japanese phrase she used [to evidence her consent to publicity] translates roughly to 'Put my face out there a little more, please.'").

283. "In an action for defamation, the plaintiff's consent to the publication of the defamation confers an absolute immunity or an absolute privilege upon the defendant. Stated differently, the plaintiff's consent constitutes a complete defense to a defamation action." 43A N.Y. JURISPRUDENCE § 105, *supra* note 269.

284. *See* Ellison & Watts, *supra* note 282.

be *unchastity*.[285] As far as Golden's statements during the promotion of the novel are concerned, most courts would not look favorably at the actionability of an oral imputation of unchastity to a woman without proof of damage.[286] However, New York, by virtue of a specific statutory provision,[287] permits an action of slander to be maintained for unchastity without the necessity of alleging or proving special damages. In New York, any words are slanderous per se that impute unchastity to a woman.[288] Iwasaki could have argued that Golden falsely associated sexual activity and prostitution to her when he wrote about sex acts performed by Sayuri as a geisha in the novel. If Iwasaki could prove these sex acts are "of and concerning" her, she could then have argued that Golden indirectly accused her of sexual activity, which would then constitute an actionable and possibly viable claim of slander under New York law.

5. Common-Law Copyright Infringement In *Hemingway*, the New York Court of Appeals spoke out quite clearly against the merits of a claim of common-law copyright for taped conversations where the speaker has not marked off the copyrightable utterance in question from the ordinary stream of speech.[289] Unless the speaker can indicate that she actually intended to mark off certain parts of the taped speech as her own literary creation, the whole taped conversation would not pass muster under copyright law, as set forth in *Hemingway* (discussed below).

---

285. *See* PROSSER, *supra* note 197, at 759 ("An accusation of unchastity was at first regarded as purely a "spiritual matter"—that is, a sin—and so was not actionable without proof of "temporal" damage, such as the loss of a particular marriage. This remained the law of England until 1891, when it was remedied as to the female sex by the Slander of Women Act of 1891 (54 and 55 Vict. Ch 51). Similar statutory changes of the common law rule have been made in a number of American states, and several courts have accomplished much the same result by holding that an imputation of unchastity to either sex is equivalent to a charge of the crime of adultery or fornication, which involves an infamous punishment or moral turpitude.").

286. *Id.* at 760.

287. CLS Civ. R. Law §77.

288. Segel v. Barnett, 34 Misc 2d 591, 226 N.Y.S. 2d 141 (Sup.Ct. Montgomery Co. 1962); Gunsberg v. Roseland Corp., 34 Misc 2d 220, 225 NYS 2d 1020 (*N.Y.*Sup. 1962); Dahm v. O'Connell, 96 Misc 582, 161 NYS 909, rev'd on other grounds 179 AD 363, 166 NYS 450 (1917). *See also* Imputations of Unchastity, Sexual Offenses, and Indecency—Slander. 16A *Am Jur. Pleading and Practice Forms (Rev), Libel and Slander*, Forms 141 et seq., cited in NY JUR DEFAM L 24, N.Y. JURISPRUDENCE, Second Edition. 43A, N.Y. JUR. 2d § 24, *supra* note 269 (discussing slanderous imputations).

289. *Hemingway*, *supra* note 267, at 256 ("Assuming, without deciding, that in a proper case a common law copyright in certain limited kinds of spoken dialogue might be recognized, it would, at the very least, be required that the speaker indicate that he intended to mark off the utterance in question from the ordinary stream of speech, that he meant to adopt it as a unique statement, and that he wished to exercise control over its publication.").

a. Estate of Ernest Hemingway v. Random House, Inc. The facts of *Hemingway* are strikingly similar to Iwasaki's case against Golden. The defendant in both cases is Random House, and both cases involve a claim to copyright infringement of taped conversations that develop into a fictionalized biography called memoirs.[290] In the *Hemingway* case, Ernest Hemingway's widow sued the publisher (Random House), and the author (Hotchner) who wrote a biography of the writer entitled *Papa Hemingway*. She sued for damages and injunctive relief on the grounds that the biography consisted largely of Hemingway's taped and confidential conversations with Hotchner. The court was called upon to decide whether conversations of a highly regarded writer may become the subject of common-law copyright even though the speaker himself did not reduce his words to a writing.[291]

Hotchner was an intimate friend of Hemingway who had frequently recorded their personal conversations.[292] Hotchner even published several articles about Hemingway based on these conversations. In the past, Hemingway had consented to the publication of these articles.[293] After Hemingway's death, Hotchner wrote *Papa Hemingway* based upon his notes and his recollections of conversations he had with Hemingway. The book, which is subtitled *A Personal Memoir*, contains lengthy quotations from these conversations.[294]

Hemingway's wife objected vigorously to the last two chapters of the book about Hemingway's suicide and mental illness. She sued Hotchner claiming four causes of action, which are strikingly similar to those in Iwasaki's case: (1) that the biography consists of literary matter composed by Hemingway and in which he had a common-law copyright (an author's proprietary interest in his literary or artistic creations before they have been made generally available to the public, also referred to as the *right of first publication*); (2) that publication would constitute an unauthorized appropriation of Hemingway's work and would compete unfairly with his other literary creations; (3) that Hotchner wrongfully used material imparted to him in the course of a confidential and fiduciary relationship with Hemingway, and (4) that the book invades the right to privacy[295] to which Mary Hemingway herself was entitled under § 51 of the New York Civil Rights Law.

The *Hemingway* court held that in order to claim a common-law copyright in a taped conversation, the plaintiff must indicate that Hemingway intended to mark off the utterance in question from the ordinary stream of speech, that he

290. *Id.* at 253 ("Subtitled 'a personal memoir,' it is a serious and revealing biographical portrait of the world-renowned writer.").

291. *Id.* at 253.

292. *Id.*

293. *Id.*

294. *Id.*

295. *Id.* at 254.

meant to adopt it as a unique statement, and that he wished to exercise control over its publication.[296] Golden could similarly assert the defense that Iwasaki never marked off portions of her taped conversation from the ordinary stream of her speech, that she did not intend to adopt portions of it as unique, and that she did not express to Golden any wish to control the publication of the taped conversations. Thus, the merits of Iwasaki's claim are weakened by the holding of *Hemingway*, and she is unlikely to have had any success in her claim of common-law copyright infringement. This is no doubt one of the primary reasons she ultimately voluntarily dismissed her Complaint even before Golden responded to it.

6. Quantum Meruit and Unjust Enrichment Defendant has a moral obligation, if not a legal one, to compensate Iwasaki for her hours spent in providing him with valuable information about the geisha life. But, if there were no oral or written agreement about compensation, there is no legal justification for her claim to quantum meruit. However, by the equity of business practice, Golden should compensate her for her services.

Golden should not have to compensate her for the profits he earned from the writing of his own book, which Iwasaki claims is unjust enrichment. If a New York court accepted the holding of the Texas court in *Matthews*, New York law would not recognize her as coauthor of this book, and therefore Iwasaki would not likely succeed on her claim of unjust enrichment.

C. What is the Likelihood That Iwasaki Would Have Succeeded on the Merits?

Iwasaki makes similar claims to those of Mary Hemingway in the *Hemingway* case. Iwasaki argues that she owns a common-law copyright to the taped conversations she had with Golden in her home. Like Mary Hemingway, Iwasaki claims Golden is unjustly enriched due to the misappropriation of her personal property. Iwasaki also similarly claims she was not remunerated for her services. As in *Hemingway*, Iwasaki bases most of her claim on the breach of an oral confidentiality agreement between Golden and herself. Iwasaki also alleges that there was a serious, confidential relationship between her and Golden that he breached. Iwasaki further claims he breached her right to privacy when he portrayed her as Sayuri and thereby misappropriated her name and likeness in the novel.

Judging from the holding of the court in *Hemingway* and the similarity of both cases, Iwasaki does not have much hope of winning. However, *Hemingway* was an easier case because the Hemingway biography containing information that Hotchner allegedly misappropriated is one of an uncontested public figure. Iwasaki is a public figure only in Japan, but she was arguably unknown to the Western world when the book first came out. However, Iwasaki became a public figure because of the publicity she created about the book. Iwasaki might have

296. *Id.* at 256.

prevailed if she claimed she is not a public figure in the United States and, therefore, has a right to privacy. However, if she claimed she is not a public figure, she could not easily win on the claim of misappropriation of her name and likeness (which has more value if she is a celebrity). Iwasaki might have prevailed if she could have persauded the court that there was an agreement of confidentiality and anonymity between her and Golden and that Golden breached that agreement by placing her name boldly in the acknowledgment of the book. However, Golden has continued to deny the existence of any such agreement.

Iwasaki's claims for misappropriation, right of privacy, breach of common-law copyright and coauthorship, and breach of contract are unlikely to succeed in view of the holdings in *Matthews*[297] and *Hemingway*.[298] Specifically, the New York Court of Appeals rejected Hemingway's similar claims for misappropriation and copyright infringement.

Iwasaki's claim for defamation-in-fiction will also probably fail because she consented to the publication and publicizing of the book, and consent is a complete bar to a claim of defamation.

VI. PRETEXT

A. Why Did Iwasaki Really File a Complaint against Golden?

Iwasaki may have been interested in just compensation, but she appears to have been less motivated by greed than by a personal mission to save herself and to save the geisha tradition. In interviews with newspaper reporters, Iwasaki revealed her personal, hidden motives for filing a Complaint against Arthur Golden, her former friend. She claims Golden told lies about her and about the geisha tradition.[299] Since the publication of Golden's book, Iwasaki has been on a mission to defend both her own reputation and the reputation of the geisha tradition, which she sees as the bastion of Japanese culture.

Like an advocate for the rights of the geisha, Iwasaki was offended by Golden's misguided association of the geisha with the prostitute, an unfortunate link that casts a long shadow of immorality over the reputation of the geishas in general and of Iwasaki in particular. Iwasaki believes that geishas are worthy of respect, not opprobrium. "Golden has mixed up the well-respected and highly educated geisha with the common prostitute in order to spice up the story for Western audiences . . . In so doing, Golden has insulted all true geishas."[300] "Although

297. *See* discussion *supra* notes 212–13 on the claim by plaintiff of coauthorship to a fictionalized biography, which was rejected by the *Matthews* court.

298. *See supra* text accompanying notes 290–96 for a discussion of the *Hemingway* case on the claim of coauthorship which was rejected by the court.

299. Norton, *supra* note 13 ("The book is lies, all lies.").

300. Norton, *supra* note 13.

some geisha quarters did engage in prostitution, most did not, and the perception that all geisha sleep with their clients is absolutely false," she insisted.[301] Iwasaki is defending the whole geisha tradition that she considers a vestige of old world Japanese culture and the key to the Japanese soul.[302] She has set it as her personal goal to correct the misguided images of the geisha. "We [geisha] are precious goods and the livelihood of the geisha houses depends on us."[303] Iwasaki sounds like an advocate for woman's human rights when she claims that geishas are "proud, accomplished women who have absolute rights over [their] own bodies."[304]

Iwasaki must also protect her own image. Having retired from the geisha life and now living in Japan as a married woman and the proud mother of two children, Iwasaki must defend her own reputation as a woman for the benefit of her family, friends, and former geisha sisters who are maligned by any association of the geisha with the prostitute. Despite much evidence to the contrary, Iwasaki insists the geishas did not perform sex for money. "The geisha world is not a place where you sell your body."[305] In short, Iwasaki does what she can to save face.

Iwasaki filed a Complaint against Golden because he offended her honor, and any slight to her personal honor is also a blow to the honor of the whole geisha profession. Golden's painting of a less-than-clear picture about the morality of the geisha is viewed by Iwasaki as a direct attack on her honor. Given Golden's duality and ambivalence about the geisha tradition (which he communicates in his novel), Iwasaki's irritation with him and the resulting legal suit were inevitable. Her Complaint is more about honor than about money. That is why initially she sought only a public apology from Golden,[306] not $10,000,000 in compensation. She also only "want[ed] her name removed from all future reprints of the book."[307] Her own lawyer stated that in Japan Iwasaki withdrew an official Complaint when the publisher there agreed to remove her name from the book's acknowledgments.[308] This response does not sound like a plaintiff motivated entirely by greed.

Iwasaki sued Golden because she felt betrayed by someone she considered a good friend. Arguably, this betrayal is a reenactment of the betrayal she felt towards her own father who sold her to a geisha house presumably to give her a

---

301. Tegler, *supra* note 9.

302. Hoh, *supra* note 35, at 46 ("[T]he geisha have retained a peculiar iconic status; some outsiders still see them as a key to unlocking the Japanese soul.").

303. Id.

304. Id.

305. Norton, *supra* note 13.

306. *Id.*

307. *Id.*

308. Mehren, *supra* note 63.

better life and to save the family's honor. There must have been some misunderstanding about how Golden would use her material because she repeatedly refers to Golden's betrayal of her confidence and trust. "He has betrayed me and my family," she said.[309] "I am angry about the way he has abused my confidence and trust. He could not have written the book without my help. This is not just a personal injury law suit. I am not just doing this for myself. His book is an insult. He has shown a total lack of respect for me, my privacy and that of all geishas."[310] This lack of respect and privacy are based on her misunderstanding that the fictional geisha is not the real geisha. She is embarrassed because Golden writes in the book that "as a young girl [the protagonist's] virginity was 'auctioned to the highest bidder,' which Iwasaki falsely assumes must refer to her own life. The selling of her virginity, that rite of passage, did not happen," said Iwasaki's lawyer.[311]

Iwasaki felt compelled to defend her own reputation as an authority on the geisha tradition because she herself (with the assistance of Rande Brown) was writing two books about her own life as a geisha and the whole geisha tradition when she filed the Complaint. Both these books were published in 2002,[312] and all the publicity surrounding Golden's book must have helped sales of Iwasaki's books.

For example, in defense of her own reputation as an author and authority on the geisha tradition, Iwasaki denies that geisha ever had to undergo the indignity of a deflowerment ceremony. "There was no money put on virginity in my circles."[313] Iwasaki's statement is true about the geisha who lived in the 1960s and 1970s, in precisely the time that Iwasaki was practicing as a geisha. But Golden's fictional geisha lived in the 1930s and 1940s when the deflowerment ceremony was a ritual that each young geisha typically endured.[314] The real geisha assumes wrongly that she is the same person as the fictional geisha, and her identification with the fictional character is the source of her anger, which is manifested in the filing of a Complaint. Iwasaki's statement denying deflowerment of the geisha as a ritual casts doubt on her being an authority about the history of geisha. Her denial of the deflowerment ceremony shows her lack of understanding of the evolution of the geisha tradition. In a different interview, Iwasaki is quoted as saying that "the system under which geisha operate was established in 1873 and has not changed since then." Nothing could be farther

---

309. *Id.*

310. *Id.*

311. Barret, *supra* note 77.

312. *See* IWASAKI, *supra* note 1; IWASAKI, *supra* note 2.

313. *Id.*

314. DALBY, *supra* note 3, at 109–10 ("Older geisha automatically say how wonderful it is that their daughters do not have to submit to *mizu-age*.").

from the truth, and studies have been done to trace the evolution of the geisha from the seventeenth century to today.

Iwasaki filed a Complaint against Golden because of a culture clash. She is Japanese, defending the old-world tradition of the geisha that she knew in 1960 and 1970; and Golden is an American writing in 1997 in the voice of a female geisha of the 1930s. This is no doubt a tour de force for a writer, but there may be moments when Golden's assumed Japanese voice does not ring true to the Japanese reader. Iwasaki—and apparently many of the Japanese readers—do not like the book because some of the details simply do not reflect their own image of themselves as they see Japan and as they remember one of their most valued traditions, the geisha. "The vulgar details it contains about unsavoury lavatories and thigh tatooes are not to Japanese taste."[315]

Iwasaki also filed a Complaint against Golden because she needed to defend herself from attacks by her geisha friends who were bound, with a seriousness of purpose, to a code of silence that she clearly breached by speaking out to Golden. The reaction of her geisha friends was so violent that she thought the only way to deflect their anger was to sue the author and place the blame on him and his breach of confidentiality. The merits of this claim are dubious.

VII. CONCLUSION

Memoirs of a Geisha by Arthur Golden deserves entry into the law and literature canon. The author writes with authenticity and engaging lyricism in the many different voices of an evolving female narrator who represents the geisha in the 1930s and 1940s. With stylistic ingenuity and an elaborate array of poetic and exotic similes, Golden paints vivid portraits of characters who populate the geisha world. His poetry in prose captures the peculiarities of Japan's geisha tradition. This book belongs in the law and literature canon because for the first time an author's narrative technique, based on voyeurism and duality, constitutes the primary motive for a lawsuit. It is not only *what* Golden says about the geisha, but *how* he says it that provokes the real geisha to sue the author and his publisher for common-law copyright infringement, breach of contract, quantum meruit and unjust enrichment, misappropriation, right to privacy, and defamation in a work of fiction.

Iwasaki's defamation-in-fiction claim against the author and publisher is difficult and fraught with contradictions flowing from her need to present evidence of both similarities and differences between herself and the main character of Golden's fictional biography. In a defamation-in-fiction case, the evidentiary simultaneity of similarity and difference puts the judge and jury in a disconcerting

315. Norton, *supra* note 13.

doublethink as they endeavor to balance the real needs of the plaintiff with the precious freedom of speech of the literary artist.

In Japan, the geisha is both revered as an artist and symbol of old-world Japanese tradition and reviled as a sex slave. Golden paints a realistic picture of the geisha and illustrates both the ugly and the beautiful aspects of the geisha tradition. For example, the recruitment of geishas by force, fraud, and deception, and the practice of selling one's own children into a life of slavery is a heinous aspect of the geisha tradition likening it to the international crime of sex trafficking. Recruitment of children for the purposes of sexual exploitation and slave labor cannot be justified by the argument of cultural relativism. Slavery is a universal crime that is universally condemned; the recruitment of children into the geisha world is a variant of sex slavery and must be eradicated. That does not mean, however, that the geisha tradition should be outlawed entirely. As Golden points out, the geisha is the bastion of Japanese culture, the symbol of the apogee of a nation, and the representation of Japan's most respected values: love of beauty and the arts. To ban the geisha entirely would be to violate the soul of Japan.

Iwasaki's own perception of the geisha does not always coincide with Golden's. Iwasaki resents Golden's dualistic portrait of the geisha, and she herself paints only a one- dimensional picture of the geisha in her own two novels published five years after Golden's. As an advocate for the geisha, Iwasaki's agenda is to preserve the sanctity of the tradition and to establish a positive image of the geisha in the mind of society. Golden has a different goal, which is to provide a historically accurate slice of the geisha life. Golden's dualist image of the geisha is realistic; Iwasaki's monolithic image of the geisha is romantic. She also shies away from the stereotype of the geisha as a courtesan, preferring to view the geisha as an artisan.

Iwasaki would have had a hard time defending her claims in court. To win the defamation-in-fiction claim, she would have had to contradict herself and prove that she both is and is not like Sayuri. Iwasaki would have had to assert that she is like Sayuri if she wanted to prove that Golden's allegedly defamatory statements are "of and concerning" herself. However, Iwasaki would also have had to assert that she is not like Sayuri if she wanted to prove the statements made in the novel are untrue.

She would also have had a difficult time making a case for both misappropriation of her name and likeness in Golden's work of fiction. For example, to be successful in her claim of misappropriation, Iwasaki would have had to assert that she is a public figure in Japan and in the United States because only a public figure has a property right to ration the use of her name and likeness in public. Iwasaki is caught in a conundrum because she also would have to assert that she is not a public figure to win her claim for defamation. In addition, even if she were found to be a public figure, her claim for defamation might fall afoul of *New York Times v. Sullivan*. That landmark case protects a writer's freedom of speech when reporting facts about public figures by requiring a show of actual malice. Moreover, it is not at all clear that *New York Times v. Sullivan* applies to works of fiction.

Iwasaki's claim for quantum meruit has equitable, if not legal, merit because she was never paid for her more than one hundred hours of taped sessions with Golden. On the other hand, her claim to unjust enrichment, which is based on a veiled claim for misappropriation of her copyrighted tapes, has no basis under New York law. She sought to receive a large percentage of the profits of the novel based on her contention that she is the coauthor. However, *Matthews* does not recognize a claim of coauthorship by an information provider of a fictionalized biography. Plaintiff's claim to the ownership of a common-law copyright in the taped conversations also has no merit based on the *Hemingway* holding.

Golden's main defense against Iwasaki's claims based on right to privacy and publicity as well as defamation is that he wrote a work of fiction whose main character is a literary creation. As a writer of fiction, he has First Amendment protections of free speech to write about information held in the public domain. This novel is not about Iwasaki, who was a geishas in the 1960s and 1970s—it is about Sayuri, who is a symbol of all geishas in the 1930s and 1940s.

Iwasaki's consent to publicity is a bar to her claims of misappropriation of her name and likeness and her right to privacy and publicity as well as her claim to defamation of her character. Defendant also has a full-proof defense against her common-law copyright claim based on *Hemingway*, which requires the claimant to distinguish any literary statements from the main stream of conversations (which Iwasaki failed to do).

The real geisha has many hidden motives for suing that go beyond mere pecuniary satisfaction. Something more than money would have to justify a famous geisha from breaking the sacred code of silence and incurring the wrath of her sister geishas in Japan. Arguably, Iwasaki's confessions to Golden were her way of expiating a deep sense of guilt about her life as a geisha. She spoke out against Golden because she is an advocate of the geisha tradition as she sees it, and she wants the rest of the world to see the geisha in that special light. After the publication of Golden's novel, Iwasaki went on a mission to defend both her own reputation and that of the geisha tradition that she continues to see as the bastion of Japanese culture. She is offended by Golden's association of the geisha with the prostitute, an unfortunate historically based link that casts a long shadow of immorality over the reputation of the geisha in general and of Iwasaki in particular. Moreover, Iwasaki needed to defend her reputation as an authority on the geisha tradition because she, herself, was writing two books on this same subject that she hoped would sell. Iwasaki also defended her reputation for moral reasons for the benefit of her family and children. She also sued Golden because he offended her honor and showed disrespect toward her by painting a less-than-totally positive image of the geisha in the novel. Any slight to Iwasaki's personal honor is a blow to the honor of the whole geisha profession. Iwasaki felt betrayed, as she once was by her father who sold her into the geisha life. Now she was betrayed by Golden, a friend whom she mistakenly assumed would be loyal enough to keep her thoughts confidential.

In addition, Iwasaki sued Golden because of a misunderstanding between them based on a culture clash. Golden is an American male writing in 1997 in the voice of a female geisha of the 1930s. To accomplish this literary feat, the author must cut through time, generations, gender, and nationality. Golden is very successful at the manipulation of these voices, especially for American reading audiences. But the Japanese readers did not appreciate some of the details he included that do not reflect the image of themselves as they see Japan. Iwasaki is offended by these cultural and perceptual differences.

Finally, Iwasaki sued Golden because she had to defend herself from attacks by her own geisha friends. To the geishas of Japan, Iwasaki's breach of the code of silence was a serious a breach of trust. Frightened and ashamed, Iwasaki tried to deflect their anger and her own humiliation by focusing her energies on a lawsuit against the author. This type of frivolous suit is not uncommon in the American courts. This novel (and the lawsuit it engenders) is of interest to the law and literature canon because it revives the defamation-in-fiction conundrum that begs the serious question of the writer's freedom of speech, and it illustrates the limits of a common-law copyright infringement action.

12. THE IMPACT OF CULTURE ON THE SEMIOTICS OF TREATY INTERPRETATION

How Pirates Read and Misread the Berne Convention*

I. INTRODUCTION

China's rampant piracy of American intellectual property[1] costs the United States billions of dollars annually.[2] Economics alone cannot explain why a country chooses to steal books, cassettes, movies, and computer programs rather than obey the law. The causes and effects of intellectual property piracy are intricately connected to, and affected by, a multiplicity of factors, including the economy of the country in which the piracy is committed, the political history and ideology of the pirating nation, the culture of the people engaged in the piracy, and the adequacy of the legal system to enforce domestic and international intellectual property laws. This chapter examines the effect of these interrelated factors on a

* This chapter is a substantially revised, updated, and expanded version of a paper presented at the American Society of International Law Conference in Washington, D.C. on Apr. 4, 1998, for the session entitled "Reading International Texts" chaired by Professor Julie Stone Peters of Columbia University. The article emanating from that presentation was published in 1999, entitled *A Hermeneutic Methodology and How Pirates Read and Misread the Berne Convention*, 17, 1 Wisc. Int'l. L.J. 1–26 (1999). I wish to thank Professors Leon Friedman, Richard Weisberg, Richard Neumann, and Julie Stone Peters for reading drafts of the original article and providing illuminating comments.

1. Seth Faison, *China Turns a Blind Eye to Pirated Disks*, N.Y. Times, Mar. 28, 1998, at D1 ("Chinese authorities have essentially given up efforts to prevent the sale of illegally copied videodisks. . . ."). *See* William P. Alford, *Making the World Safe for What? Intellectual Property Rights, Human Rights and Foreign Economic Policy in the Post-European Cold War World*, 29 N.Y.U. J. Int'l. L. & Pol. 135, 136 (1996–97) ("U.S. governmental policy toward the development of protection for American intellectual property in the PRC . . . has yielded limited results. . . ."). *See* Susan Tiefenbrun, *Piracy of Intellectual Property in China and the Former Soviet Union and its Effects Upon International Trade: A Comparison* 46, 1 Buffalo L.R. 1–69 (1998). For a more recent assessment of piracy of intellectual property in China *see generally*, Peter K. Yu, *From Pirates to Partners (Episode II): Protecting Intellectual Property in Post-WTO China*, 55, 4 Am. U. L.R. 901–91 (2006). For a contrast to the prevailing views about piracy of intellectual property see my colleague's groundbreaking work: Aaron Schwabach, *Intellectual Property Piracy: Perception and Reality in China, the United States and Elsewhere*, J. Int'l. Media & Ent. L. 65 (2008).

2. Ernest P. Shriver, *Separate But Equal: Intellectual Property Importation and the Recent Amendments to Section* 337, 5 Minn. J. Global Trade 441, 442 (1996).

nation's interpretation of an international treaty designed to protect intellectual property rights of authors and artists.

At the end of the chapter, I will provide a brief analysis of a related film entitled *Flash of Genius*. This film portrays the catastrophic impact of patent infringement on an American inventor whose patented invention (a windshield wiper for cars) is stolen by Ford and other big car companies. The movie details the grueling human drama, the difficult legal process, and the ultimate success of the inventor who represents himself in court, suing on principle alone and refusing to take offers of sizable settlements from these patent-infringing pirates.

A nation's possible responses to an international treaty include its recognition of, and decision to adhere to, the international treaty; its implementation of domestic laws in compliance with the international treaty, and its success or failure to enforce these domestic and international laws. These responses are hermeneutic signs indicating the manner in which a nation reads, interprets, and possibly misreads the legal discourse of an international treaty.

This chapter explores the role culture plays in the application of a hermeneutic method based on principles of semiotics[3] and reader-response theory.[4] The hypothesis is that culture plays a significant role in how a nation reads and interprets an international treaty. The purpose of this investigation is to decode the meaning of different cultural practices in China and the United States to determine how culture influences these nations' interpretations of texts, notably the Berne Convention[5] and its unique form of writing.[6]

Semiotics involves the decoding of cultural signs. Umberto Eco referred to semiotics as a "substitute for cultural anthropology.[7] According to Eco, "systems of meanings (understood as systems of cultural units) are organized as structures (semantic fields and axes) which follow the same semiotic rules as were set out for the structures of the sign-vehicle."[8] For example, an automobile "is not

3. *See generally* Susan Tiefenbrun, *Legal Semiotics*, 5 CARDOZO ARTS & ENT. L.J. 89 (1986) for a history of semiotics as applied to the law, and Chapter 2 of this book.

4. Post-structuralists include the reader-response critics such as H. JAUSS, LITERATURGESCHICTE ALS PROVOKATION (1970); H. JAUSS, *Literary History as a Challenge to Literary Theory*, *in* NEW DIRECTIONS IN LITERARY HISTORY, 11–41 (R. Cohen, ed. 1974); H. JAUSS, AESTHETISCHE ERFAHRUNG UND LITERARISCHE HERMENEUTIK (1977); STANLEY FISH, IS THERE A TEXT IN THIS CLASS? THE AUTHORITY OF INTERPRETIVE COMMUNITIES (1980). *See also* Susan Tiefenbrun, *Legal Semiotics*, *supra* note 3, at 147–48, note 294.

5. Berne Convention for the Protection of Literary and Artistic Works, Sept. 9, 1886, as revised at Paris, July 24, 1971, 828 U.N.T.S. 221 [hereinafter Berne Convention].

6. *See* Gary Minda, *Law and Literature at Century's End*, 9 CARDOZO STUD. L. & LITERATURE 245, 248 (1997).

7. UMBERTO ECO, A THEORY OF SEMIOTICS 27 (1979).

8. *Id.*

only an object as such but a *cultural unit* inserted into a system of *cultural units* with which it enters into certain *relationships*"[9] (emphasis added).

Yuri Lotman, the great Russian formalist who contributed mightily to the field of semiotics, also believed that semiotics embraces the study of culture. Lotman said, "Semiotics aims to study the entire range of sign systems and the various processes of communication. . . ."[10] Lotman's goal was to define a typology of cultures, both to discover universal aspects common to all cultures and to identify the specific systems that represent the "language" of medieval or of Renaissance culture.[11] According to Lotman, "a culture is a set of texts seen as a set of codes."[12] In any culture several codes exist simultaneously.[13] Lotman provided a typology of cultures across time, and he understood that there is a multiplicity of codes in any given culture, which give rise to contrasts and hybrids[14] as well as a multiplicity of valid interpretations. However, he did not go so far as to say that the multiplicity of codes produces "indeterminacy" of interpretation; he merely led the way to acceptance of many interpretations based on cultural differences and codes. Yuri Lotman, Roman Jakobson, and Umberto Eco all share the view that there is an "organic link between culture and communication,"[15] but Lotman was the first to study in depth the semiotics of culture.[16]

The focus of this investigation is to determine the role of cultural (i.e., political, esthetic, economic, etc.) factors affecting the Chinese and U.S. interpretations of the Berne Convention as well as the cultural differences between the U.S. and European conceptions of copyright. In considering the cultural factors that influence the interpretation of a treaty, this particular study does not view law as literature nor does it attempt to uncover the literature in the law.[17] Rather, the goal of this study is to explore a hermeneutic method in which the legal language of the Berne Convention is viewed as a cultural, ideological, and esthetic (if not literary) artifact. Thus, this study could legitimately be classified as a type of law and literature analysis.

After examining arguments proposed for and against the protection of author's rights, this chapter will explore the dramatic irony represented in the history and development of U.S. and Chinese adherence to the Berne Convention.

---

9. *Id.*

10. YURI M. LOTMAN, UNIVERSE OF THE MIND: A SEMIOTIC THEORY OF CULTURE x (introduction by Umberto Eco) (Ann Shukman trans., 1990).

11. *Id.*

12. *Id.*

13. *Id.*

14. *Id.* at xii.

15. *Id.* at 20.

16. *Id.* at 215, 261.

17. Minda, *supra* note 6, at 246.

It will attempt to uncover the copyright theories encoded in the language of the Berne Convention that constitute sources of cultural clashes that overdetermine the Chinese and American interpretations of the Convention. U.S. and Chinese compliance with the Berne Convention's minimum standards and other forms of responses to the Berne Convention are viewed as significant signs of these nations' respective interpretations of the Convention.

In this chapter I advance the theory that the United States has read the Berne Convention in a manner consistent with the intent of the treaty and has interpreted the implications of the minimum standards it imposes; it is precisely for those hermeneutic reasons that the United States chose not to sign or even adhere to this international treaty for more than one hundred years. In contrast, China superimposed its own specifically Chinese cultural, political, and esthetic values on the European value systems embedded deeply in the Berne Convention. In other words, China read the treaty in its own idiom and interpreted the legal discourse of the Berne Convention in a manner inconsistent with the spirit and intent of the treaty. The Chinese interpretation of the Berne Convention is evidenced by a careful study of the substance and enforcement of Chinese domestic copyright laws that were drafted to enable China to comply with the Berne Convention's minimum standards. The Chinese intellectual property laws, which are adequate in substance but ineffectively enforced, result in a high rate of piracy of foreign and, notably, American intellectual property.

II. HERMENEUTICS AND READER-RESPONSE THEORY

Professor John Ciardi once asked the significant question, "*How* does a poem mean?" which launched the literary world on a giant voyage in a new direction away from the study of history instead of text and toward the interconnected islands of stylistics, structural analysis, and ultimately deconstruction and postmodernism. This investigation begins with a similar question: "*How* does a nation interpret a treaty?" Hopefully, this question will launch legal scholars on a hermeneutic adventure into multiculturalism.

The varied responses a nation makes to an international treaty are surface signs of its interpretation. Hidden deeply below these surface signs in the interstices of the legal discourse are cultural practices that overdetermine a nation's interpretation of the law. The varied responses to the treaty are considered signs of a semantic or stylistic legal event in the discourse that triggers the response. The semantic legal event, called the *signified*, is expressed in the written language of the treaty called the *signifier*. The task of this investigation is to decode the language of the law triggering the response and to analyze the culturally determined etiology of the reader responses.

Let us consider the United States and China as reader-nations of the Berne Convention and analyze their responses to the treaty. According to reader-response theory, the reader is an average reader, something like the "reasonable man" construct, which includes government officials, legislators, informed citizens, and all those who are held accountable for drafting, obeying, and enforcing the law in question.

In China, the role of one such group of readers, the State and local government officials, is more extensive than in the United States. China's massive bureaucracy, which was already firmly in place by 1600, is harmonized by a millennium of tradition and bonded by an immense body of statutory laws that govern the daily life of China's people and especially the business practices of its State-owned companies.[18] "The hand-in-hand collusion of business and government" and the nature of the legal system in China are "at the root of structural problems"[19] that account for the general failure to enforce copyright law in China. The central government officials, province officials, and other local Chinese government officials who are the very same framers, readers, and enforcers of the Chinese domestic copyright laws are also allegedly connected to and even committing the massive pirating of CD-ROMs, videos, books, and computer software.[20] Piracy of intellectual property fits neatly into the Chinese traditional ways of doing business, which depend on directives from government officials who write and enforce the laws. For example, the fair use exceptions and vague language of the Computer Software Regulations[21] published in China in 1991 for the purpose of protecting authors' rights are tantamount to the wholesale license to pirate by the State.

III. ARGUMENTS FOR AND AGAINST PROTECTING AUTHORS' RIGHTS

The Berne Convention for the Protection of Literary and Artistic Works was concluded in 1886 due to the influence of the celebrated French poets Victor Hugo and Alphonse de Lamartine. In 1883, Victor Hugo presided over a historic meeting of the members of the *Association Littéraire et Artistique Internationale* in Berne, Switzerland that resulted in the enactment of the Berne Convention three years later.[22] Earlier in 1841, Alphonse de Lamartine spoke before the French Chamber of Deputies proclaiming the urgent need for a universal copyright law

18. JONATHAN SPENCE, THE SEARCH FOR MODERN CHINA 7–8 (1990).

19. Seth Faison, *China's Paragon of Corruption*, N.Y. TIMES, Mar. 6, 1998, at D1, D4.

20. *See* Susan Tiefenbrun, *Piracy of Intellectual Property in China*, *supra* note 1, at 37. *See also* Peter K. Yu, *supra* note 1, for an update of piracy of intellectual property in China.

21. *See infra* text accompanying footnotes 134–39.

22. Precursors of this meeting were held on Sept. 27, 1858 in Brussels where the Congress of Authors and Artists held its first international meeting. *See* Peter Burger, *The Berne Convention: Its History and Its Key Role in the Future*, 3 J.L. & TECH. 1, 11 (1988).

to protect authors' rights.[23] Hugo and Lamartine were persuasive poet/diplomats who represented the interests of creative people seeking to end the piracy of artistic works in foreign countries.[24] Thus, the Berne Convention, the doyenne of all multilateral intellectual property treaties, was born out of the felicitous marriage of law and the humanities.

Although more than one hundred nations have joined the Berne Convention to date, the United States and China refused to do so for more than one hundred years.[25] The United States and China ultimately joined the Berne Convention in 1989 and 1992, respectively, for different reasons, and for reasons that constitute the very stuff of dramatic irony!

The Berne Convention is the international intellectual property treaty with the longest history, the greatest number of adherents, and the highest level of protection.[26] The history of the Berne Convention reflects the vagaries of legal arguments that either oppose or support authors' rights protection. The Berne Convention strives to protect the rights of authors in their literary and artistic works, including books, pamphlets, writings, musical compositions, designs, and scientific works.[27] It has been periodically modernized through six revisions, and was last amended in 1979.[28] To date there are over 164 member states, with the last three important countries to accede to the Berne Convention being the United States, China, and Russia.

Protection against the widespread piracy of foreign works was the underlying cause of the enactment of the Berne Convention at the end of the nineteenth century.[29] At that time arguments raged both for and against the protection of foreign authors. Support for the protection of authors' rights is founded on the theory of creative incentive. According to this theory, an artist whose endeavors

---

23. *See* Sam Ricketson, *The Birth of the Berne Union*, 11 COLUM.–VLA J.L. & ARTS. 9, 17 (1986).

24. *See id.*

25. Russia also was late to join the Berne Convention. *See generally* György Boytha, *The Berne Convention and the Socialist Countries with Particular Reference to Hungary*, 11 COLUM.-VLA J.L. & ARTS 57 (1986) for a discussion of the failure of the Soviet Union to join the Berne Convention, opting instead to enter into bilateral treaties with other nations.

26. Ralph Oman, *The Impact of the Berne Convention on U.S. Copyright*, 455 PLI/PAT 233, 237 (1996).

27. Joseph Greenwald & Charles Levy, *Introduction to Berne Convention for the Protection of Literary and Artistic Works of September 9, 1886, Paris Text–July 24, 1971, as amended (1989), in* BASIC DOC. INT'L ECON. L.J. 711 (1990).

28. The Berne Convention was revised at Paris in 1896, Berlin in 1908, Rome in 1928, Brussels in 1948, Stockholm in 1967, and Paris in 1971. The 1979 amendment concerned only administrative matters and did not address procedural or substantive aspects of protection.

29. *See* Ricketson, *supra* note 23, at 13.

are remunerated will be inspired to create more works for the benefit of society.[30] Countries opposing protection such as the United States based their arguments against a universal copyright treaty on the need for greater public access to knowledge. Opponents of authors' rights protection argued that the activities of pirates resulted in cheaper copies and greater availability of the foreign work in developing countries where people were thirsty for knowledge; thus, less protection would be advantageous and in the public interest. This argument was the basis of the persistent refusal by the United States throughout the nineteenth century to protect foreign works.[31]

IV. PIRACY, THE BERNE CONVENTION AND DRAMATIC IRONY

Piracy[32] is the leitmotif of the Berne Convention and the springboard of its dramatic irony. The Europeans encouraged the United States to join the Berne Convention in 1886 to stop American piracy of European artistic works, primarily of British origin.[33] The United States refused to do so, claiming a belief in public access to knowledge. The U.S. attitude toward copyright protection in the nineteenth century mirrors the prevalent culture of the swashbuckling rugged individualist who would not hesitate to steal rather than buy personal or intellectual property. The United States ultimately joined the Berne Convention a century later in response to pressure by the American computer industry seeking to curb or eradicate Chinese piracy of American intellectual property. China joined the Berne Convention in 1992 primarily to stop threats of American trade sanctions, which were part of the paradox of the U.S. big-stick foreign policy toward China. The United States has continued to increase trade with China at the very same time it has attempted forcefully to curb China's escalating piracy of American intellectual property.[34]

Throughout the twentieth century and while the United States continued to refuse to join the Berne Convention (defending its position on the basis of a need to protect and increase public access to foreign works), the Chinese continued happily to pirate American CD-ROMs, movies, and cassettes. The theft of U.S. intellectual property by China escalated exponentially in the 1980s and

30. *See infra* text accompany footnotes 56–64 for a discussion of natural law theory and economic theory that relates to arguments for and against the protection of authors' rights.

31. *See* Ricketson, *supra* note 23, at 13.

32. *See id.*

33. *See* Hamish Sandison, *The Berne Convention and the Universal Copyright Convention: The American Experience*, 11 COLUM.-VLA J.L. & ARTS, 89, 91–92 (1986).

34. See Tiefenbrun, *supra* note 1, at 30.

accounted for the annual loss of billions of U.S. dollars.[35] The International Trade Commission estimated that the annual loss to the United States in all intellectual property theft was between $43 and $71 billion.[36]

In response to the piracy of important technology and artistic works, the United States adopted a big-stick policy towards China in the 1980s and 1990s. To deter piracy, the United States threatened to impose trade sanctions against China under § 301 of the Omnibus Trade and Competitiveness Act of 1988.[37] The United States placed China on a priority watch list under "Super 301".[38] The United States also threatened to impose § 337 relief under the Tariff Act of 1930.[39] In fact, the United States came close to a trade war with China in 1995 because of China's continued piracy of American intellectual property.

This big-stick policy toward China is the U.S. government's response to the American entertainment industry and the high-technology companies who lose billions of dollars each year to Chinese pirating. Nevertheless, the United States still continues to trade with China and even signed thirty-four contracts worth more than $6 billion in Beijing and elsewhere in China at the very same time it threatened severe sanctions against China.[40] Consistent with its contradictory trade policy toward China, the United States sought further protection against piracy provided in the GATT/TRIPS Agreement[41] that gave teeth to the Berne Convention and embodied its basic principles and tenets.[42] However, not being a member of the Berne Convention made it difficult for the United States to claim protection from China under the GATT/TRIPS Agreement, so the United States finally decided to accede to the Berne Convention in 1989. In response to American trade policy, China acceded to the Berne Convention on October 15,

---

35. *See* Frank Prohaska, *The 1995 Agreement Regarding Intellectual Property Rights Between China and the United States: Promises for International Law or Continuing Problems with Chinese Piracy?*, 4 TULSA J. COMP. & INT'L L. 169, 177 (1996); Rafael A. Declet, Jr., *Protecting American Intellectual Property in China: The Persistent Problem of Software Piracy*, 10 N.Y. INT. L.R. 57 (1997); and Tiefenbrun, *supra* note 1, at 34–36.

36. *See* Shriver, *supra* note 2, at 442.

37. Omnibus Trade and Competitiveness Act of 1988, Pub. L. No. 100-418, 102 Stat. 1107, at §1301.

38. 19 U.S.C. § 2242 (a)(1)(A) (containing the Special 301 provisions); 19 U.S.C. § 2420(a)(l)(A)–(B) (as amended) (containing the "Super 301" provisions). Super 301 was repealed shortly after it was enacted.

39. 19 U.S.C. § 1337 (1930).

40. *See* Tiefenbrun, *supra* note 1, at 31.

41. *See* Agreement on Trade-Related Aspects of Intellectual Property Rights, April 15, 1994, 33 I.L.M. 1197 ("TRIPS Agreement"). This Agreement, also commonly known as TRIPS, includes the requirements of GATT on national treatment and most favored nation status. TRIPS provides the standard for intellectual property protection offered by World Trade Organization member states and incorporates provisions of both the Berne and Paris Conventions (for patents and trademarks).

42. Oman, *supra* note 26, at 248.

1992 and to the Universal Copyright Convention in October 1992, as required by the 1992 China-United States Memorandum of Understanding on the Protection of Intellectual Property.[43]

Why did it take so long for the United States and China, two important players in the international economic community, to adhere to an international treaty that boasts of more than 164 signatories? The answer may be found in hermeneutics and the way a nation interprets a treaty, which is overdetermined by cultural factors and ideological differences. The history of copyright reveals the development of ideological differences among nations (i.e., the cultural, political, economic and aesthetic differences between China and the United States, on the one hand, and between each of these nations and the European nations on the other). These cultural differences influence the nation's interpretation of the Berne Convention, which can be seen in a study of the respective responses to the treaty.

V. HISTORY OF COPYRIGHT

A. System of Privileges

The history of copyright began with invention of the printing press. Censorship of the press and monopolies to print specific works quickly developed after Gutenberg's invention of the printing press appeared in 1436.[44] The printing press increased the level of copying and publishing worldwide, replacing the slaves and scribes who copied authors' manuscripts by hand.[45]

The resultant increase in the illegitimate copying of texts prompted national jurisdictions to respond with new laws and entitlements.[46] The invention of the printing press enabled "pirate" booksellers to copy books already published by legitimate booksellers. Pirate booksellers sold copied books at lower prices with neither authors nor legitimate booksellers having any legal recourse.[47] The sovereigns of Europe could not tame the thriving commerce in books and ideas.[48]

In the fifteenth century, pressure for legislation came not from authors but from booksellers motivated by pecuniary interest. They requested protection from their respective sovereigns pleading for an exclusive right known as a *privilege*. The privilege provided the bookseller with a limited monopoly and an exclusive

---

43. Memorandum of Understanding on the Protection of Intellectual Property, Jan. 17, 1992, P.R.C.-U.S., 34 I.L.M. 676.

44. *See* 1 International Copyright Law and Practice § 2-14.1 & 14.2 (Melville B. Nimmer & Paul E. Geller eds., 1988).

45. *See* Burger, *supra* note 22, at 3.

46. *See* 1 International Copyright Law and Practice, *supra* note 44, at § 2-14.1.

47. *See* Burger, *supra* note 22, at 4.

48. *See* 1 International Copyright Law and Practice, *supra* note 44, at § 2-16.

right to print and sell a specific author's manuscript for a limited time.[49] The use of privileges ended about two hundred years later in the seventeenth century.

B. Statutory Copyright

The key to the system of privileges that preceded the development of true copyright throughout the seventeenth century was in the sovereign's right to police the dissemination of works.[50] This system soon proved ineffective, and statutory protection developed. Statutes focused for the first time on the rights of authors rather than booksellers.[51] National legislators fashioned a new entitlement to be enforced by civil suit. Thus, copyright was born.[52]

Great Britain was the first nation to enact statutory protection of authors' rights in the 1709 Statute of Anne. Other European states and the United States followed soon thereafter. Economic circumstances and cultural trends made it necessary to put the theory of copyright into practice.[53] The Statute of Anne and the French Laws of 1791 and 1793, which were prototypes of copyright laws to come, secured only rights of economic exploitation.[54] Later in the nineteenth century, French judges began to enforce moral rights.[55]

VI. COPYRIGHT THEORIES AND THE BERNE CONVENTION

A. Natural Rights Theory: Economic Rights versus Moral Rights

When the focus of copyright switched from the bookseller to the author, a debate emerged as to the origin of the author's right. Under the old privilege system, the right was justified on economic grounds. Booksellers needed an exclusive right for a limited duration in order to make an adequate profit to cover the costs of a printing press and authors' manuscripts.

Authors, unlike booksellers, were creators. Many argued that copyright should protect both the author's economic and personal interests, which should be unlimited. This view establishing economic and moral rights was based on a natural law theory, according to which statutes existed only for the limited purpose of recognizing the creator's God-given rights and of endowing these natural rights with a more precise embodiment in the law.[56]

---

49. *See* Burger, *supra* note 22, at 4.

50. *See* 1 INTERNATIONAL COPYRIGHT LAW AND PRACTICE, *supra* note 44, at § 2-17.

51. *See* Burger, *supra* note 22, at 4.

52. *See* 1 INTERNATIONAL COPYRIGHT LAW AND PRACTICE, *supra* note 44, at § 2-17.

53. *See id.* at § 2-18 & 19.

54. *See id.* at § 2-21.

55. *See id.* at § 2-21. *See infra* text accompanying footnotes 59–61, 79–82, and 87–90 for a discussion of moral rights theory.

56. *See* Burger, *supra* note 22, at 6.

The natural rights approach was partially rejected in Great Britain and the United States. Under their common laws, these countries respectively recognized a copyright of perpetual duration based on property right principles. Statutes later replaced common law copyright at least for published works. The statutes did not codify natural law, and they created in authors an exclusive (but now time-limited) right to prevent others from copying their works without authorization.[57] In Britain, the Statute of Anne enacted in 1709 provided an exclusive right to copy for fourteen years.[58] The purpose of this exclusive right was to protect the economic rights of publishers who bought the authors' copyrights.

In Europe under the natural rights approach, authors always retain their personal or moral rights even if they sell their economic rights to publishers. Personal rights are inalienable. However, the U.S. Supreme Court rejected the natural law theory of copyright in 1854.[59] Because the United States did so and did not explicitly incorporate moral rights theory into its copyright legislation, the copyright laws in European *droit d'auteur* countries have been viewed to be more favorable to authors than the laws of Anglo-American countries.[60] With time, the United States has continued to incorporate moral rights into its laws, especially with the passage of the Visual Artists Rights Act.[61] The United States has also extended the period of copyright protection from the life of the author plus fifty years to the life of the author plus seventy years.[62]

Thus, modern American copyright scholars recognize two apparently conflicting copyright theories. The first dominant theory, which is based on economics, states that copyright exists solely to provide necessary remunerative incentives for the production of creative works. The second theory, which is based on natural law, considers copyright as the legal vindication of people's moral right to property in the fruits of their labor.[63] Thus, the natural rights approach views copyright protection for authors as an entitlement while the Anglo-American countries view copyright as a statutorily created privilege for the economic benefit of copyright owners.[64]

---

57. *See id.*

58. See *id.*

59. *See* Wheaton v. Peters. 33 U.S. 591, 654–68 (1854).

60. *See* Alfred C. Yen, *The Interdisciplinary Future of Copyright Theory*, in THE CONSTRUCTION OF AUTHORSHIP: TEXTUAL APPROPRIATION IN LAW AND LITERATURE 159, 159–75 (Martha Woodmansee & Peter Jaszi, eds., 1994).

61. Visual Artists Rights Act, 17 U.S.C. § 106 (1990). *See infra* text accompanying notes 141-142.

62. Eldred v. Ashcroft, 537 U.S. 186 (2003).

63. *See id.* at 161 (citing the writings of William Blackstone and John Locke). *See* 2 WILLIAM BLACKSTONE, COMMENTARIES 8; JOHN LOCKE, TWO TREATISES OF GOVERNMENT § 27 (Peter Laslett ed., 3rd ed. 1970).

64. *See* Burger, *supra* note 22, at 7.

B. Diverse Rights Theories Interrelated

Property rights theory and diverse rights theories that developed later became interrelated in the concept of copyright and are now reflected in the language of the Berne Convention. However, property theory, privacy theory, personality rights theory, and market theory underlying the notion of copyright do clash in many different ways with the American and Chinese ideologies.

1. Property Rights Theory By the end of the seventeenth century, a theory of property in works of the mind began to develop.[65] However, socialist countries such as China find it difficult ideologically to accept the notion of a private property right in works of the mind. The strangeness of the concepts of property and ownership to the Chinese mind are reflected in the remarks made in 1984 by a Chinese scholar in intellectual property who, with the amazement of an *ingenu*, stated: "We recognize that copyright is a type of property" and "we recognize that copyright, generally speaking, is a type of right that may be owned by an individual."[66]

Copyright is strongly connected to the concepts of individual inspiration and initiative, and to the act of creation, which is a materialization of human freedom.[67] Socialist nations, bound by traditional schemes of collectivism and planning, have to go through profound ideological and cultural changes before being able to accept the notion that works of the mind are private property.[68]

Some scholars maintain that China's failure to enforce anti-piracy laws stems from its deep-rooted cultural notions based in Confucianism.[69] Chinese writers, artists, and creators in all areas of knowledge have significant reverence and attachment for the past, which results in legitimized copying.[70] Moreover, China's esthetic views reflect a preference for imitation in art over innovation.

---

65. *See* 1 INTERNATIONAL COPYRIGHT LAW AND PRACTICE, *supra* note 44, at § 2-22.

66. *See* Jianming Shen, *The P.R.C.'s First Copyright Law Analyzed*, 14 HASTINGS INT'L & COMP. L. REV. 529, 556–57 (1990–91).

67. *See* George Koumantos, *The Future of the Berne Convention*, 11 COLUM.-VLA J.L. & ARTS, 225, 233 (1986).

68. S*ee id. See also* Sanford Levinson's *Political Change and the "Creative Destruction" of Public Space, in* CULTURAL HUMAN RIGHTS 341–51 (Francesco Francioni & Martin Scheinin eds., 2008). Levinson presents a very interesting and informative discussion of culture, multiculturalism, political change, and the destruction of statues that are iconic symbols of a political regime, such as the destruction of the Soviet statue of Dzerzhinsky on August 22, 1991 (the father of the secret police and the founder of the infamous gulag) signifying the end of Communism. The destruction of the statue of Sadaam Hussein when the U.S. defeated the Iraqi regime signified the end of Sadaam's oppressive regime and the victory of democracy. Levinson discusses the multiple meanings of the term *culture.*

69. *See* Declet, *supra* note 35, at 60, citing William P. Alford, *Don't Stop Thinking about Yesterday: Why There was No Indigenous Counterpart to Intellectual Property Law in Imperial China*, 7 J. CHINESE L. 3, 9 n.17 (1993) (arguing that China's lack of protection for intellectual property stems from its Confucianist cultural and legal traditions).

70. *See* WILLIAM P. ALFORD, TO STEAL A BOOK IS AN ELEGANT OFFENSE 29 (1995).

This preference for imitation flies in the face of the prohibition against reproduction and emphasis on innovation established in the Berne Convention. For example, in the eighteenth century under the Qianlong dynasty, the Emperor maintained total indifference to foreign objects, manufactures, and ideas, and objected to "ingenious" objects and innovation.[71]

Given the Chinese preference for imitation, their reverence for tradition, and their penchant for the legitimate appropriation of the creative works of others, copyright theory as it is codified in the Berne Convention seems to be on a collision course with Chinese cultural, esthetic, and political beliefs. This ideological incompatibility would explain the failure of the Chinese to properly interpret and enforce the Berne Convention that views copying as illegal.

Education in the basic value systems that underlie the Berne Convention is necessary to insure that its interpretation will be consistent with its spirit and intent. The Chinese government has implemented widespread training programs[72] to teach its people and the government agencies (which are allegedly largely responsible for committing and condoning the pirating) about the notion of private property and authors' rights. This training program is another sign of the prominence of China's own cultural identity that accounts for its specific interpretation of the Berne Convention.

2. Agency Theory of Copyright Toward the end of the eighteenth century, another theory of copyright proposed a norm for the author's relationship with the media; this theory conceptualized the agency relationship of the author to the publisher who disseminates the author's work.[73] The American and British recognition of the important role of the publisher in the creative process (which is sometimes viewed by the author as exploitative) is a source of friction between the European and American/British views of copyright protection. The agency relationship of the author to the publisher is also quite strange to the culture of communism or socialist ideology where ownership of property is held by the State.

3. Privacy Theory of Copyright By the end of the nineteenth century, a theory of privacy developed in common law copyright that afforded control over the initial disclosure of works.[74] The notion of privacy is difficult to reconcile with

---

71. *Id.* at 30.

72. Agreement Regarding Intellectual Property Rights, Feb. 26, 1995, China–U.S. 34 I.L.M. 881, 885. A State Council Working Conference on Intellectual Property Rights and Sub-Central Working Conference were established in China in 1995: "[t]o instruct and organize the relevant authorities within regions and departments in China, to provide education on and publicity for the laws regarding intellectual property rights, to foster the understanding of intellectual property rights protection among people throughout the country and to improve intellectual property law enforcement skills of leading officials at various levels of government, as well as the skills of enforcement personnel."

73. *See* 1 INTERNATIONAL COPYRIGHT LAW AND PRACTICE, *supra* note 44, at § 2-22.

74. *See id.* at § 2-23.

socialist philosophy, collectivist planning, and State control over the individual that is at the heart of the Chinese socialist economy, but which has been modified by market reforms.

4. Personality Rights Theory of Copyright The personality rights theory developed in Germany. This theory enables any natural person to protect his name, social or professional status, public reputation and image, freedom of self-expression, and privacy interests.[75] However, a difference is immediately discernable between the quality of freedom of expression that exists in socialist nations and in Western democratic nations. Moreover, the demands of uniformity imposed upon individuals by collectivism conflict with the desire to develop respect for the individual personality in Western democratic nations.

5. Market Theory of Copyright In the eighteenth and nineteenth centuries, copyright laws were intended to govern market use; they were designed to permit private suits against unauthorized use.[76] In the twentieth century, the courts, legislators, and collecting societies fashioned rights of remuneration for widespread uses of works by allowing these uses to take place pursuant to legal, compulsory, or blanket licenses.[77] In China, the socialist political system of central planning suddenly began to coexist and develop alongside an economic system involving market reforms that were instituted in 1979 under Deng Xiaoping. The simultaneity of two conflicting systems in China explains some of the confusion that besets the average Chinese reader attempting to comprehend Western copyright theories encoded in the Berne Convention.

Property, agency, privacy, personality, and market theories of copyright are not mutually exclusive and are often interrelated and reflected harmoniously in the copyright law of a nation. Anglo-American statutes tend to enumerate a "bundle" of property-like rights and remedies, calling these entitlements "copyright."[78] Other interests of the author are not thought of as "copyright." Thus, in the United States there is a certain pluralism among the legal bases of what the European law calls "moral rights."[79]

VII. CLASHES OF CULTURE

The Chinese and American delays in joining an important international treaty such as the Berne Convention are complex to explain, due in part to cultural differences between China and the United States on the one hand and among each of these nations and the European nations on the other. European nations that

75. *See id.*
76. *See id.* at § 2-24.
77. *See id.* at § 2-25.
78. *Id.* at § 2-27.
79. *Id.*

signed the Berne Convention support the principles of natural law, moral and property rights theories, and automatic protection that are reflected in the language of the Berne Convention and that conflict with American and Chinese ideologies for very different reasons.

American opposition to the concept of universal copyright protection and its continued refusal to join the Berne Convention were due, in part, to the absence of a formality provision and the insistence on moral rights in the Berne Convention, which conflicted with U.S. copyright procedure and with the interests of the book and movie industry. The United States claimed that developing countries needed greater public access to knowledge, which universal copyright protection would diminish.

European arguments for the protection of foreign works are founded in an ideology of natural law and in moral, practical, and personal interests of the author whose creative works are considered private property, whose rights to ownership are endowed naturally, and whose financial remuneration acts as an incentive to continue creating. In contrast, China has a concept of intellectual property and copyright founded in an esthetics of tradition and imitation that flies in the face of the requirements of the Berne Convention.

VIII. BERNE CONVENTION: UNDERLYING PRINCIPLES AND RIGHTS THEORIES

The Berne Convention embodies three basic principles and several different rights theories. The three basic principles are national treatment, automatic protection, and independence of protection. The Berne Convention imposes minimum standards of protection on "every production in the literary, scientific, and artistic domain, whatever may be the mode of its expression."[80]

The Berne Convention protects "economic rights" such as the right to translate, to perform, to broadcast, to make reproductions, to make motion pictures and to make adaptations and arrangements of the works.[81] The Berne Convention also provides for "moral rights" (i.e., the right of paternity and identity) protecting authors against the distortion or mutilation of their works, even after they have sold or licensed their economic rights.[82]

The Berne Convention protects developing countries that are understandably in need of gaining access to information and technology.[83] As set forth in the Berne Convention, Appendix to the Paris Act of 1971, under certain circumstances

---

80. *Id.*

81. The Berne Convention, *supra* note 5, at Article 2.

82. Greenwald & Levy, *supra* note 27, at 711–12.

83. *See* the Berne Convention, *supra* note 5, at Appendix to the Paris Act of 1971; Greenwald & Levy, *supra* note 27, at 712; Guo Shoukang, *The Berne Union and Developing*

developing countries are permitted to deviate from the minimum standards of protection with respect to the right of translation and the right of reproduction.[84] However, the developing nation that seeks reservations concerning translation and reproduction rights must institute a system of compulsory licensing and provide for just compensation to the licensor of the intellectual property in question.[85]

Each member of the Berne Union must enact national laws that afford the following rights to foreign authors: national treatment; absence of formalities; right of enforcement and seizure of infringing works; term of years protecting the author's copyright for at least the life of the author plus fifty years; very limited compulsory licenses; wide range of coverage for categories of original works; and right to control a wide range of possible uses of the protected work. These are the minimum standards required by the Berne Convention.

IX. U.S. AND CHINESE COMPLIANCE WITH THE BERNE CONVENTION'S MINIMUM STANDARDS

The principle of automatic protection and the absence of formalities presented a significant problem for U.S. compliance with the minimum standards of the Berne Convention. For many years, the United States required such formalities as notice, registration, and deposit to obtain copyright. For example, all U.S. authors seeking copyright protection had to register their works in the U.S. Copyright Office, affix a copyright notice to the protected work, and deposit their works in the U.S. Copyright Office. Failure to provide notice resulted in the work losing copyright protection and falling into the public domain.[86] These U.S. formalities fell afoul of the Berne Convention's principle of automatic protection and absence of formalities.

The Berne Convention also requires national treatment and prohibits reciprocity. National treatment is a provision contained in some treaties (mostly international commercial treaties) according foreigners the same rights, in certain respects, as those accorded to nationals. The very basis of the GATT and the WTO is the notion of according national treatment to foreign products and of protecting the principle of nondiscrimination. Under a regime of reciprocity, one country would protect foreign authors only at the level that the foreign country protects its own authors.

Countries, With Particular Reference to the People's Republic of China, 11 COLUM.-VLA J.L. & ARTS 121 (1986).

84. Shoukang, *supra* note 83, at 121.

85. GREENWALD & LEVY, *supra* note 27, at 713.

86. *See* Oman, *supra* note 26, at 237–38.

The Berne Convention does permit one instance of reciprocity with respect to the term of protection. If a country gives its own authors protection for life plus seventy years, which is longer than the Berne Convention requirement of protection during the life of the author plus fifty years, that country with the longer term does not have to give the longer term to foreign authors. This is known as the Rule of the Shorter Term[87] that blatantly discriminates against foreign authors and contradicts the Berne Convention's basic principle of national treatment. In the U.S. Copyright Act, the United States now protects its own copyrighted works for the life of the author plus seventy years pursuant to the *United States v. Eldred* Supreme Court case.

The Berne Convention bans compulsory licenses, permitting them only for developing countries. China could arguably fall into the category of a developing country. However, a compulsory license requires adequate compensation to the author and, therefore, piracy cannot be explained away as a "license."

The Berne Convention protects the author's personal or moral rights. Personal rights include the right of *paternity*, which prevents others from being named as the author (the so-called right of attribution); the right to decide whether, where, when and how to divulge the underlying work to the public (the so-called *droit de divulgation*, occasionally referred to as the right of dissemination); and the right to prevent distortions, deformations, modifications, or changes (the right to protect the integrity of the work).[88] Moral rights reflect the French or continental approach to copyright rather than the U.S. approach that does not explicitly provide the moral right in its copyright statute.[89] The United States has a weaker moral rights regime than France and other nations on the continent. In France, for example, the right of integrity gives the director of a black-and-white motion picture the power to bar the colorization of the author's work even if the author is no longer the copyright owner. However, despite a reportedly weaker moral rights regime, the United States provides other related remedies and is effectively in compliance with the moral rights requirements of the Berne Convention.[90]

X. U.S. RESPONSES TO THE BERNE CONVENTION

America's delay in joining the Berne Convention reflects a clash of cultures. In the nineteenth century, Europeans (most notably the British) deplored the lack

---

87. *Id.* at 239.

88. *See* Shen, *supra* note 66, at 532 for a discussion of moral and personal rights.

89. *See* Oman, *supra* note 26, at 240. However, moral rights are recognized in the Visual Artists Rights Act, *supra* note 61, at § 106. On the French copyright laws and French views toward moral rights, *see, e.g.*, Jane Ginsburg, French Copyright Law: A Comparative Overview (1989) and her many excellent articles on international copyright issues.

90. *See* 1 International Copyright Law and Practice, supra note 44, at § 2-27. *See* Burger, *supra* note 22, at 240.

of international copyright protection in the United States.[91] The Europeans attempted forcefully but unsuccessfully to encourage America to join the Berne Convention. Anthony Trollope accused the Americans of appropriating "the goods of other people . . . with impunity," insisting that the United States would continue to oppose international copyright protection because "American readers are the gainers . . . and this argument . . . comes not from the people, but from the book-selling leviathans and from those politicians whom the leviathans are able to attach to their interests."[92]

Charles Dickens and Anthony Trollope exchanged revealing views on the grim prospects of U.S adherence to the Berne Convention: "I discussed this matter of American international copyright with Charles Dickens, who strongly declared his conviction that nothing would induce an American to give up the power he possesses of pirating British literature . . . the American decision has been, according to his thinking, dishonest . . . American dishonesty is rampant; but it is rampant only among a few."[93]

In fact, U.S. piracy of European intellectual property was the principal reason for the establishment of the Universal Copyright Convention[94] in 1952 that paved the way for American accession to the Berne Convention. The Universal Copyright Convention was viewed as a compromise between the high level of automatic protection implicit in the Berne Convention's European concept of the *droit d'auteur* as a natural right and the conditional protection accorded to authors in American copyright law that views authors' rights not as automatic, but as a privilege obtainable only upon compliance with certain statutory formalities.[95]

Close readings of the Hearings of the Committee on the Judiciary House of Representatives in 1988[96] indicate that the U.S. delay in joining the Berne Convention had nothing to do with American indifference or its misreading of the treaty. On the contrary, America validly interpreted the importance of moral rights in the Berne Convention, which ran counter to publishers' interests and threatened to upset the existing balance between creators and proprietors, employees and employers, authors and publishers. To appease the publishers' interests, Congress took a minimalist approach to joining the Berne Convention.[97]

---

91. *See* Sandison, *supra* note 33, at 91.

92. Anthony Trollope, An Autobiography, 310–11 (M. Sadleir & F. Page eds., 1950), quoted in Sandison, *supra* note 33, at 93, note 21.

93. *See* Sandison, *supra* note 33, at 119.

94. Universal Copyright Convention, July 24, 1971, 25 U.S.T. 1341, 943 U.N.T.S. 178.

95. *See* Sandison, *supra* note 33, at 89.

96. Berne Convention Implementation Act of 1987/1988: Hearings on H.R. 1623 Before the Subcomm. on Courts, Civil Liberties, and the Admin. of Justice of the House of Representatives Comm. on the Judiciary, 100th Cong. (1987–1988).

97. *See* Oman, *supra* note 26, at 242.

Finally, the Berne Convention Implementation Act[98] went into effect on March 1, 1989 eliminating notice, recordation, and registration requirements.

XI. HOW THE UNITED STATES READS THE BERNE CONVENTION

The U.S. choice not to join the Berne Convention for more than a century after its enactment justifies the theory that the United States correctly interpreted the Berne Convention and understood that American copyright law was incompatible with many of the Berne Convention's key provisions. Moreover, the United States refused to "muster the political will to make the necessary changes."[99] As the representative of the United States at the Berne Convention's 100th anniversary in 1998 said, "We took a perverse pride in the fact that we did it our way."[100]

The Universal Copyright Convention was created in the early 1950s for the specific purpose of making it possible for the United States to join the Berne Convention. The Universal Copyright Convention established a low-level international regime requiring no change in U.S. law to bring it into the international copyright legal arena and to stop U.S. piracy of foreign works.

Once the United States joined the Universal Copyright Convention, the U.S. Copyright Office, with the encouragement of Congress, undertook the task of drafting a new copyright law that would bring the United States into harmony with most of the Berne Convention's basic provisions. The revision process began in the mid-1950s and took twenty years to conclude, resulting in the 1976 Copyright Act that brought the United States to the doorstep of Berne Convention compliance.[101]

Under the provisions of the 1976 Copyright Act, the United States dropped the 28-year term that was renewable for another 28 years in favor of the Berne Convention's "life plus 50 year term"; it expanded the breadth of subject matter protection to follow the comprehensive formulation of "literary and artistic works" as provided in Article 2 of the Berne Convention;[102] and it dropped strict

98. Berne Convention Implementation Act of 1988, Pub. L. 100-568, 102 Stat. 2853 (1988).

99. Oman, *supra* note 26, at 241.

100. *Id.*

101. *See id.*

102. Berne Convention, *supra* note 5, at art. 2: "The expression 'literary and artistic works' shall include every production in the literary, scientific and artistic domain, whatever may be the mode or form of its expression, such as books, pamphlets and other writings; lectures, addresses, sermons and other works of the same nature; dramatic or dramatico-musical works; choreographic works and entertainments in dumb show; musical compositions with or without works; cinematographic works to which are assimilated works expressed by a process analogous to cinematography; works of drawing, painting, architecture, sculpture, engraving and lithography; photographic works to which are

copyright formalities, including registration and deposit as preconditions to copyright protection and renewal after 28 years. With federal preemption, the U.S. copyright law created a national system of copyright protection simplifying the protection of foreign works in a uniform and predictable manner. It established liability for jukeboxes; and it allowed the manufacturing clause to expire.[103] It also established the complete divisibility of copyright and adopted a broad formulation of exclusive rights that met the expectations of the Berne Convention as to the scope of public performance rights and the meaning of reproduction. Finally, it moved toward a nonformalistic means of giving authors the opportunity to renegotiate unfavorable copyright assignments.[104]

Despite these changes that brought the United States very close to Berne Convention compliance, the United States took another twelve years to finally make the changes needed for compliance and ratification of the Berne Convention. This delay was due to pressure from publishers. The magazine publishers, led by Time-Life, believed that adherence to the Berne Convention would threaten their interests in favor of authors. To appease the publishers' interests, Congress took a minimalist approach to joining the Berne Convention and made only those changes to U.S. copyright law explicitly required by it.[105]

The Berne Convention Implementation Act[106] went into effect on March 1, 1989. It eliminated the requirement of copyright notice and the recordation and registration requirements for filing copyright infringement actions in federal court. It added architectural plans to the list of protected works, and it modified the jukebox compulsory license to allow the composers and the jukebox operators to negotiate the terms of the license. Most importantly, nothing in the new legislation changed the level of moral rights existing in the United States at the time of its enactment.[107]

The United States finally entered the Berne Convention in 1989, and the impact of U.S. adherence has been dramatic. The Berne Convention has acted as a brake on legislative creativity in the proverbial battle between users and creators of copyrighted works.[108] Berne Convention adherence has also prompted pro-author legislative initiatives. For example, in the nine years since joining, the United States has continued to move toward and even surpassed the high Berne Convention standards. Specifically, the United States has enacted a strong law

---

assimilated works expressed by a process analogous to photography; works of applied art; illustrations, maps, plans, sketches and three-dimensional works relative to geography, topography, architecture or science."

103. *See* Oman, *supra* note 26, at 242.

104. *See id.* at n.1.

105. *See id.* at 242.

106. Berne Convention Implementation Act of 1988, *supra* not 98. (1988).

107. *See* Oman, *supra* note 26, at 242.

108. *See id.* at 249.

protecting works of architecture, and it has adopted a higher level of moral rights protection for visual artists.[109] It made copyright renewal for pre-1978 works automatic, eliminating the last vestige of formalities. The United States also enacted a digital home recording levy that compensates composers for the home taping of their music on digital media. Finally, the United States restored copyright in foreign works that had fallen into the public domain in the United States because of a failure to comply with a U.S. formality (such as registration, notice, or renewal).

Another example of the strong impact of the Berne Convention on U.S. copyright law is its prospective application. The United States has no federal provision on *droit de suite* or the artist's resale right. To adopt such a regime, the United States would have to strictly comply with the Berne Convention's provision on this issue.[110]

The successful enforcement of Berne Convention provisions by the United States and their implementation into U.S. copyright law indicate the validity of the American interpretation of the treaty. However, certain standard U.S. business practices in dealing with copyrighted works simply do not pass muster in other Berne Convention countries. For example, the U.S. concept of work-made-for-hire is not well received in France. Moreover, differences in the very definition of certain terms in copyright law still exist, such as the definition of an *author* (the one who can collect royalties allocated for authors and who can authorize changes in a copyrighted work) is not the same in the United States and Europe. The disparity in the basic definition of key terms such as *the author* indicates that the United States prefers, in these limited instances, to read the Berne Convention in its own idiom, with reference to its own cultural, political, and economic ideology.[111]

XII. CHINA'S RESPONSES TO THE BERNE CONVENTION

China's responses to the Berne Convention include delay in joining until 1992, failure to enforce recently enacted anti-piracy laws, failure to enforce domestic copyright laws,[112] and failure to enforce the Berne Convention. China's responses to international law are often explained via simple economic principles: it is

---

109. Visual Artists Rights Act, *supra* note 61, at § 106.

110. *See* Oman, *supra* note 26, at 251.

111. *Id.* at 256.

112. *See* Authorship Right Law of the People's Republic of China, Sept. 7, 1990, 7th National People's Congress, 15th Sess. of the Standing Comm., *translated in* Jianming Shen, The P.R.C.'s First Copyright Law Analyzed, *supra* note 66, at 529 [hereinafter Authorship Right Law]; Chinese Computer Software Protection Regulations, promulgated by the State Council, June 4, 1991, effective Oct. 1, 1991, *translated in* Chinese Foreign

currently cheaper for China to steal than to buy. However, this explanation is not sufficient. China delayed joining the Berne Convention because of the strangeness to the Chinese mind of the concepts of private property and ownership.

The principle of strangeness explains why the purpose clause of the Chinese Authorship Right Law is culturally and politically overdetermined, combines individual and society interests, aims to promote "socialist spiritual civilization and material civilization," and promotes "the development and advancement of socialist, cultural, and scientific undertakings."[113] The "fair use" provisions of this law give the State the right to make unauthorized use of copyrighted materials in order to "execute official duties."[114] The language of the Chinese Authorship Right Law's purpose clause, which is overdetermined by socialist ideology, is very different both semantically and stylistically from the purpose clause of the Berne Convention, which reflects the European concern for authors' rights: "The countries of the Union, being equally animated by the desire to protect, in as effective and uniform a manner as possible, the rights of authors in their literary and artistic works. . . ."[115]

It is interesting to compare the emphasis on the protection of authors' rights encoded in the language of the Berne Convention's purpose clause and the language of the copyright clause of Article I, Section 8 of the U.S. Constitution, which almost one hundred years earlier enumerated the powers vested in the United States federal government.[116] By its choice and ordering of words, the copyright clause of the U.S. Constitution focuses less on authors' rights and more on the need to provide greater access to knowledge: "To promote the progress of science and useful arts, by securing for limited times to authors and inventors the exclusive right to their respective writings and discoveries."[117] The juxtaposition of these two clauses (in the U.S. Constitution and the Berne Convention, respectively) crystallizes the ideological differences between the American and European conceptions of copyright.

The ideological differences between the American and Chinese conceptions of copyright are even more pronounced. China is steeped in a history of Marxist philosophy that is arguably incompatible with the copyright principle of property ownership. Moreover, Marxist political theory rejects market economy principles based on the profit motif. Nevertheless, since 1979, under the leadership of Deng Xiaoping the Chinese have gradually adopted market reform tactics into their

---

ECON. L., ANALYSIS & COMMENTARY, Section 16, 15–31 (Rui Mu & Wang Guiguo eds., 1994) [hereinafter Software Protection Regulations].

113. Authorship Right Law, *supra* note 112, at Art. 1.

114. *Id.* at Art. 22.

115. The Berne Convention, *supra* note 5, at (Preamble) 223.

116. Mayer Gabay, *The United States Copyright System and the Berne Convention*, 26 BULL. COPYRIGHT SOC'Y U.S. 202 (1978–79).

117. U.S. CONST. art. I, section 8.

economic system by encouraging foreign investment in the form of joint ventures and wholly owned foreign direct investments that can—and often do—involve the sale or licensing of intellectual property.[118] Thus, the Chinese people have been indoctrinated in Marxist/Leninist ideology on the one hand, and have been required by reform policies to accept the incompatible notions of private property ownership and individual initiative for profit on the other. Chinese scholars report that the inherent contradictions between Marxism and market economy theories have led to "societal dislocation and transformation"[119] and, more importantly, to a general confusion of values among the Chinese people. This transformation and confusion of values explain, in part, the Chinese particular "reading" and understanding of copyright law and theory. This confusion coupled with the particular quality of the Chinese legal system explain the failure by the Chinese to enforce domestic and international copyright laws that require strong protection of private property rights in general, and intellectual property rights in particular.

XIII. HERMENEUTICS AND CULTURAL DIFFERENCE

Just as beauty is in the eyes of the beholder, interpretation is in the mind of the reader. As Professor Weisberg stated in his work on *Vichy Law and the Holocaust*,[120] "under any model of reading, interpretive communities control the meanings of important texts." In the long and rich cultural history of the Chinese, there is little evidence of Chinese appreciation for either private property rights or intellectual property rights. William P. Alford, one of the most respected Chinese legal scholars today, concludes that strong protection of intellectual property will be accorded by China only if its citizens gain enough access to cultural goods to develop their appreciation for a multiplicity of viewpoints, a sense of the role of private ownership, and an understanding of the part that intellectual property can play in fostering a marketplace of ideas.[121]

---

118. *See* Susan Tiefenbrun, *Joint Ventures in the USSR, Eastern Europe, and the People's Republic of China as of December 1989*, 21 N.Y.U. J. Int'l L. & Pol. 667, 743–55 (1989); and Tiefenbrun, *Piracy*, *supra* note 1.

119. Alford, *Making the World Safe for What?*, *supra* note 1, at 137.

120. Richard H. Weisberg, *Vichy Law and the Holocaust in France: Précis of a Talk to the Hofstra Conference*, *in* Law and the Arts (Susan Tiefenbrun ed., 1999).

121. *See* Rochelle Cooper Dreyfuss & Diane L. Zimmerman, *Convenors' Introduction: The Culture and Economics of Participation in an International Intellectual Property Regime*, 29 N.Y.U. J. Int'l L. & Pol. 1, 5 (1996–97), summarizing William P. Alford's presentation in the Symposium Issue, *supra* note 1, at 145: "History demonstrates quite clearly, with only the most modest of exceptions, that serious intellectual property protection requires political and economic pluralism and independent legal institutions capable of vigorously enforcing citizens' rights."

Chinese esthetics places value on imitation over innovation. Chinese writers, artists, and creators in all areas of knowledge have significant reverence for the masters of the past, and copying the works of great artists is not only condoned but encouraged.[122] The Chinese esthetic preference for imitation is difficult to reconcile with the Berne Convention's prohibition of illegitimate reproduction and its respect for innovation.

XIV. HOW CHINA READS THE BERNE CONVENTION

To comply with the requirements of the Berne Convention, a nation must pass adequate domestic copyright law. Although rudimentary copyright legislation existed in China as far back as the Song Dynasty in the tenth century,[123] China's first true copyright law, the Authorship Right Law, was not passed until 1990.[124] This law was followed by the Authorship Right Law Implementing Regulations (1991) and the Computer Software Protection Regulations (1991). China acceded to both the Berne Convention and the Universal Copyright Convention in July 1992. China ultimately joined the WTO and therefore signed and ratified TRIPS, which incorporates by reference both the Berne Convention and the Paris Convention protecting copyrights, patents, and trademarks, respectively.

A. The Chinese Authorship Right Law

It is beyond the scope of this chapter to analyze in depth the Chinese Authorship Right Law. Suffice it to say that even the title of the law (which utilizes the term *authorship* rather than *copyright*) and other linguistic anomalies that exist in it are signs of the cultural strangeness of copyright theories to the Chinese people. The Chinese framers chose to employ the word *zhuzhoquan*, which means literally "authorship right," rather than the better known and more commonly used term *banquan*,[125] which literally means "copyright." Today the two terms in Chinese are practically synonymous, connoting what is generally understood to be copyright.[126] Thus, copyright in Chinese no longer means simply the rights of printers or publishers. It symbolizes the whole bundle of rights of authors and other copyright holders, and even includes neighboring rights.[127] The Chinese readers'

---

122. *See* ALFORD, TO STEAL A BOOK IS AN ELEGANT OFFENSE, *supra* note 70, at 29.

123. *See* Declet, *supra* note 35, at 61 (citing Yiping Yang, *The 1990 Copyright Law of the People's Republic of China*, 11 UCLA PAC. BASIN L.J. 260 (1993)).

124. *See* Chinese Authorship Right Law, *supra* note 112.

125. See Shen, *supra* note 66, at 529.

126. *See* Decet, *supra* note 35, at 61, n. 24.

127. Shen, *supra* note 66, at 530.

cultural strangeness to the concept of copyright might account for their failure to enforce its provisions.[128]

The Chinese Authorship Right Law includes personal rights (moral rights) and proprietary rights (property or economic rights),[129] but these are encoded in a peculiarly socialist idiom. Thus, the law protects moral and economic rights only if the works are advantageous to the development of science, culture, and the arts.[130] For this reason, only "acceptable" works can be copyrighted under Chinese law. This same subtle form of censorship that reflects socialist ideology existed in Russia as well as in China until the fall of communism in Russia in 1991 when the entire system of intellectual property protection in Russia had to be revised.

In a sense, the Chinese concept of copyright as embodied in the Chinese Authorship Right Law is broader than the American concept of copyright because the Chinese law provides explicitly for both personal (moral) and economic rights of the author. The Chinese concept of works-made-for-hire is narrower than in American law because the Chinese Authorship Right Law adheres in theory to an author-centered ideology that is closer to the Berne Convention's European conception of copyright that protects the author's natural and moral rights.[131]

The Chinese Authorship Right Law is in compliance with the Berne Convention and even provides remedies for pirating, including civil liabilities, mediation, and administrative penalties.[132] In 1995, criminal liabilities for intellectual property infringement cases were instituted in the Chinese Supreme People's Court.[133]

B. Chinese Computer Software Protection Regulations[134]

Chinese piracy of American computer software constitutes a serious problem resulting in U.S. threats of trade sanctions and the reestablishment of Chinese anti-piracy laws. An adequate law regulating computer software does exist in China, but it is not effectively enforced. This response can be viewed as a sign of the nation's particular interpretation of the law.

The Computer Software Protection Regulations establish both personal and economic rights and guarantee the following rights to software copyright owners: the right of publication, the right of attribution, the right of exploitation,

---

128. *See id.*

129. See *id.* at 534.

130. *See* Chinese Authorship Right Law, *supra* note 112, at art. 1.

131. Shen, *supra* note 66, at 542–43.

132. *See id.* at 554 (citing to the Chinese Authorship Right Law, *supra* note 112, at art. 48).

133. *See* Letter to Ambassador Michael Kantor, Feb. 26, 1995, 34 I.L.M. 881, 883 (1995).

134. *See* Software Protection Regulations, *supra* note 112, at §16, 15–31.

the right to license and to receive remuneration, and the right to assign.[135] On their face, the Chinese Computer Software Protection Regulations appear to address every mode of piratical activity. However, the overall protection is potentially diminished by a series of broad fair use provisions[136] that are similar to the Chinese Authorship Right Law's troublesome fair use provisions. These exceptions allow for reproduction "in small quantities" of software for "such non-commercial purposes as classroom teaching, scientific research and carrying out of official duties by State agencies."[137] Because so many of China's businesses are partially State-owned, the fair use provision could be misconstrued and abused by pirates or State agencies themselves to get around the Computer Software Protection Regulations' otherwise adequate copyright protection.[138] Therefore, the fair use exceptions explicitly stipulated in the law itself, coupled with the cultural and political overdetermination of the law that implicitly places power in the hands of State agencies, account for the failure of the law to protect against piracy of computer software.

An old Chinese proverb, often quoted, sums up the Chinese perception of copyright protection: "To steal a book is an elegant offense." This proverb is founded on a metaphor whose basis of comparison is encoded in an oxymoron ("elegant offense"). The proverb can be interpreted to mean many different things, but it is above all an apt crystallization of the Chinese mind that reads copyright law in its own idiom and interprets the Berne Convention in accordance with its own cultural background.

XV. U.S. VIEWS ON PIRACY OF PATENTED INVENTIONS AS EXPRESSED IN FILM: *FLASH OF GENIUS*[139]

Piracy of intellectual property today is not confined to China and Russia. The people and corporate entitites in the United States continue to pirate their own U.S. citizen's patented inventions.[140] The theft by Ford of Dr. Robert Kearn's invention of the intermittent windshield wiper in the early 1960s is the subject of the movie *Flash of Genius*. In it, a hardworking engineering professor spends

135. Declet, *supra* note 35, at 68.

136. *See* Chinese Software Regulations, *supra* note 112, at arts. 21–22.

137. *Id.* at art. 22.

138. Declet, *supra* note 35, at 69.

139. FLASH OF GENIUS (Universal Films, 2008), starring Greg Kinnear, Lauren Graham, Dermot Mulroney, Alan Alda, Jake Abel, Daniel Roebuck, Tim Kelleher, and Bill Smirrovich. This film was based on a *New Yorker* magazine article by John Seabrook.

140. People and corporations in the United States continue to pirate their own copyrighted works, especially with regard to musical downloads off the Internet. *See Music Piracy Suit Against N.Y. Family is Settled for $7,000*, N.Y. TIMES, Apr. 28, 2009, at B4.

a good deal of his life inventing a windshield wiper and an even greater part of his life suing (by himself without the expertise of an intellectual property patent lawyer) the big car manufacturers worldwide for patent infringement of his invention. This inventor is obsessed with the indecency of piracy by rich car manufacturers who exploit the creative scientist, whose only dream in life is to invent something wonderful to help people live better.

Rather than reward the inventor, Ford and Chrysler steal with elegant duplicity the inventor's intermittent windshield wiper, claiming the wiper to be their own invention. Ford, realizing it might lose the case, offers to settle with Kearn for as much as $30 million, but the inventor stubbornly refuses to settle, risking everything to fight for his principles of fair play. This movie uncovers the realpolitik of patent infringement litigation and the illegal machinations of duplicitous manufacturers, lawyers, and businesspeople. Here the inventor is no less than a superhero who ends up winning $40 million, but who loses his job, his sanity, and even his wife in the throes of this battle.

Early in his legal fight to slew the giant Ford, Kearn dismisses (with good reason) his greedy and self-dealing lawyer. Deciding to represent himself in this uphill battle against the big car manufacturers, he asks his loving children to help him find the law he needs to win each case. This inventor mistrusts the car manufacturer who steals his invention and mistrusts his own friend who gets him the job with the car manufacturer. He also mistrusts his lawyer who prefers to get a settlement rather than fight for the principles of copyright law.

In the end, the inventor wins and wins big, and the American legal system ends up looking very good in its ability to favor the little guy in a world dominated by corporate giants. In this narrow sense, the film seems to point in the direction of an implicit adoption by the United States of moral rights principles and a return to the European doctrine of the romantic author or the mad scientist whose ambitious and noble endeavors need incentivization and recognition as well as financial remuneration.

XVI. CONCLUSION

As expressed in the film *Flash of Genius*, some people and corporations in the United States continue to pirate their own and probably foreign patented and copyrighted works. China also continues to pirate U.S. intellectual property even though it has joined the Berne Convention and has enacted adequate domestic laws to protect foreign works. Unlike the United States, China has a conception of intellectual property founded in a political theory that rejects ownership of private property. China has adopted an esthetic theory that values tradition and imitation. But Chinese politics, economic theory, and esthetics are necessarily shifting, aligning themselves more closely with the international legal discourse which is, itself, reshaped by modern conditions.

U.S. intellectual property policy has also shifted. In 1854, the U.S. Supreme Court rejected moral rights,[141] but since then the United States has slowly adopted a moral rights theory, which is reflected in the enactment of the Visual Artists Rights Act.[142] The development in China of its own technology may in time reshape its economy and alter its current economic incentive to steal rather than buy or license intellectual property. Continued efforts at education of the people and enforcement of the law are likely to realign deep-rooted cultural practices that influence a nation's interpretation of a widely accepted international treaty and that are reflected in that nation's responses to that law.

---

141. *See* Wheaton v. Peters, *supra* note 59, at 654-68.

142. *See* Visual Artists Rights Act, *supra* note 61, at § 106. The Visual Artists Rights Act constitutes landmark legislation creating moral rights for artists in the United States. It was enacted on Dec. 1, 1990 as an amendment to the copyright law that took effect on June 1, 1991. This law is analogous to the moral rights protected in the Berne Convention by protecting artists' rights of attribution and integrity in paintings, drawings, and photographs produced for exhibition, prints, and sculpture. *See id.*

PART G

CONCLUSION

It is not an easy task to draw conclusions from a life's work spanning two careers in literature and in the law. A little bit of each part of my life is reflected in the analytical method I use, in the legal issues I see illuminated in the literary texts I have chosen to study, in the exciting relationships I find in these literary and legal works, and in my constant attempt to create a balance between the content and style of the international laws and the humanities that I put under a microscope.

This book provides students with an introduction into the many complex facets of international law dramatically illustrated in literary works. International law encompasses the legal principles governing relationships between nations. International law also includes international relations, and it embraces not only nations but international organizations, multinational corporations, nongovernmental organizations, and even individuals, including women and children who invoke their human rights or soldiers and commanding officers who commit war crimes, crimes against the peace, crimes against humanity, or genocide in violation of the laws of war. Thus, international law includes international human rights law and international humanitarian laws (i.e., the laws of war).

International customary law derives from customary law and supplements codified norms. Private international law (a dangerously ambiguous term) is distinguished from public international law, and it includes international business law and international intellectual property laws. Comparative law is the scholarly study of the similarities and differences between the legal systems of different jurisdictions, as for example American or European law versus Chinese, Japanese, or Iranian law.

Many of the most controversial legal issues of today are analyzed in this book using semiotic theory. Terrorism, civil disobedience, feminism, human trafficking, use of children as soldiers, and torture, along with the predominance of a culture of violence, the piracy of intellectual property, and the role that culture plays in interpreting international treaties are some of these controversial issues. I study these issues in depth by decoding literary and cinematographic works in which these legal issues are illustrated. Terrorism is an international law crime that has exploded all over the world and caused universal consternation about national security. However, the need to protect national security and the fear of terrorism have resulted in an erosion of basic civil and human rights in countries that have been victimized by terrorists. Terrorism is intrinsically related to civil disobedience. We can imagine the need to disobey an unjust law like the Patriot Act, which arguably violates human rights. It is the perception of these kinds of relationships that occupy the focus of this book.

I have attempted to study the style of literary and legal texts, focusing on such devices as ambivalence, ambiguity, contradiction, duality, paradox, irony, satire, metaphors, and symbolism to show how writers, legislators, and politicians can avoid censorship by using coded language. My aim is to decode the international laws embedded in literary works and to reveal hidden messages about the law and the literature.

I have also uncovered many legal themes and legal jurisprudential theories represented in the language of the humanities. For example, the study of *The Pianist* is a foray into war crimes, crimes against humanity, and genocide as well as the role that music can play in the life of a victim of war. The study of Arthur Golden's *Memoirs of a Geisha* is a journey into such legal issues as defamation-in-fiction, freedom of speech, copyright infringement, common law copyright, right of privacy and publicity, misappropriation in fiction, enforceability of oral contracts, quantum meruit and unjust enrichment, prostitution, sex trafficking, and the comparative laws of Japan. The geisha tradition in Japan is part of its rich cultural heritage; however, cultural relativism cannot be a justification for practices involving torture, slavery, and violence against women. Similarly, the draconian One-Child Policy in China has resulted in the disappearance of many women and the development of an international business known as sex trafficking to meet Chinese men's demands for a bride. The violence toward women in Asia and elsewhere is part of a cultural pattern that devalues women and reflects a long-standing tradition of male-child preference.

Culture and tradition cannot justify sex trafficking of women or the piracy of intellectual property in China, even though it is interesting to note that communist ideology does not typically permit the ownership of intellectual property. Similarly, cultural differences cannot really justify the misreading of international treaties because valid interpretation must be done in conjunction with the knowledge of a treaty's historical and political context. Thus, this study shows how the Chinese read or misread the Berne Convention on copyright infringement according to their own culture that admires imitation in the arts. Like China, the United States refused to sign the Berne Convention for more than one hundred years after its enactment. But unlike China, the United States fully understood the significance of this international treaty and refused to sign it because it did not want to reduce publishers' rights!

The content of literature, film, and the law often reflect prevailing social, political, and economic conditions. Authors and filmmakers use mediated forms of communication to convey personal messages to readers and viewers about the need for social change. Legislators write laws, and lawyers and judges interpret and carry them out in order to change injustices in society. These vehicles of communication—literature, film, and the law—are sign systems reflecting infrastructural conditions that affect the rights of all people (and especially women and children) to be treated equally and justly. Important information about society, its traditions, and its hidden policies perpetuated by governments can be conveyed effectively through mediated signs. Semiotics teaches us that messages are not conveyed by words alone. A picture can be worth a thousand words. Communication happens by transmission of information through signs and symbols. This is the essence of the semiotic system. Writers speak directly to readers through words and indirectly through tropes, literary figures, and symbols that need interpretation to uncover the meanings hidden in analogies. Filmmakers communicate messages through the immediacy of pictures that create an aura of authenticity and drama. In turn, this book decodes international law through a semiotic analysis of different works in the humanities.

INDEX

Abbott, Amy Beth, 416*n*126
Abortions in China
  forced, 372–73
  sex-selective, 380–81
Actants, 68*n*282
Acteurs, 68*n*282
Adams, Samuel, 170
Adoption law, of China, 378
Adorno, Theodor, 160
Aesthetic hypothesis, 59
Afary, Janet, *Foucault and the Iranian Revolution*, 265*n*5
African Charter on the Rights and Welfare of the Child, 424
Agency theory of copyright, 539
Agents, meaning of, 94
Ahmadinejad, Mahmoud, 331
AIDS, 406
  and orphans, 408
Al-Ahram Weekly, 309
Alai, Ahmad Mir, 337
Alford, William P., 549
Alien Tort Claims Act, 452
Alimony, in Iran, 332
All-China Women's Federation, 359
Al Sharpton, 223
Amendments to Divorce Regulation (ADR) (1992), Iran, 324
American Friends Service Committee, 205
American Medical Association (AMA), 412
Anarchism, 117, 119–20
Anderson, Kevin B., *Foucault and the Iranian Revolution*, 265*n*5
Anglo-American law, 38
Annan, Kofi, 102
Anouilh, Jean, *Antigone*, 4, 9, 10, 191, 222, 244, 251–58
Anthony, Susan B., 179, 223
Anthropology
  Claude Lévi-Strauss, semiology and structuralism, 50–51
  structural, and law, 51–52
Anti-federalism, 174
Anti-Prostitution Act (1956), Japan, 481–82, 490–91
Antiterrorism Act, U.S. (1996), 84*n*6
Aquinas, Thomas
  on civil disobedience, 183, 201*n*54, 202, 213, 214, 226
  on natural law, 234–35
Arbitrariness, of sign, 41–42, 43
Argument, as sign, 36
Aristotle
  Ethics, 230
  on semiotics, 30
Arkansas Criminal Code, 91
Armed conflict, 106, 107. *See also* Child soldiering
  history of, 144–48
  law violations, basic principles of, 155–58
  The Pianist, illustrations of inadequate war laws implementation in, 151–58
  World War II international war laws failure, causes of, 148–51
Arnaud, André-Jean
  on explicit and implicit structures, 67
  and Lévi Straussian model, 64
  matrimonial and family structure analysis, 51–52
Art as self-help remedy, and restorative justice, 159–64
Articles of Confederation, 173, 174
Association Littéraire et Artistique Internationale, 531
Athenian democracy
  and Sophists, 231–32
  and tragedy, 249
Atlantic Monthly, 307
Atwood, Margaret, 308
Aufhebung, 217

Bakunin, Mikhail, 117
Banquan (copyright), 550
Barbie, Klaus, 96

Barry, Kathleen, 496*n*185
Barthes, Roland, 22, 64*n*254, 464*n*14
  "degree zero" style, 195
  Éléments de Sémiologie, 41*n*122
  on structural semiotics, 69–71
Bassiouni, Cherif, 83, 85*n*8
  definition of terrorism, 105–6
  and international terrorism contexts, 106–7
  paradox in meaning of terrorism, 114
Baudelaire, Charles, 298
Beale, Joseph, 37
Beauvoir, Simone de, 275
Bedeutung and *Sinn*, distinction between, 32
Behaviorist semiotics, 48–49
Behbahani, Simin, 311
Beijing Declaration, 358
Bellaigue, Christopher de, *In The Rose Garden Of The Martyrs*, 295*n*211
Bellow, Saul, 306
Bentham, Jeremy, 236, 238
Beres, Louis Rene, 85*n*8
Berne Convention, 16. *See also* China; Copyright
  author's rights protection, for and against, 531–33
  China's responses to, 547–49
  Chinese Authorship Right Law, 550–51
  Chinese Computer Software Protection Regulations, 551–52
  culture clashes, 540–41
  Flash of Genius, 552–53
  Implementation Act (1989), 546
  literary and artistic works, 545–46
  minimum standards, U.S and Chinese compliance with, 542–43
  piracy and dramatic irony, 533–35
  underlying principles and rights theories, 541–42
  U.S responses to, 543–45
  U.S. reading of, 545–47
Big-stick policy, of U.S., 534
Bindrim v. Mitchell (1979), 510
Birmingham News, 205
Blackstone, William, 228
Blakesley, Christopher L., 85
  and five elements, 87–88*n*17
Blood money, 313, 327–28
Bolzano, Bernard, 31, 32
Book of Acts, 206
Bork, Robert H., 9
  on civil disobedience, 185
  on *The Tempting of America*, 217
Boston Tea Party, 218
Boutwell, Albert, 204
Brandeis, J., 45
Breach of contract, 504–6
Brennan, J., 28*n*58
British Medical Journal, 381
Bromley London Borough Council v. Greater London Council, 48
Brown v. Board of Education (1954), 204, 208, 214
Buber, Martin, 214
Bunyan, John, 213
Bush, George, 92, 93, 361
Buyssens, Eric, functional linguistics, 49

Calhoun, John, 174
Canadian Anti-Terrorism Act, 99
Canadian Criminal Code, 101
Cape Town Principles (1997), 401, 421
Carr, Caleb, 107*n*103
Catachresis, 73, 74
Catechism of the Revolutionist, 122
Cattle Release Act (1872). *See* Emancipation of Prostitutes and Geisha Act (1872)
Chador, 274, 277, 281, 282, 284
Charron, William, 37
Children in Armed Conflict Protocol, 412–13, 418–21
  direct participation of hostilities restriction (Article 38(2)), 419–20
  voluntary recruitment monitoring (Article 3(3)), 419
Children's rights, 13–14
Child sexual exploitation, 399–400
Child soldiering, 14, 398–99
  abuse, 403–5
  AIDS and orphans, 408
  Allah is Not obliged, 436–41
  Beasts of No Nation, 442–45
  children as not real soldiers, 445–47
  Children in Armed Conflict Protocol, 418–21

Convention on the Rights of the Child (CRC), U.N., 416–18
Declaration of the Rights of the Child, 416
economic reasons and solutions, 410–11, 453
extent of, worldwide, 400–403
family and ethical values, changes in, 407
globalization, 407–8
human rights violations, 447–50
ILO Worst Forms of Child Labour Convention 182, 434–35
international humanitarian laws and child protection, 422–24
laws relating to use of, 412–16
military reasons for, 409
Palermo Protocol, 429–31
prevention, 450–52
prosecution of perpetrators, 453–56
PROTECT Act (2003), 428–29
protection of victims, 452–53
reasons, 406–7
Sale of Children Protocol, 421–22
slavery and international laws, 431–34
small personal weapons, increase in use of, 408
social and psychological causes of, 410
trafficking, 399
Trafficking Victims Protection Act (TVPA), 425–28
treatment as criminals, 411–12
U.S. Department of Labor recommendations, 436
voluntary and forced recruitment of children, 405–6
voluntary recruitment of, 411
warfare nature, changes in, 408–9
China. *See also* Berne Convention
Confucian view of women, 383
culture, 349–50
demographic crisis, 347–49
hermeneutics and cultural difference, 549–50
Marriage Law, 370, 377
trafficking in. *See* Trafficking
women as commodity, 383–85
women's life in nineteenth century, 389–92
women shortage and impact on men, 386–87
Chinese Authorship Right Law, 548, 550–51
Chinese Computer Software Protection Regulations, 17, 551–52
Chinese Criminal Code
sentence on abduction and trafficking (Article 240), 358
sentence on rape (Article 236), 358
Chomsky, Noam, 42, 77
Christianity and natural law, 234
Chu Junhong, 380
Ciardi, John, 530
Cicero, 233
Civil disobedience, 8–10, 88, 218
and Anouilh's *Antigone*, 251–58
arguments against, 184–85, 224
arguments for, 182–83, 224–26
Bork on, 217
constitutional right to dissent, 185–86
constitutional right to free speech, 186–89
and conflict-of-law, 226–27
deep structure of, 175–78
duality of, 179–81
Dworkin on, 219, 223
as expressive conduct, 188
Feminism and Antigone, 242–44
and free speech argument, 227
Hegel on *Antigone*, 239–42
and natural law theory, 213–16
and postmodernism, 227–28
legal positivism, 229, 231–32, 236–39
natural law, 228–36
positive connotations of, 177
protests, 223–24
purpose of, 223
Rawls on, 180, 182, 223–24, 227
in Sophocles' *Antigone*, 244–51
Thoreau on, 222
Civility, 177
Civil libertarians, 92
Civil litigation, 177
Civil rights, 177
Civil Rights Act (1964), 204

Classification system, 32
Clinton, Bill, 360
Coalition Against Trafficking in Women, 496
Coercion, definition of, 374
Cohen, Carl, 182
Cohen v. California (1971), 45–46
Colloquium requirement of defamation, 508
Committee on the Elimination of Discrimination Against Women, 359
Communication, 61
  act of, 56–57
  and mediation, 23, 24, 294
Competence, 42
Conative function, 57
Conde, H.V., *A Handbook of International Human Rights Terminology*, 149*n*99
Confessional literature, 468–69
Conflict-of-law theory, 183, 226–27
Confucian view, of women, 349, 383
Confucius and *Five Classics*, 13, 349, 383
Connor, Eugene Bull, 204, 205
Conrad, Joseph
  five elements of terrorism, representation of, 123
  ironic method, 114–18
  The Secret Agent, 4, 6, 83, 87, 114–23
  symbols of terrorism, 118–22
Conscription, meaning of, 446
Conseil d'Etat, France, 289
Constructive non-violent tension, 192
Continental law, 38
Convention on the Elimination of All Forms of Discrimination Against Women (CEDAW), 326
  child custody rights (Article 16(f)), 332
  cultural activities participation, right to (Article 13(c)), 331
  elimination of discrimination (Article 10), 329–30
  employment rights (Article 11), 330–31
  equality before law (Article 15), 331–32
  equality between men and women (Article 2), 327–28
  freedom of reproduction choices (Article 16), 356
  nationality (Article 9), 329
  social and cultural patterns of men and women (Article 5), 328
  voting rights (Article 7), 328
Convention on the Rights of the Child (CRC), U.N., 377–78, 412–13, 416
  Children in Armed Conflict Protocol, 418–21
  education interference, protection from (Article 32), 417, 444
  forced recruitment prohibition (Article35), 417
  hostilities participation restriction, (Article 38), 418, 448
  Protocol on Children in Armed Combat, 455
  Sale of Children Protocol, 421–22
Cook, Anthony and *Beyond Critical Legal Studies*, 192*n*6
Coomaraswamy, Radhika, 455
Copyright. *See also* Berne Convention
  agency theory of, 539
  history, 535–6
  market theory of, 540
  natural rights theory, 536–37
  personality rights theory of, 540
  privacy theory of, 539–40
  property rights theory, 538–39
  statutory, 536
Copyright infringement and common law copyright, 499–500, 516–18
Cornell, Saul, 174
Corporations (*personnes morales*), 98
Cosmopolis, 233
Cracow Ghetto, 142
Creative extremist, 213
Creative incentive, 532–33
Creon and Antigone, conflict between, 239, 248–49
Crimes against humanity, illustration of, 152–53
Critical legal studies and semiotics, 76–78, 137
Culler, Jonathan, 63, 64*n*257
Cultural anthropology, 5
Cultural relativism and geisha, 497–99

Dabashi, Hamid, 309
Daisy Miller, 303
Dalby, Liza, 488*n*138

Debt bondage, in geisha tradition, 483–84, 491
Declaration of Independence, U.S., 171, 173, 213, 229
Deconstruction, 44*n*136. *See also* Civil disobedience
  and difference, 211–13
  of myth of difference, 203
  resistance and revolution in United States, 169–72
  rights of resistance and national security tensions, and Constitution, 172–75
  and semiotics, 72–73
  vs. structuralism, 62–63
Defamation, 506–8
Defamation-in-fiction
  colloquium requirement of defamation, 508
  contradictions and conundrums, 511
  opinion and false statements of facts, 509
  proof of actual malice for public figure, 510
  self-censorship, 510
  claim, 474–75
Defamiliarization, 53
Defendant's response. *See also Memoirs of a Geisha*
  absence of contract, 512–13
  common-law copyright infringement, 516–18
  fair comment and free speech, 513–14
  plaintiff's consent, 515–16
  quantum meruit and unjust enrichment, 518
Deflowerment ceremony, 478, 481, 521
De Lamothe, Olivier Dutheillet, 288*n*187
Delicta juris gentium, 431–32*n*232
De Man, Paul, 64
Denotation and connotation, 31–33
Depolarization, 197
De Republica, 233
Derrida, Jacques, 72, 211
De Vattel, Emerich, 144
Dewey, John, 38–39
Diallo, Amadou, 223
Dicent, 36
Dickens, Charles, 544
Différance, 212
Differentiation and equalization, 196
Différer, 212
Dissent and civil disobedience, constitutional provision, 185–86
Distinction, principle of, 155*n*140, 157
Divine law, 235
Divorce Regulations (1992), Iran, 280
Domestic terrorism, comparison with international terrorism, 108–9
Douglas, J., 61
Droit d'auteur, 544
Droit de divulgation, 543
Due process violations, 179
Dworkin, Ronald, 5, 9, 125, 182, 185
  on civil disobedience, 223
  on creation and interpretation, 78*n*333
  and legal interpretation, 59–60
  Taking Rights Seriously, 219
Dyilo, Thomas Lubanga, 445–47

Ebadi, Shirin, 268, 279, 288, 342
  on blood money, 313
  on education in Iran, 313
  on esthetic of death, 316
  on headscarf, 312
  on interpretation of Koran, 333
  Iran Awakening, 4, 12, 264, 295, 310
  on non-interference of Americans, 314–16
  on patriarchy in Iran and male-child preference, 316–17
  on power of interpretation, 314
  on power of words, 314
Eco, Umberto, 64*n*254
  on semiotics, 4, 15, 29, 528
  Theory of Semiotics, 32*n*74
Edo regime, 480
Eldred; United States v., 543
Emancipation of Prostitutes and Geisha Act (1872), 480, 485–87
Empiricus, Sextus, 30
English Prevention of Terrorism (Temporary Provision) Act (1984, 1989), 94–95
Enlistment, meaning of, 446
Equivalence, 55

Estate of Ernest Hemingway v. Random House, Inc. (1968), 512, 517–18, 524
Eternal law, 234
European Commission of Human Rights, 292
European Convention for the Protection of Human Rights and Fundamental Freedom (ECHR)
  Article 9, 293
  Article 25, 292
European Convention on the Suppression of Terrorism, 99
European Court of Human Rights, 291, 292
Evidentiary theory, 26
Existentialism and Anouilh, 255–58
Explicit sign, 26–27

Fairness and unjust laws, 184, 215
Family laws, 321–24
Family planning, in China. *See* One-child policy
Family Protection Law (Iran), 268
Family Status Ordinance (1997), Hong Kong, 358
Fedayan-e Khalq, 267
Fedayeen, 275
Feminism and Antigone, 242–44
Feminist activism and Iran–Iraq war, 270–71
Finkelman, Paul, 174
Finnis, John, 237
Fish, Stanley, 137
Fitzgerald, Scott, *The Great Gatsby*, 300–302
Flash of Genius, 5, 18, 528, 552–53
Folk talk, 66
Footbinding, 390
Formalism, 232
Fortas, Abe, 176, 179, 186, 189
Foucault, Michael
  on global impact of Iranian Revolution, 271–72
  and language, 73–74
Foundation of the Theory of Signs, 48
Fourth World Conference on Women, 358
Fragmentation, 119
Frank, Jerome, influence of Peirce on, 37
"Free Children from War" Conference, 451
Free speech and civil disobedience, constitutional provision, 186–89
Frege, Gottlob, *Grundgesetze der Aritmetic*, 31*n*72
French Civil Code, 38
French Criminal Code, 96–97
Fuller, Lon, 39
Functional linguistics, 49

Gandhi, M.K., 179–80, 223
Geisha, 15–16, 459. *See also Memoirs of a Geisha*
  cultural relativism, 497–99
  evolution of Japanese law on prostitution, 479–82
  feminist legal theory on sex trafficking, 496–97
  history of, 482–92
  sex trafficking and slavery in, 492–96
The Geisha Reader, 488*n*138
Gendercide, meaning of, 354
General Assembly Resolution (1991, 1999), 102, 105
General public, 105
Geneva Conventions, 145, 147, 422–24, 446
Geneva Gas Protocol, 147
Genocide
  act of, 112
  definition of, 111
Gény, Francois, Peirce's influence on, 37–38
George, Terry, *Hotel Rwanda*, 6, 83, 87, 123–24
Girl Care Project, 382
Global Alliance Against Trafficking Women, 430, 497
Globalization and child soldiering, 407–8
Global terrorism, 93
Glossematics, 49
Golden, Arthur. *See Memoirs of a Geisha*
Goodrich, Peter
  on legal linguistics, 48
  on semiotics, 70
Gorji, Monir, 285
Greimas, Algirdas, 22, 54
  Du Sens: Essais Sémiotique, 68*n*282

Sémantique Structurale, 68*n*282
Grisez, Germain, 236
Griswold, Erwin, 185, 219
Griswold v. Connecticut (1965), 61*n*238
Grotius, Hugo
  on natural law, 235
  On the Law of War and Peace, 144
Ground and sign, 33

Hagiwara Sakutaro, 460*n*3
Hague Peace Conferences (1899, 1907), 149*n*104, 150
  Martens Clause in the Preamble to, 155*n*139
  on war regulation, 145–46
Hague Regulations. *See* Hague Peace Conferences
Hague Rules of Air Warfare, 147
Halberstam, Malvina, 83
Hamilton, Alexander, 170
Harlan, J., 45
Hart, H.L.A., 5
  fair play concept, 215
  and legal positivism and semiotics, 60–62
  on pure legal positivism, 238
  Positivism and the Separation of Law and Morals, 229*n*54
Hartman, Geoffrey H., 154*n*135
Hegel, G.W.F., 10, 239–42
Hejab (Islamic head covering), 264, 277, 279
  in France, 289–91
  freedom of choice factor, 281–82
  and freedom of speech denial, 280–81
  as humiliation, 284–85
  and Koran, 285–86
  meaning of resistance to, 288
  as Muslim identity, 283
  as polyvalent symbols of imprisonment and liberation, 284
  as power sign over women, 283
  as segregation, 287–88
  as sign of women's political engagement and Jihad, 283
  in Turkey, 291–94
  as virtue and honor, 282–83
  women's reaction to, 286–87
Hendricks, Lola, 204
Heraclitus, on natural law, 230
Hermann, Donald, 66
Hermeneutics
  and cultural difference, 549–50
  legal, 25, 40
  and reader-response theory, 530–31
Hesketh, Therese, 381
Hezbollah, 274
Hitler, Adolf, 151
Hjelmslev, Louis, glossematics, 49
Hobbes, Thomas, 31*n*72, 235–36
Hoene-Wronsky, Joseph Marie, *La Philosophie du Langage*, 32*n*72
Hoffer, William, *Not Without My Daughter*, 266–67*n*12
Holmes, Oliver Wendell
  on good motives, 187
  influence of Peirce on, 36–37
  on legal positivism, 238
  on natural law, 237
Holocaust
  authenticity of representation of, 154*n*135
  and memoirs writing, 142–43
Homeric epics, natural law in, 229–30
Homologoumenos te physei zen (life in harmony with nature), 233
Hotchner, A.E., *Papa Hemingway*, 517
Hughes, Donna, 321
Hugo, Victor, 531, 532
Humanity, principle of, 155*n*139, 156–57
Human rights, 131*n*18
  violations, illustration of, 153–55
  of women, 11–13, 263
Human Rights Watch, 326, 377
Human trafficking. *See* Trafficking
Hume, David, 236
Husserl, Edmund, 32

Icons, 34–35
Ijtihad, 314
Immigrants, *hijab* and, 290–91
Imperial Ordinance No.9, Japan, 480–81, 488–89
Implicit sign, 28
Imprisonment, 217–18
Index, 35
Infanticide, in China, 379–80
Injustice, King's notion of, 215

Innocent civilian, meaning of, 88–89
Integrity of work protection, 543
Intent and terrorism, 100, 105, 106
International Convention for the Suppression of the Financing of Terrorism (1999), 105
International Court of Justice, 432*n*232
International Covenant on Civil and Political Rights (ICCPR)
 arbitrary arrests and detentions, prohibition of (Article 9), 335
 degrading treatment and punishment, prohibition of (Article 7), 334–35
 equality before law (Article 26), 339
 on leaving any country (Article 12(2)), 336
 marriage and family rights (Article 23), 338
 right of peaceful assembly (Article 21), 338
 right to freedom of thought, conscience and religion (Article 18), 336
 right to life (Article 6) and violations, 333–34
 right to opinion without interference (Article 19), 337
International Covenant on Economic, Social and Cultural Rights (ICESCR), 339–41
 equal right to social and cultural rights (Article 3), 340
 right to just and favorable conditions at work (Article 7), 340–41
International Criminal Court (ICC), 113, 455
 and investigations about atrocities in Uganda, 161–62
 Rome Statute of, 111, 452
International Criminal Tribunal for the Former Yugoslavia (ICTY), 110–11,
International Criminal Tribunal in Rwanda (ICTR), 443
International humanitarian law, 130
International Labour Organization (ILO)
 Article 22, 434*n*244
 Statistical Information and Monitoring Program on Child Labor (SIMPOC), 436
 Worst Forms of Child Labour Convention 182, 399, 415–16
International Law Commission, 432*n*232
International Organization of Migration, 353
International terrorism, 84*n*6. *See also* Terrorism
 Anti-Terrorism Act and Effective Death Penalty Act's definition of, 91
 contexts, 106–7
 court for, 113
 difference with domestic terrorism, 108–9
 U.S. State Department's definition, 94
International Working Men's Association, 117
Interpretant, 33
 misunderstanding of, 34
 relationship with sign, 34*n*85
Interpretation, meaning of, 24
Iran, 263. *See also* Ebadi, Shirin; Milani, Tahmineh; Mir-Hosseini, Ziba
 Convention on the Elimination of All Forms of Discrimination Against Women (CEDAW), 326–32
 family laws, 321–24
 feminist activism and Iran–Iraq war, 270–71
 Foucault on global impact of Revolution, 271–72
 hejab. See Hejab
 International Covenant on Civil and Political Rights (ICCPR), 332–39
 International Covenant on Economic, Social and Cultural Rights (ICESCR), 339–41
 invasion by foreigners, 265–66
 marriage contract, 324–25
 new Iranian constitution and government, 273
 new Islamic Republic, birth of, 273
 public/private split in society, 276–78
 quiet revolt of women, 278
 religious and secular women in Iran after Revolution, 269–70
 religious nepotism, 275–76
 revolution against Westoxication, 266–67
 unexpected developments in women's rights, 279–80
 Women's protest, 274–75
 women's rights denial, signs of, 278–79

women's rights, as represented in humanities, 294
women's role in Revolution, 267–69
Iranian Civil Code (ICC), 321–22, 323
Iranian Family Protection Law, 322
Irigaray, Luce, 243
Irony and terrorism, 115–18
Iweala, Uzodinnma, *Beasts of No Nation*, 4, 442–45

Jackson, Bernard, 39*n*118
on Hart, 60
on law and language, 46
Semiotics and Legal Theory, 46, 65
on structuralism, 65–66, 68
Jacobs, Leslie, 188
Jakobson, Roman, 5, 22, 36*n*95
communication, 56–57
metaphor and metonymy, 55–56
James, Henry, *The Ambassadors*, 304
Japanese culture, 15
Jefferson, Thomas, 169, 171–72, 173, 183, 213, 226
Jenkins, W.A., Jr., 205
Jospin, Lionel, 289
Judge and interpretive process, 39
Juror selection, 25
Jus cogens, 431*n*232, 432*n*232, 498
Justifiable disobedience, 182
Just laws. *See* Civil disobedience

Kachka, Boris, 443
Kafu Nagai, 488*n*140
Kalinowski, Georges, 49
Kant, Immanuel, 236
Kashf-e hejab, 282
Kazemi, Zahra, 334
Kearn, Robert, 552
Keller, Thomas, on structuralism, 67–68
Kellogg-Briand Pact, 159
Kelsen, Hans, 237
Kelsenian grammar of legal structure, 42
Kevelson, Roberta, 39*n*118
Khomeini, Ayatollah, 322
on *Chador*, 274, 282
criticism from international human rights groups, 333
on dress code, 285, 286
on education to women, 269
in exile, 266
on *hijab*, 274, 282, 286, 287
on ideal Muslim women, 334–35
imposition of veil for women, 269, 282
Iran–Iraq war, 270
Islamic Republic, 273
on marriage age, 338
promise of freedom and equality to women, 268
on women's participation in cultural activities, 331
on writers and artists, 301, 312
Shari'a, 322
King, Martin Luther Jr., 4, 8, 9, 174, 176, 179, 223. *See also* Civil disobedience; *Letter from Birmingham Jail*
Kinship, Greek definition of, 250
Knopf, Alfred A., 500
Koinai ennoiai (common notions), 233
Komiteh, 274
Koran
on dress code, 285
on execution, 333
on *hejab*, 285–86
Kourouma, Ahmadou, *Allah is Not obliged*, 4, 436–41
Kristeva, Julia, 63*n*249
Kroc Peace and Justice Center, 312, 315–16

Lacan, Jacques, 75
Lamartine, Alphonse de, 531–32
Lambert, Jean-Henri, *Neues Organon*, 32*n*72
Langue, 42
Law. *See also individual entries*
and defamiliarization, 53
Greek history and Sophocles' *Antigone*, 250–51
Greek terms for, 248
Greek tragedy in debating, 249
and linguistics, 47–48
and morality, 238
narrative structures, 53–54
Peirce on, 36
and semiology, 44–45
and sign theory, 26–28
as sublanguage, 46–47
Law and Humanities Institute (LHI), 137–38

Law and literature movement, 130
  history of, 134–37
  law on literature, impact of, 134
  law-as-literature, 134, 135–37
  law-in-literature, 133–34, 135
Law of Formation of General Courts (1994), Iran, 324
Law on the Protection of Minors, 359
Law on the Protection of Women's Rights and Interests (LPWRI), 357–58, 377
Legal discourse, 45
Legal linguistics, 48
Legal positivism, 42, 44
  and natural law, 38, 235, 229, 231–32, 236–39
  and semiotics, 60–62
Legal realism, 37–39
  affinity to, 65
  Gény, 37–38
  historical perspective, 39–40
Legal relativism, 183
Legal relativity, 218
Legal semiotics, 19, 48, 49. *See also* Semiotics
  definition of, 24–25
  process, 25–28
Legisigns, 29, 34, 38
Legitimacy, of interdisciplinary method
  law and literature movement, 133–38
  narratives in *The Pianist*, 140–43
  representation, 138–40
Leniency and moral rights, 219
Letter from Birmingham Jail, 4, 9, 182, 191–92, 226. *See also* Civil disobedience
  Allegory of the Cave, 202–3
  anti-law stance of Martin Luther King and biblical background, 201–2
  codes, 193–94
  decoding of messages, 194
  difference and deconstruction notion, 211–13
  genre of, 199–200
  historical and legal context of, 203–
  interpretation and decoding, 195–96
  and intertextuality, biblical allusions, 200
  narrative structure of, 205–11
  reader role, 196–99
Levi, Primo, 143
Levinson, Sanford, 538*n*68
Lévi-Strauss, Claude, 5, 21
  semiology and structuralism, 50–51
Lewis, Bernard, 309
Lexis ®, 26
Leyla Sahin v. Turkey, 291–94
Licoln, Abraham, 213
Lieber, Francis, 40*n*119
Lieber Code (1863), 152, 156*n*142
Li Lu, 381
Linguistics
  and law, 46–48
  Busysens, functional linguistics, 49
  Hjelmslev, glossematics, 49
  Morris, behaviorist semiotics, 48–49
  Ogde and Richards, context theory of meaning, 45–46
  Saussure, 40–45
  significance of, 41*n*122
  Soviet semioticians, 50
Literal and figurative language, Focault's views on, 74
Literary and cinematographic representations, of terrorism
  Hotel Rwanda, 123–24
  Secret Agent, 123
Literary and legal discourse, reductionist dichotomy between, 128
Literary criticism
  critical legal studies and semiotics, 76–78
  new criticism, 57–62
  post-structuralism, 71–75
  Prague School, 54–55
  Roman Jakobson, 55–57
  Russian formalism, 52–54
  structural poetics, 62–71
Li Weixiong, 386
Lloyd, Lord, 95
Locke, John
  Essay Concerning Human Understanding, 31*n*72
  on natural law, 229, 236
Logocentrism, 72
London Agreement, 158, 183
Longinotto, Kim, *Divorce Iranian Style*, 4, 12, 264, 295

Lords' Resistance Army (LRA), Uganda, 404–5, 454
Lotman, Yuri, 16, 50, 529

MacArthur, Douglas, 488
Madison, James, 171
Mahmoody, Betty, *Not Without My Daughter*, 266–67*n*12
Mahr (marriage gift), 325
Maiko, 490
Man-made laws (thesis), 232
Mao Zedong, 349, 385
Maqnaeh, 277
Maria Luz ship, 485
Market theory of copyright, 540
Marriage contract, 324–25
Marriage Law (1931), Iran, 321, 323
Marshall, Rob, 463
Maternal and Infant Health Care Law, 381
Matthews v. Wozencraft (1994), 502–4, 518, 519, 524
Maurras, Charles, 244
McCulloch v. Maryland (1819), 59*n*218
Mediation
  and communication, 23, 24, 294
  and semiosis, 34*n*83
Medicine, as semiotic source, 29–30
Mehriyeh, 318
Meiji regime, 480
Memoirs of a Geisha, 4, 15, 459*n*1, 460*n*4
  breach of contract, 504–6
  confession structure and legal consequences, 468–70
  copyright infringement and common law copyright, 499–500
  damages, 511
  defamation, 506–8
  defamation-in-fiction, 508–11
  defendant's response, 512–18
  duality and narrative representation of geisha as prostitute, 475–77
  geisha and sex act in, 477–79
  as genre, and narrative tension structure, 470
  Matthews v. Wozencraft, Random House, Inc. et al., 502–4
  misappropriation of name and likeness, privacy, and publicity, 500–502
  motivation of informants, 467–68
  narrator in, 465
  reality and fiction, 467
  sex trafficking and slavery in, 470–74
  style, simile, and relevance to legal claims, 474–75
  success of, 463
  voyeurism and failure to satisfy conditions, 466–67
  voyeurism structures and mirroring in, 463–66
Memoir writing, 142–43
Meron, Theodor, 149*n*104
Metalingual function, 57
Metaphor
  code, 27
  geisha, 476
  judicial, 74
  and legal language, 45–46, 55–56
  semiotic theory, 203, 209
  structural semiotics, 194
  symbolic, 437
Metonymy, 55
Mfume, Kweis, 223
Milani, Tahmineh, *Two Women*, 4, 12, 296, 313, 319–20, 342
Military goal and terrorism, 89
Military necessity
  definition of, 156*n*142
  significance of, 155*n*138
Mill, John Stuart, 31*n*72
Miller, Hillis, 71
Millet, Kate, 275, 286
Minda, Gary, 78*n*333
Mineko Iwasaki, 15, 461. *See also Memoirs of a Geisha*
  Geisha, A Life, 459*n*1
  likelihood of succeeding against Golden, 518–19
  reasons for case against Golden, 519–22
Mine Workers Rule, 205
Minow, Martha, 182
Mirare, 490
Mir-Hosseini, Ziba, 286*n*162, 296
  Divorce Iranian Style, 4, 12, 264, 295, 317–19, 325, 342
  Marriage on Trial, 295
  Muslim Women's Quest for Equality, 315*n*359
Misogyny, 306

Mizuage, 478, 481, 490
Mojahedine-e Khalq, 267
Monosemicity, 47
Moral rights, 543
  versus economic rights, 536–37, 541
  leniency, 219
Moreno-Ocampo, Luis, 446
Morphology of the Folktale, 53
Morris, Charles, 36*n*96, 48–49
Moscow Linguistic Circle, 52
Mossadegh, Mohammed, 266
Motivation, 41–42
Muhammad, Elijah, 212
Mukarovsky, J., 54
Music, as representation, 139–40, 141, 163

Nabokov, Vladimir, *Lolita*, 299, 308, 334
Nafaqa (maintenance), 325
Nafisi, Azar, 268, 270, 342. *See also Reading Lolita in Tehran*
Narrative grammar, 68–69
Narrative structures and law, 53–54
National Action Plan to Combat Trafficking, 359, 364
National Conference of the Confederation of Geisha Houses, 487
National People's Congress Standing Committee, 357, 359
National Security Presidential Directive on Trafficking, 361
Natural law doctrine, 213–16
  Aristotle, 230
  Christianity, 234
  critics of, 236
  Grotius on, 235
  Heraclitus, 230
  history of, 229–30
  Hobbes on, 235–36
  Kant on, 236
  legal positivism, 236–39
  Locke on, 236
  meaning of, 228–29
  Plato, 230
  Rousseau on, 236
  Scholasticism, 234–35
  Sophocles, 232–33
  Stoicism, 233–34
  under Sophists and Athenian democracy, 231–32
Natural rights theory, 536–37
New criticism
  objectivity and subjectivity in legal interpretation, 59–60
  and semiotics, 58–59
  text-centered approach and application, 57–58
New York Times, 469
New York Times v. Sullivan (1964), 502, 509, 523–24
Nietzche, Friedrich, 74
Nomos (convention), 231, 232, 248
Nongovernmental organizations (NGOs), 452
Nonscientific discourse, 45
Nonviolent resistance, 170
Not Without My Daughter, 320
Nuremberg Trials, 149*nn*99,104, 152–53, 158–59, 183, 225–26, 237
Nu shu (women's writing), 389, 390
Nussbaum, Martha, 238

Obama, Barrack, 92
Object and sign, 33–34
Objectivity and subjectivity, in legal interpretation, 59–60
O'Brien, Conor Cruise, 257
Ogden, Charles, 45
Omnibus Trade and Competitiveness Act (1988), U.S., 534
One-child policy, of China, 347, 348, 350, 366, 369, 388, 393
  birth-planning workers and agent informants, 371–72
  carrot and stick coercion for compliance, 374–75
  forced abortions, 372–73
  forced sterilizations, 373–74
  recent changes, 382–83
  scarcity of women, 375–82
Open texture of legal language, 61
Opinio juris, 149*n*99
Originalism and textualism, 57
Original understanding and popular sovereignty, 173
Outsider, concept of, 197

Pahlavi, Reza Shah, 265, 266
Palermo Protocol, 351, 364, 398, 425, 429–31
  purpose of, 429–30
  section on children, 431
Paradox
  in meaning of terrorism, 113–14
  of thought and emotion, 139
Parody, in Anouilh's *Antigone*, 253–55, 256, 257
Parole, 42
Paternity right, 543
Pearson, Keir, 123
Peirce, Charles Sanders, 3, 5, 21, 28, 29
  definition of sign and interpretant, 33–34
  Dewey, influence on, 38–39
  and Frank, 37
  Gény and legal realism, influence on, 37–38
  Holmes, influence on, 36–37
  and law, 36
  on legal realism, historical perspective, 39–40
Penalty, 217
Pericles, 232, 245
Personality rights theory of copyright, 540
Personality theory and just laws, 214
Personal justice, 250
Personal rights, 543
Peters, Julie Stone, 129*n*7
Petrograd Society for the Study of Poetic Language (OPOYAZ), 52
Pffaf, William, 107*n*103
Philosophy, as semiotic source, 30–40
  denotation and connotation, 31–33
  Peirce, Charles Sanders, 33–40
  sign and interpretant, 33–34
Physis (natural law), 231, 232
The Pianist, 4, 7, 131, 138, 140–43, 151, 155
  crimes against humanity, illustration of, 152–53
  distinction principle, 155*n*140, 157
  empowerment and remedial effects of memoirs and film making, 142–43
  history as personal testimony, 140
  human rights violation, illustration of, 153–55
  humanity principle, 155*n*139, 156–57
  military necessity, 155*n*138, 156*n*142
  oppressed people symbolization, in occupied territories, 140
  proportionality principle, 155–56*n*141, 157–58
  representation differences between book and film, 141–42
  war crimes illustration in, 152
Piracy and dramatic irony, 533–35
Platform for Action, China, 358
Plato
  Allegory of the Cave, 9, 202–3
  on natural law, 230
Plessy v. Fergusson (1896), 204
Poinsot, Jean, 31*n*72
Polanski, Roman, 4, 7, 133, 138, 156
  art as self-help remedy, 162
  childhood as Jew, 142
  The Pianist, 4, 7, 131, 138, 140–43
Polarity, 55
Polis, 241, 242, 245, 247, 250
Political conflicts, international, 107
Polygamy, 325
Polysemy, 61
Popular sovereignty, 173–74
Positive law. *See* Legal positivism
Posner, Richard A., 129*n*8, 137
Postmodernism, 222*n*10
  and civil disobedience, 227–28
  and CLS movement, 78
Post-structuralism, 5, 22*n*32, 63, 67, 71, 78
  and psychoanalysis, 75
  deconstruction and semiotics, 72–73
  deconstructionist notion of difference, 73
  Foucault and language, 73–74
Powell, Colin, 426
Pragmatics, 48
Prague School, and social consciousness development, 54–55
Prenatal sex selection, 380
Privacy theory of copyright, 539–40
Privilege and copyright, 535–6
Professional Responsibility Rules, 127
Program for the Development of the Chinese Women, 359
Property rights theory, 538–39

Proportionality, principle of, 155–56*n*141, 157–58
Propp, Vladimir, 53
Prosecutor v. Sam Hinga Norman, 445
Prosecutor v. Thomas Lubanga Dyilo, 445, 446, 447
Prosser, William, 502
Prostitute and Geisha, difference between, 476–77, 484–85
Prostitution Prevention Law. *See* Anti-Prostitution Act (1956), Japan
"PROTECT Act", 361, 415, 428–29, 495–96
Provisional law, 38
Psychoanalysis and post-structuralism, 75
Public figure, definition of, 500*n*197
Public speech and civil disobedience comparison of, 182

Qualisigns, 34
Quantum meruit, 499, 505–6, 518, 524
Quasi-contract, 506*n*234

Racketeer Influenced and Corrupt Organizations (RICO), 54
Rahbari (leadership), 273
Randolph, Edmund, 171
Rape
  Beasts of No Nation, 443–44
  in conflict, 112*n*121
  sentence on, 358
Rawls, John
  on civil disobedience, 180, 182, 223–24
  on fair play concept, 215
Reading Lolita in Tehran, 4, 12, 264, 295, 297
  The Great Gatsby, 300–302
  Henry James' novels, 302–4
  literary critics on, 306–10
  literature as reflection of reality in, 299–300
  narrative structure of, 298–99
  women's human rights abuse, freedom from, 305–6
  women's loss of agency, individuality, and freedom in, 300
Reagan, Ronald, 113
Reality and fiction, 467
Reciprocity and Berne Convention, 542–43
Recreation and Amusement Association, 488
Red Cross, 145, 411
Referent, 30, 31
Referential fallacy, 138
Regulation for Control of Prostitutes (1901), Japan, 480
Representation, 127, 138–40
  of armed conflict laws, in *The Pianist*, 144
  music as, 139–40
Restorative justice
  and power of art as self-help remedy, 159–64
  self-help remedies, 132
Retributive justice
  after World War II and Nuremberg trials, 158–59
  self-help remedies, 132
Rheme, 35–36
Richards, I.A., 45, 58
Riffaterre, Michael, 64*n*253
Right of first publication, 517
Right of publicity, 501, 513*n*269, 515
Right to privacy, 513*n*269, 515
Robertshaw, Paul, 66, 74
Robinson, Mary, 431
Roman à clef, 510, 514*n*278
Rome Statute, 111, 446, 447, 452. *See also individual entries*
Roosari, 277
Rosenbaum, Thane, 154
Rousseau, Jean-Jacques, 236
Royal Greenwich Observatory, 115
Rule of the Shorter Term, 543
Russian formalism, 52–54
  defamiliarization and law, 53
  narrative structures and law, 53–54

Sale of Children Protocol, 421–22
Sankoh, Foday, 438
Saussure, De Ferdinand, 3, 5, 21, 28, 72
  arbitrary sign, 41–42
  langue and *parole*, 42
  law and semiology, 44–45
  linguistics and semiology, 43–44
  semiology, 40–41
  society and semiology, 43

synchronic and diachronic study of language, 42–43
Saussurean semiotics, 35. *See also* Structuralism
Scalia, Antonin, 57
Scholasticism and natural law, 234–35
Scholes, Robert, 58*n*210
Schwabach, Aaron, 83
Scientia sermocinales, 31*n*72
Scientific discourse, 45
Scott, Richard, 83
Secrecy and semiotics, 119
Secularism, in France, 291
See, Lisa, *Snow Flower and the Secret Fan*, 4, 13, 389–92
Segregation, 214–15
Self-censorship, 510
Self-critical awareness, 63
Self-defense and terrorism, 114
Self-determination and terrorism, 109–11
Self-immolation, in Iran, 315
Selma March (1965), 204
Semantics, 48
Seme, 49
Semiology, 29, 40–41, 70
and law, 44–45
linguistics, 43–44
and society, 43
and structuralism, 50–51
Semiosis, 34*n*83, 73
Semiotics, 28. *See also* Legal semiotics; Linguistics
anthropology, 50–52
behaviorist, 48–49
and critical legal studies, 76–78, 137
culture, 527
definition of, 23–24, 48, 85*n*11
hermeneutics and reader-response theory, 530–31
and law and literature, 131–33
legal positivism, 60–62
and *Letter from Birmingham Jail*. *See Letter from Birmingham Jail*
literary criticism, 52
medicine, 29–30
and new criticism, 58–59
philosophy, 30–40
of women's human rights in Iran, 263
Sex Discrimination Ordinance (1995), Hong Kong, 358
Sex trafficking. *See also* Geisha; Trafficking Victims Protection Act (TVPA)
complicity of corrupt officials, 367
criminalization of and reprisal against trafficking victims, 368–69
definition of, 352
domestic trafficking of women within China, 364–65
eradication of, 495
feminist legal theory on, 496–97
international trafficking into and outside China, 365–66
policy suggestions to combat, 387
and slavery, 470–74, 492–96
Shah, Mohammad Reza, 266
religious opposition to, 267
Shah, Reza, 281–82, 286, 287, 321
Shanghai Children's Welfare Institute, 377
Shari'a law, 286
and family law, 280, 321
Guardian Council, 273
reinstatement of, 322–23
women's rights, 287, 343
Shklovskvy, Victor, 53
Shura-ye negahban (Guardian Council), 273
Sign, 3–4
classification of, 34–36
and ground, 33
and object, 33–34
Peirce's definition of, 33
and symbols, 35
theory and law, 26–28
triadic relation for, 33*n*83
Signification, 28
Signified
and referent, 30, 31
in *The Pianist*, 131
and signifier, 3, 26, 30–31, 194, 530
Similarity and difference, interplay of, 198
Simpson, Mona, 307
Sinsigns, 34
Sinter, P.W., *Children at War*, 401*n*25
Slavery Convention (1926), 147, 432
Slavery Convention (1956), 432–33
Social consciousness development, 54–55

Socrates, 202*n*63, 218
  Apology, 216
  Sophists, 231
Sontag, Susan, 307
Sophists and Athenian democracy, and natural law, 231–32
Sophocles, 222, 230
  Antigone, 4, 9, 10, 191, 231, 238, 239–42, 244–51
  natural law, 232–33
South African Truth and Reconciliation Commission, 162
Southern Christian Leadership Conference (SCLC), 204, 205
Soviet semioticians, 50
Spielberg, Steven, 463
Stankiewicz, Edward, 62*n*245
Stasi Commission, 289–90
Statistical Information and Monitoring Program on Child Labor (SIMPOC), 436
Statute of Anne (1709), 536, 537
Statutory copyright, 536
St. Augustine, 201, 234
Sterilizations in China, forced, 373–74
Stewart, Potter, 84
Stoicism and natural law, 233–34
Stoic theory, 30
Storytelling, through art, 160
St. Paul, 201, 206
St. Petersburg Declaration (1868), 145
Structural anthropology and law, 51–52
Structuralism, 27*n*54, 39*n*118. *See also* Saussurean semiotics
  Barthesian semiotics, 69–71
  vs. deconstructionism, 62–63
  grammar of narratives, 68–69
  and semiology, 50–51
  theories and law, 63–68
St. Thomas, 230
Sun Tzu, 144
Symbolic speech, 186
Symbols
  and meaning, 116
  and semiotic nature, 118–19
  and signs, 35
  of terrorism, 118–22
Syntactics, 48
Système de la Mode, 41*n*122
Szpilman, Wladyslaw, 7, 131, 133, 138, 139, 153
  art as self-help remedy, 162–64
  The Pianist, 4, 7, 131, 138, 140–43

Tafazoli, Jahangir, 337
Tafsir (Koranic interpretation), 344
Tamkin (sexual submission, obedience), 325
Taney, J., 174
Tariff Act (1930), U.S., 534
Tempo Reforms, 484–85
Term employment, 485
Terrorism, 181. *See also* international terrorism
  activity, 95, 100
  group, 94, 101
  international crimes, 111–12
  literary and cinematographic representations of, 114–24
  paradoxes in meaning of, 113–14
  and self-determination, 109–11
Terrorism definition, 85*n*8, 87, 89*n*30
  Anti-Terrorism Act (1996), 91–92
  of Canada, 99–101
  of England, 94–96
  of European Nation, 99
  FBI, 93
  Financial Anti-Terrorism Act (2001), 92–93
  of France, 96–99
  of scholars, 105–8
  of U.N., 101–5
  U.S. Patriot Act (2001), 92
  U.S. State Department, 94
Terrorisme, 96
Theory and Time magazine, 386
Thirdness, 34*n*83. *See also* Mediation
Thoreau, Henry David, 9, 169, 182, 223
  on civil disobedience, 222
  On the Duty of Civil Disobedience, 191*n*3
Threatening, significance of, 101
Tiefenbrun, Susan and *Legal Semiotics*, 193*n*14
Tillich, Paul, 214
Todorov, Tzvetan, 22, 68–69
Trade-Related Aspects of Intellectual Property Rights (TRIPS), 534*n*41

Trafficking, 13. *See also* One-child policy; Sex trafficking
in China, 350–51
Chinese law, 357–60
definitions, 351–54, 366, 397, 398, 492
international instruments regulating, 354–57
U.S. laws, 360–64
Trafficking in Persons ("TIP") Report, 276*n*92, 361
on child soldiering, 425–26
division of countries into tiers, 362–64, 426–27
Trafficking Victims Protection Act (TVPA) (2000), 352, 360, 361, 414–15, 424, 425–28, 493
Trafficking Victims Protection Reauthorization Acts (TVPRA), 361
Transitional justice, 162
Translinguistics, 41
Treaty of Versailles, 147
Treaty on the Protection of Artistic and Scientific Institutions and Historic Monuments (Roerich Pact), 147–48
Tribe, Laurence, 26
Trollope, Anthony, 544
Tudeh, 267
Tulkens, J., 293, 294

Unchastity, 516*n*285
Unfair law, 215
Uniform Commercial Code, 27–28
United Kingdom Terrorism Act (2000), 95–96
United Mine Workers; United States v. (1947), 205
United Nations Children's Fund (UNICEF), 399
United Nations Educational, Scientific and Cultural Organization (UNESCO), 410
Universal Copyright Convention (1952), 544, 545
Universal Declaration of Human Rights (UDHR), 333, 339
Universal grammar, 69
Unjust enrichment and quantum meruit, 518
Unjust laws, obedience to, 184. *See also* Civil disobedience
based on fairness theory, 184
based on negative consequences theory, 184
U.N. Protocol on Trafficking, 495
Untermenschen (subhumans), 151
U.S. Constitution of 1787, 173–74
U.S. Copyright Office, 542

Velayat-e faghih (rule of the Islamic jurist), 273
Vienna Convention on Treaties, 432*n*232
Violence, definition of, 88, 100
Visual Artists Rights Act (1990), 537
Voting Rights Act (1964), 204

Walden and Civil Disobedience, 9, 191
Walker v. City of Birmingham (1967), 205
Wallace, George, 205
Wallace, William, 144
War crimes
definition of, 110
history of, 144
illustration of, 152
Warsaw Ghetto, 140, 142, 152, 157
Warsaw Rising, 163
Washington, George, 171
Washington Square, 303
Webster, Daniel, 175
Weisberg, Richard, 137
The Failure of the Word, 135
Vichy Laws and the Holocaust, 135, 549
Wei Xing Zhu, 381
West, Robin, 238, 246
Westlaw ®, 26
Westoxication, revolution against, 266–67
White, James Boyd
law and literature movement, 135
The Legal Imagination, 135
White Revolution, 266
White slavery, 494
Wiesel, Elie, 143
Wissenschaftslehre, 32*n*73
Witteveen, Willem J., 39*n*118
Women in black-and-white ethos, 300–304
Women scarcity in China, causes of, 375
infant girls abandonment, 376–78
infanticide, 379–80
non-registration of children at birth, 381–82
sex-selective abortions, 380–81

Women's Handicraft Workshop, 487
Women's human rights abuse, freedom from, 305–6
Working Group on Contemporary Forms of Slavery, 433–34
World Bank, 353
World War I, 146

Xenophobia, of Iran, 337
Xiaoping, Deng, 370

Yagman, Stephen, 107*n*103
Yakuza, 489*n*143, 493

Zeno, 233
Zhao Baige, 382
Zhuzhoquan (authorship right), 550